D1305647

real
learning
_____

a
sourcebook
for
teachers

real learning

a sourcebook for teachers

Edited by

MELVIN L. SILBERMAN

Temple University

JEROME S. ALLENDER

Temple University

JAY M. YANOFF

School District of Philadelphia

LB
1025.2
.R398
1976

Little, Brown and Company

Boston   Toronto

A398
1976

The chapter-opening art in this book
was contributed by:

Franklin Graham, age 6   Chapter 1

Louis Carpinto, age 17   Chapter 2

Suzanne Eide, age 5   Chapter 3

Simone Allender, age 4   Chapter 4

Augustus Harrington, age 18   Chapter 5

Leighanne Eide, age 10   Chapter 6

WITHDRAWN

INDIANA
UNIVERSITY
LIBRARY
OCT 1 3 1983

SOUTH BEND

Cover drawing: **Jeffrey McCain**

The cover drawing was done by a student at the
William M. Trotter School, in the Boston School
System.

Marion J. Fahey, Superintendent

Daniel S. Coughlin, Director, Title I Programs

Dr. Muriel K. Harris, Community Superintendent,
Citywide Magnet Schools, District IX

Barbara L. Jackson, Assistant Director,
William M. Trotter School

Copyright © 1976, 1972 by Little, Brown and Company (Inc.)

All rights reserved. No part of this book may be reproduced in any form or by any
electronic or mechanical means including information storage and retrieval systems without
permission in writing from the publisher, except by a reviewer who may quote brief passages
in a review.

Library of Congress Catalog Card No. 75–18410

First printing

Published simultaneously in Canada by Little, Brown & Company (Canada) Limited

Printed in the United States of America

Photos: Robert Allender
Illustrations: Randi Levy and Vantage Art, Inc.

The authors are grateful for permission to quote from the following sources:

B. Zuger, "Growth of the Individual's Concept of Self." Reprinted from the *American Journal
of Diseases of Children* (June 1952), Volume 83, p. 179. Copyright 1952, American Medical
Association.

Anonymous, "Finding the Real Self." Reprinted, by permission of the editor, from *The
American Journal of Psychoanalysis* (1949), Volume IX, pp. 5–6.

Langston Hughes, "What happens to a dream deferred?" Copyright 1951 by Langston Hughes.
Reprinted from *The Panther and the Lash,* by Langston Hughes, by permission of
Alfred A. Knopf, Inc.

Portions of this book originally published under the title *The Psychology of Open Teaching
and Learning: An Inquiry Approach.*

contents

The following is a list of the Initial Experiences and the Projects and Activities that begin and end each chapter.

activities

preface

Back in 1964, in his initial book *How Children Fail,* John Holt asked: "How can we make school a place where real learning goes on, and not just word swallowing?" As anyone who has followed the course of educational change in the past twelve years can attest, countless ideas to promote real learning have been advocated and tried. In place of the closed and prescriptive structures common to most classrooms, teachers have been seeking ways to allow students to become personally involved in the learning process and to develop inquiry skills for dealing with constantly growing and changing bodies of knowledge. The search has often been frustrating; there has been some success but not as much as many had hoped.

Effective approaches to teaching and learning simply will not come until we give up the fantasy that change is instantly possible and attainable by simple formulae. A host of issues, both theoretical and practical, face any teacher who wishes to move from the relatively straightforward arrangements existing in traditional classrooms to the complex web of relationships found in truly humane environments for learning. Our hope is that this teacher's sourcebook will, in its own small way, facilitate the constructive changes needed in education today.

This book is adaptable to the needs of various education courses, inservice programs, and individual teachers at all levels of schooling. At the same time, it is suitable for a wide range of purposes, from independent study to a program for large groups. In contrast to the typical book of readings, it contains extensive activity suggestions and guidelines for inquiring into its contents. In addition, the readings cover a broader range of issues and views than do other books on humanistic approaches in education.

To readers who are familiar with our previous book, *The Psychology of Open Teaching and Learning,* we believe you will welcome this sourcebook. This new book maintains a focus on psychological themes underlying humanistic education, yet it also moves quite boldly in the direction of classroom application. Additional topics are included such as affective learning, group processes, limit setting, and evaluation. Most of the readings reflect recent contributions to the literature. The activities provide not only interesting experiences, but also designs for considering future actions.

This book is an outgrowth of our experience in teaching undergraduate and graduate courses in the Department of Psychoeducational Processes at Temple University and in training and consulting with teachers and principals in the School District of Philadelphia. Our goal has been to create, as best as possible, conditions of real learning for our students. To enable us to develop and evaluate our efforts, we have had generous support from the College of Education of Temple University and the Exxon Education Foundation.

Colleagues and students in the Department of Psychoeducational Processes contributed significantly to the selection of readings and the creation and testing of activities. We greatly appreciate their work. Also, the staff of the Affective Education Program of the School District of Philadelphia willingly gave us exercises to adapt for the purposes of this book. We are grateful for their contributions as well as for the things we have learned in our association with them. Ann Strouse and Maxine Sullivan were most helpful in the book's preparation. To them, we owe a great deal of thanks. We also wish to acknowledge the creative suggestions of Robert Allender and the editing of Mike Masch. Finally, we are indebted to Marci Resnick for her untiring devotion to this project. Marci assisted us in many ways, from initial planning of the book to editing of the final manuscript. Above all, she was a valued critic and sensitive spokesperson for the needs of students and teachers.

real
learning
—————————
a
sourcebook
for
teachers

When our first book, *The Psychology of Open Teaching and Learning,* was published, open approaches to teaching and learning were just beginning to be used and experimented with by large numbers of teachers and students. Now, just a few years later, open classrooms have become commonplace. They are being conducted in an ever growing number of schools throughout England, America, and many other parts of the world. The phrase "open classroom" has become a familiar cultural term. Clearly, the movement for open education has grown tremendously, but not all of this growth has been synonymous with progress. Indeed, many of us long involved with the idea of open education have come to fear that it is in danger of becoming a fad rather than a serious alternative. Frequently, open education has not led to real learning.

With such widespread and sometimes indiscriminate use of open education procedures, it may have been inevitable that many naive teaching decisions would be made. Having been guilty of making many such decisions ourselves, we are well aware that serious mistakes have occurred. Too often, teachers have sought to involve students solely on the basis of their interests. Too often, the full range of human tendencies to become involved in learning has not been tapped. In some cases, group processes have not been emphasized enough. In others, choices have been given so casually that students have not felt that those choices were real options for them. Teachers have fooled themselves and their students by claiming that teachers have few, if any, personal limits. Teachers have not always defined clearly the amount of responsibility they assume, and the amount of freedom they leave to the student for self-direction. The basis for freedom in the classroom has sometimes been a desire to avoid "hassles" between teachers and students. Finally, teachers have tried to pretend that their life experience does not count in the classroom, and in some cases they have even attempted to deny that they have their own interests and values.

We can, of course, learn from these mistakes. We can recover from the narrow and simple-minded notions under which we have been operating and create conditions which open our classrooms to real learning. What it takes, above all, is a great deal of self-understanding. Unless we struggle to understand and make known our feelings, motives, and reasons for action, our students are not likely to struggle themselves to grow and learn.

The aim of this sourcebook is to facilitate a personal investigation of how one can make learning real. It contains materials which have been helpful to us in working with both preservice and in-service teachers at various levels. The readings, projects, and activities stimulate consideration of the environmental conditions and thinking skills necessary for learning. They suggest practical applications of learning theory. And they illustrate the dynamics of personal growth, the processes of group living, and the active role teachers can play

overview

in guiding students. We hope they will enable you personally to answer many of the questions and examine many of the issues that will face you as you attempt to promote real learning.

SUBJECT MATTER

Each of the six chapters of this book emphasizes a specific concern in teaching and learning. Naturally, our division is somewhat arbitrary. Overlap between chapters and subjects is inevitable. We hope that our way of organizing the book's contents works for you, but if it does not, the sequence of the chapters can easily be altered or the chapters themselves can be combined in various ways. A brief overview of the book follows.

Chapter 1: involving learners. In the first chapter we shall explore the psychological factors that encourage student involvement in learning. The emphasis is on the motivational drives and emotional needs of the learner and on the classroom conditions that are responsive to those needs. Consideration is given to both theory and practical teaching strategies.

Chapter 2: guiding thinking and learning. In Chapter 2 we shall discuss the processes by which knowledge is gained and created. The materials in that chapter should

help you to examine the ways the mind functions and to apply this information in developing effective teaching approaches. Creative ways of teaching language arts, science, mathematics, and social studies, at both elementary and high school levels, are illustrated.

Chapter 3: educating for emotional growth.
In recognition of the growing importance of the affective domain in education today, we shall focus, in Chapter 3, on goals and strategies for guiding emotional growth. Three themes in affective education are highlighted: self-awareness, responsibility, and personal values. The chapter also contains examples of the use of affective techniques in classrooms.

Chapter 4: learning to work in groups.
Chapter 4 will help you to apply group dynamics principles to the classroom. Equal emphasis is given to facilitating small group activity and to building a total community in the classroom. Strategies are described for improving interpersonal communication, decision-making, group planning, and leadership.

Chapter 5: creating freedom and limits.
Chapter 5 is designed to help a teacher to clarify his or her personal limits and to deal with the tensions freedom in a classroom may bring. Practical ideas of psychologists and educators are suggested for resolving conflicts between adults and children in a humane way. We have also included accounts of problems teachers

have faced in creating a context of freedom in their classrooms.

Chapter 6: building active teacher roles.
In Chapter 6, many of the ideas in the preceding chapters will be integrated. We shall deal with the major vehicles by which the teacher can structure, guide, and evaluate learning experiences without inhibiting student involvement and responsibility.

RESOURCE MATERIALS

Each chapter contains different types of resource materials. The purpose of these materials is to help you get more deeply into each topic. A clarification of their function may be helpful to you.

Initial experiences.
Each chapter begins with two "initial experiences" that should whet your appetite for the readings and activities presented later in the chapter. These materials also may help you assess your interests, prior knowledge, and skills relevant to the topic of study of that chapter.

Introduction.
Every chapter is introduced with remarks by the editors. This is our way of expressing the importance of the topic for each chapter and of orienting you to the kinds of information you can expect to find farther along in the chapter.

Readings.
The readings themselves have been chosen for their relevance to the

specific concerns of each chapter as well as their general contribution to the field of education. Within each chapter, there is a balance between theoretical and descriptive material. Our goal is to provide insightful ways of thinking about the problems of facilitating real learning and also to present the soundest practical ideas and strategies around at the moment. Before each of the readings, you will find brief comments orienting you to the contents of the article.

Projects and activities.
Reading is one way to gather information, but experiential activity is an invaluable source of data, too. In our view, experiencing ideas is necessary for a fuller understanding of their meaning. For example, an intellectual grasp of "defense mechanisms" and "mental sets" is not the same as experiencing one's own defensiveness when placed in a threatening situation and one's inability to solve what seems to be a simple problem. Therefore, several projects and activities in this book are geared to helping you relate personally to key concepts and ideas presented in each chapter. We also believe that teachers can gain a great deal of sensitivity and skill in facilitating learning through process-oriented activities if they have tried the activities out on themselves first. Hence, we have provided many exercises and games appropriate for adults yet modifiable for children. We have also included in every chapter at least one activity that can be

directly used in elementary or secondary classrooms.

Additional resources. A list of resource material supplements the readings and activities in each chapter. It contains books, articles, and films.

WAYS TO USE THIS BOOK

This book lends itself to a variety of uses. If you wish to use it for casual reading and as a resource for independent study, you can treat the book as a catalog by reading and doing activities that seem appealing and rejecting what is irrelevant to your personal needs. At the other extreme, the book can be seen as a curriculum guide. Thus, the materials in each chapter can be used sequentially to structure an inquiry into the subject matter of that chapter. For those instructors and students who will use this book as the basis for a course of study, we would like to share our experience in organizing and guiding student activity.

Since its beginning in 1969, The Center for Student-Directed Learning at Temple University (with which we are associated) has maintained a program to prepare teachers to involve their future students in the teaching-learning process. The plan of training and research that has been followed is intentionally quite broad. As a result, the generation of ideas about ways of structuring student-directed inquiry activities that are particularly applicable to education courses and in-service workshops has been continuous.

Out of this experience have come three basic approaches to designing a course of study that allows for active student participation. These three options, labelled *teacher-guided, group-planned,* and *individually oriented,* are based on three themes found in recent literature on education. One theme centers on the teacher as a structuring agent of the classroom. The view is that inquiry can be guided by juxtaposing activities which contain common patterns or principles, and which help to extend the students' interest in an educative direction. The way the teacher structures activity and decides on the parameters of the subject matter are seen as critical to the amount and quality of students' information processing. The second theme is based on the role of the peer group in the learning process. It is believed that student work groups can facilitate individual learning by allowing a student to communicate his ideas to others as well as learn from the insights of his peers. Successful programs in team learning and with student-led discussion groups have helped to demonstrate that learning by individual effort can be enhanced through group process. The third theme involves a stress on the organic nature of learning and the need for self-reliance. The central idea here is that students benefit from learning that is initiated by their own questions and organized by their personal timetable. The teacher's aim is to guide the student's work so that he finds the way he learns best and the problems that interest him the most.

Of course, these three themes are not mutually exclusive. The teacher-guided, group-planned, and individually oriented models, however, are each designed to emphasize one of these themes. Within the democratic classroom, the teacher-guided design basically gives the student the role of information processer and the teacher the role of structurer. The group-planned design is based on the idea that students can learn from and teach each other with the teacher's outside facilitation. The individually oriented design is aimed toward the student's self-reliant learning, with the teacher acting as a resource when needed. Empirical study of these designs has been conducted at the elementary school level (Yanoff, 1972) and at the college level (Silberman and Allender, 1973). The results of that research indicate that all three designs are viable options for the teacher whose goal is to encourage student involvement and inquiry.

Descriptions of the three designs follow. Each is written in terms of a college course in which this book is used as the text, but modifications for in-service workshops and other settings should be easily managed.

Teacher-guided design

The teacher-guided approach mainly involves inquiry activities undertaken by a class as a whole; small group activities and individual projects can be helpful at some points, but they are not critical. Reliance on large group activities ensures that the instructor has adequate opportunity to give direction, participate, criticize, and make suggestions. Initially, the instructor makes choices for the class from his or her position of expertise and early knowledge of class interests and needs. Midway through the course, he or she can make deliberate attempts to show students where they can easily contribute to the planning and direction of activities. Toward the end, students can be encouraged to do more of the planning. Throughout the course, however, students may expect the teacher to provide direct guidance, when needed.

An instructor could begin a teacher-guided class using this book by assigning the initial experiences and introduction to the first chapter and providing orienting remarks or activities. Based on students' reactions to this beginning, the instructor would select readings, projects, and activities and assign them to the class or, instead, might present alternative plans to the class for discussion and possible modification. Perhaps the first activity would be a lecture that provided some basic theory and information — as would be found in any typical course. Throughout this early period, the instructor could invite student feedback to test his or her plans against students' needs. Thus, subsequent selection of topics, readings, and activities could be based on the instructor's knowledge of the students' readiness and interests. After some weeks have passed, the instructor

could involve students more actively in planning the course. A simple way to do this is to organize a student steering committee, which meets with the instructor to select readings and activities and processes what is going on in the course. By the last weeks of the course, students could go through the entire planning process as a class, in small groups, or perhaps as individuals. Their plans would be subject to the advice and criticism of the instructor, but after some negotiation, students might take over the leadership of activities or engage in independent study. The instructor would have to intervene only when guidance was necessary or appropriate.

Group-planned design

The group-planned approach utilizes small groups that plan their own inquiry in consultation with the instructor. Each group meets regularly as a class, only occasionally meeting with the other groups or working on independent projects. Although the instructor can still give direct guidance, he or she would have to divide attention among all the groups that are formed.

Group planning implies that students would continue their work whether the instructor is present or not. Time for the instructor to help and for the group to work alone might be regularly scheduled. Such time could also include informal lectures, which can be requested by groups. In beginning to plan the inquiry, the instructor's actual direct involvement might

be minimal; in contrast, his or her role in requiring a group to defend its choices of goals, resource material, and activity plans, as well as to evaluate its ongoing inquiry is critical and time consuming. One practical way of relating to several groups in this manner would be to form within each group a rotating planning committee, which could meet with the instructor between classes. Such committees could have the responsibility of taking the rough goals and plans of its group and transform them into activities that really allow for people to inquire together. They also might assume the leadership of these activities and thus have quasi-teaching experiences within the course. In addition, when the instructor is not available, former students could act as student consultants or group facilitators.

The group-planned design creates a lot of tension. The problems students face in working together in this manner can be considerable. At the same time, the rewards are incredible. To reduce some of the initial difficulties, it may be desirable to develop some group skills before formally launching into the course. Chapter 4 in this book, Learning To Work in Groups, might be a useful resource.

Individually oriented design

The individually oriented approach employs a great deal of self-directed, indepen-

Three designs for teaching

dent study. Students are responsible to a group or class for general planning and reporting of ideas and findings, but most of their energy is concentrated in furthering a personal inquiry.

In an individually oriented course using this book, students might begin each chapter by working with the initial experiences, either as a class or in small groups. On the basis of this activity, each student can develop personal goals and negotiate them with the instructor, the rest of the class, or a small group. This negotiation allows the student to consider the relevance of the goals he or she is choosing. Once the focus of an inquiry is established, however, the student would be relatively free to develop it on an individual basis.

Except for being required to check plans with the instructor, a student could plan on his own, unless he wished to work with students who have similar interests. Although group activities (such as a lecture or a film) might be made available periodically, searching for information would typically lead to independent study. Participation in group activities would be on the basis of their helpfulness to an individual's inquiry. The resolution phase of the inquiry might bring students together to exchange information and insights, or it might remain focused on helping students to complete individual projects and come to personal conclusions. The most active tasks for the instructor are providing individual consultation and keeping the overall

	Teacher-guided design	Group-planned design	Individually oriented design
General emphasis	Teacher-designed inquiry with openness for student contribution	Facilitation of small group investigation with a focus on group processes	Encouragement of individual planning and decision-making within teacher-structured parameters
Role of the teacher	Creates overall structure of a unit of study	Negotiates group's plans and facilitates group movement	Serves as resource person and organizes the learning environment for individual activity
Teacher interaction	Content-related messages, used to confront and inform	Process interventions to encourage listening, feedback exchange, and perception checking	Communications designed to clarify and extend student's meaning
Expectations toward students	Expected to process experiences created by teacher into some personal state of resolution	Expected to work with and learn from peers	Expected to rely on self and to be aware of own direction
Nature of the peer group	Mobilized and organized frequently by the teacher for singular activities; usually formed randomly or on the basis of friendship	A stable, ongoing unit designed to achieve intense relationships; usually formed by combining people who work well together	An available source of common activity for individual students usually formed on the basis of interest
Type of learning process	Guided discovery; structured information processing	Peer teaching; group investigation	Self-directed; informal and organic

structure of the environment sufficiently organized to minimize the interference that many activities can cause for each other.

All three designs allow for some teacher guidance, small group activity, and individual initiative. However, the emphasis of each design is different, and the designs also differ along these five dimensions: the role of the teacher, teacher interaction, expectations toward students, nature of the peer group, and type of learning process. The table opposite shows these differences in emphasis. The descriptions given in the chart for each design represent the greatest differences in emphasis.

Other viable approaches can be created by interweaving the designs presented. For example, a model can be devised in which different stages of the inquiry would have a teacher-guided, group, or individual orientation. Another possibility would be gradually to change the approach over the course of the semester. Offering two or three approaches at the same time is also feasible, with some modifications. Students could choose the mode of student direction that best meets their needs. But whatever model is chosen should support and facilitate the instructor's goals. An instructor should therefore weigh the models carefully when deciding how to facilitate student direction.

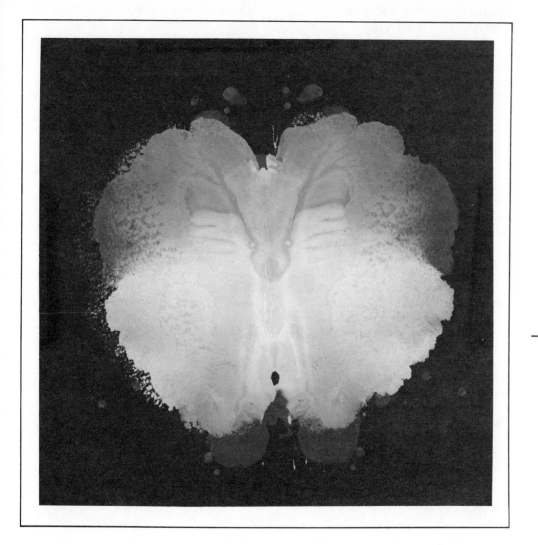

chapter
one

---

involving
learners

initial experiences

BRAINSTORMING WAYS OF INVOLVING STUDENTS

Involvement is an ambiguous term, but the feeling it connotes is unmistakable when we experience it. We may be intrigued. We defer other plans and needs. Above all, we feel connected with what we are learning and with the person with whom we are learning.

1. Imagine that you are being interviewed for a teaching position. The interviewer asks you this question: "What steps would you take to create a feeling of involvement in your classes?" How would you respond? In the chart opposite spaces are provided for you to write up to ten ideas which you think might help you to achieve involvement in your class(es). List different kinds of ideas. Some of your ideas might be associated with the physical climate of the classroom (for example, developing interest centers); some with your behavior as a person (inviting student feedback); some with the manner in which you approach teaching (using simulation games). For now, you are asked to leave the boxes in the lefthand margin blank.

2. Now that you have completed your list of ideas, consider whether any of the following statements apply:

A. This is common practice in schools today.
B. I have experienced this as a student.
C. I have tried this as a teacher.
D. I'm afraid to attempt this.
E. I would never have thought of this three years ago.

If any do, check the appropriate boxes next to the corresponding ideas. (For example, if only statements A and B are true of your first idea, check boxes A and B next to idea 1.) After you have completed the chart, share the results with other students. Think about your confidence — or lack of it — in your ability to involve the students in your classroom.

INDIVIDUAL DIFFERENCES IN LEARNING NEEDS

Different people need different conditions to involve them in learning. Some need pressure; others need a relaxation of demands. Some need a directive and highly stimulating teacher; others need a teacher who encourages and trusts them to work independently. Most conditions of learning are not universally helpful or harmful. One system for describing such diverse needs is presented by M. B. Rosenberg (1968). He identifies four learning styles: (1) rigid-inhibited; (2) undisciplined; (3) acceptance-anxious; and (4) creative. Certain behaviors exemplify each style of learning:

Rigid-inhibited
1. afraid to assert self or show initiative
2. upset by change in routine
3. becomes confused and disoriented easily
4. cannot get a job done unless others are immediately available to help

A	B	C	D	E	Ideas
					1.
					2.
					3.
					4.
					5.
					6.
					7.
					8.
					9.
					10.

Undisciplined
1. lacks tolerance for tasks the student does not enjoy
2. prone to blame teacher or external circumstances when things don't go well
3. breaks classroom rules
4. asserts independence in an obvious negative manner

Acceptance-anxious
1. tries too hard
2. wants to show off or impress others
3. excessively competitive and jealous
4. frequently seeks teacher contact and approval

Creative
1. is open to new ideas
2. shows persistence in attacking problems
3. can constructively assert himself or herself
4. able to apply what is learned to a new situation

What conditions do you think are *most* important in promoting learning involvement for students who exhibit each of these styles? You may wish to consider this question yourself and share your deliberations with others, or you may pursue the question in a more structured fashion by dividing into two or more groups and having each group present two ideas for each learning style on newsprint or a blackboard. Discussion can follow in which the lists can be compared and contrasted. To aid you in this task, here is a list of conditions of learning, from which you can select two as the most critical for each learning style.

— encouragement
— pressure
— close supervision
— rules and routines
— independence
— clear demands
  and expectations

— stimulation
— trust and
  acceptance
— competition
— rewards
— choice
— affection

Teachers continually face the task of creating and maintaining a classroom environment that stimulates involvement in learning. No single condition establishes such a climate, and yet only one critical, missing ingredient may produce disinterest among students. Furthermore, regardless of what a teacher objectively thinks he or she is doing, each student's perception of the classroom environment greatly determines the degree of involvement. Clearly, a teacher's decisions about the learning environment he or she wants in the classroom necessitates an active inquiry. It is not enough to resolve that a "relaxed," "warm," or "student-centered" climate is important. These labels describe a constellation of values, attitudes, and concrete behaviors which are meaningless unless their theoretical dynamics and their practical implications are carefully understood.

What should a learning environment provide in order to involve learners? Let us approach that question by asking the opposite question: How is openness to learning inhibited? Learners do not by any means all become discouraged in the same way, but there are some learning conditions that stifle almost every student. Although you will read a lot about these negative factors in the selections that follow, a general overview might be appropriate.

The *teachers' attitudes toward students* can often be a basic source of trouble. A great deal of research has indicated that teachers' emotional predispositions toward different students affect their actions. Typically, some students are regarded favorably, some negatively, and many others are disregarded during a good part of the school day. Although teachers feel a strong obligation to be fair and objective, the quantity and complexity of their daily interactions with students is so great that it is difficult to maintain impartiality and to curb personal feelings. When this leads to excessive evaluation and pernicious classification of students, learning is severely discouraged. Such a climate facilitates what has been described as the "self-fulfilling prophesy." This phenomenon occurs when the teacher's expectations about a student's potential and worth are actually fulfilled by the student even when the predictions are inaccurate.

Another problem is the *dominance of the teacher* in the classroom.

introduction

When teachers are obsessed with control (which usually means they have little personal control), students' intrinsic motivation and sense of individual responsibility can be squelched. Such conditions as regimentation and heavy-handed guidance oppress students and discourage learning involvement. Students' interests and needs are not accepted. Moreover, the teacher becomes the only available source of support and stimulation. Competition can, at times, encourage learning, but competition for the teacher's praise is another matter. If students are preoccupied with vying for the teacher's affection or avoiding his or her displeasure, the real business of learning takes a back seat. Although the teacher can be an important source of information, ideas, and values, students concerned with picking the teacher's brain are denied the opportunity to learn from their peers. A class in which the teacher is the fountain of all recognized knowledge lacks variety and opportunities for self-direction. A teacher who talks most of the time does not allow students to hear from others, to have moments of private reflection, or to ask their own questions.

A third source of concern is *teacher clarity*. Much learning takes place when the encounter of teacher and student is honest and stimulating. But when the teacher's "agenda" is confused or hidden, students are sidetracked into a guessing game called "what's he up to now?" Almost all teachers have nonnegotiable demands, but often they feel guilty about them and fail to communicate them clearly. Almost all teachers have learning goals in mind when they interact with students, but when they fail to share those goals openly, the students cannot evaluate the teachers' intentions and decide how well they mesh with their own. Finally, almost all teachers want to befriend their students. But when teachers continually shift in their relationship with students from playful peer to stern parent, they deny their students what Dennison has called the "natural authority of an adult," the adult who, from experience, can support, guide, and understand.

The creation of a learning environment which *does* involve students depends on the teacher's success in dealing with the conflict of safety and growth. When a person is faced with new and perhaps risky situations, he usually attempts to protect himself psychologically. If he feels that his ability to protect himself is threatened, he tends to be particularly reluctant to take on challenging experiences and often tries to remove himself from the situation. Abraham H. Maslow theorizes in "Defense and Growth" (see pages 23, 24) that with regard to safety and growth,

Every human being has both sets of forces within him. One set clings to safety and defensiveness out of fear, tending to regress backward, hanging on to the past . . . afraid to take chances, afraid to jeopardize what he already has, afraid of independence, freedom and separateness. The other set of forces impels him forward toward wholeness of Self and uniqueness of Self, toward full functioning of all his capacities. . . . In the choice between giving up safety or giving up growth, safety will ordinarily win out.

The problem we as teachers face is how to minimize the dangers and maximize the attractions of learning and personal growth so that students, rather than being defensive and self-protective, will choose to be involved. Learning is, after all, a way of experiencing new and different phenomena. Probably any learning situation is naturally anxiety provoking. How then can a teacher honor a student's need to be assured of his safety and at the same time fulfill his own responsibility to provide a challenging environment? * We hope you will find helpful answers to this question in the readings that follow.

Besides thinking about emotional support for the learner, you should also consider how his learning will be stimulated. No matter how supportive a classroom is, it may still be boring. Learning involvement depends on activity, variety, and meaning. It cannot ultimately depend on external rewards. The teacher needs to examine what materials develop interest and excitement, what physical facilities allow for interaction and private concentration, and what activities initiate and sustain student inquiry. Several selections in this chapter are concerned with these matters.

Finally, any investigation of what involves learners must consider the

---

* Teachers, of course, face the conflict of safety and growth within themselves as well. Without emotional support from supervisors, colleagues, and parents, teaching can indeed be a trying experience.

direction of learning. Who should control the learning process? To what degree, for example, should students decide what they are going to learn, what materials they are going to use, and what experiences will best enhance their learning? Consideration of the kind of freedom to create in a learning environment is important for any teacher who wants to promote growth in learning as well as emotional security. All too often, potentially exciting material fails to involve students, because the students do not have "ownership" of what is being taught. Unless the student is committed to the teacher's plans, or better yet, is initially involved in developing learning plans, even the most relevant and provocative topics may fail to maintain interest.

Silberman discusses, in general terms, the problematic aspects of school environments. His article can help you think about the negative conditions of learning that are prevalent in our schools. Drawing on literature that helped to stimulate concern and some of the changes in present-day education, he identifies such problems as the hidden curriculum, congested social environments, constant evaluation, and pervasive authority. Once this survey of problems is understood, it can be used as a background against which other articles in this chapter can be read for deeper insight and potential solutions.

MELVIN L. SILBERMAN

WHAT SCHOOLING DOES TO CHILDREN

School is the setting for a major portion of children's lives. For well over a thousand hours a year, children are influenced by what happens there. It is important, therefore, to examine what the school environ-

From *The Experience of Schooling,* edited by Melvin L. Silberman. Copyright © 1971 by Holt, Rinehart and Winston, Inc. Adapted and reprinted by permission of Holt, Rinehart and Winston, Inc.

ment is generally like for them and what aspects of it require change.

The most pervasive but often overlooked aspect of school life is its institutional quality. While it is commonly believed that the main concern of schools is instruction, schooling is a much broader experience than being taught what is contained in textbooks. Students learn not only facts, skills, and concepts but also rules of membership in a social institution. Often this learning experience may have greater impact on students' ultimate well-being than do those experiences we commonly identify with the academic curriculum. The school's rules, routines, and procedures form what has been called a "hidden curriculum" (Jackson, 1968) designed to mold individual behavior to the requirements of institutional living. This curriculum is made necessary by the fact that personal interests can rarely be accommodated in schools. Students must often yield when their own wishes and plans inconvenience other people or interfere in other ways with the efficient operation of the school. A group of students, for example, may want to finish a chemistry experiment but the school schedule calls for them to proceed to their next class. Or a request by students to rearrange their desks may have to be denied because, among other considerations, it would make it difficult for the janitor to sweep the floor.

Acquiescing to these procedural rules, however, is a painful process for most students, especially when the rules are numerous and rigidly applied. Jackson (1968)

readings

finds, for example, that whether students want to be called on in class discussion, or request the teacher's help, or use materials in short supply, they usually must wait their turn. They must also wait for each other to be quiet or get to the right page before the teacher will proceed. In addition, countless instructions and directions must be endured, even though a good number of them, according to Brenner, Hofmann, and Weddington (1964), do not refer to the academic activity at hand. Finally, spontaneous desires must often be held in abeyance until the proper time and place. Mastering the hidden curriculum is also made difficult by confusion as to what is expected when institutional requirements conflict with educational demands. It is common for students to be expected to be passive and conforming in school and yet, at the same time, intellectually curious and aggressive.

Whenever school personnel do not fully grapple with the problems of institutional living, they risk solving them in unsatisfactory ways. For example, students may be asked to line up before leaving or entering school even though less regimented ways of avoiding pushing and shoving are possible. One reason that alternative solutions are not explored is that current procedures appear to be necessary. Without giving the matter much thought, administrators cannot conceive how to manage students without recourse to the means they have instituted. To compound the problem,

classroom teachers may place an even greater value on the procedures the school principal expects them to enforce. For instance, besides dismissing students by rows, teachers might choose the quietest row first. Thus, obedience to rules of dismissal becomes a virtue in itself, quite apart from its functional necessity. When this happens, students learn to view conformity as morally right and nonconformity as morally wrong. They learn little about why rules and regulations are necessary nor how to determine when they are unnecessary. In this regard, many teachers who have allowed brief experiments in classroom government report that their students create extremely stringent and inflexible rules for themselves. One of the implications of their remarks is that children are not mature enough to handle self-government. Quite possibly, however, the students are merely exaggerating what they have been taught about classroom procedures. Their efforts to control themselves reflect the same unquestioning stance toward rule making that the school adopts. Little attention is given to understanding when classroom conditions require institutionalized procedures and how they can be planned to avoid unpleasant consequences for individual people.

Beyond the learning of rules and procedures which govern personal action, membership in school requires a set of psychological adjustments. One of these adaptations is learning to live in school without the assurance of the adult acceptance that children take for granted at

home. Teachers, after all, cannot be as intimate and patient with their students as parents can be with their children. Their energies are severely taxed by the several roles they perform for many students simultaneously.

These limitations, unfortunately, often lead to a kind of teacher favoritism. This occurs when teachers develop certain perceptions, preferences, and expectations concerning their students in order to simplify the task of relating to many children. For example, Kohl (1967) found from personal experience that by perceiving some students as defiant, unmanageable, or disturbed, he could reject their claim on his attention and still preserve his self-image as a responsive teacher. In this regard, a study by Feshbach (1969) suggests that student teachers attempt to ease the problems of classroom management by showing preference to children who are conforming and orderly over those who are independent and active. Moreover, research by Rosenthal and Jacobson (1968) supports the notion that teachers come to expect greater academic improvement in some students than in others. Such differential expectations, it could be argued, allow a teacher to channel his efforts when his energies are at a premium. As a result of this favoritism, some students are lucky enough to have teachers who believe in them, care for them, and help them learn. The students who are the victims of teachers' biased vision, however, often receive less attention and concern. What makes their neglect particularly problematic is that children often react to it in ways which confirm and perpetuate their teacher's negative perceptions and expectations.

The problem of changing how teachers perceive their students is exacerbated by the categories used in schools to describe children. When students are viewed in terms of their I.Q., achievement test scores, social class background, and conformity to classroom rules and procedures, the possibility that they will be stereotyped rather than seen as individuals is increased. All too frequently, these categories are merely used by teachers to make quick predictions about a child. If the predictions are negative, the temptation to ignore or reject him is great. Occasionally, teachers reveal instances in which they regretted the fast impression they formed of a child. After getting to know him, they had a richer view of the student as a person and were able to respond more warmly to him. Unfortunately, some children do not get a "second look" and even if they did, they may already have begun to act in ways which fulfill the teacher's initial expectations. What we need are conceptions of the teaching-learning process in which teachers would not have to depend so greatly on tight categories of perceiving children. Without this dependence, teachers might be less threatened by these traditional indices of what to expect from students and thus more open to who they really are.

A second demand made in schools is that students manage their lives in a highly congested social environment. Approximately thirty people inhabit a room which has far less space than a family enjoys in a house. We confine students to quarters in which their ability to stretch their feet, walk around, and spread out their possessions is limited. Furthermore, the ratio of students to teacher and to materials is quite high, even in the least crowded classrooms.

Because classrooms are crowded places, students are usually required to do things together most of the time. Individually, they have little opportunity for private action. Personal pursuits sooner or later conflict with the teacher's rules or the wishes of classmates. Even where the chance to be alone arises, it has been found that a student's ability to go about his business without being interrupted or distracted is virtually impossible (Jackson and Wolfson, 1968). As a result of these crowded conditions, a sense of privacy and individuality is difficult to achieve. In an environment which is essentially unresponsive to individual differences, according to Adams and Biddle (1970), one student is practically indistinguishable from another.

Paradoxically, students' failure to find psychological privacy in the classroom is frequently accompanied by an inability to interact meaningfully with each other. Because of the crowded social environment in the classroom, children are often beseeched to keep to themselves, to desist from talking with classmates, and above all, to avoid showing their work to each other. For children to ignore each other is, of course, as impossible as finding privacy.

The impact on children of spending five

hours a day in crowded classrooms cannot be easily studied. Adults, moreover, cannot fully comprehend the experience because the conditions under which they work are rarely as congested. By comparison, classrooms provide less freedom of movement, less personalized facilities, and more distraction than do most adult work settings. Despite our distance from classroom life, however, we might logically deduce that children have very little incentive to develop their own interests and plans in school. To have such incentive would require that individual students experience the classroom as a place for their own use. What is needed are ways of designing classrooms so that space can be used flexibly to create several types of physical settings in which students can learn. With greater choice as to how any activity can be organized, a classroom could accommodate a variety of purposes and thereby make it a less depersonalizing climate in which to live and work.

Schooling is, thirdly, an experience in withstanding continual evaluation of one's words and actions. Probably in no other setting is one so often judged as a person. To make matters worse, these judgments are typically voiced before an audience of peers. As Dreeben (1968) suggests, classroom praise and criticism, although intended to help the learner, may threaten him instead.

To cope with this threat to their self-respect, many students find it necessary to devote their mental energies to strategize how to avoid failure and shame. The strategies they use depend on the intensity of that threat. Those whose position in the class pecking order is secure maintain the teacher's favor by zealously complying with the academic and social expectations of the school. Others stay on the teacher's "good side" by feigning involvement, hiding misdeeds, and misinforming the teacher. The less secure the student, the more likely is he to be forced to engage in this "cheating." For students to whom classroom evaluation is an especially threatening experience, however, active attempts to impress the teacher are often too risky. So, these students, as Holt (1964) has described, actually choose failure. Saving face becomes more important to them than learning and thinking.

When we witness students in school laughing, daydreaming, or complaining, it is hard to believe that many of them are apprehensive. The problem of observing the apprehension created by classroom evaluation is that children respond to it in ways which disguise their real fears. Nonetheless, it is visible if one looks closely enough. It is reflected best in the choices apprehensive students make in the classroom. If the teacher's judgments did not threaten them, they would choose to use their mental energies to tackle new ideas rather than scheme how to hide their shortcomings.

School is a place where children are not accepted at their present stage of development. Growth is expected. But children grow only after they feel safe; that is, they will seek out new knowledge most fully when they are convinced that penalties will not be invoked if they fail. Failure itself is not anxiety producing. The persistence which infants show in their attempts to master the environment suggests that human beings are not naturally afraid of failure. It becomes problematic, though, when a person believes he will lose something of value to him (e.g., approval, good grades, a special privilege) if he does not succeed. The only way to relieve a child's anxiety about the teacher's evaluations is to assure him that they will not be held against him. The problem is how students can be evaluated so that their successes and failures are viewed as helpful information rather than as indications of reward and punishment.

A fourth condition to which students must adjust in school is the pervasive authority of school personnel. While it is true that students can make some choices for themselves, Friedenberg (1963) argues that teachers and principals have broad discretionary jurisdiction over students. They can decide what content will be in the curriculum as well as what disciplinary action to take when students do not follow rules and regulations. Even in schools where students have a voice in those matters, the privilege to do so can be withdrawn at any time. If students are dissatisfied with the school's decisions, they have no official power to press their grievances. In short, the school authorities are very much in control.

Basically, schools ask their students to conduct meaningful lives with few rights, privileges, and opportunities for responsibility and choice. Most administrators and teachers, of course, do not consciously try to be autocratic but few know how to avoid it. They rely on their authority to demand and restrict in order to carry out their educational functions. In response, students give up any sense of autonomy. They come to feel that their education is largely out of their hands. More importantly, they come to believe in the school's definition of their capacity for freedom and responsible decision-making.

One of the common fears in giving students greater control in school is that they will not act responsibly. There are many experiments in classroom freedom, however, which demonstrate that this fear is unfounded. In Kallet's experience (1966), children who attend schools in which restrictions are placed on moving and talking, activities are closely supervised, and decisions are rarely left to students, are far less self-reliant than their counterparts in freer schools.

The concern that children make wise choices may be partly invalid to begin with. It suggests that children are prone to make personally irresponsible decisions. Yet, Maslow (1968) finds that people generally make wise choices if they are truly free to do so. Only when they are frightened into making self-protective decisions, he believes, are their choices irrational.

The real problem may not be whether children can be trusted with freedom but whether it is possible in schools to allow each student to be fully free to make his own choices.

In recent years, increased attention has been given to questions concerning the school's authority over its students. Attempts have been made to lessen the distance between teachers and students, to relax regulations concerning physical appearance and other personal matters, and to reduce the number of academic requirements to which a student must adhere. But, as welcome as these liberalizing efforts may be, they have not changed the basic powerlessness of students. It is questionable whether a school can be run like a political democracy. On the other hand, by assuming the right to be autocratic, school personnel deny students the opportunity to achieve some meaningful direction over their own lives.

One of the major effects of these psychological demands of school life is to make students overly concerned about their personal well-being and thus insensitive to their relations with each other. To make matters worse, peer tensions and antagonisms are directly encouraged in many classrooms. For example, Henry (1957) has observed that it is common for teachers to ask students to evaluate each other and thus magnify the threat which classroom evaluation poses for students. According to Minuchin (1965), they also invite destructive competition among students by dominating social interaction and thereby becoming the sole source of recognition in the classroom. Furthermore, studies by Lippitt and Gold (1959) and Hawkes (1968) show that teachers influence the formation of peer cliques by their expression of differential attitudes and expectations for different children. In most cases, the antagonism, competition, and social exclusion engendered in classrooms are unintended. Hence, the tension among classmates in schools often goes unrecognized and untreated.

Even though teachers do not intend to facilitate negative relations among their students, they cannot dismiss them, as they sometimes do, by appealing to the myth that children are naturally cruel to each other. Actually, the most serious vice of children is their imitation of significant adults around them. Their identification with adult behavior patterns is evidenced by extensive modeling of their teachers. For example, students are quick to attach evaluative labels to each other. They also tend to select friends and reject others on the basis of traditional academic indices without much regard for personal qualities.

When we think of a person with character and personal strength, we think, in part, of a person who recognizes desirable qualities in others, who is loyal to those he befriends, and who is able to give help as well as receive it. We frown on a person who exploits the weaknesses of others, who submits too readily to those more powerful than he, or who envies his peers. The social attributes which students are encouraged, intentionally or not, to adopt

in schools are more likely to create the latter person. If we want schools to help children learn how to build human relationships as well as develop academic skills, we must be careful not to put students in a position which makes it difficult for them to respect and cooperate with each other.

From these remarks, one can readily sense that schooling presents challenging problems to children. They must contend with a morass of institutional rules and regulations, the personal preferences and biases of their teachers, and the crowded social conditions of the classroom. They must also learn to live with frequent public evaluation, limited rights and privileges, and tensions among peers. What children experience when confronted with these demands is difficult to pinpoint and doubtlessly varies from student to student. The testimony presented in several books and articles suggests, however, that students' feelings fall into such negative categories as uncertainty, fear, and resentment.

How concerned we are about the psychological conditions under which children live in schools depends, perhaps, on how necessary we feel are unpleasant experiences to a child's growth and development. Our concern might also depend on the extent to which we tolerate these conditions in our adult lives, in our responsibilities at work and in our relations with the major institutions of society. It might be more helpful, though, to assess the psychological quality of schooling by asking what kind of images of themselves children develop as a result of going to school. Does their schooling help them to believe in themselves, that is, to see themselves as competent, resourceful, capable of altering some parts of their environment? If we are to compel children to live at least ten years of their lives in schools, we owe it to them to explore seriously the answer to this question. If children do not form positive views of themselves as a result of their schooling, we are obligated to rethink how schools can be organized so that children will view them as a valuable resource in their lives.

In this chapter from Toward a Psychology of Being, Maslow presents the view that human beings have within them two sets of forces or needs — one that strives for growth and one that clings to safety. Although not written specifically for educators, this chapter is useful for examining the emotional needs that any learning environment must fulfill. In a long footnote, Maslow provides a good illustration of how a child naturally approaches a new experience and how an overly directive adult can inhibit curiosity. Maslow's theory has important implications about the role of choice in the learning process.

ABRAHAM H. MASLOW

DEFENSE AND GROWTH

This chapter is an effort to be a little more systematic in the area of growth theory. For once we accept the notion of growth, many questions of detail arise. Just how does growth take place? Why do children grow or not grow? How do they know in which direction to grow? How do they get off in the direction of pathology?

The answer I find satisfactory is a simple one, namely, that growth takes place when the next step forward is subjectively more delightful, more joyous, more intrinsically satisfying than the previous gratification with which we have become familiar and even bored; that the only way we can ever know what is right for us is that it feels better subjectively than any alternative. The new experience validates *itself* rather than by any outside criterion. It is self-justifying, self-validating.

We don't do it because it is good for us, or because psychologists approve, or because somebody told us to, or because it will make us live longer, or because it is good for the species, or because it will

Abridged version from *Toward a Psychology of Being* by Abraham H. Maslow. Copyright © 1968 by Litton Educational Publishing, Inc. Reprinted by permission of Van Nostrand Reinhold Company.

bring external rewards, or because it is logical. We do it for the same reason that we choose one dessert over another. I have already described this as a basic mechanism for falling in love, or for choosing a friend, i.e., kissing one person gives more delight than kissing the other, being friends with a is more satisfying subjectively than being friends with *b*.

In this way, we learn what we are good at, what we really like or dislike, what our tastes and judgments and capacities are. In a word, this is the way in which we discover the Self and answer the ultimate questions Who am I? What am I?

The steps and the choices are taken out of pure spontaneity, from within outward. The healthy infant or child, just Being, as *part* of his Being, is randomly, and spontaneously curious, exploratory, wondering, interested. Even when he is non-purposeful, non-coping, expressive, spontaneous, not motivated by any deficiency of the ordinary sort, he tends to try out his powers, to reach out, to be absorbed, fascinated, interested, to play, to wonder, to manipulate the world. *Exploring, manipulating, experiencing,* being interested, choosing, delighting, *enjoying* can all be seen as attributes of pure Being, and yet lead to Becoming, though in a serendipitous way, fortuitously, unplanned, unanticipated. Spontaneous, creative experience can and does happen without expectations, plans, foresight, purpose, or goal.* It is only when

* "But paradoxically, the art experience cannot be effectively *used* for this purpose or any other. It must be a purposeless activity, as far as we

the child sates himself, becomes bored, that he is ready to turn to other, perhaps "higher," delights.

Then arise the inevitable questions. What holds him back? What prevents growth? Wherein lies the conflict? What is the alternative to growth forward? Why is it so hard and painful for some to grow forward? Here we must become more fully aware of the fixative and regressive power of ungratified deficiency-needs, of the attractions of safety and security, of the functions of defense and protection against pain, fear, loss, and threat, of the need for courage in order to grow ahead.

Every human being has *both* sets of forces within him. One set clings to safety and defensiveness out of fear, tending to regress backward, hanging on to the past, *afraid* to grow away from the primitive communication with the mother's uterus and breast, *afraid* to take chances, afraid to jeopardize what he already has, *afraid* of independence, freedom and separateness. The other set of forces impels him forward toward wholeness to Self and uniqueness of Self, toward full functioning of all his capacities, toward confidence in the face of the external world at the same

---

understand 'purpose.' It can only be an experience in *being* — being a human organism doing what it must and what it is privileged to do — experiencing life keenly and wholly, expending energy and creating beauty in its own style — and the increased sensitivity, integrity, efficiency, and feeling of well-being are by-products" (Wilson, 1956, p. 213).

time that he can accept his deepest, real, unconscious Self.

I can put all this together in a schema, which though very simple, is also very powerful, both heuristically and theoretically. This basic dilemma or conflict between the defensive forces and the growth trends I conceive to be existential, imbedded in the deepest nature of the human being, now and forever into the future. If it is diagrammed like this:

$$Safety \leftarrow \langle PERSON \rangle \rightarrow Growth$$

then we can very easily classify the various mechanisms of growth in an uncomplicated way as

a. enhancing the growthward vectors, e.g., making growth more attractive and delight producing
b. minimizing the fears of growth
c. minimizing the safetyward vectors, i.e., making it less attractive
d. maximizing the fears of safety, defensiveness, pathology and regression

We can then add to our basic schema these four sets of valences:

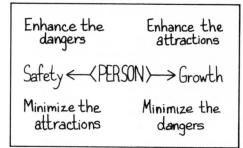

Therefore we can consider the process of healthy growth to be a never ending series of free choice situations, confronting each individual at every point throughout his life, in which he must choose between the delights of safety and growth, dependence and independence, regression and progression, immaturity and maturity. Safety has both anxieties and delights; growth has both anxieties and delights. We grow forward when the delights of growth and anxieties of safety are greater than the anxieties of growth and the delights of safety. . . .

One additional relationship between safety and growth must be specially mentioned. Apparently growth forward customarily takes place in little steps, and each step forward is made possible by the feeling of being safe, of operating out into the unknown from a safe home port, of daring because retreat is possible. We may use as a paradigm the toddler venturing away from his mother's knee into strange surroundings. Characteristically, he first clings to his mother as he explores the room with his eyes. Then he dares a little excursion, continually reassuring himself that the mother-security is intact. These excursions get more and more extensive. In this way, the child can explore a dangerous and unknown world. If suddenly the mother were to disappear, he would be thrown into anxiety, would cease to be interested in exploring the world, would wish only the return of safety, and and might even lose his abilities, e.g., instead of daring to walk, he might creep.

I think we may safely generalize this example. Assured safety permits higher needs and impulses to emerge and to grow towards mastery. To endanger safety, means regression backward to the more basic foundation. What this means is that in the choice between giving up safety or giving up growth, safety will ordinarily win out. Safety needs are prepotent over growth needs. This means an expansion of our basic formula. In general, only a child who feels safe dares to grow forward healthily. His safety needs must be gratified. He can't be *pushed* ahead, because the ungratified safety needs will remain forever underground, always calling for satisfaction. The more safety needs are gratified, the less valence they have for the child, the less they will beckon, and lower his courage.

Now, how can we know when the child feels safe enough to dare to choose the new step ahead? Ultimately, the only way in which we can know is by *his* choices, which is to say only *he* can ever really know the right moment when the beckoning forces ahead overbalance the beckoning forces behind, and courage outweighs fear.

Ultimately the person, even the child, must choose for himself. Nobody can choose for him too often, for this itself enfeebles him, cutting his self-trust, and confusing his *ability* to perceive his own internal delight in the experience, his *own* impulses, judgments, and feelings, and to differentiate them from the interiorized standards of others.*

* "From the moment the package is in his hands, he feels free to do what he wants with it. He opens it, speculates on what it is, recognizes what it is, expresses happiness or disappointment, notices the arrangement of the contents, finds a book of directions, feels the touch of the steel, the different weights of the parts, and their number, and so on. He does all this before he has attempted to do a thing with the set. Then comes the thrill of doing something with it. It may be only matching one single part with another. Thereby alone he gets a feeling of having done something, that he can do something, and that he is not helpless with that particular article. Whatever pattern is subsequently followed, whether his interest extends to the full utilization of the set and therefore toward further gaining a feeling of greater and greater accomplishment, or whether he completely discards it, his initial contact with the erector set has been meaningful.

"The results of active experiencing can be summarized approximately in the following way. There is physical, emotional, and intellectual

If this is all so, if the child himself must finally make the choice by which he grows forward, since only he can know his subjective delight experience, then how can we reconcile this ultimate necessity for trust in the inner individual with the necessity for help from the environment? For he does need help. Without help he will be too frightened to dare. How can we help him to grow? Equally important, how can we endanger his growth?

The opposite of the subjective experience of delight (trusting himself), so far as the child is concerned, is the opinion of other people (love, respect, approval,

self-involvement; there is a recognition and further exploration of one's abilities; there is initiation of activity or creativeness; there is finding out one's own pace and rhythm and the assumption of enough of a task for one's abilities at that particular time, which would include the avoidance of taking on too much; there is gain in skill which one can apply to other enterprises, and there is an opportunity each time that one has an active part in something, no matter how small, to find out more and more what one is interested in.

"The above situation may be contrasted with another in which the person who brings home the erector set says to the child, 'Here is an erector set, let me open it for you.' He does so and then points out all the things in the box, the book of directions, the various parts, etc., and, to top it off, he sets about building one of the complicated models, let us say, a crane. The child may be much interested in what he has seen being done, but let us focus on one aspect of what has really been happening. The child has had no opportunity to get himself involved admiration, reward from others, trusting others rather than himself). Since others are so important and vital for the helpless baby and child, fear of losing them (as providers of safety, food, love, respect, etc.) is a primal, terrifying danger. Therefore, the child, faced with a difficult choice between his own delight experiences and the experience of approval from others, must generally choose approval from others, and then handle his delight by repression or letting it die, or not noticing it or controlling it by willpower. In general, along with this will develop a dis-

_____

with the erector set, with his body, his intelligence, or his feelings, he has had no opportunity to match himself up with something that is new for him, to find out what he is capable of or to gain further direction for his interests. The building of the crane for him may have brought in another factor. It may have left the child with an implied demand that he do likewise without his having had an opportunity to prepare himself for any such complicated task. The end becomes the object instead of the experience involved in the process of attaining the objective. Also whatever he may subsequently do by himself will look small and mean compared to what had been made for him by someone else. He has not added to his total experience for coming up against something new for the next time. In other words, he has not grown from within but has had something superimposed from the outside. . . . Each bit of active experiencing is an opportunity toward finding out what he likes or dislikes, and more and more what he wants to make out of himself. It is an essential part of his progress toward the stage of maturity and self-direction'' (Zuger, 1952, p. 179).

approval of the delight experience, or shame and embarrassment and secretiveness about it, with finally, the inability even to experience it.*

_____

* "How is it possible to lose a self? The treachery, unknown and unthinkable, begins with our secret psychic death in childhood — if and when we are not loved and are cut off from our spontaneous wishes. (Think: what is left?) But wait — victim might even 'outgrow' it — but it is a perfect double crime in which the him-it is not just this simple murder of a psyche. That might be written off, the tiny self also gradually and unwittingly takes part. He has not been accepted for himself, *as he is.* Oh, they 'love' him, but they want him or force him or expect him to be different! Therefore he *must be unacceptable.* He himself learns to believe it and at last even takes it for granted. He has truly given himself up. No matter now whether he obeys them, whether he clings, rebels or withdraws — his behavior, his performance is all that matters. His center of gravity is in 'them,' not in himself — yet if he so much as noticed it he'd think it natural enough. And the whole thing is entirely plausible; all invisible, automatic, and anonymous!

"This is the perfect paradox. Everything looks normal; no crime was intended; there is no corpse, no guilt. All we can see is the sun rising and setting as usual. But what has happened? He has been rejected, not only by them, but by himself. (He is actually without a self.) What has he lost? Just the one true and vital part of himself: his own yes-feeling, which is his very capacity for growth, his root system. But alas, he is not dead. 'Life' goes on, and so must he. From the moment he gives himself up, and to the extent that he does so, all unknowingly he sets

The primal choice, the fork in the road, then, is between others' and one's own self. If the only way to maintain the self is to lose others, then the ordinary child will give up the self. This is true for the reason already mentioned, that safety is a most basic and prepotent need for children, more primarily necessary by far than independence and self-actualization. If adults force this choice upon him, of choosing between the loss of one (lower and stronger) vital necessity or another (higher and weaker) vital necessity, the child must choose safety even at the cost of giving up self and growth.

(In principle there is no need for forcing

_____

about to create and maintain a pseudo-self. But this is an expediency — a 'self' without wishes. This one shall be loved (or feared) where he is despised, strong where he is weak; it shall go through the motions (oh, but they are caricatures!) not for fun or joy but for survival; not simply because it wants to move but because it has to obey. This necessity is not life — not his life — it is a defense mechanism against death. It is also the machine of death. From now on he will be torn apart by compulsive (unconscious) *needs* or ground by (unconscious) conflicts into paralysis, every motion and every instant canceling out his being, his integrity; and all the while he is disguised as a normal person and expected to behave like one!

"In a word, I saw that we *become* neurotic seeking or defending a pseudo-self, a self-system; and we *are* neurotic to the extent that we are self-less" (Anonymous, 1949, p. 7).

the child to make such a choice. People just *do* it often, out of their own sicknesses and out of ignorance. We know that it is not necessary because we have examples enough of children who are offered all these goods simultaneously, at no vital cost, who can have safety and love *and* respect too.)

Here we can learn important lessons from the therapy situation, the creative educative situation, creative art education and I believe also creative dance education. Here where the situation is set up variously as permissive, admiring, praising, accepting, safe, gratifying, reassuring, supporting, unthreatening, non-valuing, non-comparing, that is, where the person can feel completely safe and unthreatened, then it becomes possible for him to work out and express all sorts of lesser delights, e.g., hostility, neurotic dependency. Once these are sufficiently catharted, he then tends spontaneously to go to other delights which outsiders perceive to be "higher" or growthward, e.g., love, creativeness, and which he himself will prefer to the previous delights, once he has experienced them both. (It often makes little difference what kind of explicit theory is held by the therapist, teacher, helper, etc. The really good therapist who may espouse a pessimistic Freudian theory, *acts* as if growth were possible. The really good teacher who espouses verbally a completely rosy and optimistic picture of human nature, will *imply* in actual teaching, a complete understanding and respect for

regressive and defensive forces. It is also possible to have a wonderfully realistic and comprehensive philosophy and belie it in practice, in therapy, or teaching or parenthood. Only the one who respects fear and defense can teach; only the one who respects health can do therapy.)

Part of the paradox in this situation is that in a very real way, even the "bad" choice is "good for" the neurotic chooser, or at least understandable and even necessary in terms of his own dynamics. We know that tearing away a functional neurotic symptom by force, or by too direct a confrontation or interpretation, or by a stress situation which cracks the person's defenses against too painful an insight, can shatter the person altogether. This involves us in the question of *pace* of growth. And again the good parent, or therapist or educator *practices* as if he understood that gentleness, sweetness, respect for fear, understanding of the naturalness of defensive and regressive forces, are necessary if growth is not to look like an overwhelming danger instead of a delightful prospect. He implies that he understands that growth can emerge only from safety. He *feels* that if a person's defenses are very rigid this is for a good reason and he is willing to be patient and understanding even though knowing the path in which the child "should" go.

Seen from the dynamic point of view, ultimately *all* choices are in fact wise, if only we grant two kinds of wisdom, defensive-wisdom and growth-wisdom. Defensiveness can be as wise as daring; it depends on the particular person, his par-

ticular status and the particular situation in which he has to choose. The choice of safety is wise when it avoids pain that may be more than the person can bear at the moment. If we wish to help him grow (because we know that consistent safety-choices will bring him to catastrophe in the long run, and will cut him off from possibilities that he himself would enjoy if only he could savor them), then all we can do is help him if he asks for help out of suffering, or else simultaneously allow him to feel safe and beckon him onward to *try* the new experience like the mother whose open arms invite the baby to try to walk. We can't *force* him to grow, we can only *coax* him to, make it more possible for him, in the trust that simply experiencing the new experience will make him prefer it. *Only* he can prefer it; no one can prefer it for him. If it is to become part of him, *he* must like it. If he doesn't, we must gracefully concede that it is not for him at this moment.

This means that the sick child must be respected as much as the healthy one, so far as the growth process is concerned. Only when his fears are accepted respectfully, can he dare to be bold. We must understand that the dark forces are as "normal" as the growth forces.

This is a ticklish task, for it implies simultaneously that we know what is best for him (since we *do* beckon him on in a direction we choose), and also that only he knows what is best for himself in the long run. This means that we must *offer* only, and rarely force. We must be quite ready, not only to beckon forward, but to respect retreat to lick wounds, to recover strength, to look over the situation from a safe vantage point, or even to regress to a previous mastery or a "lower" delight, so that courage for growth can be regained.

And this again is where the helper comes in. He is needed, not only for making possible growth forward in the healthy child (by being "available" as the child desires) and getting out of his way at other times, but much more urgently, by the person who is "stuck" in fixation, in rigid defenses, in safety measures which cut off the possibilities of growth. Neurosis is self-perpetuating; so is character structure. We can either wait for life to prove to such a person that his system doesn't work, i.e., by letting him eventually collapse into neurotic suffering, or else by understanding him and helping him to grow by respecting and understanding both his deficiency needs and his growth needs.

This amounts to a revision of Taoistic "let-be," which often hasn't worked because the growing child needs help. It can be formulated as "helpful let-be." It is a *loving* and *respecting* Taoism. It recognizes not only growth and the specific mechanism which makes it move in the right direction, but it also recognizes and respects the fear of growth, the slow pace of growth, the blocks, the pathology, the reasons for not growing. It recognizes the place, the necessity and the helpfulness of the outer environment without yet giving it control. It implements inner growth by knowing its mechanisms and by being willing to help *it* instead of merely being

hopeful or passively optimistic about it.

Our final formula then has the following elements:

1. The healthily spontaneous child, in his spontaneity, from within out, in response to his own inner Being, reaches out to the environment in wonder and interest, and expresses whatever skills he has,
2. To the extent that he is not crippled by fear, to the extent that he feels safe enough to dare.
3. In this process, that which gives him the delight-experience is fortuitously encountered, or is offered to him by helpers.
4. He must be safe and self-accepting enough to be able to choose and prefer these delights, instead of being frightened by them.
5. If he *can* choose these experiences which are validated by the experience of delight, then he can return to the experience, repeat it, savor it to the point of repletion, satiation or boredom.
6. At this point, he shows the tendency to go on to more complex, richer experiences and accomplishments in the same sector (again, if he feels safe enough to dare).
7. Such experiences not only mean moving on, but have a feedback effect on the Self, in the feeling of certainty ("This I like; that I don't for *sure*"); of capability, mastery, self-trust, self-esteem.
8. In this never ending series of choices of which life consists, the choice may

generally be schematized as between safety (or, more broadly, defensiveness) and growth, and since only that child doesn't need safety who already has it, we may expect the growth choice to be made by the safety-need gratified child. Only he can afford to be bold.

9. In order to be able to choose in accord with his own nature and to develop it, the child must be permitted to retain the subjective experiences of delight and boredom, as *the* criteria of the correct choice for him. The alternative criterion is making the choice in terms of the wish of another person. The Self is lost when this happens. Also this constitutes restricting the choice to safety alone, since the child will give up trust in his own delight-criterion out of fear (of losing protection, love, etc.).
10. If the choice is really a free one, and if the child is not crippled, then we may expect him ordinarily to choose progression forward.*

* A kind of pseudo-growth takes place very commonly when the person tries (by repression, denial, reaction-formation, etc.) to convince himself that an ungratified basic need has really been gratified, or doesn't exist. He then permits himself to grow on to higher-need-levels, which of course, forever after, rest on a very shaky foundation. I call this "pseudo-growth by bypassing the ungratified need." Such a need perseverates forever as an unconscious force (repetition compulsion).

11. The evidence indicates that what delights the healthy child, what tastes good for him, is also, more frequently than not, "best" for him in terms of far goals as perceivable by the spectator.

12. In this process the environment (parents, therapists, teachers) is important in various ways, even though the ultimate choice must be made by the child:

    a. it can gratify his basic needs for safety, belongingness, love and respect, so that he can feel unthreatened, autonomous, interested and spontaneous and thus dare to choose the unknown;

    b. it can help by making the growth choice positively attractive and less dangerous, and by making the regressive choice less attractive and more costly.

13. In this way the psychology of Being and the psychology of Becoming can be reconciled, and the child, simply being himself, can yet move forward and grow.

Each person, in his life situation, needs to finds "a place in space." This is no less true for learning environments — maybe more.

We tend to think of teaching only in accustomed ways, but Ashby helps us feel new kinds of solutions to the problem. He suggests many different kinds of places (existing, nonexisting, changing, closed, open, and more) for a creative learning environment. In addition, this article can help you get practical ideas from other articles that you read. The emphasis is not on working out logical applications, but on generating creative ideas for a learning environment.

GORDON ASHBY

A PLACE IN SPACE

You know . . . this whole business of environments and learning . . . and people . . . and things . . . all has to do with . . .

FINDING A PLACE IN SPACE

Finding a place to be . . . your place

I'd like to read you a little story about places . . .
It's called "The Table."

From *Big Rock Candy Mountain*. Reprinted by permission of the author.

He had been coming to the table now for twelve years,
Taking his place in front of his knife, fork, spoon, plate and cup.
He had been doing this, as he distinctly remembers, since the age of six.
This was his view:
Mother to the right,
Brother to the left,
Another brother to the right of mother, and father at the head of the table.
The view in front of him was always the same, silence had permeated this table arrangement for ten of the twelve years.

One day he decided to rearrange the placing of the dishes and glasses.
And even the chairs.

For some time it was startling and even disconcerting,
But it soon led to conversation and discussion.
He changed the places further in the months which followed, and eventually everyone participated in the rearrangements.

For there was much joy and excitement in finding a new place, in space.

It seems to me that the job ahead and the thing which needs doing has to do with "providing places for the living things of this earth."

And there are old possibilities which must be reinstated,

There are future possibilities which must be examined,
There are existing possibilities which must be retained,
And there are other possibilities yet to be imagined.

Many raise the question . . . "That's fine, but how do we get started?"
And to me . . . by looking at this group tonight we are started.

And once started . . . there is something we must all keep in mind.

"There are many ways of doing things . . . besides your own."

And that "change is the stuff of the universe."

With this in mind then . . . I would like to touch on some of my ideas about environments . . . or places.

As I said earlier . . . putting together environments is really a way of "seeing" . . . a way of looking at a situation . . . determining what might be done and acting on your feelings about it.

For example: let's look at existing places.

Existing places

Laundries look like laundries.
Print shops look like print shops.

Farms look like farms.
If you see a situation which looks like what is going on there, you know it immediately . . . If it does not reflect what is going on then there is a chance that something is amiss.
It's fairly sure that what is going on there they wish wasn't.
Have you ever gone to someone's home where there are three or four young children . . . and the place looks like a dentist's office.

The school certainly has much this same feeling . . .
How is it possible, that a place which is allowed to teach, and where children are allowed to learn (which means to make mistakes, fail, invent, take risks, etc.) looks like a place where everything is resolved.

How is it possible, that the first-grade classroom looks just like the ninth-grade classroom, except for the graffiti on the desks.

Non-existing places

Dreams are non-existing places.
Dreams look like dreams
Are fantasies only in books.
Dream places are new places . . . places which are not totally there but are in the process of becoming . . . dream places reflect all the things we would like to do but can't . . . because we can't fly.

Changing places

The forest is a place.
The city is a place.
The ocean is a place.
Changing places means moving spaces
. . . It means being here then being there
. . . All we need is a ride!

Closed places

Closed places are secret places.
Closed places are inside spaces.
Closed places don't open.
There is a need for closed places .·. places where you can get far away . . . and let yourself feel out your mind as well as your body . . . A place where, for a moment, you can get a hold of your life . . . and know no one else can know how.

Open places

Open places are open spaces.
Open spaces let out inside places.
Open places are never closed.
Closed places let you get hold of yourself, open places help you get hold of everything else . . . There is a real need to keep open places open . . . For Closed signs are cheap.

Hard places

Hard places are work places.
Hard places take our energy
And make our bodies part of our mind.
Hard places put us in contact with our
times . . . They make us aware of the fact
that maintaining our places in these spaces
is not paid for by the other guy . . . hard
places make us pay our dues.
For there is no such thing as a free
lunch . . .

Soft places

Soft places remind us of hard places.
Soft places give us energy
And make our bodies part of our whole.
Soft places are necessary also because animals, particularly Man, needs to have a
place out of the main stream where he
can float, without fear of being drowned.

Output places

Output places let us shout to the sky, and
let us hear what we have been thinking.
Output places are to make contact with
other members of our family.
Output places are places where we can
send our messages, make our sound, paint
our pictures. Output places let us express
what is going on in ourselves.

Input places

Input places are places to meet and greet.
Input places are necessary for guidance
for they tell us where we might be going.
Input places are the places where we find
out how we are doing. They give us the
chance to get supplies from others who
may have taken the trip before us . . . or
are able to see farther than we because
they stand on the shoulders of giants.

All these places are needed . . . It is not a
question of finding the right one . . . and
remember that in order to have places
there will be voids . . . that thing in between the places . . . There will always be
voids for that is the place provided by the
gods to expand into . . . to grow . . . to
create.

And it is the idea of continuous creation
that seems to stick in the craw of a lot of
folks these days . . . They seem to feel that
miracles have no place in the scheme of
things . . . I wonder how they explain the
presence of those things which already
exist in the universe? Now? . . . Either it
has always been here, or . . . it was created
out of nothing at some time . . . and either
way . . . it involves the miracle of creation.

In closing I would like to suggest a problem . . . an environment problem . . .

We all would like a creative learning environment . . . The problem then, to me, is
one of access, not of form . . . the problem
is:

"How do we get everyone in touch with
everyone else?"

Whew ! ! ! ! ! !

Carl Rogers describes three interpersonal
qualities in teachers that help learners: realness, acceptance, and empathic understanding. He gives examples of how teachers with whom he has been associated
have exhibited these qualities. It might be
interesting to explore how they foster the
conditions of safety and growth described
by Maslow. For example, do they affect the
way students think of themselves and subsequently act in response to the teacher?
It might also be helpful to consider what
teacher behaviors reflect personal attitudes
toward students.

CARL R. ROGERS

THE INTERPERSONAL RELATIONSHIP IN THE FACILITATION OF LEARNING

. . . It is in fact nothing short of a miracle that the modern methods of instruction have not yet entirely strangled the holy curiosity of inquiry; for this delicate little plant, aside from stimulation, stands mainly in need of freedom; without this it goes to wrack and ruin without fail.

—*Albert Einstein*

I wish to begin this paper with a statement which may seem surprising to some and perhaps offensive to others. It is simply this: Teaching, in my estimation, is a vastly overrated function.

Having made such a statement, I scurry to the dictionary to see if I really mean what I say. Teaching means "to instruct."

Abridged version of an article appearing in *Humanizing Education: The Person in the Process*, edited by Robert R. Leeper (Washington, D.C.: Association for Supervision and Curriculum Development, 1967), pages 1–9. Reprinted with permission of the Association for Supervision and Curriculum Development and Carl R. Rogers. Copyright © 1967 by the Association for Supervision and Curriculum Development.

Personally I am not much interested in instructing another. "To impart knowledge or skill." My reaction is, why not be more efficient, using a book or programmed learning? "To make to know." Here my hackles rise. I have no wish to *make* anyone know something. "To show, guide, direct." As I see it, too many people have been shown, guided, directed. So I come to the conclusion that I *do* mean what I said. Teaching is, for me, a relatively unimportant and vastly overvalued activity.

But there is more in my attitude than this. I have a negative reaction to teaching. Why? I think it is because it raises all the wrong questions. As soon as we focus on teaching, the question arises, what shall we teach? What, from our superior vantage point, does the other person need to know? This raises the ridiculous question of coverage. What shall the course cover? (Here I am acutely aware of the fact that "to cover" means both "to take in" and "to conceal from view," and I believe that most courses admirably achieve both these aims.) This notion of coverage is based on the assumption that what is taught is what is learned; what is presented is what is assimilated. I know of no assumption so obviously untrue. One does not need research to provide evidence that this is false. One needs only to talk with a few students.

But I ask myself, "Am I so prejudiced against teaching that I find no situation in which it is worthwhile? I immediately think of my experience in Australia only a few months ago. I became much interested in the Australian aborigine. Here is a group which for more than 20,000 years has managed to live and exist in a desolate environment in which a modern man would perish within a few days. The secret of his survival has been teaching. He has passed on to the young every shred of knowledge about how to find water, about how to track game, about how to kill the kangaroo, about how to find his way through the trackless desert. Such knowledge is conveyed to the young as being *the* way to behave, and any innovation is frowned upon. It is clear that teaching has provided him the way to survive in a hostile and relatively unchanging environment.

Now I am closer to the nub of the question which excites me. Teaching and the imparting of knowledge make sense in an unchanging environment. This is why it has been an unquestioned function for centuries. But if there is one truth about modern man, it is that he lives in an environment which is *continually changing*. The one thing I can be sure of is that the physics which is taught to the present day student will be outdated in a decade. The teaching in psychology will certainly be out of date in 20 years. The so-called "facts of history" depend very largely upon the current mood and temper of the culture. Chemistry, biology, genetics, sociology, are in such flux that a firm statement made today will almost certainly be modified by the time the student gets around to using the knowledge.

We are, in my view, faced with an entirely new situation in education where the goal of education, if we are to survive, is the *facilitation of change and learning.* The only man who is educated is the man who has learned how to learn; the man who has learned how to adapt and change; the man who has realized that no knowledge is secure, that only the process of *seeking* knowledge gives a basis for security. Changingness, a reliance on *process* rather than upon static knowledge, is the only thing that makes any sense as a goal for education in the modern world.

So now with some relief I turn to an activity, a purpose, which really warms me — the *facilitation of learning.* When I have been able to transform a group — and here I mean all the members of a group, myself included — into a community of *learners,* then the excitement has been almost beyond belief. To free curiosity; to permit individuals to go charging off in new directions dictated by their own interests; to unleash curiosity; to open everything to questioning and exploration; to recognize that everything is in process of change — here is an experience I can never forget. I cannot always achieve it in groups with which I am associated but when it is partially or largely achieved then it becomes a never-to-be-forgotten group experience. Out of such a context arise true students, real learners, creative scientists and scholars and practitioners, the kind of individuals who can live a delicate but ever-changing balance between what is presently known and the flowing, moving, altering, problems and facts of the future.

Here then is a goal to which I can give myself wholeheartedly. I see the facilitation of learning as the aim of education, the way in which we might develop the learning man, the way in which we can learn to live as individuals in process. I see the facilitation of learning as the function which may hold constructive, tentative, changing, process answers to some of the deepest perplexities which beset man today.

But do we know how to achieve this new goal in education, or is it a will-of-the-wisp which sometimes occurs, sometimes fails to occur, and thus offers little real hope? My answer is that we possess a very considerable knowledge of the conditions which encourage self-initiated, significant, experiential, "gut-level" learning by the whole person. We do not frequently see these conditions put into effect because they mean a real revolution in our approach to education and revolutions are not for the timid. But we do find examples of this revolution in action.

We know — and I will briefly describe some of the evidence — that the initiation of such learning rests not upon the teaching skills of the leader, not upon his scholarly knowledge of the field, not upon his curricular planning, not upon his use of audio-visual aids, not upon the programmed learning he utilizes, not upon his lectures and presentations, not upon an abundance of books, though each of these might at one time or another be utilized as an important resource. No, the facilitation of significant learning rests upon certain attitudinal qualities which exist in the personal *relationship* between the facilitator and the learner.

We came upon such findings first in the field of psychotherapy, but increasingly there is evidence which shows that these findings apply in the classroom as well. We find it easier to think that the intensive relationship between therapist and client might possess these qualities, but we are also finding that they may exist in the countless interpersonal interactions (as many as 1,000 per day, as Jackson [1966] has shown) between the teacher and his pupils.

What are these qualities, these attitudes, which facilitate learning? Let me describe them very briefly, drawing illustrations from the teaching field.

REALNESS IN THE FACILITATOR OF LEARNING

Perhaps the most basic of these essential attitudes is realness or genuineness. When the facilitator is a real person, being what he is, entering into a relationship with the learner without presenting a front or a façade, he is much more likely to be effective. This means that the feelings which he is experiencing are available to him, available to his awareness, that he is able to live these feelings, be them, and able to communicate them if appropriate. It means that he comes into a direct personal encounter with the learner, meeting him on a person-to-person basis. It means that he is *being* himself, not denying himself.

Seen from this point of view it is suggested that the teacher can be a real person in his relationship with his students. He can be enthusiastic, he can be bored, he can be interested in students, he can be angry, he can be sensitive and sympathetic. Because he accepts these feelings as his own he has no need to impose them on his students. He can like or dislike a student product without implying that it is objectively good or bad or that the student is good or bad. He is simply expressing a feeling for the product, a feeling which exists within himself. Thus, he is a person to his students, not a faceless embodiment of a curricular requirement nor a sterile tube through which knowledge is passed from one generation to the next.

It is obvious that this attitudinal set, found to be effective in psychotherapy, is sharply in contrast with the tendency of most teachers to show themselves to their pupils simply as roles. It is quite customary for teachers rather consciously to put on the mask, the role, the façade, of being a teacher, and to wear this façade all day removing it only when they have left the school at night.

But not all teachers are like this. Take Sylvia Ashton-Warner, who took resistant, supposedly slow-learning primary school Maori children in New Zealand, and let them develop their own reading vocabulary. Each child could request one word — whatever word he wished — each day, and she would print it on a card and give it to him. "Kiss," "ghost," "bomb," "tiger," "fight," "love," "daddy" — these are samples. Soon they were building sentences, which they could also keep. "He'll get a licking." "Pussy's frightened." The children simply never forgot these self-initiated learnings. Yet it is not my purpose to tell you of her methods. I want instead to give you a glimpse of her attitude, of the passionate realness which must have been as evident to her tiny pupils as to her readers. An editor asked her some questions and she responded: " 'A few cool facts' you asked me for. . . . I don't know that there's a cool fact in me, or anything else cool for that matter, on this particular subject. I've got only hot long facts on the matter of Creative Teaching, scorching both the page and me" (Ashton-Warner, 1963, p. 26).

Here is no sterile façade. Here is a vital *person,* with convictions, with feelings. It is her transparent realness which was, I am sure, one of the elements that made her an exciting facilitator of learning. She does not fit into some neat educational formula. She *is,* and students grow by being in contact with someone who really *is.*

Take another very different person, Barbara Shiel, also doing exciting work facilitating learning in sixth graders.[1] She gave them a great deal of responsible freedom, and I will mention some of the reactions of her students later. But here is an example of the way she shared herself with her pupils — not just sharing feelings of sweetness and light, but anger and frustration. She had made art materials freely available, and students often used these in

creative ways, but the room frequently looked like a picture of chaos. Here is her report of her feelings and what she did with them.

I find it (still) maddening to live with the mess — with a capital M! No one seems to care except me. Finally, one day I told the children . . . that I am a neat, orderly person by nature and the mess was driving me to distraction. Did they have a solution? It was suggested that they could have volunteers to clean up. . . . I said it didn't seem fair to me to have the same people clean up all the time for others — but it *would* solve it for me. "Well, some people *like* to clean," they replied. So that's the way it is (Shiel, 1966).

I hope this example puts some lively meaning into the phrases I used earlier, that the facilitator "is able to live these feelings, be them, and able to communicate them if appropriate." I have chosen an example of negative feelings, because I think it is more difficult for most of us to visualize what this would mean. In this instance, Miss Shiel is taking the risk of being transparent in her angry frustrations about the mess. And what happens? The same thing which, in my experience, nearly always happens. These young people accept and respect her feelings, take them into account, and work out a novel solution which none of us, I believe, would have suggested in advance. Miss Shiel wisely comments, "I used to get upset and feel guilty when I became angry — I finally realized the children could accept *my* feelings, too. And it is important for them to know when they've 'pushed me.' I have limits too" (Shiel, 1966).

Just to show that positive feelings, when they are real, are equally effective, let me quote briefly a college student's reaction, in a different course. ". . . Your sense of humor in the class was cheering; we all felt relaxed because you showed us your human self, not a mechanical teacher image. I feel as if I have more understanding and faith in my teachers now. . . . I feel closer to the students too." Another says, " . . . You conducted the class on a personal level and therefore in my mind I was able to formulate a picture of you as a person and not as merely a walking textbook." Or another student in the same course,

. . . It wasn't as if there was a teacher in the class, but rather someone whom we could trust and identify as a "sharer." You were so perceptive and sensitive to our thoughts, and this made it all the more "authentic" for me. It was an "authentic" *experience*, not just a class (Bull, 1966).

I trust I am making it clear that to be real is not always easy, nor is it achieved all at once, but it is basic to the person who wants to become that revolutionary individual, a facilitator of learning.

PRIZING, ACCEPTANCE, TRUST

There is another attitude which stands out in those who are successful in facilitating learning. I have observed this attitude. I have experienced it. Yet, it is hard to know what term to put to it so I shall use several. I think of it as prizing the learner, prizing his feelings, his opinions, his person. It is a caring for the learner, but a non-possessive caring. It is an acceptance of this other individual as a separate person, having worth in his own right. It is a basic trust — a belief that this other person is somehow fundamentally trustworthy.

Whether we call it prizing, acceptance, trust, or by some other term, it shows up in a variety of observable ways. The facilitator who has a considerable degree of this attitude can be fully acceptant of the fear and hesitation of the student as he approaches a new problem as well as acceptant of the pupil's satisfaction in achievement. Such a teacher can accept the student's occasional apathy, his erratic desires to explore byroads of knowledge, as well as his disciplined efforts to achieve major goals. He can accept personal feelings which both disturb and promote learning — rivalry with a sibling, hatred of authority, concern about personal adequacy. What we are describing is a prizing of the learner as an imperfect human being with many feelings, many potentialities. The facilitator's prizing or acceptance of the learner is an operational expression of his essential confidence and trust in the capacity of the human organism.

I would like to give some examples of this attitude from the classroom situation. Here any teacher statements would be properly suspect, since many of us would like to feel we hold such attitudes, and might have a biased perception of our qualities. But let me indicate how this attitude of prizing, of accepting, of trusting, appears to the student who is fortunate enough to experience it.

Here is a statement from a college student in a class with Morey Appell.

Your way of being with us is a revelation to me. In your class I feel important, mature, and capable of doing things on my own. I want to think for myself and this need cannot be accomplished through textbooks and lectures alone, but through living. I think you see me as a person with real feelings and needs, an individual. What I say and do are significant expressions from me, and you recognize this (Appell, 1959).

One of Miss Shiel's sixth graders expresses much more briefly her misspelled appreciation of this attitude, "You are a wounderful teacher period!!!"

College students in a class with Dr. Patricia Bull describe not only these prizing, trusting attitudes, but the effect these have had on their other interactions.

. . . I feel that I can say things to you that I can't say to other professors. . . . Never before have I been so aware of the other students or their personalities. I have never had so much interaction in a college classroom with my classmates. The climate of the classroom has had a very profound effect on me . . . the free atmosphere for discussion affected me . . . the general atmosphere of a particular session affected me. There have been many times when I have carried the discussion out of the class with me and thought about it for a long time.

. . . I still feel close to you, as though there were some tacit understanding between us, almost a conspiracy. This adds to the in-class participation on my part because I feel that at least one person in the group will react, even when I am not sure of the others. It does not matter really whether your reaction is positive or negative, it just *is*. Thank you.

. . . I appreciate the respect and concern you have for others, including myself. . . . As a result of my experience in class, plus the influence of my readings, I sincerely believe that the student-centered teaching method does provide an ideal framework for learning; not just for the accumulation of facts, but more important, for learning about ourselves in relation to others. . . . When I think back to my shallow awareness in September compared to the depth of my insights now, I know that this course has offered me a learning experience of great value which I couldn't have acquired any other way.

. . . Very few teachers would attempt this method because they would feel that they would lose the students' respect. On the contrary. You gained our respect, through your ability to speak to us on our level, instead of ten miles above us. With the complete lack of communication we see in this school, it was a wonderful experience to see people listening to each other and really communicating on an adult, intelligent level. More classes should afford us this experience (Bull, 1966).

As you might expect, college students are often suspicious that these seeming attitudes are phony. One of Dr. Bull's students writes:

. . . Rather than observe my classmates for the first few weeks, I concentrated my observations on you, Dr. Bull. I tried to figure out your motivations and purposes. I was convinced that you were a hypocrite. . . . I did change my opinion, however. You are not a hypocrite, by any means. . . . I do wish the course could continue. "Let each become all he is capable of being." . . . Perhaps my most disturbing question, which relates to this course is: When will we stop hiding things from ourselves and our contemporaries? (Bull, 1966).

I am sure these examples are more than enough to show that the facilitator who cares, who prizes, who trusts the learner, creates a climate for learning so different from the ordinary classroom that any resemblance is, as they say, "purely coincidental."

EMPATHIC UNDERSTANDING

A further element which establishes a climate for self-initiated, experiential learning is empathic understanding. When the teacher has the ability to understand the student's reactions from the inside, has a sensitive awareness of the way the process of education and learning seems *to the student*, then again the likelihood of significant learning is increased.

This kind of understanding is sharply different from the usual evaluative understanding, which follows the pattern of, "I understand what is wrong with you." When there is a sensitive empathy, however, the reaction in the learner follows something

of this pattern, "At last someone understands how it feels and seems to be *me* without wanting to analyze me or judge me. Now I can blossom and grow and learn."

This attitude of standing in the other's shoes, of viewing the world through the student's eyes, is almost unheard of in the classroom. One could listen to thousands of ordinary classroom interactions without coming across one instance of clearly communicated, sensitively accurate, empathic understanding. But it has a tremendously releasing effect when it occurs.

Let me take an illustration from Virginia Axline, dealing with a second grade boy. Jay, age 7, has been aggressive, a trouble maker, slow of speech and learning. Because of his "cussing" he was taken to the principal, who paddled him, unknown to Miss Axline. During a free work period, he fashioned a man of clay, very carefully, down to a hat and a handkerchief in his pocket. "Who is that?" asked Miss Axline. "Dunno," replied Jay. "Maybe it is the principal. He has a handkerchief in his pocket like that." Jay glared at the clay figure. "Yes," he said. Then he began to tear the head off and looked up and smiled. Miss Axline said, "You sometimes feel like twisting his head off, don't you? You get so mad at him." Jay tore off one arm, another, then beat the figure to a pulp with his fists. Another boy, with the perception of the young, explained, "Jay is mad at Mr. X because he licked him this noon." "Then you must feel lots better now," Miss Axline commented. Jay grinned and began to re-build Mr. X. (Adapted from Axline, 1944.)

The other examples I have cited also indicate how deeply appreciative students feel when they are simply *understood* — not evaluated, not judged, simply understood from their *own* point of view, not the teacher's. If any teacher set herself the task of endeavoring to make one non-evaluative, acceptant, empathic response per day to a pupil's demonstrated or verbalized feeling, I believe he would discover the potency of this currently almost non-existent kind of understanding.

Let me wind up this portion of my remarks by saying that when a facilitator creates, even to a modest degree, a classroom climate characterized by such realness, prizing, and empathy, he discovers that he has inaugurated an educational revolution. Learning of a different quality, proceeding at a different pace, with a greater degree of pervasiveness, occurs. Feelings — positive and negative, confused — become a part of the classroom experience. Learning becomes life, and a very vital life at that. The student is on his way, sometimes excitedly, sometimes reluctantly, to becoming a learning, changing being.

This chapter from Bruner's book Toward a Theory of Instruction is of great value to anyone who is considering the psychological conditions that stimulate learning. Bruner's view is that human beings possess internal motives that can be channeled effectively into educational activities. He discusses in some detail intrinsic sources of motivation such as curiosity, competence, identification, and reciprocity. You may find it helpful, as you read this article, to reflect on past learning experiences, in school and in other circumstances, in which you felt very involved. Do the factors Bruner describes adequately explain your involvement?

JEROME S. BRUNER

THE WILL TO LEARN

The single most characteristic thing about human beings is that they learn. Learning is so deeply ingrained in man that it is almost involuntary, and thoughtful students of human behavior have even speculated that our specialization as a species is a specialization for learning. For, by compari-

Reprinted by permission of the publishers from Jerome S. Bruner, *Toward a Theory of Instruction*, Cambridge, Mass.: The Belknap Press of Harvard University Press, Copyright © 1966 by the President and Fellows of Harvard College.

son with organisms lower in the animal kingdom, we are ill equipped with pre-pared reflex mechanisms. As William James put it decades ago, even our instinctive behavior occurs only once, thereafter being modified by experience. With a half century's perspective on the discoveries of Pavlov, we know that man not only is conditioned by his environment, but may be so conditioned even against his will.

Why then invoke the idea of a "will to learn"? The answer derives from the idea of education, a human invention that takes a learner beyond "mere" learning. Other species begin their learning afresh each generation, but man is born into a culture that has as one of its principal functions the conservation and transmission of past learning. Given man's physical characteristics, indeed, it would be not only wasteful but probably fatal for him to reinvent even the limited range of technique and knowledge required for such a species to survive in the temperate zone. This means that man cannot depend upon a casual process of learning; he must be "educated." The young human must regulate his learning and his attention by reference to external requirements. He must eschew what is vividly right under his nose for what is dimly in a future that is often incomprehensible to him. And he must do so in a strange setting where words and diagrams and other abstractions suddenly become very important. School demands an orderliness and neatness beyond what the child has known before; it requires restraint and immobility never asked of him before; and often it puts him in a spot where he does not *know* whether he knows and can get no indication from anybody for minutes at a time as to whether he is on the right track. Perhaps most important of all, school is away from home with all that fact implies in anxiety, or challenge, or relief.

In consequence of all this the problem of "the will to learn" becomes important, indeed exaggerated. Let us not delude ourselves: it is a problem that cannot be avoided, though it can be made manageable, I think. We shall explore what kinds of factors lead to satisfaction in "educated" learning, to pleasure in the practice of learning as it exists in the necessarily artificial atmosphere of the school. Almost all children possess what have come to be called "intrinsic" motives for learning. An intrinsic motive is one that does not depend upon reward that lies outside the activity it impels. Reward inheres in the successful termination of that activity or even in the activity itself.

Curiosity is almost a prototype of the intrinsic motive. Our attention is attracted to something that is unclear, unfinished, or uncertain. We sustain our attention until the matter in hand becomes clear, finished, or certain. The achievement of clarity or merely the search for it is what satisfies. We would think it preposterous if somebody thought to reward us with praise or profit for having satisfied our curiosity. However pleasant such external reward might be, and however much we might come to depend upon it, the external reward is something added. What activates and satisfies curiosity is something inherent in the cycle of activity by which we express curiosity. Surely such activity is biologically relevant, for curiosity is essential to the survival not only of the individual but of the species. There is considerable research that indicates the extent to which even nonhuman primates will put forth effort for a chance to encounter something novel on which to exercise curiosity. But it is clear that unbridled curiosity is little more than unlimited distractibility. To be interested in everything that comes along is to be interested in nothing for long. Studies of the behavior of three-year-olds, for example, indicate the degree to which they are dominated from the outside by the parade of vivid impressions that pass their way. They turn to this bright color, that sharp sound, that new shiny surface. Many ends are beyond their reach, for they cannot sustain a steady course when the winds shift. If anything, they are "too curious." They live by what psychologists have long called the laws of primary attention: attention dominated by vividness and change in the environment. There has been much speculation about the function of this early and exhausting tempo of curiosity. One neuropsychologist, Donald Hebb, has suggested that the child is drinking in the world, better to construct his neural "models" of the environment. And, it is plain that a stunted organism is produced by depriving an infant of the rich diet of impressions on which his curiosity normally feeds with such extravagance. Animals raised in homogenized environments show crippling deficits in their later ability to learn and to transfer what they have learned. Children "kept in the attic" by misguided or psychotic parents show the same striking backwardness. Indeed, even the children who have suffered the dull, aseptic environment of backward foundling homes often show a decline in intelligence that can be compensated only by vigorous measures of enrichment. So surely, then, an important early function is served by the child's omnivorous capacity for new impressions. He is sorting the world, storing those things that have some recurrent regularity and require "knowing," discriminating them from the parade of random impressions.[1]

But if attention is to be sustained, directed to some task and held there in spite of temptations that come along, then obviously constraints must be established. The voluntary deployment of curiosity, so slowly and painfully mastered, seems to be supported in part by the young child's new-found capacity to "instruct himself," literally to talk to himself through a sustained sequence. And in part the steadying force seems to be the momentum of concrete overt acts that have a way of sustaining the attention required for their completion by shutting off irrelevant impressions. In time, and with the development of habitual activities, and of language, there emerges more self-directed attention, sometimes called derived primary attention. The child is held steady not so much by vividness as by the habitual round of activity that now demands his attention. Little enough is known about how to help a child become master of his own attention, to sustain it over a long, connected sequence. But while young children are notoriously wandering in their attention, they can be kept in a state of rapt and prolonged attentiveness by being told compelling stories. There may be something to be learned from this observation. What makes the internal sequence of a story even more compelling than the distractions that lie outside it? Are there comparable properties inherent in other activities? Can these be used to train a child to sustain his curiosity beyond the moment's vividness?

Observe a child or group of children building a pile of blocks as high as they can get them. Their attention will be sustained to the flashing point until they reach the climax when the pile comes crashing down. They will return to build still higher. The drama of the task is only its minor virtue. More important is the energizing lure of uncertainty made personal by one's own effort to control it. It is almost the antithesis of the passive attraction of shininess and the vivid. To channel curiosity into more powerful intellectual pursuits requires precisely that there be this transition from the passive, receptive, episodic form of curiosity to the sustained and active form. There are games not only with objects, but with ideas and questions — like

Twenty Questions — that provide such a disciplining of the channeling of curiosity. Insofar as one may count on this important human motive — and it seems among the most reliable of the motives — then it seems obvious that our artificial education can in fact be made less artificial from a motivational standpoint by relating it initially to the more surfacy forms of curiosity and attention, and then cultivating curiosity to more subtle and active expression. I think it is fair to say that most of the success in contemporary curriculum building has been achieved by this route. When success comes, it takes the form of recognition that beyond the few things we know there lies a domain of inference: that putting together the two and two that we have yields astonishing results. But this raises the issue of competence, to which we must turn next.

For curiosity is only one of the intrinsic motives for learning. The drive to achieve competence is another. Professor Robert White puts the issue well:

According to Webster, competence means fitness or ability, and the suggested synonyms include capability, capacity, efficiency, proficiency, and skill. It is therefore a suitable word to describe such things as grasping and exploring, crawling and walking, attention and perception, all of which promote an effective — a competent — interaction with the environment. It is true, of course, that maturation plays a part in all these developments, but this part is heavily overshadowed by learning in all the more complex accomplishments like speech or skilled manipulation. I shall argue that it is necessary to make competence a motivational concept; there is *competence motivation* as well as competence in its more familiar sense of achieved capacity. The behavior that leads to the building up of effective grasping, handling, and letting go of objects, to take one example, is not random behavior that is produced by an overflow of energy. It is directed, selective, and persistent, and it continues not because it serves primary drives, which indeed it cannot serve until it is almost perfect, but because it satisfies an intrinsic need to deal with the environment.[2]

Observations of young children and of the young of other species suggest that a good deal of their play must be understood as practice in coping with the environment. Primatologists describe, for example, how young female baboons cradle infant baboons in their arms long before they produce their own offspring. In fact, baboon play can be seen almost entirely as the practice of interpersonal skills. Unlike human children, baboons never play with objects, and this, the anthropologists believe, is connected with their inability to use tools when they grow up. And there is evidence that early language mastery, too, depends on such early preparation. One linguist recently has shown how a two-year-old goes on exploring the limits of language use even after the lights are out, parents removed, communication stopped, and sleep imminent.[3]

The child's metalinguistic play is hard to interpret as anything other than pleasure in practicing and developing a new skill. Although competence may not "naturally" be directed toward school learning, it is certainly possible that the great access of energy that children experience when they "get into a subject they like" is made of the same stuff.

We get interested in what we get good at. In general, it is difficult to sustain interest in an activity unless one achieves some degree of competence. Athletics is the activity par excellence where the young need no prodding to gain pleasure from an increase in skill, save where prematurely adult standards are imposed on little leagues formed too often to ape the big ones. A custom introduced some years ago at the Gordonstoun School in Scotland has become legendary. In addition to conventionally competitive track and field events within the school, there was established a novel competition in which boys pitted themselves against their own best prior record in the events. Several American schools have picked up the idea and, while there has been no "proper evaluation," it is said that the system creates great excitement and enormous effort on the part of the boys.

To achieve the sense of accomplishment requires a task that has some beginning and some terminus. Perhaps an experiment can serve again as a parable. There is a well-known phenomenon known to psychologists by the forbidding name of the Zeigarnik Effect. In brief, tasks that are interrupted are much more likely to be returned to and completed, and much more likely to be remembered, than comparable tasks that one has completed without interruption. But that puts the matter super-ficially, for it leaves out of account one factor that is crucial. The effect holds only if the tasks that the subject has been set are ones that have a structure — a beginning, a plan, and a terminus. If the tasks are "silly" in the sense of being meaningless, arbitrary, and without visible means for checking progress, the drive to completion is not stimulated by interruption.

It seems likely that the desire to achieve competence follows the same rule. Unless there is some meaningful unity in what we are doing and some way of telling how we are doing, we are not very likely to strive to excel ourselves. Yet surely this too is only a small part of the story, for everybody does not want to be competent in the same activities, and some competencies might even be a source of embarrassment to their possessors. Boys do not thrill to the challenge of sewing a fine seam (again, in our culture), nor girls to becoming competent street fighters. There are competencies that are appropriate and activating for different ages, the two sexes, different social classes. But there are some things about competence motives that transcend these particulars. One is that an activity (given that it is "approved"), must have some meaningful structure to it if it requires skill that is a little bit beyond that now possessed by the person — that it be learned by the exercise of effort. It is probably the combination of the two that is critical.

Experienced teachers who work with the newer curricula in science and mathematics report that they are surprised at the

eagerness of students to push ahead to next steps in the course. Several of the teachers have suggested that the eagerness comes from increased confidence in one's ability to understand the material. Some of the students were having their first experience of understanding a topic in some depth, of going somewhere in a subject. It is this that is at the heart of competence motives, and surely our schools have not begun to tap this enormous reservoir of zest.

While we do not know the limits within which competence drives can be shaped and channeled by external reward, it seems quite likely that they are strongly open to external influence. But channelization aside, how can education keep alive and nourish a drive to competence — whether expressed in farming, football, or mathematics? What sustains a sense of pleasure and achievement in mastering things for their own sake — what Thorstein Veblen referred to as an instinct for workmanship? Do competence motives strengthen mainly on their exercise, in whatever context they may be exercised, or do they depend also upon being linked to drives for status, wealth, security, or fame?

There are, to begin with, striking differences among cultures and between strata within any particular society with respect to the encouragement given to competence drives. David McClelland, for example, in writing about the "achieving society," comments upon the fact that in certain times and places one finds a flowering of achievement motivation strongly supported by the society and its institutions and myths alike.[4] Emphasis upon individual responsibility and initiative, upon independence in decision and action, upon perfectibility of the self — all of these things serve to perpetuate more basic competency motives past childhood.

But cultures vary in their evaluation of *intellectual* mastery as a vehicle for the expression of competence. Freed Bales, for example, in comparing Irish and Jewish immigrant groups in Boston, remarks that the Jewish, much more than the Irish, treat school success and intellectuality as virtues in their own right as well as ways of upward mobility.[5] The reasons can be found in history. Herzog and Zborowski, in their book on eastern European Jewish communities, suggest that the barrier erected against Jews' entering other professions may have helped foster the cultivation of intellectual excellence as a prized expression of competence.[6]

A culture does not "manage" these matters consciously by the applications of rewards and reproofs alone. The son of the rabbi in the eastern European *stetl* was not punished if he wished to become a merchant rather than a Talmudic scholar, and, indeed, if he chose to become the latter he typically went through long, extrinsically unrewarding, and arduous training to do

so. More subtle forces are at work, all of them fairly familiar but too often overlooked in discussing education. One of them is "approval." The professional man is more "respected" than the manual worker. But that scarcely exhausts the matter. Respected by whom? Contemporary sociologists speak of the approval of one's "reference group" — those to whom one looks for guides to action, for the definition of the possible, for ultimate approbation. But what leads *this* individual to look to *that* particular reference group?

What appears to be operative is a process we cavalierly call identification. The fact of identification is more easily described than explained. It refers to the strong human tendency to model one's "self" and one's aspirations upon some other person. When we feel we have succeeded in "being like" an identification figure, we derive pleasure from the achievement and, conversely, we suffer when we have "let him down." Insofar as the identification figure is also "a certain kind of person" — belongs to some group or category — we extend our loyalties from an individual to a reference group. In effect, then, identification relates one not only to individuals, but to one's society as well.

While this account is oversimplified, it serves to underline one important feature of identification as a process — its self-sustaining nature. For what it accomplishes is to pass over to the learner the control of punishment and reward. Insofar as we now carry our standards with us, we achieve a certain independence from the

immediate rewards and punishments meted out by others.

It has been remarked by psychologists that identification figures are most often those who control the scarce psychological resources that we most desire — love, approval, sustenance. Let me skip this issue for a moment and return to it later.

The term identification is usually reserved for those strong attachments where there is a considerable amount of emotional investment. But there are "milder" forms of identification that are also important during the years of childhood and after. Perhaps we should call those who serve in these milder relationships "competence models." They are the "on the job" heroes, the reliable ones with whom we can interact in some way. Indeed, they control a rare resource, some desired competence, but what is important is that the resource is attainable by interaction. The "on the job" model is nowhere better illustrated than in the manner in which the child learns language from a parent. The tryout-correction-revision process continues until the child comes to learn the rules whereby sentences are generated and transformed appropriately. Finally he develops a set of productive habits that enable him to be his own sentence maker and his own corrector. He "learns the rules of the language." The parent is the model who, by interaction, teaches the skill of language.

In the process of teaching a skill the parent or teacher passes on much more. The teacher imparts attitudes toward a subject and, indeed, attitudes toward learning itself. What results may be quite inadvertent. Often, in our schools, for example, this first lesson is that learning has to do with remembering things when asked, with maintaining a certain undefined tidiness in what one does, with following a train of thought that comes from outside rather than from within and with honoring right answers. Observant anthropologists have suggested that the basic values of the early grades are a stylized version of the feminine role in the society, cautious rather than daring, governed by a ladylike politeness.

One recent study by Pauline Sears underlines the point.[7] It suggests that girls in the early grades, who learn to control their fidgeting earlier and better than boys, are rewarded for excelling in their "feminine" values. The reward can be almost too successful, so that in later years it is difficult to move girls beyond the orderly virtues they learned in their first school encounters. The boys, more fidgety in the first grade, get no such reward and as a consequence may be freer in their approach to learning in later grades. Far more would have to be known about the other conditions present in the lives of these children to draw a firm conclusion from the findings, but it is nonetheless suggestive. There are surely many ways to expand the range of competence models available to children. One is the use of a challenging master teacher, particularly in the early grades. And there is film or closed-circuit television, opening up enormously the range of teachers to

whom the student can be exposed. Filmed teaching has, to be sure, marked limits, for the student cannot interact with an image. But a kind of pseudo interaction can be attained by including in the television lesson a group of students who are being taught right on the screen, and with whom the student can take common cause. Team teaching provides still another approach to the exemplification of a range of competences, particularly if one of the teachers is charged specially with the role of gadfly. None of the above is yet a tried practice, but pedagogy, like economics and engineering, often must try techniques to find not only whether they work, but how they may be made to work.

I would like to suggest that what the teacher must be, to be an effective competence model, is a day-to-day working model with whom to interact. It is not so much that the teacher provides a model to *imitate*. Rather, it is that the teacher can become a part of the student's internal dialogue — somebody whose respect he wants, someone whose standards he wishes to make his own. It is like becoming a speaker of a language one shares with somebody. The language of that interaction becomes a part of oneself, and the standards of style and clarity that one adopts for that interaction become a part of one's own standards.

Finally, a word about one last intrinsic motive that bears closely upon the will to learn. Perhaps it should be called reciprocity. For it involves a deep human need to respond to others and to operate jointly with them toward an objective. One of the important insights of modern zoology is the importance of this intra-species reciprocity for the survival of individual members of the species. The psychologist Roger Barker (1963) has commented that the best way he has found to predict the behavior of the children whom he has been studying in great detail in the midst of their everyday activities is to know their situations. A child in a baseball game behaves baseball; in the drugstore the same child behaves drugstore. Situations have a demand value that appears to have very little to do with the motives that are operative. Surely it is not simply a "motive to conform"; this is too great an abstraction. The man who is regulating his pressure on the back of a car, along with three or four others, trying to "rock it out," is not so much conforming as "fitting his efforts into an enterprise." It is about as primitive an aspect of human behavior as we know.

Like the other activities we have been discussing, its exercise seems to be its sole reward. Probably it is the basis of human society, this response through reciprocity to other members of one's species. Where joint action is needed, where reciprocity is required for the group to attain an objective, then there seem to be processes that carry the individual along into learning, sweep him into a competence that is required in the setting of the group. We know precious little about this primitive motive to reciprocate, but what we do know is that it can furnish a driving force to learn as well. Human beings (and other species as well) fall into a pattern that is required by the goals and activities of the social group in which they find themselves. "Imitation" is not the word for it, since it is usually not plain in most cases what is to be imitated. A much more interesting way of looking at what is involved is provided by the phenomenon of a young child learning to use the pronouns "I" and "you" correctly. The parent says to the child, "You go to bed now." The child says, "No, you no go to bed." We are amused. "Not *me* but *you*," we say. In time, and after a surprisingly brief period of confusion, the child learns that "you" refers to himself when another uses it, and to another person when he uses it — and the reverse with "I." It is a prime example of reciprocal learning. It is by much the same process that children learn the beautifully complicated games they play (adult and child games alike), that they learn their role in the family and in school, and finally that they come to take their role in the greater society.

The corpus of learning, using the word now as synonymous with knowledge, is reciprocal. A culture in its very nature is a set of values, skills, and ways of life that no one member of the society masters. Knowledge in this sense is like a rope, each strand of which extends no more than a few inches along its length, all being inter-

twined to give a solidity to the whole. The conduct of our educational system has been curiously blind to this interdependent nature of knowledge. We have "teachers" and "pupils," "experts" and "laymen." But the community of learning is somehow overlooked.

What can most certainly be encouraged — and what is now being developed in the better high schools — is something approximating the give and take of a seminar in which discussion is the vehicle of instruction. This is reciprocity. But it requires recognition of one critically important matter: you cannot have both reciprocity and the demand that everybody learn the same thing or be "completely well rounded" in the same way all the time. If reciprocally operative groups are to give support to learning by stimulating each person to join his efforts to a group, then we shall need tolerance for the specialized roles that develop — the critic, the innovator, the second helper, the cautionary. For it is from the cultivation of these interlocking roles that the participants get the sense of operating reciprocally in a group. Never mind that this pupil for this term in this seminar has a rather specialized task to perform. It will change. Meanwhile, if he can see how he contributes to the effectiveness of the group's operations on history or geometry or whatnot, he is likely to be the more activated. And surely one of the roles that will emerge is that of auxiliary teacher — let it, encourage it. It can only help in relieving the tedium of a

classroom with one expert up here and the rest down there.

At the risk of being repetitious, let me restate the argument. It is this. The will to learn is an intrinsic motive, one that finds both its source and its reward in its own exercise. The will to learn becomes a "problem" only under specialized circumstances like those of a school, where a curriculum is set, students confined, and a path fixed. The problem exists not so much in learning itself, but in the fact that what the school imposes often fails to enlist the natural energies that sustain spontaneous learning — curiosity, a desire for competence, aspiration to emulate a model, and a deep-sensed commitment to the web of social reciprocity. Our concern has been with how these energies may be cultivated in support of school learning. If we know little firmly, at least we are not without reasonable hypotheses about how to proceed. The practice of education does, at least, produce interesting hypotheses. After all, the Great Age of Discovery was made possible by men whose hypotheses were formed before they had developed a decent technique for measuring longitude.

You will have noted by now a considerable de-emphasis of "extrinsic" rewards and punishments as factors in school learning. There has been in these pages a rather intentional neglect of the so-called Law of Effect, which holds that a reaction is more likely to be repeated if it has previously been followed by a "satisfying state of affairs." I am not unmindful of the notion of reinforcement. It is doubtful, only, that "satisfying states of affairs" are *reliably* to be found outside learning itself — in kind or harsh words from the teacher, in grades and gold stars, in the absurdly abstract assurance to the high school student that his lifetime earnings will be better by 80 percent if he graduates. External reinforcement may indeed get a particular act going and may even lead to its repetition, but it does not nourish, reliably, the long course of learning by which man slowly builds in his own way a serviceable model of what the world is and what it can be.

In a critical analysis of our schools, Thelen argues that the teacher should use the natural tendencies of children to involve them in learning, rather than suppressing and ignoring those tendencies. He discusses how natural tendencies potentially fit together within a coherent, sequential model of inquiry for use in the classroom. The use of groups within his framework also illustrates how Maslow's concepts of safety and growth can be dealt with at the same time. Principles for generating inquiry-oriented learning experiences given in the article deserve careful reading. Particularly helpful is Thelen's discussion on using confronting activities to initiate an inquiry.

HERBERT A. THELEN

THE EDUCATIVE PROCESS

To be able to direct our own thinking about a body of phenomena, we need to assert a proposition about how we intend to seek understanding. I submit that the most significant and inclusive proposition for illuminating the study of teaching is that *in any situation there are some tendencies "going our way" and some going in other ways.* The teacher's job is to maximize the first and minimize the second. He must set such conditions as are under his control in such a way that whatever educable tendencies the child has become actualized to a greater extent than tendencies in other directions. But — and here is something many teachers would like to forget — the teacher has to deal with *both* sorts of tendencies, for conflict between the two

Abridged and reproduced by special permission from *The Journal of Applied Behavioral Science,* "Some Classroom Quiddities for People-Oriented Teachers," by Herbert A. Thelen, pages 274–81. Copyright © 1965, NTL Institute for Applied Behavioral Science.

Previous publication: Earlier draft under same title in *Bulletin of the Bureau of Social Service* (Lexington, Ky., College of Education), June 1964, 36 (4), 39–52.

types is the normal condition of the learner at the beginning of a new unit or activity; and the teacher's behavior decides which kind of tendency will dominate. To a high degree, the art of the sophisticated teacher manifests itself in the ability to capitalize on the wide range of natural tendencies that exist in the class: to work with them rather than suppress them and to teach the child socially constructive, higher-reward behaviors through which his tendencies can be expressed. Thus, for example, behaviors which express resistance and opposition to the work and to the teacher are capitalized on by one teacher and their energy is channeled into useful learning; whereas another teacher attempts to punish or suppress them. One teacher accepts any and all responses as challenges and weaves the contradictory and inconsistent behaviors of the students into a reality-seeking dialogue; whereas the other teacher acts like a censor, calling the responses he wants "relevant" and the others "irrelevant." For his students, the experience is one of continually trying to guess what the teacher has in mind — up to the time when they find out that the reward they can get is incommensurate with the effort. (From then on, they simply seduce the teacher into giving his lecture, which is what he really has been wanting all along. But who listens?)

What, then, are these "natural tendencies" and under what conditions do they occur? Let us "walk through" a lesson being taught in the classroom.

Consider first the natural tendencies through which persons get "involved." At the beginning of a lesson, the teacher hopes to get the students "involved," interested, intrigued, "ready" to learn more. The tendencies he needs to facilitate are those through which the student "takes on" some part of the environment and has thoughts and feelings about it. There are (at least) three tendencies that can be capitalized on: (a) if stimuli are too sparse, the tendency is to "fill out" the picture by speculation (projection); (b) if stimuli are overwhelming, the tendency is to select certain ones and ignore others; (c) if stimuli violate expectations, the tendency is to try to rationalize away the inconsistency.

The teacher capitalizes on these tendencies, respectively, when he (a) presents a chemical demonstration silently and then asks the students to decide what were the hypotheses, the data, and the conclusions; or when he hands the student a document and asks him to reconstruct the way of life and community out of which the document came. To "overwhelm" (b) calls for a "rich" experience: a field trip, a dramatic movie, an exciting role-played scene. The invitation that unleashes the tendency is simply the question: What is the thing that strikes you as most important (significant, interesting, troublesome, and so on) about the field trip, movie, or other? That is, given all these things we might talk about,

what things do you have the most need to talk about? The third tendency (c) is set in motion when expectations are violated: the demonstration that doesn't work, the prediction that fails, the behavior that is unexpected. Professor Bruner thinks that children have intuitive feelings about such things as levers and weights; and when the yardstick balance tilts up instead of down, the pupils become highly "involved." Any unaccustomed behavior of the teacher will involve the students and preoccupy them; and if the unaccustomedness is related to the subject discipline, it may develop readiness to learn; but if it is related to interpersonal manners, it is more likely to develop readiness to react defensively to the teacher — which is not the same thing.

In short, speculation, selection, and resolution of inconsistency are behaviors most persons "normally" engage in when given the opportunity. To get the students to do these things, the teacher must give them the chance; and he does this by carefully arranging the input from the environment.

The two most usual ways to prevent these normal tendencies from taking over are: (a) to make oneself (i.e., the teacher's person) the object of concern, and this is easily accomplished by threatening behavior which arouses interpersonal anxiety; and (b) to do all the work oneself, so that the students really have no role at all except that of bystanders.

Consider second the tendency of "involved" persons to seek "meaning."

When most persons are "involved" in something, they tend to want to talk about it with certain other persons. These other persons do not normally include the teacher; the other persons are peers, and, more especially, friends. The need, following initial involvement and arousal, is to "get hold" of the experience both emotionally and conceptually, and this requires one to formulate thoughts and name the feelings one has. This is a risky enterprise, and it calls for interpersonal support from someone who has neither the power nor the inclination to engage in reprisals for what may turn out to be deviate or antisocial thoughts and feelings. In a classroom, after getting the children involved, the teacher actualizes this second tendency most effectively when he asks them to select themselves into small groups to compare notes and decide what they think and feel about the confronting involvement situation.

The tendency to associate with others in order to cope with one's own feelings, doubts, and anxieties is the fundamental cause of "friendship" or "psyche" groups, such as bull sessions. When members of a large group, such as a class, are forced to associate with one another day after day, smaller psyche groups form; students, we say, begin to "relate" to one another interpersonally; and, especially when the lesson is dull, they fill in the void and the anxiety it produces by talking with one another. (This annoys many teachers, and they seek advice on "classroom management"; they hope to suppress this busy-buzz, this "inattentiveness," these cliques. A tug of war develops between teacher and class, and the teacher is likely to resort to threats and punishment: he makes and enforces "rules," preaches, punishes by making the lesson even duller. In short, he tries to suppress a very basic and very natural tendency instead of either arranging to capitalize on it or by setting conditions under which the tendency is minimized.)

Consider third the tendency to seek closure amidst semi-conflicting and untested opinions. After finding out that one has many different ideas, and that his friends have additional ideas, one seeks to know what is "right" or "true." That is, to seek authority (authorization, legitimization) for an answer rather than to leave the perceptual-cognitive field wide open. But this is not a strong tendency because the psyche group, through its "acceptance" of ideas and its nonreprisal basis of operation, actually encourages toleration of all personal or subjective opinions — which is why it works so well in encouraging people to formulate and express their ideas. In effect, for the truth-seeking (or rationalizing) tendency to be strong, we have to reverse the field of the small subgroups. This reversed field can be found in the *class-as-a-whole*, a miniature society with an authoritative leader, with interpersonal competition for recognition and scarce rewards (grades) and (most important for learning) with a sense of common purpose in planning and carrying out activities. To distinguish it from the psyche group, Jen-

nings named it a sociogroup; or it could also be called a "work" group.

When the teacher brings the class back together, he has the problem of capitalizing on the wide range of ideas the students have just formulated and rehearsed with one another. There are three ways in which he might proceed. He could ask the class what they think is the *right* answer to some question that was presumably introduced along with the confronting stimuli: What do you think this document is? What was the purpose of the silent demonstration I showed you? In the ensuing discussion, he would respond (in effect) with "right" or "wrong" to whatever the students said. He would, presumably, be noting which students were right or wrong, and they would understand that this would influence their grades. He would also, probably, compliment the right ones and ignore, correct, or punish the wrong ones. A second possibility would be to ask for the *best* answer, thus inviting students to try to "top" one another. Focus on the right answer appeals to desire for certainty, whereas focus on the best answer invites competition.

Seeking authoritative answers and competing with others are indeed natural human activities. But encouragement of these by the teacher is less educative than a third possibility which depends on the sociogroup's sense of common purpose. Under common purpose, cooperation rather than competition is dominant; for the members join forces to cope with some situation, achieve some objective, meet

some demand made on the group as a whole. The chief requirement for the cooperative situation is that each individual believes that he needs the others in order to do something he needs or wants to do: in other words, he is a member of the group in order to put his contributions together with those of others in order to get something done that he cannot do by himself. If the others are to help him in this undertaking, then it follows that they, too, must value the undertaking (for some reason); and to proceed effectively, there must be some agreement on what the undertaking is and what its purposes are. It is by no means required that the individuals must want or value the undertaking for all the same reasons (which is lucky, because such a condition never occurs); but it is required that there be public agreement and understanding of at least the conditions external to the group that their activity is to change.

Thus, for example, the class can agree to design and carry out an experiment. This requires that they decide what objects to manipulate through what actions, but it does not require that all the students achieve or even seek the same personal gratifications. To one individual, the experiment is a situation in which to imagine himself a scientist; to another, it means checking some hunches against nature; to a third, it might mean mostly taking on a challenging task and completing it successfully. Cooperation, then, is the coordination of roles taken by the students as members of the group, not the development of identical personal views and feelings.

We conclude, then, that following the free exchange in subgroups, the teacher should draw out the opinions of the students and then invite the group to plan some further activity. In the planning discussion, opinions are neither *right* nor *best;* they are useful. And the reward comes not from the teacher as authoritative expert nor as encouraging father but rather from the satisfaction of influencing the class through its adoption of or "building" on one's ideas. The teacher's role under these conditions is that of methodologist-consultant, helping the class put its ideas together, confronting them with further facts in order to get them to sharpen, qualify, or assess the usefulness of their ideas.

So far, we have considered three tendencies: (a) the tendency of persons to get "involved" under certain conditions; (b) the tendency of psyche groups to form from "involved" persons so they can come to terms with their own involvements; and (c) the tendency, in sociogroups, to assess ideas and give them some backing more authoritative than personal hunches. These tendencies, properly encouraged, produce some of the most important activities of educational learning.

The class, like most other groups, either alternates or blends the two characters,

psyche and socio. The artistic teacher knows when to "push" on the task and when to "break the tension" by encouraging more intimate and expressive behaviors. The student has a place in both the psyche and socio structures: sociometrically, he is part of a friendship network; in relation to tasks, he has a reputation and a range of roles that people come to expect of him. To be secure, he needs to know (or at least not be anxious about not knowing) his place in *both* structures.

Let us look at the teacher's use of the sociogroup to help students follow up the ideas they expressed in their small psyche groups. I think that seeking authoritative "truth" (right answers) and competing with others for scarce rewards (best answers) may well express tendencies in *individuals,* but I do not believe that carrying out these activities is a legitimate or natural purpose of groups. Groups do not get together to see who is right, and they do not get together merely to engage in intermember competition. These things can go on in groups, but then only for reasons that should not exist in the classroom. Granted that individuals want authority and want to compete — or at least some of them do, an effective voluntary group seduces the authority only when it needs to agree on some assumption that cannot be tested within their experience and yet has to be settled in order to be able to take further steps in planning; and it engages in intermember competitive struggles only when it has not yet developed satis-

factory leadership. On the other hand, planning and carrying out activities together and on behalf of the individuals is, of course, the whole rationale for society.

This reading will be helpful to those who want to involve students at the elementary school level. (If you read it along with the following reading, which presents applications at the secondary level, you will probably be able to imagine a whole range of possibilities for all grades, from K through 12.) Hassett and Weisberg help us to break with some of the typical assumptions we hold for traditional classrooms. They see the use of classroom space as an important aspect of a creative learning environment. As you read this article, try to think of examples of "turn-on agents" and "interest areas" that would apply to the students you might be teaching.

JOSEPH D. HASSETT AND ARLINE WEISBERG

CLASSROOMS COME IN ALL SHAPES AND SIZES

Teachers respond with some of the following answers when confronted with the question, "How do you relate the environment to your classroom?" "I teach a unit on pollution"; "I motivate a cleanup campaign"; "We go for a nature walk"; or "We plant seeds in the spring." Relating the environment to the classroom involves a great deal more in environmental education than taking children outdoors or making them aware of the degradation of the environment. On the one hand, it involves creating an exciting, pleasant, motivating classroom environment for the child to work and discover in, and on the other hand, utilizing the positive elements in

From Joseph D. Hassett and Arline Weisberg, *Open Education: Alternatives Within Our Tradition*, © 1972. Reprinted by permission of Prentice-Hall, Inc., Englewood Cliffs, New Jersey.

the child's home environment as links or turn-on agents to work towards meaningful education experiences. To accomplish this, it is necessary to make some changes in the basic physical structure of the classroom.

One way to begin this process would be to start with one corner of the room. Designate that area as the "child center," the "discovery area," or the "project area." If no corner is available, then a space marked off by a table, a large cardboard carton, or an unused easel would do for a beginning. (See Figure 1.) Discuss with your children the kinds of material they like to "mess about" with. Observe the

things they bring to school or carry in their pockets and brainstorm the learning possibilities of these objects. In the lower grades it is fruitful to begin with a pile of "junk": boxes, bags, cardboard rollers, bits of colorful fabric, wood shavings, sticks, scissors, or paste. See what kinds of things the children fashion from these objects. Give the children space to display their projects and time to talk about them. Furnish the children with a way to record the details of the various projects. Set aside a specific hour each week for a specific number of children to work in the discov-

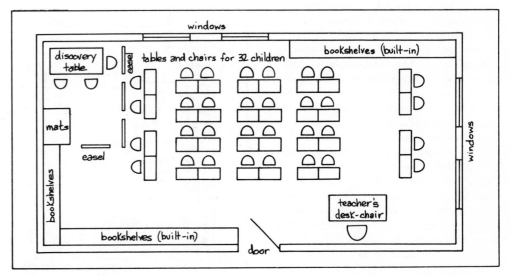

Figure 1.

ery area. Choose a time when the entire class is working on individual work or programmed instruction or a quiet activity. Train the children to use the area and stress "Take care, clean up, and share."

As the children begin to use the materials creatively and to become involved in projects, they will spill out of the area into other sections of the classroom. They will need more room to work, to store unfinished projects, and to proudly display accomplishments. By this time the teacher is also more comfortable with the change that is taking place and he is no longer threatened by the gradual alteration of his physical surroundings. The classroom must be rearranged to allow for more freedom of movement and more child-centered areas within the confines of four walls. It is possible to create flow, interest, excitement, and privacy within the four walls of the classroom, and still maintain a classroom in which traditional programs can coexist with environmental education.

Most of the space in the traditional classroom is taken up by the desks and chairs. Is it absolutely necessary, or even desirable, to have a desk and a chair for every child to use for the entire day? It is only necessary if the teacher is committed to keeping all of the children confined to their seats all day. Perhaps half the tables and chairs can be used to form interest centers in the four corners of the room, with bookcases, easels, or panels as dividers. Perhaps there can be a reading cor-

ner with mats on the floor, and an art corner with paper runners that can be disposed of at cleanup time. (See Figure 2.) Most of the New York City classrooms are provided with movable furniture that can be used for a variety of purposes in the course of the day.

When the need arises for drawing the entire class together for a sharing period or to teach a particular skill, it is a fairly simple matter to pick up the paper runner in the center and gather the chairs and mats to the center of the room. If writing is necessary, inexpensive clipboards serve as a writing surface and help children keep their papers together until they are ready to transfer them into a notebook or an

envelope. A clipboard with a string fastened to it (so it can be hung about the child's neck) serves as a portable writing surface and leaves the child's hands free to work on his project. . . .

Some teachers prefer to start the change in the physical environment with a small corner and gradually branch out; others prefer to start with the entire class at once. One of the teachers in our workshop arranged his tables and chairs into four groups of eight children each. (See Figure 3.) Based on his observations of the children's interests, he collected four different groups of materials: group 1 — tangram puzzles, protractors, Cuisenaire rods, task cards; group 2 — fabrics, dyes, detergents,

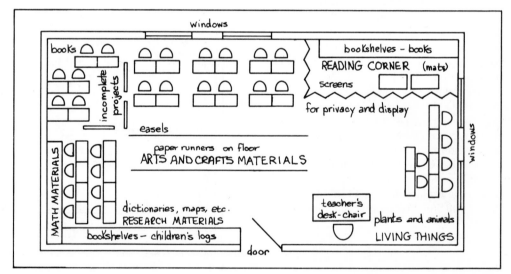

Figure 2.

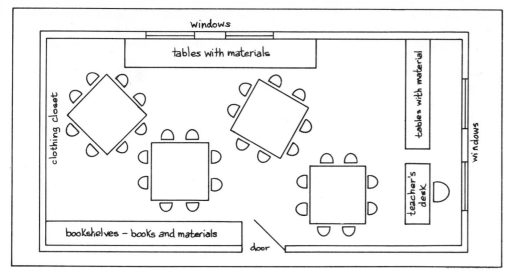

Figure 3.

their leisure-time preferences are, and what their aspirations are. Take note of things they are playing with in the desk as they *seem* to be listening to the social studies lesson. If tiny model cars turn on second-grade Johnny, then consider what other materials might be grouped with model cars to lead Johnny into a learning experience. Perhaps some clay to build a road or blocks to build a bridge might help him learn how people travel in a big city. In a fifth-grade classroom that uses model cars as a turn-on, some of the children might be interested in exploring pollution, advertising campaigns, or motors. The turn-on agent is the bridge from teacher to child. Exploration of the turn-on agent leads to the development of learning experiences.

Although the turn-on agents will vary with the age level and academic level of the children, certain materials have proved to have universal appeal. Most children, regardless of age or reading ability, respond to an animal in the classroom. There is a wide variety of animals to choose from, and the care of an animal is an educational experience.

One sixth-grade class adopted a guinea pig. They looked up the history of the guinea pig and located the guinea pig's indigenous areas on the map. One group avidly read about the care and comfort of guinea pigs so they could provide him with an adequate home. Another group weighed, measured, and listened to his

bleaches; group 3 — various size pieces of wood, tools, nails, how-to books for making things; group 4 — geoboards, pattern pieces, shapes. Each group of eight children formed an interest center. The tables and bookshelves were filled with scales, thermometers, measuring devices, writing materials, paints, rulers, empty jars and bottles, books — in short, basic materials that a child might need to pursue an interest or complete a project. One of the first topics of discussion with the entire class was techniques for communicating while keeping the noise level down. The children devised an elaborate set of signals. Certain pupils were elected to alert the others when the noise level was getting

too high. Each day a short discussion period was held to evaluate the day's work. . . .

The most important initial element in the success of the environmental education approach is the selection of the materials. How does the teacher ascertain what specific materials will turn on the thirty-four or thirty-five different individuals who challenge his creativity every day? The first and most obvious way is to get to know your children. With the younger children, discuss their interests with them, observe them at play, notice the kinds of things they bring to school and carry in their pockets. With the older children, circulate a questionnaire designed to find out what heartbeat to make sure he remained in good health. Rusty the guinea pig became the inspiration for drawing, creative writing and, ultimately, a film. The children were motivated to investigate other animals. The class concern for the guinea pig involved all the disciplines — reading, mathematics, social studies, science, hygiene, art, and group interaction.

Construction materials and tools attract many children. Building is an activity with a very definite foreseeable conclusion, and it affords a good feeling of success when the project is complete. Along the way it requires creativity, reading directions, proper handling of tools, measuring, and making judgments. The completed construction may then lead to a new interest; for example, the finished table can serve as a base for a puppet theater, or the counter for a rock sale.

Odd bits and scraps of fabric, paper and string, grouped with paper bags, sticks, odd socks, paper plates, and other materials from which puppets can be constructed, may lead to a variety of skills and interests. Many children will verbalize more readily behind the mask of a puppet. The development of language arts skills is increased through the writing and dramatizing of puppet shows. Scenery adds a new dimension to the activity. A modern scene, a scene of long ago, a scene in a foreign country, these make social studies live for the child. The researching and copying of different kinds of costumes help him to become aware of how other people live. Role playing is an effective tool in helping children play out some of their aggressions.

Other teachers have successfully used spinning tops, rocks, shells, macaroni, and foreign money as turn-on agents. These may not necessarily interest your class. Perhaps something that is your hobby will be successful with your children because of your own enthusiasm. Think of the learning experiences in learning how to cook or to sew, in collecting stamps, making pottery, or raising tropical fish and you realize that you have the entire environment to draw from.

Once the teacher has observed her children and selected her materials, there is an operational sequence that has proven helpful in many classrooms. In the workshops, we call step one "helping your children develop a rapport with materials." The second step is "brainstorming the materials." This process enables the teacher not only to be aware of the educational possibilities of the turn-on agent, but to be prepared with questions, supplementary materials, and suggestions to help the children in their explorations.

Let us now consider a hypothetical situation. A fourth-grade teacher has arranged her room so that she has space for three interest areas. After observing her children, she has decided upon model cars, sand, and fabrics as possible turn-on agents. Her second task is to investigate these materials herself and to brainstorm all the learning experiences she can imagine. This process of brainstorming is one of the most valuable tools in the use of this method. As you work with a material such as sand, let your mind associate freely with all the possibilities involving sand. No matter how farfetched or ridiculous some of them may sound, make note of all the possibilities. Then group your possibilities into areas of exploration; some will be discarded as improbable, some as too sophisticated for the grade level, while others will lend themselves to grouping or clusters. These groupings or clusters are leads to the kinds of questions you will ask, the kinds of suggestions you will make, and the kinds of supplementary materials you will select. Practice brainstorming. It is a valuable activity for any kind of teaching. The three charts below are examples of the brainstorming process (see Figures 4, 5, and 6).

This brainstorming and elimination process enables the teacher to anticipate the problems, to prepare other materials to group with the turn-on agent, and to prepare questions and activity cards to guide those children who need a great deal of direction. This final chart, which we call a flow chart, is only a guide, not a rigid plan. Some of the flow areas will be discarded as uninteresting or unsuitable to the age level of the children. Some children may go off in a totally unanticipated direction, and the teacher will have to expand her thinking to include their needs. The flow chart also enables the teacher to provide for books, an integral part of each interest area.

The teacher is now ready to take the third step, to introduce the materials to the children and review the routines and

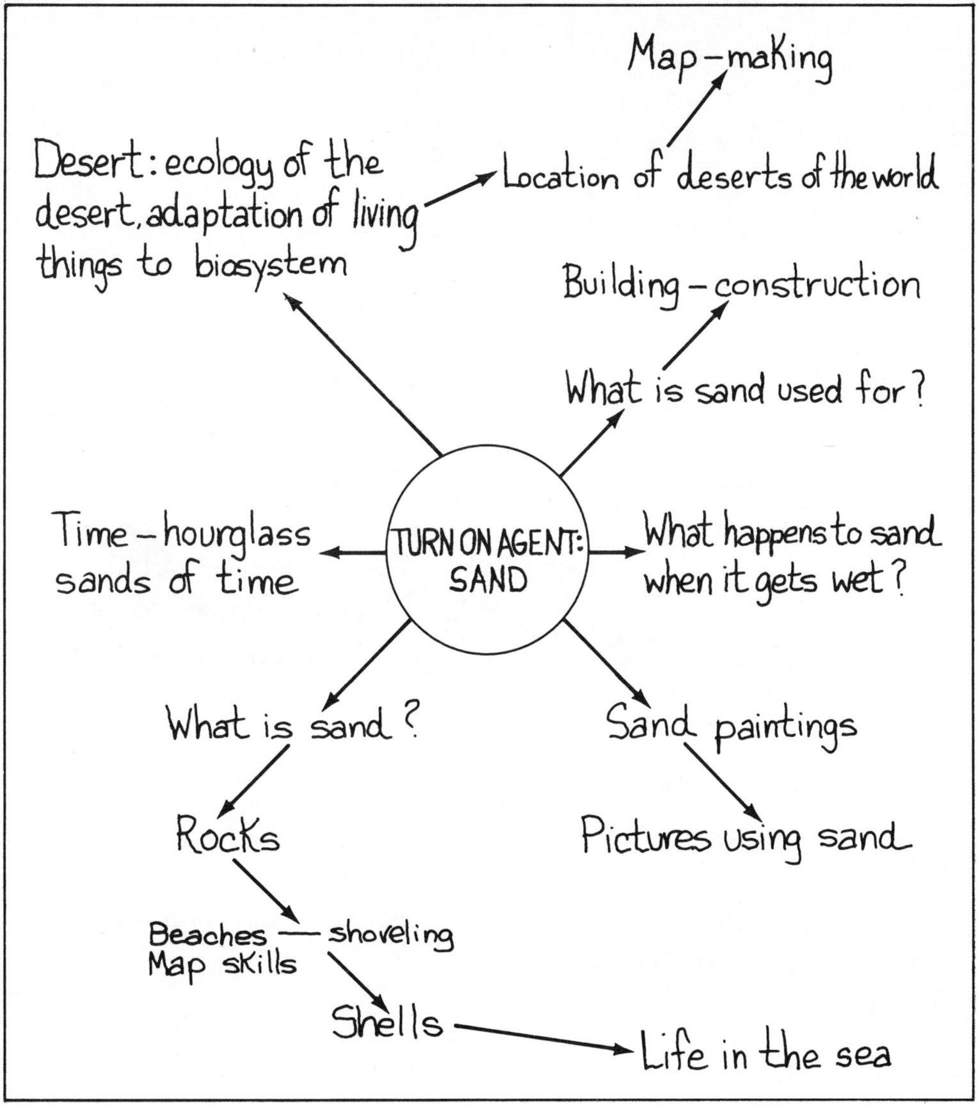

Figure 4.

responsibilities for using them. A time limit should be set for the initial experience, providing enough time for the children to choose an area, become acquainted with what's available, start to "mess about," and go through the routine of cleanup. At least twenty minutes time at the end of the session should be provided for calling together the entire group and evaluating the experience. Many clues to a more satisfactory experience the next time will come from the children themselves.

"But," says the first-grade teacher, "this is no help to me. My children cannot read, they are not mature enough to make judgments, and they need constant direction. It will never work." How shall we deal with this problem? Think in terms of some of the concepts we want the first-graders to develop: light/heavy, hard/soft, bright/dull, colors, size, and number. Consider how the exploration of many manipulative materials can lead to the development of these concepts. A cup of sand and a cup of water on a balance scale, bits of colored fabrics pasted on a collage, and tiny cars running through a street of blocks are valuable activities; a first-grader can learn the meaning behind these concepts from experience. A young child learns by repeating a process over and over again. If the materials are readily available, the child may experiment until he himself is satisfied that he understands enough to verbalize about what he has experienced. Then picture books can be made, articles labeled, and experiences acted out.

On a table in a first-grade classroom there are various-sized magnets, paper clips, clothespins, corks, pins, thumbtacks, plastic discs, buttons, and fasteners. A pan of water is also provided. Children can experiment in several directions. They can find out which objects sink and which objects float. They can investigate which objects are attracted by the magnet, or if the magnet pulls through water. If some children choose to tell about what they have experienced, the teacher can incorporate their observations into an experience chart. Others who prefer to draw about their discoveries can combine their drawings to form a short picture book, and the teacher may help with writing the captions. Still other children may elect to demonstrate or act out their experiences.

There is a distinct possibility that the initial turn-on materials may not produce the desired outcomes. This indicates not a failure of the method, but a misjudgment on the part of the teacher. Perhaps these particular children need materials more relevant to their daily environment or their own individual personalities. A walk around the neighborhood or a discussion of the objects the children carry in their pockets might prove fruitful. Perhaps these children would be intrigued by something totally *alien* to their environment, such as a telescope or an iguana.

If the child is to have freedom of choice, and if the motivating materials are to foster valuable learning experiences, then a great variety of materials is necessary. We

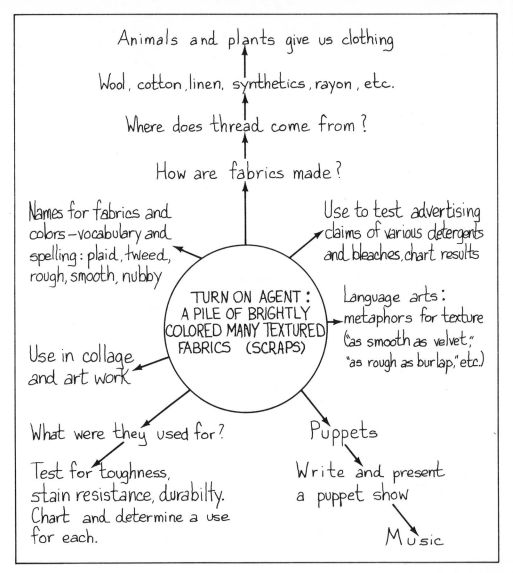

Figure 5.

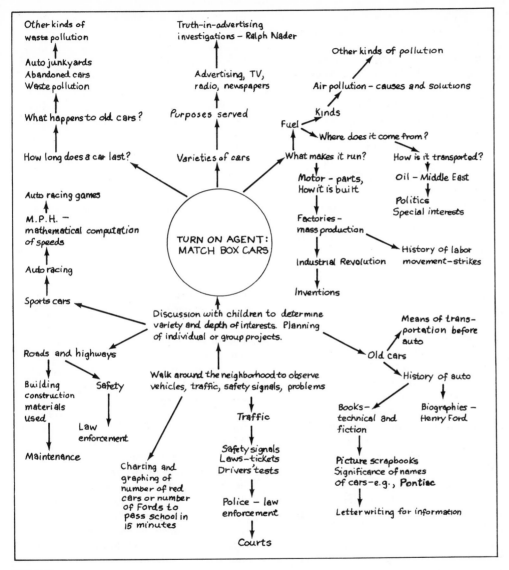

Figure 6.

Other kinds of waste pollution

Auto junkyards
Abandoned cars
Waste pollution

What happens to old cars?

How long does a car last?

Auto racing games

M.P.H. — mathematical computation of speeds

Auto racing

Sports cars

Roads and highways

Building construction materials used

Safety

Law enforcement

Maintenance

Truth-in-advertising investigations – Ralph Nader

Advertising, TV, radio, newspapers

Purposes served

Varieties of cars

Other kinds of pollution

Air pollution – causes and solutions

Kinds

Fuel

Where does it come from?

What makes it run?

Motor – parts, How it is built

Factories – mass production

Industrial Revolution

Inventions

How is it transported?

Oil – Middle East

Politics
Special interests

History of labor movement–strikes

TURN ON AGENT: MATCH BOX CARS

Discussion with children to determine variety and depth of interests. Planning of individual or group projects.

Walk around the neighborhood to observe vehicles, traffic, safety signals, problems

Charting and graphing of number of red cars or number of Fords to pass school in 15 minutes

Traffic

Safety signals
Laws–tickets
Drivers' tests

Police – law enforcement

Courts

Means of transportation before auto

Old cars

History of auto

Books – technical and fiction

Biographies – Henry Ford

Picture scrapbooks
Significance of names of cars–e.g., Pontiac

Letter writing for information

are aware of the cuts in the educational budget, and we have fielded many queries from teachers and principals. The most common question is, "Where can I get materials?" The school building itself is a gold mine of materials. We walk through building after building and see shelves of supplies covered with dust. Your first source of supply is your school: the science materials in the closet, the arts and crafts materials, paper, paste, scissors, string, and the standard math materials. Another source of supply is junk: egg cartons, fabric scraps, boxes, jars, paper rollers, tubes, broken clocks, radios, and so on. One teacher sends a "treasure-hunt" note through her school once a month and is deluged with supplies. "I am looking for empty spools, paper-towel rollers, pop sticks, and empty jars." Free and inexpensive materials available are listed in booklets in the school library. A teacher's parents can be helpful, especially if they work in factories, and might supply scraps of wood, leather, and Styrofoam packing materials. Become a saver and a collector. A construction site or a rubble heap in your neighborhood may be a valuable source of materials and deserves investigation. You may discover something as interesting as the tiles Deborah brought into her third-grade classroom, which led to an entire project.

Purchase basic items when money is available, such as a good spring scale, balance scales, and a terrarium. Catalogs from the suppliers of school materials are invaluable. They not only provide ideas about the potential use of materials, but many of the materials can be duplicated by the children themselves using available scrap materials. Upper-grade classes can construct balance scales for use by the entire school. One very enterprising teacher removed the "rockers" from an old rocking chair and used them to construct two balance scales for her class. A wire coathanger and paper cups make a simple balance. The construction of the material itself is a learning experience. It requires planning, following directions, and trial and error. The classroom should become a workshop in which each child is encouraged to try his powers and develop his skills. Trial and error becomes a positive experience because the child has an opportunity to learn from his failure and try again.

A great source of materials is the outdoors itself. The physical environment of the classroom may be enclosed by four walls, but the children must learn to envision their environment as encompassing all of nature, all of the neighborhood, and all of the home. We extend the physical environment to include these elements by having the children bring in materials from home and from the neighborhood. To balance the confines of the neighborhood, it is periodically necessary to take the children to other environments — for example, the ghetto child to a "natural area," to collect materials and impressions that

can be brought back into the classroom and investigated further. How can the inner-city child envision what life was like when the Indians roamed New York City if he has never had the chance to explore the ecosystem of a natural area? Pictures and words won't do it, but walking in a dense growth, finding wild berries, and coming upon small animals will help to convey the impression to his senses.

Teachers have often said, "But you don't know my children. Changing the physical environment of the classroom will make them insecure. They will become disruptive. I have children who won't do one thing unless I keep after them. The children will fight and steal." No one denies that these problems happen. They occur in any method of teaching. But we would like to add one very essential ingredient to the school situation, and that ingredient is trust. Trust in the natural curiosity of children; trust in your ability to help them into new routines; and trust in their ability to learn, given the right stimulation. Get out of their way for part of the day and trust that they will choose some activity on their true level of operation, and from there you can guide them forward. Aim for the kind of physical environment that allows not only individual differences in ability, but also individual differences in personality. Give them a controlled opportunity to deal with their aggressions, hostilities, and antisocial traits in the classroom.

Environmental education necessitates a gradual physical change in the classroom

environment. The goal is to move from a teacher-dominated physical environment to a child-centered one. Take a good look at your classroom, note its limitations, but don't let them stop you. Focus on the areas possible for interest centers. Explore the interests and capabilities of your children. Discuss with them the routines and responsibilities for working in a new way. Select your turn-on agents and brainstorm them. Gather your materials and let your children try the new method. Evaluate with your children the effectiveness of the first trial and improve with each successive discovery period.

This article is a description of the author's own teaching experience. Bender applies concepts of the open classroom to teaching English at the high school level. She achieves a high degree of involvement through different kinds of subject-related and method-oriented structuring. Special areas of the classroom are used to focus on reading, writing, newspapers, periodicals, dreams, and spelling and vocabulary, each in a unique way. To ensure that the enterprise does not become chaotic, she has maintained files, points, records, and systematic evaluation and feedback schedules. Her article is a good example of how we can be aware of Ashby's different kinds of places in space. As you read this article, imagine comparable applications for other high school subjects.

IRENE BENDER

OPEN ENGLISH

My first few years in the classroom were spent traditionally. I was the teacher-as-imparter-of-knowledge — and wisdom and understanding. We did Shakespeare, Word Wealth, Spelling Demons, Compositions, and Noun Clauses. For the most part, I loved it and was good at it. My classes were lively, dramatic, loaded with papers, homework, and lots of tests. What happened was that it slowly dawned on me that I was not so much a teacher as a performer. And the name of the show was "Five Acts a Day." This meant that I literally had to be "on stage" for each of my five classes each day, and when I wasn't the class fell apart. All the energy, creativity, direction, motivation, evaluation, and stimuli came directly from me to all the kids. I operated on the premise that if a teacher is creative, and really puts out every period, then she's bound to have successful classes. In short, I had to assume all the responsibility for everyone's learning (and loving it) or *not* learning.

I might have continued to accept that premise, except that it became fairly obvious that with all I was putting out, I was only reaching perhaps five kids per class.

From The School District of Philadelphia, *Open Education Curriculum and Instruction . . .* 1, no. 1 (Dec. 1972); 1, no. 2 (June 1973). Copyright © 1976 by Irene Bender. Reprinted by permission.

Something was wrong. I was beginning to feel:

1. The rewards weren't worth it.
2. Besides not reaching most of the kids, I was *losing* them.
3. I was only one person out of 35–40 in the classroom. Why did everything have to come from me?
4. What I was teaching them was not particularly important.
5. I had to find a better way. . . .

. . . I wanted first of all to stop performing, and to stop short-circuiting the flow of communications and relationships in the classroom. I wanted to feel more comfortable with myself while teaching, and to stop viewing kids as merely sentence splicers without knowing a whole lot more about them. I wanted them to start learning about themselves and the ways they do things, so that they could start to feel more control over who they were and what they did. I wanted to reduce the discrepancy between what happened in the real world and in school. I wanted them to work together more, independently of me. I wanted time to talk to kids individually, and time for them to talk with each other. As interested as I was in affective growth, I was nonetheless interested in the basic thinking, reading, and writing skills; I wanted most of all to organize a program in which these components could be balanced. I wanted a classroom that could engage kids in discovering what they were about so that they could share impressions,

feel less impotent in school and in life, as well as make more sense out of school and life.

Once the goals became clear, the job was to create a classroom with the kinds of organization and structure that would develop a climate for the learning experiences, the relationships, and the behaviors I desired. To accomplish this, stations in the following language arts-oriented activities were placed around a large rectangular room:

Reading. This consisted of a huge table on which were arranged a variety of hard cover novels, anthologies, short stories, biographies, essays, and poetry. These were collected and displayed on the basis of interest and variety, genre, level of difficulty, and length — trying as much as possible to get an array of all of the above characteristics. On this table we placed from five to ten copies of each book, which came from our English bookroom. We filled an adjacent bookcase with single copies of books contributed by faculty, book salesmen, students, parents, visitors, and all of our relatives. There were also two revolving wire stands on which we placed $100.00 worth of the best paperback books we could find. The reading area also contained several folders with lists of reading activities, plus our "lie-down-and-read" section, compliments of the gym department (mats) and our school nurse (for the bedspreads that covered the mats).

Writing. On a few pushed-together desks we placed a folder with activity lists and directions, some pencils, writing paper, and a nearby typewriter.

Newspapers. This area consisted of a podium, the top of which was used for activity lists and directions plus one copy of each of the three major daily newspapers. On the shelves inside we kept old newspapers, Sunday editions (local papers and *The New York Times*), and various community papers.

Periodicals. Although we operated without any budget, one of the ways in which the administration supported us was to direct us to pieces of furniture and equipment that, although assigned to our school, were not in use. The paperback stands mentioned before are an example, as are our magazine racks. On these racks we placed copies of whatever we could beg or borrow. Again, we ran a faculty drive, we plundered the basements of family and friends, and accepted donations from our school library and the offices of doctors and dentists (those with sympathetic nurses).

Drama. We placed this station as far as we could from the reading area. There were opportunities here for kids to give speeches, read plays, and do improvisations, role playing, and pantomiming. On a big low table we placed lots of play an-

thologies and "Scope" magazines, which became very popular. Close to this table was a small area enclosed by three portable bulletin boards. This area was used for the dramatic activities listed above. Between the reading materials and the enclosed area was a desk with all the appropriate instructions and activities.

Spelling / vocabulary. Against one wall on a work table we placed several grammar texts, lots of dictionaries, some vocabulary books, pencils, paper, and specific worksheets for vocabulary, spelling, and word work. All of the references were used by students working in other activities as they were needed.

———

At each center there were approximately twenty-five activities for each area. Some were designed for individual work, some for small groups, while others could be done in pairs. Most could be converted to service any number of students, though we encouraged them to consider no more than six when working in small groups. These activities were initially teacher-constructed and were predominantly value-oriented and "affective" as those were the orientations of the teachers. As soon as the activities had been designed, and the stations were complete, the students were given instructions about how the room was to operate: Each student would get a manila folder which he would use for keeping his written work — the work he did in response to activities in the various areas.

His work would provide the basis for individualization in that the teachers would use the work in evaluating, diagnosing, and prescribing with each student. The more work a student did, the more points he collected, the higher his grade would be, since point accumulations were translated into letter grades on report cards. Essentially, then, students would be rewarded for effort, and to the extent that learning followed effort, they were rewarded for learning.

Because the work in each student's folder became so important in the learning process, we decided on the following routines:

1. All work would be kept in a file cabinet in the classroom at the end of each period. We wanted to be able to take home whole folders to evaluate at home in order to get a sense of any student's progress as well as "mark" any particular papers.

2. All students were required to accumulate points in at least five areas per report period, but by the end of the school year they must have worked in each area at least once. In this way students were forced to expose themselves to each aspect of the language program as it had developed thus far.

3. Because we placed no grade on student work, we required their work in ink, neatly done, and student-checked. Student checkers were used in our room for several reasons. First, we wanted to get the best quality of our students' work as possible. We wanted to evaluate the work without

the carelessness, the misspellings, the omitted words, etc. Secondly, we wanted to attach some "status" to having basic language skills — student checkers were given points for checking. Also, we wanted to encourage students to begin to share their work with others in our attempt to make it a student-centered room, and finally, we wanted to encourage a climate of student cooperation rather than competition where the responsibility for learning was not owned by the teacher alone, but a shared venture by all the classroom participants.

4. Once the work was selected, completed, and checked, it went into the student's folder where the teacher could evaluate it. Depending on the student's needs, interests, skills or lack of skills, the teacher praised, corrected, suggested, commented, prescribed and appropriately reacted to the work. Points were or were not given for the activity; the teacher might have wanted a student to rewrite a section of the paper before points were assigned, or the teacher might have wanted to increase the points for an outstanding work, or a student might have been asked to complete an exercise from a grammar book with relation to some writing problem in the paper, or the paper might have been worthy of the designated points as it was. In this way, each student and his writing personality was handled individually. Moreover, the teacher could comfortably spend time individually with each student and she was confident that all of her other students were working.

For many months, this comprised a large part of our program and routine. Most student/teacher relationships were formed through this process, and this individualized approach helped to set a climate for learning, for taking a student "where he was" and helping him from that point toward his personal direction rather than towards some "group" goal that fitted no one in reality. Through this process, we grew to know and understand our students not just as spellers, comma-splicers, etc. but as "whole" human beings, which is how they came to perceive us as well.

Because of our interest in value clarification and affective education, we scheduled time for students to participate in small group discussion, role-plays, fantasies, "magic-circle" activities, "gripe" sessions, value-clarifying exercises, and mirroring and feedback devices. We sometimes held these in the area designated for "dramatic" activities when it wasn't being used, or on the gym mats, or within the room in chairs or the floor, away from wherever the hubbub of activity was for the day. At these sessions, we required students at least to participate in terms of listening: One of our fears concerned losing those students who seemed to be desperately lost and forgotten.

These group activities constituted the second major "routine" of our project. Often we used the concerns raised in the students' works as the basis for our affective group sessions as well as concerns, fears, doubts, frustrations, and problems we heard as we related with the students

individually. In keeping with our goals, we tried to balance the cognitive, the skill-centeredness with the affective domain.

To summarize thus far, anyone walking into our room at a given time might see any of the following: students thinking and writing individually, in pairs, or small groups; eight students looking for and through activities; six students reading a play; ten students with a teacher having a discussion; fifteen students, five of whom might be lying on the gym mats, all with various kinds of reading materials in their hands; four students having a discussion of their own; a few pairs of students talking quietly; a teacher with a student going over work, with two or three students waiting or even participating in the evaluation; five pairs of students working in the student checking capacity with other students; three students walking around trying to borrow a pen or paper; four students working at the spelling and vocabulary area; a few students browsing at each center — through magazines, books, and newspapers; three students who appear to be daydreaming and one good-natured soul who is sweeping!

Flowing into and interacting with these routines were some special features that evolved because the need came, a problem developed, an idea grew. . . . We had "bonus days." On certain days, students seemed under- or over-stimulated and needed help in "getting themselves together." So, reflecting the practices of many of students' favorite television game shows, we doubled the points on certain days. This meant that any twenty-five point activity was worth fifty, but on that day only. Those days were exciting, for students had to concentrate their efforts in order to get the work in that day!

There also were "environment" days. We believed that students should be aware of their learning environment, care about it, plan for it — in short, notice it, and help to structure it in terms of their own desires and needs. On environment days, we brainstormed ways in which "this room could help us learn better," or "things we could have to make this room more interesting and exciting." During these times we also talked about re-arranging the room furniture for the sake of variety or efficiency; we also dealt with the issue of room neatness. Sometimes students made posters, painted signs, designed mobiles, and cleaned on these days.

On a table near the usually obscured teacher desks were five small boxes, each with a different color construction paper covering, each with a slot in the center big enough to insert a three by five card, and each with a different number on it designating each class period. These were the "Mail Boxes." Each student was required each week to write to us. In our open situation, we were fearful of losing contact with shy individuals, we wanted to incorporate as many devices to keep the lines of communication open for all students, and we wanted each student to evaluate

his progress himself, in so much as this was indicative of self-conscious learners and assuming responsibilities for one's behavior in the classroom. We asked students to write to us in informal letter style; each was to tell us how he felt about what happened in English throughout the week, what problems he had, how successful he felt, suggestions for the program's improvement; students could also write or ask us things that weren't "English" related. We had one rule: Please don't ask or tell us anything that you would prefer we didn't ask or tell you! Through the "Mail Boxes" we had a chance to learn about students and their lives in a way that doesn't occur in most classes; besides evaluating their week's progress they commented on our clothing, hair style, they gave feedback on our moods, methods of teaching and non-verbal behavior. But also, they asked questions — What kind of car did we drive? How many children do we have? Why are we doing this kind of English? What did we think about the Angela Davis trial? Could they have this kind of English next year? And on the back, we answered the cards and perhaps asked them questions. We used the opportunity to give them feedback — you seem upset; What a great looking outfit you wore! Haven't seen much work from you recently; If you enjoyed that book, you might like one by Salinger. . . . Thus we established a running dialogue with students; it kept us in tune with what was happening within our students, and provided us with a way to humanize the curriculum.

Between each report period we had sev-

eral days of feedback and evaluation. In agreement with our notions that learning is a shared responsibility between the teacher and his students, we "regrouped" periodically to assess as a group where the kinks were, what was working well, what was getting boring, what we had outlived our need for; in short, where are we, and where do we go from here. During these times, no folders were passed out, and no one worked on projects or activities — everyone's participation was required.

Toward the end of the year, we moved about a third of the kids off daily points and into long range study projects. The idea was to give kids a process for finding any information that might be important for them to find for whatever purpose. Through this process they raised questions about areas of special interest to them, decided on which questions they would address themselves to, gather information through reading, interviewing, visiting places and finally answer their original questions via some project that would show that their research had some value for them. Some of the topics kids explored were: Astrology, Marriage, Abortions, Driving Ed., Drugs, Pregnancy, Genghis Khan, Stewardesses, Communism, Teaching, Fashions, Religion, Carpentry, Birds, Black Poetry.

There were trips: Kids went independently to hospitals, schools, offices, garages, libraries and factories in their efforts to work on special reports and projects.

We tried also to bring the community into the classroom as well as get the kids into the city: We had a drug rehabilitator, a representative from SEPTA,* a psychiatrist, and even a spokesman from the Mormon Church. None of these people lectured to kids; all talked informally, answered questions, arranged for follow-up activities and explored their fields.

We also hooked more kids into the tutoring program which consisted of our students tutoring neighboring elementary children in reading and math skills, or acting as classroom aides. We wanted our kids to feel how it is to be the teacher, and we trained our students in skills like "eye contact," body language — in short, we reviewed communications and relationships.

This, then, presents the basics of what we wanted to accomplish and how we tried to get there.

* Southeastern Pennsylvania Transportation Authority.

projects and activities

STIMULATING CURIOSITY

While curiosity may be a dangerous thing for cats, it is a primary motivating force for human learning. As Jerome Bruner states in his article, "The Will To Learn" (pp. 36–43), "Curiosity is almost a proto-type of the intrinsic motive." It stands to reason, therefore, that when a teacher can appeal to a student's curiosity about a learning topic, he possesses a powerful means of involving the student.

Procedure

Listed here are topics typically studied in elementary and secondary schools. For each topic, your task is to generate questions which might arouse curiosity. The following questions on Shakespeare might be useful as an example.

Topic: Shakespeare

1. How could Shakespeare write so many plays?
2. Why did Shakespeare use such fancy English?
3. How did Shakespeare know what Julius Caesar and Brutus said to each other?
4. If Shakespeare were alive today, do you think he would be famous?

TO BE OR NOT TO BE...
THAT IS THE QUESTION

After you have finished, share your questions with a partner to find out if your questions arouse curiosity in him. If at all possible, interview elementary and secondary students as well: ask them what interest any of these topics holds for them.

Topic: The Civil War

1. _____

2. _____

3. _____

4. _____

Topic: The Weather

1. _____

2. _____

3. _____

4. _____

Topic: The Metric System

1. _____

2. _____

3. _____

4. _____

Topic: The Origin of Words

1. _____

2. _____

3. _____

4. _____

SAFETY AND GROWTH

Maslow's article "Defense and Growth" (pp. 22–28) suggests that growth is most likely to occur "when delights of growth and anxieties of safety are greater than the anxieties of growth and the delights of safety." This activity is designed to test the meaning of these factors.

Procedure

Imagine under what conditions each event listed below would encourage students to take risks for the sake of personal growth rather than to avoid risks and become closed to learning. We have provided what we feel is one negative (closed, threatening) idea and one positive (open, safe) idea for each event. See if you agree with them and then try to generate other ideas.

1. **Coming into a class for the first time**

   Closed, threatening

   a. Talk about the new student in front of the whole class.

   b. _____
   _____

   Safe, open

   a. Ask a student to serve as a support buddy for the new student.

   b. _____
   _____

2. **Standing up to make a speech in a class**

   Closed, threatening

   a. Invite other students to criticize the delivery.

   b. _____
   _____

   Safe, open

   a. Have the student ask questions of the rest of the class on the quality of his speech.

   b. _____
   _____

3. Discussing one's ideas with classmates

Closed, threatening

a. Make all students tell their ideas.

b. _____

  _____

Safe, open

a. Allow a student to pick any other student to share ideas with.

b. _____

  _____

4. Wanting to ask a question in class

Closed, threatening

a. Expect the student always to ask *relevant* questions.

b. _____

  _____

a. Allow students to write their questions, whenever they occur, on an index card and put them into a question box.

b. _____

_____

5. Taking a test

Closed, threatening

a. Make it clear that the student's grade is on the line.

b. _____

_____

Safe, open

a. Allow a student to go to a private test file and take a test confidentially to see how well he or she knows something.

b. _____

_____

A NOTE FROM A BELEAGUERED TEACHER

All too often, a teacher works alone. She has little opportunity to plan with other teachers, to observe them teaching or to receive their emotional support. This isolation can be very dangerous for it can blind a teacher from new insights and alternative behaviors. In this activity, you will help a teacher who has gotten stuck in her relationship to students and is reaching out for help. The situation may not be entirely believable, but you can stretch your imagination if necessary.

Procedure

The following note describes the plight of a high school history teacher who has failed to involve her students. After reading the note, ask yourself what learning conditions you think this teacher may have either created or ignored. You might also imagine that this teacher has previously sought your help. How would you respond? As a guide for your answer we have included the response of a student from Temple University. How do you react to her suggestions?

Dear Colleague:

I have been thinking a lot about a high school history class that I am scheduled to teach for the fall semester. This time I want things to be different, but how? In previous classes, the students seemed to be putting forth the least amount of effort possible. For example, every time I asked challenging questions, they would sit and stare. Rarely was anyone willing to take a stab at the answer. If a student was called on, he would often shrug his shoulders and pretend he hadn't the faintest idea how to answer. Another example of the students' lethargy involved the reading assignments. I began many classes by asking if anyone had questions about what he read. Was there anything that wasn't understood? Rarely did students volunteer questions and yet when I proceeded to ask my own questions about the assignment, I often found that key ideas in the reading were not properly understood. What was really puzzling was that these students, on the surface, are ideal to teach. They are college-bound and bright. They came from the highest ability track in the school. What's more, I had taken special pains to make the class relevant. The readings and the class activities revolved around topics that should have been of considerable interest to my students — racism, war, ecology, etc. I wonder what I can do this time to involve my students more effectively?

Dear Beleaguered Friend:

Your letter relating to your "sleepwalking" high school students caught my attention. I have felt the same frustration faced with those blank stares in response to what I had thought would be an exciting, provocative question or activity. Especially when working with a group of "ideal" students who resist any involvement in the class or subject, one can become so frustrated that alternative solutions or changes evade one.

I think you have a very good start for an exciting classroom situation because you have sought out relevant material that should interest these students. Clearly, it is not the material that is preventing their involvement. Perhaps there are things you can do with the material and with the students as individuals that can change the atmosphere in your room.

Being high school students, these kids have many years of programming behind them that has put their imagination into hibernation. They have learned that the ideal student is passive. They absorbed this to the point that they will not react to the most provocative topic. And you are in the front of the class, expecting them to be aggressive, imaginative, and inspired in a situation where these attitudes are discouraged.

First of all, their commitment to the class is essential. No one student felt risky enough to volunteer an idea or reaction because they were facing you and their fellow students as isolated individuals. As a unified group, where they were not putting themselves on the line to have their thoughts and persons accepted or rejected, but rather were sharing ideas with everyone, more risk and involvement and growth would be possible. Perhaps the letter that I'm responding to should have been addressed to them, your students, making clear to them that their expectations and needs were important to you and necessary to a definition of anything that would take place within that room. The burden to get things rolling in your classroom seems to be on your shoulders. Transferring the responsibility to them could instigate independent thinking, searching, curiosity, and growth in the social

environment, where they are infrequently demanded to use these faculties.

REMEMBERING SCHOOL

We have had many encounters with teachers and classrooms during our school experience. Some are remembered with excitement and fondness, others with resentment and perhaps hate. This activity focuses on those memories.

Procedure

1. Remember a room in a school where you wrote your name as a child. In the box provided here, write your name holding the pencil or pen in the "wrong" hand and imagine that room. Then draw a floor plan. Put in the desks and chairs and everything else found there. How does it feel to be that pupil again? Tell somebody else.

2. Look back at encounters you have had with teachers and examine the qualities they had that encouraged or limited students. As you think back on your schooling, you may find the following list of experiences helpful. Try to remember if these experiences ever happened to you.

— A teacher discussed a weakness of yours in front of other students.
— You needed some help in solving a difficult problem, and the teacher encouraged and helped you to think out the problem yourself.
— You overheard your teacher say something about you to another teacher.

— A teacher told you he understood what you were feeling.
— You were excited about a project, but no one gave you encouragement.
— A teacher told you something personal about himself that made you respect him.
— You were asked to think for yourself and then were criticized for your thoughts.
— A teacher told you that he would trust a decision you were to make for the class.
— You needed time to finish an assignment, but the teacher claimed that it was necessary to move on.
— After you openly expressed your dislike for a class activity, the teacher eagerly asked you to recommend some changes.

3. Now, write down a similar list of experiences that you would like your students to write when remembering you (for example, "He helped us to clarify our problems but always left the decisions up to us").

a. _____

b. _____

c. _____

d. _____

e. _____

ASSESSING INVOLVEMENT

Whether you, as a teacher, feel that things are going well or poorly in your class, it is often helpful to collect data from students about their feelings of involvement and to watch for behaviors that indicate their involvement. This activity will suggest some ways to collect such data.

Procedure

The following two data-collecting methods have been designed and used by the editors of this book to assess involvement in an undergraduate course in educational psychology. Respond to them if they are appropriate to your personal circumstances or modify them accordingly. After you have completed both description and the questionnaire, share your responses with others. See if there are differences in involvement in your group. Then discuss how these methods could be adapted for use with elementary and secondary school students. How would you simplify the wording? Could you design a data-gathering activity suitable for children who cannot read? What uses would you see for collecting this information? Would you be willing to inform the class of the results?

THE COURSE DESCRIPTION[1]

Imagine that another student has said to you, "I'll probably have to take your (ed. psych.) course next semester. Could you tell me what it's been like for you?" How would you respond? Write for fifteen minutes.

INVOLVEMENT BEHAVIOR QUESTIONNAIRE[2]

This questionnaire is designed to gather information about what has been happen-

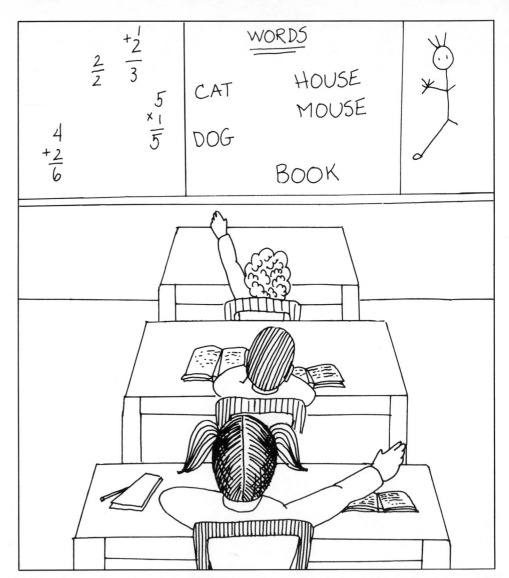

ing to you in the course *during the past week*. Below are nine statements which may or may not reflect your behavior and feelings last week. Respond *only* to statements that represent your experience.

The following key should be used in responding to the statements:

YES?   I think that happened but I'm not absolutely sure.
YES   Yes, that did happen.
YES!   That *really* happened.

1. I came to class with ideas I wanted to explore.

 YES?_____   YES_____   YES!_____

2. During class I was mentally stimulated.

 YES?_____   YES_____   YES!_____

3. I found myself thinking about class at a later time.

 YES?_____   YES_____   YES!_____

4. I listened with interest to other people's ideas.

 YES?_____   YES_____   YES!_____

5. I wanted to share my ideas with other people in the class.

 YES?_____   YES_____   YES!_____

6. I looked forward to coming to class.

 YES?_____   YES_____   YES!_____

7. I looked over related readings before coming to class.

 YES?_____   YES_____   YES!_____

8. I used, in a teaching situation, something I had become aware of in class.

 YES?_____   YES_____   YES!_____

9. I talked about the class to someone.

 YES?_____   YES_____   YES!_____

DEVELOPING INITIAL ACTIVITIES

Teachers are faced with the problems of starting a new unit and trying to get students interested enough and involved in the subject matter. According to Thelen (see pp. 43–46), initial activities which invite speculation are a way of engaging learners. This activity is based on that principle.

Procedure

1. Here is an initial activity from a unit entitled "The Survival of Animals in Our World Today," written for elementary school children. Read it and think about

the kinds of questions and issues it might raise in children's minds.

What would you do if:

1. You saw a person chasing birds away.
2. An animal was afraid of you.
3. You saw a cockroach in your house.
4. There was not enough food for the birds in winter.
5. A threat of bears was possible while you were on a camping trip.
6. Flies were swarming on some meat left uncovered in the sun.
7. You were walking through a woods and discovered a snake.
8. You caught a fish that by law was too small to catch.
9. You knew someone who was not kind to animals.
10. You were hungry and found a dead rabbit in the woods.[1]

2. Pick a topic you could teach. Now try to develop an initial activity that will get students involved, maximize their interest, get them to ask many questions, and start them thinking about the topic. Remember, the activity must have problematic situations embedded in it or it must generate questions that students will want to answer in the future. An initial activity can take place over one day or several, depending on your purposes and goals.

[1] From "The Survival of Animals in Our World Today" by Jay M. Yanoff and Donna S. Allender (mimeographed, 1973).

additional resources

BOOKS AND ARTICLES

Bettelheim, Bruno. *Love Is Not Enough.* New York: The Free Press, 1949.

Brophy, Jere E., and Good, Thomas L. *Teacher-Student Relationships.* New York: Holt, Rinehart and Winston, 1974.

Combs, Arthur; Avila, Donald; and Purkey, William. *Helping Relationships.* Boston: Allyn and Bacon, 1971.

Daniels, Steven. *How 2 Gerbils, 20 Goldfish, 200 Games, 2,000 Books and I Taught Them How to Read.* Philadelphia: Westminster Press, 1972.

de Charms, Richard. "The Making of Pawns in the Classroom," Paper presented at the Annual Meeting of the American Psychological Association, 1970.

Erikson, Erik H. "Identity and the Life Cycle," *Psychological Issues* 1, no. 1, Monograph 1. New York: International Universities Press, 1959.

Good, Thomas L., and Brophy, Jere E. *Looking In Classrooms.* New York: Harper and Row, 1973.

Gorman, Alfred E. *Teachers and Learners: The Interactive Process of Education.* Boston: Allyn and Bacon, 1969.

Gross, Ronald, and Osterman, Paul. *High School.* New York: Simon and Schuster, 1971.

Holt, John. *How Children Fail.* New York: Pitman, 1964.

Jackson, Philip W. *Life In Classrooms.* New York: Holt, Rinehart and Winston, 1968.

Jourard, Sidney W. *Self-Disclosure.* New York: Wiley, 1971.

Jourard, Sidney W. "Fascination: A Phenomenological Perspective on Independent Learning," *The Theory and Nature of Independent Learning.* Scranton, Pa.: Intext Educational Publishers, 1967.

Leacock, Eleanor Burke. *Teaching and Learning in City Schools.* New York: Basic Books, 1969.

Marin, Peter. "The Open Truth and Fiery Vehemence of Youth: A Sort of Soliloquy," *The Center Magazine* 2, no. 1 (1969): 61–74.

Maslow, Abraham H. *Toward a Psychology of Being.* New York: Van Nostrand Reinhold, 1968.

Maslow, Abraham H. *The Farther Reaches of Human Nature.* New York: Viking Press, 1971.

Minuchin, Patricia; Biber, Barbara; Shapiro, Edna; and Zimiles, Herbert. *The Psychological Impact of School Experience.* New York: Basic Books, 1969.

Nyberg, David. *Tough and Tender Learning.* Palo Alto, Calif.: National Press Books, 1971.

Rosenthal, Robert, and Jacobson, Lenore. *Pygmalion in the Classroom.* New York: Holt, Rinehart and Winston, 1968.

Schrank, Jeffrey. *Teaching Human Beings: 101 Subversive Activities for the Classroom.* Boston: Beacon Press, 1972.

Silberman, Charles. *Crisis in the Classroom.* New York: Random House, 1970.

Silberman, Melvin L., ed. *The Experience of Schooling.* New York: Holt, Rinehart and Winston, 1968.

Stacey, Judith; Bereaud, Susan; and

Daniels, Joan, eds. *And Jill Came Tumbling After: Sexism in American Education*. New York: Dell, 1974.

Women on Words and Images. *Dick and Jane as Victims: Sex Stereotyping in Children's Readers*. Princeton, N.J., 1972.

FILMS

Building Class Involvement. Media Five, 1011 North Cole Avenue, Suite F, Hollywood, CA 90038.

A fifth-grade class demonstrates a technique called "lead-up activities" which is used to increase listening and involvement among students.

Growing up Female. The Eccentric Circle, Box 1481, Evanston, IL 60204.

How women are conditioned to accept stereotyped roles.

Maslow and Self-Actualization. Psychological Films, 205 West 20th Street, Santa Anna, CA 92706.

Two films in which Abraham Maslow discusses the theory of self-actualization; one film deals primarily with honesty and awareness and the other film with freedom and trust.

The Cave. Stephen Bosustow Productions, 1649 Eleventh Street, Santa Monica, CA 90404.

A cartoon account of the parable of Plato's cave. This film can be used to

stimulate discussion on the social pressures which inhibit learning involvement.

What They Want to Produce, Not What We Want to Become. Educational Development Center, 39 Chapel Street, Newton, MA 02160.

How aspects of traditional education confine children's learning.

chapter
two

guiding
thinking
and
learning

initial experiences

ALTERNATIVES IN TEACHING

All too often, teaching means that a teacher shows or tells a student how to understand or do something; the student merely watches. What is imparted may be heavily determined by the way *the teacher* understands the concept or skill. Little effort is made to relate to the student's background and knowledge. To break away from this teaching approach is most difficult even if one realizes that it may not be helpful to learners.

We would like to encourage you to develop different ways of teaching the same concept or skill. Pick a concept or skill from the list shown here and plan how you would teach it using the three teaching procedures that follow. (If you wish, you can get three people together and divide up the work so that each of you teaches the concept or skill a different way.) If possible, teach the concept or skill to real students, or use colleagues who will play student roles.

— telling time
— a proper golf, tennis, or baseball swing
— use of the dictionary
— finding the lowest common denominator with fractions

— learning how magnets work
— the difference between inflation and recession
— the purpose of the conjugation of verbs in different languages

Teaching procedure I: creative explanation

You should do most of the talking or demonstrating, but unlike most lecturers, try to:

1. allude to the students' previous experiences and existing knowledge
2. employ a combination of visual, auditory and tactile stimulation
3. use helpful analogies to make your point

For example, if you were teaching children about objects that float or sink, you could explain and demonstrate the weight and density of various objects and how they react to being placed in containers of water varying in volume. Refer to floating and sinking objects one might observe daily in the environment.

Teaching procedure II: guided activity

Give the students a well thought out sequence of questions, tasks, and exercises that leads to an ultimate conclusion. You may ask them to do a series of brief experiments. For example, have the students make a series of predictions as to what happens to the water level when you put various objects into a glass.

Teaching procedure III: messing around

Provide the students with an environment and written or tangible materials to play with and allow them to discover for themselves. You may assist and converse, but do not expect the student to reach any level of immediate success. For example, provide reference books and objects for experimentation with which students can explore. Encourage them to ask questions as they work.

TIMES OF MAXIMUM LEARNING

What is taught is not necessarily learned. What is learned is not necessarily what is taught. We probably have all had experiences that attest to these statements. During the following task, we will discover some of the possible reasons for this lack of correlation.

1. Divide into groups of no more than five people. Each person should tell the other members of his group his answers to each of these questions.

a. Think of a time in your life when you learned something that you retain to this day. You may have learned it in school or anyplace else. Tell the group about it. You may have had a major insight or learned to do something you could not do before. What happened? What did the teacher (if one was present in this situation) do or not

do to facilitate your learning? How did you feel about what you learned? How did you feel about the teacher?

b. Think of a time when you were asked to learn something, but no matter how hard you tried, your mind seemed blocked. What happened? What did the teacher in this situation do or not do to facilitate your learning? How did you feel about what you were trying to learn? How did you feel about the teacher?

Think about the questions for a few minutes before you begin. Each participant should limit his response to the group to five minutes. If a group is not available, you may write down your impressions.

2. As a group, compare these two experiences. On a large piece of paper, draw a line down the middle and on one side list all the factors your group can identify as leading to maximum learning. On the other side, list the reasons for minimal learning. These positive and negative factors might have related to the teacher's behavior, your behavior, the learning climate, or any other aspect in learning. Try to make descriptive rather than evaluative remarks. (For example: "The teacher used many graphics to show a point" is descriptive, whereas "The teacher was interesting" is evaluative.) When other groups have completed this chart, you may want to compare maximum learning experiences.

introduction

Have you ever memorized information for a test and found that when the time came for the test, you could remember the page the information was on but not the facts themselves? Did you ever walk down the street, meet someone you knew well, but fail to remember the person's name at that moment? Or, have you ever tried to solve a problem and given it up after great effort only to have the solution pop into your head when you were attending to something else? These are all examples of tricks our minds play on us.

What accounts for these mental breakdowns, and what implications for teaching can we draw by considering their cause? Thinking seems to be going on in our minds all the time. Our brain does not function like a tape recorder or telephone switchboard, simply accumulating information by some associative process. More accurately, incoming information is continually being tested, reformulated, and acted upon. With such wear and tear, breakdowns are inevitable. But, on the other hand, our brain is a very powerful organ. It is so "gifted" that, with it, a child can learn the complexities of a language without benefit of systematic instruction! Moreover, each person's mind is unique. When each of us tastes, smells, sees, or hears something for the first time, each experiences it differently. None of us have had the same previous experiences by which to test or compare this incoming data. This uniqueness partly explains why students are not always ready at the same time to begin to read and why some learn number facts before others. It also accounts, to a degree, for some students' ability to interpret a poem in greater depth than others or to take a motor apart and repair it when others cannot. We, as teachers, must learn how to take into account and work with the unique and continual information processing going on in our students' minds. For example, we need to reflect on what occurs when we *flood* students with our own thoughts (however insightful they are) or when we rely too often on "let me show you how" demonstrations and explanations. What happens to students when they are put into a position of sustained, passive listening and observation? As teachers, we must also consider the effect a student's past learning experiences have on his view of new concepts and problems. If we fail to understand our students' frame of reference, we may not be aware of the cognitive assumptions that block their understanding. Finally, we must realize that the incredible brains our students possess may be put to inappropriate use if most of the demands we make involve memorization. We should be aware that a student's success in retrieving information depends largely on how well it was processed and stored in the first place.

We believe that teaching should not be a matter of pouring information, concepts, and patterns of thinking into another person's head (and expecting them back in return). Rather, it should be a way of working with students to facilitate their acquisition of information and their processing of meaningful ideas about the world. Unless we understand how students perceive and solve classroom learning problems, how can we develop principles to guide them?

As a start, we find it useful to view learning as the reorganization of knowledge into new or more differentiated ways of apprehending phenomena. Obviously, the worst thing one can do when someone is trying to juggle and rearrange facts and concepts is to interfere by pressure or overdirection. Sometimes it is best simply to leave students alone to "mess around" and figure things out themselves. At other times, there are many teaching behaviors that can help information processing. Presenting ideas in a multisensory way, encouraging speculation and prediction, providing concrete activities, using role-playing and gaming techniques, stimulating question asking, are all ways of facilitating learning. Whatever behaviors you use, keep in view the goal of allowing students to use their powerful minds so that they become increasingly able to reorganize their experience.

One consideration which we feel deserves special attention in this chapter is the tempo of students' thinking. Spurred by expectations to produce rather than to reflect, many students think impulsively. Typically, they come to answers quickly without first exploring the questions and problems they are facing and the kinds of information that would lead them to solutions. Many educators recognize this issue when they push for a spirit of "inquiry" in classrooms. Inquiry is, perhaps, best defined as a mental (and emotional) attitude which delays judgment, encourages a sense of playfulness with data, and allows ideas and skills to sink in gradually. Many of the materials that follow are devoted to developing this willingness to slow down the thinking process.

The readings in this chapter were selected to give you both theoretical and practical guidance. They begin by examining the nature of thinking. The following questions are explored: Under what conditions does thinking become blocked? By what processes do we learn new ideas and skills? In what ways do children think differently at various stages of development? Ways of facilitating inquiry and discovery are also presented with discussion of how these teaching procedures contrast with other methods. Following these considerations, strategies of guiding thinking and learning are depicted by vignettes involving actual elementary and secondary teachers and students. The teaching techniques used in these accounts differ considerably. Some stress creative ways of explaining concepts to students, whereas in others the teacher asks questions more often than he or she explains. Student activity is highly directed in a few of the vignettes. In others, the teaching is nondirective. Despite this diversity, we think these are *all* examples of teaching that encourages information processing and the reorganization of experience.

Yanoff's article provides an overall understanding of cognitive functioning. It contains both a systematic analysis of the input, integration, output, and feedback processes of the brain, and some implications of the functioning of these processes for teaching. The ideas presented here are important background for most of the discovery and inquiry models of learning. You may also find the clear organization of this article useful in organizing the ideas and suggestions in other articles in this section.

JAY M. YANOFF

THE FUNCTIONS OF THE MIND IN THE LEARNING PROCESS

A teacher needs to understand the functions of the mind to facilitate learning. Intellectual skills can be taught best when they are based on a model of thinking. This article will present such a model and indicate its implications for educational practice.

Two popular ways that have been used

From *The Psychology of Open Teaching and Learning* by Melvin L. Silberman, Jerome S. Allender, and Jay M. Yanoff (Boston: Little, Brown and Company, 1972), pp. 114–21. Reprinted with permission.

to conceptualize the cognitive process are to compare it with a telephone switchboard and a computer. In the switchboard model, one person dials a number (the stimulus) and the message is sent to the receiving party who answers (the response). The contact is direct. The connection between the stimulus and the response does not alter the system between. The connection is specific and the line can be disconnected when the call is completed. No call can be made unless the wires are linked and there is no principle that making a call does anything fundamental to any of the wires except those involved in the call.

The switchboard model, however, is limited in several ways. It fails to recognize the brain as the primary organ of learning; rather it focuses on the stimulation and the response. We have all had experiences when learning has taken place even though we could not make a specific response. If this model is placed into educational practice, it serves to teach what is offered by the teacher or the materials he uses. There is no way that this model can account for creative or imaginative thinking. It is also limited by a teacher's means of reinforcing an answer (response). In this model, routine, conventional thinking tends to be reinforced and creative and inventive behavior is not.

The computer model allows for a more comprehensive examination of thinking in the learning process. In this model, information is fed into a computer. The computer stores the information in memory banks for later recall. When given the appropriate directions, the computer prints out information that it has stored. The programmer's final command to the computer is to stop. In this model the brain is viewed as a total, active system with memory drums and feedback. The more information that is stored, the more useful the computer becomes. But the computer model in some ways is also incomplete since it does not account for the ability of the brain to seek data, act on its own, and stop when finished (all of which a computer cannot do). What is needed, then, is a model that avoids some of the inadequacies of the switchboard or computer models, one that offers a more comprehensive analysis of cognition in the learning process.

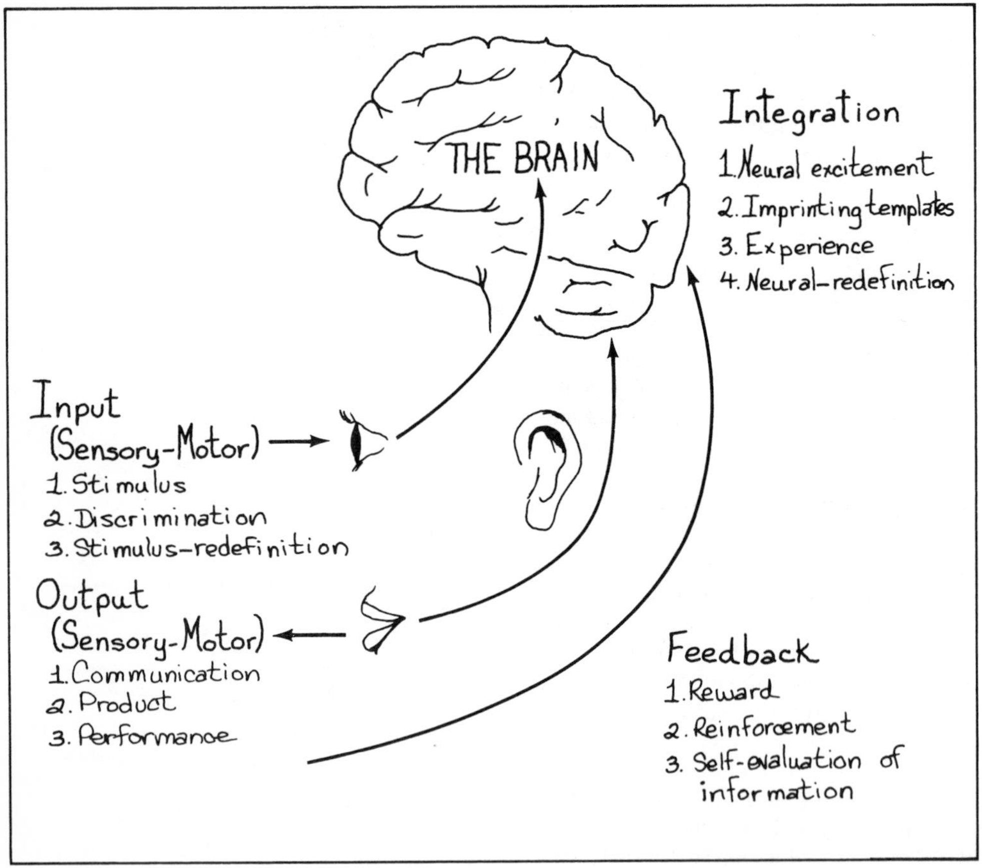

Figure 1. Model of cognition

A MODEL OF COGNITION

The model in Figure 1 is a basis for conceptualizing what takes place in the thinking-learning process. It is based on the practical experiences of the author as well as various theoretical foundations presented by Allender (1967), Getman (1962), Hebb (1949), Hill (1963), Kephart (1960), Osgood (1953), Penfield (1969), Piaget (1954, 1969), and Simpson (1968). The process is separated into the following major functions:

1. input — the stimulation of the sense organs for reception of information to be sent to the brain
2. integration — the process by which the brain receives information, acts upon it, and initiates some reaction
3. output — the sensory-motor application of messages sent from the brain for action in the environment
4. feedback — the realization by the brain that appropriate output has been given

Input

Perception and learning have been investigated by Bartley (1969), Getman (1962), Osgood (1953), Piaget (1969), and Simpson (1968). Their work supports the notion that the perceptual system provides the input for the cognitive processes. The sense organs feed the brain its information. Cognition begins here, with appropriate perception.

Look at the dots below.

Light energy travels from the paper and stimulates the retina in your eye. Just as the optic nerve transforms light into electrical impulses and carries the information from your eye to the brain, the other sense organs take in data and transform it into language the brain can understand. The role of the sensory organs is to receive the stimuli: the eyes for seeing, the ears for hearing, the nose and mouth for smell and taste, the skin for touch, and the entire body for awareness in space or kinesthesia. When there is a stimulus available, the sense organs can be activated. They are then able to transform the information into messages for the brain. This is similar to the way data is fed into the computer. If no stimulus exists, however, there can be no perception. Sight begins when the eyes are stimulated by light rays. If there is no light, there can be no sight. If, on the other hand, the eye itself does not function

properly, sight will be impaired. In each of the perceptual modes there are two essential elements: (1) a well functioning organ and (2) adequate stimulation.

The sensory organ itself has the ability to become a discriminating unit. When you compare dots A and B, your eyes discriminate the difference in the degree of light stimulation between the two. The degree of discrimination is impaired in individuals with color blindness. There is a breakdown in the process which does not allow the brain to receive the color messages properly.

In the sensory system, wherever organs exist in pairs (eyes and ears), the pair must function together to allow for accurate perception. Try catching a ball with one eye closed. Your depth perception is impaired because you are receiving information with only one eye. When you use both eyes you receive information from three dimensions; one eye transmits only two dimensions. Getman (1962) has shown the necessity of activating both eyes for accurate visual input. When the perceptual system operates efficiently, the organs receive the stimuli, discriminate, and pass accurate messages to the brain. This process can be called *stimulus redefinition*.

Integration

Integration is the process by which the brain receives electrical impulses, the redefined stimuli, and acts upon them. The brain has the power to scan its memory

bank to see if the incoming data is congruent with any prior experience. If the stimulus will fit into a previously formed category, the brain can act upon it. However, if the information is new, the impulses are newly imprinted. The mind seeks to find a likeness or a fit of information before it forms a new imprint.

Think about an *arfnif*. Does an *arfnif* fit into any previous categories you know? Is it a food? Animal? Fish? Emotion? Sport? Since *arfnif* does not fit into these categories, you might assume that it is a nonsense term. Your brain will make a new imprint of it. The next time you encounter *arfnif* you will not necessarily imprint, as it is a part of your prior experience.

When you imprinted *arfnif*, a new concept or idea took shape in your mind. Allender (1967) would maintain that you have formed a new "mental template" in this imprinting process. A template is a pattern that allows one to reproduce a specified shape. In the case of the brain, a template allows one to record an idea or experience. In more concrete terms, templates form the structure of the mind. We can represent the brain as a series of unlimited, interrelated templates. As data bombards the mind, it (1) recalls previously formed templates, (2) connects previously formed templates, or (3) develops new templates.

Piaget (1954) uses the term "assimilation" to describe that process in which incoming data fits previously formed templates. When new templates are formed, he calls the process accommodation. Real learning takes place in accommodation. Studies by Hebb (1949), Miller, Galanter and Pribram (1960), and Penfield (1969) stress the inherent activity of the brain as well as its function as an information processing system. Different from the computer, which can only store data, templates allow the brain to test and evaluate all incoming stimuli. The brain accepts, acts upon, or in many cases, screens stimuli at a conscious and an unconscious level.

Stop reading for a moment and listen to the sounds around you. Your mind has screened out or filtered these distracting stimuli and allowed you to concentrate selectively upon your reading. If the mind accepted all stimuli equally, one would be overwhelmed with the chaos of input to the point of inaction. Unlike the video-tape machine, which records all visual and auditory stimuli, the mind maintains order and sanity by selecting that data to which it wishes to attend.

The mind is not only a receptive mechanism but also a seeking instrument. In a totally dark room, your brain seeks light. In silence, your brain seeks noise. The brain has the need to reach out into the environment and experience stimuli.

Individuals seek to involve more than one sensory mode to conceptualize reality. Simpson (1968), Bush and Giles (1969), Kephart (1960), and Getman (1962) advo-cate multisensory approaches to learning. The more senses that are involved in each experience, the better able an individual is to develop reality templates. Visual input alone is unsatisfactory, so we ask to feel the fabric, to taste the candy, and to smell the flower. The young child learning to read finds more satisfaction from reading aloud than from merely following the words with his eyes. Think how many senses are employed when you consider buying a new car!

The brain also has the ability to initiate action and to stop action by its own will. The mind is able to rearrange the templates that have been assimilated and accommodated to initiate its own new templates. What is truly unique is the ability of the mind to *stop* thinking of one idea and make a shift to a completely new one. By its own choice, the mind can direct itself to start or stop particular processing. This ability differentiates it from the computer, which must be directed by the programmer who tells it what to do and how to do it. Man's thinking must always be an input to the computer. The integration process in a computer cannot reach the potential of the mind. There has never been a creative computer because it cannot reorder or change its action without being directed to do so.

Creative individuals are those who have developed skills for making the mind initiate. For a man to think creatively and develop new ideas, he must take existing templates and restructure them. One must "break mental sets" — think beyond reality to be truly creative. Penfield (1969) pro-poses that the mind and the individual are one and the same. The child is able to reach out with his mind and condition his own cortex. These complex functions of the integrative process differentiate man from all other animals, as well as from the computer.

Output

To date, there is no known way to accurately measure the cognitive process. Output gives us some indication. Output is the expression of ideas or templates from the brain that have been redefined as electrical impulses. These impulses have been carried to the neuro-muscular system, where they are redefined and exhibited in three ways: (1) communication, (2) product, and (3) performance. Communication may be any form of language-based interaction. Products are typically the construction of an idea. A student's answer on a written test or his art project are forms of output expressed as products. Performance is an exhibition of an ability, such as singing a song and giving a speech. Combinations of more than one of these modes of output are used to express sophisticated thinking. Generally speaking, we judge an individual by his output.

Everyone has more in his mind than can possibly be demonstrated by his output. We have ideas in our heads, but because our output is always somewhat limited, we have all experienced frustration. There have been times when we felt that we were judged unfairly by our output — when we could not adequately express what we were really thinking. One may have heard a comical story, but when trying to retell it to another person, it does not sound funny. Perhaps you have tried to draw a picture of something, but you find that the product is not an accurate representation of what . you see. One cannot fully explain love, and yet he knows that it is very real to him. Poets find they must say less in order to say more.

From the time the brain triggers a response, there is no way the output system can increase the expression of that response before it is expressed. Concepts are lost through an inability to express an idea in oral language. Muscular coordination keeps one from drawing what he has visualized or from running as fast as he wishes. Inability to transfer sounds heard into sounds reproduced keeps one from singing as he would like. Output can never fully represent what has occurred in the integrative process.

An individual can improve the expression of his thinking. Simpson (1968) and Getman (1962) contend that the more a person exercises and trains the sensory-motor mechanisms of expression, the more closely he is able to match his output with his thinking. Individuals have a basic need for expression, to facilitate their mental processes, to identify self, and to test reality.

Feedback

Feedback is the recycling of an individual's thinking. Hill (1963) suggests that the feedback system operates like a thermostat. When the temperature falls, the thermostat turns on the furnace to make the temperature rise. When the temperature rises to a certain point, the thermostat turns the furnace off. The temperature in the room is the input of the system and the activity of the furnace is the output. The effect of the output is fed back into the system as input.

Feedback involves adjustments in the cognitive process. The action is often so quick and automatic that the individual is unaware of it. When a person sings, hearing is his feedback. He can adjust his singing according to what he hears.

When an individual produces some output, feedback fixes the template. Reward and reinforcement are examples of feedback similar to that of the thermostat. They can be defined as whatever strengthens the tendency for a particular response to follow a specific stimulus. Programmed materials have been developed to give students a bit of information immediately followed by reinforcement. We have even seen the advent of behavior modification with its emphasis on output and reward feedback.

The major feedback agent, however, is the individual's self-evaluation of information. This process allows the individual to continually test ideas and deal with

higher cognitive processes. Pribram (1964), in challenging the need for external feedback, contends that within the brain, feedback involves (1) a test of readiness with regard to input, (2) an operation that seeks to match the test, (3) a retest to see whether a match was made, and then (4) an exit from control. Real learning, memory, and recall are increased when the learner can evaluate himself and is sensitive to his own needs for input or stimulation.

Through active engagement with his environment, an individual is able to learn a wide range of concepts and develops a complex cognitive structure. Man will, when he has not been made apathetic by deprivation, aroused by threat or frustration, or damaged in any way, naturally seek to understand his world.

SOME IMPLICATIONS FOR TEACHING

Since information is fed to the brain through the senses, a learning environment should provide multisensory stimulation. It should allow a student to explore and manipulate. By providing such multisensory experiences in the classroom, the teacher allows the student to learn through his strongest perceptual mode. If a child shows auditory strength, a phonetic approach may be best for teaching reading. The whole-word approach may be best for teaching the visually oriented child. An environment that is responsive to the child's individual input and processing styles allows him to seek the means by which he can deal most effectively with his environment. Some children learn best through listening, others through seeing, and still others through physical manipulation. It is important then that each experience in school involve as many of the senses as possible. Through a wide range of experiences, man will develop the templates that will give order to a complex world.

Just as the teacher must provide multisensory stimulation, too much distracting input can hinder learning. Some students find it hard to function in the classroom with its mass of stimuli. The teacher should provide places where a student can work quietly and at his own rate. The teacher and the student together can determine the optimal levels of stimulation and what levels are distracting. Intense noise levels and visual distractions keep children from being able to concentrate. The use of divided sections in the classroom, carpeting, and elimination of interruptions by intercoms and bells cut down distractions. The teacher, the biggest distraction in the classroom, should temper the extent of his verbal bombardment. Even the teacher's desk should be moved from the front of the room so that it is not distracting. The teacher should be a facilitator not a distractor.

It is important that teachers be aware of the degree of perceptual input in their classrooms to be able to provide optimal stimulation while minimizing distractions. When the teacher provides an environment that is flexible for himself and his students, it can be adapted to an individual child's cognitive style.

The difference between seeing and visualizing provides a good example of the significance of integration to the thinking process. Of importance is not only that the child can see but also that he can utilize and interpret the information being fed to his brain. Seeing is only input, while visualization combines input with integration. In schools, most of a student's information is received through vision and audition. Persons should use extreme care when evaluating a child's vision or audition so that acuity is not mistaken for understanding.

Teachers often complain about a child's short attention span and his inability to concentrate. One must agree that most lessons in school are just too long. One way to view a child's attention span is to consider the concept of time. A short wait in a doctor's office may seem like hours, while at a sporting event or in a lively discussion, hours seem to pass like minutes. When students can choose areas they wish to study, when they are actively involved in the planning process, when they are able to make decisions concerning areas which effect them, and when they are able to implement their decisions, their attention span increases.

Creativity involves the most advanced integrative processes. Teachers need to provide experiences where children can sense problems, formulate strategies, review resources, and seek resolutions. This discovery or inquiry approach provides the individual with problem-solving skills which help develop his potential for creative thinking. He must utilize previously formed resources to develop new ideas. A new and creative idea is greater than the sum of the mental templates from which the idea has been drawn. A major concern of teachers should be ways to enhance the thinking of children. Experience in problem-solving situations provides a student with the necessary skills to think about his changing environment. After a problem is sensed, the person must formulate an attack for the solution. He must determine what he is seeking and how he will find resolution.

The more formulation activities that a teacher can present to students the better able they will be to attack future problems. These problem-solving activities encourage students to use their minds to the fullest.

One consideration in development of thinking skills is the process of coming to resolution. The brain has the capacity to make decisions quickly — sometimes, too quickly. The teacher is often faced with the problem of slowing down the process. Instead of asking for recall which necessitates quick responses, the teacher should ask students to consider alternative ways of thinking. This forces students to use more templates and thus develops the process of creative thinking. The teacher can facilitate this process by letting students brainstorm or hypothesize as many alternative answers as they can.

Products have short lives, while process skills allow the individual to adapt to many varied situations. One of the teachers' main functions should be to allow for, encourage, and facilitate creative thinking. Schools for thinking will produce students who think.

As the aim of education turns more toward creative thinking, new modes of evaluation must be developed and implemented. Testing situations should encourage a student to utilize his thinking processes rather than to repeat specific answers. Measuring the degree of impact may be an effective way to evaluate the relationship between classroom experience and learning. As the classroom becomes more open, new alternatives for expression of output become available. Instead of the traditional recall of ideas, teachers can provide exciting challenges for students to pursue. These experiences should be designed so that each student can have some self-measure of success.

A teacher certainly can evaluate and be helpful to students, but the testing experience should provide for each individual to work at his best. He should not be compared to others. Examples of testing that utilize this concept are: (1) The teacher asks students what problems they sense and encourages them to pursue some conclusions, as opposed to, students solving the teacher's problems. (2) The student

develops his own workbooks, which he uses instead of the standardized ones. (3) The student is asked to hypothesize and theorize about real situations. For example, What would the world be like if the Spanish Armada had not been defeated? Activities such as these only begin to open the minds of students. The teacher should continually search for better ways to explore the workings of the thinking process. Teachers should use caution to avoid the pitfalls of classrooms where recall and recitation are the foremost means of student expression. Joint planning and evaluation by student and teacher can help to promote potential output.

If the classroom is to become a place where students can exhibit many forms of expression or output of ideas, the teacher must provide an environment that eliminates repression and encourages expression. The classroom should be supplied with varied media, perceptual-motor games, manipulative devices, nonrestricting materials, and problem-solving tasks. The classroom should be a forum for expressing ideas, feelings, and insights.

If the teacher is to play the role of a helping person, he must provide means by which students can express what is in their heads. A piece of art work can be seen as having as much expression of self as a dialogue. Each mode of output should be seen as an attempted exposure of oneself to the world. When this exposure is received with acceptance, reassurance, and support, the student is more willing to risk further display of self.

Self-evaluation is the most valuable form of feedback. When an individual can critically evaluate his own thinking, greater growth is achieved. Emphasis should then be taken off reward and reinforcement and directed toward a student's own evaluation.

Students gain confidence and are willing to risk more when they have experienced success. The teacher should help students to have successful experiences and build upon them to develop a positive self-image. A confident person is willing to take more risks, which in turn provide more experiences and allow him to develop more templates. Positive feedback builds templates which encourage more templates to be built, while negative feedback deters templates from being formed. A teacher must encourage the positive, constructive forms of feedback that allow for more cognitive growth. Such feedback may include asking students to consider how much they think they learned, asking them what is still confusing to them, asking at what point they got stuck in thinking, asking how they feel about the class, and asking what would make learning better for them. The teacher is then able to respond to individual or group needs.

The feedback system is not merely a collection of stimulus-response units but is a continually ongoing process returning to the integration level. It makes the learner examine for himself, whether he senses his learning is on the right track or gone astray, and allows him to make the decision to change.

SUMMARY

Man's brain is a powerful instrument. It not only receives data but is also able to reach into the environment for sensory feeding. Man's senses are not as keen as other animals'. Birds see better, dogs have better hearing, and deer are able to detect odors more easily. Man is not the strongest animal, nor is he the fastest. The ability of his mind differentiates man from all other animals. He uses language, creates and initiates — all from within the functionings of his mind. He cannot store information at the rate of the computer, but he can think. And thinking gives him power.

Schools must be oriented to help children learn the skills of thinking so that they can either intelligently adapt themselves to the environment or change it. To be able to make the changes necessary for better learning, teachers must consider how information is received by the senses, the way the mind uses data, and the means of expression that people have. Then, and only then, can the teacher provide a learning environment that is responsive to each child's cognitive functioning.

Conklin focuses on one major problem of teaching and how the mind functions: integration. He says, "In every case the pupil alone can integrate the parts into a single whole. This act of integration is private and cannot be forced or guaranteed by anyone but the pupil himself." He uses examples to show how teaching can be viewed as breaking down skills, understandings, and attitudes into parts and how learning can be viewed as putting them back together so they work for you. You may be interested in considering your own integration process as you put ideas of this article together for yourself into a meaningful whole. At the end of the article you will find some unusual but helpful principles of teaching.

KENNETH R. CONKLIN

WHOLES AND PARTS IN TEACHING

Teachers are utterly dependent on their pupils for success. No matter how knowl-

Reprinted from *The Elementary School Journal* (December 1973): 165–71 by permission of The University of Chicago Press. Copyright © 1973 by the University of Chicago Press.

edgeable and skillful a teacher may be, he can impart knowledge to a pupil only if the pupil cooperates. Knowledge is produced by the knower's private, free, and active exercise of intelligence: knowledge cannot be delivered in finished form by someone else. The phrase "learning by discovery" is redundant, because learning comes only through discovery. Plato, St. Augustine, and St. Thomas Aquinas demonstrated the use of this principle in teaching adults knowledge of absolutes. Here we are more concerned with the use of this principle in teaching children ordinary understandings, skills, and attitudes. Most teachers may agree that they need their pupils' active cooperation. Yet, certain teaching methods that are now gaining widespread popularity conflict with the idea that pupils are intelligent creatures whose active cooperation is necessary to the success of teaching, while some valid methods based on this premise are ignored or misused.

WHOLES AND PARTS

Why is it that knowledge cannot be delivered from teacher to pupil in finished form? Because what can be delivered is always one level below what is intended. The explanation is the same whether we are talking about skills, understandings, or attitudes: a teacher must communicate by breaking down his subject matter into smaller pieces and conveying the pieces to the pupil. The teacher depends on the pupil to put the pieces back together for himself in the correct manner. Let's take some examples.[1]

To teach the skill of writing, we have pupils practice subskills. Pupils learn to hold a pencil, to shape individual letters, and to make connections between letters. We depend on the pupil to integrate these subskills into the smooth performance of the skill of writing. If a pupil has trouble writing, we point out the things he is doing wrong and have him practice doing them correctly one by one. Then we can only hope that he will be able to work these particulars properly into the total task.

All skills are taught by breaking them into subskills. Swimming is broken down into floating, breathing, arm-stroking, and leg-kicking. Reading is broken into recognizing letters, diphthongs, syllables, and small words. For every skill, teachers require pupils to practice subskills, but depend on pupils to integrate subskills into the smooth performance of the total skill.

To help a pupil understand a generalization ("red"), we deliver some particulars (stoplight, apple, rose). To convey the notion of an abstract concept ("money"), we deliver some concrete examples (pennies, quarters, dollar bills). To teach the attitude of "respect for the flag," we instruct pupils to keep the flag from touching the ground, we teach them to say the Pledge of Allegiance, and we teach them to sing "The Star-Spangled Banner."

These examples demonstrate a general principle: all skills, understandings, and attitudes are taught by breaking a whole into its parts and having pupils master the parts.

In every case the pupil alone can integrate the parts into a single whole. This act of integration is private and cannot be forced or guaranteed by anyone but the pupil himself.

Thus, a whole is greater than the sum of its parts. The whole is not merely the collection of its parts, but also the properly organized integration of them. The whole gives meaning to the parts, and it is the intuitive grasping of this meaning that enables a pupil to integrate the parts. Teacher and pupil have reverse roles: a teacher breaks a whole into deliverable parts and presents them to the pupil, whose task is then to accept the parts, internalize them, and integrate them.

Excessive concentration on the parts can block the internalizing and integrating processes. For this reason rote memorization and recitation must stop before deeper understanding can begin. When we concentrate on the parts we block the view of the whole; likewise, when we focus on the whole we temporarily forget about the parts. Pupils studying a foreign language must memorize vocabulary and grammatical rules. But as long as a pupil must refer consciously to what he has memorized, he will not read or speak fluently. The breakthrough to fluency (understanding without translation) occurs when the pupil stops paying attention to the subsidiary elements of grammar and vocabulary, and starts paying attention to his internalized sense of meaning. Smooth performance is always crippled by worrying about subsidiary elements in skills, under-

standings, and attitudes. Analysis and piecemeal mastery of parts can be helpful, but only if the separate masteries are reintegrated into the whole.

A whole can be broken into parts, each of which can be broken into subparts, ad infinitum. Likewise, anything regarded as a whole may later turn out to be only part of a still greater whole. A teacher's task, then, is not only to break a whole into parts for delivery to a pupil, but also to decide which level of the analysis is best for the pupil being taught. More mature pupils are able to understand concepts at a higher level of abstraction and are distracted and frustrated if a teacher requires close attention to particulars at too low a level. Likewise, immature pupils are unable to comprehend subject matter that is presented at too high a level.

FALLACIES IN FAVORITE METHODS

We have seen why rote memorization and recitation may be detrimental to a pupil's progress if continued for too long. The pupil's attention remains focused on the parts, and he is prevented from integrating them into awareness of the whole, which is the object of instruction. Almost everyone today agrees that rote learning can be useless or even harmful if carried to excess. But some recent fads in teaching methods depend on rote learning. Large numbers of new teachers have apparently learned by rote that rote learning is bad, without understanding why it is bad and how these popular methods are derived from it.

One popular technique is called "small-step learning." The idea is to break up subject matter into the smallest conceivable bits and feed them to pupils bit by bit. Even the most dull pupil can understand these bits; and so, we reason, we can feed a child all the bits, thereby making him understand the big idea.

What happens at best is that the pupil memorizes all the bits and gives them back to us on demand. The real test of understanding is to see whether a pupil can tell us a bit that was not told to him. That would demonstrate that he had integrated the bits we gave him into a greater whole and had generated the new bit out of that whole. But if we give the pupil all conceivable bits in the first place, we cannot rely on the fact that he gives us one back as proof that he understands the whole.

Programmed materials, teaching machines, and other forms of small-step learning are based on rote learning. As already noted, excessive concentration on the parts can cripple the process of integration, while analysis that is too simple for a pupil will bore, frustrate, and mislead him. Small-step learning can help slow learners and may occasionally improve the efficiency of bright pupils who get stuck at some point, but small-step learning can help only if the size of the steps and the level of delivery are carefully selected for the individual.

Behavior modification is another popular technique that can block higher-level understanding. In using this method, teachers give unruly or inattentive pupils praise, tokens, or pieces of candy for doing small tasks or parts of tasks correctly. Pupils can be rewarded for keeping silent for five minutes, or raising their hands in response to a teacher's question, or getting to class on time.

There are ethical questions about behavior modification that go beyond the scope of this paper. For example, we may criticize behavior modification as a form of materialistic bribery that leads to brainwashing. What concerns us here, however, is that the behavior that is rewarded must be short-term, physically observable, and precisely specified. Thus, behavior modification is a form of small-step learning and is subject to the criticisms developed earlier. Pupils have their attention focused on little pieces instead of what is important, so that integration to a higher level of awareness is blocked.

The same criticisms apply to some current efforts to improve the overall effectiveness of schools. In the arrangement known as "performance contracting," a corporation signs a contract with a school guaranteeing that by the end of a specified period every pupil will achieve a promised level on a standardized test. The corporation receives school-tax money for each child who succeeds, but must refund the money for each child who fails. The profit motive operates to create extra effort and efficiency in teaching. However, all the effort goes into achieving the goals written into the contract.

In performance contracting or in any form of performance-based education, the goals must be stated as specific, observable, short-range behaviors. Performance-based education is the newest version of teaching for the test. The chief flaw is that teachers and pupils are distracted from large-scale, important, general goals when their attention is focused on a list of nitty-gritties that only partially define the goals. The growing new fad called "performance-based teacher education" is especially hazardous to the profession of teaching. Professors who educate teachers are under increasing pressure to focus instruction on the least important, least generalizable elements of teaching. The long-term result of performance-based teacher education will be the production of a generation of teachers who lack professional judgment and flexibility. Instead of professionals who understand the complexities of educational problems, we shall have semiskilled craftsmen who can only reproduce a limited set of behaviors.

SOME GOOD METHODS OVERLOOKED

We have seen that the teacher's task is to break a whole into its parts and deliver the parts, while a pupil's task is to receive the parts and integrate them. The teacher depends on the pupil to do the integrating, which is of necessity a private act of creative intelligence. No teacher can do the integrating for a pupil. But teachers can sometimes prod pupils or lead them toward integration.

One way of promoting integration is to shock the pupil by doing or saying something unexpected. For example, pupils who have carefully practiced each procedure to be followed in case of fire may understand and integrate those procedures when the bell rings for an unannounced fire drill. Seventh-grade pupils studying rules of etiquette may suddenly discover how to follow those rules when attending their first school dance.

A less traumatic way of fostering integration is to have the pupil witness the correct performance of the whole, in the hope that he can model or imitate that performance. Thus, a pupil who is practicing pronunciation of foreign phrases begins by paying attention to specific movements of his own lips and tongue, but then watches and listens to a native speaker.

Since integration is internal and private, the best a teacher can do is to prod or lead a pupil toward his own discovery. But shock and modeling are not the only techniques available. We have seen that correct selection of the teacher's level of delivery is important: focusing attention at too low a level cripples integration. Can focusing attention at a level slightly too high promote integration? The answer is yes, but the explanation is complex.

Wholes have parts, which have subparts,

and so on. The phenomenon called "plateau learning" can now be accounted for. When pupils are learning how to type, they make steady gains in speed for a while but then make almost no further gains in speed despite much additional practice. At this point pupils are at a plateau: they must integrate subsidiary skills to a new level of wholeness before additional practice will improve speed. Then, once again speed improves with practice for a while until another plateau is reached. Plateau learning occurs in reading, mathematics, and other areas where skills are involved. The developmental stages described by Freud for personality, by Piaget for cognition, and by Kohlberg for moral reasoning might be regarded as plateaus.

When a pupil has reached a plateau, shock and modeling are two ways of hastening a breakthrough. Another way is to encourage pupils to "play around" with the whole above the plateau even though they have not completely mastered its parts. There is some evidence to suggest that when a pupil plays with a whole, its parts draw together. The reason is that a part derives its significance or meaning from belonging in the whole. Unmastered parts become more understandable when they are viewed in context.

Three paradoxical but useful principles of teaching may now be stated as applications of what has been said here:

1. A skill or a concept of moderate difficulty may be learned more easily when

studied only tangentially, as part of a more difficult skill or concept, than when studied directly. For example, pupils who are having difficulty with arithmetic may learn it painlessly when they study mechanical drawing or modern algebra in some of the "new math" programs. Pupils who have difficulty learning the grammar of a foreign language, or even the standard form of their native language, may improve their scores on grammar tests by stopping the direct study of grammar and learning some conversations by means of audiolingual methods. Pupils or employees can carry out instructions more effectively when told the purposes they serve.

2. Intuitive notation systems can facilitate faster learning of organized subject matter than standard notation systems, even counting the time required for pupils to transfer from the intuitive system to the standard system. For example, pupils learn to read English faster when the phonetically appealing initial teaching alphabet is used than when the ordinary alphabet is used, even counting the time needed later to change from the initial teaching alphabet to the standard one. As another example, pupils can learn how to program computers by writing programs for a while in the code system that is most intuitively appealing to them: ordinary English (that is, their native language); then, having mastered the general skill of programming, pupils can easily learn and apply new code systems such as FORTRAN and COBOL.

3. Pupils whose basic ideas are mistaken sometimes learn high-level correct ideas faster if encouraged to build a false system based on their mistaken ideas than if the pupils are shown their mistakes and required to start all over with correct ideas. This principle is obviously a corollary of the previous one, since the pupil's mistaken basic ideas are probably intuitively appealing to him. The point is that if a pupil is to gain a sense of depth or logical hierarchy, he will have to master the skill of moving from one plateau of parts to the integration of those parts into a whole at the next plateau. This skill may be mastered more easily if the pupil starts with ideas, even though mistaken, that seem natural to him. For example, in mathematics it is important to know how to reason from axioms to more complex theorems; once this skill is mastered pupils may make rapid progress regardless of which axioms are chosen as starting points. Pupils can learn to construct grammatically correct sentences even if their spelling is incorrect. Indeed, nonsense words can be used as in

> 'Twas brillig, and the slithy toves
> Did gyre and gimble in the wabe.[2]

Teachers are utterly dependent on their pupils for success in teaching skills, understandings, and attitudes. Teachers deliver parts, but only pupils can integrate the parts to achieve personal knowledge of the whole, which is the object of instruction.

A whole may be only part of a still greater whole. At any level, focusing on parts for too long may cripple the process of integrating them into their whole. Small-step learning, behavior modification, and performance-based education can therefore be detrimental to a pupil's deeper achievement. Shock, modeling, and teaching slightly above a pupil's level can help him master difficult parts and rise to higher plateaus.

Piaget's thinking has become so important to education that no discussion of guiding, thinking, and learning would be complete without thoughtful consideration of his ideas. Ginsburg and Opper review many of his central concepts and theories and show general guiding principles for education that emerge from them. This reading will be of particular interest to those who (will) teach elementary school children. The nature of children's thought and language, their need for active learning, the importance of novel experience, the use of self-regulation in learning, and other important facets are directly related in this article to problems of teaching and learning.

HERBERT GINSBURG
AND
SYLVIA OPPER

PIAGET:
IMPLICATIONS
FOR
EDUCATION

In [this selection], we will consider some general implications of Piaget's views for education. While Piaget himself has hardly dealt with the problems of education or with other practical applications of his work, it is clear nevertheless that his theories are particularly relevant for educational practice. Piaget's investigations into the development of a number of logical, physical, and mathematical notions, as well as other aspects of the child's thought, implicitly contain a number of ideas which, if suitably exploited and developed, could prove valuable to educators and educational planners. The potential of his findings for education has so far scarcely been acknowledged, and it is only fairly recently, during the past ten years or so, that psychologists and educators have begun to appreciate the importance of Piaget's the-

From Herbert Ginsburg and Sylvia Opper, *Piaget's Theory of Intellectual Development: An Introduction,* © 1969. Reprinted by permission of Prentice-Hall, Inc., Englewood Cliffs, N.J.

ories. Attempts are currently being made in various countries, especially in Great Britain, to modify existing school programs in line with the discoveries of the Geneva group, and these attempts could profitably be extended to other parts of the world. We will therefore attempt to extract from his theories a number of general principles which may be of value to the educator. It should be emphasized at the outset, however, that our intention is not to propose particular curricula or materials on the basis of Piaget's work. We will not describe, for example, a teaching sequence on number or on logical implication; rather, our concern is with general guiding principles which emerge from Piaget's psychological research. The implementation of these principles requires the special skills of the educator, not the psychologist.

DIFFERENCES BETWEEN ADULTS AND CHILDREN

Piaget's theory as a whole suggests a proposition, which, although quite general, should have important consequences for education. The proposition is that the young child is quite different from the adult in several ways: in methods of approaching reality, in the ensuing views of the world, and in the uses of language. His investigations concerning such matters as the concepts of number, or verbal communication, have enabled Piaget to contribute to a change, indeed one might almost say to a metamorphosis, in our ways of looking at children. As a result of his work we have become increasingly aware that the child is not just a miniature, although less wise adult, but a being with a distinctive mental structure which is qualitatively different from the adult's. He views the world from a unique perspective. For example, the child below the age of 7 years truly believes that water, when poured from one container to another, gains or loses in quantity, depending on the shape of the second container. For him there is no inconsistency in stating that a given amount of water gains or loses in quantity merely by being poured from one container to another. Or in the case of number, the young child, although able to count to 20 or more, has no conception of certain fundamental mathematical ideas. He may think, for example, that a set of five elements contains more than a set of eight elements, if the physical arrangement of the sets takes on certain forms.

These and many other unexpected discoveries concerning the child's notions of reality lead us to the surprising recognition that the child's world is in many respects qualitatively different from that of the adult. One reason for the child's distinctive view of reality is a distinctive mental structure. The young child (below about 7 or 8 years of age) centers his attention on limited amounts of information; he attends to states rather than transformations; he is egocentric, and fails to take into account other points of view; and he is incapable of forms of thought, like reversibility, which allows symbolic manipulation of the data

of experience. Even the older child (between 7 and 11 years), although capable of fairly subtle mental operations, is strongly tied to concrete situations. He reasons best only about immediately present objects, and fails to take into account the possibilities inherent in a situation.

One result of the child's cognitive structure is a view of reality which seems chaotic and unnatural to the adult. Another consequence is that the young child's use of language is different from the adult's. That is, the words that the child uses do not have the same meaning for him as for the adult. This point has sometimes been overlooked in the past. It was usually assumed that if a child used a particular word, this word naturally would convey the same meaning as when an adult used the same word. Adults believed that once a child has learned the linguistic label for an object, he has available the underlying concept. But Piaget has shown that this is often not the case. The child does learn his words from the adult, but assimilates them into his own mental structure, which is quite different from the adult's. The words "same amount to drink," for example, are interpreted in one way by the 4-year-old, and in another way by the adult. Only after a period of cognitive development does the child use these words and understand them in the same way as the more mature person.

The implication of this very general proposition — that the young child's thought and language are qualitatively different from the adult's — is also very general. It must follow that the educator must make a special effort to understand the unique properties of the child's experience and ways of thinking. The educator cannot assume that what is valid for him is necessarily valid for the child. For example, while the educator himself may learn a great deal by reading a book or listening to a lecture, similar experiences may be far less useful for the young child. While the educator may profit from an orderly arranged sequence of material, perhaps the child does not. While the educator may feel that a given idea is simple and indeed self-evident, perhaps the child finds it difficult. In short, it is not safe to generalize from the adult's experience to the child's. The educator's assumptions, based as they often are on his own learning experience, may not apply to children. What the educator needs to do is to try to improve his own capacity to watch and listen, and to place himself in the distinctive perspective of the child. Since the meaning expressed by the child's language is often idiosyncratic, the adult must try to understand the child's world by observing his actions closely. There are no easy rules or procedures for the educator to use in order to understand the child. What is needed chiefly is considerable sensitivity — a willingness to learn from the child, to look closely at his actions, and to avoid the assumption that what is true or customary for the adult is

also true for the child. The educator needs to interact with the child in a flexible way in order to gain insight into the latter's current level of functioning. With this attitude — a willingness to observe the child, to learn from him — the educator can begin to understand the child, and tailor the educational experience to the child's needs.

ACTIVITY

Perhaps the most important single proposition that the educator can derive from Piaget's work, and thus use in the classroom, is that children, especially young ones, learn best from concrete activities. We have seen throughout this book that Piaget places major emphasis on the role of activity in intellectual development, especially in the early years of life. In Piaget's view, one of the major sources of learning, if not the most essential one, is the intrinsic activity of the child. The child must act on things to understand them. Almost from birth, he touches objects, manipulates them, turns them around, looks at them, and in these ways he develops an increasing understanding of their properties. It is through manipulation that he develops schemes relating to objects. When new objects are presented, the child may at first try to apply to them already established schemes. If not successful, he attempts, again through manipulation, to develop new schemes; that is, new ways of acting on and thereby comprehending the world. This understanding may not be on a verbal

level. In fact, verbal understanding is not usually accomplished at the outset; it takes a long time. The child must begin by acting on objects, that is, by manipulating them. Over a period of time, these overt, sensorimotor schemes can become internalized in the form of thought. Still later the child may be able to express on a verbal level the notions he has developed on the basis of interaction with the world.

For these reasons a good school should encourage the child's activity, and his manipulation and exploration of objects. When the teacher tries to bypass this process by imparting knowledge in a verbal manner, the result is often superficial learning. But by promoting activity in the classroom, the teacher can exploit the child's potential for learning, and permit him to evolve an understanding of the world around him. This principle (that learning occurs through the child's activity) suggests that the teacher's major task is to provide for the child a wide variety of potentially interesting materials on which he may act. The teacher should not teach, but should encourage the child to learn by manipulating things.

Acceptance of the principle of active learning requires a considerable reorientation of beliefs concerning education. Teachers (and the public at large) usually consider that the aim of education is to impart knowledge of certain types. According to Piaget's theory, this conception is in error for several reasons. First, teachers can in fact impart or teach very little. It is true that they can get the child to *say* certain things, but these verbalizations often indicate little in the way of real understanding. Second, it is seldom legitimate to conceive of knowledge as a *thing* which can be transmitted. Certainly the child needs to learn some facts, and these may be considered *things*. But often the child does not learn facts if the teacher transmits them; the child must discover them himself. Also, facts are but a small portion of real knowledge. True understanding involves action, on both the motoric and intellectual levels. Consider for example the understanding of class properties. A traditional view might propose that the child learns some facts about classification; for instance, that a square is a geometric form. Piaget's view, on the other hand, argues that understanding of classification consists of a sequence of activities. First the child physically sorts or otherwise manipulates objects. He feels various forms and in this way, among others, perceives the differences among them. He may put different forms in different places. Later, he can sort the objects solely on a mental level. He does not need to separate things physically, but he can do it mentally. Later still, he can perform inclusion operations on the (imagined) classes of objects. He can consider that a hypothetical class includes and is "larger than" its constituent sub-class. Thus, knowledge of classification does not merely involve facts, but actions as well: physical sorting, mental sorting, mental inclusion operations. Furthermore, most of these actions are non-verbal.

The teacher's job then is not so much to transmit facts or concepts to the child, but to get him to act on both physical and mental levels. These actions — far more than imposed facts or concepts — constitute real knowledge. In this connection it may be useful to conceive of the child's understanding in terms of three levels.

The first of these levels is motoric understanding. Knowledge at this level implies that the child can act directly on objects and manipulate them correctly. He can adjust his movements to fit the properties of the objects, and thus indicate that he has understood them at the level of motor responses. For instance he can move objects, or lift them up, or turn them around. Another level of understanding is that of internal activity on an intuitive basis. The child performs actions on the objects in a very abbreviated and internal manner. Because the activity can be performed so much faster on a mental level than on an overt level, the child is able to do more in a given period of time. He is also no longer limited by spatial and temporal restrictions. Finally, there is the level of verbal understanding. The child is able to deal with concepts on an abstract verbal level, and he can often express his mental operations in words.

Several important comments can be made concerning these levels of understanding. First, the higher levels — intuitive and verbal — depend upon the lowest; that is, the motor. Manipulation of things is a prerequisite for higher, verbal understanding. The young child cannot jump to the higher levels before establishing a basis

in concrete manipulation. Therefore, concrete experience should precede learning from verbal explanations or written materials. Second, these different levels need not necessarily be restricted to given ages. It is unlikely, for example, that the preoperational child is completely intuitive in his approach, or that the adolescent is completely verbal. Rather it seems probable that at a given period of development one mode of understanding will predominate over, but not exclude the rest. For both these reasons, that is, the priority of concrete manipulation and the presence of all modes of understanding at all age levels (at least beyond infancy), children must have a chance to be active in the classroom, to touch and feel things, to find out what they do, to explore, and so forth. This is what real knowledge is about.

COGNITIVE STRUCTURE, NEW EXPERIENCE, AND SELF-REGULATION

Piaget's theory stresses the interaction of current cognitive structure and new experiences for the arousal of interest and the subsequent development of understanding. One way of putting the matter is to say that interest and learning are facilitated if the experience presented to the child bears some relevance to what he already knows but at the same time is sufficiently novel to present incongruities and conflicts.

If you will, recall the moderate novelty principle as an example which was discussed in the case of infancy (but applying to older children as well). Piaget's proposition is that the child's interest is aroused when an experience is moderately novel; the experience is not so radically novel as to be unassimilable into current cognitive structure; and it is not so familiar as to surfeit the child. This principle is relativistic: the experience does not contain in itself any intrinsic properties of interest. Rather, interest derives from the interaction between the state of the child's mind and the thing to be known.

Equilibration theory emphasizes that self-regulatory processes are the basis for genuine learning. The child is more apt to modify his cognitive structure in a constructive way when he controls his own learning than when methods of social transmission (in this case, teaching) are employed. Do recall Smedslund's experiments on the acquisition of conservation. If one tries to teach this concept to a child who does not yet have available the mental structure necessary for its assimilation, then the resulting learning is superficial. On the other hand, when children are allowed to progress at their own pace through the normal sequence of development, they regulate their own learning so as to construct the cognitive structures necessary for the genuine understanding of conservation.

These principles, if taken seriously, should lead to extensive changes in classroom practice. They imply, first, that teachers should be aware of the child's current level of functioning. Unless such an assessment is made, the teacher will find it difficult to judge what is apt to arouse the interest of his students. Second, the principles imply that the classroom must be oriented more toward the individual than the group. Since there are profound individual differences in almost all areas of cognitive development, it is unlikely that any one task or lesson will arouse the interest of or promote learning in all members of the class. For some children the task may be too easily assimilated into current mental structures, whereas for other students the problem may require a greater degree of accommodation than the student is at present capable of mastering. The result is boredom for the first group and confusion for the second. Third, children must be given considerable control over their own learning. Some may need more time than others to deal with the same material; similarly, children may approach the same problem in different ways.

To promote interest and learning, then, the teacher should tailor the curriculum to the individual. This means that the group should effectively be disbanded as the only classroom unit, that children should often work on individual projects and that they should be allowed considerable freedom in their own learning. Several objections are usually raised to this sort of proposal. First, if this were done, how could the teacher assure that all the children learn some common, required material? The answer is that he could not, unless the children's interests overlapped. But why is it essential for all children always to learn the same things? Second, under an individual learning arrangement, would not the children just waste their time or engage in mere play? This attitude, shared by many teachers, reveals a derogatory opinion concerning children's intellectual life, and a lack of faith in them. The attitude is clearly wrong too. Piaget has shown that the child is quite active in acquiring knowledge, and that he learns about important aspects of reality quite apart from instruction in the schools. In the first two years of life, for example, the infant acquires a primitive understanding of causality, of the nature of objects, of relations, of language, and of many other things, largely without the benefit of formal instruction or adult "teaching." One need only watch an infant for a short period of time to know that he is curious, interested in the world around him, and eager to learn. It is quite evident, too, that these are characteristics of older children as well. If left to himself the normal child does not remain immobile; he is eager to learn. Consequently, it is quite safe to permit the child to structure his own learning. The danger arises precisely when the schools attempt to perform the task for him. To understand this point consider the absurd situation that would result if traditional schools were entrusted with teaching the infant what he spontaneously learns during the first few years. The schools would develop organized curricula in secondary circular reactions; they would develop lesson plans for object permanence; they would construct audio-visual aids on causality; they would reinforce "correct" speech; and they would set "goals" for the child to reach each week. One can speculate as to the outcome of such a program for early training! What the student needs then is not formal teaching, but an opportunity to learn. He needs to be given a rich environment, containing many things potentially of interest. He needs a teacher who is sensitive to his needs, who can judge what materials will challenge him at a given point in time, who can help when he needs help, and who has faith in his capacity to learn.

LIMITATIONS AND OPPORTUNITIES

There are certain limitations on what the child can learn. His thought develops through a series of stages, each showing both strengths and weaknesses. Any one stage is characterized by the ability to perform certain actions typical of the particular stage, and, on the other hand, by the propensity to commit certain typical errors. Intellectual development is a progressive process. New mental structures evolve from the old ones by means of the dual processes of assimilation and accommodation. Faced with novel experiences, the child seeks to assimilate them into his existing mental framework. To do this, he may have to adjust and modify the framework, or

accommodate to the requirements of novel experience. New knowledge is never acquired in a discontinuous fashion, but is always absorbed into preexisting structures in such a way that prior experience is used to explain novelty, and novelty is adapted to fit previous experience. Mental development is more than a mere accumulation of isolated and unrelated experiences; it is a hierarchical process with the later acquisitions being built upon, and at the same time expanding upon the earlier ones.

One implication of the stage theory is in a way "pessimistic." Since intellectual development seems to follow an ordered sequence — a sequence which, until proof of the contrary, appears to be universal — the young child is incapable of learning certain kinds of concepts. It would serve no purpose, for instance, to try to teach a child of the preoperational period the principle of inertia, or any other abstract notion which requires the existence of reasoning at a formal operational level. A current trend prevails in the United States which believes that it is possible to teach anything to a child of any level of development, providing the appropriate method is used. Piaget's findings tend to stress the contrary. Certain things cannot be taught at any level, regardless of the method adopted. It is of course possible to accelerate some types of learning to a certain extent by use of suitable environmental stimuli. For instance, if a child of the preoperational period is fairly close to achieving the structure of concrete operations, suitable physical experience may expedite

the process, with the result that the structure may be acquired somewhat earlier than if no such experience had been presented. But presentation of the same experience to an infant would not have the same effect. The infant lacks much of the experience and mental development necessary to achieve concrete operations and would consequently not have available an appropriate mental structure into which he could fruitfully assimilate the planned experience. In all likelihood, the infant would assimilate the experience to fit his own level of understanding. He might learn something from it, but not what the teacher had had in mind. The experience, therefore, although being suitable to accelerate the achievement of concrete operations for the preoperational child, would have quite a different effect on the infant. The effects of experience are limited, then, by the intrinsic ability of the child at a particular stage of development.

Thus, one aspect of Piaget's stage theory is "pessimistic"; that is, it assumes that there are some things children cannot learn. But there is an "optimistic" side to his theory too. At each stage of development the child is capable of certain forms of thought, and he has spontaneously developed certain notions of reality. For example, Piaget has found that concepts of topological geometry (distinctions between closed vs. open figures, etc.) develop in the child before those of Euclidean geometry (measurement of angles, distances, etc.) and projective geometry (measurement of perspectives, coordinates, etc.). Understanding of topological notions appears fairly early in life, whereas the child only begins to understand the notion of Euclidean and projective geometry at around 7 years of age. Thus, while the 5-year-old may be incapable of learning projective concepts, he has already developed an intuitive understanding of topological notions. Each stage of development is characterized by both strengths and weaknesses.

There are several implications stemming from Piaget's proposition concerning the strengths and weaknesses of each stage of development. First, as we have already stressed, the teacher must try to be aware of the child's current level of cognitive functioning. To some extent the teacher can rely on Piaget's discoveries for this information. But Piaget's work is not sufficient, since it covers only a limited number of the subjects which are usually studied in schools. Therefore, the teacher himself must make an assessment of his students' capabilities. Even if revelant research were available, the teacher must still perform such an assessment since it is extremely likely that there are wide individual differences with respect to the understanding of any concept at almost any age level. The teacher's job is not easy. He should not place great reliance on standardized tests of achievement. Piaget's clinical method has shown that the child's

initial verbal response (the type of response that is given to a standard test) is often superficial and does not provide a reliable index of the real quality of his understanding. Tests often tap only the surface, and they also often test the wrong things. Again the teacher must observe the children carefully and attempt to discover both their intuitive competence and weakness in any area.

Second, once the teacher has some awareness of the child's current level of functioning, he can make available to the child experiences which facilitate development. For example, in the case of geometry, the teacher might first present his students with opportunities to learn about topological concepts (these opportunities would not, of course, involve teaching, but perhaps acquiring materials which emphasize topological distinctions and at which the child, under the teacher's general guidance, can work on independently). If such an arrangement were followed, the young student would feel comfortable with topological notions. His available mental structures would assure understanding of some topological concepts and others could be elaborated without great difficulty. Thus, his first school experiences with geometry should build upon and exploit what he already knows in an intuitive way.

SOCIAL INTERACTION

In Piaget's view, physical experience and concrete manipulation are not the only

ways in which the child learns. Another type of experience leading to understanding of the environment is social experience, or interaction with other persons, be they peers or adults. The effects of this type of experience, although almost negligible during the first few months of life, become increasingly important as the child grows older. We have pointed out earlier that one of the prime deterrents to an objective understanding of reality is the child's egocentric thought. He cannot view things objectively at first because he can only see them as related to himself. The very young child assimilates external events directly into his own action schemes. Things are only relevant to the extent that they concern his own private preoccupations. He cannot view objects or events from any other perspective besides his own. This egocentrism naturally prevents the child from gaining an objective view of objects or of persons. Gradually, as the child becomes capable of decentering his attention, as he begins to focus on various aspects of reality simultaneously, as he comes to understand another person's point of view, then he gains a more objective knowledge of reality.

One method which promotes the relinquishing of egocentrism is social interaction. When one child talks to another he comes to realize that his is not the only way of viewing things. He sees that other people do not necessarily share his opinions. Interaction inevitably leads to conflict and argument. The child's views are questioned. He must defend his ideas, and he must justify his opinions. In doing this he is forced to clarify his thoughts. If he wants to convince others of the validity of his own views, his ideas must be expressed clearly and logically. Other people are not as tolerant of his inconsistencies as he is himself. So we see that, apart from the more commonly stressed affective side of social interaction, or the need to get along with other people, there is an important cognitive component. Social experience not only helps people to adjust to others at an emotional level, it also serves to clarify a person's thinking and helps him to become in some ways more coherent and logical.

In both types of experience, physical and social, the teacher can help the child to develop his potential for activity. By providing a variety of objects which the child can manipulate, the teacher provides a setting for the empirical discovery of physical properties of things or the opportunity for understanding at the motoric or intuitive level. By providing the opportunity for social interaction, the teacher promotes an exchange of opinions which ultimately leads to understanding or learning at the verbal level.

It should be made clear that social experience is not independent from physical experience. Verbal exchange of opinions is not feasible on certain subjects until the prior physical experience which gave rise to the opinion has occurred. In fact during the early stages of development, it seems that physical experience, or motor activity, plays a relatively more important role than

language in the discovery of reality. Once the child has acted on an object or a situation, language can then serve as a major tool to internalize the experience into a compact category of experience. But the child's activity or experience is of paramount importance especially during the early stages of development.

The implication of Piaget's view is that social interaction should play a significant part in the classroom. Children should talk with one another. They should converse, share experience, and argue. It is hard to see why schools force the child to be quiet, when the results seem to be only an authoritarian situation and extreme boredom. Let us restrict the vow of silence to selected orders of monks and nuns.

Shulman examines the ideas of Bruner and compares them with Gagné's concepts of the learning process, thus allowing you to see two contrasting views of the role of discovery in learning. This article also provides helpful illustrations of the kind of teaching-learning procedures each view implies. It is important to become aware of why and when a teacher would select these different approaches. Examine the utility of each for your own learning. Then, keeping in mind what you think children ought to learn in school, ask yourself what strategy would best fit your teaching.

LEE S. SHULMAN

PSYCHOLOGICAL CONTROVERSIES IN TEACHING

The popular press has discovered the discovery method of teaching. It is by now, for example, an annual ritual for the Education section of *Time* magazine to sound a peal of praise for learning by discovery (e.g., *Time*, December 8, 1967). *Time*'s hosannas for discovery are by no means unique, reflecting as they do the educational establishment's general tendency to make good things seem better than they are. Since even the soundest of methods can be brought to premature mortality through an overdose of unremitting praise, it becomes periodically necessary even for advocates of discovery, such as I, to temper enthusiasm with considered judgment.

The learning by discovery controversy is a complex issue which can easily be oversimplified. A recent volume has dealt with many aspects of the issue in great detail (Shulman and Keislar, 1966). The controversy seems to center essentially about the question of how much and what kind of

Adapted from the article "Psychological Controversies in the Teaching of Science and Mathematics," by Lee S. Shulman, *Science Teacher* 35 (1968): 34–38, 89–90. Reprinted by permission.

guidance ought to be provided to students in the learning situation. Those favoring learning by discovery advocate the teaching of broad principles and problem-solving through minimal teacher guidance and maximal opportunity for exploration and trial-and-error on the part of the student. Those preferring guided learning emphasize the importance of carefully sequencing instructional experiences through maximum guidance and stress the importance of basic associations or facts in the service of the eventual mastering of principles and problem-solving.

Needless to say, there is considerable ambiguity over the use of the term *discovery*. One man's discovery approach can easily be confused with another's guided learning curriculum if the unwary observer is not alerted to the preferred labels ahead of time. For this reason I have decided to contrast the two positions by carefully examining the work of two men, each of whom is considered a leader of one of these general schools of thought.

Professor Jerome S. Bruner of Harvard University is undoubtedly the single person most closely identified with the learning-by-discovery position. His book, *The Process of Education* (1960), captured the spirit of discovery in the new mathematics and science curricula and communicated it effectively to professionals and laymen. His thinking will be examined as representative of the advocates of discovery learning.

Professor Robert M. Gagné of the University of California is a major force in the guided learning approach. His analysis of *The Conditions of Learning* (1965) is one of the finest contemporary statements of the principles of guided learning and instruction.

I recognize the potential danger inherent in any explicit attempt to polarize the positions of two eminent scholars. My purpose is to clarify the dimensions of a complex problem, not to consign Bruner and Gagné to irrevocable extremes. Their published writings are employed merely to characterize two possible positions on the role of discovery in learning, which each has expressed eloquently at some time in the recent past.

In this paper I will first discuss the manner in which Bruner and Gagné, respectively, describe the teaching of some particular topic. Using these two examples as starting points, we will then compare their positions with respect to instructional objectives, instructional styles, readiness for learning, and transfer of training. We will then examine the implications of this controversy for the process of instruction in science and mathematics and the conduct of research relevant to that process.

INSTRUCTIONAL EXAMPLE: DISCOVERY LEARNING

In a number of his papers, Jerome Bruner uses an instructional example from mathematics that derives from his collaboration with the mathematics educator, Z. P. Dienes (Bruner, 1966).

A class is composed of eight-year-old children who are there to learn some mathematics. In one of the instructional units, children are first introduced to three kinds of flat pieces of wood or "flats" (Figure 1). The first one, they are told, is to be called either the "unknown square" or "X square." The second flat, which is rectangular, is called "1 X" or just X, since it is X long on one side and 1 long on the other. The third flat is a small square which is 1 by 1, and is called 1.

After allowing the children many opportunities simply to play with these materials and to get a feel for them, Bruner gives the children a problem. He asks them, "Can you make larger squares than this X square by using as many of these flats as you want?" This is not a difficult task for most children and they readily make another square such as the one in Figure 2.

Bruner then asks them if they can describe what they have done. They might reply, "We have one square X, with two X's and a 1." He then asks them to keep a record of what they have done. He may even suggest a notational system to use. The symbol $X^\square$ could represent the square X, and a + for "and." Thus, the pieces used could be described as $X^\square + 2X + 1$.

Another way to describe their new square, he points out, is simply to describe each side. With an X and a 1 on each side, the side can be described as $X + 1$ and the square as $(X + 1)(X + 1)$ after some work with parentheses. Since these are two

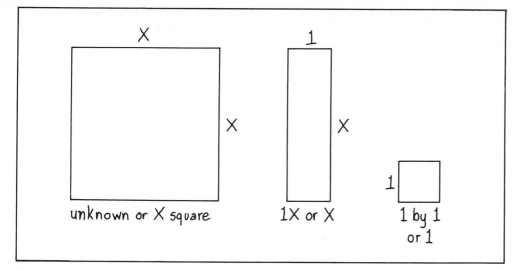

Figure 1.

ing in the outside world and some models or templates that he already has in his mind. For Bruner, it is rarely something *outside* the learner that is discovered. Instead the discovery involves an internal reorganization of previously known ideas in order to establish a better fit between those ideas and the regularities of an encounter to which the learner has had to accommodate.

This is precisely the philosophy of education we associate with Socrates. Remember the lovely dialogue of the *Meno* by Plato, in which the young slave boy is brought to an understanding of what is involved in doubling the area of a square. Socrates maintains throughout this dialogue that he is not teaching the boy any-

basic ways of describing the same square, they can be written in this way: $X^\square + 2X + 1 = (X + 1)(X + 1)$. This description, of course, far oversimplifies the procedures used.

The children continue making squares and generating the notation for them. (See Figure 3.)

At some point Bruner hypothesizes that they will begin to discern a pattern. While the X's are progressing at the rate of 2, 4, 6, 8, the ones are going 1, 4, 9, 16, and on the right side of the equation the pattern is 1, 2, 3, 4. Provocative or leading questions are often used Socratically to elicit this discovery. Bruner maintains that, even if the children are initially unable to break the code, they will sense that there is a pattern and try to discover it. Bruner then illustrates how the pupils transfer what they have learned to working with a balance beam. The youngsters are ostensibly learning not only something about quadratic equations, but more important, something about the discovery of mathematical regularities.

The general learning process described by Bruner occurs in the following manner: First, the child finds regularities in his manipulation of the materials that correspond with intuitive regularities he has already come to understand. Notice that what the child does for Bruner is to find some sort of match between what he is do-

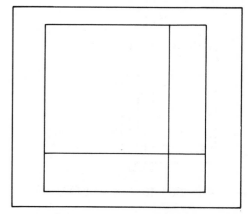

Figure 2.

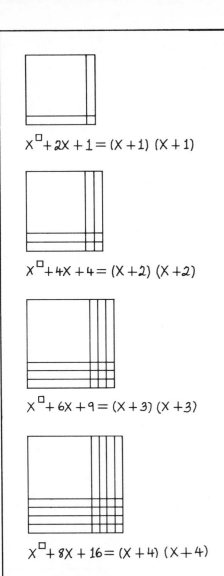

$X^\square + 2X + 1 = (X + 1)(X + 1)$

$X^\square + 4X + 4 = (X + 2)(X + 2)$

$X^\square + 6X + 9 = (X + 3)(X + 3)$

$X^\square + 8X + 16 = (X + 4)(X + 4)$

Figure 3.

thing new; he is simply helping the boy reorganize and bring to the fore what he has always known.

Bruner almost always begins with a focus on the production and manipulation of materials. He describes the child as moving through three levels of representation. The first level is the *enactive level,* where the child manipulates materials directly. He then progresses to the *ikonic level,* where he deals with mental images of objects but does not manipulate them directly. Finally he moves to the *symbolic level,* where he is strictly manipulating symbols and no longer mental images of objects. This sequence is an outgrowth of the developmental work of Jean Piaget. The synthesis of these concepts of manipulation of actual materials as part of a developmental model and the Socratic notion of learning as internal reorganization into a learning-by-discovery approach is the unique contribution of Jerome Bruner.

The Process of Education was written in 1959, after most mathematics innovations that use discovery as a core had already begun. It is an error to say that Bruner initiated the learning-by-discovery approach. It is far more accurate to say that, more than any one man, he managed to capture its spirit, provide it with a theoretical foundation, and disseminate it. Bruner is not the discoverer of discovery; he is its prophet.

INSTRUCTIONAL EXAMPLE: GUIDED LEARNING

Robert Gagné takes a very different approach to instruction. He begins with a task analysis of the instructional objectives. He always asks the question, "What is it you want the learner to be able to do?" This *capability* he insists, must be stated *specifically* and *behaviorally.*

By capability, he means the ability to perform certain specific functions under specified conditions. A capability could be the ability to solve a number series. It might be the ability to solve some problems in non-metric geometry.

This capability can be conceived of as a terminal behavior and placed at the top of what will eventually be a complex pyramid. After analyzing the task, Gagné asks, "What would you need to know in order to do that?" Let us say that one could not complete the task unless he could first perform prerequisite tasks *a* and *b*. So a pyramid begins (Figure 4). But in order to perform task *a*, one must be able to per-

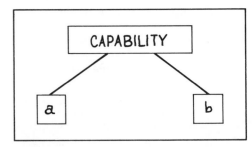

Figure 4.

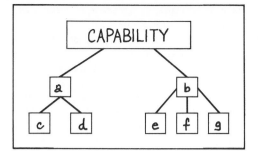

Figure 5.

form tasks *c* and *d* and for task *b,* one must know *e, f,* and *g* (Figure 5). So one builds a very complex pyramid of prerequisites to prerequisites to the objective which is the desired capability.

Gagné has developed a model for discussing the different levels of such a hierarchy. If the final capability desired is a *problem-solving* capability, the learner first must know certain *principles.* But to understand those principles, he must know specific *concepts,* and prerequisite to these are particular *simple associations* or *facts* discriminated from each other in a distinctive manner. He continues the analysis until he ends up with the fundamental building blocks of learning — classically or operantly conditioned responses.

Gagné, upon completing the whole map of prerequisites, would administer pretests to determine which have already been mastered. Upon completing the diagnostic testing, the resulting pattern identifies precisely what must be taught. This model is particularly conducive to subsequent pro-

graming of materials and programed instruction. When prerequisites are established, a very tight teaching program or package develops.

Earlier, we discussed the influences on Bruner. What influenced Gagné? This approach to teaching comes essentially from a combination of the neo-behaviorist psychological tradition and the task analysis model that dominates the fields of military and industrial training. It was precisely this kind of task analysis that contributed to successful programs of pilot training in World War II. Gagné was trained in the neo-behaviorist tradition and spent the major portion of his early career as an Air Force psychologist.

NATURE OF OBJECTIVES

The positions of Bruner and Gagné take very different points of view with respect to the objectives of education. This is one of the major reasons why most attempts at evaluating the relative effectiveness of these two approaches have come to naught. They really cannot agree on the same set of objectives. Any attempt to ask which is better — Michigan State's football team or the Chicago White Sox — will never succeed. The criteria for success are different, and it would be absurd to have them both on the same field competing against each other.

For Gagné, or the programed-instruction position which can be derived from him, the objectives of instruction are capabil-

ities. They are behavioral products that can be specified in operational terms. Subsequently they can be task-analyzed; then they can be taught. Gagné would subscribe to the position that psychology has been successful in suggesting ways of teaching only when objectives have been made operationally clear. When objectives are not clearly stated, the psychologist can be of little assistance. He insists on objectives clearly stated in behavioral terms. They are the cornerstones of his position.

For Bruner, the emphasis is quite different. The emphasis is not on the *products* of learning but on the *processes.* One paragraph from *Toward a Theory of Instruction* captures the spirit of educational objectives for Bruner. After discussing the mathematics example previously mentioned, he concludes,

Finally, a theory of instruction seeks to take account of the fact that a curriculum reflects not only the nature of knowledge itself — the specific capabilities — but also the nature of the knower and of the knowledge-getting process. It is the enterprise par excellence where the line between the subject matter and the method grows necessarily indistinct. A body of knowledge, enshrined in a university faculty, and embodied in a series of authoritative volumes is the result of much prior intellectual activity. To instruct someone in these disciplines is not a matter of getting him to commit the results to mind; rather, it is to teach him to participate in the process that makes possible the establishment of knowledge. We teach a subject, not to produce little living libraries from that subject, but rather to get a student to think mathematically for himself, to consider matters as a historian does, *to take part in the process of knowledge-getting. Knowing is a process, not a product.* (Bruner, 1966, p. 72. Italics mine.)

Speaking to the same issue, Gagné's position is clearly different.

Obviously, strategies are important for problem solving, regardless of the content of the problem. The suggestion from some writings is that they are of overriding importance as a goal of education. After all, should not formal instruction in the schools have the aim of teaching the student "how to think"? If strategies were deliberately taught, would not this produce people who could then bring to bear superior problem-solving capabilities to any new situation? Although no one would disagree with the aims expressed, it is exceedingly doubtful that they can be brought about by teaching students "strategies" or "styles" of thinking. Even if these could be taught (and it is possible that they could), they would not provide the individual with the basic firmament of thought, which is subject-matter knowledge. Knowing a set of strategies is not all that is required for thinking; it is not even a substantial part of what is needed. *To be an effective problem solver, the individual must somehow have acquired masses of structurally organized knowledge. Such knowledge is made up of content principles, not heuristic ones.* (Gagné, 1965, p. 170. Italics mine.)

While for Bruner "knowing is a process, not a product," for Gagné, "knowledge is made up of content principles, not heuristic ones." Thus, though both espouse the acquisition of knowledge as the major objective of education, their definitions of *knowledge* and *knowing* are so disparate that the educational objectives sought by each scarcely overlap. The philosophical and psychological sources of these differences will be discussed later in this paper. For the moment, let it be noted that when two conflicting approaches seek such contrasting objectives, the conduct of comparative educational studies becomes extremely difficult.*

INSTRUCTIONAL STYLES

Implicit in this contrast is a difference in what is meant by the very words *learning by discovery.* For Gagné, *learning* is the goal. How a behavior or capability is learned is a function of the task. It may be by discovery, by guided teaching, by practice, by drill, or by review. The focus is

---

* Gagné has modified his own position somewhat since 1965. He would now tend to agree, more or less, with Bruner on the importance of processes or strategies as objectives of education. He has not, however, changed his position regarding the role of sequence in instruction, the nature of readiness, or any of the remaining topics in this paper (Gagné, 1968). The point of view concerning specific behavioral products as objectives is still espoused by many educational theorists and Gagné's earlier arguments are thus still relevant as reflections of that position.

on *learning* and discovery is but one way to learn something. For Bruner, it is learning *by discovery.* The method of learning is the significant aspect.

For Gagné, in an instructional program the child is carefully guided. He may work with programed materials or a programed teacher (one who follows quite explicitly a step-by-step guide). The child may be quite active. He is not necessarily passive; he is doing things, he is working exercises, he is solving problems. But the sequence is determined entirely by the program. (Here the term "program" is used in a broad sense, not necessarily simply a series of frames.)

For Bruner much less system or order is necessary for the package, although such order is not precluded. In general Bruner insists on the child manipulating materials and dealing with incongruities or contrasts. He will always try to build potential or emergent incongruities into the materials. Robert Davis calls this operation "torpedoing" when it is initiated by the teacher. He teaches a child something until he is certain the child knows it. Then he provides him with a whopper of a counterexample. This is what Bruner does constantly — providing contrasts and incongruities in order to get the child, because of his discomfort, to try to resolve this disequilibrium by making some discovery (cognitive restructuring). This discovery can take the form of a new synthesis or a new distinction. Piaget, too, maintains that cognitive development is a process of successive disequilibria and equilibria. The child, confronted by a new situation, gets out of balance and must accommodate to achieve a new balance by modifying the previous cognitive structure.

Thus, for Gagné, instruction is a smoothly guided tour up a carefully constructed hierarchy of objectives; for Bruner, instruction is a roller-coaster ride of successive disequilibria and equilibria until the desired cognitive state is reached or discovered.

READINESS

The guided learning point of view, represented by Gagné, maintains that readiness is essentially a function of the presence or absence of prerequisite learning.

When the child is capable of d and e in Figure 6, he is by definition ready to

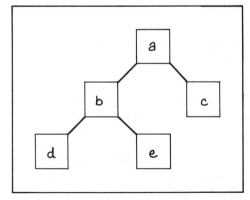

Figure 6.

learn b. Until then he is not ready. Gagné is not concerned with genetically developmental considerations. If the child at age five does not have the concept of the conservation of liquid volume, it is not because of an unfolding in his mind; he just has not had the necessary prior experiences. Ensure that he has acquired the prerequisite behaviors, and he will be able to conserve (Gagné, 1966).

For Piaget (and Bruner) the child is a developing organism, passing through cognitive stages that are biologically determined. These stages are more or less age-related, although in different cultures certain stages may come earlier than others. To identify whether the child is ready to learn a particular concept or principle, one analyzes the structure of that to be taught and compares it with what is already known about the cognitive structure of the child at that age. If they are consonant, it can be taught; if they are dissonant, it cannot.

Given this characterization of the two positions on readiness, to which one would you attribute the following statement? ". . . any subject can be taught effectively in some intellectually honest form to any child at any stage of development." While it sounds like Gagné, you recognize that it isn't — it's Bruner! (1966, p. 33). And in this same chapter he includes an extensive discussion of Piaget's position. Essentially he is attempting to translate Piaget's theories into a psychology of instruction.

Many are puzzled by this stand, including Piaget. In a recent paper delivered

in the United States, he admitted that he did not understand how Bruner could make such a statement in the light of Piaget's experiments. If Bruner meant the statement literally; i.e., *any* child can learn *anything,* then it just is not true! There are always things a child cannot learn, especially not in an intellectually honest way. If he means it homiletically, i.e., we can take almost anything and somehow resay it, reconstruct it, restructure it so it now has a parallel at the child's level of cognitive functioning, then it may be a truism.

I believe that what Bruner is saying, and and it is neither trivial nor absurd, is that our older conceptions of readiness have tended to apply Piagetian theory in the same way as some have for generations applied Rousseau's. The old thesis was, "There is the child — he is a developing organism, with invariant order, invariant schedule. Here, too, is the subject matter, equally hallowed by time and unchanging. We take the subject matter as our starting point, watch the child develop, and feed it in at appropriate times as he reaches readiness." Let's face it; that has been our general conception of readiness. We gave reading readiness tests and hesitated to teach the pupil reading until he was "ready." The notion is quite new that the reading readiness tests tell not when to begin teaching the child, but rather what has to be done to get him more ready. We used to just wait until he got ready.

What Bruner is suggesting is that we must modify our conception of readiness so that it includes not only the child but the subject matter. Subject matter, too, goes through stages of readiness. The same subject matter can be represented at a manipulative or enactive level, at an ikonic level, and finally at a symbolic or formal level. The resulting model is Bruner's concept of a spiral curriculum.

Piaget himself seems quite dubious over the attempts to accelerate cognitive development that are reflected in many modern math and science curricula. On a recent trip to the United States, Piaget commented,

... We know that it takes nine to twelve months before babies develop the notion that an object is still there even when a screen is placed in front of it. Now kittens go through the same stages as children, all the same substages, but they do it in three months — so they're six months ahead of babies. Is this an advantage or isn't it? We can certainly see our answer in one sense. The kitten is not going to go much further. The child has taken longer, but he is capable of going further, so it seems to me that the nine months probably were not for nothing.

It's probably possible to accelerate, but maximal acceleration is not desirable. There seems to be an optimal time. What this optimal time is will surely depend upon each individual and on the subject matter. We still need a great deal of research to know what the optimal time would be. (Jennings, 1967, p. 82.)

The question that has not been answered, and which Piaget whimsically calls the "American question," is the empirical experimental question: To what extent it is possible through a Gagnéan approach to accelerate what Piaget maintains is the invariant clockwork of the order? Studies being conducted in Scandinavia by Smedslund and in this country by Irving Sigel, Egon Mermelstein, and others are attempting to identify the degree to which such processes as the principle of conservation of volume can be accelerated. If I had to make a broad generalization, I would have to conclude that at this point, in general, the score for those who say you cannot accelerate is somewhat higher than the score for those who say that you can. But the question is far from resolved; we need many more inventive attempts to accelerate cognitive development than we have had thus far. There remains the question of whether such attempts at experimental acceleration are strictly of interest for psychological theory, or have important pedagogical implications as well — a question we do not have space to examine here.

SEQUENCE OF THE CURRICULUM

The implications for the sequence of the curriculum growing from these two positions are quite different. For Gagné, the highest level of learning is problem solving, lower levels involve facts, concepts, principles, etc. Clearly, for Gagné, the appropriate sequence in learning is, in terms of Figure 7, from the bottom up. One begins with simple prerequisites and works up, pyramid fashion, to the complex capability sought.

For Bruner, the same diagram may be appropriate, but the direction of the arrow would be changed (Figure 7). He has a pupil begin with *problem solving*. This process is analogous to teaching someone to swim by throwing him into deep water. The theory is that he will learn the fundamentals because he needs them. The analogy is not totally misbegotten. In some of the extreme discovery approaches we lose a lot of pupils by mathematical or scientific drowning. As one goes to the extreme of this position, he runs the risk of some drownings. For Gagné, the sequence is from the simple to the complex; for Bruner one starts with the complex and plans to learn the simple components in the context of working with the complex.

It is unclear whether Bruner subscribes to his position because of his concept of the nature of learning or for strictly motivational reasons. Children may be motivated more quickly when given a problem they cannot solve, than they are when given some little things to learn on the promise that if they learn these well, three weeks from now they will be able to solve an exciting problem. Yet, Bruner clearly maintains that learning things in this fashion also improves the transferabil-

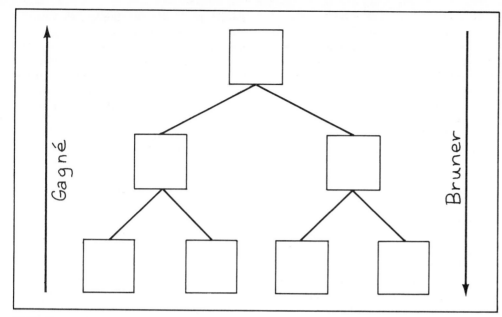

Figure 7.

ity of what is learned. It is to a consideration of the issue of transfer of training that we now turn.

TRANSFER OF TRAINING

To examine the psychologies of learning of these two positions in any kind of comprehensive form would require greater attention than can be devoted here, but we shall consider one concept — that of transfer of training. This is probably the central concept, or should be, in any educationally relevant psychology of learning.

Gagné considers himself a conservative on matters of transfer. He states that "transfer occurs because of the occurrence of specific identical (or highly similar) elements within developmental sequences" (Gagné, 1966, p. 20). To the extent that an element which has been learned, be it association, concept, or principle, can be directly employed in a new situation, transfer will occur. If the new context requires a behavior substantially different from the specific capability mastered earlier, there will be no transfer.

Bruner, on the other hand, subscribes to the broadest theories of transfer of training. Bruner believes that we can have massive transfer from one learning situation to another. Broad transfer of training occurs when one can identify in the structures of subject matters basic, fundamentally simple concepts or principles which, if learned well, can be transferred both to other subject matters within that discipline and to other disciplines as well. He gives examples such as the concept of conservation or balance. Is it not possible to teach balance of trade in economics in such a way that when ecological balance is considered, pupils see the parallel? This could then be extended to balance of power in political science, or to balancing equations.

Even more important, for Bruner, is the broad transferability of the knowledge-getting process — strategies, heuristics, and the like — transfer whose viability leaves Gagné with deep feelings of doubt. This is the question of whether learning by discovery leads to the ability *to* discover, that is, the development of broad inquiry competencies in students.

What does the evidence from empirical studies of this issue seem to demonstrate? The findings are not all that consistent. I would generalize them by saying that most often guided learning or expository sequences seem to be superior methods for achieving immediate learning. With regard to long-term retention, the results seem equivocal, with neither approach consistently better. Discovery learning approaches appear to be superior when the criterion of transfer of principles to new situations is employed (Worthen, 1968). Notably absent are studies which deal with the question of whether general techniques, strategies, and heuristics of discovery can be learned — by discovery or in any other manner — which will transfer across grossly different kinds of tasks.

Why is transfer of training superior in the discovery situation when the learning of principles is involved? There are two kinds of transfer — positive transfer and negative transfer. We call something positive transfer when mastery of task X facilitates mastery of task Y. Negative transfer occurs when mastery of task X inhibits mastery of task Y. Positive transfer is a familiar notion for us. Negative transfer can be exemplified by a piece of advice baseball coaches often give their players. They tell them not to play golf during the baseball season because the baseball swing and the golf swing involve totally different muscles and body movements. Becoming a better golf swinger interferes with the baseball swing. In psychological terms there is negative transfer between golf and baseball.

What is needed for positive transfer is to minimize all possible interference. In transfer of training, there are some ways in which the tasks transferred to are like the ones learned first, but in other ways they are different. So transfer always involves striking a balance between these conflicting potentials for both positive and negative transfer. In discovery methods, learners may transfer more easily because they learn *the immediate things less well*. They may thus learn the broad strokes of a principle, which is the aspect most critical for remote transfer, while not learning well the detailed application of that specific principle, which could interfere somewhat with successful remote transfer.

If this formulation is correct, we are never going to find a method that will both allow for tremendous specific learning of products and broad transfer, because we are dealing in a closed system in which one must make a choice. To the extent that initial learning is well done, transfer is restricted. The instructor may have to decide which is more important — an immediate specific product or broad transfer — and choose his subsequent teaching method on the basis of that decision. This is a pessimistic view, and I hope that future studies might find it flawed.

In this excerpt from How Children Learn, Holt discusses what goes on in his mind when thinking through problems or listening to the explanations of others. He gives several vivid examples of how he grasped an insight or worked out a solution even though his mind resisted con-tinued productive functioning. Holt is **also very adept at putting himself in the role of a child learning new concepts and provides a likely explanation of how language and other new learning occurs. After reading this excerpt, you will probably find it helpful to restate in your own words the factors that, according to Holt, contribute to effective thinking.**

JOHN HOLT

THE MIND AT WORK

One of the puzzles we had in my fifth-grade class was a geometrical puzzle called *Hako*. You began with a number of thin, flat, rectangular plastic pieces arranged a certain way in a shallow box. The aim was to slide them around, without turning them or lifting them out of the box, so as to finish with the largest piece, a square, at the opposite end of the box from which it started. Though I spent many hours on it, I was never able to do it. This exasperated me. What exasperated me even more was that I seemed to be able to prove that the puzzle was impossible — though I knew it was not. Like most people, I be-

From *How Children Learn* by John Holt. Copyright © 1967 by Pitman Publishing Corporation. Reprinted by permission of Pitman Publishing Corporation.

gan by moving the pieces around in a kind of blind, haphazard way. Before long, and unwisely, I grew impatient with this. There were too many possible moves, this could go on forever. The thing to do was use the brain and figure it out. So, moving the pieces very carefully, and analyzing each move, I deduced that in order to get the large piece from the top to the bottom, certain other things had to happen along the way. There had to be a point at which certain of the pieces were going up past the big piece while it was going down. Then, still carefully analyzing, I showed that this could only happen if certain other pieces moved in certain ways. Finally, I proved that they could not be moved in those ways. Therefore the problem was impossible.

The trouble was, I knew it wasn't impossible. Companies don't sell impossible puzzles; they would be sued, or worse. Besides, the puzzle had been mentioned in the *Scientific American*. Besides that, and worst of all, some students had done it. With all my heart I wanted to believe that they had lied or cheated, but I could not convince myself; they weren't the type. I remember thinking furiously, "I suppose anyone could do this puzzle if he were willing to sit in front of it like a nitwit, moving the pieces around blindly, until just by dumb luck he happened to get it. I haven't got time for that sort of thing." More to the point, I felt above that sort of thing.

I went back to the puzzle many times, hoping that I would find some fresh ap-proach to it; but my mind kept moving back into the little groove it had made for itself. I tried to make myself forget my supposed proof that the problem was impossible. No use. Before long I would be back at the business of trying to find the flaw in my reasoning. I never found it. Like many other people, in many other situations, I had reasoned myself into a box. Looking back at the problem, and with the words of Professor Hawkins in my ears, I saw my great mistake. I had begun to reason too soon, before I had allowed myself enough "Messing About," before I had built a good enough mental model of the ways in which those pieces moved, before I had given myself enough time to explore all the possible ways in which they could move. The reason some of the children were able to do the puzzle was not that they did it blindly, but that they did not try to solve it by reason until they had found by experience what the pieces could do. Because their mental model of the puzzle was complete, it served them; because mine was incomplete, it failed me.

In one of the classes I previously shared with Bill Hull, we worked a good deal with a three-dimensional puzzle named *Soma*, also described and discussed in the *Scientific American*. In this, twenty-seven cubes of wood were glued together to make six four-cube pieces and one three-cube piece. The aim was to use these seven pieces to make various other shapes, beginning with a cube and other simple shapes, and going on to more complicated shapes such as the Tunnel, the Bathtub, the Castle, etc. It was a splendid puzzle, one of the very best I have ever seen, among other reasons because children can work on it at many different degrees of difficulty.

My first meeting with this puzzle was embarrassing. A person familiar with it can make the cube in less than half-a-minute in any one of several different ways. By the time I started trying to make the cube, a number of the children were able to do it in about fifteen seconds. My first effort took me about fifty minutes. I tried to keep my struggles out of the sight of the children, but there were some pointed questions. Fortunately I was able to avoid falling into the trap of analyzing too soon, perhaps only because I could not see how to. Unable to think of any "sensible" way to proceed, I fiddled with the pieces, trying to fit them this way and that, making mistakes, working myself into dead ends, going back and starting again. One of the frustrating things about this particular puzzle is that if you have it almost right, you know you have it entirely wrong. When you find yourself saying, "If this piece just looked like that piece, I could do it," you have to start almost from the beginning. By many such trials and errors, retrials and corrections, I was finally able, like many of the children, to build up a good mental model of the way these pieces worked. With this model I could tell, without having to try it out, that a certain piece, or even combination of pieces, would not go in a certain spot, and could see several pieces in advance when I was going wrong. Before long I became one of the class experts.

Such experiences suggest a reason why so much that seems to me trivial, misleading, or downright false, has been written about child psychology. The psychologists, on the whole, have not done enough of Professor Hawkins' "Messing About." They have not seen enough children in their native habitat — homes, schools, playgrounds, streets, stores, anywhere. They haven't talked or played with enough of them, or helped them, or comforted them, or coerced them, or made them pleased, or excited, or rebellious, or angry. Unless he is very fortunate, a young psychologist is very likely to have his head stuffed full of theories of children before he has had a chance to look at any. When he does start looking at them, it is likely to be in very special laboratory or testing situations. Like many teachers, he may not recognize the many ways in which children betray anxiety, because he has never seen them in a situation in which they were not anxious. Also, like me trying to do the puzzle, he may be so much a prisoner of his theories that he cannot see anything that does not fit into them.

For such reasons I would like to stress again what I said very early in my book. My aim in writing it is not primarily to persuade educators and psychologists to swap new doctrines for old, but to persuade them to *look* at children, patiently, repeatedly, respectfully, and to hold off making theories and judgments about them until they have in their minds what most of them do not now have — a reasonably accurate model of what children are like.

I should add, too, that I am not trying to deny the importance of close, deductive, analytical, logical reasoning. In its proper place, it is a useful, powerful, often essential tool. I am only trying to say that out of its place, it is likely to be not only useless but harmful, and that its place is not everywhere. It works when we have a very limited amount of evidence, all we are going to get, and from it have to reconstruct the past — find out who committed a crime, or how and why an accident took place, or what is ailing in a particular man, or machine. It works when we can limit and isolate, one by one, the variables we have to deal with. Thus the skilled repairman, trying to find out why a machine is working badly, checks its various elements, one by one, until he finds the one that is causing the trouble. Thus the scientist, meeting a new phenomenon in the lab, changes, one by one, the conditions of the experiment until he finds the one that seems to affect the phenomenon. And we use this kind of reasoning to check our hypotheses, our theories or hunches about why things work as they do. We say, "If this theory is true, then certain other things ought to happen,"

and then we find out whether in fact they do happen. If they do, the theory is confirmed, temporarily, at least. The story is told of Einstein that, after the observations of some astronomers seemed to have confirmed his Theory of Relativity, a woman congratulated him on his theory having been proved right. He said, "Madam, a thousand experiments can never prove me right; a single experiment can prove me wrong." Even when the facts seem to support our reasoning, we must, like Einstein, not assume that we have found the final truth.

But if there are times and places and conditions where this kind of reasoning is useful, there are others where it does not work at all. If the experience before us is completely new and strange; if there is much new material to be observed, material that doesn't seem to fall into any recognizable pattern or order; if we cannot tell what are the variables that influence the situation, much less isolate them, we will be unwise to try to think like a detective, or a scientist in a laboratory.

Some years ago, some sociologists were trying to draw analogies between the behavior of molecules in a gas and the behavior of human beings in society, and from there between the laws that describe or explain the behavior of gasses and comparable laws that would supposedly describe and explain the behavior of human beings in society. This is a very good example of how not to use the scientific method. In such situations, we must use our minds very differently. We must clear them of preconceived notions, we must suspend judgment, we must open ourselves to the situation, take in as much data as we can, and wait patiently for some kind of order to appear out of the chaos. In short, we must think like a little child.

It may be useful to describe a few situations in which I had to, and was able to, make myself think this way. One bright summer day some friends took me to the Haystack School of Arts and Crafts in Maine. There, for the first time, I saw a hand loom. One of the teachers had it out in the sunshine, on one of the many broad, wooden terraces that look down a hill and over the sea. She was setting it up for some weaving, and my hosts gathered around to talk about what she was doing and was planning to do.

After looking at the machine a while, and listening to this informed talk, I felt the faint beginnings of anxiety. A hand loom is a very open machine; all the parts of it can be clearly seen. It seemed to me that after some careful looking and reasoning I ought to be able to figure out how this machine worked. But I couldn't. It looked like nothing but a jumble and confusion of little parts, wires, and scraps of wood. None of it made any sense at all. Nor could I think how to make sense of it. Where to begin?

In such situations we tend to have a defensive reaction, which I began to sense in myself. Confronted with what it cannot grasp, the mind tends to turn away, to shut it out. We say to ourselves, "Oh, well, who cares about looms and weaving, anyway?" We seek the relief of thinking about something that we can grasp and understand. Having learned to recognize this protective and cowardly strategy, I would not allow myself to use it. I thought, "Come on, now, quit acting like a scared kid." I examined the loom more carefully, and began to ask myself intelligent questions. What's this for? Where does this lead? But no use. It remained as much a mystery as ever. The anxiety grew, with a little shame added. Some of this was caused by not being able to make sense of the loom. Some was caused by my feeling that as a supposedly fairly intelligent man I ought to be able to make sense out of it. Like children in school, I was worried by the fear of not being able to live up to my own concept of myself. Finally, I knew that everyone else around me knew how that loom worked, and knew that I didn't. I could almost hear them thinking, "Funny about John, he's usually pretty smart about most things, yet that simple loom, that you would think anyone could understand, is too much for him." Then, to make matters worse, they began to try to help by giving explanations. They spoke with that infuriating mixture of indulgence and impatience with which the expert always explains things to the non-expert. It is always gratifying to be able to understand what someone else cannot; and more gratifying yet to make yourself his benefactor, by explaining it to him; and still more gratifying — unless you are required to make him understand — if in spite of your explanation he con-

tinues not to understand. In this spirit my friends began to say, "It's really very simple; this piece here . . ."

After a certain amount of this I said, rather sharply, "Please stop talking about it, and just let me look at it." I thought to myself, "Remember what you have learned about learning. Be like a child. Use your eyes. Gag that teacher's mouth inside your head, asking all those questions. Don't try to analyze this thing, look at it, take it in." And shutting out of mind the knowing conversation of the others, I did so. Now and then the voice inside would begin to ask questions. I silenced it, and for sometime went on looking.

There were many other things to see: potters, print makers, and most exciting of all, glass blowers. After seeing them all, we started home. And as we drove a most extraordinary thing began to happen. I was not thinking about the loom; as my host was a potter, we were talking mostly about the pottery. But as we talked, a loom began slowly to put itself together in my mind. There is no other way to describe it. Suddenly, for no reason, the image of a particular part would suddenly appear in my consciousness, but in such a way that I understood what that part was for. When I say "understood," I don't mean that some kind of verbal explanation went along with it. I mean that I could see what the part was for and what it did, I could almost see it doing its work. If I had been building a loom and had had that part in my hand, I would have known where to put it.

This loom-building process was very slow. It would be interesting to have a record of the order in which the parts of this loom appeared and assembled themselves, but I have none. Sensing that something important was happening in the non-verbal, non-conscious part of my mind, I did not want to look too hard at the process, lest I bring it to a stop. Also, I had no way of knowing, at any time, how much further it would go. When the first part of the loom appeared in my surprised consciousness, I had no reason to believe that other parts would later appear in the same way. However, they did, some during our trip home, others during the rest of the day, some even the following day. By the end of that day, a loom had made itself in my mind. There was a working model of a loom in there. If I had had to build a loom, I would have known at least roughly what parts were needed and where they went. There was much about the loom that I didn't know, but I now knew where knowledge left off and ignorance began; knew the questions I needed to ask; knew enough to be able to make sense of the answers. Some of what people had told me, trying to explain the loom, came back to me, and now I could see what their words meant.

Explanations. We teachers — perhaps all human beings — are in the grip of an astonishing delusion. We think that we can take a picture, a structure, a working model of something, constructed in our minds out of long experience and familiarity, and by turning that model into a string of words, transplant it whole into the mind of someone else. Perhaps once in a thousand times, when the explanation is extraordinarily good, and the listener extraordinarily experienced and skillful at turning word strings into non-verbal reality, and when explainer and listener share in common many of the experiences being talked about, the process may work, and some real meaning may be communicated. Most of the time, explaining does not increase understanding, and may even lessen it.

A few years ago I spent an evening, at Bill Hull's house, in the company of a number of people who were all interested in teaching mathematics to children. For most of the evening we talked about things we had done in classes, or were thinking of doing. As the party began to break up, one of the group, a most distinguished visitor from abroad, confessed that although most of the materials he had developed for children dealt with numbers and numerals, or with algebra, his own real love was geometry. Not the old-fashioned plane geometry that most people have met in school, but a much more advanced and exotic geometry. Memory tells me that he called it projective geometry, though it didn't sound like the only projective geometry I had

ever read about. I asked him what he liked so much about this branch of mathematics. He replied that it was the beauty and simplicity of the theorems. "Such as what?" I asked. It was a mistake. His eyes flashed with enthusiasm. Such as the proof that intersection of two quartics is a twisted cubic. Seeing a glazed look in my eyes, he began to sketch the proof. I held up a hand, laughing, and said, "Whoa, wait a minute, I've never even heard of these things, I don't know what a quartic or a cubic is, much less a twisted cubic." Too late. The teaching fit was on him. He began to "explain." As he saw that I still did not understand, he began to grow exasperated — like most teachers when their "explanations" are not being understood. "It's really very simple!" he said, as his hands sketched complicated shapes in the air. I was amused, but appalled. Here was a really great teacher, who for years had been working with young children trying to find ways to have them experience and discover, with hands and eyes, the relationships of mathematics. Yet in spite of his long experience, he believed so strongly in the magic power of explanations that he thought he could drop me into the middle of an advanced and complex branch of mathematics, in which I had absolutely no knowledge or experience, and with a few words and waves of the hand make the whole thing clear.

Jerome Bruner has said that one thing that happens in school is that children are led to believe they don't know or can't do something that they knew, or could do, before they got to school. I have seen this demonstrated many times, but never as vividly as in the following example, quoted from the prospectus of the Green Valley School, in which George von Hilsheimer writes:

One of our art associates once conducted an experiment in her art resources classroom. As the children entered the classroom they found construction paper on the desks. The teacher held up a folded fan — like those you and I have made many times — "Know what this is?"
"Oh, yes!"
"Can you make one?"
"Yes! Yes!"
Every child quickly made the little fan. The teacher then read from the book the instructions on how to make the fan. She read slowly, with proper emphasis and phrasing. The instructions were well designed to be clear to the fifth grade mind. After reading, the teacher asked the children to make the fans again. Not one child could make a fan. The teacher sat at each desk and tried to get the children to go back to the first way they had made the fan (with the fan still lying on the desk). They could not.
There have been many such experiments in educational psychology. Unfortunately, few teachers and even fewer school systems take such evidence seriously. We do.

Such stories make many defenders of the system angry. They say, "But human knowledge is stored and transmitted in symbols. We have to teach children to use them." True enough. But the only way children can learn to get meaning out of symbols, to turn other people's sym-

bols into a kind of reality or a mental model of reality, is by learning first to turn their own reality into symbols. They have to make the journey from reality to symbol many times, before they are ready to go the other way. We must begin with what children see, do, and know, and have them talk and write about such things, before trying to talk to them much about things they don't know. Thus, given children who knew how to make a paper fan, it might not be a bad idea at all to ask them to try to tell someone else how to make one, without using any gestures, as if they were talking over a phone. I used to ask fifth-graders how they would explain over the phone the difference between right and left, to someone who could speak English but did not happen to know those words. Such games are exciting and useful. But when we do what we do most of the time in school — begin with meaningless symbols and statements, and try to fill them with meaning by way of explanations, we only convince most children either that all symbols are meaningless or that they are too stupid to get meaning from them.

Perhaps the greatest dangers of becoming too bound up with symbols, too symbol-minded, if I may be allowed the phrase, is that we don't know how to give them up, get them out of the way, when they are of no use to us. We become addicts. There are times when words, symbols, only get between us and reality. At such times, we must be ready to let them go, and use our minds in more ap-

propriate ways — more childlike ways.

Such an experience took place not long ago when I was visiting A. S. Neill at Summerhill School in England. The weather was terrible, the public rooms of the school were deserted, the students were all in their rooms, so there was nothing much to see around the school. Neill himself was laid up in his room with a painful attack of sciatica, and was eager for company. So we had a long and very interesting talk. More than once, thinking I had taken enough of his time, I got up to go, but he waved me back in my chair, where I was more than glad to stay.

At about three o'clock his brother-in-law came in, and asked if he could use the TV to watch the England-Scotland rugby match. Neill asked me if I knew anything about rugby. I said I didn't; he said he didn't either. We decided to watch the game. Before it had gone on two minutes, I found myself in the same panicky confusion that had gripped me when I looked at the loom. Rugby is a hard game for a novice to understand. It is like a crazy combination of soccer and football, just enough like either one to be misleading. As I watched, the teacher-voice in my head began to ask, "Why did he do that? Why did he put the ball there? Why is he running that way?" And so on. But there were no answers.

After a few futile minutes of this, I saw that this was the loom situation again. I didn't know enough about the game to be able to reason about it. No use to ask questions. Neill couldn't answer them. His brother-in-law — a taciturn man — wouldn't. Anyway, I didn't know enough to know what questions to ask. The only thing to do was to turn off the questions and watch — like a child. Take it all in. See everything, worry about nothing. This is what I did. When the voice inside began to yammer, I silenced it. At half-time I seemed to know no more than at the start. Everything that happened on that field surprised me. During the half the announcers, as in every land, talked learnedly about the play during the first half. Not a word they said made any sense. I listened, like a child listening to adult conversation, taking in the words without knowing or caring what they might mean. Soon the second half started, as puzzling as the first. Then, suddenly, about ten minutes into the period, the patterns of the game all fell into place. Like the loom, the game put itself together in my mind. I suddenly found that I knew what the players were doing, what they were trying to do, what they might do next, why the plays the announcer called good were in fact good, why the mistakes he pointed out were in fact mistakes. There was still much I didn't know, details of the game, rules, penalties. But I knew enough to ask about them, and to make some sense out of the answers.

Not long afterwards, I had another chance to think like a child. Going south from London on a train, I found myself in a compartment — a small, closed-in section seating eight passengers — with a Scandinavian couple. They were talking rapidly in their native language, of which I understood nothing. For a while, I paid no attention, looking at England through the train window, and thinking my own thoughts. Then, after a while, it occurred to me that this was an interesting opportunity to listen to language as a baby listens to it. Still looking out the window, I began to pay close attention to what they were saying. It was very much like listening to a complicated piece of modern music. I have discovered, after hearing many concerts and records, that the best way to listen to strange and unfamiliar music, to keep your attention focussed sharply on it, is to try to reproduce the music in your mind — instant imitation. In the same way, I was trying to reproduce in my mind, as soon as I heard them, the sounds made by these people as they talked. I didn't get them all, but I got many of them. Also, though I wasn't looking for patterns — there wasn't time for that — I was alert for them, so that when a sound or word came along that I had heard before, it made an extra impression. It was an interesting and absorbing exercise. By the time forty minutes had passed, and I had reached my stop, I had begun to feel, and almost recognize, a few of the sounds and words in their talk. Perhaps this kind of raw listening would be useful for students studying a foreign language. We might have a record, or a tape, of a voice reading a particular passage, first at rapid conversational speed, then more slowly, finally so slowly that each word could be heard separately. From listening to such tapes, students might become sensitive to the relation between the separate sounds of a language and the sound of the flow of the whole language.

Applying some of the principles that stem from the more theoretical articles in this chapter, Hawkins discusses three phases of teaching, to which he attaches the symbols ○, △, and □. In words, the phases are: messing about, multiple programming, and formal and informal lecturing. Each phase is geared to a different aspect of how the mind functions; the total approach is responsive to the different stages of learning that a student is likely to go through. Although Hawkins' examples are all related to the teaching of science, try to imagine how the ideas would apply to other subjects.

MESSING ABOUT
IN SCIENCE

"Nice? It's the only thing," said the Water Rat solemnly, as he leant forward for his stroke. *"Believe me, my young friend, there is* nothing *— absolutely nothing — half so much worth doing as simply messing about in boats. Simply messing,"* he went on dreamily, *"messing — about — in — boats — messing —"*
— From The Wind in the Willows

My outline is divided into three patterns or phases of school work in science. These phases are different from each other in the relations they induce between children, materials of study, and teachers. Another way of putting it is that they differ in the way they make a classroom look and sound. My claim is that good science teaching moves from one phase to the other in a pattern which, though it will not follow mechanical rules or ever be twice the same, will evolve according to simple principles. There is no necessary order among these phases, and for this reason, I avoid calling them I, II, and III, and use instead some mnemonic signs which have, perhaps, a certain suggestiveness: ○, △, and □.

Abridged version of article "Messing About in Science," by David Hawkins, *Science and Children*, 2, no. 5 (February 1965): 5–8. Reprinted by permission.

There is a time, much greater in amount than commonly allowed, which should be devoted to free and unguided exploratory work (call it play if you wish; I call it work). Children are given materials and equipment — *things* — and are allowed to construct, test, probe, and experiment without superimposed questions or instructions. I call this ○ phase "Messing About," honoring the philosophy of the Water Rat, who absentmindedly ran his boat into the bank, picked himself up, and went on without interrupting the joyous train of thought:

— about in boats — or *with* boats. . . . In or out of 'em, it doesn't matter. Nothing seems really to matter, that's the charm of it. Whether you get away, or whether you don't; whether you arrive at your destination or whether you reach somewhere else, or whether you never get anywhere at all, you're always busy, and you never do anything in particular; and when you've done it there's always something else to do, and you can do it if you like, but you'd much better not.

In some jargon, this kind of situation is called "unstructured," which is misleading; some doubters call it chaotic, which it need never be. "Unstructured" is misleading because there is always a kind of structure to *what* is presented in a class, as there was to the world of boats and the river, with its rushes and weeds and mud that smelled like plumcake. Structure in this sense is of the utmost importance, depending on the children, the teacher, and the backgrounds of all concerned.

Let me cite an example from my own recent experiences. Simple frames, each designed to support two or three weights on strings, were handed out one morning in a fifth-grade class. There was one such frame for each pair of children. In two earlier trial classes, we had introduced the same equipment with a much more "structured" beginning, demonstrating the striking phenomenon of coupled pendula and raising questions about it before the laboratory work was allowed to begin. If there was guidance this time, however, it came only from the apparatus — a pendulum is to swing! In starting this way I, for one, naively assumed that a couple of hours of "Messing About" would suffice. After two hours, instead, we allowed two more and, in the end, a stretch of several weeks. In all this time, there was little or no evidence of boredom or confusion. Most of the questions we might have planned for came up unscheduled.

Why did we permit this length of time? First, because in our previous classes we had noticed that things went well when we veered toward "Messing About" and not as well when we held too tight a rein on what we wanted the children to do. It was clear that these children had

had insufficient acquaintance with the sheer phenomena of pendulum motion and needed to build an apperceptive background, against which a more analytical sort of knowledge could take form and make sense. Second, we allowed things to develop this way because we decided we were getting a new kind of feedback from the children and were eager to see where and by what paths their interests would evolve and carry them. We were rewarded with a higher level of involvement and a much greater diversity of experiments. Our role was only to move from spot to spot, being helpful but never consciously prompting or directing. In spite of — because of! — this lack of direction, these fifth-graders became very familiar with pendula. They varied the conditions of motion in many ways, exploring differences of length and amplitude, using different sorts of bobs, bobs in clusters, and strings, etc. And have *you* tried the underwater pendulum? They did! There were many sorts of discoveries made, but we let them slip by without much adult resonance, beyond our spontaneous and manifest enjoyment of the phenomena. So discoveries were made, noted, lost, and made again. I think this is why the slightly pontifical phrase "discovery method" bothers me. When learning is at the most fundamental level, as it is here, with all the abstractions of Newtonian mechanics just around the corner, don't rush! When the mind is

evolving the abstractions which will lead to physical comprehension, all of us must cross the line between ignorance and insight many times before we truly understand. Little facts, "discoveries" without the growth of insight, are *not* what we should seek to harvest. Such facts are only seedlings and should sometimes be let alone to grow into. . . .

I have illustrated the phase of "Messing About" with a constrained and inherently very elegant topic from physics. In other fields, the pattern will be different in detail, but the essential justification is the same. "Messing About" with what can be found in pond water looks much more like the Water Rat's own chosen field of study. Here, the implicit structure is that of nature in a very different mood from what is manifest in the auterities of things like pendular motion or planet orbits. And here, the need for sheer acquaintance with the variety of things and phenomena is more obvious, before one can embark on any of the roads toward the big generalizations or the big open questions of biology. Regardless of differences, there is a generic justification of "Messing About" that I would like, briefly, to touch upon.

This phase is important, above all, because it carries over into school that which is the source of most of what children have already learned, the roots of their moral, intellectual, and esthetic development. If education were defined, for the moment, to include everything that children have learned since birth,

everything that has come to them from living in the natural and the human world, then by any sensible measure what has come before age five or six would outweigh all the rest. When we narrow the scope of education to what goes on in schools, we throw out the method of that early and spectacular progress at our peril. We know that five-year-olds are very unequal in their mastery of this or that. We also know that their histories are responsible for most of this inequality, utterly masking the congenital differences except in special cases. This is the immediate fact confronting us as educators in a society committed, morally and now by sheer economic necessity, to universal education.

To continue the cultivation of earlier ways of learning, therefore; to find *in school* the good beginnings, the liberating involvements that will make the kindergarten seem a garden to the child and not a dry and frightening desert, this is a need that requires much emphasis on the style of work I have called ◯, or "Messing About." Nor does the garden in this sense end with a child's first school year, or his tenth, as though one could then put away childish things. As time goes on, through a good mixture of this with other phases of work, "Messing About" evolves with the child and thus changes its quality. It becomes a way of working that is no longer childish, though it remains always childlike, the kind of self-disciplined probing and exploring that is the essence of creativity.

When children are led along a common path, there are always the advanced ones and always the stragglers. Generalized over the years of school routine, this lends apparent support to the still widespread belief in some fixed, inherent levels of "ability," and to the curious notions of "under-" and "over-achievement." Now, if you introduce a topic with a good deal of "Messing About," the variance does not decrease, it increases. From a conventional point of view, this means the situation gets worse, not better. But I say it gets better, not worse. If after such a beginning you pull in the reins and "get down to business," some children have happened to go your way already, and you will believe that you are leading these successfully. Others will have begun, however, to travel along quite different paths, and you have to tug hard to get them back on to yours. Through the eyes of these children you will see yourself as a dragger, not a leader. We saw this clearly in the pendulum class I referred to; the pendulum being a thing which seems deceptively simple but which raises many questions in no particular necessary order. So the path which each child chooses is his best path.

The result is obvious, but it took me time to see it. If you once let children evolve their own learning along paths of their choosing, you then must see it through and *maintain* the individuality of their work. You cannot begin that way

and then say, in effect, "That was only a teaser," thus using your adult authority to devalue what the children themselves, in the meantime, have found most valuable. So if "Messing About" is to be followed by, or evolve into, a stage where work is more externally guided and disciplined, there must be at hand what I call "Multiply Programmed" material; material that contains written and pictorial guidance of some sort for the student, but which is designed for the greatest possible variety of topics, ordering of topics, etc., so that for almost any given way into a subject that a child may evolve on his own, there is material available which he will recognize as helping him farther along that very way. Heroic teachers have sometimes done this on their own, but it is obviously one of the places where designers of curriculum materials can be of enormous help, designing those materials with a rich variety of choices for teacher and child, and freeing the teacher from the role of "leader-dragger" along a single preconceived path, giving the teacher encouragement and real logistical help in diversifying the activities of a group. Such material includes good equipment, but above all, it suggests many beginnings, paths from the familiar into the unknown. We did not have this kind of material ready for the pendulum class I spoke about earlier, and still do not have it. I intend to work at it and hope others will.

It was a special day in the history of that pendulum class that brought home to

me what was needed. My teaching partner was away (I had been the observer, she the teacher). To shift gears for what I saw as a more organized phase of our work, I announced that for a change we were all going to do the same experiment. I said it firmly and the children were, of course, obliging. Yet, I saw the immediate loss of interest in part of the class as soon as my experiment was proposed. It was designed to raise questions about the *length* of a pendulum, when the bob is multiple or odd-shaped. Some had come upon the germ of that question; others had had no reason to. As a college teacher I have tricks, and they worked here as well, so the class went well, in spite of the unequal readiness to look at "length." We hit common ground with rough blackboard pictures, many pendula shown hanging from a common support, differing in length and in the shape and size of bobs. Which ones will "swing together"? Because their eyes were full of real pendula, I think, they could *see* those blackboard pictures swinging! A colloquium evolved which harvested the crop of insights that had been sowed and cultivated in previous weeks. I was left with a hollow feeling, nevertheless. It went well where, and only where, the class found common ground. Whereas in "Messing About" all things had gone uniformly well. In staff discussion afterward, it became clear that we had skipped an essential phase of our work, the one I am now calling △ phase, or Multiply Programmed.

"Messing About" produces the early and indispensible autonomy and diversity. It is good — indispensible — for the opening game but not for the long middle game, where guidance is needed; needed to lead the willing! To illustrate once more from my example of the pendulum, I want to produce a thick set of cards — illustrated cards in a central file, or single sheets in plastic envelopes — to cover the following topics among others:

1. relations of amplitude and period
2. relations of period and weight of bob
3. how long is a pendulum (odd-shaped bobs)?
4. coupled pendula, compound pendula
5. the decay of the motion (and the idea of half-life)
6. string pendula and stick pendula — comparisons
7. underwater pendula
8. arms and legs as pendula (dogs, people, and elephants)
9. pendula of other kinds — springs, etc.
10. bobs that drop sand for patterns and graphs
11. pendulum clocks
12. historical materials, with bibliography
13. cards relating to filmloops available, in class or library
14. cross-index cards to other topics, such as falling bodies, inclined planes, etc.
15.–75. blank cards to be filled in by classes and teachers for others

This is only an illustration; each area of elementary science will have its own style of Multiply Programmed materials, of course, the ways of organizing these materials will depend on the subject. There should always be those blank cards, outnumbering the rest.

There is one final warning. Such a file is properly a kind of programming — but it is not the base of rote or merely verbal learning, taking a child little step by little step through the adult maze. Each item is simple, pictorial, and it guides by suggesting further explorations, not by replacing them. The cards are only there to relieve the teacher from a heroic task. And they are only there because there are apparatus, film, library, and raw materials from which to improvise.

☐ PHASE

In the class discussion I referred to, about the meaning of *length* applied to a pendulum, I was reverting back to the college-teacher habit of lecturing; I said it went very well in spite of the lack of Multiply Programmed background, one that would have taken more of the class through more of the basic pendulum topics. It was not, of course, a lecture in the formal sense. It was a question-and-answer, with discussion between children as well. But still, I was guiding it and fishing for the good ideas that were ready to be born, and I was telling a few stories, for example, about Galileo. Others could do it better. I was a visitor, and am still only an amateur. I was successful then only because of the long build-up of latent insight, the kind of insight that the Water Rat had stored up from long afternoons of "Messing About" in boats. It was more than he could ever have been told, but it gave him much to tell. This is not all there is to learning, of course; but it is the magical part, and the part most often killed in school. The language is not yet that of the textbook, but with it even a dull-looking textbook can come alive. One boy thinks the length of a pendulum should be measured from the top to what he calls "the center of gravity." If they have not done a lot of work with balance materials, this phase is for most children only the handle of an empty pitcher, or a handle without a pitcher at all. So I did not insist on the term. Incidentally, it is not quite correct physics anyway, as those will discover who work with the stick pendulum. Although different children had specialized differently in the way they worked with pendula, there were common elements, increasing with time, which would sustain a serious and extended class discussion. It is this pattern of discussion I want to emphasize by calling it a separate, ☐ phase. It includes lecturing, formal or informal. In the above situation, we were all quite ready for a short talk about Galileo, and ready to ponder the question whether there was any relation between the way unequal weights fall together and the way they swing together when hanging on strings of the same length. Here we were approaching a question — a rather deep one, not to be disposed of in fifteen minutes

— of theory, going from the concrete perceptual to the abstract conceptual. I do not believe that such questions will come alive either through the early "Messing About" or through the Multiply Programmed work with guiding questions and instructions. I think they come primarily with discussion, argument, the full colloquium of children and teacher. Theorizing in a creative sense needs the content of experience and the logic of experimentation to support it.

———

I have put ◯, △, and ☐ in that order, but I do not advocate any rigid order; such phases may be mixed in many ways and ordered in many ways. Out of the colloquium comes new "Messing About." Halfway along a programmed path, new phenomena are accidentally observed. In an earlier, more structured class, two girls were trying obediently to reproduce some phenomena of coupled pendula I had demonstrated. I heard one say, "Ours isn't working right." Of course, pendula never misbehave; it is not in their nature; they always do what comes naturally, and in this case, they were executing a curious dance of energy transference, promptly christened the "twist." It was a new phenomenon, which I had not seen before, nor had several physicists to whom, in my delight, I later showed it. Needless to say, this led to a good deal of "Messing About," right then and there.

What I have been concerned to say is only that there are, as I see it, three major

phases of good science teaching; that no teaching is likely to be optimal which does not mix all three; and that the one most neglected is that which made the Water Rat go dreamy with joy when he talked about it. At a time when the pressures of prestige education are likely to push children to work like hungry laboratory rats in a maze, it is good to remember that their wild, watery cousin, reminiscing about the joys of his life, uttered a profound truth about education.

———

In this excerpt, a student-teacher gives a detailed report on his experience in teaching traditional aspects of elementary mathematics in a humanistic way. This reading uses specific classroom experiences to show how teachers can guide their students in inquiries that involve the students personally. Here, involvement is ensured by focusing on the children's own bodies as an object of measurement while the teacher guides them through concepts of the inch, the foot, and the yard. As an exercise, analyze the ways in which events of this classroom experience, and of that in the next article on secondary level education, are examples of theoretical principles that have appeared in the earlier articles of this section.

AL RODRIGUEZ

———

MATHEMATICS FOR THE HUMAN CLASSROOM

My task here is to relate how certain traditional goals were achieved in a humanistic setting. While personal and academic knowledge were both ongoing in this classroom, I am focusing primarily on a process that leads to a meaningful understanding of specific academic concepts. The learning situation blossoms into its fullest potential when interaction between the participants is authentic, the atmosphere is human, and the concepts are concretely experienced.

I developed a series of activities that brought elementary children into a real encounter with linear measurement. More specifically, in concrete ways I introduced concepts of inch, foot, yard, and mile, and the usage of these concepts in measuring objects. I invited each child to approach his physical self, his body, from the single dimension of linear distance. This process recognizes the child's capacity to become personally involved

From Clark E. Moustakas and Cereta Perry, *Learning to Be Free*, © 1973. Reprinted by permission of Prentice-Hall, Inc., Englewood Cliffs, New Jersey.

in sharing in the unfolding of a meaningful experience.

The preparatory experience (presented to the entire classroom) included an introduction to linear measurement through mathematical filmstrips,[1] available in our unit program at Merrill-Palmer. A brief question-and-answer period followed which centered on the units of inch, foot, yard, and mile.

Can anyone show me how much an inch is? Have you ever seen anyone measure something in inches? Who was the person? What was the person using to measure the object? How did the person measure the object? What did he do?
Does anyone know how much a foot is? Show me how long a foot is with your hands. Is that longer or shorter than an inch? Find an object in the classroom that you can measure in inches. Find an object in the classroom that you can measure in feet. What parts of your body can you measure in inches? What parts of your body can you measure in feet?
How much is a yard? Show me. Have you ever heard of anything measured in yards? What was the object? Is a yard longer than a foot? How about an inch?

The unit of a mile was discussed with reference to the distance that each child lived from the school. For example, Joseph's house was approximately three-quarters of a mile from school. He had to leave his house earlier than any other child to get to school at 9:00 A.M. because he had to walk farther.

In the next session, the classroom teacher and I divided the children into two groups with approximately twelve students in each group. After discussing the limits in our group activity, I probed the children to find out if they understood the relationship between inch and foot.

Miller, can you tell me what this is? Does anyone know what it is? Has anyone seen someone use it? Have you ever used this, Katrina? Yes, it is a ruler. What kind of ruler is it? An inch? A foot? A yard? Can you show me how much an inch is with your fingers? Is the length of this ruler the same length as an inch? Is it the same length as a foot? What do these little black marks and numbers mean? How much is it from the end of the ruler to the line with the number "1" near it? Can you make the same distance with your fingers? Now make the distance of an inch. Yes, they're both the same. How many of these inch distances are on the ruler? How many inches are there in a foot? Is the foot the same size as twelve of these inch units? Let's count them again.

Next, I invited each child to search the classroom and bring back an object that was an inch long. We discussed each object in terms of what it was and its distance in inches. We accepted only those objects which were either an inch long or an inch wide. To demonstrate that the numbers on the ruler represent the sum of an object's inch units, I directed the children to line up their objects in a chain. Each child knew that his object was an inch in distance. Two objects then linked together were two inches. I asked, "What is the number printed on the ruler nearest to the end of our second object?" I continued the procedure until the series of objects distanced twelve inches. "How long is our chain of objects? One foot or twelve inches?" To test if the children understood the relationship between the printed numbers and the sum of inch units, I randomly broke off the chain and asked, "How long is our chain of objects now?" Then I asked a number of individual children to make the chain an x-amount of inches in distance. This was repeated many times.

The next session dealt with acquainting each child with the fundamentals of measuring.

Now, I would like each of you to go back to your desk and bring back a pencil or a crayon to draw with. Lamar, would you also bring back sheets of green drawing paper for everyone.
Let's sit in our circle while we wait for everyone to come back.
I cannot talk when everyone is talking, so I will wait a couple of minutes for you to finish up whatever you want to say. I really want to continue because we are going to measure something very interesting, something that none of you have ever measured before.
I am going to divide you into four groups with four people in each group.
Now that your groups are established, I would like each of you to draw a picture of yourself.

After each child completed his drawing, I gave the following directions:

Here are rulers for each group. Can you measure the different parts of your body? If you want to, you can work all together or in pairs. I will visit each group and help you with any problems you are encountering.

With each of the small groups, I asked the following questions:

What person are you measuring now? What part of her body are you measuring? From where to where on her body are you measuring?

If the group needed direction in measuring, I first asked, "Would you like me to help you with what you are doing?" If anyone needed help, I gave the person a specific responsibility. For example, in measuring the length of Curtis' body, Dennis showed from which two points we were going to measure. Dennis held two rulers (one on top of another lengthwise) while Venzetta connected two more foot rulers. Melissa stood on a chair and added a fifth ruler which went beyond the length of Curtis' body. Melissa was also responsible for finding the number that was closest to the top of Curtis' head. Curtis, during the measuring, was responsible for keeping his body as rigid and straight as possible, being careful not to move the slightest fraction. Melissa told the number of inches that were on the last ruler and we added on the number of feet represented by the other four rulers. Curtis was four feet and five inches. I then showed Curtis how to make arrows on his drawing to represent the distance we measured. With the group's assistance he wrote down the numerals and the unit labels for the length of his body. The same procedure was followed for measuring others in the group; the measurement roles were rotated. This collective effort ended our preparatory experience.

Benjamin, Miller, Katrina, Paulette, today I'm going to be working exclusively with you in the cloakroom. We will be making a life-size poster outline of someone's body and labeling the different parts in inches and feet. Before we start, I would like to talk with you about the limits that will be necessary for you to work within if I am to be with you. Why don't we sit around in a circle so everyone can see each other? Tell me, what are the things you think we won't be able to do?

Miller: Not everyone talks.
Al: Why not?
Miller: Because no one can hear.
Al: Yes, I also get confused when everyone is talking at once because I can't really hear what each person is saying. I also don't like to be interrupted when I am talking to someone. I would prefer that you hold your questions or comments until the person and I are finished. I, in return, will not interrupt when two other people are having a conversation.

Okay, quietly go back to your desks and bring back your crayons. If you don't have any, borrow some from a friend. Katrina, would you also bring the rulers.

I would like all of you to decide amongst yourselves who is going to be outlined. We only have time enough to do two people today and there are four of you. I am going to get the paper and materials ready. I'll come back when you have made the decision of who is to be drawn.

————

Have you come to a decision yet?

How did you come to your decision? Katrina, do you agree that Benjamin and Paulette are to be outlined? Miller, do you agree that

Benjamin and Paulette are to be outlined? Who's first?

What's this? Yes, it's a ruler, a foot ruler. What is it used for? How can one measure with it? What are these lines and numbers for? Does anyone remember how much an inch is? Can you do it with your hands? And a foot, how much is that? How long would one foot and one inch be? Katrina, can you be the foot and Miller, can you be the inch? Let's put them together.

What color shall we use to outline Benjamin?

Benjamin, lie down on this paper and place your body in just the way you want to be outlined. Make every part of your body stiff now, every muscle, your head, neck, shoulders, arms, hands, fingers, chest, stomach, thighs, knees, calves, ankles, feet, toes. Everything stiff like cardboard so we can trace around it. Make your body heavy so it can't be moved.

Everyone else, carefully, lightly trace slowly around his body. Try not to move anything except the crayon you are using.

————

Benjamin, we are finished. When you feel like getting up, we can continue with the rest of our project.

Let's all make the lines real dark now so we can see the whole outline.

Benjamin, what part of your body would you like to measure? How are you going to measure it?

Benjamin lined up the rulers beginning at the heel and stopping when the rulers had passed the head of his outline.

How many complete rulers do you have laid down? And how many inches of the one that isn't complete? How tall is your outline in feet and inches? That's right, how did you figure that out?

Now, I'll draw an arrow from the tip of his heel and another arrow from the tip of his head. What is the space between the two arrows for? Can you write in feet and inches how long the outline is? Does anyone know how to spell *feet*? Does anyone know how to spell *inches*?

Now each of you can find a part that interests you and measure it.

The children proceeded to measure parts of Benjamin's body.

Paulette, can I measure part of the outline with you?

Does anyone see a part of the outline that we haven't measured yet? Let's do it!

Everyone ready to color?

Benjamin, there is a mirror on that desk. You can use that to see what your face looks like, then you can shape and color what it looks like to you.

The rest of us will color the other parts. I think I'll color the left shoe.

Does anyone feel that the picture needs more coloring? Why don't we stop then.

Here are some tacks I found. Where do you think we can tack our picture up? I really like it.

How tall is Benjamin according to this outline? Where does it say that? What do those arrows mean?

What part did you measure, Katrina? How did you measure it? How wide is his hand? Did you use the foot unit? What two points did you measure from?

Our group decided to limit the discussion of the finished outline of Benjamin until we had completed the outline for Paulette. The same procedures were used for Paulette's outline. We tacked both outlines up and discussed how they differed. I invited each child to share with us the part that he had measured. While looking at the crude outlines and seeing the look of pride and accomplishment on the children's faces, I felt certain that they had learned what measurement was all about.

The perspective that I have been writing from is limited. Mathematical concepts were only part of the experience. Creativity, personal and honest interaction, joy, self-awareness, group collectiveness, sharing, involvement, self-expression, caring — these human qualities were reflected in every session. Life had been created in the classroom with learning that was alive and exciting. The children were fully involved, valuing and seeking what they were learning, enjoying the process, and not wanting it to end.

———————

"What happens to a dream deferred?" This excerpt is a detailed report of a teacher's use of classroom inquiry in teaching poetry to high school students. One might imagine that involvement is ensured by the subject matter of the poem (by Langston Hughes), but clearly much more is going on. The teacher, by guiding the discussion in a directed way, helps the students as a class to write a com- parable poem of their own. You will see at the end of the reading that it is really a good poem. How might you use what you've learned in this article to guide learning of other subject matter in a similar way?

MARGARET CLARK, ELLA ERWAY, AND LEE BELTZER

———————

EXCERPT FROM *THE LEARNING ENCOUNTER: THE CLASSROOM AS A COMMUNICATIONS WORKSHOP*

Mr. Tharp: Remember the poem we read together and discussed yesterday? (*Class nods and responds, "Yes."*) Remember the feelings we said we felt after hearing the poem? Paulette, would you read the poem again for us . . . and let's try to recall some of those feelings and ideas.

From *The Learning Encounter: The Classroom as a Communications Workshop*, by Margaret Clark, Ella Erway, and Lee Beltzer. Copyright © 1971 by Random House, Inc. Reprinted by permission of the publisher.

Paulette (reading from a mimeographed sheet the class received the day before):

What happens to a dream deferred? [1]

> *Does it dry up*
> *like a raisin in the sun?*
>
> *Or fester like a sore —*
> *And then run?*
> *Does it stink like rotten meat?*
> *Or crust and sugar over —*
> *like a syrupy sweet?*
>
> *Maybe it just sags*
> *like a heavy load.*
>
> *Or does it explode?*

Mr. Tharp: Thanks, Paulette.

Paulette: Oh — did everybody hear me today . . . 'cause yesterday Robert said he couldn't hear me the last time.

Robert: I heard you good this time. But when something explodes . . . like . . . that's big, like a ball.

Mr. Tharp: Is that the kind of explosion that happens in this *dream?*

Paulette: No.

Mr. Tharp: Then why do you think he uses those words? Words like "dry up" and "fester"?

Richard: I don't know, but I forgot what "deferred" means.

Paulette (spontaneously): Put off . . . not right now . . . maybe you can do it later, but you're not sure. . . .

Richard: Well all right. But gettin' back to those words about rotten meat. I don't

[1] In Langston Hughes, *The Panther and the Lash* (New York: Knopf, 1951).

really know . . . but when *I* dream, it don't stink.

Mr. Tharp: Well, Richie, what *do* you dream about? . . .

> *(General laughter that builds in the part of the room where Richard is sitting)*

Mr. Tharp: How many of you remember dreaming?

> *(Hands begin to go up, some rather cautiously. Finally all but about seven hands are up.)*

Mr. Tharp: What about the others? Don't you . . . when you sleep . . . don't you remember something that you dreamt during the night?

Joseph (who was one of the seven who did not raise his hand): Martin Luther King had a dream . . . we talked about it on his birthday. . . .

Mr. Tharp: Yes . . . well try to remember some of the things we said and try to think about your own dreams . . . the ones you have while you sleep . . . or maybe you can think of dreams like Martin Luther King's if you didn't have a dream last night or the night before. Why don't we write about our dreams? *(To George)* You raised your hand, didn't you? *(George nods.)* You others? Okay?

Janet: I haven't had no dreams. . . .

Mr. Tharp: Night before last? Night before? Night before that? *(She shakes her head "No" through all these questions; the class giggles and breaks into general laughter.)* Okay. How about trying a dream like Martin Luther King's?

Janet: Well . . . like . . . Okay, I guess I can try. . . .

Mr. Tharp: Okay. Now. What I want you to do is simply to talk about the dreams in writing. Write a dream that you had . . . either the dream you had last night or the night before. Put it down as you remember it . . . or a dream you had last year . . . or, like Janet, perhaps something you imagined during the day: a daydream. And while you're writing, try to remember everything, even the feelings you had if you can remember your feelings during the dream. Let's see what we come up with . . . and then maybe you'll want to read your dreams to the class . . . some of you . . . all right? So could we try? Remember, if you need to, find a dream, like Martin Luther King. Everyone got paper and something to write with?

> *(A general noisy scramble until everyone gets necessary materials)*

Mr. Tharp: Okay. Take it easy now, and let's try to get those dreams.

> *(The following interval of ten to fifteen minutes is generally quiet, reflecting the students' concentration on the work. When some noise occurs, usually due to a student's finishing his writing, Mr. Tharp suggests that the student try reading the dream aloud but very quietly to himself. Finally all students seem to be done.)*

Mr. Tharp: Okay? Okay . . . everybody

done? Paul? Done? Okay. Now . . . would anyone like to share his dream with the rest of us?

(Tentative pause)

Mr. Tharp: No one? How about you, Tom?

Tom: Well . . . okay . . . Once upon a time I had a dream. . . . I had a dream at one time about the prisons. . . . Like Martin Luther King I have a dream that one day I will make it to the bottom of the mountain. I think I am free because no one can stop me from being free at all and nobody gonna free me. They may try their best, but they won't get nowhere. The end.

(Immediate audible response of enthusiasm in the room at the end of the reading; a scattering of applause that provokes giggles)

Mr. Tharp: How about another? Jack, do you have anything you want to read to us? *(Jack nods "Yes.")* All right.

Jack: I had a dream. I want to be a millionaire. And I want to have a free family, and I want to be free. People should have a dream because a dream may come true, and I hope that everyone had a dream.

Sophie (without being called on specifically): "My Dream." One night I dreamed that I was a queen and I was having a birthday party and then all at once I was looking out the window. You see I thought I was crawling on the floor. Then when I got outside, I was jumping up and down saying, "I want a rose."

(A palpable silence holds the class for a moment)

Mr. Tharp: Another? Fine Merryl.

Merryl: When I was five years old, I dreamed there was a peanuts . . . I mean a peanut . . . it was going to get me, and soon I woke up and saw that it was only a dream. When I woke up my mother about the peanut, she gave me a glass of water I asked for.

Mr. Tharp: Atria, do you have a dream to read? Feel free to read it. I mean it. Go right ahead.

Atria (hesitantly): One night I had a dream that my sister was in the bed with me and she was walking around the house with no head.

Maria (quickly, obviously having gained courage from Atria's reading): One night when I went to bed, I dreamed a . . . that . . . that a big dog was after me and I never woke up. I just kept on running until I started screaming on my mother's bed. My mother thought I had a bad dream.

Harris (also joining spontaneously when he judged Maria had finished): I had a dream that I was a millionaire and lived on a boat with my own studio . . . and I had Batman and Robin on my show.

Mr. Tharp (obviously wooing a small Puerto Rican girl in the back of the room): Do you have a dream? We'd like to hear from you. Do you have one?

Brenda (very quietly and hesitantly at first, but increasing vocal intensity as she continues): Once I had a dream about that I was a horse in a country. My master was Mr. . . . (name unheard). He let his friends ride me. Some of his friends were fat. This lady came and asked him can she ride me down the street. My master said yes. She jumped on me, and I took her down the road. I was so tired I jumped and she fell off. On the way back she had to walk.

Mr. Tharp: Maurice, would you like to add yours?

Maurice: Can I sing mine? *(The class responds in mixed fashion; but most students urge him to sing his dream.)* So . . . now . . . everyone listens to my dream. *(He sings the following and accompanies himself on his desk, as if on the bongo drums.)* "This Is Black." Black is not the color of one's skin. It is a state of mind. It is an unyielding desire and fight for freedom and self-determination. It is deep feeling and . . . *(word lost in desk drumming)* We all are people . . . people. . . . It is a love for the lovable regardless of their race or color or religion. It is an understanding and avoidance of the advocate of hatred. It is a deep and sensational expression called soul. It is a knowledge of one's history to build a greater future. Blackness is not the color of one's skin. Are you black?

(The class applauds spontaneously with enthusiasm.)

Mr. Tharp: Hey Maurice that was great . . . just great . . . all of you. Wait. Let's try something now. I am going to give you an incomplete thought, and each of you tries to finish it. I mean . . . well . . . if I said, "The leaf falls from the tree like . . ." you would finish the sentence with . . . for instance *(obviously seeking help from the class)*. . . .

Merryl: Like gentle rain from heaven?

Mr. Tharp: Great. Another possibility?

Francia *(her first contribution all period)*: Like a word that said fall is here. . . .

Mr. Tharp: Yes . . . yes . . . very good . . . exactly . . . okay . . . now . . . Erica, would you go to the board and be our secretary? *(Erica goes)* And I'll give you a beginning. When you think of a way to finish the comparison, the idea, hold up your hand, and let Erica call on you. Be patient so she can write them down. Okay . . . so here it is . . . okay Erica? . . . Okay . . . "A dream deferred is like. . . ."

(As Erica writes on the board, students whisper and then pause with no response.)

Mr. Tharp: "A dream deferred is like . . ." any ideas? Raise hands. There. Erica, call on them as you are ready. And let your feelings help. Remember those dreams and that song. Okay. . . .

(Hands start going up. Over a period of about twenty minutes, with some further facilitating, the following list was compiled on the blackboards around the room.)

"A dream deferred is like . . ."

1. a meal skipped
2. a sore that festers *(This response provoked laughter, and one student asked Mr. Tharp: "Is that fair? To use the other thing . . . the other poem?" After brief discussion, the class decided to try to be original.)*
* 3. a sky with no sun
* 4. a child without play
* 5. a woman without a man
6. a man without a woman
7. an unpleasant duty
* 8. a "joint" without a match
9. a dreamer's sleep
10. a miscarriage
*11. "I wish I could help!" *(A spontaneous utterance by a student searching in vain for a simile)*
12. an old maid
*13. a smile with no happiness
14. anger without a gun
15. anger with a gun
*16. losing your deferment
*17. trying to put it out of your mind
*18. believing in peace
19. a list without end *(Provided by Erica, humorously; the class laughed and continued.)*
*20. still being hungry
*21. an empty room
22. an impossible wish
*23. a place ya can't go
*24. having nowhere to go
*25. not being able to go
26. being chained and slowly killed
27. opening a beautiful canteloupe and finding the inside rotten *(After this, students were heard to whisper, "What is a canteloupe?" A student explained the fruit with a drawing to those ignorant.)*
28. a Pandora's box *(similar reaction to "Pandora" as to "canteloupe"; explanation followed.)*
*29. reaching out with nothing to touch

Mr. Tharp: Others? Okay . . . great . . . now. . . . Would someone read the whole list so far?

Erica: Let me. Okay?

Mr. Tharp: Fine. Go ahead. *(Erica reads clearly from the board.)* Now, Erica, stay right there. Okay. Now let's vote to see how many of these most of us feel really complete the idea best . . . the idea "A dream deferred is like. . . ." You can vote as many times as you like. Just be sure you vote for ones you really dig . . . those you might have written to express yourself. . . . Dig? Okay. . . .

(Erica reads each one, and whenever a majority of hands goes up, she places an asterisk, as above, next to the item.)

Mr. Tharp: Okay. Everyone. Let's see what we've got. Erica, erase the ones we've omitted from the final list. *(She does.)* Now everyone, let's read together what we've written. *(The class, in unison with Erica leading, reads the following.)*

"A dream deferred is like . . ."

a sky with no sun
a child without play

a woman without a man
a "joint" without a match

"I wish I could help!"
a smile with no happiness

losing your deferment
trying to put it out of your mind
believing in peace

still being hungry

an empty room

a place ya can't go
having nowhere to go
not being able to go —

"A dream deferred is like . . ."
reaching out with nothing to touch.

(The line groupings, punctuation, and reuse of title at end grew out of meaning desired after several unison readings.)

Mr. Tharp: Well . . . what have we done? What have we got?

Paulette: We've written out our own poem, and I like it better than the one about festering . . . *(general sounds of agreement).*

Mr. Tharp: Shall we give it a name? *(Much chatter; spontaneous suggestions such as "That's Life," "Living," "Hate," and "Bed-Stuy")* No name? Let's vote. How many want to leave it the way it is? *(Majority of the hands goes up.)* Okay. We don't need a name.

Janet: We can each give it our own name . . . is that okay?

Mr. Tharp: Why not? Okay, let's try reading it. . . .

(At this point the bell for fire drill interrupts.)

The Allenders describe a set of programmed materials that departs radically from the typical format. The materials allow students to play the role of a mayor of a small town and to develop inquiry skills. They encourage participation in open-ended learning activities in which the problems and their solutions are not predetermined. Try to imagine how you would use these materials in the classroom if you were teaching social studies. Also, try to imagine how you would use materials like these in the subjects with which you are most familiar.

DONNA S. ALLENDER AND JEROME S. ALLENDER

I AM THE MAYOR: INQUIRY MATERIALS FOR THE STUDY OF CITY GOVERNMENT

If you were the mayor of a small city in the West, you could say, "I am the Mayor"

Adapted from The Teacher's Manual for *I Am the Mayor: Inquiry Materials for the Study of*

and you would know what a mayor does. For those of you who are not or never have been a mayor of a small city in the West, this manual should be used for a briefing about the job and its responsibilities.

These materials allow you and your students to be the mayor of a small western city. They were written to teach about city government. But they were also written to do something more. With the inquiry materials, you will be able to teach inquiry skills. The best introduction is for you to pretend you are a mayor. This section will act as your briefing session for being Mayor of Tinker, Colorado, and for being the teacher of other mayors.

So, imagine yourself as a mayor and that you have just received a letter (Figure 1).

You are expected to make some kind of decision about this letter. But you have been asked to support a proposal about which you know nothing. If you accidentally made a good decision at this moment, it would have to be a lucky guess. Before you make a decision, you should collect information about the suggestions which come up in Mr. Vale's letter. Before you can collect information you will have to sense embedded problems and formulate questions which will direct you to useful information. You will of course

---

City Government (Philadelphia: Center for the Study of Federalism, Temple University, 1971). Reprinted by permission of the Center for the Study of Federalism.

```
                              512 South Sun Street
                              Tinker, Colorado
                              April                      320
The Mayor
City Hall
Tinker, Colorado


Dear Mayor,
The Business Club of Tinker wants the City to build a
new parking lot in downtown Tinker. We feel the City     321
Council should carefully study Tinker's need for
another lot in that part of town. If there were more     322
parking spaces open during the shopping hours, people
from towns around Tinker would be more interested in
coming to Tinker to shop. We would be pleased if you     323
would be in favor of the idea when we bring it up at
a City Council meeting.                                  324

                              Yours truly,


                              Lee Vale
                              Tinker Business Club        325


                  I want to make a decision.             812
```

Figure 1.

want then to locate the information that answers your questions.

Look at the letter again and notice that sentences are numbered in the right margin. This numbering system allows you to request sets of questions having to do with problems embedded in the sentences. For example, if you thought there was a problem embedded in the second sentence of the letter, you would turn to page 322 (Figure 2) and find these questions.

One of the information files which you can receive to search for answers to the questions [in Figure 2] is page 599 (Figure 3).

If your particular question wasn't anticipated, you can ask it anyway. You turn to . . . page 300 (Figure 4) the Index of Files, and you can track down the type of information you need.

Suppose you have gathered all the information you need or all that is available. In the broad sense it is necessary for you to come to some kind of decision and in general there are several types of decisions available to you. You can delay action. You can request more information, or you can take action. (See Figure 5.)

Examples of these alternatives are in Figures 6, 7, and 8.

What a student does as Mayor of Tinker resembles a major part of what he would do as a real mayor. He receives letters, memoranda, and reports to which he can respond; he has files on general information, departments, current business, and correspondence to allow him to make reasonable decisions. Because students are not really mayors, they are not expected to be familiar at first with any of the information and to help them they are provided with sets of questions and alternative decisions from which to choose. The purpose of the materials is to enable teachers to realistically involve their students in the process of inquiry.

In the modern world it is difficult for a teacher to decide what body of facts and concepts should be taught in a social studies curriculum. There is no one authoritative source of information. Textbooks and encyclopedias are not always accurate. Concepts without conflicting arguments rarely exist to explain the complex happenings of our daily lives. More and more each person is required to search and sift among a multitude of facts and figures to form knowledge that is meaningful and useful for daily life. No teacher can ever fill a student's mind with enough information — each student must learn how to find and use his own set of data about the world. Moreover, students will not forever remain students and they will not always have a teacher to choose texts and curriculum which decide for them what information they should know, or what conclusions are important. It is important that the students with whom you work have the opportunity to learn to inquire. They should be able to sense problems, formulate questions, and search for information before coming to decisions. *I Am the Mayor* gives students the opportunity to do this.

DESCRIPTION OF I AM THE MAYOR

There are four major sections to *I Am the Mayor*, and they are:

1. The Mayor's Work
2. The Mayor's Questions
3. The Mayor's Files
4. The Mayor's Decisions

Each problem found in "The Mayor's Work" can be followed through with related Mayor's Questions leading to in-

---

<u>322</u>

How many parking lots are there in downtown Tinker? I would like to see a map of downtown Tinker.	File 4	Page 363
How many parking spaces are available in downtown Tinker now? I would like to see the Traffic and Parking Chart.	File 16	Page 599
Are there other letters about the need for more parking in Tinker? I would like to see the Mayor's letters about parking.	File 20	Page 785
My question is not here. I want to see a list of all my files.		Page 300

Figure 2.

<u>599</u>

	1950	1960	Last year
Cars in Tinker	2,000 cars	2,500 cars	3,000 cars
Parking downtown	300 spaces downtown	500 spaces downtown	500 spaces downtown
Stop lights	6 stop lights	10 stop lights	10 stop lights
Time to drive through downtown Tinker	3 minutes	6 minutes	10 minutes

Figure 3. City growth chart: traffic and parking

Figure 4. Index of files

```
                                                          812
I don't want to do anything about this message
    right now.                                             903
I need to find out something that is not in my files.     904
I would like to do something about this right away.        905
```

Figure 5.

formation in the Mayor's Files and finally with the selection of a decision from the Mayor's Decisions.

1. "The Mayor's Work" . . . consists of letters, messages about telephone calls, reports, and a local newspaper. They directly draw the mayor's attention to matters concerning the scouts, school safety, trees, zoning, park development, street repair, a new airport, electric power, and water pressure; the mayor is confronted indirectly with several other local matters. The work can be received and handled in several ways. It does not invite yes and no answers or quick decisions.

2. "The Mayor's Questions" . . . are sets of questions which follow from each piece of work and are intended to help students formulate problems they sense in the work. There are from six to ten sets of questions for each piece of "The Mayor's Work." Each page of "The Mayor's Questions" has three questions and a direction to go to the main index in the event that a question desired by the student is not included on the page. There are no correct questions on any page. The value of a question can only be evaluated in terms of what the student needs to know and what he or she already knows. There can be several good reasons given for choosing each question. Generally, they are written to include a specific question, a more general one, and a very general question on each page.

3. Each question leads to a piece of information or to a specific file. The information is all contained in the section called "The Mayor's Files." . . . We have tried to construct a filing system for the student mayors which contains information on many aspects of a city and a city government — not only those that pertain to the work. The files include the mayor's calendars, a history, laws of Tinker, maps of the city, general information bulletins, records and reports of city departments, budgets and financial statements, committee information, city council records, city growth charts, the city plan, and letters to both the mayor and the other city officials of various departments. There is ample information available concerning each piece of "The Mayor's Work." Some of the information is relevant to several pieces of work. Some is applicable to only one. An attempt has been made to make the kinds and amount of information available as broad as possible. This allows for the development of various types of inquiry behavior. The information does not offer a definite or correct solution to any problem. A variety of information can be combined and evaluated by the mayor before a decision is reached.

4. There are two parts to the set of decisions. First the mayor must choose a type of decision. . . . The mayor may choose to do nothing now, ask for more information, or take some action. When the mayor has chosen one of these types of

903

A. Do what you think best with this.
B. Put this where it belongs in my files.
C. Put this with work to be done later today.
D. I want to keep this on my desk for a while.
E. I want to put it somewhere else:

_____

_____

_____

_____

Figure 6.

904

A. Ask the Business Club to find out how many parking
   spaces a city the size of Tinker should have.
B. Call the Police Department and ask for all information
   they have about parking problems in Tinker.
C. Find out what it costs to build parking lots.
D. I need to know something else:

_____

_____

_____

Figure 7.

905

A. Write Mr. Vale that his group should do what is best for the city.
B. Write Mr. Vale and ask him to find someone to do a study of how many more people could come to Tinker to shop.
C. Write Mr. Vale that I will be in favor of the City building a new parking lot when it is brought up at the Council meeting.
D. I want to do something else:

_____

_____

_____

_____

Figure 8.

decisions, the exact decision must be specified. . . . Each of these decision pages provides a choice of six prewritten decisions and an opportunity to write an original one, if the student chooses.

There are no correct decisions. It may be possible that any one would be a good decision under certain circumstances. The decisions range from very active to very inactive behavior. The correctness of any particular decision can only be judged against the standards the individual sets. They will be affected by the mayor's philosophy of government, by the amount of data available, by the feelings of the community as he sees them, and by what is legally and financially possible for a mayor or government to do. Some of these standards can be determined somewhat objectively, but others are very subjective.

We have therefore included no correct decision sheets for each problem. It is our hope that each child's decisions will be given full consideration. This is not to imply there can be no criticism or controversy. On the contrary, there will be both. A "good" decision reached by poor methods could be criticized by a teacher or fellow students as only a chance occurrence. A decision which has no rhyme or reason in terms of the information received would need a strong defense by the mayor who made it. We would like to emphasize evaluation which requires all the decisions to be the same for the same problem is not suitable for these inquiry materials.

It is recommended that the materials be used as an individual learning tool rather than for large group instruction. They are most effective when each child can go through his own process of being Mayor from start to decision. Actually, the materials have never been tested in a situation where a whole class plays Mayor together. Perhaps it would be fun sometime for a large group to go through one of the problems together. However, one of the great values of the materials is that they allow the child maximum freedom to act as an individual and work at his own pace. It would be wasteful not to take advantage of this quality when many materials exist which are designed for use with a large group.

There are several arrangements which can be made for an individual to play Mayor. There is no reason to believe that any one is a great deal better than another. It is more likely that one method will be more suitable for a specific child or group of children. The development and maturity of the children will be a consideration as will the financial situation of the school.

1. A child can use the Mayor materials by himself. He can draw out the file he needs and record his own path through the materials. He would be responsible for refiling the materials as he finishes with them. It is possible that several children could be using the box at one time, especially if they are considering different problems. Multiple copies of important files and the ten problems make it feasible for several children to work on one problem.

2. One child can act as Mayor while another acts as secretary to him. The secretary would give him the pages he asks for, refile the pages, and record the pages he used on the record sheet. This method would free the student from thinking about the clerical aspects of the process. It can also be of value to the secretary, who can closely view another person's inquiry process. (A carrel which simulates a mayor's and secretary's office is available.)

3. A teacher's helper could act as secretary to several children at one time. She could keep records for each Mayor and keep the files in order.

4. A small group could work together using their consensus for making choices. One of them could be chosen as recorder and another as file keeper.

There may be several other arrangements which classes could develop together. This is encouraged. The method which is best suited to the needs of the individual is best for teaching with the Mayor materials.

MENTAL ILLUSTRATIONS

When trying to describe something to another person, we often find ourselves lost for words or unable to break mental sets. One way of helping someone to understand what you are trying to explain is to give an illustrative example. A graphic picture with simplified characterizations often helps in describing a complex notion.

Procedure

1. Look at the picture on the next page and examine each part carefully. Notice how the illustrator has represented the interior workings of an automobile as if they were familiar items in the home.

2. This exercise can be done in a small group or alone. Try to think of something other than an automobile that moves and has parts; it may be a piece of machinery, like an air conditioner, or something nonmechanical, like the human heart. What familiar objects might you use to illustrate its parts? Have each person pick the same object and draw its parts independently. When all the drawings are complete, compare the results; they will probably be quite different.

Processing questions

a. How did you decide on the representations you used?
b. What was unique about your illustration?
c. If your mind was blocked, or you were unable to produce a part, how did other people's pictures help you?
d. How did the illustration shown here and those you drew help you in understanding a concept?

3. Now that you have made an illustration, you will have an opportunity to try another form of description. For this activity, there should be at least eight people, all seated in a circle. One person starts by getting into the middle of the circle; he should decide on a piece of machinery he wishes to pantomime. Once he has decided, he will select one part of that machine and move his body as if he were that part. For example, if he decides to be a clock, he might stand in the middle, bend down and swing both hands as if he were the pendulum on a grandfather's clock. After this first person begins to move, the other people in the group join in the center when they figure out what the machine is. Each person pantomimes a different part. There should be no talking, although sounds sometimes are helpful (clapping of hands for the tic-toc of the clock, for instance). When all the people in the group are involved and moving together, stop and see if everyone was thinking of the same machine; then

projects and activities

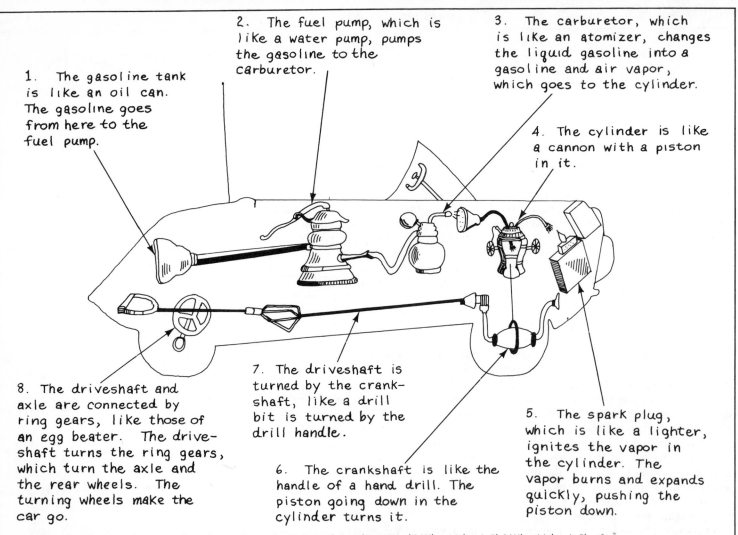

1. The gasoline tank is like an oil can. The gasoline goes from here to the fuel pump.

2. The fuel pump, which is like a water pump, pumps the gasoline to the carburetor.

3. The carburetor, which is like an atomizer, changes the liquid gasoline into a gasoline and air vapor, which goes to the cylinder.

4. The cylinder is like a cannon with a piston in it.

5. The spark plug, which is like a lighter, ignites the vapor in the cylinder. The vapor burns and expands quickly, pushing the piston down.

6. The crankshaft is like the handle of a hand drill. The piston going down in the cylinder turns it.

7. The driveshaft is turned by the crankshaft, like a drill bit is turned by the drill handle.

8. The driveshaft and axle are connected by ring gears, like those of an egg beater. The driveshaft turns the ring gears, which turn the axle and the rear wheels. The turning wheels make the car go.

Adapted from illustration by Joe Kaufman from *What Makes It Go? What Makes It Work? What Makes It Fly? What Makes It Float?*
Copyright © 1971 by Western Publishing Company, Inc. Used by permission of the publisher.

find out what they were doing to imitate a particular part. This activity is fun and will generate lots of laughter, so enjoy yourself while doing it. Try repeating at least five or six times, with a different person beginning each time.

Processing questions

a. When did you know what the machine was? How many parts (persons) were needed before you knew?
b. How did your part move? Would anyone else do that movement differently?
c. How did your movement affect other people's movement?
d. How could this activity be adapted for use in your classroom?

VARIED WAYS
TO PLAY
CHESS, CHECKERS,
AND
OTHER GAMES

When you play games like chess and checkers, you do a lot of thinking. In the following activity you will examine such mental exercise under various conditions. We hope you will learn something about how the mind works and discover some important implications for teaching.

Procedure

Choose a game to play with another person in which thinking and strategizing is essential. Besides chess and checkers, backgammon, tic-tac-toe, and most card games are excellent possibilities. Play the game three times, each time observing one of the following conditions.

1. Play the game without discussion and try to concentrate on your thinking. For

example, think about the moves you make and why you make them. What are your strategies? Can you anticipate your opponent's moves or plan your future moves ahead of time? What happens to you when you do this?

2. Play the game again *as fast as possible,* not allowing time to think between moves. No discussion!

3. Find partners and play the game so that each pair acts as one player. Instead of one individual coming to a decision, the two partners must come to a consensus about each of their moves.

Processing questions

a. What did you have to think about before you could make your next move during the first round?

b. When you played as fast as possible, did the increase in pressure affect your error rate?

c. How did playing with a partner increase the difficulty of a decision?

d. What implications for teaching can you derive from this activity?

PLANNING
A
LESSON

To a teacher, a plan can be like a traveler's map. It may be quite structured and detailed with an end product or destination in view. But, just as a traveler may stop a little longer to see a sight or try a new road, a teacher can also vary a lesson while he is actually teaching it. One thing is certain: when one uses a lesson plan, one should consider how the mind works to maximize the learning process of students. In the following activity, you will have a chance to work on this skill.

Procedure

Imagine that the following case study formed the basis of a lesson you wished to present to your students. Could you get students at any age to relate to this material? What would you do with this material? How would you teach it?

On the subtropical north coast of Australia lives a tribe of native hunters and fishermen called the Yir Yoront. Like most primitive Australians, long cut off from other cultures, the tribe enjoyed great stability. Customs and beliefs were standardized, and before any change was accepted, a myth had to be invented which

proved that one's ancestors did things that way, and thus the change was really no change at all.

Up to the turn of the century, the tribe was still living in the Stone Age. An important tool, a short-handed stone ax, was used to build huts, cut firewood and make other tools for hunting, fishing and gathering wild honey. The stone heads came from a quarry 400 miles to the south, and were obtained from other tribes in an annual intertribal fiesta. The handle was fitted with great skill and care and attached with bark and gum. The completed article — or artifact — was far more than a tool. It had become a symbol, a totem, a sign of the owner's masculinity, to be cherished and handed down and loaned only with the greatest circumspection. The stone ax was not only useful, it was a kind of keystone in the belief of the Yir Yiront.

About 1900, steel axes began to filter in along the tribal trade routes. They were welcomed at first as more efficient; one could cut down a tree much faster. By 1915, missionaries were distributing the steel axes as gifts and rewards. If a man worked especially hard, he might get an ax, and so might his wife or young son. The missionaries hoped by this means to induce people to plant and fence gardens and improve their diet.

The idea was excellent, but it overlooked the culture concept. The steel ax destroyed a most important symbol in the belief system of the tribe. A man lost his importance and dignity; his very masculinity was threatened without his stone ax. Women and children, now possessing axes themselves, became independent and disrespectful. The entire system of age, sex and kinship roles was thrown into confusion. The old trade relations were disrupted and the intertribal fiesta was robbed of significance and charm. Stealing and wife lending increased. The ancient totem system was shattered, for it could not be decided whether the steel ax should be a totem of the Sunlit Cloud Iquana Clan, as the stone ax had been since time out of mind, or the totem of the Head-to-the-East Corpse Clan. . . .

Anthropologists, studying the situation in the 1930's, found that the culture had not broken down so completely as in the case of certain other tribes more exposed to western influences, but it was shaky and insecure. The major reason was the change in the composition of one artifact, from stone to steel, and a change technically for the better.[1]

Some questions you may want to consider in developing your plans are:

a. What do I need to know about my students before I ever begin to plan?
b. What thinking processes will I ask students to use in this lesson?
c. How will I begin the lesson?
d. What kinds of activities might help my students to understand this culture?
e. How will I get feedback about students' learnings?

MENTAL MEASUREMENTS

There are many tests on the market which profess to measure mental func-

[1] From *The Proper Study of Mankind,* Revised Edition by Stuart Chase, pp. 112–113. Copyright 1948, 1956 by Stuart Chase. Reprinted by permission of Harper & Row, Publishers, Inc.

tioning. Have you noticed the variety? Have you ever seen what the tests really measure? The following activity is designed to give you an opportunity to compare several tests of mental functioning and to determine their use and applicability for the classroom.

Procedure

This project will require out-of-class work. You will need to obtain some, if not all, of the following tests of mental activity as well as the instruction manuals for administration:

— Wechsler Intelligence Scale for Children (WISC)
— Bender Gestalt
— Illinois Test of Psycholinguistic Abilities (ITPA)
— Harris Goodenough Draw-a-Man Test
— Torrance Test of Creativity
— Purdue Perceptual-Motor Survey
— Vineland Social Maturity Scale

Examine each test and administration manual carefully.

Processing questions

a. What is each test measuring?
b. What common school activities are similar to the items on these tests?
c. What criteria for intelligence and creativity are used in these tests?

d. What would the results of each test tell you, as a teacher, to do with a student?
e. Which test would you find most useful to you in your teaching?

REORGANIZING PERCEPTION

Look at the woman in the picture. This ambiguous picture has been used exten-

sively in psychological experiments and human relations training. Typically, participants are asked to relate their feelings and opinions about the woman. The catch is that the drawing can be viewed in two different ways: some people see an old woman; some, a young woman. Instead of using this drawing for its usual purpose (examining stereotyping and group pressure on perception), you can use it as the basis for an interesting teaching experience.

Procedure

1. You will need two volunteers in this activity and any number of observers.

2. One volunteer is to be a teacher. He or she should be a person who can see both the old and young woman in the drawing.

3. The other volunteer is to be a student. He or she should be able to see only the young woman in the drawing.

4. The teacher should try to show the student how to "see" the old woman. Any way of accomplishing this goal is accepted.

5. After the student has seen the old woman, the observers should tell the teacher *in as descriptive terms as possible,* what he or she did in coping with the student.*

* A "student" may see the old woman all of a sudden before the teacher has said or done very

6. As long as time permits, have more rounds of teaching (with new volunteers) and observation.

7. Discuss the relationship between teaching behavior and changes in perception. Were any teaching behaviors harmful or helpful in loosening up the students' perceptions of the drawing? How many different ways can you think of for the teacher to help the student in this situation?

ONE- AND TWO-WAY COMMUNICATION

The lecture approach is a classic example of one-way communication. A person who is being "lectured at" faces the formidable task of deciphering the lecturer's message without opportunity to stop and question what is being said. We all know this but frequently we lose sight of this knowledge when we are demonstrating and explaining. The following exercise is created to increase your awareness of that phenomenon and at the same time, to reflect on the potential hazards of

much. If this happens, replace this student with someone else.

two-way communication (which may account for our frequent choice of one-way communication).

Procedure

1. You will need a communicator and a small, even-numbered group of listeners.

2. The communicator should begin by turning his back to the group and describing a house or apartment in which he or she has most recently lived. The listening group is not allowed to ask questions.

3. When the description is finished, the listening group should divide up in pairs. One member of the pair should then describe the house or apartment to his or her partner (who, in turn, listens without comment).

4. The communicator should then face the listening group and describe another house or apartment he or she has either lived in or visited. This time, the group may ask as many questions of the communicator as they wish.

5. Following step 4, the listening group should again divide into the same pairs. This time, the listening partner from step 3 should describe the house or apartment to his or her mate.

6. The group can then compare notes on the accuracy of their descriptions under the two conditions and the level of frustration they experienced while they listened to the communicator. The com-

municator should also share with the group his or her feelings about communicating under both conditions.

SWAPPING TEACHING IDEAS

The notion that teaching is simply "telling information" is largely discredited. To really help a student understand something often requires imagination and creativity. We invite you to share creative teacher ideas with your colleagues.

Procedure

You may want to create a "swap shop" of teaching ideas in one of several ways. For example, you can limit yourselves to one topic, to a single subject, to a particular level of schooling, or to a specific teaching approach (for example, inquiry). It may even work without any limitations.

Each participant is responsible for bringing to the swap shop a few unorthodox teaching ideas. If it is possible to write up these ideas and to duplicate copies, the group can create its own book of ideas. The ideas can come from several sources:

1. readings in this book
2. articles from instruction-oriented magazines such as *Learning, Instructor, Grade Teacher, Scholastic Teacher,* etc.
3. your own teaching experience
4. other teachers

The best way to present these ideas is to try them out on each other. The group

members can react to each idea by discussing the following:

— I think this idea is useful because . . .
— I would be concerned about using this idea because . . .
— This idea can be modified by . . .

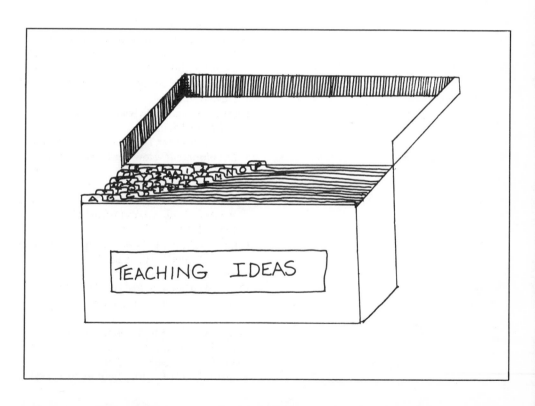

TEACHING IDEAS

additional resources

BOOKS AND ARTICLES

Ashton-Warner, Sylvia. *Teacher*. New York: Simon and Schuster, 1963.

Bruner, Jerome S. *The Process of Education*. Cambridge, Mass.: Harvard University Press, 1961.

Bruner, Jerome S. *On Knowing: Essays for the Left Hand*. New York: Atheneum, 1966.

Bruner, Jerome S. "The Act of Discovery," *Harvard Educational Review* 31(1961): 21–32.

Crutchfield, Richard S. "Nurturing the Cognitive Skills of Productive Thinking." *Life Skills in School and Society*. ASCD 1969 Yearbook, Washington, D.C.: Association for Supervision and Curriculum Development.

Farnham-Diggory, Sylvia. *Cognitive Processes in Education: A Psychological Preparation for Teaching and Curriculum Development*. New York: Harper and Row, 1972.

Furth, Hans G., and Wachs, Harry. *Thinking Goes to School: Piaget's Theory in Practice*. New York: Oxford University Press, 1974.

Gagné, Robert M. *Essentials of Learning for Instruction*. Hinsdale, Ill.: The Dryden Press, 1974.

Gattegno, Caleb. *What We Owe Children*. New York: Outerbridge and Dienstfrey, 1970.

Guilford, J. P. "Factors that Aid and Hinder Creativity." *Teacher's College Record* 63 (1962): 380–92.

Hilgard, Ernest R., ed. *Theories of Learning and Instruction*. NSSE 63rd Yearbook. Chicago: University of Chicago Press, 1964.

Joyce, Bruce, and Weil, Marsha. *Models of Teaching*. Englewood Cliffs, N.J.: Prentice-Hall, 1972.

Kohl, Herbert. *Reading, How to: A People's Guide to Alternative Methods of Learning and Testing*. New York: E. P. Dutton, 1972.

Mallan, John T., and Hersh, Richard. *No G.O.D.'s in the Classroom, Inquiry into Inquiry*. Philadelphia: W. B. Saunders, 1972.

Miller, George A.; Galanter, Eugene; and Pribram, Karl. *Plans and the Structure of Behavior*. New York: Holt, Rinehart and Winston, 1960.

Mosston, Muska. *Teaching: From Command to Discovery*. Belmont, Calif.: Wadsworth Publishing Co., 1972.

Postman, Neil, and Weingartner, Charles. *Teaching as a Subversive Activity*. New York: Dell Publishing Co., 1969.

Scheerer, Martin. "Problem Solving." *Scientific American* 208 (April 1963): 118–28. Reprint Available from W. H. Freeman and Company, 660 Market Street, San Francisco, CA 94104.

Schrank, Jeffrey, ed. *The Seed Catalog: A Guide to Teaching/Learning Materials*. Boston: Beacon Press, 1974.

Schwebel, Milton, and Raph, Jane. *Piaget in the Classroom*. New York: Basic Books, 1973.

Shulman, Lee S., and Keislar, Evan R., eds. *Learning by Discovery: A Critical Appraisal*. Chicago: Rand McNally, 1966.

Siegel, Lawrence, ed. *Instruction: Some Contemporary Viewpoints*. Scranton, Pa.: Educational Publishers, 1967.

Stiles, Lindley J., ed. *Theories for Teaching*. New York: Dodd, Mead, 1974.

FILMS

A Time for Learning. University at Large, 71 West 40th Street, New York, NY 10018.

Jerome Bruner describes his views on discovery learning and presents a discovery-oriented unit called *Man: A Course of Study*.

Information Processing. CRM Productions, 1330 Camino Del Mar, Del Mar, CA 92014.

A very funny film about memory and how people process information.

Jean Piaget on Memory and Intelligence. Davidson Films, 3701 Buchanan Street, San Francisco, CA 94123.

Piaget gives his views on memory and intelligence and talks about his experiences observing children's thinking.

Learning about Thinking. Phoenix Films, Inc., 743 Alexander Road, Princeton, NJ 08540.

Depicts teachers observing and putting into use Piagetian tasks with children.

Learning is Searching. Psychological Cinema Register Audio-Visual Aid Library, Pennsylvania State University, University Park, PA 16801.

Illustrates the use of a discovery approach in elementary social studies.

Why Man Creates. Pyramid Film Producers, P.O. Box 1048, Santa Monica, CA 90406.

This creative film allows the viewer to examine conditions that allow people to create.

chapter
three
_____

educating
for
emotional
growth

initial experiences

RELATING TO STUDENTS' CONCERNS

Many educators today are urging the use of "confluent" learning experiences. These are activities which blend cognition and affect or, in other words, build knowledge through thinking and feeling. Sometimes, in this method of teaching a teacher will use students' personal concerns as a point of departure for "hooking" into the regular school curriculum. But these concerns are legitimate content in their own right.

Here are some familiar topics of study in schools:

— money — the value of commodities and services
— natural resources — the energy crisis
— biology — the human body

By yourself or with others, identify personal concerns (value conflicts, social attitudes, fears and doubts) that these topics might trigger in students. If possible, think about ways to gear your teaching into helping students become aware of these concerns. The following examples might be useful.

Topic: The study of occupations — vocational choice

— What occupations do I value?
— What occupations affect my daily life?
— What occupations best suit my personality, my interests, my skills?

— Can anything block my pursuit of vocational goals?
— I'm a woman. How will that affect my chances?
— I'm black. How will that affect my chances?
— What are some things I can do now to overcome obstacles I've identified?

Topic: Measurement — height and weight

— How tall am I? How much do I weigh?
— How does my height and weight affect me and the way others see me?
— I'm big. Does this mean I'm a threat to people? Does it mean I can't ask to be hugged? How can I show people that sometimes I feel small?
— I'm small. Does this mean people will always want to take care of me? Does it mean I'll always get pushed around? How can I show people that sometimes I feel big inside?

A "TOGETHER" PERSON — MY VIEW

Among psychologists and psychiatrists, there is incredible disagreement about what constitutes a healthy personality (for example, compare the views of Freud, Rogers, Szasz, and Laing). How can we say who is healthy and who is sick? Are Zorba the Greek and Yossarian (of *Catch 22* fame) insane or really "together"? As difficult as this question is, we feel it is an important one for teachers who wish to promote emotional growth in the classroom. Without a conception of psychological health, you may find it hard to develop goals and priorities as an "affective" teacher.

Describe your view of a "together" person. Look at yourself and reflect on other people you know. Or if you wish, read the following description by an undergraduate student at Temple University.

Many people, both adults and children, are unable to make independent decisions and act on them. When in an uncomfortable situation they often respond: "He did it," "It's not my fault!" "Why do these things always happen to me?" A child will throw crayons without thinking because they were thrown at him, or adopt a role at home or in the classroom because he thinks it is expected of him. A teenager involved with his friends in drugs or vandalism will be resentful at being caught rather than reevaluating his involvement. And adults often spend their lives in unsatisfying jobs or relationships. These people do not feel personally responsible for their own lives and actions — they think undesirable things happen to them because of outside forces. Such an attitude takes all energy away from growth, positive activity, and the search for self-fulfillment — qualities that mark the healthy personality.

The cause of the problem is that these "unto-

gether" people are not in touch with their own needs and feelings. The healthy person understands his or her needs. He can recognize his personal feelings and perhaps anticipate his reactions to given situations. It is only by being

able to reach and examine that people can clearly see their way to defining their own goals. To satisfy their own needs, immediate or long-term, they must first know what they are about.

A "together" person knows that the responsibility for his actions rests on his own shoulders: neither the devil nor anyone else "made him do it." But for the healthy person this responsibility is not a terrible burden; it is an opportunity to make the most of his potential. He knows that his own decisions and life plan (whether the long-range goals of an adult for his future or the day-to-day goals of a child) can shape his actions positively. He can confront situations with energy and enthusiasm. It is he who decides whether to participate in one activity or another, he who decides how to react to a problem or provocation or "golden opportunity."

A healthy personality, by being in touch with his needs and feelings, his good qualities and his weaker characteristics, can make independent choices in his own interest. Rather than feeling manipulated by people outside him, he can act on his own.*

* By Sivia K. Katz. Reprinted with her permission.

introduction

We often talk about "getting ourselves together." Usually, we mean to suggest many different things when we say this: gaining control over ourselves and our impulses, arranging our lives so that we can do the things we really want to do, becoming more aware of our surroundings, and so on. What we mean specifically depends on who we are and what our situation is. To a great extent, the new and growing emphasis in schools today on what is called affective, confluent, or humanistic education is based on the same idea of getting ourselves together and the various meanings we give it.

Before going on, we should ask ourselves a basic question: Why the need for a new emphasis at all? Is it because our old ideas about education were inadequate, or because the environment in which education takes place has changed?

Not surprisingly, the answer lies somewhere between the two. In part, the emphasis on affective education is simply a balancing act, a rectification of the overemphasis on cognitive concerns in American education which was triggered by the "Sputnik era." But, more importantly, it is a response to the new and increasing need to facilitate personal decision-making at a time when society presents the individual with an ever-growing, ever-changing number of options.

For all sorts of reasons, historical and technological, this is the kind of society we live in today, probably the most complex and bewildering society human beings have ever had to cope with. More and more, it is becoming a society of choices, in which it is increasingly acceptable to have long hair or short, no children or many, heterosexuality or homosexuality. In many cases, we find ourselves able to entertain many choices, when not so long ago we might have thought we had none. This relaxation of established norms of behavior provides us with both opportunities and problems. We have a chance to increase our human potential. Yet we also endanger our sense of direction and identity as formed by our culture's past. Although some may argue that options are inherently good, in reality they are only a means to an end. How we work with options, and how children who are born into such a state of cultural flux work with them, is the subject of this chapter.

Besides talking about getting ourselves together, people often stress self-awareness. Knowing oneself means being aware of one's needs, wishes, feelings, fears, and doubts. Why is this task considered so important? And why is it so difficult? A digression into the drama of child development might help provide an answer.

According to Piaget, children begin life with little or no sense of separation from others. People do things because of them and they do things because of others. This combination of omnipotence and dependence allows for behaviors which most adults can envy, such as risk-taking and spontaneity. In their own way, very young children are "self-actualizing" or "fully-functioning," open to experience, and unafraid to make mistakes. But then the inevitable cognitive change occurs, and young children come to realize that the world and they are separate. As they separate from the world, children frequently lose some of their prior state of certainty and begin the painful inquiry: Who am I? As anyone who has observed young children from two to five years of age knows very well, a process of "trying on new hats" then begins. Some days, children decide to be mischievous, whereas other days they may be slavishly obedient. Sometimes, they role-play an "inventor," yet other times they can't do anything without complete help. Now, while this process is unfolding, children are likely to get constant feedback from parents and teachers as to which "hats" these adults like and dislike. By this process, parents and teachers influence the self-images of their children. The only lines of defense children have to these powerful adult messages are repression, projection, or introjection. They either bury them deep within themselves, ascribe them to others (like siblings or classmates), or passively accept them. These events often leave children confused about who they really are. Although children earlier could not clearly differentiate themselves from others in a cognitive way, they now fail to do so emotionally. Children may in this way begin a lifelong process of denying ownership of their feelings, needs, and desires, assuming instead that *others* are responsible for what they want and who they are.

The above scenario may be altered, but only with difficulty. It takes a huge degree of self-awareness and sensitivity on the part of teachers and parents. For instance, there *are* ways of talking to children which minimize the chance that they will receive detrimental feedback, but none of these communication formulae work unless the adult who uses them is fairly clear himself about who he is. Children who have been subjected to this process of self-denial can also overcome it through personal exploration. "Awareness" exercises may be of some help. But it would be foolish to expect that personal growth activities will produce sudden insights. Only a steady, perhaps lifelong, process of awareness will have real pay-off.

Educating for emotional growth, then, is a difficult enterprise, but by no means a futile one. Evidence of its worth is the serious attention being given to affective education by many educators and psychologists. The bibliography at the end of this chapter attests to the burgeoning interest. A great deal of literature is now available to help teachers, and instructional media focusing on the development of human potential is also plentiful. In our opinion, any serious teacher can now develop safe and appropriate ways of helping the personal growth of students. But such an effort will require a great deal of personal examination, study, and experience.

The readings and activities in this chapter have been designed to assist this process of examination, study, and experience in four ways: (1) by examining what is psychological health, (2) by considering what educational goals are important in guiding emotional growth, (3) by helping you to be more aware of yourself, and (4) by acquainting you with strategies teachers have used to sensitize students to their feelings, concerns, and values, and to help students develop personal growth skills.

readings

This excerpt from the introduction of Brown's book, **Human Teaching for Human Learning**, is a concise theoretical statement that serves as a basis for understanding the articles that follow in this section. Brown's major contention is that education needs to be confluent; a joining together "of the affective and cognitive elements in individual and group learning." Brown argues that most of us have the habit of denying our feelings. As a result, we are cut off from much of our positive life energy. This problem underlies much of the need for confluent education. You may wish to test Brown's ideas in terms of your own personal emotional growth and development.

GEORGE ISAAC BROWN

EXCERPT FROM
HUMAN TEACHING
FOR
HUMAN LEARNING

At home, first graders watch a Jacques Cousteau television special on turtles. They

From *Human Teaching for Human Learning* by George Isaac Brown. Copyright © 1971 by George Isaac Brown. Reprinted by permission of The Viking Press, Inc.

see the frigate birds eat most of the eggs the turtles lay. The next day in class their teacher has them play the roles of turtles and frigate birds. They not only "do" this but also talk about how they feel as they do it. And they talk about similar feelings they've had in other situations. They write stories and learn to read and to spell new words. Can first graders understand tragedy? Can they experience tragedy as part of the condition of nature and life? Can they be the stronger for this? And can they learn "readin', 'ritin', and 'rithmetic" as well as they would in a conventional lesson — perhaps better? . . .

We are now at a new threshold. Simultaneously emerging in our time are a number of approaches to the extension of human consciousness and the realization of human potential. Some are dangerous, some are irresponsible, and some are exciting, holding great promise. There are a variety of exploratory practices and theories that can be grouped under the taxonomic umbrella of humanistic psychology. These have been the largest resource for work in the new area of confluent education.

Confluent education describes a philosophy and a process of teaching and learning in which the affective domain and the cognitive domain flow together, like two streams merging into one river, and are thus integrated in individual and group learning. The term "affective" . . . refers to the feeling or emotional aspect of experience and learning. And the more familiar "cognitive" refers to the activity of the mind in knowing an object — to intellectual functioning. Schools have focused almost exclusively on cognitive learning.

One hears much about relevance today. How, then, do we know when something is relevant? It is relevant when it is personally meaningful, when we have feelings about it, whatever "it" may be. There has been concern in the educational establishment for motivating learners, but this is usually only fancy wrapping on the package. If the contents of the package are not something the learner can feel about, real learning will not take place. We must attend not only to that which motivates but to that which *sustains* as well.

The position of most educators at all levels is that the primary function of schools is to teach the learner to be intellectually competent. The position is described by those who hold it as realistic, hardheaded, and a number of other fine-sounding things. Our belief is that this position is instead most unrealistic and illusionary. Oh, yes, it would greatly simplify matters if we could somehow isolate intellectual experience from emotional experience, but at the moment this is possible only in textbooks and experimental designs. The cold, hard, stubborn reality is that whenever one learns intellectually, there is an inseparable accompanying emotional dimension. The relationship between intellect and affect is indestructibly symbiotic. And instead of trying to deny this, it is time we made good use of the relationship. Indeed, the purest, highest form of abstract thinking is coupled with congruent feelings on the part of the thinker, even in the grossest sense of pleasure, boredom, or pain. Or, as Michael Polanyi has observed, it is the passion of the scholar that makes for truly great scholarship.

The more of reality a person has available to him, the more effective he becomes in work, in play, and in love. What has happened to most of us is that we have learned to continually substitute fantasies for reality. This is aggravated by the fact that we share many of these fantasies; that is, they are socially reinforced. This is a large and complex area. But here is a somewhat oversimplified description of how the substitution of fantasy for reality can occur.

As children, we are unable to separate the acts we do from the feelings or impulses that accompany them. When we are punished for a naughty act, we also assign the punishment to the feelings that precipitated and sustained the act. What we feel is thus as bad as what we do. As we become socialized or learn to behave in acceptable ways, we not only restrain our "bad" acts but also repress our "bad" feelings. There are a number of psychological mechanisms that enable us to do this, but whatever the means we use, we are forced to deaden ourselves. We must deny feeling. The more we deaden our bad feelings, the more we deaden all feeling, for apparently we have no way of selecting for elimination only those unacceptable feelings. The deadening is an over-all process. As the process of deadening persists, we lose touch to the extent that we are no longer aware of what we really do feel. We eventually reach a point where we have little choice about how we behave, for, deprived of feelings to tell us what we want or don't want, we react primitively, compulsively, ritualistically. It is not surprising, then, that without access to their feelings a large number of people really do not know what they want.

We do not suggest as an ideal the hedonistic, anarchistic individual who expresses his feelings no matter what, where, when, or who. This sort of person is as "out of it" as the one who has no feelings. A healthy individual has a mind and uses it — not to deny the existence of feelings but to differentiate how, when, and with whom it is appropriate to express feelings spontaneously from occasions when one must wait. When he chooses to postpone or control the *expression* of his feelings, however, he does not at the same time deny to himself that *they exist.*

The denial of the existence of genuine feelings has three unfortunate effects, which are related. These are the replacement of real feelings by pseudo-feelings — feelings we *think* we have — the fear of change, and the substitution of fantasy and illusion for reality.

An outgrowth of our struggle to keep certain feelings from emerging into consciousness is the preservation of our precious self-concept. We experience ourselves in certain ways and struggle mightily to preserve that status quo. Change is a threat, for if we open ourselves to new experience and thus allow for change to occur, we must in that opening give up control. That is precisely what we have steeled ourselves against for many years.

One way we avoid change is by creating with our minds imaginary catastrophes that might happen if we were to move into the unknown of new experience. We terrify ourselves, or at least think we are terrified. And in order to stay the way we are or the way we conceive ourselves to be we dissipate huge amounts of psychic energy in manipulating our environment — especially other persons in our personal universe — so that it will respond to us in terms of our self-concept. We believe we "need" others to support, to judge, to punish, to advise, to order, to do an infinite number of things for us that we ostensibly cannot do for ourselves. We are thus out of touch with our own strength and resources. We all do need others. But it is absurd and wasteful to believe that we need others to do things we are perfectly capable of doing ourselves — to refuse to take responsibility for ourselves and for what we do or could

do. We imagine both what some people will do to us and what others must do for us. In each case this is an illusion that accompanies the fantasy of our own limitations.

The obvious waste of living in fantasy in contrast to reality is illustrated by the story of the student who finally got a date with a girl he had been hotly pursuing for two months. He had an exam the next day, so he made the date for nine o'clock, planning to study from seven until nine. He sat down to study, and instead, for two hours, thought about what he was going to do on the date. Then he went out with the girl, and spent the rest of the evening worrying about the exam for which he had not studied.

This example may seem of minor significance. But if we magnify it by how often and how much we keep ourselves out of the present by either hanging on to the past or anticipating the future, the enormity of this waste becomes readily apparent. The only reality we can experience is the reality of the moment. All else is fantasy, something we create for ourselves. We grow and mature through reality experiences. False alternatives merely reinforce our status quo, help keep us stuck.

Bessell discusses an important aspect of emotional growth: awareness of feelings, thought, and behavior inside oneself and

in others. Expanding the views of Brown that we saw in the first reading (pp. 145–147), Bessell argues that conscious knowledge of one's personal impulses leads to wiser choices of action with regard to oneself and to others. Bessell and his colleagues have thus created The Human Development Program for school use. It centers on a once or twice weekly gathering of teacher and students — known as "The Magic Circle" — which promotes affective learning by encouraging children to express thoughts, feelings, and attitudes about themselves and others.

HAROLD BESSELL

AWARENESS

To have awareness is to know what one is really seeing, hearing, thinking, feeling, saying, and doing. If a person is fundamentally aware, he has all his inner and

From *Methods in Human Development — Affective Theory Manual, 1973 Revision,* by Harold Bessell. Reprinted with permission. The Human Development Program was created and developed by Uvaldo Hill Palomares Ed.D, Geraldine Ball M.S., and Harold Bessell, Ph.D. For information on materials and training write Human Development Training Institute, 7574 University Avenue, La Mesa, California 92041.

outer channels or receptors open. If he sees that someone he is talking to is slouching with boredom or stiffening with fear or anger, he knows that he sees it and feels that the listener is in fact bored, angry or hurt. He hears what people tell him; he *listens* to what people tell him and how they say it, and he doesn't garble it or "reinterpret" it so that it sounds the way he would *like* it to sound. If he has sadistic fantasies, grotesque desires, or grandiose dreams, he knows it. He knows also that they are just that: fantasies, desires, and dreams. If he resents his mother, he doesn't convince himself that he loves her; if he is afraid of the dark, of tall blondes, or of losing his wife, he knows it. If he has said something which has pleased or hurt someone, he knows it. If he picks his nose when he is depressed or scowls when he is flattered, he knows it. In other words, he is or exists in feeling contact with himself. His state of being is fully receptive to the inner and outer environments, and he is therefore prepared or equipped to function *responsively* or *responsibly* in relation to himself and to others.

Normal children of preschool and kindergarten age are highly aware in this sense. Very little gets in the way of their perception; very little is filtered or blocked on the way in or on the way out. Around the first grade or about age six, children begin to close to themselves and to others, to bury or mask their feelings and thoughts, subtly and usually unconsciously distorting their expressions and their actions. This happens partly because children, just when their need for it is greatest, are not provided with what we might call *an approved language of feeling*. Instead, they are faced with a vast organized effort to get them to name and describe an external world and to manipulate the symbols of an abstract one. Because nobody *talks about* fantasies or dreams or feelings of helplessness, fear, worthlessness, loneliness, anger or pleasure, children often conclude that what is going on inside them is unique, suspect, or unsayable. They decide or sometimes are even told that great chunks of their experience are strange and unacceptable, and that they themselves are therefore strange, unlikeable, and unacceptable. Nobody can bear to feel unlikeable and unacceptable, and so all sorts of tiny iron curtains start falling into place, partitioning the child's experience and his sense of himself. By the time the child is ten years old, he is no longer whole; he is defensive, withdrawn, cagey, self-segregating. He is, in fact, neurotic. . . .

Children are first and foremost creatures of feeling, and in the schools they feel mostly afraid, lonely, and resentful. No teacher can get anywhere worth getting with children unless she realizes this. The schoolchild is a pool of fear, and this fear — of rejection, of ridicule, of putdowns, of failure — has a tidal ebb and flow. If the tide of fear is high, the child just won't talk; he may "forget" or fidget or daydream or even poke somebody, but the two things he won't do is talk and learn. If the tide of fear is low, the child's natural instincts to assert himself and to gain approval will prevail, and he will try to do what is expected of him *even* though he is still afraid of saying or doing the wrong thing.

Nursery school or kindergarten children can be lonely almost to the point of devastation, because they are separated from the crucial adults in their lives, their parents — their basic source of warmth and protection. Young children instinctively and unerringly regard their parents as their lifeline, and when this lifeline is unplugged they are correctly terrified and desolate, and they have no way of knowing that the connection is not permanently severed. *Later*, even mere hours later, has no meaning for the child; *now* is what he understands and essentially only now. If this lifeline is not quickly plugged into another significant adult whom the child can respond to as a source of warmth and security, he will be recurrently desolate and insecure. Older children have the same need for closeness and warmth and protective attention, but if they don't get it, they don't respond with intense biological alarm; they are just lonely.

Children are resentful for two reasons. First, they have built-in drives to become more powerful and capable, and these drives are frequently "powered" by anger. Conditions of severe helplessness and powerlessness are intolerable to the human animal from the day of birth on, and anger or rage is what makes a child get out of his cradle and a subtler form of the same anger is one part of what has carried man some quarter of a million miles from his planetary home. People chafe at *all* restrictions, and restrictions perceived to be unnecessary, meaningless, or spiteful generate intense resentment. The typical school setting has been one of the most restrictive and unresponsive environments ever devised. Secondly, children perceive quite accurately that adults in general and many teachers in particular *do not care very much about their feelings.* This indifference or neglect is frequently interpreted — usually incorrectly — as active hostility. Most human beings intuitively or instinctively respond like-to-like: in the felt presence of hostility, they become hostile; in the presence of fear, they become afraid; in the presence of happiness, they become happy; in the presence of loving-kindness, they become loving and kind.

The solution to all this should be obvious. Teachers must be *aware* of the children's fear, loneliness, and resentment. They must encourage children and reduce the fear-tides; they must provide children with the needed adult interest and protective caring attention; they must reduce the child's resentment by taking a genuine interest in his feelings and by removing restrictions which needlessly deny him freedom, responsibility, and competence. Little of this can be done *directly,* however, and little of it can be done immediately. You cannot directly *tell* a

child that you know he is afraid, lonely, or angry, because he can become severely anxious: you know him too well, you are getting too close to the quick. You have to allow him to reveal these things in his own time, when he feels ready and safe and willing to share these feelings with you and with his peers. You cannot tell a child to be afraid of rejection, put-down, or ridicule; you must *show* him slowly and patiently that you do not expect perfection, that it is safe and acceptable for him to open up and try, that nobody will laugh, at least not too much or cruelly. You can *show* him that you care about him, and you can *show* him that you are willing to listen to him. If you show him, he will believe you, and cease to hate you.

ESCAPE FROM AWARENESS

Sigmund Freud began it all by identifying in people a tremendous force which he named *repression.* Human beings have all sorts of instinctual survival, reproductive, and pleasure-seeking impulses. Since not all these impulses can be granted consummation if society is to have some degree of peaceful and effective organization, these inherent urgings are denied expression by the authority agents of society, mainly parents and teachers employing different forms of restraint, reprimand or punishment. When the forces of the instincts come into conflict with the blocking forces of society, the child appre-

hends danger and experiences feelings of anxiety. Since anxiety is an extremely disagreeable feeling, the child, having only a fuzzy, budding comprehension of what is happening, automatically inhibits his own natural instinctual impulses. This unconscious suppression of impulse is what Freud called repression.

Repression has desirable and undesirable effects. The repression of destructive impulses serves to protect us from each other. It also tends to create dammed-up energy in the person who is repressing some impulse. Such dammed-up energies could, according to Freud, have beneficial consequences when sublimated or "translated" into some creative avenue of expression. When they remained dammed-up, however, these energies would eventually express themselves in what Freud called *symptom formation* — they would emerge in twisted form as hysterical paralysis, obsessions, phobias, compulsions, nightmares, or psychosomatic "diseases" like migraine, ulcers, impotence, and so forth.

Thus while repression promotes at the surface level peaceful and constructive interactions with society, it can also cause much subterranean personal misery. Freud discovered that treatment was possible, however; it turned out that in many individuals old impulses which had once been repressed could be remembered and could be expressed verbally. This calling-up or verbal regurgitation Freud called catharsis or cleansing: it meant that the impulse could be revived under conditions of adequate control and didn't have to be acted out behaviorally. Even though the impulse was just "spoken out," enough dammed-up energy was released so that the tell-tale symptom diminished or disappeared. This discovery of Freud's constituted one of the most significant breakthroughs in our understanding of human nature. It suggested that people could remain fully aware of the various destructive impulses without having to act them out behaviorally. This has turned out to be the case: if people retain full awareness of their potentially dangerous impulses and are allowed to express them verbally under controlled conditions, many of the harmful side-effects of repression can be lessened or avoided altogether. And all this suggests to me what people would be like if they could remain fully aware — strong, stable, responsible, character-ful, healthy, *beautiful*.

Usually, those impulses that achieve the fate of repression have tended to deserve it; they are usually potentially disruptive ones. Does this mean that we will encourage disruption? The answer is decidedly "NO." We must keep in mind the important difference between the *unconscious* restraint of impulse and the *conscious* restraint of impulse. When restraint is repressive or unconscious, deliberately self-controlled behavior is at a mini-

mum. When restraint is conscious, people know what they are doing and why.*

Our objective is not merely to preserve and increase awareness. Rather, our objective is to increase the responsible and self-controlled handling of the potential antisocial impulses which inevitably arise in all children. To accomplish this important objective, we *encourage* the natural, honest, verbal expression of potentially harmful impulses but simultaneously *discourage* their behavioral expression.

Once the teacher has mastered this guiding principle, she can proceed comfortably and responsibly to promote self-awareness in her children.

ORGANIZING ONE'S EXPERIENCE

Awareness can be divided quite simply (and artificially) into two parts, internal and

* "Impulse" has been a very useful word in conceptualizing adaptive conflicts. It is a word which blends the concepts of feeling and thought, and most accurately conveys the notion of urgings toward some activity in the environment. In fact, we use this word a great deal in more advanced Levels of the HDP, in the mastery units. However, for the purposes of promoting a more articulate awareness in four- and five-year-olds, we temporarily sacrificed accuracy for the more important benefit of increasing understanding by using the more easily grasped terminology of "feelings" and "thoughts." Actually, feelings and thoughts are better thought of as derivatives of an impulse.

external: the child can be aware of those events that happen *inside* him, and those events that originate or happen *outside*, out in the world somewhere or in other people.

The events themselves can be divided into three kinds: feelings, thoughts, and behavior. We can also categorize these events according to purpose or effect: we can say simply that all feelings, thoughts, and behavior tend ultimately either to promote human pleasure and survival or to produce pain and extinction.

For very young children — especially for four- and five-year-olds — we have to simplify language radically, of course. For them, we talk about events that are basically "good" (tending to promote pleasure and survival) and contrast these with events that are basically "bad" (tending to cause pain, danger, and ultimate extinction). If the teacher is interested in a comprehensive study of the fascinating subject of the role of adaptation in survival, she is referred to the works of Weston LaBarre and Theodosius Dobzhansky.[1]

"Good" and "bad" have no direct moral connotation in the Human Development Program. While considerate behavior is to be encouraged at all times, we believe that it is preferable to avoid possible conflicts of values and focus our attention upon providing the child with some understanding of what leads to human benefit and what tends to be detrimental as the child is now able to see it. In time, all children come to their own conclusions about what is morally right and wrong. Instead, the terms "good" and "bad" refer in the HDP to the way in which *the person having the experience feels about it*. Thus, for a three-year-old going out in the street would be "good" because that is what he wants to do. But his mother would naturally see this activity as "bad" because she knows of its dangers: she would, to understate it, feel badly if the child got hit by a car and was injured or killed, and her anxiety about this is a distinctly "bad" feeling.

The following table shows a simple scheme for designating experience in terms of its origin, nature and significance. The child who knows this "periodic table" of experience can thus orient himself in a universe which contains himself and other people. He can quite literally get a grip on his experience.

The importance of *shared* experience cannot be overstressed. The investigator chiefly responsible for calling our attention to the vital significance of experiencing oneself as different and therefore possibly inferior is Alfred Adler.[2] Later, Harry Stack Sullivan made this a central concept in his thought: he found that great numbers of people felt that they were "different" from each other in some unpleasant way, and he labelled this notion the "delusion of uniqueness."[3] As children, we learn about ourselves by comparing ourselves literally thousands of times with other children and with adults, to see if we are doing things right or behaving acceptably or learning the right things. Comparison is an inevitable perceptual yardstick. Children can very easily draw the wrong conclusions about what others are thinking, feeling, and doing, and can thus develop feelings of self-scorn and inferiority which will severely damage their self-concept, their performance in the classroom, and their chances for happiness and personal effectiveness in life. Our task is to promote realistic comparison as a useful adaptive force, and then to promote its constructive utilization as a tool for healthy personality development. . . .

LANGUAGE AND AWARENESS

We must take special note of the core tool of awareness, namely language. Language is a crucial vehicle for feelings and thoughts, and for placing behavior in a frame of reference and perspective. The early developmental aspects of language have been reviewed by Otto Fenichel as follows:

The ability to recognize, to love, and to fear reality is developed in general before the learning of speech. But it is the faculty of speech that initiates a further decisive step in the development of reality testing.

Words allow for a more precise communication with objects, and also for making more precise the anticipation by trial actions. This anticipation of action now becomes thinking proper and consolidates consciousness finally. Of course there already had existed a consciousness without words. . . . But his is merely the undifferentiated predecessor of thinking. . . . Schilder has shown that every single thought be-

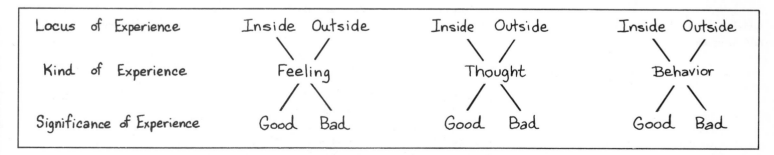

Locus of Experience	Inside Outside	Inside Outside	Inside Outside
Kind of Experience	Feeling	Thought	Behavior
Significance of Experience	Good Bad	Good Bad	Good Bad

fore formulation, has gone through a prior wordless state. The acquisition of the faculty of speech, of the understanding that certain noises are used as symbols for things, and of the gradual capacity for rational use of this faculty and understanding is a decisive step in the formation of the ego. . . .[4]

The vital role of the Magic Circle in dispelling delusions of uniqueness and in keeping the child's awareness of himself and others open and fresh cannot be fulfilled in a communications vacuum. Children desperately need to be provided with a vocabulary and a syntax that relate to the nitty-gritty of their experience. Far more important than learning how to spell c-a-t is learning how to say, "I feel bad because they didn't let me play with them," or "What Johnny said made me feel good." The early Levels of the Human Development Program are therefore built around verbal communication in general and around the language of personal feelings and thoughts in particular.

GENERAL PRINCIPLES OF AWARENESS

We may sum up the quality of awareness in a series of general principles:

— *Awareness means that the person has open channels for receiving information. His degree of awareness is his degree of openness or receptivity.*

— *The aware child is usually able to discriminate amongst classes of events and organize his experience.* He recognizes an event as occurring within or without, and can subcategorize the event as a feeling, thought or behavior. He usually recognizes the probable value direction of an event: he knows whether an event is essentially negative or positive in terms of pleasure or survival.

— *The aware child is an effective communicator.* He is able to convey with accuracy his perception of the events in his internal and external environment. He can verbally indicate whether he feels good or bad, whether his thoughts are good or bad, and whether his behavior is constructive or destructive. He can discover and can say verbally if another person feels good or bad, if another's thoughts are pleasant or unpleasant, and if another person's behavior is constructive or destructive.

— *The aware and effectively communicating child knows about and can verbally describe the similarities and differences among people.* He is accepting and tolerant of these similarities and differences.

Sometimes unnoticed and sometimes forgotten, responsibility is an important part of affective education. No matter how good a teacher is, the student has the ultimate responsibility for learning. Two sides of this problem are presented by Castillo: The student needs to recognize his or her responsibility; but, in order to promote such awareness, the teacher must share control over the learning environment with students. This excerpt is particularly useful for the way in which it shows the connection between the cognitive and the affective, between learning and responsibility, and between teaching and giving up control.

GLORIA A. CASTILLO

RESPONSIBILITY

Attending to responsibility is vital in making learning confluent. It directly or indirectly provides for experiences that allow the child to assume responsibility for his learning. I generally start with lessons aimed at self-awareness, because only someone who knows what is happening to him will be able to tune in to what is happening to others. In a classroom I expect a great deal of learning to occur as a result of the presence of other children, other adults, others' ideas as presented in books, etc. All this must move into the child's awareness for the development of

From *Left-Handed Teaching: Lessons in Affective Education* by Gloria A. Castillo. © 1974 by Praeger Publishers, Inc., New York. Excerpted and reprinted by permission.

responsibility. When each child assumes responsibility for what happens to him to his full capacity, when he can choose that which will give him the most satisfaction, when he can move from one appropriate response to the next, smoothly and easily, then teaching and learning are together in one meaningful whole, with the teacher and the child learning from and teaching each other equally.

Many teachers are alarmed when I speak of a child's having responsibility for himself. But it is the child who does or does not learn, read, do math, cooperate, sit quietly, play vigorously, etc. I cannot be responsible for him in that final step. This does not mean that I can allow the child to do anything he wants, whenever he likes. I do not believe in allowing children to be only where and what they are. To teach is to show the child that more is possible. I feel that I have something to teach, and I want to teach it. And as I am engaged in teaching, I want the child to be engaged in what is happening to him. This will allow for a wide variety of responses. He may just go along with me, or he may become actively involved or he may need additional information or help. I have a structure to work in, the confluent model, and I strive to provide a learning environment that will allow the child to define his own structure, but always within limits. I do not believe that a child wants or needs license. He needs to know that no matter what he does, he will be safe. No matter how confusing things may get, there will be a time of

clearing. He needs and wants freedom, and with that comes responsibility.

Children, and adults as well, do not feel much responsibility for things over which they experience no control. Within the space of responsibility, therefore, I try to develop the concept, "I control myself." This is achieved, in part, by asking over and over again, "What are you doing" and "Who is doing that?" It is also developed by enhancing the child's sense of his ability to make himself felt in his world. The classroom is a large part of a child's world, and so it is necessary to give him some of the responsibility involved in creating that world. Even a kindergartner can be invited to share his ideas on "What do you need a teacher to do for you?" There are real things that a child needs an adult to do for him, and at the same time there are many things a child can be responsible for all on his own. People do not become responsible at a certain age. Responsibility involves lifelong learning. It is not a "subject" but an ongoing process.

It is possible to have many levels of awareness and responsibility in the same class at the same time. Even the youngest school-age child can be given his share of responsibility. Consider the following examples.

"My mother makes me dump the garbage."
"How does she make you dump the garbage?"
"She tells me to."
"Who dumps the garbage?"
"I do."
"Well, could you not dump it?"

"No. I have to do it or I'll get in trouble. She makes me do it."
"How does she make you do it? Does she take you over there and put your hands on it?"
"No. She makes me, and if I don't, I get in trouble."

"I have to be nice to my sister."
"Who is nice to your sister?"
"I am."
"Who makes you do that?"
"I do. I have to do that because if I don't, my father really gets angry, and I don't like my father to get angry, so a long time ago I decided that I would make myself be nice to my sister."

In the first example, the child seems to be very much aware of what his mother does and as yet does not see what he does in that situation. He is like a robot, with his mother the master controller. In the second example, the child realizes the rewards of doing what his father wants him to do. He does not express the hopelessness, the powerlessness, of the first child. He does something he has to do in order to get something he wants. He has some control over the kind of relationships he has with his sister and with his father, and he is aware of that control.

It is necessary to seek ways to permit the child to have control in the cognitive domain also. When a child is permitted to be aware of what is happening to him, when he takes responsibility for what does and does not happen to him, he can and will make the personal translations from the cognitive domain to his own being. A fourth-grade girl brought her math paper to me stating, "I can't do math." I asked her to find *what* in math she couldn't do. It didn't take long for her to discover that what she couldn't do was master a few multiplication facts. She could add and subtract, borrow and carry. She put aside her paper and said, "I need to work on these four multiplication facts." She left the assignment until she was sure of those facts and then completed it in a very short time. Later in the day she told me, "I like math now. I discovered what I needed to learn, and I learned it."

In helping a child to take responsibility and be in control in the cognitive domain, it is necessary to tune in to his readiness/ awareness level. If the material is too far removed from the skills he now has, if it is too foreign to his own readiness/aware-ness level, he will not be able to relate to it. It is important to identify what the child already knows that will help him to master new materials. What else in the curriculum might be related to new cognitive experiences? What activities can the child engage in to test out his ideas? A child at any age can be remarkably adept at designing methods for answering these and other questions that will emerge from cognitive materials. He satisfies his own needs for learning while involving himself naturally and easily in his play and free-time activities. There is no reason he

cannot be allowed to do so within the limits of the classroom.

Giving control to children is not easy for most teachers to do. We have been taught by teachers who were in control of us, and we have been taught to be con-trollers. Experimentation with allowing children to be in control and with various kinds and amounts of control by teacher and class is a necessary part of confluent education.

Each teacher will have to deal with this issue in his own way. No one can take that final step for him. All I can do is to share some of my experiences, some of my successes, some of my failures.

Once a group of teachers was working with this problem, meeting once a week to discuss what was happening. There were reports of everything from complete bed-lam to great success. One teacher had nothing to say for more than a month. Then she came in all excited, proudly re-porting, "My confluent program has begun. I kept in mind that the worse thing that could happen would be that the whole class would fall apart. I started a lesson and the whole class did fall apart. I got angry but shared my feelings with the class. They were frustrated with me, feeling that I assured their failure with my attitude. We had quite a discussion, and it was very hard for me to listen to what they had to say. We stayed with it and worked out new directions and now we are really moving along together."

Her decision was to face giving up con-trol, to listen to what the children had to

offer, and to allow herself to be uncom-fortable for a while in order to "move along" with her class. There is a fine line between losing control and giving up con-trol. In this case, the teacher actually gained control by giving up control, by sharing it with the class.

A teacher will have to find ways to dis-cover what his children feel, what they think about when they are not made to think about school subjects, what they do with themselves when they are free. Con-tinuing questions a teacher must ask the learners are: "How do you feel about this?" and "What do you already know that makes you feel that way?" Also, the questions that people always ask them-selves, such as "Who am I?" "What can I do about things?" "Who am I really con-nected to?" "How do I fit into the scheme of things?" must be explored constantly. This may not be easy. Children have learned very well that the teacher is the source of power in the room and that they must somehow say what must be said in words that he will allow. For example, I had been doing morning lessons on taking responsibility for one's actions for about a week when suddenly one after-noon two boys began an all-out fist fight. Before I could stop them, one had a bloody nose and both were in tears, more of rage than pain. Calmly, I asked what had happened. I got the usual, "He started it." Then, thinking back to our morning lessons, I asked, "What are you feeling now?" Since both boys were still obviously upset and quite angry, I was amazed and confused when one replied: "Sorry." I asked, "How do you know that you are sorry?" He answered: "My mother says to say I'm sorry." This child had learned the words he was "supposed" to say after a fight, but he had no words of his own to express the enormous amount of feeling that went along with the act, or, if he had them, he knew that they were not to be used in this classroom.

Then I asked, "What *might* you feel when you are fighting?" This seemed less threatening than "What *do* you feel?" but still neither boy responded. Others in the class, however, were quite stimulated and very willing to share their ideas since they had not, at that moment, been involved in fighting.

This incident gave me a great deal of material to work on. I realized that these boys were not yet willing to go very far in stating their responsibility, assuming that they were aware of what they were doing. Only when the involvement was at a distance could they respond — they could answer such questions as "What might you feel?" instead of "What do you feel?" and "How does someone else feel?" Knowing this, I continued with readiness/awareness techniques. I found all kinds of opportunities to ask "What are you doing now?" and "Who is doing that?" We stopped during regular activities to finish the statement "Now I am . . ." or "Now I feel . . ." When children got into fights or quarrels, I had them talk to each other, not to me, about what was happening now, and not about what had happened

earlier. When a child said "I can't," I asked him to say "I won't." In every way possible I helped, and at times even forced, the children to be aware of their own existence in the here and now.

About two weeks after the fight, one of the boys involved delighted me when he walked in from recess and proudly announced: "I had a fight with John. I gave him a bloody nose. I feel powerful. I feel good." By this I do not mean to say that I encourage fighting. But dealing with fights is part of being a teacher, and I do need to know what fighting does for a child so that I can help him find more acceptable ways to get the same rewards he gets from fighting, whatever they may be. So it was necessary to allow this child to experience his power in an acceptable manner. In every possible way, I helped him to become aware of his power to deal with curriculum (e.g., solving math problems), his power to influence others in the class, the multiple ways in which he affected us, and ultimately the power he used on himself to avoid solving his conflicts with his fists.

In the foregoing case, we had been exploring our feelings in general, allowing them to be present in the classroom, and we had been exploring ways of acknowledging those feelings verbally and nonverbally. It was not until weeks later that this boy was able to express those feelings as his own. One cannot just go through a set of lessons and come out responsible. But by listening, tuning in, going back to less threatening responses, leaving more

risk and more involvement always available, applying skill, intuition, and knowledge, the teacher can direct lessons that allow for a continuing spiral of taking responsibility, having both more difficult and more easily reached levels equally available for himself and the children. The doing becomes a trying, an experiment with the environment to find out what it is like. There is always something new to be learned, some new awareness, some new way of taking responsibility for one's life to be discovered.

There is nothing we can say about this reading. You'll see.

BUD CHURCH

SILENCE
MAKES
THE HEART
GROW LOUDER

Ron was the kind of kid who would have been better off wrestling with his teachers

Reprinted with permission from the October, 1970, issue of *Media and Methods* magazine, 134 N. 13th St., Philadelphia, Pa. 19107. © North American Publishing Company.

literally rather than academically. He liked to argue, but he didn't feel comfortable unless he could push you in the chest a couple of times, punch at your shoulder, maybe slap you on the arm. Ron really liked to make contact. Then he was happy.

One morning in homeroom he skipped up to me, jabbing toward my chin, and announced that he didn't have much use for cowards who avoided the draft. I suggested in my most carefully considered verbal way that cowardice might not be the sole motive for resisting involvement in Vietnam. I took my share of pokes for that, and then with a gentle elbow in the stomach Ron switched the bout to police being tougher on law and order. I couldn't let that pass either without some wordy qualifications. When the bell rang Ron socked it to me and we parted on a note of inconclusiveness. Knowing how frustrated Ron felt about discussions that couldn't be pinned flat to the floor, I was just a little on guard when he came back later in the morning for English.

The bell for the class hadn't rung yet. Ron was outside the door talking quickly to the students as they entered the room. Each one nodded his head. Some smiled a little. Something was up.

I casually pressed myself against the wall and worked my way near the door. "Don't say anything, even if Mr. Church calls on you," Ron was telling them. So that was it. An old trick on teachers. And

a neat one. Every teacher deserves to have it happen now and then.

The class sat down and looked at me, absolutely quiet. The bell blasted for a second, then died. No one stirred. I stood in the center of the semicircle I taught in, saying nothing. I slowly turned my head studying each stiff face a few seconds, looking for a crack. No one flinched. They had me.

Well, time to go to Plan B, as my colleagues in the car pool put it when our wives suddenly decide they all need a car the same day. I sat in an empty seat in the semicircle and waited. I waited, and they waited. And it was perfectly still. I had never experienced such a calm. I confess I couldn't take it. Suddenly I went to the board and without looking at any of them wrote: "Silence is beautiful." Then I sat down with them.

A girl was looking at me curiously, a girl who never contributed much to class, who was considered dull-average. On an impulse I tossed the chalk to her. She looked at it a second, and I waited for her to scoff and throw it back. But she didn't. She went to the board and slowly wrote something like "I don't like to talk." As she was walking to her seat a boy jumped up and grabbed the chalk from her and wrote under my sentence, "That's a lot of crap." He placed the chalk on a desk. It didn't sit there long. Ron jumped forward and swept up the chalk with a deft movement as he skipped past the desk toward the board.

I don't exactly remember what was put

up, but every member of that class put something on the board. Many put several things. Two dozen different kinds of handwritings — tiny cursive scrawls, bold square manuscript, sweeping loops of letters, one written painfully upside down, others in circles and mushrooms and rainbows. A few were obviously connected in a chalky conversation; others were just scraps of poems or song verses or graffiti. Never a word was spoken.

The end of the period came. We were at a high anyway. Every bit of board was covered. There was much crammed in, for reading between the lines. The students left as quietly as they had come. I'm not sure how long it was before I said anything to anyone. When I did the words came stumbling and harsh.

The teacher in me wasn't able to let such precious possibilities rest. I had to try it on a class. That, I knew, would be another bucket of bullfrogs altogether. Contrived, artificial, phoney — it would only work once, I warned myself; but I pushed the advice away as teachers so often do, determined to ruin a good thing if I must.

I selected an entirely different kind of class, an advanced class, the hot-shots of the school — always talking, always testing and parrying and stumping and in general flapping their verbal banners in front of their squads of studied reflections.

They came in jabbering, some arguing about whether student council really was a viable force in the school and others convinced that Hamlet's problem was

Freudian and even Shakespeare probably didn't know it.

When the bell rang they obeyed smoothly, turning with rapt attentiveness to the business of the class. I looked at the students carefully, touching the eyes of each one briefly, then went and sat among them. I said nothing. They waited. It was always my move in this class for then they'd know how to gauge a successful response (something they were masters at for they had spent eleven years learning it). I at least had that going for me. This time it was my conspiracy.

Finally I gave the chalk to a girl conspicuously two desks away from me. She took it. It was very quiet. She sensed that breaking the silence was inappropriate, for even advanced students underneath all those years of achievement are sensitive human beings. I didn't look at her. Finally she went to the board and wrote, "I don't know why, but I know how." She brought the chalk back to me. I gave it to someone else. He went up and wrote, "What is the sound of one hand clapping," stolen but appropriate. Then it happened again, all over the board — in corners, at angles, shared thoughts and private quips, anger and tenderness. A few in this class, unlike the other one, didn't go up (which says something, I think, in its silent way). I joined in, too, answering a comment I couldn't resist, or just balancing out the composition with smudges of chalk in empty spaces.

In the last ten minutes of this class we talked about it. It's funny how that had to happen. No one really wanted to, but I told them what had occurred in the other class, and none of them told me to shut up; and they, too, couldn't help but verbally reflect on the experience. It was kind of a shame.

Something similar happened the next time I tried it. A friend of mine, David Kranes in the English Department at the University of Utah, had arranged for me to visit the University to talk about teaching. Most of my role was informal. I went from class to class, usually made up of undergraduates, getting feedback about how they looked at the years of schooling they had gone through, sharing some of my frustrations at getting kids to be more alive, and in general elated by the responsiveness of these young people to the prospect of education in America being something more than eulogized drudgery.

One evening over beers I told Dave about the silent lessons, and he urged me to try it in one of his classes. So the next day Dave introduced me to the group he had selected, mumbling something about how I was going to take the class for the period, and I got up and went to the board. I looked out at the class for a minute, scattered around an old biology room in which the seats were bolted to the floor in ancient rows, and then I wrote: "I am Mr. Church. 'Bud' will do. Who are you?" I picked out a coed who looked both alert and pretty and walked over to her seat and gave her the chalk. She got up, more on reflex than anything else, and I sat in her place. She went slowly to the board, paused for a moment, then wrote, "I'm Theresa. What's going on?"

She came back to me and gave me the chalk. I got up. Everyone was watching me closely. No one had spoken. I walked way to the back of the room and gave the chalk to a boy sprawled over two or three chairs. He got up as casually as he had been sitting and shuffled up to the board and wrote, "I'm suspicious." Then he came back and gave me the chalk.

So this one was going to be a chess game for awhile, I thought, moves between me and the class. Well, that's the college game, so let's play it. I gave the chalk to another girl. She wrote, "I'm Shauna, but I'm suspicious too." She gave the chalk back to me. I went up and wrote, "Is everyone at U. of U. suspicious? All I want to do is get to know you." I left the chalk up in the front of the room this time. Without much pause a boy went up and wrote, "I'm not suspicious but I'm curious." Another boy took the chalk and wrote, "I'm curious, too, about why we don't use the board on the other wall?" The next person went to the board on the other wall. Before we were through most of the board space on both walls was filled up, and arrows were drawn all over, including across a painted wall from one board to the other.

Finally a boy got up and stomped up to the chalk board and began collecting all the chalk, even an almost full box of it that was on a table. Then climbing over chairs and desks he went in a straight line for an open window, extended his hands out of it ceremoniously, and dumped every piece of chalk down two stories on whatever was below.

The class laughed heartily but no one said a word. A boy near me wrote on a piece of paper, "Can we continue with pencil and paper?" and passed it to me. As I was writing, "Go ahead!" Dave jumped up and found one tiny stub of chalk on the floor that had been missed, a piece bigger in diameter than length. He hastily wrote on the board, "What the hell is going on!" I went over to a far corner of one of the boards and wrote, "Make Love, Not Grades." Meanwhile the paper was going around the room, and other students took the scrap of chalk and were still going on, ignoring my attempt to be cute, picking up more thoughtful or witty threads.

Finally Dave interrupted. He felt that in the final ten minutes the class ought to know me and how all this had started. The class was upset at the interference. This college class was upset! It was beautiful. They didn't care about who I was, at least not via the noises we call "speech." They felt that the sounds of words were flat after what had gone on. We looked at the board. Again, all kinds of messages were there for him who had eyes to see. As one boy put it, for the first time in his ex- perience in a college class he felt he had

gotten to know the anonymous students who sit around him, the ones with whom he had engaged in classroom skirmishes but seldom communication, as well as the ones who never spoke. Their walks to the board, their handwriting, the look in the eyes after as they walked back, the set of their mouths, said things. Something had sprung open in unique messages. The students were almost sad when it ended. So was I.

I teach fourth grade now. Naturally I have tried the silent treatment. It came one day when I had put a four line poem on an overhead transparency and had pro- jected it on the screen at the beginning of the class without saying anything. I sim- ply put it up there for them to read aloud, to comment on if they wished, to wonder about. I hadn't planned to do anything but that for a minute or two, perhaps fielding questions if they had any, but in general just starting off the morning.

But it became silent very quickly, and stayed that way. Each student read it to himself and then waited. And I wondered, do I dare try? I went to the board and wrote: "What word do you like best in the poem?" Hands went shooting up, and even a couple of words were called out, but I went to a boy and gave him the chalk and sat in an empty chair. He got up and went to the board without any hesitation and wrote, "Dragon." I went up and wrote "Why" and he wrote, "Be- cause it's neat." By then some students were asking each other if I had laryngitis, and some students were clamoring about

wanting the chalk so they could write on the board, and I wrote, "Mark, would you be willing to read the poem aloud?" He did. One boy was very confused and kept asking, "Why isn't he talking?" I gave the chalk to him. He shook his head and gave it back. I think he was sorry later.

I turned off the overhead and wrote on the board a question I had gotten from somewhere: "Which are you more sure of, tomorrow or gravity?" A boy named Jimmy Holman, an itchy boy who finds it hard at any time to stay still, darting in and out of ideas and trouble, the kind our education system creates and will break or alienate before grade 8, ran up and took the chalk from me and carefully wrote, "Gravity." Then Jimmy tapped the pointer on the board and began to lecture: "First I have to draw two pictures like this" ("Yes, Mr. Hol- man," someone chided), and he drew one picture of a man standing on earth, and another of a man upside down above the earth. "This is gravity," he said point- ing to the first one and, turning to the second, he said, "this isn't."

I still didn't say anything. When I was pressed again about why didn't I talk I went to the board, spanked Jimmy away with the pointer, and wrote, "Words are walls." "That doesn't make sense," a girl commented. I wrote, "If it makes sense to you, thumbs up. If it doesn't, thumbs down." (By now as I wrote each word on the board the class was saying it in unison.) I put my thumb up. About half the class put their thumbs up. I put my thumb down, and the other half put theirs down. So I wrote, "Can words say I love you?" A girl came up and wrote, "I love you means I love you." I guess even Gertrude Stein would be proud of that at nine-years-old.

The spoken word is a delight; it has a magical power. But how easily that delight is dulled, that power abused. We crush the magic in all the deceptive and banal talkings of each day. Words are still poor symbols that can be twisted to block meanings and experiences instead of heightening them.

In school, especially, we spread out a flat desert of sound on fertile young ears, baking them dry day after day with what we call education. The hot sun of "communication skills" and "language arts" beats down year after year until even a possible oasis of sparkling language becomes for the student a poisoned well. To say nothing in that dry atmosphere of talk becomes nourishment; an important kind of learning about language and its limitations takes place.

Even as I write this the words are beginning to come numb. Enough of justification. "The rest is silence."

Harmin, Kirschenbaum, and Simon believe that education must be concerned with facts, concepts, and values. Here they

clarify some of the ways in which it is possible to "teach" values. To begin with, they point out that "students do not need any more values imposed upon them. They do need to learn the skills that will help them develop their own values." This is done by helping students learn to choose and prize their beliefs and behaviors and to act on their beliefs. Value clarification methods have been widely used in many education programs throughout the country.

MERRILL HARMIN, HOWARD KIRSCHENBAUM, AND SIDNEY B. SIMON

THE GOAL OF VALUES-CLARIFICATION

— Connie, ten years old with big brown eyes and long, dark hair, talks about herself and about her mother who is on

Excerpted from *Clarifying Values Through Subject Matter* by Harmin, Kirschenbaum and Simon, copyright © 1973 Winston Press, Inc., 25 Groveland Terrace, Minneapolis, MN 55403. All rights reserved.

welfare. She says, "I'd like to find out what I want to be. I'd like to find a job and earn enough money to have my own apartment and to buy a car. I don't want an expensive apartment, like for a hundred-thirty dollars a month, but one for about ten dollars. Then I could take care of my mother."

— Fourteen-year-old Tim moved from the city to a small town where he was dropped from all the school teams because he had let his hair grow long. The administration even threatens to expel him from school.

— Bill is not doing well in his inner-city school. When his mother visits the school, the teacher tells her that Bill daydreams in his class. The teacher adds, "But why should you worry how he does? The boy will never get out of the ghetto anyway."

— A group of older teenagers complain about their urban neighborhood. If two or three boys congregate on the corner, the police accuse them of making trouble and threaten them. The hamburger joint on the corner kicked them out because adults complained that they made too much noise. They are welcome only in bars. There is no place else in the neighborhood where they can get together.

— Returning from a weekend at the lake, the Schmidts discover that friends of their fifteen-year-old daughter used their apartment for an unchaperoned party. Mary's friends threatened to exclude her from all their activities unless she gave them the apartment key.

These situations raise questions of values. Each situation clearly illustrates that arriving at values is a difficult, often painful, process; one that requires frequent choices between conflicting alternatives.

Too often schools supply only a knowledge of facts, concepts, or cognitive skills. Yet this knowledge is not enough to equip young people for coping with problems in today's pluralistic and complex society. Young people have become aware that their schools are failing them, and an increasing number of students are no longer willing to tolerate a curriculum that does not acknowledge their needs, interests, and concerns. Schools, as well as homes, must offer young people a way to develop a set of values upon which they can act and base their lives.

How do young people acquire a set of values? Are we to tell them what to value and how to live, over and over and over again, in the hope that they will listen? No. None of us can be certain that our values are right for other people. And even if we believed they were right, our own choices could not possibly apply to all the diverse values problems and dilemmas young people will encounter. Students do not need any more values imposed upon them. They *do* need to learn the skills that will help them develop their own values. For this reason it is more effective to teach a *process of valuing* than it is to teach one set of values.

Louis E. Raths, in *Values and Teaching*, outlined a process of valuing composed of seven subprocesses. The subprocesses help persons of all ages to make choices which are both personally satisfying and socially responsible. As students build the total process into their lives, they need less and less to be told what is desirable or how to act.

The seven subprocesses, based on choosing, prizing, and acting, are outlined here.

Choosing one's beliefs and behaviors

1. Choosing freely. If we are to live by our own values system, we must learn how to make independent choices. If we are able only to follow authority, we will be ineffectual when authority is silent or absent, when it gives up conflicting directions, or when our emotions impel us in contrary directions.

2. Choosing from alternatives. For choice-making to have meaning, there have to be alternatives from which to choose. If there are no alternatives, there are no choices. The more alternatives available, the more likely we are to value our choices. Generating and considering alternative choices is necessary for clarifying and refining values.

3. Choosing after thoughtful consideration of consequences. We need to learn to examine alternatives in terms of their expected consequences. If we don't, our choice-making is likely to be whimsical, impulsive, or conforming. By considering consequences, we lessen the chance of those consequences being unexpected or unpleasant.

Prizing one's beliefs and behaviors

4. Prizing and cherishing. Values inevitably include not only our rational choices, but our feelings as well. In developing values we become aware of what we prize and cherish. Our feelings help us determine what we think is worthy and important, what our priorities are.

5. Publicly affirming. When we share our choices with others — what we prize and what we do — we not only continue to clarify our own values, but we help others to clarify their values as well. It is important to encourage students to speak out about their beliefs and their actions in appropriate ways and circumstances.

Acting on one's beliefs

6. Acting. Often people have difficulty in acting on what they come to believe and prize. Yet, if they are to realize their values, it is vital that they learn how to connect choices and prizings to their own behavior.

7. Acting with some pattern. A single act does not make a value. We need to examine the patterns of our lives. What do we do with consistency and regularity? Do these patterns incorporate our choices and prizings? If our life patterns do not reflect our choices and prizings, we then must reconsider our priorities or change our behavior in order to actualize those priorities.

Collectively, these seven subprocesses comprise the total valuing process. Students who have built the process of choosing, prizing, and acting into their lives have learned an approach to living which is uniquely their own. The process will serve them effectively as they are confronted with controversial issues, values choices, and life dilemmas.

Ideally, teaching extends beyond the facts level and the concepts level to include this valuing process at the third level — the values level.

If you let it, this article can be a very active trip. In a meeting at a religious education conference, Simon presents his ideas along with a series of exercises for his audience. Try them as you read the account. Here you will learn how values and emotional

growth are very much related. We all have values, but many of us find it difficult to talk about them, to consider modifying them, and consciously to act on them. Sidney Simon tries to, and asks you to do the same. The major problem is to get over our resistance to expressing and evaluating our values. In many ways we have been negatively educated for emotional growth, but Simon gives us experimental possibilities for altering ourselves. In this way, he hopes you will learn how to teach your students something about value clarification.

SIDNEY SIMON

VALUES
AND
TEACHING

This is really not a lecture, but a demonstration. We're going to have a chance to see some students working on some value clarification exercises, and not only some students, but from among you teachers — to come and join the student panel.

But I think it's only fair that we ask the students to reveal some of their values

Reprinted from the March/April 1973 issue of *Religious Education* by permission of the publisher, The Religious Education Association, 409 Prospect St., New Haven, Conn. 06510.

and take some chances and risks for their values, and I will reveal some of mine, and we also ask some of you to reveal some of yours.

Let me share a few very simple things out of my own life with you; I really would like you to come to know me, because as you see me working with students, I think it will add to the creditability of what I am trying to do.

One of our values at the Simon House in Amherst, Massachusetts is that we have a "No Smoking" sign on the door, so that when people walk into our house, the first thing they see, instead of a "Welcome" mat, right near the doorbell is "NO SMOKING, CANCER CONTROL IN PROGRESS." (Size 8½ × 11, in red and white). When entering the house above the living room door, there is another sign "NO SMOKING — SMOKING IS HAZARDOUS TO MY HEALTH." Now I hope you can quickly identify what trouble that causes in one's life when we post a "NO SMOKING" sign on our house. People get terribly insulted; they won't come; some do not return, and take it as a personal affront as if you directed that deliberately at them. Yet for my value system, I feel so strongly in need to live a long productive life; and I want for our 4 children to live in a home with a man who not only *says* but *tries* to do what he values.

My wife and I felt we could do nothing less than post that sign, but it causes a lot of trouble when you try to live life values. We do not provide ash trays in our house; we let people feel uncomfortable while they search for a place to put their ashes in their cups or in their pockets, hoping they would get the hint that this house wouldn't tolerate smoking. When you put a sign up, you stand up and be counted in a way that is sometimes very scary. That's one of our values, and I fear that I may even have angered some of you because of my imposition upon your own lives, as I sound "holier than thou" and tell you that if you come visit us, you will not be allowed to smoke.

Another example given was where we park our car, as far away from the center door of any supermarket or discount store. Is that a value? We, at Simon's, think so! Reasons:

1. You can always find your car.
2. You never get your fenders bumped.
3. You never feel guilty to let your door swing open and dent someone else's car. There just is no one out so far.
4. The Simons buy less, because of the prospect of the distance to carry.

I really think it works, and one of our values is to reduce the materialism in our own lives, and I think our kids get the hang of it.

Here's another one. Again, it may or may not threaten you, but it is one of *our* values and I believe that everybody should have it; it works for us, and I'll say it rather strongly because I feel it rather strongly, but it need not work for you. I I offer it as an alternative for you to consider and then reject if it is not your style.

At our house, the grown-ups do not watch any television at all. I haven't seen, in our house, a newscast for maybe 10 years. True, I've missed some beautiful and important things. My priorities are that there are other things I'd rather do with my eyes and with my time and with my attention. Actually I'm quite critical of television, I need to feel that if I am critical, I must take a stand, and I want my children to see that stand of their Father and their Mother. I see television as a narcotic, and probably just as bad, just as debilitating, just as addictive as some of the drugs we are frightened about that the students in the universities, colleges and high schools are moving towards; and I see these addicted on many different levels. For one thing, it very subtly, to my way of thinking and to my value system, makes spectators out of us, and I don't want to be a spectator to life. I think of that "Auntie Mame" quote: she says "Life is a banquet, and the poor S.O.B.'s are mostly starving!" That's really grim when you think of that. I see television in that way. I see it as generating that BUY ME, GET ME syndrome which I see growing in so many of the children we teach. Because television really nourishes them to believe that they're not beautiful if their hair hasn't been shampooed or dyed or tinted. And that they really couldn't hope to win anybody to love them if they perspire, and if their bad breath should emerge, they are destined to a life of loneliness and despair. It teaches them that perhaps the only reason for being is to enter into fantasy and to get your view of reality from someone's 35 second blast on the newscast of whose tragedy is up for the day. I don't want my life to be numbed with that kind of view of life, and so I've chosen to watch none. I've not been very successful with our children in that area, and it is one of the ongoing negotiations that a family goes through of "How much is enough?" I've resisted the sneaky temptation to steal a tube and claim that the set is broken and will get it repaired. But I've admired one family who has their television in a dark, damp basement and has a rule that no food can be taken down there.

I've revealed some of my values with you, and now maybe you know me a little better; you won't necessarily *like* me better, but you *know* me better, and it is as we learn to review our values that we come to know ourselves better too. Sidney Jourard, in *The Transparent Self* has written: "Until man learns to disclose himself, he cannot know himself. Until he is willing to make himself transparent, other people cannot get close to him." And I'm moved by that, as I personally do not want to live a lonely life. I do not want to live a life where I do not know love and do not know about giving love. I want to reveal myself wherever and ever I can, because I do indeed wish to know *who I am,* and have other people know *who I am.*

I want to help you help me, help us learn something about knowing who you are. And now I ask each of you to take a blank sheet of paper and enter into a very short value clarifying exercise. I want to ask you to list any 10 things in your life, any 10 at all, which you *love* to do. What are 10 things in your life you *really love* to do. The only requirement is that you love to do it. I want now to take you through a little process looking at your values. This is what value clarification is all about. I have such a list of 10 things I love to do, but my list is mine, and yours is yours. I would not impose my list on you in saying that you should do as I do, but I'll always tell you, with a quiet dignity, what's on my list because I like the notion that we have almost an obligation as human beings to share our lives and to let people look into what we disclose.

Go down your list, and just for the fun of it put a dollar ($) sign if any time you do any one of the 10 things that cost $3.00 or more. What do you love to do, and how many of them cost more than $3.00. Now the next one is a little tricky. Put the number "5" in front of any item which you are pretty sure would *not* have been on your list five years ago. Is your life changing, in any way, that 5 years ago some of these items would not have been on your list? Does that make sense? Some people will have 10 "5's" and some won't have any. Here's another — put the letter "F" for Father — if he, at your age, would have enjoyed doing the things you list; put a minus sign before any of the items you would not be willing to have announced to this crowd.

What did you learn about YOU?

— I learned that I ——— (spend too much money, etc.)
— I relearned that I ———
— I see that I ———
— I noticed that I ———
— I affirm that I ———

. . . I'll ask you a series of 10 questions, and they are all things you are either for or against, or in the middle. It is called VALUES VOTING, and you're going to be asked to show, with your hands, where you stand. So if you're for it, raise your hand. If you're against it, go thumbs down. If you're thoroughly against it, grit your teeth and move your thumbs down to show you're very much against it. If you're *very for it* look like a helicopter. If you don't know where you stand, or don't care to tell us, then fold your arms, which means you pass. And I want to make it clear that in all these value exercises you have the right to pass on any question — you are not obligated or forced to answer.

1. How many of you brush your teeth before breakfast?

2. How many of you prefer winter to summer?
3. How many of you are more religious than you were three years ago?
4. How many of you met someone in your life who cheated at monopoly?
5. How many of you had a parent who said, "I'll give you something to cry about!"
6. How many of you have ever seen the inside of a *Playboy* magazine?
7. How many of you have ever used the words — even in a joke or in jest — "nigger," "Watts," "Polack," "Kyke" or one of those words?
8. How many of you cry in the movies?
9. How many of you made at least 50% of the Christmas presents you gave this past year?
10. How many of you use a spray deodorant?

You must be confused about what's happening. What I've done is that I have asked a random series of questions. . . . Why a value clarifying teacher does it is that he simply wants to be able to get on the floor of the classroom more and more topics. We don't need to talk about this because it's based again on the notion that till people learn to disclose, they don't know themselves; and the basis for it is that if we get people to trust this classroom until more and more gets disclosed, we'll be working more for value clarification.

We could take time to talk about any of those questions and we could take the whole period, but if all you have time for is to ask the 10 questions, that's okay. And what I do at this point is I ask some student to volunteer to bring in a list of 10 questions. I make up the first list and then the students do it from there on. Somebody always has his list of 10, and kids begin to ask the most beautiful questions — really important to them.

Now I have a somewhat more complex strategy called *RANK ORDERS*. Here's what happens in this one — I'm going to give you three things to think about, and you are to say them back to me in your own personal rank order; say the *WORST FIRST*, then the *SECOND WORST* NEXT, and the *THIRD WORST* LAST (the third is the one you like best of all three).

I'm thinking of a kind of funny one. It has to do with Thanksgiving at your house. Just think of that time of year when all the children come around for a festive dinner complete with the turkey and all the trimmings. And your Mother comes out and says "Look — I'm really tired — *this* Thanksgiving is a drag! I'm not cooking this year! We're sending out for Pizza, and that's it!"

Now just imagine: the family gets around the table and cut the pizza. "Pass me the one with anchovies" someone says. "I'll take the one with sausage." Or she comes out and she says "This Thanksgiv-ing stuff is really for the birds; I don't believe in it, and all this 'togetherness' is really overrated. Look! You like Thanksgiving? Here's Ten Dollars. You wanna go out? Buy yourself some cranberries and have a good time." She gives you $10.00 and says "Just leave me alone, will ya?" (some Thanksgiving, huh? Really cheers you up!) *Third alternative:* On the other hand, she makes the complete dinner; she really does it up right. The family runs in; there's stuffing and pumpkin pie. The family sits down at the table, says a prayer, and in 11½ minutes later, yes, 11½ minutes later, they've eaten the whole dinner and they've all gone in to watch a football game.

And that's 3 choices of Thanksgiving.

And the question is: Which is the worst? Second worst? Third worst?

You'll share how you get to that answer, and why you think the way you do. I'll ask you to start.

1. $10.00 — completely give up the ideal
2. football game — no unity in the family, no appreciation of what the mother does
3. pizza scene — they did get together, sat down, ate and shared

What we now have is a new RANK ORDER really, from the different people's suggestions, and that's where they grow, out of the kids' lives, the kids' suggestions. I am moved by that simple pizza, that $10.00, that 11½ minutes, because it brings up to me the idea that each of these kids really have ahead of them 60 or 70 Thanks-givings. But do these people believe that they can shape what Thanksgiving is going to be like? That is one of the most crucial values questions.

Can we shape our lives to make it *cause* the way we want it to be? You may get 60 chances to shape Thanksgiving. Maybe we should make a list of ten things we'd love to do on Thanksgiving, and then face the complex political problem of "Can we get our families to go along with what we'd love to do?" How *do* we move a family? We talk to more and more kids who feel they don't have a chance to shape their lives at all. They can't shape school, they can't shape their work, they can't shape war, they can't shape politics. We think a rank order helps in that.

Let me show you another to start off. What about these 3 things?

1. Would you like to be able to cry easily when you are uptight, and need what tears can bring to release? Would you like to get better at that?
2. And the other is to be as angry on the *outside* as you are on the *inside*. That means, if you're really angry at some-one, at something somebody did to you, you don't say, "oh, that's all right, I didn't mind that. It didn't hurt at all." But there is an honesty to what's on the outside and what's on the inside.
3. To boldly ask for affection when you

need affection. You might hear someone say "Hey, I'm really scared; hold me." "Oh, I need a backrub worse than anything in the whole world — give me a backrub?" But to be able to really come up to somebody and ask for what you really want.

I want to share with you about the book *Love Story*. I was riding on a plane, reading the book, and cried uncontrollably. The passenger sitting next to me went to the Stewardess to see what was wrong, and the Stewardess came and I told her I was just reading a very beautiful book, and that I was very moved, and the Stewardess just snuck away. The book has allowed more people to cry than the movie.

With my class, I put all the people who took crying first, and place them all together; those who chose anger together, and those that chose affection together. All have a chance to talk together, and maybe for the whole period. The next day I'd put one person from each group together and make a little trio and they'd have an opportunity to say "Now you see life differently than I do. What have you to share with me, and what can I teach you?" And it gets to be a model how we work together; where people take a stand with their openness to other people's alternatives to hear what they have to say.

Another direction is to ask the student if there is somebody who *really* wants to ask for help in one of these three things.

And someone says, "I really want to learn more about this crying," and he takes his chair up and he sits facing the group, and what the group then does to whoever takes that chair (it's sometimes called the hot seat but it is a very important seat) is to share out of their own lives, and they must use the first person pronoun "I." They say they have learned about crying, and he can ask a question, but he listens to their alternatives, and then he decides which ones he wants to do something about, and then somebody will say, "I want to learn more about how to show my anger, or how to control my anger." And people share, but they must use the first person and they do not give advice as much as they tell about their own lives. I wish I could get into your heads and wonder what you'd think about this if this were to go on in *your* school. What we're advocating is that, if you want to move ahead in value clarification, you must get people to talk about this.

It goes one more step. We could ask people what they'd want to learn how to do more than these 3, and as soon as we get another we can do rank order, and in fact this is what I want to ask you. Can you think of something that you'd' like to learn how to do *more* than to cry, show your anger outside as well as inside, or boldly ask for affection? (Take, for an example, a boy going out who wants to dress a certain way, but his Mother wants him to dress the way she wants him to be seen, etc. etc.)

The Mother would like to hear things like this:

— My! You have such a nice looking son!
— You have a son with such integrity!

or

— You have a son who is so successful!

I realize it is possible to be nice, and be successful, and have integrity, but it is interesting where we put our pressures and to see what you and your principals put out in your memos; it tells a lot about what you value. And when you are a parent, to see what you fuss over; it tells a lot about what you value, and as a teacher what you nag about.

A neat thing is to rank in order what you want from the children you teach, what you want them to become, and see if there is any consistency between what you nag about and what you say you want them to become.

———

I want to ask you all to be thinking about the idea of sending a Telegram to someone in your life, not a famous person, but someone in real life, and the first 3 words of the telegram are "I URGE YOU." This is what you do —

1. Tell us whom you're sending it to.
2. What the message is (15 words or less).

3. You *must* sign your name. Don't sign an interested mother or a concerned teacher.

EXAMPLES GIVEN BY DEMONSTRATORS

I'd send it to my sister. She's the oldest in the family, and she always pushed me around. I'd say

I urge you to stay involved in Catholic education, because we need teachers who are concerned, who are important to young people. We need to have a person who is going to be as convinced as you are. Don't retire.

    Greetings from the Church of St. Rose
    Joe

I would send mine to one of my sisters — a teacher at school, and I would say:

I urge you to stop worrying about what people think of you and to start being yourself if you want to be happy. Someone who really loves you.

    Sister Cecile

I would send a telegram to my 16-year old sister, because I discovered last Sunday night that she was messing with drugs and I've known about this from my 18-year old brother, Kevin:

I urge you, Wendy, to talk to your brother Kevin, just as much as you can, and keep talking; same to your brother, David — talk to anybody you can.

    Brother John

I urge you, Richard, to remain what you are in spite of what's happening now.

    Your Patty

This one is to my sister — a young girl 17 years old who is expecting a baby in about 6 weeks. It happened in her last semester of high school. Her husband and she are very much in love.

I urge you to continue with your courage because you really are living in what you believe, and it is very difficult, for you, now, because everybody doesn't believe what you believe.

    Your loving sister, Kathy

Send this to my friend to tell her to keep going in what she is doing:

I urge you, Joanne, to please be yourself, stay yourself. I love you as you are.

    Ruth

From this, we can see our students beginning to put trust in their lives with us and then they'll begin to do the other things, to grow into a value clarifying class. They begin to ask us for some help. They borrow from each other's lives without it ever being imposed upon them. They borrow really good things, I think. They almost never borrow the destructive things. It requires a certain kind of climate, but it comes very fast if you are willing to get into it.

———

Let's do 2 last things. We'll go through the list 3 times, up and down the line.

You begin. Here's what we'll do: What we're going to ask you to do is to make "I wonder" statements.

— I wonder why ———
— I wonder how come ———
— I wonder what would happen if ———
— I wonder why I ———

Let what comes to the top of your head, and don't censor it; whatever comes out, let your wonder be. You don't have to be profound, or be a genius. Just sit and let it happen.

Examples
1. I wonder what all these people here are thinking about us, and what kind of impression they are getting of the local high school kids.
2. I wonder if I've been too harsh on our own kids about television watching.
3. I wonder what has happened that we are all interested in values, and where they were before.
4. I wonder why God loves me as much as he does, because I have so many proofs to put my fingers on that it just doesn't make sense.
5. I wonder what will happen when I get back to my classroom after being out for awhile and having learned all the things that I have learned.
6. I wonder why I feel that it's important to learn about openness and sharing and never feel quite able to do it.
7. I wonder how many books or articles one has to write before one feels successful.

8. I wonder why it's so hard for me to accept compliments.

There was enough meat in those wonder statements for a whole year of search and inquiry and values. In all the time that I have been doing my wonders, I have yet to hear a child ask — I never heard him wonder — "what are the 7 products of Argentina?"

I urge some of you to read the stories of John Cheever. One of his most recent is *Bullet Park* and the one I love best is the collection of short stories *The Housebreaker of Shady Hill.* John Cheever writes about the people who have been to the Ivy League Colleges and have won the high-paying job that they have struggled for since they were in Kindergarten making finger paints. And he shows their lives as shot full of alcoholism, infidelity, distance between their children, and going to work they hate each morning. I think there is a desperate, desperate need for value clarification.

Do you have the time and energy to do one last thing? I want to involve the whole group, if I can. It's kind of an interesting thing. Here I have what looks like a Coat of Arms, a shield. Imagine this on your wall as a large plaque. This is your *personal* Coat of Arms, and it has 6 sections. In each section I'm going to ask you to make a very crude picture. You have to use drawings. In the 6th block, you're allowed to use three words, that is the only place you are allowed to use words. (This is not an *art* lesson, but is a *values* lesson).

1. In the first block, draw a picture of one thing that you are good at. What are you good at? (Example: skiing, swimming, etc.)
2. In the next block, draw your biggest success of the past year (example: cap and gown, learning to drive a car, etc.).
3. What was the biggest personal failure of this past year? Life is made up of rhythms of successes and failures, and on your Coat of Arms you have to draw a failure of the past year. What will the picture represent?
4. What is one thing that you will not budge on? That you are so deeply committed to, that you will not budge, even torture. Can you draw a picture of that?
   Incidentally, would you want to change your Coat of Arms as you think of it more and more? This is like the first draft.
5. If you were told that you had 1 year to live and you could be sure, guaranteed a success in anything that you undertook, could you draw a picture to represent what you would undertake? ONE YEAR TO LIVE AND GUARANTEED SUCCESS. What would you choose for it? That's really something to think about because today is the first day of the rest of your life. Remember: life is a banquet, how come so many people are starving?
6. Three words that you would want people to say about you. It can form a sentence, or be 3 separate words, so on your personal Coat of Arms would be *those three words.*

I want to close by saying a poem to my family. It's my way of being and showing my gratitude. It's very important to me:

Some day my eyes will be closed forever,
Death is a frightening word to me.
I cannot want to live the unlived life
I want to fly NOW, while I still have the wings
*   of Life,*
The only problem is —
I don't know which direction to soar.

And I think that describes me — and you — and a lot of others. I hope you will join my way to help people know which way to fly.

These excerpts by Janet Lederman are from what one might call an "experiential book." They reflect the author's awareness of her own feelings: awareness of responsibility, the here and now, feelings that are hard to express, and the feelings of others are brought to life in a "dialogue" that Janet is having within herself. She holds this dialogue to help herself and she asks her students to try it as a way of becoming aware and responsible for their actions. Get into her style as you read

and then try thinking and feeling this way yourself. Ask yourself how this exercise could help you.

JANET LEDERMAN

EXCERPTS FROM
ANGER
AND THE
ROCKING CHAIR

Games, puzzles, records, building tools, building blocks,
wood,
trucks,
easels and paint.
The walls are bare when first you come.
Here is a folder.
You may decorate it if you wish.
Then, pin it on the waiting wall.
There is your name for all to see.
You exist for me.
But how do you exist for you?
You say, "I'll beat him up; then he'll know who I am."
Anger.

From *Anger and the Rocking Chair — Gestalt Awareness with Children.* Copyright © 1969 by Janet Lederman. Used with permission of McGraw-Hill Book Company.

Anger.
That is real for you.
But anger is not usually acceptable in school.
You play "bully."
You play "helpless."
You say,
"I won't."
"I can't."
"You can't make me."
"You're not my mama."
Steve, you walk in an hour late.
Norma, you won't talk.
You respond to "a school."
You respond to "a schoolroom."
You respond to "a teacher."
"I won't."
"I can't."
    Each of you carries your own expectation. Each of you has his own image. Each of you tries to avoid what is happening "now."
    Reggie, you fling open the door, stomp in, look around, go over to Steven and you hit him.
    "What are you doing, Reggie?"
"Nothing."
    "What did you just do to Steven?"
"Steven looked at me."
    "What did *you* do to Steven?"
"Steven's a baby."
    "What did you do to Steven?"
"Hit him." (You are smiling slightly.)
    "Yes, now put that into a sentence starting with the word 'I.'"
"I hit Steven." (Your slight smile is now a big smile.)
    I have introduced you to the "now."

I am also building your awareness, Reggie. I am trying to make you aware of what *you* are doing. I am trying to make you aware of your existence. I will continue with this process, for you will not accept awareness easily.
    "What are you doing now, Reggie?"
"Now I am hitting Norma."
"Now I am yelling at you."
"Now I am learning to write."
"Now I am hugging you."
    Reggie, I will try to make you aware of your existence every time you write a story or paint a picture. I will try to make you aware of your existence by having you look into a mirror. And, Reggie, I have a Polaroid camera ready when you do something you thought impossible.
    "What are you doing now, Reggie?"
"Sawing a piece of wood for my boat."
    "Who is sawing the wood?"
"I am sawing a piece of wood for my boat."
    "How are you working?"
"Quietly and not bothering anyone else."
    "Who is working quietly and not bothering anyone else?"
"I am working quietly and not bothering anyone else."
    "Have a piece of candy, Reggie."

———

You are children, children who still need your mothers. You protect your mothers. "Nobody calls my mother a name."
    Troy, you walk into the room, you look at me, and you yell, "You don't do anything right, you black bitch!"

We all gather in a circle at the rocking chair. I start talking about getting angry at the people with whom we live.

"How do some of the people you live with make you angry?"

"My brother tears my books."

"My father whips me."

Soon Troy, you say, "My mother didn't cook my hamburger enough."

I ask you to come sit next to me. You walk over and sit down. You have a frown on your face. There is an empty chair in front of you.

"Troy, pretend your mother is sitting in that empty chair in front of you. Tell her what you are angry about. You may say anything you want to say, since she is not really here."

Troy, you begin, "Mama, you know this meat is raw. I hate raw meat."

Troy, sit in the other chair and pretend to be your mother. What does she say?

"I didn't know it was raw."

"Now be Troy again."

"Mama, you don't do anything right."

"Now be your mother."

"I wash your clothes. I iron your shirts so you'll look good for school."

"Now be Troy again."

"I know. But I can't eat this hamburger. I'm going to throw it away and make another one."

You continue with this dialogue. You tell your mother what you resent and also you tell her what you appreciate. Your mother is not destroyed. Next, you begin to expand your word; instead of throwing the hamburger away, you discover other "possible" solutions for the situation.

"Troy, look at the children in the room; look at me. What do you see? Is there anyone here you are angry with?"

You look around the room, you smile, you become somewhat shy. You are aware of yourself; you are aware of others. Your anger is finished. You can see us.

Troy, you answer, "No, I'm not mad at anybody. Can I take the ball out at recess?"

Patrick, you run into the room yelling, "She took away our ball. That Mrs. Brown is a bitch. I didn't do anything."

I suggest you come up to the chair next to me; put Mrs. Brown in the empty chair and tell her what you are angry about. When you start to play the "blaming game," I suggest you bring the situation into the "now" and have an encounter with whomever you are blaming. Depending on what you can accept, I either stop you with the awareness of both sides of the situation or you go on to explore other possible ways of behavior which may be more appropriate to the situation.

———

This is another action-oriented excerpt. Mr. Hillman, the teacher, lets us in on one of his high school English classes. He is very concerned with affective education and he tells us, through a report of an actual classroom dialogue, what he does to make it happen. Putting theory into action, he deals with a classroom conflict by focusing on it with an interpersonal experi-

ence (called the "positive bombardment exercise") meant to help his students express their feelings. At the same time, he relates the ensuing discussion to the class's academic work. This is a good example of teaching that is related to helping students with their developing values. Try to imagine what you would do in a similar situation. Could you relate it to a subject you have prepared to teach?

AARON HILLMAN

ONE DAY IN A HIGH SCHOOL

"Mr. Hillman?"

"Yes, Bella."

"Carlos keeps saying bad things to us."

"Have you talked to him about them?"

"I told him to shut up, but he won't."

"Carlos, what do you say?"

"Girls are crazy. I don't like girls."

"Do you believe that, Bella?"

"Yes, I do. He wouldn't talk like that if he didn't."

"He likes girls, Mr. Hillman."

From *Human Teaching For Human Learning* by George Isaac Brown. Copyright © 1971 by George Isaac Brown. Reprinted by permission of The Viking Press, Inc.

"How do you know, Grant?"

"He talks about them all the time."

"Yes, but the girls say he doesn't say nice things."

"Mr. Hillman."

"Penny."

"He just doesn't know how to talk to girls. He likes girls, but he doesn't know how to talk to them."

"That's a good point, Penny. In our play, *Death of a Salesman*, that's one of the problems the family has. They talk to each other but they don't know how to talk. Each one is talking and saying something, but he means something else. Would you like to work on that idea for a minute?"

Instant suspicion. You can hear their fears blocking the openings.

"I would like you all to form groups of four. Arrange your chairs so that you are in groups of four facing each other."

"Do we have to?"

"This time, yes. I think you will like this exercise."

Some groups are quickly formed. But there are enough students so that we get mixed groups. Even those groups who know each other can profit from this.

"Now, for the next ten minutes I want you to talk to each other and to say nothing but positive things about each other. That is, good things. You must not make any bad remarks to each other. Look at the other people and say good things only. O.K., let's begin now."

They grin at each other. Some are looking embarrassed. They are very slow in getting started. Bella and Penny are moving very well. Two different races expressing the good they feel about each other. Voices come from all over.

"I like the way you comb your hair." One boy to another; his grin is self-conscious, but I think he means it.

"You have a good personality."

"You always seem to be happy about things. What makes you so happy?"

"Don't ask questions of each other, friends. Just say whatever comes into your mind that is good about the other person."

"You get good grades."

"Dolores, you have pretty brown eyes."

"Amanda always dresses beautifully."

"You can sure drive that wagon, Bobby. You can really lay down a patch."

Tremendously exciting, vibrant, alive, and warm with good feeling. The kids are enjoying this exercise and really telling each other what they like about each other.

"All right, friends. Let's hold up for a minute. Now move the chairs so we are all facing each other in a circle. That's good. Now, can we share our experiences?"

"It was kind of hard to say something nice."

"Yeah, it seemed easier to make some other kind of remark."

"I felt embarrassed when they were talking about me. It was uncomfortable."

"We are not used to that, are we?"

"No, we don't do it much."

"Did anyone sense or hear somebody saying something nice when he really meant something else?"

"Carlos didn't say anything."

"He didn't speak, you say?"

"Yes."

"He wasn't speaking, but he was saying something. What was it?"

"He couldn't say anything nice about someone."

"Yet some of you believe that he likes girls even when he doesn't say nice things about them."

"He just can't say nice things even when he believes them."

"Pat told me he liked my figure, but he laughed."

"Did that mean he didn't like your figure?"

"No, but he said it nasty."

"You believe he was telling you something else then?"

"He sure was!"

"I liked doing that. I felt good. Can we do it again sometime?"

"Certainly. You can even do it yourselves when you are together. Try it sometime. You will like it."

"That's for girls."

"While we are seated in this circle, let's continue the exercise a different way. All of us together, let's say positive things about each other. For example, I would like to say to Carlos that I enjoy reading his writing, that I think he is intelligent, and that his smile is one that is delightful to see."

Carlos is grinning. The other boys are grinning at him.

"You are the best teacher I've ever had, Mr. Hillman."

"Thank you, Bella. That's very warm to hear."

"Luke is too quiet, but he is very handsome."

Luke looks as though he would like to run. Amanda is grinning at him. They are all feeling the joy of conveying joy and feel the peace that comes from being liked or having good things said about them. They are relaxed now, and the words tumble from many lips. Eddie and Dave are still quiet. I imagine they didn't say a word even in the small group. They cling to each other for protection.

"You can see, friends, that it isn't really hard to see nice things in others or to tell them so. Somehow we don't seem to find it easy to talk this way. It always seems easier to say things that hurt. But how much better it would be if we could speak to each other and say what we like. That doesn't mean love. We like a lot of people. When you feel like saying something mean, ask yourself first if there isn't something nice you can say. You'll be surprised at the difference. And see if you can learn to look behind what people say to understand what they really mean. We often say things in a way that doesn't agree with the words. It is just what we were saying about the play. The people were talking to each other, but they were not hearing. Now, for the rest of the period let's just talk to each other about

that. Say nice things, talk about the exercise, or anything you want, but really listen to each other and understand."

They are all moved by the class as I am moved as I sit here. I could take them all in my arms and shout.

One sentence from Castillo makes a good dictum: "Take the specific cognitive goals presented in teaching materials and look for ways to express them in terms of values, concerns, feelings." In this excerpt, we begin to see some of the classroom "how to" aspects of the ideas presented by other authors in the preceding readings of this section. Castillo suggests that cognitive and affective goals can be connected by looking for the parts of the content that are exciting to you, by finding involving activities that help students experience intellectual concepts, and by relating the experience to aspects of the real world. Her examples are taken from the primary classroom; your job is to imagine other examples that would fit the students you are preparing to teach.

GLORIA A. CASTILLO

BLENDING COGNITIVE AND AFFECTIVE LEARNING

The cognitive domain represents intellectual content for the year: the what and how of my teaching responsibilities. What am I hired to teach? What are the cognitive goals of this grade level? What materials are available in the form of textbooks, teachers' guides, state frameworks? To begin with, I go over these materials thoroughly. In any unit, any subject, there are so many concepts, so many things to teach, that I have to make choices. From all that is available, I begin by choosing those items that stir some excitement in me. It may be that I disagree with the author's viewpoint, or it may be that I agree but want to add my own information, my experience, to the material, or it may be that I find the material exciting just the way it is. In any event, it is important that I choose to work with ideas that stimulate me. If I am not excited

From *Left-Handed Teaching: Lessons in Affective Education* by Gloria A. Castillo. © 1974 by Praeger Publishers, Inc., New York. Excerpted and reprinted by permission.

about learning, I certainly cannot get the children excited about learning.

While still in the cognitive domain, I . . . ask some questions of myself. What affective experience can I provide to go along with the cognitive material? What readiness/awareness must the children have to be able to grasp the cognitive concepts that will be presented? What new knowledge will the children be responsible for acquiring? Many of these questions can be answered in behavioral-objective terms, and in the cognitive domain they can often be taken right out of the textbooks I am working from.

For example, while working on a math unit on geometric shapes, one of the goals is to have the children name and identify a triangle and a circle. An effective experience for primary children would be to have them "become" a triangle. I would ask, "How can you move? Where are your angles? Can you become a circle now? What do you have to do with your body to change it from a triangle to a circle? How can you move as a circle?"

I would provide many opportunities for the children to become aware of the angles of a triangle and the roundness of a circle. I would help them to identify other things in the environment that are like circles or triangles. "The clock is round like the circle. The legs of the chair and the floor make a triangle."

In considering the readiness/awareness aspects of the lesson, I might present only one shape at a time for very young children and more complicated shapes if triangles and circles seem too simple for the group. I might also have to allow the children opportunities to "become" objects before asking them to become shapes.

Once I have made my cognitive selection, I move my thinking to the affective domain. This represents the emotional content that will be explored. It is based on the interests and concerns of the children, on their readiness/awareness, on the level of responsibility they can assume, and on the interest and concern elicited directly by the cognitive content I have chosen to work with. It is the affective domain that gives meaning and relevancy to the rest of the program. It acts as the "supercharger," supplying life to the learning situation and energy for working in the other parts of the model.

In the affective domain, I must provide the children with some way to experience the cognitive concepts, or at least some of them. I do this primarily in two ways. One, I set up a situation so that the children can "live out" the experience in the classroom setting. This allows the children to bring their own here and now to the learning experience and provides opportunities for them to touch, see, hear, move. In math, for example, I once read the children a delightful story that illustrated the need for a standardized length when using the term "foot." Then,

before issuing rulers, I had each child remove his shoes and socks, step into a pan of washable paint, and then step off six "feet." We compared the various "definitions" of six feet that resulted and discovered differences. We then discussed the mass confusion that would result if each of us used the same term but used a different "foot" to define it. We imagined how different things would look if each of several men building one house used his own foot as the measure rather than a standard foot. Each child then measured out six standard feet and compared it to *his* "six feet." He then determined how many more of his feet he would need in order to measure the same as the standard six feet. From there, I pointed out that a ruler is much easier to handle than a true representation of a foot and gives each of us the same definition of the word, at least in the mathematical sense. Later I discovered that this "lesson" had repercussions throughout the year. Often children would discover on their own that two or more of them might be using the same term but defining it differently, and that it was this difference that was causing difficulties between them, not a difference in beliefs, values, or judgments.

The second, and perhaps more difficult, way of working in the affective domain is to have the child imagine how living out an experience relates to his real world, his here and now. This is more difficult because it requires both dealing with the imaginary setting and bringing it back to the child's real world. There is an abundance of good materials available for getting the child into imaginary settings. However, most of it stops short of adding the child's here and now to the experience. Take the classic "store in the classroom." A child may spend weeks moving about in a make-believe store. Certainly he has a wonderful time with it, and a great deal of mathematics gets reinforced by the selling and buying that goes on. But how much more valuable the store would become if it were brought back into the child's life by providing him with a wide range of opportunities for discovery of self, particularly by asking him "now" and "how" questions: "Now what are you doing?" "Now what are you feeling?" "How do you experience that feeling?" "Who else is in the store with you now?" "How do you feel about his being there?" "How is the store like other places you know about?" "How would you like to change the store? Now change it." The possibilities are limited only by available time and possible limiting cognitive concepts. As before, there is so much that can be taught, it is necessary to make decisions.

Some of the questions I would explore are: What rules did you need to keep the store working? How did you know that? What happened when those rules weren't followed? How did you feel then? What do you need from a store? What do you need in order to buy things? What happens if you need or want something and you don't have money or stamps?

How did you feel as owner of the store? How did you feel as a worker? An older child, in the fifth to eighth grade, can deal with issues that are current in stores today — rising food costs, the effects of strikes or boycotts, the creation of vacant downtown areas by movements of people, the problem of consumer information, truth in labeling, and so on.

It is necessary to find ways to relate the make-believe store to the child's own life; otherwise it remains at a simulation-game level. The modern supermarket is something that directly affects the life of the community it serves. Studying it affectively can help even a primary child begin to grasp what it means to live and grow up in a democracy with a capitalistic system. It can be another means for him to learn and discover how to cope with twentieth-century ways of life.

Take the specific cognitive goals presented in teaching materials and look for ways to express them in terms of values, concerns, feelings. For example, in reading, a typical objective in the teachers' manual is to evaluate a character in a story. A child can role-play the character and then go on to explore ways in which he himself is like and unlike the character. He can answer all or some of the following questions: How did you feel being that character? What could you do as that character that you cannot do as yourself? What do you do that is like what the character did? What do you do that is different? What else might you be if you were that character? The affective dimen-

sion of the lesson consists of allowing for the child's exploration of the emotions available in him that are evoked by the cognitive experience of reading the story.

The affective domain is the heart and soul of the learning experience, just as the cognitive domain is the thinking, intellectual part. They are directly interrelated. The cognitive domain stimulates the affective domain, and, once the child is involved in affective experiences, new cognition arises.

Lacey and Nessen present the most radical view in this chapter. They argue that students need to have at least one course in the "curriculum" which is directed more toward personal emotional growth than toward traditional curricular goals. They realize that when a teacher focuses on sensitive, powerful novels and films (for example, in an English course) important personal issues can be raised. Merely raising issues in this way does not satisfy the authors, however. Sometimes, Lacey and Nessen say, students need a laboratory situation in which they can explore personal questions and participate in group exercises designed to help them in dealing with feelings. Learning about this critical aspect of our everyday lives (and the Pandora's box that it is) is left out of our schools. It is certainly worth

wondering whether personal growth should be a major focus in education.

RICHARD A. LACEY
AND
RICHARD S. NESSEN

TEACHING IN PANDORA'S BOX

Have you ever designed a lesson to get kids to expose their real feelings about themselves or their society and then, having succeeded, wondered what to do with it all? Have you ever felt anxious when the kids in your class started discussing things they really care about? Are there some things about your students that you'd rather not have been told — especially in public? All that authentic emotional content is often scary: once you've got it, how do you handle it? When a kid starts talking about how he really feels about himself, others and society, how are we going to help him to deal with those enormous forces within him that are shaping and causing his behavior?

This article is published for the first time in this book. Copyright © 1976 by Richard A. Lacey and Richard S. Nessen.

Any teacher who has asked himself these questions is teaching kids, not content. Although it is justifiable for a student to begin exploring his personal problems by studying how writers, filmmakers, and others have sought artistically to bring order into the chaos of daily living, that is only a start. What is needed is a curriculum that deals with the immediate concerns of students — not analogous to those concerns, or paradigm solutions to those problems, but real experiences that address the individual student's immediate concerns about who he is, how he gets along with others and what power he has in society.

A kid experiences all kinds of battles in his own mind about these concerns, but nowhere in school is there a place to talk about and experiment with alternatives in these battles. What we are suggesting and implementing at the University of Massachusetts is a classroom laboratory where students and teachers deal directly with these problems and concerns — a laboratory where they ask, "Who am I?" "How do I get along with others?" and "What control do I have over my fate in society?" in a structured, productive way. For example, if a student is beginning to question his own identity he might examine what equations he uses to judge himself. He might ask:

— What do my clothes tell me and others about me?
— Does my size prescribe the way I behave, and if so, how?

— Does the way I perceive and judge my whole body dictate my behavior?
— If I am tall and I slouch, what consequences does this have in my relationships with other people, and do I like those consequences?
— If I am uncomfortable about the answers to such questions, how do I change the equations I have about myself?
— If I want to think of myself as a warm, loving, responsible person, what things do I have to do, wear and say that will satisfy that equation for me?

Here is a place where a student can experiment with alternatives in behavior, dress and life style to see what effect changes have and to examine whether he wants to incorporate them into his daily behavior. If a student questions his relations with other people, possibly he should examine the dynamics of his interactions. Possibly he should ask himself:

— How do others see me?
— How does my voice — my walk — my posture — affect others?
— How do I want other people to see and treat me?
— What part do I play in relationships with others? Am I most often the leader? A follower? Do I do most of the talking? Am I usually quiet even when I feel strongly about something?
— What effects do my strategies have in my relationships with others? What can I do to make my relationships what I want them to be?

This laboratory gives a student a place to experiment with new behaviors in order to give him some control over what happens in his relationships.

If a student is beginning to question whether he has any control over his fate in his class, school, family, or community he might ask:

— Do I have any influence on those around me?
— Must I wear particular kinds of clothes in order to get the kind of position I want?
— Does the length of my hair affect my chances of joining a group?
— Are there any skills I can learn which will aid me in getting what I want?

The laboratory is a place where the student can develop strategies to deal with such issues. In order to experiment successfully, he must learn to describe his problems accurately, for one aim of the experiments is to learn to ask the proper questions.

The appeal of such novels as *A Separate Peace*, *The Catcher in the Rye* and *Lord of the Flies* in English and social studies testifies to the urgency of the personal concerns which the writers treat artistically. From these novels students develop an abstract awareness of many of the dynamics of trusting and find resonances in their own lives. In *A Separate Peace*, the problem of trust between Gene and Finny, in *Lord of the Flies* the problem of trust between Ralph and Piggy, and in *The Catcher in the Rye* the problem of trust between Holden and everyone he encounters raise many questions which guide a student to increasingly concrete

understandings of abstract ideas. He may ask with Gene, What is the truth contained in the "level of feeling deeper than thought?"; or with Ralph, Is Man savage?; or with Holden, What is a real person?

The insights that these kinds of questions generate about the human predicament, though often moving, are primarily cognitive. They are most moving, moreover, when the analogies to the readers' own lives are close. Nevertheless, they are still, analogies. They do not suggest directly new behaviors and patterns which might aid students in answering their most immediate and pressing questions. The problem of how to apply the awareness to everyday living demands a different kind of curriculum altogether.

Students must ask, "Whom do I trust?" "Under what circumstances should I trust?" "How can I become trustworthy?" But they are not equipped to answer these questions systematically, much as they may try, so that they can make the kinds of distinctions and decisions which the literature implies they must make if they are to act on the implications of their insights. It is important to expose and confront those feelings in the security of a laboratory situation. Here a student can explore his own feelings about trust, perhaps with the perspective of the novels in mind. The stress, however, is not upon understanding a particular artist's vision in conventionally academic products such as composition, valuable as that is, but rather upon the appropriation of the

values and actions of trust in actual immediate behavior.

Our aim is to enable kids to get in touch with the feelings themselves and the consequences of the behaviors those feelings produce. If a novel helps the student to do this, good; and if the exercises in the lab help him to read more perceptively we welcome the dividend. However, the goal of our curriculum is to help kids in dealing with feelings.

The theme of *A Separate Peace* further illustrates our distinction. Gene perceives his world as a jungle; in his obsession with winning he refuses to trust, even though he tries to convince himself that he believes otherwise. His actions, however, betray him, and not until he actually discloses his Self can he find a new, trusting vision which he inherits from his victim, Finny. Any student in today's school-jungles can empathize with Gene's feelings of jealousy, guilt, and hatred. Yet Gene's salvation is an inaccessible solution, and the experience of reading the novel does not in itself change attitudes and behaviors. The student may have gained insight into his own attitudes, but the novel provides him with no way to deal with them.

Because film provides more concrete examples of behavior than fiction can, it comes closer to supplying alternatives, either directly or by implication. Still, though, the student must depend upon analogy. In *The Loneliness of the Long*

Distance Runner, for example, which also treats the theme of trust and acceptance, Colin Smith's clothes, facial expressions, gestures, movements, postures, and voice inflections provide a rich texture of impressions of a character, but do not indicate feasible alternatives. Colin's behavior, after all, depends upon his unique perception of his experiences, and the director's intention is to interpret those perceptions cinematically. We may feel empathy, but we maintain our distance.

The film shows how Colin's final rebellion grows from far more than simple defiance of authority; it is a deliberate decision based upon a clash of personal and institutional values; Colin refuses to sell his soul. One approach to studying the film is to ask whether Colin's tactics succeed in his terms. Throughout the film, does he know what he wants in his relationships, and does he get it? Exactly how? Did he have alternatives?

There are some alternatives implied through other characters in the film. Furthermore, the brief conversation of the straight boys from the visiting team suggests that Colin's situation is not so atypical as it appears; all students, including the viewers, face similar situations; it is a small step to *No Reason to Stay,* where the analogies are even closer.

However close the analogies may be, though, they are necessarily exaggerated. Despite ample selective details of behavior the filmmakers distort reality to create art.

In both of these immensely popular films the student may empathize with protagonists, study their specific behavior and its consequences, and think about his own choices and values. However, he must still depend upon analogy, and while he may clarify his own values he must still face the personal problems of whether to trust and be trustworthy, and how to survive.

How can we provide conditions in which students can learn to trust and be trustworthy — Holden's and Gene's dream — yet still survive? Most teenagers will suffer. However, the results of their suffering are usually antithetical to what we say ideally we want kids to learn. Despite the experience of literature, kids often learn, "Don't trust! Appear trustworthy, but watch out for Number One." If kids must suffer while they grow, can we make that suffering productive?

The Blind Walk is a laboratory technique which allows kids to experience concretely the dynamics of trust. It puts them in a situation in which they must trust; they cannot go through the exercise without trusting. They can resist it by not taking part, but if they participate they must expose how they go about the act of trusting.

A sighted person leads a blindfolded person on a walk — inside, outside, wherever he wishes. He has him experience running blind, walking blind, going upstairs and downstairs blind, touching trees, windows, walls — whatever — silently. As the exercise progresses each stu-

dent gets to experience both trusting and being trusted.

Through this exercise the student begins to see that different people have different feelings and behaviors about trust. He finds that there are alternatives to his feelings and behaviors. There are different ways to know trust and different ways of accepting it. The student might ask himself, "If I felt I couldn't trust some people but could trust others, perhaps I can discover when I can and can't trust, what risks I am willing to take, and how I am willing to take them. Am I willing to try what I saw others do in the same situation?" In this exercise each student has the opportunity to try on new behaviors which he has seen exhibited by his peers and see how they feel. Now he has some real experienced behaviors from which to choose.

Often a student has difficulty understanding and dealing with rejection and acceptance by his peers. If he reads *Lord of the Flies* he will see Piggy being accepted, respected, rejected, and persecuted by different individuals and groups on the island. The consequences of Piggy's behavior: death. The reader may empathize with Piggy, or perhaps with Ralph, whose ambivalence toward Piggy may reflect his own. Again, however, the novel does not suggest any specific behavioral alternatives to the student — alternatives such as eye contact, voice modulation or anything else that might fit into the individual student's unique repertoire. What is needed is a situation in which the student's feelings of concerns over acceptance or rejection become explicit so that he may experience different alternatives in dealing with those feelings. He may try on new behaviors when faced by acceptance or rejection and see what consequences his behaviors have. He may then choose among alternatives. Any of the suggested alternative behaviors that students create themselves or which are created by others are never to be considered recipes that could work for everyone. They are individual, unique patterns and responses suited to an individual student's needs and abilities.

An exercise which aids kids in making their feelings of rejection and acceptance explicit is called in-group/out-group. In it, a group of six people form a tight circle while a seventh person attempts to break into that circle, using any strategy he can think of. All those on the inside must make a decision whether to allow him to enter. Usually he will experience all of the outsider's feelings of rejection, and those forming the circle will experience all of the feelings involved in having the power to accept or reject a new member. In this situation the student has the chance to confront his feelings and to try many of the strategies available to him until he finds one or more that work. When the exercise is over, there is a discussion of both the strategies used and the feelings caused by the behavior of the group and the new member.

The emphasis in the experiment is on the student's ability to make choices about his attitudes and behavior. In this exercise we are asking the student to choose among the different strategies that occur and see if, armed with new behaviors, strategies and attitudes which he has chosen to acquire, he can make transfer to situations outside the laboratory.

The variety of exercises that will work is already considerable and is continually growing as teachers explore possibilities. For example, there is a "personal universe" exercise which helps students to discover how to view and evaluate their bodies; there is a "here and now" feedback language which allows students flexibility and precision in the feedback which they give to one another; there is a game called "Amnesia" in which students examine their clothes, room, etc., as if they had amnesia and wanted to reconstruct what kind of person they were. They make explicit the environmental cues they use in processes of self-evaluation. To date there are at least five hundred exercises which successfully deal with students' individual concerns and problems.

We are not suggesting that this is merely a better way to teach English and social studies, or even that these approaches should necessarily be incorporated in academic curricula. We believe instead that these approaches constitute a departure from the academic curriculum. We advocate not discarding the academic curriculum — far from it — but instituting a concurrent affective curriculum. This way the values of both kinds of content will enhance rather than compete with one another. . . .

Some might wonder if these issues that we have raised aren't particularly risky — potentially explosive and controversial. Is it wise to raise them in the classroom?

Our answer to this question is reflected in our title: Pandora's box is in every classroom and every student, and it's been open a long time. Not to deal with it is to abdicate from the responsibility which is entailed by asserting that the content of the classroom is the kid. Because emotions and attitudes have so much to do with a student's ability to cope with his environment and to make decisions for himself, we believe that it is our responsibility as teachers to aid him productively and systematically.

This article by Gerald Weinstein is an appropriate last reading for this chapter. Having been exposed in previous readings to several concepts, strategies, and activities in affective education, you may be feeling a need to tie things together. Much of that work you will, of course, have to do by yourself, but Weinstein's model for a humanistic psychological curriculum might prove really helpful. The purpose of his model, to paraphrase Weinstein, is to provide a way of selecting which personal growth activities to use, in what

sequence, for what people, and for what purposes or goals. He illustrates his model by describing a college course entitled "Education of the Self," but you should be able to adapt it to any level of education.

GERALD WEINSTEIN

THE TRUMPET: A GUIDE TO A HUMANISTIC PSYCHOLOGICAL CURRICULUM

There is now a plethora of affective procedures which are the offsprings of the human potential movement. Many of these can be adapted for educational programs and curricula, and represent a major breakthrough in affective pedagogy. For the first time, educators have at their disposal a huge resource bank of imaginative, experiential teaching procedures

From *Theory Into Practice* 10, no. 3 (June 1971): 196–203. Reprinted with permission.

that can be integrated into most traditional curricula and can provide source materials for curricula aiming directly at psychological growth, i.e., humanistic psychological curriculum.

With every innovation, however, there arises a host of issues. One that I have found overwhelming is the very fact that there are now so many alternative procedures from which to choose. We could easily, if we were willing to take the time, list at least 2,000 exercises — and in turn, many of the 2,000 could be extended into a variety of adaptations. But what do we do with so many possibilities? How do we go about selecting which to use, in what sequence, for what people, and for what purposes or goals?

In an attempt to answer some of these questions, in 1967 a group of us came up with a strategy for selecting and sequencing affective activities that would lead to the expansion of an individual's response patterns. The strategy was called "The Trumpet" (Figure 1). We chose that metaphor primarily for its shape. One begins at the narrow end and comes out at the wide — signifying an expansion of awareness. It is assumed that an educational experience is one that aids the learner in helping himself grow. Some of us asked if the name implied forcefully "blowing" someone through planned experiences, which didn't sound very humanistic, but we decided to take responsibility for that connotation. The Trumpet, through successive adaptations and revisions, began to take many forms,

the most elaborate of which is described by Terry Borton in *Toward Humanistic Education: A Curriculum of Affect*.[1]

In structuring a course at the University of Massachusetts entitled "Education of the Self" we have found our particular revision of the Trumpet to be extremely helpful. This article will describe the strategy and the way it has been applied. However, before I proceed, I would like my evaluation-focused readers to know that we have *not* made any careful evaluation of either the course or the Trumpet; it is strictly in a developmental phase. In our attempt to create psychological curriculum, we are trying to find out what we are trying to accomplish and how we should fashion experiences to reach those ends before we can begin to say whether or not certain goals may be reached through a particular strategy.

"Education of the Self" is a laboratory course aimed at self-exploration. The content is the "uniquely-experiencing self" that enters the course. It is not a course that deals primarily with external knowledge — that is, knowledge about the world out there — but primarily with internal knowledge — knowledge of the world within. It emphasizes subjective rather than objective knowledge, but retains both. Basically it attempts to develop self-observation skills. It has a greater intrapersonal than interpersonal focus and aims more at identity clarification skills than at relational ones. The course encourages each individual to become a natural scientist who, instead of observing

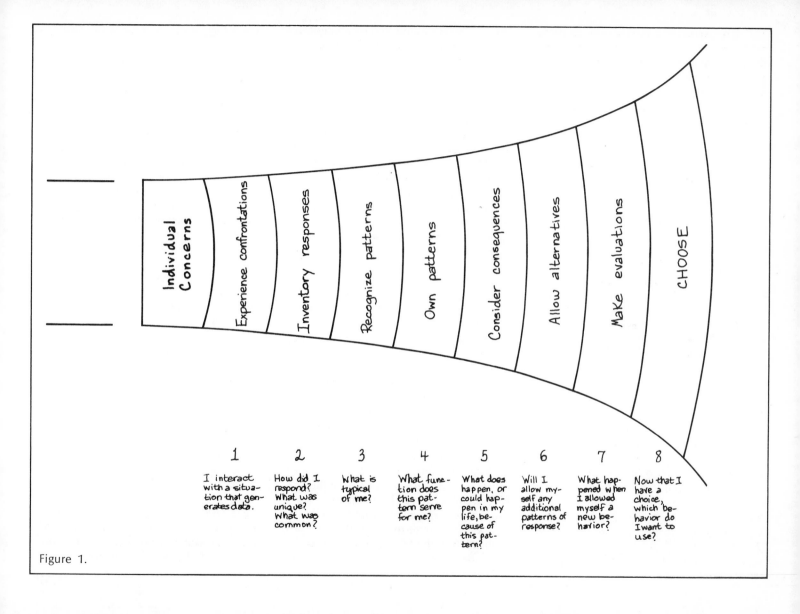

Figure 1.

the behavior of objects, animals, or other people, focuses on himself. The initial processes taught in the course might be described by such terms as "introspection" or "conscious reflection."

Assignoli, in his book, *Psychosynthesis*, considering an aspect of his work on self-realization, states:

The self is there all the time, what is lacking is a direct awareness of its presence. Introspection is a means for developing the awareness . . . directing the mind's eye, or observing functions upon the world of psychological facts, of psychological events, of which we can be aware.

Through introspection we acquire a more focused and clear awareness of what William James called the mind-stream, ceaselessly flowing within ourselves. It could also be called the attitude of the observer, the inner observer. . . . If we turn our ability to observe inward we realize that there is actually an inner world of phenomena, at least as manifold and varied as the outer world, and that through the development of observation it becomes more definite to the observer.[2]

Our hypothesis is that the more a person becomes aware of his self-responding-to-self system, the more choice he may have in responding to himself, or that when "The stability, the permanency of the observer is realized . . . he becomes aware that he cannot only passively observe but also influence in various degrees the spontaneous flow, the succession of the various psychological states . . . thus

one has to actively discriminate between the contents of the field of consciousness and its center — that which creates the self."

So much for the rationale and general aims of the course. Now we turn to the Trumpet.

The Trumpet represents a cognitive map whereby one can carefully determine the flow, phasing, or sequencing of a series of affective learning activities. Each block, moving from left to right, involves its own special set of activities. "Education of the Self" is a sixteen-week course, which meets once a week for three hours. It is divided into three phases:

— first four sessions — Trumpet blocks 1 and 2
— next eight sessions — Trumpet blocks 3, 4 and 5
— last four sessions — Trumpet blocks 6, 7 and 8

There are at least two basic ways of using the Trumpet in terms of content. One way is to identify a theme, concern, or topic, such as sex roles, conformity to other's perceptions, self-judgment, or communication, and follow this theme through the various steps of the Trumpet process. The other way is to leave the content open-ended and let the themes and issues arise spontaneously from the procedures or exercise material. We approach "Education of the Self" through the latter mode, while our curriculum develop-

ment for public schools has used the former mode.

CONFRONTATION — GENERATION OF DATA (1)

The student, through an exercise, real experience, or in reaction to a specific piece of material, confronts himself as he reacts to a particular phenomenon. Many of the structured exercises from the human potential movement are utilized here. Every exercise, however, is treated as more than just an affective experience; most are treated as data-generating devices for the individual student. The exercises may range from very common or routine experiences such as asking students at the first session to reflect on how they went about positioning themselves in the room to more unusual ones such as having each imagine his body as a geographic continent and asking himself such questions as: Where are my recreation areas, my unexplored areas, my polar regions, my equator? The students are asked to record data either in a journal or on 3×5 cards concerning their unique and/or common response.

Several criteria are used in selecting exercises for the initial confrontations. Different exercises are used with the open-ended mode than with the theme mode. Choices are narrowed when following the theme mode as most of the exercises would be selected for their potential for generating data about a particular issue.

Another criterion is the experience of the participants. Since most exercises could be classified on a low- to high-risk continuum, depending on the degree of self-disclosure and privacy of content, one would attempt to match this criterion to the degree of readiness of the participants to engage in high-risk activity.

To the degree that a trainer regards group trust as a necessary component for personal growth, it may become another criterion for exercise selection. What procedures and activities would create the most trust in a group situation so that individuals could *comfortably* view their own *uncomfortableness*? This may sound paradoxical but it serves as an important distinction for our work. Most individuals come together with heavy patterns of resistance. When asked to confront them more resistance usually occurs. When confronted in a negative, challenging way, resistance is likely to increase. Most of our initial exercises attempt to focus on positive aspects of self. In addition, we attempt to insure that no one at this stage overtly judges anyone else's responses. We ask the students to attempt to view each other's responses as simple phenomena, just as we ask them to learn to view their own. Thus, *initially,* we purposely avoid some of the "hair cutting," "stripping down the defenses," "telling it like it is" interactions that may serve well in groups whose functions and purposes are different from ours.

The last criterion deals with skills. Students need practice with some of the language of communication and self-awareness that will help them progress through the Trumpet. Examples:

1. Learning to communicate the now of awareness through phrases such as:

   — Right now I am aware that . . .
   — Now I see — hear — feel . . .
   — I sense that . . .

2. Learning to state one's demands, resentments and appreciations directly.

In addition, skills involve learning to:

1. introspect, to describe one's inner state
2. speak directly to others using first and second person
3. feel a feeling rather than think a feeling

Exercises are selected to teach the students the skills utilized in the processes of the Trumpet.

UNIQUE AND COMMON RESPONSE — INVENTORYING (2)

When someone is asked to observe himself, what is it he is to observe? We break self-observation into three basic areas: (1) feelings or sensations, (2)

thoughts, and (3) actions or behaviors. The general pattern of questioning that occurs during or immediately following a confrontation goes somewhat as follows:

Feelings

— What sensations and feelings am I experiencing or did I experience?
— Where in my body am I experiencing or did I experience them?
— How intense are/were they?

Thoughts

— What sentences are/were running through my head?
— What is/was the internal monolog or dialog?
— Am/was I having any fantasies?
— What are/were they?
— Am/was I rehearsing? What is/was the script of the rehearsal?

Actions

— What did I actually do or what am I doing — with my body — my expression?
— Did I move? Did I remain silent? Did I talk?

The answers to these questions represent one's unique response. When some of these responses are shared with the group, the individual gets some idea not only of how he is distinctly responding, but also of what he has in common with other responders.

As an example of how this works, let us follow an exercise. A very common practice in "Education of the Self" is for people to select partners and work in dyads for varying periods of time. For some, the experience of selecting or being selected is anxiety-producing. We use such a situation by telling the group at the outset that they will be asked to choose someone they hardly know for dyad work. Immediately following that statement we ask students to make a journal entry and respond to such questions as: When you heard what was expected of you, what did you experience? Was there any fear? What did you do with your eyes? What were you saying to yourself?

After they've had time to write their entry they are told to get their partner, find some space and sit down together but not talk. When this is done they are again asked to make a journal entry: What did you do? Did you initiate an action? Did you choose, or did you wait to be chosen? What sentences did you tell yourself when making the decision? What, if anything, was scary about the choice?

After making the entry they are asked to share their response, first with their partner, and later with the group at large so that the range of responses can be seen.

"Education of the Self" differs from many group experiences in that more attention is given to this conscious inventorying through guided introspection and reflection. This is a way in which cognition can serve affect. The work of Malamud and Machover (1965) for this phase of the Trumpet seems parallel:

The leader, therefore, encourages students to notice their behavior and their inner experiences with a minimum of obstructive self-judging, defensiveness, or ambitious straining for results. ... During the initial experiments the leader encourages members to share their reactions without pressing them to analyze what happens. He is content to draw the group's attention to the dramatic diversity of responses that are reported and to the varied difficulties experienced by members in their effort at "simply seeing what happens." [3]

I want to re-emphasize a point made above, the point about "not analyzing." We follow one of the principles of Gestalt training which maintains that when people focus on the "why's" of their reactions they avoid their reaction. By becoming literary or computer-like about their experience, they *talk* it away from what is really happening; it becomes a mere intellectual exercise. The emphasis in inventorying is on the words HOW is it happening, WHAT are you doing and HOW are you doing it, WHEN is it happening and WHERE is it happening, rather than WHY is it happening.

The first four sessions of "Education of the Self" involve a variety of confrontations with the students documenting the data described above in their journals. This sets the stage for the next step of the Trumpet — Recognizing Patterns.

RECOGNIZING PATTERNS (3)

As an undergraduate, I had a course in which I was placed in a neighborhood center and put in charge of a recreation program for a group of youngsters. In addition to developing a program for and with them, I was instructed to select a child from the group and observe him carefully. I was to record, on 3 × 5 cards, examples of his *behavior* — not my interpretations, but nonjudgmental descriptions of things he did. I was asked to record 12–15 cards per session. After an entire semester, I had a collection of approximately 120 cards. I sorted the cards into groups of similar behaviors to see what patterns emerged. I still remember the frustration I experienced with all of the seemingly disconnected pieces of behavior I had collected until, as I began sorting and grouping, the *gestalts* began to occur. It was an exciting experience to sense, through the emerging patterns, the unity of a person's needs and actions.

This is the goal for this phase of the Trumpet. We would like the student, who, in the past four sessions, has been collecting data on himself from what many times seems like a series of disconnected activities, to take a look at the forest rather than the trees. And so now come questions that help him focus on this: What is typical of me? As I sort my data into groups of responses, what patterns emerge? What have I presented to the people in this class that is usual for me to present to others? What are the characteristic modes of my responses in this class? How do I typically respond to directness, to nonverbal activities? Is there a pattern to my internal dialog? How have I expressed my resistances?

Students are asked to develop their own pattern profiles based on the data generated in the class. These profiles are then shared with their support group members so that the patterns can be classified and verified. (Support groups of 6—10 members are formed during the fourth session; they are permanent until the conclusion of the course.)

Exercises used at this phase are focused on pattern inventorying. A game called "In the Manner of the Person" is an example. Each member of the support group in turn asks the other members to mirror or act out a typical responding mode of the initiating member. I would say to someone in my support group, "Joe, would you walk around this group in the manner of ME? Mary, would you get into an argument with George and argue in the manner of ME? Jack, would you pretend you're looking into a mirror and respond to yourself in the way you feel I respond to myself?" Thus I would get some perceptions of others about my own patterns of behavior.

OWNING PATTERNS (4)

Once one begins to acknowledge his patterns he has to face the problem of ownership. A great deal of our energy seems to be used for rejecting aspects of ourselves that we don't like. This energy is expended in denial; i.e., we are not racist, we are not selfish, we are not angry or hostile. We busily attempt to evict members of our internal family. A common tendency, when certain of our patterns come to the foreground, is to be dissatisfied. We want to change them — we want to change us — the pattern doesn't fit our ideal image. If one is so busy disowning what he is, he cannot really change, for he is never in real contact with the aspect of self he wants to change. Thus the aim at this phase of the Trumpet is to help the individual to acknowledge and accept all of his patterns.

One way of approaching this task is to examine how the particular patterns serve the individual. Perls (1969)[4] talks about the means-whereby and the end-gain. My end-gain may be the satisfaction of hunger, a singular objective, but the ways in which I can satisfy my hunger are numerous. I can swallow a pill that supplies me with all my nutrients, I can eat simple fare, or I can approach the task as a gourmet. Our patterns represent some means-whereby that we have selected from a whole host of possibilities to achieve some particular end-gain. Perls tells of a therapist who was able to help homosexuals see more clearly that their end-gain was orgasm and that the homosexual route was one means-whereby they had selected for the end-gain. The felt-knowledge of this concept, says Perls, had a releasing effect for the individual who then felt that he could, if he so desired, expand his repertoire of means-whereby.

If the student can see what he wants to accomplish with a particular pattern, he gets in contact with his desires. By seeing his pattern as something with which he is attempting to serve himself (whether effectively or not is not the question here), he may more easily own the pattern.

One pattern that emerged from one of my students was the tendency to contribute only rarely to group discussions. She typically played it safe. The way she stopped herself from contributing was through an internal dialog that sounded something like this: "Hm — I really don't agree with what the last person said, but I'm not sure that I'm right. I'd better wait and think about it more — until I'm more certain. I'd hate to just blurt out something foolish and perhaps become an object of ridicule. Yes, I'll wait. Darn it — another person said just what I was going to say — why was I so afraid of saying it? Nothing happened to him. Oh well, I guess I didn't lose anything."

Her pattern of self-restraint in discussions was a means-whereby she attempted to reach some end-gain. With some help the girl located an end-gain, which preserved her ideal image of being intelligent or appearing so to others. By not exposing herself, she claimed, she couldn't be evaluated as stupid. This leads us to the next step in the Trumpet — Consequences.

CONSEQUENCES (5)

How effective is my pattern in achieving my *end-gain*? The student in the preceding example would begin to explore the effects of the pattern. She might ask the group with whom she is working, "How do you experience my silence in group discussion?" Someone might say, "I experience you as a very wise and thoughtful person who doesn't talk for the sake of talking, but only speaks when she really has something to say and so I really listen to you when you do speak." Thus the student might feel that her pattern is creating the effect she desires. Now let us further suppose that in addition to the above feedback she receives the following: "I experience you as someone who is frightened and hiding, and as someone who is easily intimidated." Or, "I get the impression that you're not very bright — otherwise you would have more to say."

Although the feedback has become a bit complicated and difficult to assimilate, the main point is that almost any pattern is successful to a point — it must be fulfilling something in order for it to be retained by the individual. It is, however, only *one* way to get there, and, because it may not be *wholly* effective, the person may be motivated to expand his repertoire.

Another method for examining the consequences of a pattern is to have the person, as well as the others in the group, fantasize his future with the supposition that the subject's particular pattern was frozen, that it could never be any different, could never be amended, and was the major pattern by which the person related to others. They would be encouraged to fantasize positive as well as negative consequences.

It is at this point in the Trumpet sequence that the individual decides whether or not he is motivated enough to work on the next phase — Allowing Alternatives.

ALLOWING ALTERNATIVES (6)

Questions asked at this point include: In some situations my present patterns serve me well, but in others, they fall short of my intended effects; what else do I have in my response repertoire? To what extent have I consciously chosen the patterns I find in myself? Have I really decided to be shy, extroverted, passive, aggressive, closed or open, or are these patterns I happen to find myself wearing and then find good reasons for their existence? Some people claim that they have chosen not to reveal their true feelings to anyone else. When asked, "Could you reveal your true feelings to someone if you wanted to?" they would reply in the affirmative. If they were further asked, "Have you ever revealed your true feelings to anyone?" and they

replied that they hadn't, the final question would be, "Then how do you know you could even if you wanted to?"

It is my hypothesis that if a person has singular patterns without having experienced alternatives, he really doesn't have much choice. "I can be honest whenever I want to. The reason I'm not is because I don't trust anybody enough to be honest with them." A person who has never or rarely been honest about himself to another doesn't really have the choice of being honest, since he has never practiced it.

So the task is to find out which responses one will allow oneself to experiment with.

The students now negotiate contracts with their support group for their personal experiments. They may be simple or complex, from "Tonight I'd like to experiment with being an initiator" to "How can I go about not putting myself down so much?" The group serves as a consultant in helping the person construct his project as specifically as possible and then helping him evaluate the results.

Many of the activities at this point parallel what DeRopp calls, "The Outer Theater of Self."

Outer Theater takes many forms. Its most practical and valuable form involves the attempt to play, in the daily affairs of life, some role that is slightly different from that which one plays mechanically. There is nothing esoteric about this. People attempt to use the technique every time they make a resolution to experiment with their behavior patterns. The resolutions are almost invariably broken because man ... does not have enough inner unity to play any unfamiliar role consistently. The timid person who resolved to do some roaring and table pounding for a change slips, without even noticing, back into his usual meek performance, betrayed by habitual postures, habitual facial expressions, habitual tones of voice which he does not recognize or have enough power to change. For his repertoire of gestures and facial expressions determines the role a man plays and he who would change the second must have enough self-mastery to change the first.

The practical student of Creative Psychology uses Outer Theater not to gain friends and influence people, nor to give what is loosely known as a "good impression." His aim is to gain self-knowledge, to understand the limitations imposed by his type, to determine how far these limitations can be extended.[5]

It is here that some of the Gestalt exercises dealing with opposites are most useful. George Isaac Brown, in some of his Gestalt training sessions, has individuals pair up. Their instructions are as follows:

Choose one role that you play. Sit facing your partner. Carry on a conversation while being that role. Now, what is the polarity of that role? Be that opposite role now, and continue the conversation. Now, try to visualize a role that represents a midpoint between the two poles and continue the conversation in that role.

A more existential approach is to have a person stop wherever he is at the moment and take inventory: What am I doing, thinking, feeling? Then imagine himself being the very opposite. He then tries to act out this picture, noticing what his resistances and difficulties are while trying to contact what the opposite being supplies that he misses in his original being.[6]

EVALUATION AND CHOICE (7 AND 8)

There is a great deal of risk involved in experimenting with one's response system. The most obvious, of course, is the intrapersonal one. Deviation from a pattern that has become so much a part of one's life is bound to be fraught with tension. But the greater risk, perhaps, is the possibility of the new responses alienating others, especially those with whom one is intimately involved. For example, suppose a student, John, decides to experiment with stating his demands more clearly and directly to others. Instead of manipulating people into offering him help, he begins asking for it. In addition, he will try to express his resentments rather than harbor them. He goes home and tries it with his wife. She is shocked by his new behavior. It is something strange, a pattern for which there is no precedent. She may not see the value of this "straight" talk and react quite negatively. Even though he explains what he is trying to do, she may not accept it. He may get a similar response from his friends, who "like the old John better." Thus he must evaluate his experimental responses on a number of levels in terms of the consequences. Is it worth alienating close associates? Could this be considered an initial reaction by others who might eventually accept his behavior? How does behaving that way make him feel inside? More powerful, more himself, or less so? These questions and others are all part of the evaluation stage of the Trumpet, and should be thoroughly explored by the student with his support group.

It is from the careful evaluation of the experimental behaviors that one makes his decision, which is his *Choice*, to keep all, part of, or none of his new response. Even if he chooses none, he has now chosen, and the act of choosing is the valued end-state of the Trumpet.

projects and activities

GETTING IN TOUCH WITH YOURSELF IN THE HERE AND NOW

Affective educators place a great deal of stress on self-awareness. Sensitivity to one's feelings and surroundings is seen not only as a key to personal growth, but also to better interpersonal relations. The exercises below are simple procedures for heightening awareness. They can be used with people of all ages. See if they help you increase your awareness of yourself and others. If you choose to do all of them, don't rush from one to the other. Talk awhile about what you're experiencing, then take a few deep, slow breaths and resume the activity.

Procedure

1. Sit in a circle. Each person in turn should describe how he is feeling so far today by comparing himself to a car, a fruit, or a famous personality. For example: "I feel like a sports car whose engine is racing and every once in a while skips in its timing." Allow any participant the right to pass or postpone his contribution.

2. Sit in a large group circle or in sub-group circles of four members. Everyone should take a few deep breaths. Participants are asked to state anything they know about themselves *right now* or any way they are aware of someone else in the group. For example: "Now I am sitting on an uncomfortable chair. Now I hear the rain pelting the windows. David is wearing jeans. Gail is looking at her feet."

3. As a group, choose a record, a poem, a story, a newspaper article, or anything else you can think of which involves active listening. Appoint a leader to read the following instructions: "Close your eyes and think about some place you've been in today. What was it like? . . . How did you feel there? . . . Would you like to be there rather than where you are now? . . . Open your eyes and listen while this record is playing [or "while I read" — proceed with record or reading]. Now close your eyes again. Go back in your mind to some place you would rather be. . . . What is there? How does it feel there? . . . Open your eyes again. Once more, listen to the record [or reading]. Whenever you feel the need to withdraw, allow yourself to do so. Whenever your senses flow the other way, attend to the here and now." Continue the record or reading, listening for ten or fifteen minutes.

Processing questions

a. How difficult was it to get in touch with your feelings and your immediate environment?

b. Do you feel any differently about your-self?

c. How would you do these exercises with your own students? Why would you use them? Why not?

LOOKING AT
YOURSELF
AND
SEEING HOW
OTHERS
VIEW YOU

Self-understanding involves being aware of behavior we repeat over and over again. We can gain this awareness by ourselves, but other people may help us, too. The purpose of the following exercise is to identify some of your personal characteristics and have the opportunity to receive feedback from others as to how they see you.

Procedure

1. This exercise is appropriate for a large group in which people know each other fairly well. Someone in the group is assigned the job of giving instructions. He

or she calls out one of the following adjective pairs.

— adventuresome/cautious
— critical/accepting
— lazy/energetic
— creative/non-imaginative

— even-tempered/moody
— optimistic/pessimistic

2. Each participant decides which of the two adjectives describes himself the best. The leader designates a corner of the room to which all people who have chosen one of the adjectives must go as well as another corner of the room for those people who have chosen the contrasting adjective.

3. When the group has divided itself, participants should form subgroups of two or three and reveal why they have gone to that corner of the room and if they are at all surprised by the presence of anyone else in the subgroup.

4. After a few minutes, the leader calls out another adjective pair and follows the same procedure as before. The exercise is completed when all the adjective pairs have been given.

Processing questions

a. Write down your self-profile created by this exercise and ask yourself: what opposites, if any, exist in your personality? (for example, are you lazy and adventuresome?) Was this self-profile true of you five years ago? Do you think it will change five years from now? Did you have a hard time assigning yourself positive attributes?

b. What can you learn about the personality profile of the whole group by the way people divided themselves up?

PROJECTION
AND
INTROJECTION

One of the ways we avoid "owning" our feelings and behavior is by attributing them to someone else. This mechanism of defense has been called "projection." By contrast, "introjection" is the process by which we allow others to define us. In the following exercises, you should be able to gain some skill in sorting out the real you, your projections, and the perceptions of yourself given to you by others. <u>Don't</u> <u>rush</u>!

Procedure

1. In a small group, each member should pick (but not reveal to others) an item in the immediate environment and, taking turns, describe himself to the others

This sequence of activities was originally designed by The Philadelphia Affective Education Development Program, Norman A. Newberg, Director.

in the group *as if he were that object.* Each should report how he looks, how he might seem to others, and how he might feel if he were alive. For example, a table: "I have a flat surface. People put things on me. I like to support people (their belongings, their elbows and hands, and sometimes their feet)."

When each person has had his turn, write down to the best of your ability, the things you said about the object you described. Ask yourself which statements are in any way true of yourself (for example, do you like to support people?). If you wish, you may share this part with others in the group. (As a variation, you might select one object and have everyone in the group "project onto it.") *

2. Someone should read the following instructions while others close their eyes. Take a few minutes to review in your mind the former teachers you had. Remember how they looked and what you did in their classrooms. Choose the one teacher who sticks in your mind the most. Listen to that teacher talking to you. Remember a positive or negative message he or she frequently said to you. Repeat it in your head a few times. Now, walk around to other people in the room and introduce yourself by stating that message in the first person. For example: "Hi. I'm Jack Green. I'm too smart for my own good." The other

* This first exercise is very effective with younger students. For children in the early grades, it would be best to eliminate the second part of the exercise.

person should introduce himself or herself in the same manner ("Hi. I'm Shirley Brown. I am always cooperative."). When everyone has made the rounds, do this introduction exercise again, except this time, lay the message on someone else by beginning with "you." For example: "Hi. I'm Jack Green. You are too smart for your own good." Vary your intonation with different people. (You can also have a person lay the message on you, and you may choose to reply, "No, I'm not!")

3. Think about a person who is either your superordinate or subordinate (teacher, student, boss, employee, parent, child) *who bothers you a great deal.* Describe that person to someone else. Tell them what he or she does that really bothers you.

Now, ask yourself if you are, in any way, like this person? If you would like, share your conclusions.

Processing questions

a. Do you easily project yourself onto others?
b. Do you carry, inside you, self-defining messages from parents and teachers?
c. How did you feel introducing yourself to others?
d. Are there aspects of people who bother you which you find in yourself?

ROLE PLAYING STUDENTS WITH POSITIVE AND NEGATIVE SELF-CONCEPTS

How does it feel to express personal confidence or personal doubt? The following role-playing exercise is designed to help you understand these feelings of young students and to explore your own behavior in a cooperative situation.

Procedure

1. The role playing works best with one or more groups of *six* players. Begin by writing the word "positive" on three slips of paper and the word "negative" on three slips of paper. Fold the six slips of paper and put them in a hat. Each role player picks out a slip of paper but does not reveal to the others the word he or she has picked. If you picked "positive," your job will be to role play a student with

a positive self-concept (however you define it). If you picked "negative," your job will be to role play a student with a negative self-concept (however you define it). You will not know beforehand what role the other group members are assigned although you do know that three members have picked "positive" and three have picked "negative."

Scene: a fifth-grade class. You are in a group discussing plans for developing a science fair for your school. Your job is to consider how the fair will be set up and how students will be encouraged to participate.

2. When the role playing is over, each player might pick out one other member of the group and describe the behaviors which that member exhibited in the role-playing skit. (In this manner, each role player's behavior is described by another member of the group.) Next, each role player can discuss, in turn, the problem he encountered, if any, portraying the assigned role. Each role player might also discuss these two questions: (1) "Did I ever react this way when I was younger?" and (2) "Have I ever seen younger children react this way?" It might be interesting to combine with another group of role players who did the same exercise and exchange experiences. Also, it might be helpful, if time permits, to re–role play the situation, this time exchanging roles.

PERSONAL GROWTH SKILLS

When you enter almost any classroom, you are bound to witness quick attempts by the teacher to "socialize" students by off-to-the-side counseling and preaching. This approach often invites resistance because students feel that they are required to change instantly. Personal growth, like any other learning process, is slow. It also requires the development of several skills.

Procedure

1. Listed here are personal growth skills that psychologists and educators wish to be taught in schools. Select two skills from this list which you see as most important in the classes in which you might currently be teaching or in which you expect to teach.

— developing trust
— making choices
— taking responsibility for one's own behavior
— describing feelings
— giving and receiving affection and praise
— clarifying personal values
— considering the values of others
— giving and receiving helpful criticism
— setting realistic goals
— appreciating one's own accomplishments and strengths
— active listening

— being aware of the "here and now"
— identifying personal needs and preferences
— being spontaneous
— taking a leadership role

2. Think of several ways to aid students in developing each of the two skills. You might be creative and invent a special game, a role-playing exercise, a creative writing assignment, or a research project. Or you might develop ideas you would use regularly in the classroom. The following illustration might be useful as a model.

Skill: Sharing

— Arrange for students to have a pot-luck meal together once a week.
— Invite students, at the end of the school day, to share what they have learned.
— Assign small teams of students to be responsible for classroom jobs.
— Have the class do research on ways of redistributing income and wealth.

A CONFLUENT LEARNING EXPERIENCE

Bread can be seen as a symbol of life, of love, of creation. It can be explored as a

This experience is based on a teaching plan developed by Linda Rappaport. Reprinted with permission.

scientific inquiry — its changing forms, the chemistry of yeast. It can be the basis for a mathematical problem, the recipe, the feeding of many, cost analysis, etc. Bread can be an affective vehicle — for sharing, integrating, identifying with self and with others. In the following learning experience you will use bread in each of these ways. Try this experience with a group of children or your peers. You might also use this teaching plan as a model to generate your own confluent learning experiences.

Procedure

1. Planning. a. Class brainstorms: If the class were to bake bread together, what would they need? List everything that is needed, ingredients and utensils.

b. Have everyone look at the completed list and choose an item with which to identify. Each person should imagine how that item fits into the bread-making process and write down in a personal diary how he is like the item he chose.

c. Solicit volunteers to bring whatever items they can from the list. Everyone should bring aprons or wear clothing appropriate to working with flour.

2. Baking. You may use any recipe, but follow this process:

a. Mixing the sponge: This step involves obtaining water which is 85–105 degrees, dissolving yeast, adding sweetening, and beating flour. Use amounts determined by your recipe. Ask yourself the following questions: What is happening? What is gluten? What is yeast? What brings yeast to life? What kills yeast?

If no one knows the answers, find them during the next 45–60 minutes, which are needed for the sponge to rise. Use reference books or create an imaginative theory. All ideas, hypotheses, answers, and research should be aired before going on to the next step.

b. Folding in oil, salt, and dry ingredients: After the ingredients are added in the bowl, every person should get a portion of dough, and access to the flour required in their recipe and *all* knead together. Add as much flour as you *feel* is needed. Each person must find his or her own way of bringing the dough from a sticky state to a smooth, shiny, elastic form. You may help one another knead for 10–15 minutes, always repeating the same procedure, being aware of the feel of the dough under your hands, the tension in your fingers and wrists.

Then blend your dough with the dough of the rest of the group. Knead together. Set bread to rise again for one hour. Discuss how you felt during this process. Write these feelings in your diary.

c. Punching down bread and shaping the loaves: Everyone should take a turn — hearing the air escape, feeling the softness. This takes 5 minutes. Each group divides

dough equally among group members. Individuals form their own loaves. Each person should decorate his or her own loaf with initials, decorative slits, braiding, egg wash, sesame seeds, etc. Then set the bread to rise once more, this time for 45 minutes. During this period you can: write a composition on a topic of your choice, inspired by the bread-making experience thus far; or do general research on bread (how matzoh was created; various baking methods and ovens in other times; breads from other countries).

Loaves are then placed in ovens to bake. During this time, you can clean up and do some group processing. How did your group work together? Analyze your own role in the group. How do you feel about working with these people?

Answer these questions in your diary: What did I learn today? What did I learn about me? What did I learn about someone else? When the bread is finished, share in any way which seems appropriate.

3. Time to share further reactions. Choose again one of the items used in bread-making, as you did before our experience yesterday. (Refer to your diary entry.) Follow your progress and behavior throughout the process of bread-making. How were you used? What did people do to you? How did it make you feel? How did you change? Did you enjoy performing in your role? Did you give pleasure, or receive it? Record your reactions in your diary.

POSITIVE BOMBARDMENT CIRCLE

In the reading by Aaron Hillman (pp. 169–171), he says to his students, "It isn't really hard to see nice things in others or to tell them so. Somehow we don't seem to find it easy to talk this way. It always seems easier to say things that hurt. But how much better it would be if we could speak to each other and say what we like." In his article, he gave an account of his use of a "positive bombardment circle" with high school students. Below are instructions for using this exercise with younger children. Try this approach with your peers, as well.

Procedure

1. The class sits in a circle. One child is given a special place to sit (on a chair if everyone else is on the floor). The teacher focuses attention on that child. For example: "Today we're doing the I-like-you game with Al. I want you to think about

This version of the positive bombardment circle exercise was written by Sonya Shulkin, Silvia Smith, and Shelley Reibstein of the Philadelphia Affective Education Program. Reprinted with permission.

Al for a minute. Think about what you've done with Al and what you've seen Al do. Try to get in touch with something you really like about Al." Al calls on people to contribute. The children then tell Al directly what they like about him: "Al, I like the way you build castles." "I like the way you smile." The teacher should also take part. The teacher records each statement and the name of the person who said it. At the end of the circle, the teacher asks Al one thing he likes about himself.

2. The teacher then takes a photo of Al (preferably a Polaroid). Later he will mount the picture on a big piece of cardboard and print all the statements, and who said them, around it. (For example, "Bob says: 'I like the way you draw stars.'") The teacher reads the board back to Al the next day and any other time he wants to hear it. By the end of the year each child should have a positive bombardment board to take home.

3. To encourage children to focus on behavior, read a favorite story (for instance, *The Cat in the Hat Comes Back*) and do a positive bombardment on one of the characters. (For example: "If the cat was your friend, what would you like about him? Pretend he's sitting in this chair. Tell him what you like.")

AL

BOB SAYS: I like the way you build with me.
CATHY SAYS: I like your smile.
MRS. JONES SAYS: I like the way you always finish something you start.
BILL SAYS: I like your shoes.
MARY SAYS: I like your hair.

additional resources

BOOKS AND ARTICLES

Alschuler, Alfred; Tabor, Diane; and McIntyre, James. *Teaching Achievement Motivation*. Middleton, Conn.: Education Ventures, 1970.

Berman, Louise. *New Priorities in the Curriculum*. Columbus, Ohio: Charles E. Merrill, 1968.

Bessell, Harold. "The Content is the Medium: The Confidence is the Message," *Psychology Today* 1, no. 8 (1968): 32–61.

Bessell, Harold, and Palomares, Uvaldo. *Methods in Human Development*. San Diego, Calif.: Human Development Training Institute, 1967.

Borton, Terry. *Reach, Touch and Teach*. New York: McGraw-Hill, 1970.

Brown, George. *Human Teaching for Human Learning: An Introduction to Confluent Education*. New York: Viking Press, 1971.

Brown, George, ed. *The Live Classroom: Innovation Through Confluent Education and Gestalt*. New York: Viking Press, 1975.

Castillo, Gloria A. *Left-Handed Teaching: Lessons in Affective Education*. New York: Praeger, 1974.

DeMille, Richard. *Put Your Mother on the Ceiling: Children's Imagination Games*. New York: Walker, 1967.

Fagen, Joen, and Shepherd, Irma Lee, eds. *Gestalt Therapy Now*. Palo Alto, Calif.: Science and Behavior Books, 1970.

Felker, Donald W. *Building Positive Self-Concepts*. Minneapolis: Burgess, 1974.

Flynn, Elizabeth W., and LaFasco, John F. *Designs in Affective Education: A Teacher Resource Program for Junior and Senior High*. New York: Paulist Press, 1974.

Gazda, George M. *Human Relations Development*. Boston: Allyn and Bacon, 1973.

Hamachek, Don E. *Encounters with the Self*. New York: Holt, Rinehart and Winston, 1971.

Harmin, Merrill; Kirschenbaum, Howard; and Simon, Sidney B. *Clarifying Values through Subject Matter*. Minneapolis: Winston Press, 1973.

Hawley, Robert C., and Hawley, Isabel L. *A Handbook of Personal Growth Activities for Classroom Use*. Educational Research Associates, Box 767, Amherst, MA 01002, 1972.

Hendricks, Gay, and Wills, Russell. *The Centering Book: Awareness Activities for Children, Parents and Teachers*. Englewood Cliffs, N.J.: Prentice Hall, 1975.

James, Muriel, and Jongeward, Dorothy. *Born to Win*. Reading, Mass.: Addison-Wesley, 1971.

Jones, Richard M. *Fantasy and Feeling in Education*. New York: New York University Press, 1968.

Laing, R. D. *Knots*. New York: Pantheon, 1970.

Lederman, Janet. *Anger and the Rocking Chair: Gestalt Awareness with Children*. New York: McGraw-Hill, 1969.

Lyons, Harold C., Jr. *Learning to Feel — Feeling to Learn*. Columbus, Ohio: Charles E. Merrill, 1971.

McCaslin, Nellie. *Creative Dramatics in the Classroom,* 2d ed. New York: David McKay, 1968, 1974.

Moustakas, Clark E. *Finding Yourself, Finding Ourselves.* Englewood Cliffs, N.J.: Prentice-Hall, 1974.

Perls, Frederick. *Gestalt Therapy Verbatim.* Lafayette, Calif.: Real People Press, 1969.

Raths, Louis E.; Harmin, Merrill; and Simon, Sidney B. *Values and Teaching.* Columbus, Ohio: Charles E. Merrill, 1966.

Rubin, Lewis J. *Facts and Feelings in the Classroom.* New York: Walker, 1973.

Simon, Sidney; Howe, Leland; and Kirschenbaum, Howard. *Values Clarification: A Handbook of Practical Strategies for Teachers and Students.* New York: Hart, 1972.

Stevens, John O. *Awareness: Exploring, Experimenting, Experiencing.* New York: Bantam Books, 1971.

Strom, Robert, and Torrance, Paul E. *Education for Affective Achievement.* Chicago: Rand-McNally, 1973.

Weinstein, Gerald, and Fantini, Mario D., eds. *Toward Humanistic Education: A Curriculum of Affect.* New York: Praeger, 1970.

Zahorik, John, and Brubaker, Dale. *Toward More Humanistic Instruction.* Dubuque, Iowa: William C. Brown, 1972.

FILMS

Choices and Conflicts. Stephen Bosustow Productions, 1649 Eleventh Street, Santa Monica, CA 90404.
A series of situations presenting a choice and/or conflict.

Journal into Self. Western Behavioral Sciences Institute, 1150 Silverado Street, La Jolla, CA 92037.
A documentary of an intensive basic encounter group led by Carl Rogers and Richard Farson.

Making a Decision is . . . Churchill Films, 662 North Robertson Boulevard, Los Angeles, CA 90069.
Presents numerous personal decisions one makes in life.

Sessions in Gestalt Therapy. Film Distribution Center, 6304 University Avenue, San Diego, CA 92115.
A series of 11 films documenting the work of Frederick Perls, the founder of Modern Gestalt Therapy.

The OK Classroom. Media Five, 1011 North Cole Avenue, Suite F, Hollywood, CA 90038.
Thomas Harris demonstrates Transactional Analysis techniques and their applications to facilitating emotional growth in the classroom.

chapter
four

---

learning
to work
in groups

initial experiences

DYNAMICS OF THE CLASSROOM GROUP

You have probably been in some groups that turn you on and others that turn you off. The reasons may vary, however, from situation to situation. In some groups, you may have liked or disliked the leader or your own role. The communication between members in one group may have been very free whereas in another group it may have been constrained. Other factors may have contributed to your feelings. The same factors also operate in classroom groups.

Here are five components of group functioning in the classroom.

1. Leadership. The guiding force in a group. Leadership can be appointed from sources outside the group or it can emerge from within a group.

2. Norms. The rules and expectations by which the group operates. Norms can be both explicit and implicit. There may be people within a group who oppose its norms.

3. Roles. The developing positions people assume in a group. We all have an effect on the group whether we are the loudest talker or are silent, whether we are a leader or a follower.

4. Decision-making. The means or processes by which resolutions affecting the group are made. Some groups make decisions rapidly and some slowly and deliberately. They use a variety of processes such as majority vote or consensus testing.

5. Communication. The interaction patterns between the leader and members of the group and among the members themselves. Communication can be both verbal and nonverbal. Some ways of communicating induce defensiveness; others do not.

In this activity, you are to examine a class in which you are presently a student or a teacher. Using each of the five components of groups listed above, describe how that aspect of your class manifests itself. Try to be descriptive rather than evaluative. For example, under leadership, "the teacher resolves any interpersonal differences between students" is descriptive, whereas, "I like her style," would be evaluative.

When you have completed this analysis, project ahead and imagine how these components could operate ideally in your class. For example, you may have described decision-making as coming from only a few influential (most talkative) members of the class, but you would like a mechanism to survey all student needs. When you have generated some ideal ways in which the above components of group functioning might appear, brainstorm some strategies for implementation in your class.

COHESIVENESS IN THE CLASSROOM

Cohesiveness is a central concept in the study of group dynamics. Although theorists in the field have several definitions of cohesiveness, the most usual one is a sense of community in a group. This sense of community exists when group members feel attracted to one another and when people feel that they are a part of the group. It also means that the group has a feeling of commitment: the individuals feel responsible to the group, and the group feels responsible to its individual members.

Assume, for a moment, that a teacher complained to you that her class seemed to lack cohesiveness. The group was ridden with private friendship cliques and many students had no friends at all. When the teacher asked students to clean up the room some students would always shout out, "But, I didn't make this mess!" Seldom was the word "we" uttered in the classroom. During group discussions,

students hardly listened to each other. Interruptions and "put-downs" were constant. Without knowing anything further about the class, what would you speculate are possible reasons for this lack of community in the classroom?

Divide into small groups and have each group generate three possible factors. Then assemble as a large group and report your ideas. Discuss strategies the teacher might use to remedy the situation.

introduction

Even though every group is unique, common patterns of behavior exist across groups. The more you know about what to expect in the classroom group, the better prepared you will be as a teacher to handle the situations that arise. What "groups" are you likely to encounter in a classroom? Actually, a group exists any time you, the teacher, relate to a student, any time you interact with a small group or a total class, and any time students talk, play, or work together, without your influence. In short, group dynamics are occurring whenever people are involved with each other.

It is as important for your students to learn how to work in groups as it is for you to understand group dynamics. More people lose jobs because of their inability to get along with their boss and peers than for their lack of skill. This means that if schools can educate students to get along with others and learn to work together, they will be assisting those students in their future employment. Moreover, we are told that in the next ten years, close to sixty percent of all jobs in the industrialized nations of the world will involve services to other people. Industry has become highly mechanized, and thus less people are needed to operate machinery. With a shorter workday and workweek, people will need more recreational and other free time services. Society will demand more people with human relations skills. Therefore, schools need to help students learn about the dynamics of people as well as things.

Building groups in a classroom also has direct benefits for the teacher. A strong peer community can relieve the teacher from being the sole motivator and disciplinarian. When the peer community becomes a base of power in a classroom, the students do not view themselves as powerless. The wall between teacher and students weakens. Teacher and students can then work together to determine the rules acceptable to both. There is not only an open exchange of ideas and feelings, but also a sense of trust. Because responsibility is shared, peer influence is used in a constructive manner and self-disciplining is possible. Again, because the base of influence is not centered on the teacher, but on the classroom community as a whole, the effect on the individual tends to be more significant. Think for a moment about how many people are motivated by a group to achieve what they find impossible to do alone. Weight

Watchers and Alcoholics Anonymous are just two examples of this phenomenon. The same principle operating there can be applied to the classroom. This is not to say that everyone will be excited about the same thing at the same time. On the contrary, what is exciting is the different viewpoints, the brainstorming, and the resolution of conflicts which occur when every person knows that he or she has a share in the decision. Group motivation, of course, can be a coercive force, but if properly generated, is a vital method of creating ideas and stimulating inquiry. Students learn to build on the thoughts and ideas of their classmates and the teacher learns to build on the ideas of the students. The class also does not have to carry out all activities as a group. It can just as easily initiate ideas for small groups or individuals to work on and develop.

Strange as it may seem, many "open classroom" teachers do not work hard at creating a learning community. Admittedly, these teachers use small group activities, but when problems arise or interest wanes, the practice is quickly abandoned. A sense of belonging to the group, of responsibility to the group (and of the group's responsibility to the individual) often are not major concerns. This state of affairs may result from an overemphasis on individualized instruction and the satisfaction of personal needs. Although personalization is indeed an important educational goal, group skills also need to be developed. When students are asked most of the time to pursue their own interests and master skills alone, they become unable to work with others, to help others grow, and to pool resources for learning. We believe that students can be encouraged to do things for groups as well as for themselves. Their personal learning will not be diminished. It should only be strengthened.

Of course, a sense of community does not develop overnight in a classroom. It begins the first day of class and continues to be built over the year. You cannot expect your efforts to encourage sharing among classmates in the middle of the school year to be effective unless students have become accustomed from the beginning to group living. Building a peer community means the teacher's constant attention to four dimensions of group processes: influence, attraction, norms, and communication.[1]

Influence has to do with power, control, and purpose. It is doubtful that a person will invest in a group unless he or she can influence its direction or, at least, contribute to the group. At first glance, this notion may conjure images of group members fighting for leadership. Actually, it means only that members have the opportunity to share their needs and resources. In an effective group, the roles people play can be varied and meaningful. In a classroom group, the teacher, even though he or she has the greatest potential for leadership, needs to disperse leadership and other roles of influence. This process can be started by encouraging students with high interpersonal influence to work for the benefit of the total classroom community.

Attraction allows group members to fulfill their need for interpersonal affiliation. In an effective group, individual members require some close friends in order to feel secure and comfortable. Without such friends, they can feel lonely, worthless, and anxious. If they are respected and liked by at least some others in the group, they are more likely to behave in a manner that makes them worthy of the liking and respect of others. The teacher's role, promoting attraction of group members for each other, is to discover ways of communicating the strengths, whether physical, social, or intellectual, of each student so that he or she is able to attract friends. This does not need to be done directly; a great deal can happen by the way the teacher organizes the students for activity.

Norms are the attitudes and behavior patterns in a group; they may either help or hinder the group process. When, for example, students create a shared expectation that they will assist each other in pursuing academic work, they have developed a helpful norm of support. When, on the other hand, they develop a pattern of competition and exclusion in the total group, a harmful norm has begun which can break down the sense of community in a classroom. Teachers can encourage the development of helpful norms by the model they set in their attitude and behavior toward the class and by helping the class to clarify and modify norms that do not have widespread agreement or that have outlived their usefulness.

Communication, both verbal and nonverbal, is the vehicle by which group members express their intentions. In an effective group, members will convey clearly their thoughts and feelings and express themselves in ways that do not make others feel defensive. The other side of communication is listening. A group that tunes out members, interrupts, or does not allow for maximum participation is unlikely to be productive. A teacher can facilitate clear and nondefensive communication as well as active listening by using communication exercises and by establishing helpful ground rules for group discussion.

In the readings that follow, all these dimensions of group life will be discussed in detail. Although some group dynamics literature is not applicable to classroom life, the readings we have chosen all have potential usefulness to teachers. You are urged to participate in the group activities presented in this chapter as well as those published elsewhere. Experiential learning is very valuable for teachers inquiring into group processes and their application to the classroom. You may think that the group behavior of schoolchildren is not the same as that of adults. We have found, however, that the processes are remarkably similar. We hope you will gain many practical ideas for immediate classroom use from participation in these activities.

readings

"The Workshop Way of Learning" provides a clear structure for thinking about the use of groups in teaching. The order of a group's business is reflected in Kelley's subtitles: The Goal, The Plan, The Try, The Check-Up, The Plan Revised, and Try Again. It is fascinating to realize that this article was written in the 1950s before a group process approach to learning was even a gleam in anyone's eye. Yet Kelley provides a lot of down-to-earth insight for any teacher who wants to use groups as an integral part of his teaching. Whether you are taking a course or teaching a class (or both), you could test these ideas directly for their present-day applicability.

EARL C. KELLEY

EXCERPT FROM
THE WORKSHOP WAY OF LEARNING

A true learning situation is a problem-solving situation. It is common in life outside of school on an individual basis. The individual starts with wanting to do something. He has a goal which is his own

Abridged from pp. 35–42, 43–46 *The Workshop Way of Learning* by Earl C. Kelley. Copyright 1951 by Harper & Row, Publishers, Inc. Reprinted by permission of the publisher.

and therefore worthy, in his opinion. He figures out how he wants to go about it. Then he proceeds to try to do it the way he decided would be most likely to succeed. If he seems not to be achieving his goal, he stops and asks himself whether or not there was anything wrong with his plan. He revises his plan and tries again. This time he may succeed, or he may have to change his plans again. If he cares enough about his goal, he will continue to contrive until he reaches it. It is simply a matter of having a goal held to be worthy, making a plan which seems likely to achieve the goal, trying the plan, evaluating the failure, replanning, trying it again, revised in the light of experience and achievement. This is what we all do all of the time, and it is the essence of the learning situation.

The only place in life where we do not follow the typical learning procedure, oddly enough, is in school, where people are presumably assembled for the express purpose of learning. This defection is complete, from the first grade to the doctor's degree. In school the goal is furnished by the teacher, and may or may not be worthy to the learner. Whether the learner holds it to be worthy or not is a matter of little or no concern to the teacher. The plan of attack is given by the teacher, and the teacher watches to see that the plan is carried out as directed. There is no need for evaluation along the way because the plan is sure to work, since it has worked many times before. Achievement is automatic as long as the tested plan is followed, but satisfaction of achievement is lacking because the goal was not one which the learner really cared about in the beginning. He has been denied the adventure of contriving. The learner has come in for the least interesting part of the process, and there is little in it for him except work. He has missed the exhilaration of holding a worthy goal and achieving it.

Successful group work would be easy if it were not for the fact that other people are involved; in other words, it would be easy if it were not group work. Arriving at a common goal and releasing the energies of several people in a concerted attack on the problem is the difficulty. It is also the point of greatest reward, because each individual enriches all of the others, and the profit to each member of the group is far greater than in solitary action. But the steps are the same, and are simple. If they are kept in mind, the complexity of joint action will be the only complexity involved.

THE GOAL

No group can accomplish anything until it has figured out what it wants to do. This seems elementary, but many a group has failed because it never clarified its goal. This, then, becomes the first order of business. The group must stick to the clarification of its goal until everyone in the group knows what the group wants to do and accepts it as worthy.

Establishing a goal which all can accept is not easy. It may call for a good deal of compromise. There is the advantage that the people in the group are together because they have a common general interest. But what one individual sees in a general topic may be quite different from what another sees, and this needs to be carefully worked out. It may come about that one person is unable to accept the goals of the great majority. This person may need to withdraw from the group and join another, or get the counsel of a staff member as to where in the total workshop there may be a spot where his present felt needs are apt to be met.

The topic which has brought the group together is often too general to put people to work. It needs to be made specific, so that each member can see something that he can do about it. Energy is released on specifics, not on generalities. We usually have one or more groups meet together to work on the problem of democracy in the classroom. The popularity of this topic, which nearly always emerges from the total group and is never injected by the staff, shows that many teachers earnestly desire to learn how to get rid of the autocratic methods they have inherited, and teach more democratically so that their children will have some preparation for citizenship in a democracy. But the topic itself will never motivate anyone to action.

One group, met together around this topic, made it specific by listing some questions which gave the members

places to take hold. Some of these questions follow. "How can I organize my class so that every member will have a chance to contribute? How can I find out what goals my learners can accept? When and how can I use small group techniques? How do I go about teacher-pupil planning? How can I work with my pupils democratically without having them get out of control? What kind of planning can young children do?" This list of questions made the general topic meaningful, and gave the members of the group ideas as to how they could begin. It sent them to books, to staff members, and to colleagues for information.

The specific goal of the group should be arrived at through consensus. This means that it is talked through and modified until every member of the group can accept it as worthy. No group can succeed if there is a minority which cannot accept what the group is going to do. Such minorities will exist if the chairman resorts to voting as a means of gaining a decision. Parliamentary practice — the motion, the second, the vote — can ruin any group that is planning to work together, because it divides the group instead of bringing it together. Full discussion, understanding, and compromise can achieve goals which all can accept and on which all can spend themselves. This is consensus.

Once the specific goal or goals have

been agreed upon, they need to be put into writing, and copies need to be supplied each member. These written goals should be constantly in front of the group and regularly referred to; all planning should be done with these goals clearly in mind.

THE PLAN

Having agreed upon what the group is to do, the next step is to plan how it is going to do it. This will probably involve a long-time plan and a short-time plan. The group can lay down ways of going about the whole thing so that the semester will end with achievement. This is essential, but it does not tell each individual what he can do about it tomorrow.

The short-time plan has to do with what the group is going to do next Thursday evening, and what each member can do between meetings so that he can be a more useful member of his group. Without this short-time plan, the members will come back in a week just the way they went out, so far as the group project is concerned. They will have missed the opportunity to increase their value to their fellows.

What members do between meetings so that the goals will be brought nearer will take on many forms. The first thing many of us think of is reading. And indeed it may be that the member may

profit by looking up some literature on the topic to be considered. This is only one way of preparing to be a good member the next week, however, and may not be the most fruitful way. Some other and more promising experiences are that he may try something in his class, or he may talk to others whose experience and judgment offer something, or he may consult his students who are the consumers. He may profit most of all, on occasion, by thinking about the problem himself, and coming to some tentative conclusions in that way. When he feels that he has made progress in that way, he will gain respect for his own thinking. Many of us have been trained not to respect our own thinking but to feel that we have to depend on the thinking of others. This leads us to acceptance on authority, whether what the authority says makes sense or not. We are particularly inclined to accept if the "authority" has succeeded in getting his ideas printed. We have undue reverence for the printed page, not realizing that the author is usually just another person like ourselves who has accumulated material and had it printed.

The long-time plan needs to be put in writing. The short-time plan need not be. The last few minutes of every session should be devoted to what the group is going to do at the next meeting, and what individual members can do to make the next meeting successful. Of course if the group already knows what it is going to do, then this short planning

session is not needed, but in most instances it will be.

THE TRY

Now we put into operation the plans we have made. Here contriving which bears directly on the goal begins. This will probably extend over a number of meetings.

THE CHECK-UP

All members of the group, and particularly the chairman, must watch the try, to see whether the goal is likely to be reached by what is going on.

It is not altogether a matter of approaching the goal, although that is important. There are other factors and conditions to be watched. Is there general participation? Has every member been involved? Is the morale of the group good? Are the members becoming better acquainted and coming to enjoy each other's company more? Is the attendance of the group good? Do they work their full time at each meeting, or do they usually adjourn early? Do members of the group begin to find that there are errands they have to do which cannot be done any time except when the group meets? Are they at a loss as to what to do when the meeting starts?

Some of these symptoms may reveal the fact that the plan is not working.

The members of the group had at one time expressed interest in what was projected, and if that interest has evaporated, it seems likely that the plan needs to be reconsidered.

THE PLAN REVISED

When symptoms indicate that all is not well, a session is needed to discuss the reasons. This discussion should be as frank and free as possible. To the degree that it can be done, every member's ideas should be brought out. If poor attendance is a problem, it might be helpful if the recorder would notify each member by mail that a gripe session has been scheduled. Disaffected members are more likely to show up for a gripe session than a work session, especially if the work sessions have been unrewarding.

In this session, the weaknesses of the plan as it has operated can be brought out, and revision can be made so that the members will feel that it will now work. It may be necessary to discard the old plan and substitute a new one. The defects of some of the personalities may come out in such a way that they can be accepted, and these persons may learn from this how to become better group members. Some may have driven others away by their talkativeness, others may have failed to do anything to make the group succeed.

This check-up meeting ought to have the help of a staff member unless the presence of the staff member reduces freedom and frankness. This should not be the case if the staff has succeeded in establishing the proper relationships with the workshop members. If the members of the group feel that a particular staff member is the cause of the breakdown, then the group will do better by itself or with another member of the staff. The chairman should be in the best position to decide whether a staff member should attend and who it should be.

TRY AGAIN

Further contriving is now in order, in the light of what has been learned and through the use of the revised plan.

There is no way to tell how many times the plan of action may need to be revised. As in life, we can never be sure that any projected action will take us where we want to go. No plan can ever be said to be a good plan until it is put to the test through concrete action and has brought the results which the plan was intended to bring.

In the contriving, which is the putting of a projected plan into action — with the struggle and frustration which is usually entailed — the greatest amount of learning occurs. In order for real learning to come about, the group must have freedom to plan wrongly, and to learn through action that they have planned

wrongly. More is to be learned by making mistakes in planning and execution than in perfect performance.

Of course this can be carried too far. If a group makes so many mistakes in planning and execution that it never gets anywhere, never makes any progress, feeings of futility will eventually dissipate the energies of the members and the group will disintegrate. This will not ordinarily happen. If a group pursues a fruitless path for a time, this experience should show it a better path, not a worse one. But there is nothing to be gained by artificially forcing better planning. There is more learning to be gleaned from finding out that the group cannot do what it projected than there would be in having an outsider do its planning for it.

In most cases, when the end of the semester comes, the goal will have been achieved, and the satisfaction which comes from ultimate success after much contriving will be felt. The significance of the goal will lose some of its importance, because the process will assume greater importance. The possession of the achieved goal will bring satisfaction, to be sure, but no specific set of materials or ideas can become as important, once achieved, as the contriving which brought the goal into being. The skill acquired in working with other people will abide with the individual members of the group long after the materials constituting the goal become outgrown and insignificant.

This skill is the one thing we can be sure will be needed by all human beings in a social world, and this is especially true of teachers.

One of the human values to come out of successful group operation is that the members will continuously grow in their respect for each other. They will continuously get to know each other better, and to find value in each other. Out of their contriving and frustration there will grow a group solidarity, with everyone belonging. The members will discover, often to their surprise, that these are really remarkably fine people they have been thrown with. A sort of "one for all, all for one" blood brotherhood comes, which often means much to people who by habit and training have been solitary workers, and who have felt growth stunted through the loneliness of the human spirit. . . .

. . . Criticisms of the group process are frequently heard. They come from people who have been members of groups which have failed to achieve their goals and have therefore failed to bring satisfaction to the participants, and from those who have never tried to be members of groups. They sometimes come from people who drop in on a group once, and, being unable to see where the group started or where it is going, go away without any notion of what has been going on. It is doubtful that such people are really motivated by an honest desire to see what is going on, since they would never want their own work to be judged by such a brief spot sample without orientation.

Many of the criticisms are true in specific cases. We cannot guarantee a successful experience to anyone, any more than he can guarantee it to himself when he attempts something outside of school. Some groups never do get anywhere. The main consolation is that all teachers must work on a percentage basis, and there is no teacher anywhere who has no students who did not profit.

The critics say that there is a great deal of confusion in the group process. This is true. There is confusion wherever real learning, with genuine contriving, goes on. This is true even when people are working by themselves, and it is multiplied when it involves a number of people. The only time there is no confusion is when one person establishes the goal for all, and enforces the action toward it. Democratic procedures require the involvement and consultation of many people, and this results in confusion, or what may appear to be confusion to the superficial observer. The more people involved, the more contriving, the more confusion, and the more learning. In education, beware the machine which runs too smoothly!

Sometimes we hear that group work is nothing more than a bull session, where everybody has his say and nothing eventuates. Some groups do this, and while there is some profit in such sessions, they are likely to play themselves out, and become less and less fruitful. The difference between good group work and a bull session is that in group work the group has an agreed-upon goal, a plan, and is working toward the goal as best it can. A bull session has no goal and no plan.

Some feel that if thrown upon their own, students, even mature teachers, will not work. No one will ever do anything unless someone makes him do it. This is a very commonly held belief among teachers at all levels, and often a teacher who is a student at the university believes this of his own students while resenting it when it is applied to him as a student. The democratic faith calls for a belief in the general rightness and goodness of people, and one who lacks faith in other people lacks the first requisite for democratic teaching. It is true that a person will balk, or be lazy, when forced to pursue the purposes of another. But it makes no sense to assume that he will not spend his energy in the pursuit of his own purposes. The trick to getting people to spend their energies, then, is in finding ways by which purposes acceptable to them can be arrived at. When we hear a teacher proclaiming that other people are lazy while he is not, we are puzzled to know where and how he came into possession of such virtue, while others were denied it. The only tenable position on this matter for anyone to take, it seems, is that no one has a corner on virtue, that people will move when they see something which to them seems worth moving on, and that if they are lazy and perverse, it is best to look to see what goals fail to move them.

Some say that when a group works together all they get is pooled ignorance, and that nothing times nothing is still nothing. There is more than one fallacy revealed by such a statement. In the first place, the members of the group are not ignorant. Each has a lifetime of unique experience back of him, and each has a unique contribution to make. People have been adversely conditioned for so long that the student himself may be persuaded that he is of no value. It may therefore take time and patience to bring him out so that his experiential background can become useful to his fellows. The person who believes in democracy must believe in the unique worth of every individual and must seek ways of making that worth come out, and only an autocrat could possibly say that a whole group of people have nothing to contribute.

In the second place, the contributions of the members of the group may seem trivial to an outsider, particularly if he holds himself to be superior. But no problem is trivial if it is of concern to the individual at the time. This is precisely the place to start, and it is indeed the only place where a start can be made. As growth takes place, and as the self-confidence of the members grows, the nature of the problems under consideration will also grow, and they will become more and more significant when judged in relation to the total educational scene.

This discussion of the groups has been an oversimplification, but is written in the hope that it will be of help to struggling groups. If group members will watch just two things, a great part of their trouble and the danger of failure will be obviated. The first is to have a specific goal stated in writing for the semester, to which they frequently refer and in the light of which they do their planning. The second is never to adjourn a meeting without knowing what they are going to do at the next meeting, and what each individual can do between meetings so that he will come back prepared to do his part for its success.

A well-known principle of mental hygiene is that the individual must have a worthy task, a plan, and freedom. . . . This is what the group must have, and the enthusiasm of group members who have come through a successful group experience is due, we believe, to that fact.

This excerpt from Schmuck and Schmuck's new book provides sound practical ideas and specific exercises for using groups as a part of teaching. At the same time, the authors' ideas are comprehensive enough to give you a general framework within which to think about all the readings in this chapter. The first half of the excerpt describes five communication skills: paraphrasing, behavior description, description of feelings, impression-checking, and feedback. The second half details four stages of group development and gives group activities that can be used to help bring about each stage. Try to do any of the activities which are appropriate to your learning (or teaching) right now.

RICHARD A. SCHMUCK AND PATRICIA A. SCHMUCK

A PRACTICAL GUIDE TO GROUP DEVELOPMENT

The ingredients necessary for the development of whole-person relationships

Reprinted from *A Humanistic Psychology of Education: Making the School Everybody's House* by Richard A. Schmuck and Patricia A. Schmuck by permission of Mayfield Publishing Company, formerly National Press Books. Copyright © 1974 by Richard A. Schmuck and Patricia A. Schmuck.

and I-Thou transactions in a group are the skills and abilities of members to communicate their thoughts, feelings, and impressions directly. Because effective communication is so crucial to the development of humanized learning climates, we will begin by summarizing the important skills and exercises that can be used in schools to maximize effective communication. Next we will briefly review the four developmental stages that learning groups move through on the way to humanization and suggest exercises and procedures that can be used to highlight the issues of group development at each stage.

An "exercise" (or simulation) is a structured game-like activity designed to produce group processes that participants can then easily understand *because* they have just been experienced in the game. Each exercise is designed to make salient a certain type of group process. The exercise is not intended to match the complexity of reality but rather to enable members to learn the advantages or disadvantages of specific forms of group behavior. In brief, each exercise has a particular content and product.

The term "procedure," on the other hand, refers to a group activity that does not, in itself, entail a specific content to be learned, but rather allows a group to accomplish its work more effectively. A procedure can be used for a variety of tasks or purposes. For example, certain forms of decision-making (such as majority vote) or problem-solving sequences are procedures. Whereas exercises typically are carried out only once or twice by a learning group, procedures can and should be used regularly throughout the life of a learning group.

Although our ideas are presented in a sequential format, we wish to emphasize that group development is also cyclical. Thus, exercises that are used at the beginning of a group's life to resolve membership issues, for instance, may also be appropriate at a later time because of the fact that questions about belonging can arise repeatedly during the life of a group. The suggestions we present are meant only to be examples. We have not set out to prepare a comprehensive catalogue of activities, although we have tried to include a variety of techniques for humanizing learning groups. Some of our ideas are treated in detail; others are described only briefly, with a reference to where the reader can find additional details. . . .

Our primary criteria for including the activities here are three: first, that the techniques relate primarily to issues of on-going group processes and development, and not to curricular material to be learned; second, that the techniques may be used by anyone — administrator, teacher, or student — with a small amount of previous experience in working with learning groups and a modicum of time and energy; and finally, that the techniques require only materials easily found in most schools. All of our suggestions can be tailored to fit learning groups of all ages.

SKILL TRAINING IN VERBAL COMMUNICATION

The main purpose of the skills that follow is to enhance the clarity of communication between persons. Such skills can also help a group in achieving closeness, interpersonal acceptance, shared influence, and collaborative decision-making. These skills should prove invaluable in helping the learning group to become collaborative and cohesive.

We think that the skills should be practiced one at a time, first as exercises and later as recurring procedures. Initially, the skills should be practiced in a gamelike atmosphere; later the same skills should be used as part of the regular class interchange and monitored by student observers to see whether they are being used appropriately and effectively.

Below are brief synopses of five different verbal communication skills, some ideas on how to use them in exercises, and an observation sheet that can be used when the skills are being tried out as part of a group procedure. All students should be shown the observation sheets and given some practice before the skills are used as a learning group procedure. A student's initials can be recorded whenever he performs one of the basic skills. After the learning group has had some experience with both the skills and the observation sheet, student observers can be selected to monitor any class discussion. The student observers should report their findings and the student participants should discuss their own effectiveness in using the skills.

Paraphrasing

Paraphrasing is the skill of reiterating the essence of what another person has said in one's own words. If performed properly it shows a regard for what the other person has said and a desire to mirror the other's thoughts accurately. Useful lead-ins to paraphrasing are "I understand you said. . . ." and "Did I read you to say . . . ?" The functions of paraphrasing in a learning group are twofold: to insure that one has understood the communication, and to demonstrate to the other that he has been understood.

One paraphrasing exercise can also be used to achieve feelings of inclusion. In this exercise one student talks to another on his own feelings about coming into the group and the second attempts to paraphrase him. After paraphrasing to the first student's satisfaction, the second student discusses his own feelings on the same topic and is likewise paraphrased. This exercise works very well during the first meeting of a learning group and can be extended in various ways to help create a more accepting atmosphere. For instance, the pairs can be collected into foursomes and, after further discussion and paraphrasing, into eight-person groups, and so on, until the whole group is discussing feelings of acceptance and practicing paraphrasing. The educational leader should participate equally as a member of the learning group.

Behavior description

The skill of behavior description involves noting some of the overt behaviors of another person *without* impugning motives and without trying to generalize about or interpret the other's actions. Looking beyond behavior for psychological interpretations often is a cause of miscommunication and defensiveness. Some differences between behavior description and the assignment of motives are clarified by the following examples. "Paul and Mary have talked most during this discussion," and "That is the third time you have interrupted," are behavior descriptions. "Paul and Mary are the only ones who understand the idea," or "Why don't you listen to what I'm saying," are not behavior descriptions but *interpretations* of behavior, and are likely to create defensiveness and to close off dialogue.

Members of a brand new learning group can practice the skill of behavior description in an exercise in which they try to list all those behaviors at the first meeting which made inclusion and involvement easy. They can also list those behaviors that seemed to get in the way of achieving feelings of inclusion and membership. These listings can be done by pairs or small groups, or by the entire group. All three group formations can be used in sequence.

Practice in behavior description generally only works well in regard to recent and relevant behaviors. One should be careful not to use behaviors that were performed too long before, since memories are faulty and too often the actual behaviors have been lost, with only the interpretation remaining. The ideal procedure is to discuss behaviors that have just occurred.

Description of own feelings

The direct statement of one's own feelings is probably the least used skill of communication, and its lack of use can cause considerable misunderstanding in a group. It is true that a direct statement of one's feelings places a person in a vulnerable position with others, especially if there is little trust between them. Because trust is an unknown quantity in many learning groups, feelings tend to get expressed in indirect ways and so are often misunderstood. The following examples illustrate differences between direct and indirect expressions of feelings. Direct expressions of feeling are: "I feel embarrassed," "I feel pleased," or

"I feel annoyed." These same emotions are often indirectly (and thus ambiguously) expressed by blushing or giggling, or saying, "That's OK" or "Forget it!" Anger, which can be directly expressed in such statements as "That makes me angry," (or annoyed or hurt) is often indirectly expressed by simply withdrawing or by characterizing the other person, as in the statements, "You're mean" and "Why do you do such awful things?"

A poignant instance of the indirect expression of feeling occurred when Allen, our four-year-old son, went to receive a gamma globulin injection against hepatitis. He was well prepared and, at the beginning, not very afraid. His composure broke down, however, when he saw the needle, and he broke into tears. The nurse quickly administered the shot before he could become very agitated, but his immediate response was an angry and teary "You're a bad lady." Such an indirect expression can be accepted and understood from a four-year-old; when it occurs between adults or between a teacher and a student the results may not be as amusing.

A useful exercise early in a group's existence is to ask students to express in various ways their feelings regarding inclusion and then in general discussion to practice making the distinction between direct feeling descriptions and indirect feeling expressions. The exercise begins as each student jots down on a card a description of the feelings he has at present about his place in the group. He then sets the card aside. The leader should explain the entire exercise to the students so they will know how the cards will be used. The next part of the exercise utilizes nonverbal expressions of feeling about one's part in the group. The group stands in a large circle and each student (and the educational leader) in succession places himself in relation to the circle according to how he feels about his membership in the group. A student can also direct the group to move so that his feelings will be expressed clearly. For instance, a focal individual might get in the middle of the circle and direct the members to crowd in closely around him. By contrast, a student might direct the circle to move to one end of the room while he goes to the other end. Next, the nonverbal indirect-feeling expressions are discussed in small groups. The discussions should emphasize the direct description of one's feeling about inclusion. Finally, the students share their previously prepared descriptions of feeling by taping them to the wall for all to see. After some conferring about these responses in twos and threes, all the members of the group discuss how they might enhance one another's feelings of inclusion and membership.

Impression-checking

This skill involves checking one's impressions of another's psychological state in a tentative fashion. It is similar to paraphrasing, except that it concerns the interpretation of the *feelings* and *internal processes* of another rather than his words and overt behaviors. Impression-checking is inevitably tentative; it should be used to free the person described so that he will respond by describing his *own* feelings directly. The students and leader should avoid implying disapproval when checking impressions. Some effective impression-checking statements are: "I get the impression that you are angry with me. Are you?" and "You appear uninterested in your work today. Is that right?" Some ineffective impression checks are: "Why are you angry at me?" or "Why don't you like to do what you're supposed to be doing?" These questions make assumptions which may arouse defensiveness and dishonesty.

The most appropriate time to practice impression-checking early in a learning group's life is soon after an exercise on behavior description has been completed. Students can then use their perceptions of one another's behavior as grist for forming their impressions. For example, after some listing of behaviors that were helpful and unhelpful to the development of feelings of inclusion, small groups can discuss their estimates of the feelings that might have been behind such behaviors. In this way, the practice is theoretical and relatively nonthreatening. Immediately after, members of the small groups can pair off and practice actual impression-checking by seeing whether they have accurately read some of each other's feelings as aroused by the discussion.

Feedback

Feedback involves the giving and receiving of information about how people are affecting one another. It may involve any of the four communication skills, such as *paraphrasing* ("Did I understand you to say that . . . ?), *behavior description* ("This is the fourth time you've asked me that. Can you say more about your question?"), *descriptions of own feelings* ("I felt very good when you asked my opinion."), or *impression-checking* ("You seem to feel very strongly about the point you were making. Do you?"). The person who receives feedback should be free to use it or not, as he or she chooses. In a learning group, feedback should be given only after careful assessment of the needs of the student receiving it. If feedback is to communicate and engage the student in thought and dialogue, it should arise from a concern for him and not from a need for catharsis on the part of the sender. Feedback is instructive and useful when it is specific and concrete rather than general. Often we do not realize the consequences of our behavior: feedback makes people aware of such consequences. For instance, many students (and adults) often interrupt others. Specific feedback such as, "This morning I have been annoyed because you have

cut me off two times — once when I was . . . and then when I . . . " can help others become aware of the consequences of their behavior and provide an opportunity to try to change. It is also important that the sender check to see if the message has been received correctly ("Do you understand why I have been annoyed?").

Feedback should be given after all the four previously mentioned communication skills have been practiced and can be used routinely. Perhaps the best time for feedback regarding issues of inclusion and membership is at the end of the learning group's first two weeks. It is important, of course, that the feedback is constructive and helpful and not traumatic or damaging at this early stage of the group's development. The leader might ask students to write down a few questions about themselves and then choose individuals from whom they would like to receive feedback. Each group should have a student observer whose job is to make sure that all participants are following procedures for constructive feedback.

Feedback should become a routine procedure in the learning group. It is especially important that the educational leader take an equal part in the process. It is good practice to set some daily or at least weekly time aside for discussions. Not only do such discussions help to build feelings of inclusion and membership in the group, but they are also ideal occasions for practicing the four communication skills.

Figure 1 is an observation sheet that

can be used to monitor communication skills during the regular activities of the learning group and to remind students of their importance.

DEVELOPMENTAL STAGES AND PRACTICAL SUGGESTIONS

We turn now to a discussion of four stages of learning group development, offering exercises and procedures that may be used to highlight the important issues of each stage and to facilitate the development of humanized relationships at each stage.

Stage 1: establishing feelings of inclusion and membership

A friend we knew well was very ambivalent about the birth of her first child. Since she had hoped to accomplish many more tasks before becoming a mother, she did not look with favor toward the birth of the child. While she continued to feel resentful and unhappy after the birth, she also gradually grew more fond and attached to the baby. She resolved her ambivalent feelings in a unique manner, surprising especially to those who did not know her well. She openly expressed her resentment to the baby with words, "You messed up my life," "You're a little nuisance," or even

Figure 1. Observation sheet for communication skills

The table within the figure contains the following:

Jot down in the boxes the initials of those who use the skill.

	Time								
Evidence of Listening									
A. Paraphrases									
B. Makes a point relevant to the discussion									
Contributions									
A. Makes a direct description of feeling									
B. Describes another's behaviors									
C. Contributes an idea or suggestion									
Impression-Checking									
A. Checks the feeling of others									
B. Paraphrases to understand									
Feedback									
A. Tells how others affected him									
B. Asks others how he is affecting them									

"I hate you," while at the same time communicating love and care nonverbally. All of her hostile statements were emitted in tones of endearment and tender affection. She soon settled her ambivalence and accepted the baby both verbally and nonverbally. There is a happy ending to the story: the baby is now a happy healthy child. What the mother uttered apparently was not as important as *how* she said it or the nonverbal cues that she emitted.

At the first stages of group development the specific verbal statements of members are often not as important as the feeling tones and the behavioral patterns that take place. While we do not advocate that leaders should dump their inner conflicts and psychic turmoils verbally onto members at the first meeting, we do think that the way in which the educational leader behaves does have a stronger effect than what is said. A teacher who begins by saying, "You are important and I want to hear what you have to say," but who at the same time curtails discussion among the students will have communicated a different message from that of the words.

Consistency between an educational leader's verbal and nonverbal behaviors is especially important during the very first meetings of a learning group. At the beginning, most students are reticent, anxious, and very concerned about the impressions the teacher and their peers will have of them. Since this new interpersonal situation is at least somewhat ambiguous, the students look to their educational leader for cues on how they are expected to behave. Thus, typically the students scrutinize the leader's behavior very carefully. Most first meetings of a learning group do tend to go smoothly and harmoniously, at least on the surface. All students and the leader attempt to present the best possible images of themselves.

During the first period of group development, by virtue of the traditional position of authority, the educational leader takes on extraordinary power for setting the tenor of the group's future. The leader can set the stage for whole-person relationships, I-Thou transactions, and close collaboration; or for distant role relationships, I-It transactions, and one-way influence; or for something in between. Not until later in the group's development do the members have sufficient information to decide whether the educational leader's behaviors are worth following, ignoring, or rejecting. What is crucial for humanization, then, is that the educational leader take the initiative to help the members of his learning group toward establishing feelings of inclusion and membership.

Herbert Kohl (1969) illustrated two ways in which teachers view their role in the first stage of group development by telling of two classrooms on the first day of school. The first teacher had spent much time arranging her classroom room to appear attractive. On the first day of school, she explained her rules and regulations to the students and informed them of the classroom procedures they would follow. Contrastingly, in the second classroom the teacher had not prepared any particular presentation. She had decided to leave the classroom as she found it the week before and to spend the first day encouraging students to decide how to arrange the physical space. Kohl argued that a year-long pattern for student involvement was already being established on the first day of school in each class. We concur with his view.

The primary theme of the first stage of development in a learning group involves "belongingness": membership. Questions such as "Will they accept me?" "Will they like me?" "Who are they?" and "Can I get close to them?" are asked implicitly and preconsciously by all students. Some learning groups, of course, never do develop past this stage, so that such questions remain unanswered throughout the life of the groups. In such groups the students remain formally distant and unconnected; interaction is subdued; goals usually are not discussed, except perhaps when the teacher announces what they should be; and the group structure is characterized by isolated students taking separate turns to interact with the teacher.

We cannot be precise about the length of time it takes for learning groups to achieve feelings of inclusion and membership. The intensity of the striving for inclusion and its eventual resolution depend on the amount of time the students spend together, the past familiarity of students,

the ages of the students, and their previous experience in working out some of the developmental isues in a learning group. However, we believe that every learning group must first resolve the basic issues of membership in some way, even though the resolutions will take on quite different forms and patterns. . . .

Activity: where do I belong? Members stand up and mill around the center of the room. Without verbal communication they are asked to divide up into subgroups of four people each. The rule of four to a subgroup is very useful unless the number in the entire group does not allow for this kind of division. As a subgroup becomes too large, members are asked to leave it to form another one. The educational leader should not talk or suggest where students should move; he should just remind them of the rule of four to a group. After the groups have been formed, the students discuss how this entire process felt, how it felt to have to leave one group and join another, and in general their reactions to forming and reforming groups. The educational leader might ask: Was it easier to move toward some groups and not others? Were there verbal or nonverbal messages of acceptance or rejection given? If so, what were they like?

After the subgroups have had a chance to discuss each individual's experience, the entire group should then discuss what the exercise means for the whole learning group, insofar as the group will be working together for a long time. The students should be encouraged to construct a list of behaviors that communicate acceptance of others and those that communicate rejection. The group might also make a list of feelings that students have when they are not accepted or when they do not feel part of a learning group. Finally, the students can discuss what they might do to help new student members feel more at ease and become a part of the learning group. . . .

Stage 2: establishing shared influence and collaborative decision-making

After the students and educational leader have built some sense of security and belonging, two kinds of "power struggles" typically become prominent in a learning group. One has to do with testing the formal leader's power limits and typically involves the psychodynamics of dependency and counterdependency. The other concerns the pecking order of the student peer group and involves the psychodynamics of domination and autonomy.

Traditionally the pattern has been for the teacher to maintain *all* important power in the classroom. Beneath the surface of a controlled classroom, unresolved interpersonal conflicts and tensions exist

between the teacher and students and also within the student peer group. Teachers of such classes have been warned, "Don't smile before Christmas." This means that if they can maintain formal control during the first four months of school, they have a good chance of avoiding disruptions or attempts to gain control. They also prevent the development of a humanized climate in the learning group, however.

Those teachers who manage to "keep the lid on," not only waste energy in policing students' interactions, but also tend to miss the excitement — as well as the pain — of getting genuinely close to their students. Conflict over how things will operate and who will make decisions is very natural. After all, such conflicts arise in all human relationships: between child and parent, friends, and spouses, and also in churches, communities and communes, and nation-states.

Attempts to control can be clearly at certain stages of child development. There are the invincible and incorrigible two- or three-year-olds who struggle with their parents as they discover ways to be autonomous and independent. "I do it myself" the child says, as he or she persistently and incapably tries to button a shirt, or "You go away" as the child touches a forbidden object. The child hears the word "no" over and over as he or she attempts to establish an independent position in the world. Of course, the child's attempts at autonomy and influence are mixed with wishes for love, acceptance, and security. Part of the control issue for the youngster

involves testing the limits of love and acceptance.

A similar development of acceptance and control occurs in learning groups. One common question among T-group trainers is whether the trainer has managed to "stick it out" with his group or if he has been kicked out. In learning groups a similar issue arises. How the leader's role in the group will be resolved depends in part on how the group has developed during its first stage. The educational leader who has maintained all power by "not smiling before Christmas" will most likely produce a well ordered, formal (possibly even pleasant) classroom where no student makes an obvious attempt to gain power. Such classrooms, however, also tend to produce students who feel alienated from classroom life and school. There will not be many public influence struggles, except for a few attempts to test the authority of the leader.

We do not intend to imply that educational leaders who have encouraged closeness, "belongingness," and shared leadership in the beginning stages of the learning group's life will have an easy time during this second stage. After all, their norms support public discussions of conflict and "clearing the air," and the movement toward collaborative decision-making and shared influence can produce a great deal of tension. An example of the difficulty comes from the innovative Adams High School in Portland, Oregon. From the beginning great effort was made at that school to increase dialogue and collaborative decision-making between staff and students. Apparently these efforts were successful in bringing a feeling of community to the school: While other schools were suffering from delinquency, drug problems, racial conflicts and the like, Adams stood out for its cohesiveness and high morale. Yet, during its second year of operations, there were several attempts — both from students and faculty — to write and rewrite a constitution and to change the governmental structure. Apparently the difficulty was not in establishing collaborative power as much as in defining the structures to maintain it. In other words, the logistics of shared influence and collaborative decision-making are extremely cumbersome even when the norms and attitudes support them. Even if successful structures for collaboration can be built, they will not be utilized without some conflict and interpersonal struggles. The important criterion for humanization is that this struggle is carried on openly and honestly, and that the individual students and staff members are heard and respected. . . .

Activity: the learning group steering committee. The steering committee is a procedural structure for implementing representative democracy; it is one way of trying to disperse influence among the students. The primary purpose is collaboration in decision-making; the primary procedure is for a small group of representatives to solve problems and propose

innovative actions to the entire learning group.

The very first arrangements for implementing such a group should be decided upon either by the educational leader or by the learning group as a whole. However, since many students will not have a very clear idea of what is possible, the educational leader should be the most active in launching the steering committee. Successful examples that we have observed have provided for a rotating membership with the terms of some students overlapping for purposes of continuity. If the membership is rotated, eventually all students in the learning group will have an opportunity to take part. The terms of service should not be shorter than two weeks nor longer than two months. The steering committee is charged with suggesting goals, rules, and procedures, and final decisions are made by the whole group. Naturally, the educational leader should decide whether to reserve veto power and should announce that decision to the steering committee at its first meeting.

The educational leader should remember that the communication skills of paraphrasing, behavior description, description of feelings, impression-checking, and feedback are very useful, and perhaps necessary, for successful participation in the steering committee. Also, some practice in "clearing the air" and in collecting diagnostic data will be useful prerequisites to the group. In short, some maturity of understanding and skill about inclusion

and membership is basic to effective collaboration among the students.

One teacher met with the steering committee three times a week during lunch hours. She actively trained the students beforehand in communication skills and reminded them to use the skills in the group. She also helped the committee establish agendas and clear decision-making procedures. Later in the school year, she gave still more power to the committee and became much less involved as the initiator and prodder. Students became group conveners and began carrying virtually all of the discussion.

As an example of committee influence on learning procedures, let us consider a high school general science class studying plants. The steering committee has gathered information that students are bored and disinterested in this topic and the teacher is concerned that students are not mastering the material. The steering committee may have made a diagnosis of the problem after several students complained to them about the topic. They may then have gathered more information by having each student fill out a short questionnaire and by talking to the teacher. The problem posed to the steering committee is: How can we make the study of plants more interesting and at the same time help the students to master the information prescribed by the teacher or curriculum guide. The steering committee may think of several alternative plans: (1) have more field trips so students can see plants in their natural habitat, (2) have the teacher make up a list of specific competency requirements so that students know what is expected of them, (3) have speakers from conservation groups or local nurseries come in to discuss the importance of plants, (4) set up a simple plant laboratory in the school so students can conduct their own experiments. The steering committee could bring the statement of the problem and the list of alternatives to the entire learning group concerned with plants. The entire group would decide which, if any, of the options they would pursue. The final procedure for decision-making would depend on the learning group; if it were a class involving several hundred students and several teachers, the decision might be made by majority opinion; if the group were small it might strive for consensus: everybody is willing to go along with the plan decided upon, even if some were in disagreement with it.

Although the establishment of a learning group steering committee may be a complex procedure for achieving shared influence and collaborative decision-making, it is the sort of structure that we believe will be useful in humanizing schools. Prior to establishing a steering committee, however, it may be necessary to help the students gain knowledge and skill in using influence processes. . . .

Stage 3: pursuing academic and individual goals

We have friends who helped establish the New School, an alternative school located in Spokane, Washington. In the beginning stages, the staff, parents, students, and consultants spent hours in seemingly endless talk, making decisions about running the school, until all were on edge, frustrated, tired, and feeling as if the talk had been fruitless. These feelings lasted almost until Thanksgiving vacation, when a student finally noted a breakthrough. "At last," he exclaimed, "We have come to a decision. We have finally decided who will empty the ash trays."

To some people, analysis of such an "unimportant" decision may seem belabored and inconsequential. For the New School in its first months of operation the decision was monumental in the importance of its implications. This seemingly unimportant decision was the first one in which all the decision-making processes had taken a visible and concrete form. In fact, this decision set a precedent for many later decisions. By implication, the decision meant (1) that all people should be involved in making certain decisions, (2) that some maintenance chores had to be accomplished, and (3) that somebody had to be responsible for carrying out necessary maintenance chores. In working out this seemingly unimportant decision the group had developed a crude sense of responsibility to establish a division of

labor to maintain the organization itself. The New School is now in its fourth year; it has rules and regulations about emptying ash trays and community meetings no longer focus on such concerns, except when members are not doing their jobs. However, the school has kept the precedents set down by its first decision. Learning is carried out when an inventory of individual's objectives is taken, plans of action are decided upon, and someone is assigned responsibility to make sure those plans are carried out.

Learning groups within public schools are not in the position of creating a new institution; consequently many of their concerns are not the same. Public schools operate within a framework of "givens" laid down by the school board, as well as community or fiscal concerns, and they usually do not include "ash tray" issues. Yet humanized learning groups within the public schools do take time to discuss issues of procedure and decide on precedents for how they will function.

Teachers who are concerned about finishing the formal curriculum may ask, "But aren't such discussions a waste of time?" Learning groups are not ready to work diligently and productively on academic and personal growth until they have settled the issues of group membership and interpersonal influence at least to some degree. This does not mean that learning groups have merely to "sit and rap" for their first few months of existence. Some academic work, of course, is done during the early stages of group development, but not so much as during this third stage.

One third grade teacher in a public school put the case very neatly when she described to us her three-stage design for the year. The first stage generally lasted from the beginning of school until December. Students carried out the usual tasks of skill development and reading but her primary goals were helping the students to feel comfortable with one another, to work independently, to make collaborative decisions, and to learn how to be cooperative. She visualized January through May as the period of high academic productivity. During these months, students set their own goals and developed many projects that emphasized various academic skills. May and June were primarily given over to evaluating progress by students and teacher, setting goals for the students' next year at school, and getting the students ready to work with their next teacher.

One frequent complaint we hear from teachers in traditional classrooms is that they waste too much time policing interactions in the learning group. To us, such complaints of unruly and undisciplined students indicate that the first two stages of group development have not been resolved to a sufficient degree to allow academic work and personal growth to become predominant themes. In our experience, students who have achieved feelings of membership along with the skills of shared influence and collaborative decision-making do not have the great number of discipline problems that plague traditional classroom groups.

The third stage of group development is a "high production" period; it is the time when the norms and procedures established during the first two stages come to fruition in the attainment of academic and personal goals. This stage is most closely visible in a learning group which comes together for a short time to fulfill a specific function, such as a project. By the third stage the students should know each other well and have an understanding of one another's resources. They have settled some of the leadership questions and are ready to set clear goals, divide tasks, and set deadlines for completing the tasks.

During this stage the antagonistic pulls between the production goals of the group and the students' feelings will become obvious and persist as a problem intermittently.... Research by Parsons and Bales (1955) showed that groups tend to swing back and forth between a focus on task and a focus on the social-emotional issues. Some meetings are almost totally given over to individuals' feelings while others are directed toward production.

We believe concerns about students' satisfactions and feelings should take up a good deal of time in learning groups, and that the time taken is not wasted in terms of academic learning. It is imperative that social-emotional issues are handled if learning groups are to work productively.

Learning groups that ignore the basic pulls and tugs between members' goals and class academic goals will not be successful in their production efforts and will be missing a significant part of their productivity — the personal growth element.

The third stage is by no means all "sweetness and light," with students diligently and efficiently working on their goals. Group development is cyclical as well as linear. Some hours or days, even at the height of productivity, will be filled with intense conflicts between students about improper participation or incompleteness. Also, a learning group may come to a collective decision with which a minority disagrees strongly. Such conflicts, of course, should be publicly dealt with immediately. It should be kept in mind that short-term groups which are part of a larger body will themselves reflect in microcosm the developmental sequence of the larger group.

For students who have already developed some trust and skill in communication and group decision-making, the key problems of the first two stages can be resolved quickly and easily. Unfortunately, public schools do not usually provide opportunities to learn about group development, so that teachers with a group-skill orientation must spend much time developing students' decision-making skills — even for deciding such simple issues as who will empty the ash tray....

Activity: cross-age tutoring. In this procedure an older student tutors a younger one in some academic area. The actual tutoring procedures can vary considerably; for instance, the older can take the younger student to the library, read to him, or teach him specific lessons, such as in reading or arithmetic.

Most of the research on cross-age tutoring indicates that it is the *older* student who gains more from the tutoring relationship; an older student, for example, who has trouble with reading may well be assigned to a beginning reader, or an older student who has problems in math may benefit from teaching simple mathematical skills. Patricia Schmuck, for example, used a group of junior-high-age boys with severe reading disabilities to tutor elementary students in reading, and found that the reading skills of the older boys, as well as their understanding of personal problems, were greatly enhanced. . . .

Stage 4: keeping the learning group adaptive

Healthy learning groups, like healthy students, eventually reach a condition of adaptive maturity. For the healthy student reaching such a state is not synonymous with completion, but rather a state of heightened readiness for continuous growth and for the regularized broadening of competencies, skills, and interests.

Adaptive maturity involves confronting the options in one's life, the ability to respond with choices, and the courage to accept the consequences of one's decisions. John Gardner (1963) applied the term "self-renewal" to this kind of adaptive procedure. Self-renewing groups can continue to form new purposes and procedures out of their own internal resources and they have the competence to adopt new processes when the old ones are no longer functional. They are termed "mature" because the members accept the responsibility for their life as a group and are continuously striving to improve it.

Although this description may sound appealing, self-renewing learning groups are not easy to live in. They face a continuous array of human problems such as intermittent feelings of exclusion and alienation, power struggles and resentments, and frustrated goal-striving. While they afford much satisfaction and comfort to the members, they do not allow for complacency. While they support individual growth and insight, they also are confrontative and challenging.

Indeed, from one point of view, adaptive learning groups can be seen as having many contradictions. They are always the same, but yet they are changing. There is no end, no point of completion. Each day, like every other day, brings its miseries and frustrations along with its small joys and miracles. Allan Watts (1961) said it well: "The people we are tempted to call clods or boors are just those who seem to find nothing fascinating in being human;

their humanity is incomplete, for it never astonished them." (P. 130.) . . .

Activity: strength-building exercise. This exercise aims at building self-esteem and identification with the learning group by publicly sharing students' favorable characteristics and identifying the group's resources. This exercise can be used several times during the school year to keep students informed of the group's resources as well as their growth. It should not, however, be introduced too early, because it requires a modicum of basic trust. We have found that it often is difficult for students to express openly to one another their strengths. Young children and even many adults respond to this exercise with "It's not nice to brag." It must be clear, however, that the exercise is important in keeping the learning group's ability strong.

Students are given a large sheet of newsprint paper and asked to put their name at the top and to list at least three things that they consider as personal strengths. Sample items are: I obey the rules, I listen to others, I help, I can blow a bubble, I don't get angry fast, I can tie my shoes, I'm pretty smart, I get good grades, I like people, I read a lot, I can build a motor, I know about dinosaurs, I ski well, etc.

Each student then tapes his or her paper to the wall for all to see. The students move about reading the papers. Each student lists at least one additional strength on everyone else's paper. Written statements may be repeated or not, depending on the group's decision. Next, the learning group divides into subgroups to discuss how each student's strengths can be used in the group. One student, for example, may be a resource for another student or for the entire group. The exercise may lead to a new project or it may mean nothing more than a new appreciation of the various strengths of students. The strengths of students, once they are shared as a resource, can be used at various times during the life of a learning group.

A variation on this exercise is to list weaknesses next. The same method can be followed but the discussion can include ways in which students' strengths can be used to help others with their weaknesses.

Continuing the thread of discussion of the previous excerpt, Hunter adds another theoretical dimension for improving the work of learning groups. She also includes practical exercises for applying her ideas. Based on earlier work by Benne and Sheats, Hunter's article contains a description of three kinds of behavior in groups: task-oriented, maintenance-oriented, and self-oriented. The first two kinds of behavior must be learned for successful group work; the last must be avoided. The exercises help to develop ways to observe group behavior, listening skills for improving group behavior, and alternatives for dealing with group conflict. The next time you are participating in a group discussion, ask the members of the group to try one of these exercises and see for yourself whether it can be useful to you for facilitating a group's development.

ELIZABETH HUNTER

IMPROVING GROUP PRODUCTIVITY

There is a wide variety of helpful behaviors one can utilize in group meetings, and many of these behaviors must be consciously learned. That is, many of us do not own these behaviors naturally — we must quite consciously acquire and practice them at first. As we "try on" new behaviors, and as we want to use them to improve our participation in groups and further the work of the groups in which we are involved, we will begin to adopt these new behaviors rather naturally. No matter how natural behavior may become, however, we will *always* need

From *Encounter in the Classroom* by Elizabeth Hunter. Copyright © 1972 by Holt, Rinehart and Winston, Inc. Reprinted by permission of Holt, Rinehart and Winston, Inc.

to be conscious of how we are participating in groups and of how others are behaving, if the groups in which we work are to be productive and satisfying.

In group meetings it is common for participants to share ideas or opinions and to ask others to further explain what they have introduced. Most people do not think of sharing feelings, however, or of summarizing what has happened or bringing in persons who have not participated or helping the group continue to explore alternatives rather than quickly latch on to the first workable solution offered. Many people actually interfere with the work of the group, without necessarily meaning to do so, by dominating the conversation and preventing others from participating or by attempting to smother controversy which needs to surface and be faced before any workable solutions can be achieved....

GROUP MEMBERSHIP ROLES

The following list of group roles is presented in three parts. The first has to do with behaviors that further the work, or task, of the group; the second has to do with maintaining the group as a smoothly functioning unit; and the third defines some roles called personal, because they cater to self-oriented needs which interfere with the work of the group.[1]

Group Task Behavior:
Conduct That Furthers the Work
of the Group

1. *Initiating.* Proposes aims, ideas, action, or procedures.
2. *Informing.* Asks for or offers facts, ideas, feelings, or opinions.
3. *Clarifying.* Illuminates or builds upon ideas or suggestions.
4. *Summarizing.* Pulls data together, so group may consider where it is.
5. *Consensus Testing.* Explores whether group may be nearing a decision; prevents premature decision-making.

Group Maintenance Behavior:
Conduct That Helps the Group Function
Productively

1. *Harmonizing.* Reconciles disagreements, relieves tension, helps people explore differences.
2. *Gate Keeping.* Brings others in, suggests facilitating procedures, keeps communication channels open.
3. *Encouraging.* Is warm and responsive; indicates with words or facial expression that the contributions of others are accepted.
4. *Compromising.* Modifies position so group may move ahead; admits error.
5. *Giving Feedback.* Tells others, in helpful ways, how their behavior is received.

Personal or Self-Oriented Behavior:
Conduct That Interferes with the
Work of the Group

1. *Aggressing.* Attacks, deflates, uses sarcasm.
2. *Blocking.* Resists beyond reason, uses hidden agenda items which prevent group movement.
3. *Dominating.* Interrupts, asserts authority, overparticipates to point of interfering with others' participation.
4. *Avoiding.* Prevents group from facing controversy; stays off subject to avoid commitment.
5. *Abandoning.* Makes an obvious display of lack of involvement.

EXERCISES IN OBSERVING, ANALYZING, AND CHANGING GROUP BEHAVIOR

POP: process observation practice

Divide into separate groups of participants and observers. If your room is small, you may have to have just one group of about ten participants, with everyone else observing (taking turns, so that observers may also, at some time, become participants). If your room is large enough so that several different conversations can be easily heard, you can have a number of groups going at one time, with eight or ten participants, and a like number of observers. Observers may operate in one of several ways:

1. Each observer may select a certain participant to observe, and concentrate on him, noting into which category each of his statements fall.
2. All observers may note all behaviors of the entire group of participants.
3. One third of the observers may note all task behavior, one third may tally maintenance behavior, and the other third will watch for self-oriented behavior in participants.

If the decision is to watch the behavior of several persons, it will be useful to put tally marks for each participant's statement using a sheet marked out as in Figure 1, with the initials of the participants at the top and the behavior at the side.

The participants will discuss a topic which calls for solutions or decisions and one which will provoke differing opinions. Any current local, national, or international problem may be used; and problems that are particularly relevant to the discussants are always appropriate; for example:

1. The assignments in this course should consist of _____.
2. The method of grading and evaluation in this course (my school, education in general) should be _____.
3. The education department (this college, our schools) would be vastly improved if _____.

Task Behavior	B.H.	L.C.	C.B.	D.R.	S.W.
1. Initiating					
2. Informing					
3. Clarifying					
4.					

Figure 1.

Allow twenty to thirty minutes for this discussion.

Observers will give feedback to participants, using the data they have gathered based on group membership roles. More time will be required for total group feedback (all observers together giving feedback to all participants) than if one observer talks with one participant. You might allow ten to fifteen minutes for total group feedback or four to five minutes for individual feedback.

Participants will continue their group discussion for fifteen to twenty minutes more, this time trying for new behavior. For example, if a participant does not usually do any gate-keeping or encouraging, he might try these.

There will be a second feedback period. This time, even if observers are concentrating on individuals, allow some time for talking about the performance of the total group.

Switch, so that observers become participants, and vice versa. It is usual to continue the same topic of conversation, but this is not necessary.

Behavior by the label

About ten participants will sit in a circle. There will be a sign in front of each, with one or two role behaviors written on both the front and back (so all can see). For example, one person's label may say "summarize" and "clarify"; another's may say "give feedback" and "encourage"; another "dominate"; another, "abandon the group" (obviously engage in daydreaming, read a newspaper, back chair away from the group and look out the window, and so on). Those playing self-oriented roles should not overdo them to the point of parody but should make them realistic. Everyone else will observe.

Select a topic and discuss it for about ten minutes.

After the ten minutes is up, everybody will move one seat to the right and take on a new role according to the sign now in front of him. The discussion will continue for ten more minutes.

Everyone will switch one seat to the right once more and continue for ten more minutes.

Spend ten minutes or so discussing how the participants felt in the various roles.

Process observation, on and on

Every time you have a class discussion of any length (or a faculty meeting, or, in fact, any meeting of an on-going group) ask one or two persons to serve as process observers and allow five to ten minutes at the end of the discussion for feedback on behavior. This is particularly worthwhile because you will receive feedback about your behavior in real situations.

Process observation for the private eye

Whenever you are in a group of any kind, try to observe what is going on by noting the various roles that people play.

You can observe process in any group: work groups, social groups, family groups, and so on.

For children

The same categories for looking at group behavior can be used with children, though perhaps the terminology should be changed. For example:

Work Behavior

1. has new ideas or suggestions
2. asks for or gives information
3. helps to explain better
4. pulls ideas together
5. finds out if the group is ready to decide what to do

Helping Behavior

1. helps people get together
2. brings other people in
3. shows interest and kindness
4. is willing to change own ideas to help group
5. tells others in good ways how they are behaving

Troublesome Behavior

1. attacks other people
2. won't go along with other people's suggestions
3. talks too much
4. keeps people from discussing, because does not like arguments

5. shows that he does not care about what is happening

A LISTENING EXERCISE

Divide into groups of from five to ten persons, depending upon how many groups can operate in your room and still be heard. The smaller the space, the smaller the groups have to be in order for conversation to be heard. This exercise may be carried out with the total group; however, the larger the group, the fewer opportunities there will be to participate.

Select any topic for discussion which is controversial and in which participants are interested. A current political or education issue or a class or college issue is suitable.

Anyone may begin the discussion and say whatever he wishes to say on the topic. The second person to speak must repeat the essence of what the first person has said — that is, he doesn't have to give a verbatim repetition, just the main idea or ideas. Then he must check out with the first speaker to be sure he has repeated correctly. A nod from the first speaker or an "okay" will be enough of a sign to indicate that the message has been correctly interpreted.

The second speaker may then go on and state his own point of view.

When the second speaker finishes, the third speaker must repeat what the second speaker has said and check out with him before he can go on to have his

say. Each speaker repeats *only* the message of the person immediately preceding him, and anyone may speak — do *not* take turns around the circle. If a person cannot repeat what was said before, he is not permitted to offer his own point of view.

Here is a sample of what might occur. The topic: *Women are the most oppressed human beings on earth.*

"Well, I don't believe that women are oppressed at all, so I think the topic is silly. Women have as much chance as anyone else; in fact, they have it better than men in many ways because they are more apt to have their own way, be supported by someone else, and, in general, be taken care of."

"You said that you don't think women are oppressed, and the topic is silly, and, in fact, women in many ways are better off than men, because they have their own way and so on. Okay? Well, I don't agree with you, I think that women are terribly oppressed, and to make things worse, most of them don't even know that they are oppressed. It's true that women aren't necessarily poor and they have as much in the way of food, shelter, and clothing as men, but they are definitely discriminated against in other ways. They are taught from birth that they are inferior to men — but they are also taught that this is a good thing!"

"You said that you think women are very much an oppressed group, and what makes their oppression even worse than it might be otherwise is that they are taught that it's good to be discriminated against in the ways that they are. Well, I agree, and I'll give you an example, which I heard just today. Some women were talking together before my last class, and one asked another what kind of list she had been making, saying that she appeared to be so well organized. The other said she was figuring out her checkbook, and the first said — *proudly,* mind you! — that her husband didn't allow her to fiddle with their checkbook! She was delighted to think that she was so feminine she didn't have a mind adequate to deal with figures!"

"Well, you said that you agree that women are oppressed, and you gave an example of a woman who was proud to say that her husband, in essence, told her she was too stupid to have access to their checkbook. I also think that women *are* really discriminated against, and I also believe that in most instances they are so brainwashed that they don't even know that their lives could be different. They think it's a mark of honor and success to be known as Mrs. John Smith rather than to have a name and identity of their own!"

"But that's ridiculous and anyway why shouldn't . . ."

"Wait a minute! you didn't repeat."

"Oh, yes. Well, you said that women are brainwashed and . . . well, I can't remember, so I guess I don't get a turn."

"Well, she said that women are so brainwashed that they don't realize that they are oppressed, and they don't realize

that they don't even have the same degree of identity that men do. Well, I disagree, and I believe that women are not brainwashed, and what's more I believe that women dominate this country. Everybody knows that American women are very bossy and they run the men, not the other way around. Besides, how can they be the most oppressed group when there are people who are actually *starving* or who can't live in certain neighborhoods!"

"Boy! Where have you been lately! Women . . ."

"You didn't repeat what I said. . . ."

For children

This listening exercise may be used for short periods of time with even young children.

THE GAME OF LIFE[2]

This is a game to be played by six groups. A group may have as few as two members, but each group should have approximately the same number of players. The simplest way to make groups for this exercise is to have the total group count off by sixes, and then each person will join with all those holding the same number. That is, all the 1's will become a group, all the 2's, and so on. One person must remain out to act as the control person, to be the timekeeper, observer, and scorekeeper.

Object: Win as much as you can.

Procedure: This learning experience is like a game and has ten plays. On every play each group chooses either Y or X without necessarily knowing what the other groups have chosen and writes its choice on a slip of paper. All slips are handed to the control person, who tallies them and announces the results. For example, if four groups have chosen X and two have chosen Y, control will say, "X's win $4, Y's lose $8."

After plays four, six, and ten there will be a ten minute discussion and negotiation session at which one representative from each group will be present. The representatives discuss whatever they wish to. This representative may change from session to session or may be the same person each time. The sessions will be held out of the hearing of the groups, and the control person will serve as observer. *This game may seem complicated, but as you play you will see that it is easily understood.* Each group's payoff (winning or losing) depends on the combination of all six choices. (See also Figure 2.)

Payoff Possibilities

choices	payoffs
— All choose X	— All lose $2
— Five choose X	— X's win $2
— One chooses Y	— Y loses $10
— Four choose X	— X's win $4
— Two choose Y	— Y's lose $8

Approximate Time	Play	Check One		Payoff	
		X	Y	Won	Lost
5 minutes	1				
3 minutes	2				
3 minutes	3				
3 minutes	4				
5 minutes *	5†				
3 minutes	6				
5 minutes *	7‡				
3 minutes	8				
3 minutes	9				
5 minutes *	10§				

Total won

Total lost

SCORE   Won minus lost

* These plays are preceded by a negotiation session.

† The payoff doubles on this play.

‡ The payoff triples.

§ The payoff is multiplied by ten.

Figure 2. Score sheet

— Three choose X   — X's win $6
— Three choose Y   — Y's lose $6

— Two choose X   — X's win $8
— Four choose Y   — Y's lose $4

— One chooses X   — X wins $10
— Five choose Y   — Y's lose $2

— All choose Y   — All win $2

When the game is over

This game was described as a learning experience. Discuss as a total group what you have learned. Some things you might consider are:

1. What does "you" mean?
2. What were some of your feelings about winning and losing?
3. What were some of your feelings about competing and collaborating?
4. What analogies can you draw between this game and life in classrooms?
5. Compare what the winnings of the *total* group might have been with what they actually were.

For children

This game can be played with children, but you will have to decide, as always, whether or not your particular class is old enough to benefit from the experience. You may want to simplify the rules by doing away with doubling and tripling winnings, and you might also want to have a negotiation session after *every* play, changing negotiators. This would help everyone to understand the implications of the playing of X's or Y's.

One of the major difficulties that can block successful group accomplishments is defensive communication. This well-known article by Gibb outlines the kinds of defensiveness one might expect to find in a poorly functioning group. Gibb also discusses their more positive counterparts which he calls "supportive communication." He distinguishes carefully between them in ways that might give you practical help in becoming a better group member. We tend to blame the other guy for lack of communication. Gibb points out how this attitude takes energy away from the real job of figuring out how to improve communication. Learning how to use supportive communication is a skill everyone needs.

JACK R. GIBB

DEFENSIVE COMMUNICATION

One way to understand communication is to view it as a people process rather

From *Journal of Communication*, 11, no. 3 (1961): 141–48. Reprinted with permission.

than as a language process. If one is to make fundamental improvement in communication, he must make changes in interpersonal relationships. One possible type of alteration — and the one with which this paper is concerned — is that of reducing the degree of defensiveness.

DEFINITION AND SIGNIFICANCE

Defensive behavior is defined as that behavior which occurs when an individual perceives threat or anticipates threat in the group. The person who behaves defensively, even though he also gives some attention to the common task, devotes an appreciable portion of his energy to defending himself. Besides talking about the topic, he thinks about how he appears to others, how he may be seen more favorably, how he may win, dominate, impress, or escape punishment, and/or how he may avoid or mitigate a perceived or an anticipated attack.

Such inner feelings and outward acts tend to create similarly defensive postures in others; and, if unchecked, the ensuing circular response becomes increasingly destructive. Defensive behavior, in short, engenders defensive listening, and this in turn produces postural, facial, and verbal cues which raise the defense level of the original communicator.

Defense arousal prevents the listener from concentrating upon the message. Not only do defensive communicators send off multiple value, motive, and affect cues, but also defensive recipients distort what they receive. As a person becomes more and more defensive, he becomes less and less able to perceive accurately the motives, the values, and the emotions of the sender. The writer's analyses of tape recorded discussions revealed that increases in defensive behavior were correlated positively with losses in efficiency in communication.[1] Specifically, distortions become greater when defensive states existed in the groups.

The converse, moreover, also is true. The more "supportive" or defense reductive the climate the less the receiver reads into the communication distorted loadings which arise from projections of his own anxieties, motives, and concerns. As defenses are reduced, the receivers become better able to concentrate upon the structure, the content, and the cognitive meanings of the message.

CATEGORIES OF DEFENSIVE AND SUPPORTIVE COMMUNICATION

In working over an eight-year period with recordings of discussions occurring in varied settings, the writer developed the six pairs of defensive and supportive categories presented in Table 1. Behavior which a listener perceives as possessing any of the characteristics listed in the left-hand column arouses defensiveness, whereas that which he interprets as having any of the qualities designated as supportive reduces defensive feelings. The degree to which these reactions occur depends upon the personal level of defensiveness and upon the general climate in the group at the time.[2]

Evaluation and description

Speech or other behavior which appears evaluative increases defensiveness. If by expression, manner of speech, tone of voice, or verbal content the sender seems to be evaluating or judging the listener, then the receiver goes on guard. Of course, other factors may inhibit the reaction. If the listener thought that the speaker regarded him as an equal and

Table 1. Categories of behavior characteristic of supportive and defensive climates in small groups

Defensive climates	Supportive climates
1. Evaluation	1. Description
2. Control	2. Problem orientation
3. Strategy	3. Spontaneity
4. Neutrality	4. Empathy
5. Superiority	5. Equality
6. Certainty	6. Provisionalism

was being open and spontaneous, for example, the evaluativeness in a message would be neutralized and perhaps not even perceived. This same principle applies equally to the other five categories of potentially defense-producing climates. The six sets are interactive.

Because our attitudes toward other persons are frequently, and often necessarily, evaluative, expressions which the defensive person will regard as nonjudgmental are hard to frame. Even the simplest question usually conveys the answer that the sender wishes or implies the response that would fit into his value system. A mother, for example, immediately following an earth tremor that shook the house, sought for her small son with the question: "Bobby, where are you?" The timid and plaintive "Mommy, I didn't do it" indicated how Bobby's chronic mild defensiveness predisposed him to react with a projection of his own guilt and in the context of his chronic assumption that questions are full of accusation.

Anyone who has attempted to train professionals to use information-seeking speech with neutral affect appreciates how difficult it is to teach a person to say even the simple "who did that?" without being seen as accusing. Speech is so frequently judgmental that there is a reality base for the defensive interpretations which are so common.

When insecure, group members are particularly likely to place blame, to see others as fitting into categories of good or bad, to make moral judgments of their

colleagues, and to question the value, motive, and affect loadings of the speech which they hear. Since value loadings imply a judgment of others, a belief that the standards of the speaker differ from his own causes the listener to become defensive.

Descriptive speech, in contrast to that which is evaluative, tends to arouse a minimum of uneasiness. Speech acts which the listener perceives as genuine requests for information or as material with neutral loadings is descriptive. Specifically, presentations of feelings, events, perceptions, or processes which do not ask or imply that the receiver change behavior or attitude are minimally defense producing. The difficulty in avoiding overtone is illustrated by the problems of news reporters in writing stories about unions, communists, Negroes, and religious activities without tipping off the "party" line of the newspaper. One can often tell from the opening words in a news article which side the newspaper's editorial policy favors.

Control and problem orientation

Speech which is used to control the listener evokes resistance. In most of our social intercourse someone is trying to do something to someone else — to change an attitude, to influence behavior, or to restrict the field of activity. The degree to which attempts to control produce defensiveness depends upon the openness of the effort, for a suspicion that hidden motives exist heightens resistance. For this reason attempts of nondirective therapists and progressive educators to refràin from imposing a set of values, a point of view, or a problem solution upon the receivers meet with many barriers. Since the norm is control, noncontrollers must earn the perceptions that their efforts have no hidden motives. A bombardment of persuasive "messages" in the fields of politics, education, special causes, advertising, religion, medicine, industrial relations, and guidance has bred cynical and paranoidal responses in listeners.

Implicit in all attempts to alter another person is the assumption by the change agent that the person to be altered is inadequate. That the speaker secretly views the listener as ignorant, unable to make his own decisions, uninformed, immature, unwise, or possessed of wrong or inadequate attitudes is a subconscious perception which gives the latter a valid base for defensive reactions.

Methods of control are many and varied. Legalistic insistence on detail, restrictive regulations and policies, conformity norms, and all laws are among the methods. Gestures, facial expressions, other forms of nonverbal communication, and even such simple acts as holding a door open in a particular manner are means of imposing one's will upon another and hence are potential sources of resistance.

Problem orientation, on the other hand, is the antithesis of persuasion. When the sender communicates a desire to collaborate in defining a mutual problem and in seeking its solution, he tends to create the same problem orientation in the listener; and, of greater importance, he implies that he has no predetermined solution, attitude, or method to impose. Such behavior is permissive in that it allows the receiver to set his own goals, make his own decisions, and evaluate his own progress — or to share with the sender in doing so. The exact methods of attaining permissiveness are not known, but they must involve a constellation of cues and they certainly go beyond mere verbal assurances that the communicator has no hidden desires to exercise control.

Strategy and spontaneity

When the sender is perceived as engaged in a stratagem involving ambiguous and multiple motivations, the receiver becomes defensive. No one wishes to be a guinea pig, a role player, or an impressed actor, and no one likes to be the victim of some hidden motivation. That which is concealed, also, may appear larger than it really is with the degree of defensiveness of the listener determining the perceived size of the suppressed element. The intense reaction of the reading audience to the material in the *Hidden Persuaders* indicates the prevalence of defensive reactions to multiple motivations behind strategy. Group members who are seen as "taking a role," as feigning emotion, as toying with their colleagues, as withholding information, or as having special sources of data are especially resented. One participant once complained that another was "using a listening technique" on him!

A large part of the adverse reaction to much of the so-called human relations training is a feeling against what are perceived as gimmicks and tricks to fool or to "involve" people, to make a person think he is making his own decision, or to make the listener feel that the sender is genuinely interested in him as a person. Particularly violent reactions occur when it appears that someone is trying to make a stratagem appear spontaneous. One person has reported a boss who incurred resentment by habitually using the gimmick of "spontaneously" looking at his watch and saying, "My gosh, look at the time — I must run to an appointment." The belief was that the boss would create less irritation by honestly asking to be excused.

Similarly, the deliberate assumption of guilelessness and natural simplicity is especially resented. Monitoring the tapes of feedback and evaluation sessions in training groups indicates the surprising extent to which members perceive the strategies of their colleagues. This perceptual clarity may be quite shocking to the strategist, who usually feels that he has cleverly hidden the motivational aura around the "gimmick."

This aversion to deceit may account for one's resistance to politicians who are suspected of behind-the-scenes planning to get his vote, to psychologists whose listening apparently is motivated by more than the manifest or content-level interest in his behavior, or to the sophisticated, smooth, or clever person whose "oneupmanship" is marked with guile. In training groups the role-flexible person frequently is resented because his changes in behavior are perceived as strategic maneuvers.

In contrast, behavior which appears to be spontaneous and free of deception is defense reductive. If the communicator is seen as having a clean id, as having uncomplicated motivations, as being straightforward and honest, and as behaving spontaneously in response to the situation, he is likely to arouse minimal defense.

Neutrality and empathy

When neutrality in speech appears to the listener to indicate a lack of concern for his welfare, he becomes defensive. Group members usually desire to be perceived as valued persons, as individuals of special worth, and as objects of concern and affection. The clinical, detached, person-is-an-object-of-study attitude on the part of many psychologist-trainers is resented by group members. Speech with low affect that communicates little warmth or caring is in such contrast with the affect-laden speech in social situations that it sometimes communicates rejection.

Communication that conveys empathy for the feelings and respect for the worth of the listener, however, is particularly supportive and defense reductive. Reassurance results when a message indicates that the speaker identifies himself with the listener's problems, shares his feelings, and accepts his emotional reactions at face value. Abortive efforts to deny the legitimacy of the receiver's emotions by assuring the receiver that he need not feel bad, that he should not feel rejected, or that he is overly anxious, though often intended as support giving, may impress the listener as lack of acceptance. The combination of understanding and empathizing with the other person's emotions with no accompanying effort to change him apparently is supportive at a high level.

The importance of gestural behavioral cues in communicating empathy should be mentioned. Apparently spontaneous facial and bodily evidences of concern are often interpreted as especially valid evidence of deep-level acceptance.

Superiority and equality

When a person communicates to another that he feels superior in position, power, wealth, intellectual ability, physical characteristics, or other ways, he arouses defensiveness. Here, as with the other sources of disturbance, whatever arouses feelings of inadequacy causes the listener to center upon the affect loading of the statement rather than upon the cognitive elements. The receiver then reacts by not hearing the message, by forgetting it, by competing with the sender, or by becoming jealous of him.

The person who is perceived as feeling superior communicates that he is not willing to enter into a shared problem-solving relationship, that he probably does not desire feedback, that he does not require help, and/or that he will be likely to try to reduce the power, the status, or the worth of the receiver.

Many ways exist for creating the atmosphere that the sender feels himself equal to the listener. Defenses are reduced when one perceives the sender as being willing to enter into participative planning with mutual trust and respect. Differences in talent, ability, worth, appearance, status, and power often exist, but the low defense communicator seems to attach little importance to these distinctions.

Certainty and provisionalism

The effects of dogmatism in producing defensiveness are well known. Those who seem to know the answers, to require no additional data, and to regard themselves as teachers rather than as co-workers tend to put others on guard.

Moreover, in the writer's experiment, listeners often perceived manifest expressions of certainty as connoting inward feelings of inferiority. They saw the dogmatic individual as needing to be right, as wanting to win an argument rather than solve a problem, and as seeing his ideas as truths to be defended. This kind of behavior often was associated with acts which others regarded as attempts to exercise control. People who were right seemed to have low tolerance for members who were "wrong" — i.e., who did not agree with the sender.

One reduces the defensiveness of the listener when he communicates that he is willing to experiment with his own behavior, attitudes, and ideas. The person who appears to be taking provisional attitudes, to be investigating issues rather than taking sides on them, to be problem solving rather than debating, and to be willing to experiment and explore tends to communicate that the listener may have some control over the shared quest or the investigation of the ideas. If a person is genuinely searching for information and data, he does not resent help or company along the way.

CONCLUSION

The implications of the above material for the parent, the teacher, the manager, the administrator, or the therapist are fairly obvious. Arousing defensiveness interferes with communication and thus makes it difficult — and sometimes impossible — for anyone to convey ideas clearly and to move effectively toward the solution of therapeutic, educational, or managerial problems.

This reading by Underwood is a straightforward description of the ways in which groups can and do make decisions. No matter how well a group has developed interpersonally, there comes a time when specific decisions need to be made. Our experience has shown us that members of groups are very often naive about what options they have for decision-making. Underwood discusses "one man rule," "handclasp," "strong minority," "majority rule," "consensus," and "unanimous agreement." With these options clearly in mind, any of us should be able to help the groups with which we are working to make decisions. It might be useful to try to think of examples in which each decision-making approach would be optimal.

WILLIAM J. UNDERWOOD

GROUP DECISION-MAKING

Anytime two or more people collaborate they make decisions. Many of these decisions are so minute and occur so rapidly that they are not consciously perceived as decisions. An example is the decision of who will talk in what order. Another is how long to talk about something, and still another is how to change a subject. Ordinarily we think of decisions as focused and explicit choices among alternatives. Regardless of whether the decisions are subtle or obvious, some method must be used. In group work certain methods have been identified as being typical. This essay will describe several typical methods and suggest some criteria by which decision methods may be evaluated.

ONE MAN RULE

In a traditional classroom the teacher makes decisions about homework assignments, examinations, and grades. In

This article is published for the first time in this book. Copyright © 1976 by William J. Underwood.

groups with appointed leaders, the leader may unilaterally decide when to meet, what to discuss, and when to quit. These are clear examples of the one man rule method of making decisions.

The one man rule can be used in cases other than by appointed leaders. Any particularly influential member may state a proposal which is acted upon without further consideration. An example can be drawn from a typical occurrence at the beginning of a T-group. An individual may say, "I think we should all introduce ourselves. My name is John Jones." He then looks to the person on his left who introduces himself and introductions proceed around the circle, action being taken on one man's decision. It is not infrequent in participative groups that individuals holding considerable power influence the course of events rather unilaterally.

It should be pointed out here that in the study of decision-making in groups a question is often raised as to whether such a thing as a one man rule in fact exists. The argument goes that when members fail to object to a proposal and then act on it, they have by their actions shared in the making of the decision. This argument is based on two false assumptions. One is that silence means consent. The fallacy is that silence may not mean consent at all. It may represent fear, caution, shyness, confusion, uncertainty, or resistance. The second assump-

tion concerns action and states that if people act in accord with the decision, they must agree with it. But, as with silence, people may act on a decision for different reasons than agreement. They may act reflexively without thinking, they may act to demonstrate that the decision is a poor one, and they may act because at the moment they can't think of anything else to do. Given such a variety of possibilities, it is a gross exaggeration to assume only consent from either silence or actions.

HANDCLASP

In this method the decision is made for the group by two people. It is a verbal handclasp and works like this:

Member A: I think each of us ought to say what he has learned from the group so far.
Member B: Say, that's a good idea. I'll start if it's O.K. with you.
Member A: Sure, go ahead.
Member B: O.K., then we'll all take turns.

A more sophisticated version is where two members have engaged in a lengthy argument about something the group might do. After a while one of the arguers says, "You know, I'm beginning to see your point. I'm ready to try it your way. Let's do it." Often, the remainder of the group who have been silent will immediately fall into action. Sometimes another member will voice an objection or suggest another alternative. He is

usually quieted by both the handclaspers saying pointedly, "Look, we've already hashed this to death, let's go on with it."

STRONG MINORITY

Often a few members who are more vocal in the group than others will consider among themselves a course of action and reach a decision about it. They will then initiate the action expecting others to follow suit. An objection at this point by another is likely to be attacked along the lines of, "If you had something to say, why didn't you say it during our discussion?" They conveniently overlook the fact that during their discussion it may have been quite difficult for a less verbal member to intrude.

MAJORITY RULE

The majority rule method is so much ingrained in our social custom that it is often regarded as *the* best decision-making method. Its operation is quite well understood and it is equated with democratic principles. Critical examination of the majority rule method can, however, reveal rather serious shortcomings. Some of these warrant discussion.

1. It is often used as a means of curtailing discussions. If a proposal is advanced and a majority is immediately available, the decision is sometimes made with little or no consideration of alternatives. If a majority is not

immediate, discussion often proceeds only to the point where a majority is available.

2. It can limit the forecasting of consequences. There often is an implicit assumption that the fact of majority agreement itself represents sufficient validity. This notion is exemplified by the adage, "Ten million Frenchmen can't be wrong."

3. It equates resources with numbers: The procedure does not allow for the possibility that the best resources for the decision at hand may reside in only one person or in the minority.

4. It makes the assumption that the losing minority will accept the decision made. This assumption is based on a notion of fair play: that a loser should be a good sport. It is a psychological fallacy that the simple fact of a majority decision is sufficient to undo minority feelings of opposition. Studies of past decision commitment have vividly demonstrated that it is only the majority that are really committed to a majority rule decision.

5. It's the majority, not the minority, who prefer the majority rule method. One simply never hears a person who perceives himself to be in the minority call for a majority rule vote.

CONSENSUS

Consensus as a decision method lies somewhere between majority rule and unanimous agreement. It avoids the limitations of majority rule and doesn't require the extent of agreement of unanimous agreement. It has a number of distinct advantages in group work and consequently has gained considerable popularity in informed group circles.

Briefly, consensus requires *approval* rather than agreement. In effect it says that it is not necessary for all members to *agree* that a particular alternative is the best choice, but it is necessary that *every* member *approve* the choice. The test of a consensus is when every member of the group can honestly and voluntarily say that he is willing to approve a particular alternative because either (1) he thinks it is the best alternative, or (2) he thinks due consideration has been given and it is now better to proceed than to debate longer. Involved in the notion of consensus are some critically important features.

1. One member is sufficient to block action. Consensus requires the approval of *every* member.

2. Member approval must be voluntary and free of coercion. This entails a serious, honest, and real decision on the part of each member. Simply "going along" with no particular involvement or going along to avoid pressure is *not* real consensus.

3. Therefore, each member must feel and act in a sense of deep responsibility.

4. Arriving at a consensus requires that

the point of view of every member be fully developed and considered.

5. It requires that members refrain from persuasion and other pressure tactics.

6. It requires that the group commit itself fully to the norm that it will take whatever time is necessary and not use time pressure as an escape.

Reviewing these features can leave an impression that achieving a true consensus must be a nearly impossible task and rather costly in terms of the time involved. It is certainly true that consensus is a more difficult method than those identified before it. But it is also true that a group having developed considerable skill can make decisions by consensus rather expeditiously. The key to consensus is interpersonal skill. The consensus procedure frees people from the use of those interpersonal behaviors which cause others to be defensive, which reduce trust, which destroy effective communication, and which generate competition. Attempting to make group decisions by true consensus is revealing of one's ineptness at interpersonal effectiveness. Consensus requires that the dignity of the individual be given maximum value; that divergent and opposing points of view be treated with sincere interest; that feelings as well as reason be included as legitimate data; that every group member be made to feel that he has been fully heard, is considered important, and is entitled to keep his honest opinion. A group operating at such a level of skill will find its members committed to the group's progress and willing to approve action.

UNANIMOUS AGREEMENT

It is obviously impossible in many instances to obtain a truly unanimous agreement. It requires that every member actually agree in his own thinking on the same course of action as every other member. In actuality there are probably rather few true unanimous agreements. Most decisions made in the name of unanimous agreement likely contain degrees of agreement including some shadings of reservation. Obviously unanimous agreement would represent the maximum of potential commitment for follow-through action.

CRITERIA FOR DECIDING ON A METHOD

It is safe to say that there is no one best method for making group decisions. One can think of contexts for each method over others. For example, an emergency such as a theater fire would hardly be the occasion for consensus or majority rule. It would probably be most effective for one man with a loud, commanding voice to simply order patrons out of the various exits.

The criteria listed below are some of the salient dimensions for considering decision methods. The list is not intended to be exhaustive.

1. *Time.* How much time is available to invent and test alternatives and to seek the nuances of members' opinions, knowledge, and feelings?
2. *Criticalness.* How critical is the decision? Whether to buy peanuts or popcorn is of a different order than whether to commit a person to prison.
3. *Commitment.* If commitment is defined as voluntary determination to follow through as decided, it becomes important to know who, or how many, need to be committed to what degree. In a decision to use nuclear weapons every one of the Joint Chiefs of Staff and the President must be fully committed. A supervisor who will carry out his own decision need not commit his subordinates.
4. *Skill.* As highlighted in the discussion of consensus, that method requires considerable interpersonal competence. Unless there is a learning objective, the method of consensus would be meaningless frustration for people with average interpersonal skills.
5. *Resources.* If one or two people have the resources and others do not, wider participative methods are pointless unless other objectives are present.

POLL VERSUS VOTE

There is a misuse of polling in groups which is unfortunate. It goes like this:

Member A: Why don't we take a poll to find out where people stand on issue X.
Group: O.K., let's do that.
Member A: Well, it looks like all but two think it's a good idea so I guess that makes our decision for us.

What Mr. *A* has done here is to call a thing by one name at one instance and then switch the concept at the next. First he asked for a poll. As he knows, a poll is a description of how things stand. People are only being asked to indicate their current opinion. But then having seen their opinions, Mr. *A* switched the concept to one of a vote — a decision-making procedure.

This happens so frequently in groups that people have become reluctant to poll unless they're really ready to vote. Polls can be used to provide very valuable information to a group. For example, by a show of hands a group can instantly see its split on any issue; by how high hands are raised, a group can measure the degree of member involvement, or influence, or any other group characteristic. It can be useful then carefully to distinguish between a poll and a vote and to prevent the Mr. *A*'s from getting away with switching concepts.

Gillespie offers an important dictum. He says, "Good group work doesn't happen by accident; it is the result of skillful teaching and sensitive observation on the part of the teacher." This article is a more practical version of many of the theoretical concepts that have been presented in the preceding readings of this chapter. Guidelines and examples of good process questions are given. Process questions allow a teacher to help student groups learn how to support individual efforts and group goals. The teacher, after careful observation, uses the process questions as a means of constructive intervention. It will probably not be difficult for you to think of examples of groups you were working in recently that could have productively used some time for answering questions like these about the group's process.

DAVID B. GILLESPIE

PROCESS QUESTIONS: WHAT THEY ARE AND HOW TO ASK GOOD ONES

"I've been putting my kids into groups, all right, but they just mess around until I

This article is published for the first time in this book. Copyright © 1976 by David B. Gillespie.

come over and tell them to get back to work." "Whenever I put my students into groups, all they do is bicker and fight over who is responsible for what, and why so-and-so is dumb and is holding them back, and wouldn't it be nice if they could just throw him out of the group. It's no wonder that I'm on the brink of giving up and going back to a straight lecture method of teaching."

These statements and many like them reflect teachers' frustrations with trying to help their students work together in small groups. Working in groups would logically seem to be a more efficient way of operating in the classroom; students could help each other learn, leaving the teacher free to answer only the most difficult questions. In fact, however, group work turns out to be a waste of time for many teachers and students. How *can* a teacher help his or her students work efficiently and cooperatively in small groups? Is it possible to help kids work well together without making them dependent on the teacher to keep an eye on them all the time?

Good group work doesn't happen by accident: it is the result of skillful teaching and sensitive observation on the part of the teacher. It is an unfortunate truth that very few of us know much about what makes the difference between groups that work well and those that are characterized by constant fighting. We usually talk vaguely about the personalities in the group, or a "good" or "bad" leader, and rarely get more specific about why any

particular group works (or doesn't work) well together. Actually, good group work is the result of the members' learning many specific skills which are different from those needed to work alone or those needed to follow directions. Yet very little is done *directly* about teaching students how to function well in a small group setting. Merely putting students together in small groups and expecting them to work well is akin to putting a city kid on a farm and expecting him to know how to take care of the animals all by himself: it doesn't have anything to do with his personality, or whether or not he happens to like animals — he simply doesn't have the experience or the skills necessary to do the job. Similarly, students in the typical classroom do not have the experience or skills to work well in groups, and until they do, there is no point in talking about whether or not they "like" to work in groups or if their personality "fits" group work.

So — how can the teacher begin to teach his or her students some of the skills necessary for good group work? One way is to make sure that the students always take a good, useful look at how they worked together at the end of any given group task. This "post mortem" of group work is usually called processing, because the group is taking a look at its process — *how* it worked — rather than looking at what it produced. Even those teachers who have had group dynamics courses and know about processing rarely seem to value it or take it seriously as a way of teaching group skills. This is probably because they haven't seen it done effectively, or felt its impact on a group that they were a member of themselves. General talk along the lines of "Well, how did we work today?" is rarely helpful. But when a group (along with the help of the teacher at first) can take a careful look at the *specifics* of what went well and what went poorly, then it is making progress. To be able to help a group do this, a teacher has to be an acute observer of what happens within the group, and be ready with the right kinds of questions to pose to the members once they have completed the task. These questions are generally referred to as "process questions." From the teacher's point of view, there are two kinds of process questions: general ones that can be anticipated, and specific ones that are raised by how a group is actually working. "What could you do differently next time?" is a question that can almost always be asked of a group after it has finished a task; and a teacher doesn't have to be in on much of the group's work to know if that would be a helpful question. "What did anybody do to get you off the track?" is a question that probably could not be anticipated, however; a teacher would have to wait and see if the group got off the track or not before asking it.

Let's suppose that a teacher's class has just finished 15 minutes of small group work, and he is pleased with how some of

it went, but he is also disturbed about how some of the students failed to cooperate. What does he say or do? What question would be most helpful for the groups to answer among themselves? Here are some guidelines.

1. A good process question is *clearly separate from the task.* Many times a very good question is asked of a group, but some of the members are still thinking about the actual work being done, and don't answer it at all. *All* the group members must understand that they are no longer trying to decide where they are going on the class trip, or putting together a project on the Civil War, or whatever. Instead, they are now talking about *how* they were deciding or putting together. This is sometimes difficult, especially if the task was an energizing one and some of the members still haven't gotten in their last word. Be on the lookout for questions like "What were you doing in this group?" This is a question that could be answered in terms of the task — for example, "Well, teacher, we were trying to decide between going to New York or to the mountains." That answer says nothing about the process of the group, yet it *is* an answer to the question. It is more helpful to ask "How did you go about deciding?", which then focuses the group on its process.

One of the ways of avoiding this problem while teaching the skill of processing is to give groups tasks that are not too important at first. Hypothetical problems or decisions for the group are more help-

ful in the beginning — that way the members will be able to let go of the task and focus on how they worked together. "If you were *Time* magazine's editors, who would you pick for man of the year?" is a better beginning task than "Where shall we go on the class trip?" As the group members become more adept at looking back at how they worked, the tasks can become more difficult and meaningful.

2. A good process question is *nonprescriptive:* it tells the group neither what it is doing right nor what it should be doing differently. "Why weren't you listening to each other?" (asked in a punitive tone) is really a statement that the group should have been listening better; it is not helping the members grapple with the issue themselves, the way a question like "How much did you feel listened to?" might. There is a big difference between the effects that prescriptive and nonprescriptive questions have on a group: the prescriptive will tend to make the group dependent on the teacher to tell them how to improve ("They just mess around until I come over and tell them to get back to work"). This leaves virtually no way for the group to learn and grow — and any growth that does occur will be the result of the teacher's pushing rather than of *active* learning on the part of the student. A nonprescriptive question is one that tests or checks out an assumption about how the group was working, instead of telling the group. For example, if a teacher sees one group member making jokes during the task, he might assume that the student's behavior was

getting in the way of the group's work, and ask a question like, "Johnny sure did slow you down with his jokes, didn't he?" and put his perception on the group. Asking a question like, "To what degree did everybody take the work seriously?" allows the group to focus on the same issue. Yet *this* question leaves room for the members to say, "Yes, Johnny's jokes were just the thing we needed then," or, "No, we sure *did* get off the track when Johnny started cracking his jokes."

3. A good process question *touches an issue (or issues) significant to the group.* Here the keen observational skills of the teacher become important. If he asks a process question that really doesn't get to the point of what was going on in the group, then it will be of little help. If one member of the group has clearly been dominating the discussion, and the teacher doesn't ask a question about the equality of participation, then he has missed an opportunity. With practice, this skill can become more subtle. For example, it may be that a group has had a hard time listening to each other, and has been working on the issue. Then along comes a session when they listen well. Is the issue of listening no longer significant? Just the opposite. Now is the time for the group to look very closely at what it is that they did that helped them to listen better than before, so that they can build on that learning, and not let the skill be lost, just when it is within their grasp. In a situation like this, a teacher would need to have at least two process questions ready: "How well

did you listen to each other today?" and then, if the answer shows that they in fact *did* listen better (checking out the teacher's assumption), the next question would be "What did anybody do to help you listen better?"

4. A good process question is *evocative — that is, it generates usable data.* If a question is asked in such a way that it gives *all* the members an equal chance to answer, then more information is made public for the group to consider. For example, in the paragraph above, the question "How well did you listen today?" could be answered by the bully in the group (who hadn't been listening to anybody but himself) with "Yeah, we listened just fine," and that would be the end of it. Changing the question to "On a scale from one to ten, how well did you listen to each other?" directly involves each group member, and has them share their perceptions, which may be very different from those of the rest of the group. It is then the group's responsibility to deal with any discrepancies among the various members' perceptions that may have been brought out by the question. (Think of the effect on the group if the bully rates the group's listening at 8 or 9 and all the other members at 2 or 3.) Data that is elicited by a process question is usually more usable by the group if it is specific rather than general. So, looking at the example in the paragraph above, "Why did you listen well?" is less likely to be helpful than "What did anybody do to help you listen better?" because it does not push for spe-

cific answers. An answer to "Why did you listen well today?" could be something like, "Well, we seemed to be more relaxed." This answer suggests little that the group could do to repeat the success. On the other hand, "What did anybody do to help you listen better?" encourages answers like, "Bill asked me to repeat what I said when others were talking." An answer like that will then validate Bill's helpful behavior, and he now knows *specifically* what he did to help the group work better together (which means, of course, he knows something he can do *again* to help the group work better).

5. A good process question *stresses a balance between positive and negative.* If all a group talks about in processing its own behavior is how badly it did, then chances are that the members will soon weary of the exercise, since no one likes to punish himself over and over. Conversely, if the group spends all its time patting itself on the back, chances are the members are avoiding some issues that are hindering their work. There should be the expectation that whenever a group takes a look back at its own behavior, both good and bad will be discussed. "What is one positive and one negative adjective that would describe how your group worked today?" is a question that sets a tone of looking at both sides of the issue right away. This is important because a group can get in a rut of punishing each other after an activity or, on the other side, making a pact of polite-

ness, where "I won't knock you if you won't knock me."

If a teacher tries to keep these guidelines in mind when asking process questions, his class will be more likely to make improvements in how they work in groups — consciously, and, it is hoped, on their own. Helping a group improve rarely means giving suggestions or orders; they will simply have to come back to the teacher for the next suggestion or wait for the next order. None of this will work, of course, if it is done on an infrequent or ir-regular basis. A group has to be in the habit of processing its work so that it can easily deal with both the positive and neg-ative behaviors of its members whenever they come up. It is punitive to wait for the worst meeting in a while to ask a process question; dealing with the poor examples of working together is the most difficult, and people just do not build the skills necessary while trying to solve the most difficult cases. Besides all else, good processing depends on the group mem-bers' trusting of each other enough to be able to say what really was going on, and that trust will not be built in one or two sessions. Perhaps the best way to build trust is through processing especially good sessions; this gives group members the opportunity to recognize each other's strengths while learning the skill of pro-cessing at the same time.

The longer a group *regularly* takes a look at how it works, the more skilled it will become at understanding the prob-lems it is having and doing something about them. This means that ultimately members should be able to see what is go-ing on within the group, and ask helpful process questions themselves, without de-pending on an outside observer. At this point, the group can learn and grow on its own.

NONVERBAL PICTURE DRAWING

Group activities are often analyzed by the verbal interaction that takes place. However, there are pictorial ways to show the group's dynamics. The following activity will allow you to examine just such interaction. It is easy to use this activity with elementary and secondary students.

Procedure

1. Divide into groups of three to six members. You will need different color crayons or felt tip pens and a large sheet of paper. Each person selects a different color to use in this activity. There should be no talking while planning and doing the drawing. The object of the activity is to draw a picture of something as a group.

2. Examine the picture and discuss the following questions:

a. What can you see in the picture that tells you something about the way you worked? For example, is there any evidence you were competitive? disorganized? controlled?

b. Which color is seen most often? Who dominated the picture drawing?

c. What happened when you wanted to draw one thing and the others in your group wanted something else?

d. Did you achieve your goal?

e. What were some helpful things that happened in the group? Not helpful?

f. If you did a different picture, what would you like to see?

3. Display the pictures drawn by all the groups. Discuss the similarities and differences in group style reflected in the drawings. (For example, some groups may have worked in a very unified way, whereas other groups may have allowed for individual expression.)

4. Imagine that these drawings were done by different groups in an elementary or secondary class. Which group would you prefer as a teacher?

GETTING INTO GROUPS

The most difficult time in the life of a group is often its beginning. People are anxious. They do not know how to act and react. What is their role? What are the norms? Whom can they trust? The following exercises are designed to "break the ice" in a group. Read them and try a few in small or large groups. Use them with your students.

the inner circle should move clockwise so that each person advances to the next person on his right in the outer circle. For the next two minute period, talk about a good movie you saw recently. Continue to rotate in this manner every two minutes and change the topic of discussion according to the following list:

— God
— your most cherished possession
— a favorite hobby
— your childhood
— recurring dreams
— your worst teacher
— open classrooms

3. Write down on a sheet of notebook size paper (8½ × 11 inches) a list of your personal strengths and skills (for example, "I'm a caring person" or "I'm good with my hands"). Pin or tape the paper to you as you would a name tag and mill around the room as if you were at a cocktail party. Meet other people and read their personal descriptions.

4. Gather together a lot of newspaper and tape. As a group, build a tower as high as you can. Then, build a train as long as you can.

5. Form a circle, hold hands, *but* make one break in the chain of people. One of the two people who has a free hand should be designated the leader. He or she should start walking under or stepping over any clasped hands in sight. Each person in the line should follow. The leader

Procedure

1. Stand in a circle. Choose one person to go to the middle of the circle. Everyone in the circle should find out the name of the person to his immediate right and left. The person in the middle should point to someone in the circle and say either "right, bumpity, bump, bump, bump" or "left, bumpity, bump, bump, bump." The person pointed to must say the name of the person on his right or left before the "bumpity, bump, bump, bump" is com-

pletely uttered. If he fails to do so, he goes into the center and the first person in the center takes his place in the circle. Before resuming, the person who is joining the circle should find out the names of the people to his immediate right and left. Repeat this process till most people get a chance to be in the center.

2. Form an inner and outer circle with the same number of people in each circle. For two minutes, exchange with the person opposite you your views on what makes a good teacher. When two minutes are up,

should weave in and out of the group in a snake-like fashion so that the entire group becomes a twisted human pretzel. Look for every opportunity to increase the twists in the pretzel. Then unravel yourselves without letting go of each other's hands.

GROUND RULES FOR GROUP DISCUSSION

Group discussion is often unproductive and unsatisfying. Participation is not widespread. Some group members are too wordy. People interrupt. The group strays off the topic. No one really listens to what people are saying. The ground rules below are helpful in alleviating these problems. Following them may feel awkward at first, but if a group sticks with them, they should work.

Procedure

Conduct a discussion on a controversial topic or a matter of importance to your group. Try, at different times, to incorporate as many of the procedures as you can from the list below. When you are finished, discuss which ground rules were helpful and why. Which ones would help younger students?

— Strictly limit each person's contribution to 15 seconds.
— Require people to wait three seconds to speak after one person has finished.
— Allow no person to speak until he or she has accurately paraphrased the contribution of the preceding person.
— Allow no one to speak a second time until everyone in the group has spoken once.

— When a person finishes speaking, make sure he or she finds out who wants to speak next and selects one of those people to continue the discussion.
— Appoint an observer whose function is to interrupt the group discussion whenever he or she feels people are not listening or straying off the topic.
— Appoint a monitor whose job is to summarize the group discussion every ten minutes.

ROLES
PEOPLE
PLAY

Each individual in a group assumes different roles in problem situations. The following activity will ask you to involve yourself in a task and to be aware of the various roles that people play while accomplishing the job.

Procedure

1. Each of the attributes listed here may or may not be important in your estimation of an effective teacher. Rank the entries in terms of their importance as you see them. Begin by putting a 1 by the adjective that you think is most important for the teacher.*

* When using this activity with younger students, substitute a task involving decision-making that is appropriate to their age group.

_____ knowledgeable   _____ critical
_____ humorous   _____ cautious
_____ adventuresome   _____ insightful
_____ tough   _____ creative
_____ even-tempered   _____ empathetic
_____ compassionate   _____ strong
_____ energetic   _____ facilitative
_____ curious   _____ assertive
_____ tactful   _____ loving
_____ expressive   _____ challenging

2. After each person has completed ranking, form groups of six to eight members. Each group will decide which are the three most important and the three least important attributes of a good teacher. There is one stipulation. You are to make decisions by consensus only. This means that each attribute must be agreed on by each group member before it becomes a part of the group decision. Consensus is difficult to reach. Not every choice will meet with everyone's complete approval. Try, as a group, to make each choice one with which all group members can at least partially agree. Here are some guidelines to use in reaching consensus:

a. Avoid changing your mind only in order to reach agreement and avoid conflict. Support only solutions with which you are able to agree somewhat, at least.
b. Avoid "conflict-reducing" techniques. Do not use majority vote, averaging, or trading in reaching decisions.
c. View differences of opinion as helpful rather than as a hindrance in decision-making.

Place your final choices on a separate sheet of paper. You have 30 minutes in which to reach your decision.

3. Now, the focus of this activity will shift from a group task to a processing of your group's experience. There are many ways to take a look at how your group functioned during the consensus task. We think it would be useful to examine the role people played according to the table on p. 222 of Hunter's article, "Improving Group Productivity." In the space at the top of the chart on this page, write in each person's name in your group including your own.* Now think back over the consensus task and check (✓) under each person's name the roles that person played in this time period. You may check many roles for each person. When everyone has finished, compare your results.

Processing questions

a. Who was the most influential member of your group? What roles did this person play? Who was least influential?
b. How was leadership determined? Who wrote the final choices?
c. How did you like the role you played in this task? How is it similar or different from the roles you play in other tasks or groups?

* Substitute the chart on page 224 when doing this activity with younger children.

Names	1	2	3...
Initiating			
Informing			
Clarifying			
Summarizing			
Consensus testing			
Harmonizing			
Gate Keeping			
Encouraging			
Compromising			
Giving feedback			
Aggressing			
Blocking			
Dominating			
Avoiding			
Abandoning			

DEFENSIVE
AND
SUPPORTIVE
CLIMATES

We seldom like to be in groups that make us feel defensive. It's a tremendous relief to be with people who support us and let us be ourselves rather than force us to hide behind masks. The following activity will allow you to experience the differences in being a part of supportive and defensive situations.

Procedure

1. Read the table in "Defensive Communication" by Jack R. Gibb (pages 227–231). Notice how defensive behaviors are pitted against their supportive counterparts.

2. Study the article carefully to understand what each of these terms means to the author. Then, form groups of six to eight participants. Role play as many of the following situations as you can. Appoint one or two group members to observe for each role-playing situation. These observers should report which of the defensive and supportive behaviors from the above table they observed in the group role playing. If possible, replay each situation with the goal of increasing supportive behaviors.

Situation 1. A fifth-grade teacher is asking his or her class to suggest what can be done about food being thrown in the lunchroom.

Situation 2. A high school physical education department chairperson is conducting a meeting of the department faculty concerning the inclusion of sex education in the curriculum.

Situation 3. A college student association is holding a meeting for the purpose of adopting a position on a credit/no credit grading system versus a traditional system.

3. If time permits, discuss how the idea of a defensive and supportive group climate can be explained and demonstrated to elementary or secondary students.

DIAGNOSING
CLASSROOM
NORMS

A norm is a shared feeling in a group about the ways members should behave or feel. Norms can be explicit or implicit. In other words, they can be openly stated in the group or they may be adhered to even though no one ever publicly agreed to them. It is often helpful for students to discuss openly and to clarify the norms operating in a classroom. By doing this, they can reflect on how people are expected to behave and they can make desirable changes or additions if needed. The following is a partial list of group norms identified by an undergraduate class:

1. Class starts ten minutes late.
2. It is O.K. to share personal feelings.
3. Decisions are made without checking out how everyone in the group feels.
4. No one is responsible for doing assigned readings.
5. Any colorful and expressive language is acceptable.

Class discussion of these norms resulted in agreement to change some of the behavior patterns that created difficulty for a few members of the class. Instructions to diagnose the norms in your learning group follow.

Procedure

This activity should be done with an ongoing group. It can easily be modified for elementary and secondary classrooms.

1. Begin by writing down formal and informal norms you, as an individual, think operate in your group.

OUR CLASS NORMS

1. Class starts ten minutes late.
2. It is o.k. to share personal feelings.
3. Decisions are made without checking out how everyone in the group feels.
4. No one is responsible for doing assigned readings.
5. Any colorful and expressive language is acceptable.

2. Share your responses with others in a small group and make a chart together which represents the consensus of your group as to the norms which exist.

3. Get together with other small groups and combine your charts into one, using a large sheet of paper.

4. Identify the norms which are a help and a hindrance to your group. (This activity can be repeated weekly; if desired, by making additions and deletions to the large chart and discussing plans to change some of the norms).

Processing questions

a. Was there a lot of disagreement about the norms in your group? If so, why?
b. What was the feeling tone in your group as you discussed the results of the activity?
c. What criteria were used to decide which norms were helpful and not helpful?
d. Has your level of commitment to your group changed any?

additional resources

BOOKS AND ARTICLES

Backman, Carl, and Secord, Paul. *A Social Psychological View of Education*. New York: Harcourt, Brace and World, 1968.

Bany, Mary, and Johnson, Lois V. *Classroom Group Behavior*. New York: Macmillan, 1964.

Cartwright, Dorwin, and Zander, Alvin. *Group Dynamics*. New York: Harper and Row, 1969.

Chesler, Mark, and Fox, Robert. *Role Playing Methods in the Classroom*. Chicago: Science Research Associates, 1966.

Fox, Robert; Luszki, Margaret B.; and Schmuck, Richard. *Diagnosing Classroom Learning Environments*. Chicago: Science Research Associates, 1966.

Hawkes, Thomas H. "Grouping." In *Teacher's Handbook,* edited by Dwight Allen and Eli Seifman. Chicago: Science Research Associates, 1971.

Henry, N., ed. *The Dynamics of Instructional Groups*. Chicago: National Society for the Study of Education. 59th Yearbook, part 2, 1960.

Hunter, Elizabeth. *Encounter in the Classroom*. New York: Holt, Rinehart and Winston, 1972.

Institute for Development of Educational Activities, Inc. *Learning in the Small Group*. Suite 950, 1100 Glendon Avenue, Los Angeles, CA 90024, 1971.

Johnson, David. *The Social Psychology of Education*. New York: Holt, Rinehart and Winston, 1970.

Johnson, David W., and Johnson, Roger T. *Learning Together and Alone: Cooperation, Competition and Individualization*. Englewood Cliffs, N.J.: Prentice-Hall, 1975.

Luft, Joseph. *Group Processes: An Introduction to Group Dynamics*. Palo Alto, Calif.: National Press Books, 1970.

Miles, Matthew B. *Learning to Work in Groups*. New York: Teachers College Press, Columbia University, 1959.

Napier, Rodney W., and Gershenfeld, Matti K. *Groups: Theory and Experience*. Boston: Houghton Mifflin Co., 1973.

Northwest Regional Educational Laboratory. *Interpersonal Communications*. Tuxedo, Park, N.Y.: Xicom, 1969.

Pfeiffer, J. William, and Jones, John E. *A Handbook of Structured Experiences For Human Relations Training*. Vols. 1–3. Iowa City: Iowa University Associates Press, 1970.

Schmuck, Richard A. "Helping Teachers Improve Classroom Group Processes." *Journal of Applied Behavioral Science* 4, no. 4 (1968); 401–35.

Schmuck, Richard A.; Chesler, Mark; and Lippitt, Ronald. *Problem Solving to Improve Classroom Learning*. Chicago: Science Research Associates, 1966.

Schmuck, Richard A., and Miles, Matthew. *Organization Development in Schools*. Palo Alto, Calif.: National Press Books, 1971.

Schmuck, Richard A., and Schmuck, Patricia A. *Group Processes in the Classroom*. (2nd ed.) Dubuque, Iowa: Wm. C. Brown, 1975.

Schmuck, Richard A., and Schmuck, Patricia A. *A Humanistic Psychology of Education: *Making the School Everybody's House*. Palo Alto, Calif.: National Press Books, 1974.

Stanford, Gene, and Dodds, Barbara. *Learning Discussion Skills Through Games*. New York: Citation Press, 1969.

Thelen, Herbert A. *Dynamics of Groups at Work*. Chicago: University of Chicago Press, 1954.

FILMS

A Circle of Love. Contemporary Films, 330 West 42nd Street, New York, NY 10036.

Narrated by Walter Cronkite, this film focuses on the processes taking place in a small group.

Carl Rogers: On Facilitating a Group. American Personnel and Guidance Association Film Sales, 1607 New Hampshire Avenue, N.W., Washington, DC. Rogers discusses the factors he feels are important in facilitating a group. A segment of a group conducted by Rogers is included.

I Dare You. National Instructional Television, 1111 West 17th Street, Bloomington, IN 47401. Depicts kids daring a girl to do something dangerous in order to join their group.

The Beginning. Stephen Bosustow Productions, 1649 11th Street, Santa Monica, CA 90404. Animated film dealing with group pressures on individual behavior.

chapter
five

---

creating
freedom
and
limits

initial experiences

TEACHERS' NEEDS AND VALUES

A large part of developing a personal approach to freedom in the classroom is becoming aware of your own needs and values. Merely assuming that you prefer freedom in your classroom may lead to confusion and indecision. The following initial activity may sharpen your understanding and raise questions about yourself in relation to freedom in the classroom.

1. Assume that you have told your students that there will be a 45-minute period every day with a large degree of choice. At that time, they will be free to select learning activities throughout your classroom and a wide variety of materials with which to work. The students seem enthusiastic and willing to undertake this "experiment" in freedom. As the days go on, however, you're aware that most of your students relate to this "choice time" in a mindless way. Quite a few of the students wander aimlessly around the room. Others stay almost exclusively with one activity. The remainder seem to choose activities at random and flit from one to the other. Yet, to your amazement, few students are complaining. Many even tell you that they haven't had as much fun in school before. Whenever you suggest that rules and boundaries be set up for this time period, they resist like mad. They feel you are not giving the experiment a chance.

We would like you to explore your feelings about what is happening in your classroom. Avoid any action ideas. Instead, ask yourself these questions: How satisfied or dissatisfied do you feel about the present state of affairs? What do you really wish had happened in your class during this experiment in freedom? How do you feel about your students now? If you are uncomfortable about their behavior, what "freedoms" would you be willing to remove to get the class functioning the way you want it to be? Write down your responses to these questions.

2. Compare your personal reflections with others', if you wish. Out of this process, clarify your own values and needs and identify questions you still face. A good way of sharing this information is to sit in a circle with others and share your completions to the following stems:

— I learned today that I . . .
— I feel that . . .
— I wonder whether . . .

CONFLICT CLINIC

Sometimes, we might wish as teachers that some magical specialist would come into our class and solve our problems. A clinic for solving conflicts that arise with students could be very helpful. Actually, there are many new approaches for dealing with the problems of discipline (some aspects of them are presented in the readings in this chapter). These approaches are helpful because they are all based on concepts other than the use of arbitrary authority. They tend to promote a dialogue between the teacher and the students. Even though good teaching assumes the development of common goals between teachers and students, conflicts can still arise. Teachers need positive approaches to deal with these conflicts. The following tasks are meant to help you begin to think about what these approaches might be like.

1. Divide into two groups. (If you are part of a fairly large class, create four groups, but have two groups paired with each other.) In each group, identify a tough classroom problem, related to the behavior of children and adolescents, to present to the other group. The problem can come from someone's experience as a teacher or as a student. Enough detail should be included to help the other group really believe that this is a problem anyone might face, today or tomorrow, in his or her own classroom. If possible, the presentation should be in the present tense. For example, "John is walking into the room. He is twenty minutes late. He says, 'Did anyone see my lunch?'. . ." You might consider acting out the situation for the other group.

2. After each group presents its problem to the other, reconvene your own group and assume that you are specialists from a "conflict clinic" asked to help the other group with its problem. Brainstorm, invent, come up with a creative solution to the problem posed by the other group. Meet together again and exchange solutions. If time permits, try to role play the situation and act out the solution. End the activity by discussing and evaluating the solutions generated.

introduction

No doubt we've pushed (and the readings in this book stressed) the importance of freedom as a condition for real learning. Freedom in learning comes from nurturing the potential of each individual. It gives the learner open-ended possibilities. And freedom means that the student doesn't have to suppress his or her own feelings, or have a teacher around all the time. But now we need to consider more carefully the conflicts that can arise between teachers and students (and between students themselves). Teachers who offer freedom to students should be aware that their personal goals may not be accomplished and even that chaos might result. Students might not necessarily study and learn subjects that give the teacher a sense of accomplishment. In the extreme, it is possible for students to be intentionally mean and destructive. Whenever people interact, one person's freedom can create another person's limits.

In general, the only way in which freedom can be increased in the classroom is to balance all the priorities that are involved. It is highly probable, otherwise, that a radical increase of one sort of freedom will sharply delimit other freedoms. Students and teachers operating without boundaries and structures to guide their interaction can become absurd. For real learning to occur, new kinds of freedom for classrooms and new ways for teachers and students to work together are needed.

What is often missed in the formula for freedom in a classroom is careful consideration of the teacher's values. We've been justifiably concerned with students' needs, but what about the teacher's? What are the conditions that allow for satisfying and creative teaching? How can a *teacher* be free? As important as it is for students to find their place in the learning environment, it is equally important for all teachers. Teachers must make conscious efforts to know what kinds and how much of their personal needs will be gratified. The ways in which leadership will be exercised must also be determined.

In our opinion, the limits that create freedom for everyone in a learning situation must initially be developed on the basis of the teacher's authority. Authority is involved whenever a teacher decides on a body of information or skills that students will study. Authority is also basic to any judgments by the teacher about unacceptable behavior in the classroom. A teacher who wants a democratic classroom may not need absolute authority to control behavior. However, such an approach to teaching does not negate basic responsibilities for determining the limits within which the focus of any learning activity can be called relevant and within which student-to-student and student-to-teacher behavior can be called appropriate. From this point of view, limits are the action side of freedom. A teacher who simply discards his or her accustomed authority will create freedom without direction and will find no place to express his or her own uniqueness as a human being.

What are the conditions of meaningful freedom? One of the conditions mainly involves goals. As a teacher begins to teach a class, a course, or a topic, there is a need for the teacher and the students to explore their goals together. This exploration, with give and take, can lead to the development of common goals. But using only talk can be disastrous. There is also a need for activities that encourage interaction between the teacher and the students, the students with each other, and the students with the subject matter. It is not helpful to suggest a "do what you want" attitude. Freedom in that sense can sometimes be more limiting than no freedom at all — as evidenced by the joke about an early version of a progressive class, in which a child says, "Teacher, do I have to do what I want today?" A teacher, through discussion and open-ended initial activities, can create a real sense of freedom wherein exciting possibilities for learning can be seen by everyone.

A second important condition mainly involves expectations. These are not expectations in the future sense, like goals; rather, they are concerned with moment-to-moment functioning and interacting. Expectations are relevant to how students learn as well as how they relate to the teacher and each other. They are essentially a combined statement of a teacher's minimum and maximum needs for helping students learn productively. Their implications for the student should sound something like this: "All you have to do is meet these expectations and everything else will take care of itself"; and "If you don't meet these expectations, you are breaking one of the very few rules that have been made for this class." We have often started our college course with the following three expectations: (1) students will miss very few classes; (2) students will take turns outside of class time to help plan class activities; and (3) students will read what they assign themselves in small groups. Students who meet these three expectations rarely come into a serious conflict of needs with other aspects of the course. Expectations such as these, when met, tend to promote such a positive interaction between students, the teacher, and the subject matter that whatever direction a student's personal inquiry takes, it is less likely to be in conflict with the needs of others.

A discussion of the conditions of meaningful freedom, to be complete, also requires us to consider how reasonable limits can be enforced. In the traditional classroom, it is often assumed that students will naturally want to go beyond the limits that have been set. This assumption can be replaced by the notion that people, children as well as adults, would prefer not to be in conflict with other people. If a teacher starts out with more mutual understanding than traditionally exists, he or she can use seemingly weak ways of enforcing limits, with success.

A teacher can begin by making his or her resentments clear. Something is going on that is annoying, the teacher says so, and the something stops. When students are concerned with the teacher's needs, and when the "something" isn't critical to their needs, a teacher's resentments can be enough to effect a change. Similarly, a teacher can go further by making his or her demands clear. Gestalt therapy has shown that people are most likely to cooperate when they meet with clear demands. Interestingly, the demands don't have to come from someone who has authority. Apparently, most people, including children, are interested in meeting needs of others when doing so doesn't involve a whole lot of moralizing, "shoulds," or guilt.

Stronger ways of enforcing limits include heavy bargaining and the use of real power. Bargaining (like stating resentments or demands) may not seem to be an effective means of expressing authority, but it is very effective when connected with stopping "business as usual." When a teacher feels that the activity of a classroom is far outside reasonable limits, discontinuing regular class activities until new agreements have been made is important. As part of the bargaining process or as part of a strategy for improving human relations, the teacher has to withhold doing regular activities until an adequate reciprocal relationship is developed. The teacher's ultimate power involves judging whether or not someone may continue to be part of a class group. This is a minor decision when it only involves a particular learning activity, but it is an awesome one when it involves something like requiring a student to change schools. There are times, in any kind of classroom, when the disruptive behavior of even one child can make the positive efforts and work of everyone else meaningless.

These, then, are some of the means for enforcing limits. The advantage of using them is that they tend to build positive relationships. Consequently, the better the relationship between teacher and students, the less need there will be to use the stronger means. In this way, a positive cycle is started. When teachers begin to view students as cooperative spirits involved in a common venture, the students will also begin to view themselves in this way. Their behavior will then support the teacher's initial view.

In this chapter, some of the readings delve more deeply into the concept of freedom, others into the concept of limits, and some into the intersection of the two concepts. Some are theoretical and some are practical. The readings and the exercises are intended to help you develop personally relevant ways of creating new kinds of freedom and limits for the students you will teach.

readings

After you have read this excerpt from **Experience and Education**, you may find it hard to believe that there have been so many mistaken notions of open education. Dewey made it very clear, back in 1938, that freedom in education does not mean "conduct dictated by immediate whim and caprice." Freedom, as a means to an end, refers to increasing alternatives for observation, judgment, framing purposes, evaluating desires, etc. Freedom of physical movement is also considered important because it is the way in which the teacher can gain knowledge of individual students and because it is part of natural learning processes. Dewey emphasizes, though, that freedom must not be treated as an end in itself. You will see in the readings that follow how this recurring issue must be continually resolved for every kind of problem that develops.

JOHN DEWEY

THE NATURE OF FREEDOM

At the risk of repeating what has been often said by me I want to say something

From *Experience and Education* by John Dewey (New York: Macmillan, 1963). Copyright, 1938 by Kappa Delta Pi, an honor society in education. Reprinted with permission.

about the other side of the problem of social control, namely, the nature of freedom. The only freedom that is of enduring importance is freedom of intelligence, that is to say, freedom of observation and of judgment exercised in behalf of purposes that are intrinsically worth while. The commonest mistake made about freedom is, I think, to identify with freedom of movement, or with the external or physical side of activity. Now, this external and physical side of activity cannot be separated from the internal side of activity; from freedom of thought, desire, and purpose. The limitation that was put upon outward action by the fixed arrangements of the typical traditional schoolroom, with its fixed rows of desks and its military regimen of pupils who were permitted to move only at certain fixed signals, put a great restriction upon intellectual and moral freedom. Strait-jacket and chain-gang procedures had to be done away with if there was to be a chance for growth of individuals in the intellectual springs of freedom without which there is no assurance of genuine and continued normal growth.

But the fact still remains that an increased measure of freedom of outer movement is a *means*, not an end. The educational problem is not solved when this aspect of freedom is obtained. Everything then depends, so far as education is concerned, upon what is done with this added liberty. What end does it serve? What consequences flow from it? Let me speak first of the advantages which reside potentially in increase of outward freedom. In the first place, without its existence it is practically impossible for a teacher to gain knowledge of the individuals with whom he is concerned. Enforced quiet and acquiescence prevent pupils from disclosing their real natures. They enforce artificial uniformity. They put seeming before being. They place a premium upon preserving the outward appearance of attention, decorum, and obedience. And everyone who is acquainted with schools in which this system prevailed well knows that thoughts, imaginations, desires, and sly activities ran their own unchecked course behind this façade. They were disclosed to the teacher only when some untoward act led to their detection. One has only to contrast this highly artificial situation with normal human relations outside the schoolroom, say in a well-conducted home, to appreciate how fatal it is to the teacher's acquaintance with and understanding of the individuals who are, supposedly, being educated. Yet without this insight there is only an accidental chance that the material of study and the methods used in instruction will so come home to an individual that his development of mind and character is actually directed. There is a vicious circle. Mechanical uniformity of studies and methods creates a kind of uniform immobility and this reacts to perpetuate uniformity of studies and of recitations, while behind this enforced uniformity individual tendencies operate in irregular and more or less forbidden ways.

The other important advantage of increased outward freedom is found in the very nature of the learning process. That the older methods set a premium upon passivity and receptivity has been pointed out. Physical quiescence puts a tremendous premium upon these traits. The only escape from them in the standardized school is an activity which is irregular and perhaps disobedient. There cannot be complete quietude in a laboratory or workshop. The nonsocial character of the traditional school is seen in the fact that it erected silence into one of its prime virtues. There is, of course, such a thing as intense intellectual activity without overt bodily activity. But capacity for such intellectual activity marks a comparatively late achievement when it is continued for a long period. There should be brief intervals of time for quiet reflection provided for even the young. But they are periods of genuine reflection only when they follow after times of more overt action and are used to organize what has been gained in periods of activity in which the hands and other parts of the body beside the brain are used. Freedom of movement is also important as a means of maintaining normal physical and mental health. We have still to learn from the example of the Greeks who saw clearly the relation between a sound body and a sound mind. But in all the respects mentioned freedom of outward action is a means to freedom of judgment and of power to carry deliberately chosen ends into execution. The amount of external freedom which is

needed varies from individual to individual. It naturally tends to decrease with increasing maturity, though its complete absence prevents even a mature individual from having the contacts which will provide him with new materials upon which his intelligence may exercise itself. The amount and the quality of this kind of free activity as a means of growth is a problem that must engage the thought of the educator at every stage of development.

There can be no greater mistake, however, than to treat such freedom as an end in itself. It then tends to be destructive of the shared cooperative activities which are the normal source of order. But, on the other hand, it turns freedom which should be positive into something negative. For freedom from restrictions, the negative side, is to be prized only as a means to a freedom which is power: power to frame purposes, to judge wisely, to evaluate desires by the consequences which will result from acting upon them; power to select and order means to carry chosen ends into operation.

Natural impulses and desires constitute in any case the starting point. But there is no intellectual growth without some reconstruction, some remaking, of impulses and desires in the form in which they first show themselves. This remaking involves inhibition of impulse in its first estate. The alternative to externally imposed inhibition is inhibition through an individual's own reflection and judgment.

The old phrase "stop and think" is sound psychology. For thinking is stoppage of the immediate manifestation of impulse until that impulse has been brought into connection with other possible tendencies to action so that a more comprehensive and coherent plan of activity is formed. Some of the other tendencies to action lead to use of eye, ear, and hand to observe objective conditions; others result in recall of what has happened in the past. Thinking is thus a postponement of immediate action, while it effects internal control of impulse through a union of observation and memory, this union being the heart of reflection. What has been said explains the meaning of the well-worn phrase "self-control." The ideal aim of education is creation of power of self-control. But the mere removal of external control is no guarantee for the production of self-control. It is easy to jump out of the frying-pan into the fire. It is easy, in other words, to escape one form of external control only to find oneself in another and more dangerous form of external control. Impulses and desires that are not ordered by intelligence are under the control of accidental circumstances. It may be a loss rather than a gain to escape from the control of another person only to find one's conduct dictated by immediate whim and caprice; that is, at the mercy of impulses into whose formation intelligent judgment has not entered. A person whose conduct is controlled in this way has at most

only the illusion of freedom. Actually he is directed by forces over which he has no command.

As if he were directly responding to Dewey's demands, Holt shows how the distinction between a structured and an unstructured educational environment is meaningless. All human interaction is guided by structure — different kinds of structure. In the traditional classroom, there are few choices, and the overall environment is "inflexible, rigid, and static." It is a relatively simple structure. An open classroom by comparison, says Holt, is complicated, but the structure is flexible and dynamic. The point of any structure is to help you get things done. He supports his argument by showing how the functioning of a free society and a free class are similar. The excerpt can be used as a theoretical point of reference for the more practical readings that follow.

JOHN HOLT

EXCERPTS FROM
FREEDOM
AND BEYOND

One group of words, that twist and hide truth and understanding, is "structured — unstructured." Almost everyone who talks or writes about learning situations that are open, free, noncoercive, learner-directed, calls these situations "unstructured," and their traditional authoritarian, coercive, teacher-directed opposites "structured." People who support open learning use these words in this way as much as people who oppose it. It is a serious error. There are no such things as "unstructured" situations. They are not possible. Every human situation, however casual and unforced. . . has a structure.

If two men meet by chance on the street and for half a minute talk to each other, that meeting has a structure, perhaps even a very complicated one. Who are the two men? What is their relationship to each other? Are they more or less equals, or does one have some kind of power over the other? Is the encounter equally welcome to both of them? If not, why? If so, is it for the same reasons? Does one of

From Freedom and Beyond by John Holt. Copyright © 1972 by John Holt. Reprinted by permission of the publishers, E. P. Dutton & Co., Inc.

them want the other to do something? Does he think the other wants to do it? Is he willing to do it?

We could ask dozens, scores, perhaps even hundreds of such questions. The answers to any one of them will have something to do with the structure of that meeting on the street. And the structure of this meeting exists within many other structures. For each man it is a small part of a life that has many other things in it. The meeting happens at a certain time and place, on a certain kind of street in a certain kind of town, in a culture in which these men, depending on their economic and social class, are expected and expect themselves to act in a certain way.

All of us live, all the time, within structures. These exist in their turn within other structures within still larger structures, like Chinese boxes. This is just as true of children. They live in the structure of a family; beyond that in a neighborhood, about which they feel in a certain way. This child also lives in the structure of his friends, of his school. His life is much influenced by the geography and climate of the land around him. If he grows up on the coast of southern California, his life will be very different than if he lived on a ranch in northern Wyoming. Children are not indifferent to these structures. They sense them, intuit them, want to know about them, how to fit into them, how to make use of them. We do not need to *put* structure into children's lives. It is already there. Indeed, we might well say of many children, including many poor city kids, that there is far too much structure in their lives, too many situations in which they must constantly worry about what is the right thing to do and whether they want or dare do it, or refuse to do it. What they often need, as Paul Goodman has so well pointed out, is a chance to get away from it all — more solitude, time, and space.

There are certainly great differences between the traditional classroom and the open or free classroom that I and many others are urging. But this difference is not made clear at all by calling these classes "structured" or "unstructured." Or even by pointing out that the open class has if anything *more* structure than the traditional, not less. Let us instead speak of two different kinds of structure, and to see how they differ. We might say that the structure of the traditional classroom is very simple. There are only two elements in it, only two moving parts, so to speak. One is the teacher and the other is the students. The children may be all different but in such a class their differences do not make any difference. They all have the same things to do, and they are all expected to do them in the same way. Like factory workers on the assembly line, or soldiers in the army, they are interchangeable — and quite often expendable. The second thing we can say of this structure is that it is inflexible, rigid, and static. It does not change from the first day of school to the last. On the last day as on the first, the teacher is giving out information and orders, and the children are passively

receiving and obeying or refusing to obey. The third thing we can say of this structure is that it is arbitrary and external. It does not grow out of and has nothing to do with the life and needs of the class, what the children want, what the teacher has to give. It is dropped on them from above like a great glass box. The teacher is as much a prisoner and victim of this structure as the children. He has little more to say than they about what it should be, and can do little more than they to change it.

By contrast, the structure of the open class is complicated. It has as many elements as there are teachers *and* children in the classroom. No two of these elements are alike, and their differences make all the difference, since no two children will relate to the class and teacher, or make use of them, in quite the same way. Secondly, the structure is flexible and dynamic. The relationship of each child to the teacher and to the class changes from day to day, and may change enormously in the course of a year. Indeed the nature of the whole class may change. Finally the structure is organic, internal. It grows out of the needs and abilities of the children and teachers themselves. They create this order, in ways vividly described by James Herndon in *The Way It Spozed to Be,* or George Dennison in *The Lives of Children....* When and because they create it, the order works. By that I don't mean that it looks neat and pretty; it often does not. I mean that it helps people to get things done, helps them to live, work, and grow. It does not squelch life. It enhances it. . . .

I once rode into New York from the airport with an angry cab driver. The mayor had just named a new chief of police, and he had *brought him in from outside.* What about all those guys who have been waiting in line? What did he have to go *outside* for? he kept saying furiously. Where is justice in the world if, after you've waited all those years for your turn, they move some joker from nowhere in ahead of you? What's the point of doing what you're told if at the end you don't get your reward?

Small wonder that for practical, everyday talk, real talk as opposed to political oratory, we have had to invent a substitute word for "freedom," a spiteful, mean-spirited word that lets us say right out what we really feel. The word is "permissiveness." "Permissive." One result is that when some of us urge freedom for children or for learners, we find ourselves arguing about whether children should be allowed to do *anything* — torture animals or set buildings on fire. If we say No we are then told that we don't really believe in freedom after all. Or people say, the idea of freedom for children is nonsense, children need limits. All such talk illustrates a great confusion about freedom, a confusion I have already touched in what I have said about structure. It implies that freedom means the absence of any limits or constraints, and that such a state is both desirable and possible; that the idea of freedom is opposed to the idea of limits, the idea of liberty opposed to the idea of law, so that you have to be for one or the other; that a free society or government and a tyranny are not different in kind but only in degree.

As there is no life without structure, so there is no life without constraints. We are all and always constrained, bound in, limited by a great many things, not least of all the fact that we are mortal. We are limited by our animal nature, by our model of reality, by our relations with other people, by our hopes and fears. It is useless to ask if life without constraints would be desirable. The question is too iffy even to think about — what is important is not whether there are limits but how much choice we have within those limits. A man in prison has some things he can do, and others he can't. So has a man outside. The man in the prison cell has *some* choice; he can stand, sit, or lie down; sleep, think, talk, or read; walk a few steps in this direction or that. But the two men are not equally free or equally limited. It is playing with words, and bad play, to say that we are all prisoners, or that the man in the cell is free.

There are two ways in which one person may limit the choices, the freedom of action, of another. He can say, You Must Do This. Or he can say, You Must Not Do This. They are not the same, and are not equally restricting. I did not really see, though it is plain enough, until Ivan Illich pointed it out in a small seminar at MIT, that telling people what they *may not* do, if you are clear and specific, allows them much more freedom of choice and action than telling them what they *must* do. Proscriptions are better than prescriptions. One mother says to a child, "Go out and play, if you want, but don't cross the street, don't play in the street, don't climb that little maple tree, don't play in that abandoned house, and stay out of Mrs. X's garden." Another mother says, "Time to go to your swimming lesson, or to Little League." No question about which child has the most choice.

Obviously — and I say it only to spare people the trouble of pointing it out — it is possible to say You Must Not in such a way that it destroys all freedom of action.

Mother may I go to swim?
Yes, my darling daughter.
Hang your clothes on a hickory limb.
But don't go near the water.

The idea of limits is not of itself opposed to the idea of freedom. The difference between a free community or society and a tyranny — this is another way of saying what I tried to say about structure — is not that one has limits while the other does not. It is that in a free society you can find out where the limits are; in a tyranny you can never be sure. A society has moved well along toward tyranny when people begin to say (as many of our citizens do), "Better not do that, you might get into trouble." The free citizen says, "What do you mean, *might* get into trouble? If the law doesn't specifically tell me I *can't* do it, then I damn well *can* do it." The framers of our Constitution understood that an important part of what makes a tyranny is that its power is *vague*. It has no limits. You can never tell when it will move in on you. What is wrong with imaginary crimes like being un-American, counterrevolutionary, or uncooperative in school, is that you can't tell in advance what they mean. You only find out you've done wrong after you've done it.

In short, a free community differs from an unfree one, first, in that its rules are mostly of the Don't Do This rather than the Do This kind, and secondly, that it is clear and specific what you must not do. The second is as important as the first. People in our Congress often introduce and too often pass laws which would make it a crime to, let us say, undermine the morale of the armed forces, or threaten the American Way of Life, or conspire to create a riot and so on. Such laws are tyrannical, in effect *and intent*. They do not tell us what we must not do. What they tell us is that if we do any one of thousands of unspecified things, someone may *later* decide to call what we did a violation of the law. Such laws say, don't do anything that the government might not like. What we want of our laws instead is that they be as negative and as specific as possible. "Don't play where it's dangerous" is not as good as "Don't play in the abandoned house."

Finally, we don't want too many of these laws, because they will narrow too much our freedom of choice. Here the seeming conflict between the idea of freedom and that of limits or law sometimes becomes real. But it would be foolish and mistaken to say merely the fewer laws, the better. What really counts is the amount of choice they leave us.

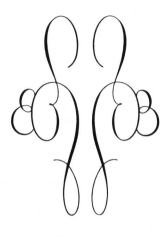

This excerpt from Dreikurs, Grunwald, and Pepper's book deals with that difficult matter that worries every teacher, namely, discipline. The first of several readings related to the problem, this one details some basic causes of misbehavior: the need for attention, power, and revenge, and the desire to display deficiencies. In their view, it is important to think about the causes before deciding what action to take to ease a troublesome situation and help a child. Think about how you might set limits for children in ways that would not aggravate these causes.

RUDOLF DREIKURS, BERNICE BRONIA GRUNWALD, AND FLOY C. PEPPER

FOUR GOALS OF MISBEHAVIOR

It is natural for an educator to seek an understanding of the reason for a child's behavior if it is necessary to correct it. Our description of the four goals of disturbing behavior offers the teacher an opportunity to understand the psychological motivation of the child, instead of groping in the dark as to why the child behaves as he does. It permits the teacher to develop diagnostic skills and psychological sensitivity. . . .

The child may try to get *attention*, to put others in his service, since he believes that otherwise he would be lost and worthless. Or he may attempt to prove his *power* in the belief that only if he can do what he wants and defy adult pressure can he be somebody. Or he may seek *revenge*:

Abridged from pp. 17–20 *Maintaining Sanity in the Classroom* by Rudolf Dreikurs, M.D., Bernice Bronia Grunwald and Floy C. Pepper. Copyright © 1971 by Rudolf Dreikurs, Bernice Bronia Grunwald, and Floy C. Pepper. Reprinted by permission of the publisher.

the only means by which he feels significant is to hurt others as he feels hurt by them. Or he may display actual or imagined *deficiencies* in order to be left alone: as long as nothing is demanded of him, his deficiency, stupidity or inability may not become obvious; that would mean his utter worthlessness.

Whichever of these four goals he adopts, his behavior is based on the conviction that only in this way can he be significant. His goal may occasionally vary with circumstances; he may act to attract attention at one moment, and assert his power or seek revenge at another. He can also use a great variety of techniques to obtain his goal; and, conversely, the same behavior can serve different purposes.

These four goals of disturbing behavior can be observed in young children up to the age of ten. It is difficult for parents and teachers to recognize that the child's disturbing behavior is directed against them. In early childhood, the status of the child depends on the impression he makes on adults. Later, he may develop different goals to gain social significance in his peer-group, and later still, in adult society. But these original four goals can still be observed in people of every age and period of life; only then, they are not all-inclusive. One must keep in mind that status and prestige can be achieved, frequently more easily, through useless and destructive means than through accomplishments.

1. The attention-getting mechanism . . . is operative in most young children. It is characteristic of our culture that we provide few opportunities to our young to establish their social position through useful contribution. Whatever has to be done in the family is done by parents or older siblings. Seeing no chance to gain status through constructive contributions, the child may seek proof of his acceptance through what he can get from others, through gifts, through affection, or at least through attention. Since none of these increase the child's self-reliance and belief in his own strength, he seeks constant new proof lest he feel lost and rejected. He may try first to get his satisfaction through socially acceptable and pleasant means. When these methods no longer prove effective, when a younger sibling steals the show, or adults expect the child to give up his childish behavior he will try any other conceivable method to put others in his service and to get attention. Humiliation, punishment or even spanking do not matter as long as he achieves his purpose. He prefers them to being ignored; then he is sure that he is lost and has no place.

2. Parents and teachers try to stop the child from demanding service and attention. He should stop his annoyance and take on responsibility for himself. When they then try to control the child, they reach a deadlock through the child's attempt to overpower them, or at least to resist their control. The child feels accepted and worthwhile only when he can do whatever he wants, and thereby refuse to do what he is supposed to do. Any adult who lets himself be drawn into a struggle for power with a child is lost. In any instance, the child will win out, with the exception of a few short-lived episodes where the adult succeeds in beating the child down. Parents and teachers pay dearly for such successes. They convince the child even more that power is all that counts in life. And he can prove that he has the means to defeat them. He is not restricted in his fighting method by any sense of responsibility or moral obligation. He is creative and inventive. The adults cannot match their wits with him because they have only very limited means at their disposal to overpower him, while the child can constantly create new and unexpected tactics which are deadly in their aim. They know where to hit. Any adult who tries to control and impose his will on the child has been born fifty years too late. He could have done so successfully in a more autocratic society, when society supported adults in their efforts. Today, there is neither a society that lets the adult abuse the child, nor a child who, in his sense of his own equality, lets an adult impose his will on him and control him. Once a power conflict ensues, the relationship between child and adult can only further deteriorate and the child may move to the next goal, revenge.

3. For children who feel utterly rejected, who have lost their faith in society and in themselves, the problem of having any significance cannot be solved through

their getting attention or demonstrating their power. The fight between such a child and adult society is too violent, too painful and at the same time, too entrenched, to permit any other avenue than mutual revenge. The only role that such a child feels able to play is to get even with those who hurt him. And once the child has established such a policy for himself, he proves to be quite capable of evoking from adults the kind of treatment which then justifies his thirst for revenge. He knows very well where he can hurt the most, and he takes advantage of the vulnerability of his opponents. He regards it as a triumph when he is considered vicious. Since this is the only triumph he thinks he can obtain, it is the only one he seeks. The degree to which such a child can stir up everyone in his reach justifies to him the feeling of triumph.

4. The intense fight between adult and child leads to complete discouragement, either to the full negation of social participation, as in the revengeful child, or to the full denial of any capacity. The child who first became passive and deficient in order to get special service and attention, eventually reaches the point where he is so convinced of his being an utter failure that he does not even try any more. Under these circumstances, the child wants nothing more than to be left alone. As long as nothing is asked of him, he can still appear as a member of the group. Then he hides himself behind a display of real or imagined inferiority, which justifies his resignation. By avoiding participation and

contribution, he thinks he can avoid more humiliating and embarrassing situations.

There are no definite rules in regard to the child's choice of a goal, or of the means by which he can obtain it. By and large, each disturbing child has reached an equilibrium, which guides all his actions. In most cases, we find the disturbing child in the pursuit of one of the four goals. Sometimes he has not settled yet, and so we find the child in between attention and power, or in between power and revenge, or between attention through passive means or giving up in defeat. Some children are so rich in their creativity that they can switch from one to the other goal and actually operate on all four of them, to the distress of adults who are dumbfounded by the unexpected changes in the child's behavior. Sometimes the child may have one goal at home and another at school and still another with his friends. In each instance, one has to be able to recognize the child's goal and to deal with it.

———

Redl's article combines theory with some practical advice. In contrast to Dreikurs, Grunwald, and Pepper, who focus on the younger child, Redl discusses aggression and violence in older children and adolescents. Redl emphasizes the need to understand that there are different causes of similar misbehaviors. One of his main

points is that the teacher should particularly avoid doing anything that will further aggravate a situation. Five practical "hints" are given, which are likely to be useful to anyone who will teach.

FRITZ REDL

AGGRESSION IN THE CLASSROOM

There's plenty of minor aggression in the classroom that nobody objects to. The real problem is the aggression that prevents good teaching and good classroom life. This aggression comes primarily from three areas.

First, it is an input from the home or from the community. A teen-ager gets hopping mad at his old man, but he doesn't dare let off steam until he gets to school. Now, the teacher didn't produce the aggression, but it's there and he's got to handle it.

Second, is the discharge from within. Some youngster sits there daydreaming, and all of a sudden during a wild fantasy,

From *Today's Education*, September 1969, pp. 30–32. Reprinted with permission.

he thinks of something that upsets him and he conks his neighbors on the head. None of them have done anything to him, and the teacher hasn't either. Something just burst out from within. (If youngsters are seriously disturbed, most of the aggression comes from way within, and neither they nor anyone else knows why.)

Third, the aggression is engendered right there in the classroom. It may be triggered either by what the teacher does that's right but that doesn't happen to fit the kid, or by God knows what — the kid's reaction to the group or to other kids, or to something that maybe the teacher wouldn't have done if he had stopped to think. But anyway, it's reactive to something in the environment at the moment.

———

Now, if I were a classroom teacher, I would like to know how much of which of those three packages is exploding before me, because it makes a difference in terms of long-range planning. It also makes some difference in terms of what to do at the moment. Most of the time we are not sure, but different sources of aggression smell different when we are confronted with them. Experienced teachers develop an uncanny skill at sensing "This is something the kid brought with him. I've got to help him recover from it before he acts it out." The outsider, though, wouldn't know.

Some aggression does not affect us di-

rectly because certain youngsters may be model pupils in the classrooms, but then after school they may go out and rape or murder someone. So a youngster may be full of sick aggression without being a classroom problem.

On the other hand, there may be a great kid sitting over there who's bored stiff. He likes you a lot, but he gets mad at the fact that you bore him stiff. Finally, he's just had it, and he runs out and slams the door. A normal youngster like that whose aggression is classroom-produced is our problem. Too often, an article on aggression in the classroom concentrates on a few examples of youngsters who should have been in a mental hospital for the last 10 years anyway and ignores all the other kids who bother us.

The term *aggression* is so overused now, you've got to watch out for it. Don't ever let anybody trap you into discussing aggression without first asking him: "Listen, brother, which aggression are you talking about? What actually happened?" Because aggression has a wide range — all the way from reacting to boredom to wrestling at the wrong time in the wrong place with another pupil.

Discharge of surplus energy or of displaced needs from the home or neighborhood; loss of control in the face of seductive equipment like a slingshot or a knife or whatnot; personal battles with adults, other kids, the group, or the teacher — all these fall under the heading of aggression.

The way Joe or Jane expresses aggres-

sion, while not the end of what we're looking for, certainly should be the starting point. Unless you know what lies behind their behavior, you will have trouble knowing how to handle it. Sometimes you may understand perfectly well how come. So the question then is what do you do to help him, which is a separate matter from knowing what was cooking to begin with.

———

I want to give special warning here not to make aggression synonymous with violence. The two are not the same, although they are obviously related. There is a theme in violence that we can legitimately call aggression. On the other hand, not all violence comes from aggressive drives. The behavior is aggressive, but the basis may be quite different. Let me give a few illustrations of violence that does not spring from aggression.

Panic coping. A kid may get scared stiff, so scared that he doesn't know what to do anymore. So he does something violent; he tears something apart. The fact that the behavior is violent is important. But this child is not hyperaggressive; he is frightened and desperate.

The need to be heard. A frequent source of violence is the feeling that nobody listens. The child finally concludes that the only way to get someone to listen is to be violent enough. So when other avenues are blocked off, violence is a substitute for verbal and nonverbal communication.

The desire to display guts. If a kid is supposed to be tough, how can he show it? Who is going to believe it? "I'd better not let them know I'm scared. So I've got to find ways to show I'm brave." In order to do this in a peaceful life, he's got to create problems.

Demonstrating loyalty to the group code. This source of violence is not originally meant to be aggression for aggression's sake. ("If the rest of my gang thinks school is no good, I'd better show that I'm with them. So I put a thumbtack in the teacher's chair. I don't hate the teacher; too bad it's her rear that gets stung. But I'm a regular guy and I'm going to prove it.")

Risk taking — to study survival skills. For instance, how can a boy know if he can run fast enough to outrun the cop, unless he swipes something first? Or else picks a rat out of an ash can, swirls it by the tail, throws it in somebody's first-floor window, and then hops over the garage roof fast before they can catch him? A kid has to know how good he is in handling a dangerous assignment.

The stink and the dust produced in the decay of group psychology. If a group suddenly gets anxious or panicky or wild or disorganized or elated or mad at each other, you get a lot of behavior that involves violence but that did not start as aggression. Although Joe and Jane may be doing something, they're not doing it as Joe and Jane but as members of a group.

Last on my list of violence that does not start with aggression but is secondary to it is, of course, *an invasion of societal turmoil from the outside.* Someone or something in the community ties a package of emotional TNT to the back of a kid and it blows up in the classroom. The kid responsible wasn't originally aggressive; he carries the whole load of community or neighborhood or subgroup aggression. As his teacher, you're just an innocent bystander. What he does has nothing to do with the way you taught him or whether you bawled him out or flunked him.

In short, there is some relationship between violence and aggression, but not a simple one. For teachers it's very important to begin to sense the difference between Joe's being loaded with personal anger at what you just did and the explosion that results when his TNT package goes off at a given time. They are different problems.

———

Now let me give a few abbreviated hints of what to do about various kinds of child behavior — hints that are not fancy enough to be written up much in books.

First, you sometimes need to get kids off the hook. The aggressive behavior is beginning but without having really been planned, and if you get pupils off the

hook *now,* they don't have to continue. Another way of putting it is that you sometimes need to cut a contagion chain without making a big deal out of it. And in most cases knowing how to do this is very important in dealing with a normally well-behaved child as well as with a wild one.

Take Joe, for example. He's sitting over there shaking imaginary dice, and at the moment you're not too bothered. You catch his eye and he stops, but only momentarily. After a while everybody else gets interested. You want to cut that contagion chain now, because if you wait another five minutes, you'll have a mass problem on your hands.

If you interfere too early, everyone thinks you're a fusspot, a dope, or chicken, and you only aggravate things. If you don't interfere at the right time, you'll have trouble. Getting Joe off the hook at the right moment will stop his behavior without a big scene, and the rest of the group will not be too heavily afflicted. This skill of cutting contagion chains without making too much of a mess is, I think, one of the most important for anybody who deals with groups.

———

A second important technique for the practical handling of aggression in the classroom is signal interference. Signal interference in time saves nine. Very often teachers underestimate the possibility of stopping minor forms of misbehavior quite casually before the kid gets too carried away by it. They don't take the behavior seriously, because it isn't bothersome enough. So they wait until it does get bothersome enough, and by that time the situation is tense, the kid is already off his noodle, and anything they do now will have an explosive effect.

The big problem is that most teachers lack a good inventory of preaggression signals for their pupils. In some youngsters, the signals are easy to spot. Others apparently go aggressive all of a sudden from nowhere. That's because the teacher's radar doesn't pick up their signals. But if the teacher works at it, after a while he begins to get the messages from all around the room. One kid, for example, gets glassy-eyed and sits there quietly in a certain rigid position. If the teacher goes over and taps him on the shoulder, he'll go up like a rocket. Two minutes ago, if the teacher had gone around and said, "Come on, let's start working," that would have been fine.

A good many teachers — particularly those who are new to the classroom — do not know enough about the physiological and gestural signals that indicate the work-up to aggressive behavior. Everybody with experience understands them, but conveying this understanding to the other guy is hard. Apparently we don't think it's important because we don't have any fancy lingo for it, but if I were a beginning teacher, that's the kind of information I would like to have.

If you send me a kid with an unknown aggression work-up potential, I'd like to get to know that kid and figure out what he looks like before he goes off the handle. After that, I can tell at a glance that this is the moment to go over to him.

In observing classrooms and watching teachers with disturbed youngsters, I am constantly amazed at the terrific skill people with experience develop, and they can't ever explain it. What's more, they don't even mention it. They think it isn't worth discussing.

Let me describe one incident I observed.

A kid is sitting stiffly at his desk, obviously determined that he "ain't gonna do *nothing.*" The teacher walks over to him, pats him on the shoulder, and says: "Now, how about it? You don't feel so good, huh?" And he doesn't say anything. What does she do then? She says: "OK, I'll come back in a while. Maybe by then you'll be feeling better." That's all. She doesn't push him. ("Why don't you . . . ? What's the matter with you? What kind of family do you come from, anyway?")

She uses her judgment, and sooner or later he's over the hump. His face clears up; his posture is relaxed. Then she comes over and puts the pencil in his hand and he starts working.

———

Now, number three: Watch out for the choreography of the dare. In our present society we all have an insatiable, unquenchable thirst for tribal rituals. We still perform tribal dances. Take this scene:

We have what looks like a relatively normal classroom at the moment. Here is Joe back there, who wishes I'd leave him alone. But he knows I'm a nice guy, that I've got to make a living, after all. And I'm pretty harmless, though a little crazy, maybe.

Still, somehow, the noise gets too loud, and I finally say: "Listen, you, you'd better stop that now." Then maybe things get worse, and maybe by this time I'm angry, too. So I say: "All right, now, if you can't be quiet here, why don't you go out and cool off?"

Let's assume I'm relatively lucky in my diagnosis, and the youngster gets up and moves to the door, but on the way he mumbles something under his breath. If I ask him what he said, he probably feels he has to lie — so I make a liar out of him. Or if he is decently honest, I have to send him to the principal.

The foregoing is one way the scene can be played. But it also can be played differently. If Joe is sensitive of his prestige in the group, and I happen to have adults looking over my shoulder, then both of us become involved in a tribal dance. He has to say, "Make me," and I have to say, "All right. I'll make you." So either I try to bounce him or I call the principal or whatnot. Then for three weeks, lots of procedures go on — all nonsensical and having nothing to do with the original issue. Joe's become a discipline case, almost.

What I've described here is a personal interaction, a limit-setting process of a very simple nature, really. Most of the time it works like a charm, but in the second instance it became a tribal dance. If I were a principal assigning teachers to study halls or other large groups, I would like to know how vulnerable they are to the tribal dance routine, because in a dare situation the pressure is terrific. If you send me a kid who is tough, I don't mind. But I would like to know how involved this kid is in a tribal dance.

You see, some kids who are plenty tough don't fall for that kind of nonsense. In fact, some of my best delinquents would never be so stupid as that. If I really challenged them, they would think: "All right, so let the guy have his little victory for a change. So what! So I get out. I'm tough enough. Nobody will think I gave in." If, however, the youngster isn't really tough enough, but has to pretend he is, then he has to do the tribal dance in order to impress the others with his plumage or whatever.

This is a big danger. And many a teacher could avoid many a large discipline problem if he were able to recognize the first drum beats of a tribal dance. Very often we push relatively tough kids who mean well into tribal dances because we are unaware of the position they are in. At other times, we do not interfere when we should because we are too afraid we'll provoke a tribal dance when actually we wouldn't.

So the tribal dance is a whole phenomenon — separate from the usual problem of discipline — that is a rather deep psychological problem.

———————

Number four: Watch out for the subsurface effect. Whatever I do also has a side effect, and it is not always visible right now. If we are aware of what else happens besides the immediate effect of what we do, we won't simply say, "Because I blamed him for being noisy or because I praised him for being quiet, everything is hunky-dory right now."

So it's important to look with one eye to the possible nonvisible side effect. I can do something about it afterwards, but only if I'm on the lookout for it. Like that boy we've been talking about. Let's say he leaves the room and doesn't start the tribal dance. In that case, I'll want to make sure we have a brief get-together afterwards to tell him that I appreciate his doing what I asked and that I'll defend his reputation with the rest of the kids. I'll say that there are no hard feelings; it was just that I couldn't let him get so loud in class. That's all; nothing more.

———————

If you have to live with aggression, at least try not to breed it. We breed it, of course, by exposing even otherwise normal boys and girls to experiences, to space arrangements, to life situations that invariably produce inner frustration.

For instance, if I bore a youngster, I expose him to frustration. Or, if I have to delay giving help that is needed — say, a boy over there is stuck in the middle of a long division problem, and I can't get to him for a while because I have to be over here with the others. Sooner or later he's had it, and he gets mad.

Or I may breed aggression if I intervene with too little sympathy. If a youngster is doing something interesting, something he likes, do I say, "Get going this minute. Do you want to be late again?" when I could just as well say, "Look, I'm sorry to have to break that up, but you know we've got to get out now."

One final point: Don't forget that from time to time, your own aggression will start showing. As you probably are aware, your hostile feelings and how you deal with them make a story no less complex and touchy than the one just presented. That your anger may be righteous and justified is not the only issue. You must ask yourself some questions: How does my anger make me behave in the classroom? Which (if any) of the behaviors it produces in me seem helpful in reducing youngsters' aggressive feelings, and which ones just make matters worse? Figuring this out requires clear thinking and real objectivity, but it is worth the effort. Your professional obligation is to handle your own aggression in such a way that the individual pupil or the class can manage the spillover effect.

The following is an excerpt from Gordon's book, *Parent Effectiveness Training*. Although it is written for parents and their children, it seems very likely that his advice will be equally helpful for teachers. The previous two readings (by Dreikurs, Grunwald, and Pepper, and by Redl) focused more on dealing with misbehavior as it arises, but here we also see a long-range approach for coping with persistent problems. The heart of the "no-lose method" is that it is not based on authoritarian control. Rather, through a series of problem solving steps, the teacher and the student or students can expect to come to a solution agreeable to both. The uniqueness of this approach is that it might become a way for the teacher and students to set limits together — even anticipating some "misbehavior."

THOMAS GORDON

SIX STEPS
OF THE
NO-LOSE METHOD

It has been helpful for parents to understand that the no-lose method really in-

Copyright © 1970 by Dr. Thomas Gordon. From the book *Parent Effectiveness Training* by Dr. Thomas Gordon. Published by Peter H. Wyden, Publishers. Used with permission of the publishers.

volves six separate steps. When parents follow these steps, they are much more likely to have succesful experiences:

— Step 1: identifying and defining the conflict
— Step 2: generating possible alternative solutions
— Step 3: evaluating the alternative solutions
— Step 4: deciding on the best acceptable solution
— Step 5: working out ways of implementing the solution
— Step 6: following up to evaulate how it worked

There are some key points to be understood about each of these six steps. When parents understand and apply these key points, they avoid many difficulties and pitfalls. Even though some "quickie" conflicts get worked out without going through all the steps, parents do better when they understand what is involved at each stage.

STEP 1: IDENTIFYING AND DEFINING THE CONFLICT

This is the critical phase when parents want the child to become involved. They have to get his attention and then secure his willingness to enter into problem-solving. Their chances of doing this are much greater if they remember to:

1. Select a time when the child is not busy or occupied or going someplace, so he won't resist or resent being interrupted or delayed.
2. Tell him clearly and concisely that there is a problem that must be solved. Don't pussyfoot or be tentative with such ineffective statements as, "Would you like to problem-solve?" or "I think it might be a good idea if we tried to work this out."
3. Tell the child clearly, and as strongly as you feel, exactly what feelings you have or what needs of yours are not being met or what is bothering you. Here it is critical to send "I-messages": "I have been upset when *I* see the kitchen *I* have worked hard to clean get all messed up after you have your after-school snack"; or "*I* am worried about *my* car getting smashed up and you getting hurt if you continue to drive faster than the speed limits"; or "*I* feel it is unfair to *me* to do so much of the work around the house when you kids might help out."
4. Avoid messages that put-down or blame the child, such as "You kids have been sloppy about the kitchen," "You're being reckless with my car," "You kids are a bunch of free-loaders around this house."
5. Be very clear that you want them to join with you in finding a solution *acceptable to both*, a solution "we both can live with," in which nobody loses and both of your needs will be met. It is critical that children believe that you are sincere in wanting to find a no-lose

solution. They must know that the "name of the game" is . . . no-lose, not more win-lose in a new disguise.

STEP 2: GENERATING POSSIBLE SOLUTIONS

In this phase, the key is to generate a *variety of solutions*. The parent can suggest: "What are some of the things we might do?" "Let's think of possible solutions," "Let's put our heads to work and come up with some possible solutions," "There must be a lot of different ways we can solve this problem." These additional key points will help:

1. Try first to get the kids' solutions — you can add your own later. (Younger children may not come up with solutions initially.)
2. Most important, do not evaluate, judge, or belittle any of the solutions offered. There will be time for that in the next phase. Accept *all* ideas for solutions. For complex problems you may want to write them down. Don't even evaluate or judge solutions as being "good," because that may imply that others on the list are not so good.
3. At this point try not to make any statements conveying that any of the offered solutions would be unacceptable to you.
4. When using the no-lose method on a problem involving several children, if one doesn't offer a solution, you might have to encourage him to contribute.

5. Keep pressing for alternative solutions until it looks as though no more are going to be suggested.

STEP 3: EVALUATING THE ALTERNATIVE SOLUTIONS

In this phase, it is legitimate to start evaluating the various solutions. The parent may say, "All right, which of these solutions look best?" or "Now, let's see which solution we feel is the one we want?" or "What do we think of these various solutions we have come up with?" or "Are any of these better than the others?"

Generally, the solutions get narrowed down to one or two that seem best by eliminating those that are not acceptable to either parent or the kids (for whatever reason). At this stage parents must remember to be honest in stating their own feelings — "I wouldn't be happy with that," or "That wouldn't meet my need," or "I don't think that one would seem fair to me."

STEP 4: DECIDING ON THE BEST SOLUTION

This step is not as difficult to work through as parents often think. When the other steps have been followed and the exchange of ideas and reactions has been open and honest, a clearly superior solution often emerges naturally from the discussion. Sometimes either the parent or a child has suggested a very creative solution that obviously is the best one — and is also acceptable to everyone.

Some tips for arriving at a final decision are:

1. Keep testing out the remaining solutions against the feelings of the kids with such questions as, "Would this solution be okay, now?" "Are we all satisfied with this solution?" "Do you think this one would solve our problem?" "Is this going to work?"
2. Don't think of a decision as necessarily final and impossible to change. You might say, "Okay, let's try this one out and see if it works," or "We seem to agree on this solution — let's start carrying it out and see if it really solves our problems," or "I'm willing to accept this one; would you be willing to give it a try?"
3. If the solution involves a number of points, it is a good idea to write them down so they won't be forgotten.
4. Make certain it is clearly understood that each one is making a commitment to carry out the decision: "Okay, now, this is what we are agreeing to do," or "We understand, now, this is to be our agreement and we're saying we're going to keep to our part of the bargain."

STEP 5: IMPLEMENTING THE DECISION

Frequently, after a decision is reached there is a need to spell out in some detail exactly how the decision will be implemented. Parent and kids may need to address themselves to *"Who is to do what, by when?"* or "Now what do we need to do to carry this out?" or "When do we start?"

In conflicts about chores and work duties, for example, "How often?" "On what days?" and "What are to be the standards of performance required?" are questions that often must be discussed.

In conflicts about bedtime, a family may want to discuss who is going to watch the clock and call time.

In conflicts about the neatness of the children's rooms, the issue of "how neat" may have to be explored.

Sometimes decisions may require purchases, such as a blackboard for a message center, a clothes hamper for the child, a new iron for daughter, and so on. In such cases it may be necessary to determine who is to shop for these, or even who is to pay for them.

Questions of implementation are best delayed until after there is a clear agreement on the final decision. Our experience is that once the final decision has been reached, the implementation issues are usually worked out rather easily.

STEP 6: FOLLOW-UP EVALUATION

Not all initial decisions from the no-lose method turn out to be good ones. Conse-quently, parents sometimes need to check back with a child to ask if he is still happy with the decision. Kids often commit themselves to a decision that later proves difficult to carry out. Or a parent may find it difficult to keep his bargain, for a variety of reasons. Parents may want to check back after a while with, "How is our decision working out?" "Are you still satisfied with our decision?" This communicates to kids your concern about their needs.

Sometimes the follow-up turns up information that requires the initial decision to be modified. Taking out the trash once every day might turn out to be impossible or unnecessary. Or, coming in at 11:00 P. M. on weekend nights proves to be impossible when the kids go to a double-feature movie. One family discovered that their no-lose resolution of the chore problem required their younger daughter, who agreed to wash the evening dishes, to work on an average of five to six hours a week, while the older daughter, whose job it was to do a weekly clean up of their common bathroom and play-room, needed only to work three hours a week. This seemed unfair to the youngest, so the decision was modified after a couple of weeks' trial.

Of course, not all no-lose conflict-reso-lution sessions proceed in an orderly fashion through all six steps. Sometimes conflicts are resolved after only one solu-tion has been proposed. Sometimes the final solution pops out of someone's mouth during Step 3, when they are evalu-ating previously proposed solutions.

Nevertheless, it pays to keep the six steps in mind.

THE NEED FOR ACTIVE LISTENING AND "I-MESSAGES"

Because the no-lose method requires the involved parties to join together in prob-lem-solving, effective communication is a prerequisite. Consequently, parents must do a great deal of active listening, and must send clear "I-messages." Parents who have not learned these skills seldom have success with the no-lose method.

Active listening is required, first, because parents need to understand the feelings or needs of the kids. What do they want? Why do they persist in wanting to do something even after they know it is not acceptable to their parents? What needs are causing them to behave in a certain way?

Why is Bonnie resisting going to nursery school? Why does Jane not want to wear the plaid raincoat? Why does Freddy cry and fight his mother when she drops him off at the babysitter's? What are my daugh-ter's needs that make it so important for her to go to the beach during the Easter vacation?

Active listening is a potent tool for help-ing a youngster to open up and reveal his real needs and true feelings. When these become understood by the parent, it is often an easy next step to think of another way of meeting those needs that will not involve behavior unacceptable to the parent.

Since strong feelings may come out during problem-solving — from parents as well as youngsters, active listening is critically important in helping to release feelings and dissipate them, so that effective problem-solving can continue.

Finally, active listening is an important way to let kids know that their proposed solutions are understood and accepted as proposals made in good faith; and that their thoughts and evaluations concerning all proposed solutions are wanted and accepted.

"I-messages" are critical in the no-lose process so kids will know how the parent feels, without impugning the character of the child or putting him down with blame and shame. "You-messages" in conflict-resolution usually provoke counter "You-messages" and cause the discussion to degenerate into a nonproductive verbal battle with the contestants vying to see who can best clobber the other with insults.

"I-messages" also must be used to let kids know that *parents* have needs and are serious about seeing that those needs are not going to be ignored just because the youngster has his needs. "I-messages" communicate the parent's own limits — what he cannot tolerate and what he does not want to sacrifice. "I-messages" convey, "I am a person with needs and feelings," "I have a right to enjoy life," "I have rights in our home."

Social-problem-solving meetings are yet a broader approach to the problem of discipline, which has been discussed in the three previous readings. Utilizing many of the principles that have been suggested, Glasser shows how making such meetings a regular part of the classroom and school program can be an important positive step forward. The emphasis is on a group problem-solving as opposed to punishment or fault-finding. Glasser says that in such meetings children learn that "they can use their brains individually and as a group to solve the problems of living in their school world." Try out a meeting like Glasser describes in a group with which you are currently working and see what potential it might have for your teaching.

WILLIAM GLASSER

SOCIAL-PROBLEM-SOLVING MEETINGS

The many social problems of school itself, some of which lead to discipline of the students, are best attacked through the use

Abridged from pp. 122–124, 127–132 *Schools Without Failure* by William Glasser M.D. Copyright © 1969 by William Glasser. Reprinted by permission of the publisher.

of each class as a problem-solving group with each teacher as the group leader. Teachers in their faculty meetings will do essentially the same thing that each class does in the classroom meeting: *attempt to solve the individual and group educational problems of the class and the school.* When children enter kindergarten, they should discover that each class is a working, problem-solving unit and that each student has both individual and group responsibilities. Responsibility for learning and for behaving so that learning is fostered is shared among the entire class. By discussing group and individual problems, the students and teacher can usually solve their problems within the classroom. If children learn to participate in a problem-solving group when they enter school and continue to do so with a variety of teachers throughout the six years of elementary school, they learn that the world is not a mysterious and sometimes hostile and frightening place where they have little control over what happens to them. They learn rather that, although the world may be difficult and that it may at times appear hostile and mysterious, they can use their brains individually and as a group *to solve the problems of living in their school world.*

School children have many social problems, some of which may call for discipline, some not. Under ordinary conditions, because there is no systematic effort to teach them social problem solving, school children find that problems that arise in getting along with each other in school are difficult to solve. Given little help, children tend to evade problems, to lie their way out of situations, to depend upon others to solve their problems, or just to give up. None of these courses of action is good preparation for life. The social-problem-solving meeting can help children learn better ways. . . .

The social-problem-solving meetings should be conducted according to the following guidelines that have proved effective both in the public schools and at the Ventura School for Girls, where I first used this technique. Although better guidelines may be developed as the meetings progress, the following should give a good start.

All problems relative to the class as a group and to any individual in the class are eligible for discussion. A problem can be brought up by an individual student about himself or someone else, or by the teacher as she sees a problem occur. In a school with a unified faculty involved with each other and with all school problems, subjects for discussion can be introduced in any class by any student or any teacher, either directly by a note to the group or indirectly by an administrator with knowledge of the problem. In addition to school problems, problems that a child has at home are also eligible for discussion if the child or his parents wish to bring them up.

To adults reading this book, my suggestions may seem strong. As adults, we usually either struggle with our own problems in privacy with little help from friends and family, or we keep our problems under the rug and try to act as if they don't exist. Thus it may sound as if I am demanding too much of small children. Having held meetings for several years, I have found that children do not think that discussing their problems openly is as difficult as we adults do. The children are concerned because they are learning to deny the existence of their problems. They would much rather try to solve them, and school can give them a chance to do so. Before they come to school, children discover that it is reasonable to try to solve problems. We must be careful, therefore, not to do as we do too often at present: extend our adult anxieties and inadequacies to children and thereby teach them to be evasive as they grow to maturity. In my experience, a class of six-year-olds will freely discuss difficult problems, even one such as stealing (ordinarily a very emotional subject for older children and adults), and try to work out a solution. A solution may require more than just trying directly to get the child to stop stealing, although this of course is the ultimate goal. A solution may include the discovery in the meeting that a child steals because he is lonely, hungry, or jealous, and the working out of ways to correct these causes. Teachers learn during meetings that small children can stand only small temptations. Teachers who do not ade-

quately safeguard lunch money, for instance, are subjecting children to temptation that they may not have the strength to withstand. If children can find a reasonable solution at age six and can concomitantly learn the value of honesty, it is likely that they will never steal again. If someone does steal in a school where discussions are a continuing part of the school program, the stage is set for solving the problem later. The students know that the purpose of all discussion is to solve problems, not to find fault or to punish. Experience in solving social problems in a non-fault-finding, nonpunitive atmosphere gives children confidence in themselves as thinking, worthwhile people.

We have stated that the social-problem-solving meeting is open for any subject that might be important to any child, teacher, or parent related to that class or school. *The discussion itself should always be directed toward solving the problem; the solution should never include punishment or fault finding.* The children and the teacher are oriented from the first meetings in the first grade that the purpose of the meeting is not to find whose fault a problem is or to punish people who have problems and are doing wrong; rather the purpose is to help those who have problems to find better ways to behave. The orientation of the meetings is always positive, always toward a solution. When meetings are conducted in this way, the children learn to think in terms of a solution — the only constructive way to handle any problem — instead of the typical adult way soon learned by school children — fault finding and punishment. The pseudo solution of problems through fault finding is one of the most worthless pursuits continually to occupy all segments of our society. Its constant companion, punishment, is equally ineffective.[1] Punishment usually works only the first time, if at all. After the first time it works only with successful people, who ordinarily don't need it. Much more often punishment serves as an excuse for not solving a problem rather than leading toward a solution.

It should also be understood that many problems arise that are not readily solvable, that have no single right answer, whose best solution might be a not-so-bad alternative. Sometimes these more difficult problems can be discussed over and over again with little seeming to happen and causing the class and the teacher to become discouraged. A class bully who pushes other children on the playground, dominates the games, and is physically abusive in and out of class often presents such a difficult problem. It seems that the more he is discussed, the less effective the discussion proves to be; the solutions offered by the class work poorly. Even for such a serious problem, the strength of the classroom meetings can be used in two ways. First, often the solution to the problem of such a child lies not so much in coming up with an exact answer, but in the discussion itself. As individual members talk about him, as they see his faults and shortcomings, they become less frightened

and less able to be intimidated. Allowing the problem to come out into the open for discussion increases the strength of the bullied students so that gradually, sometimes almost imperceptibly, though the bully's behavior hasn't changed, it becomes less destructive because the others now have more strength. Second, after he is discussed several times, discussion of the bully might be avoided. Unless he does something worthwhile or constructive, he is not talked about; if he does something constructive, it is mentioned. This technique removes the attention that he is getting through aggressive behavior and focuses on constructive, positive actions. The teacher might say, "There is no sense talking about Johnny because he is doing the same thing that everyone is complaining about. Let's wait until we can talk about something else he might do that the class would like." Johnny, hearing this and needing attention, will often improve his behavior.

It is important, therefore, in class meetings for the teacher, but not the class, to be nonjudgmental. The class makes judgments and from these judgments works toward positive solutions. The teacher may reflect the class attitude, but she should give opinions sparingly and make sure the class understands that her opinions are not law. Each child learns that he is important to every other child, that what he says is heard by everyone, and that his ideas count. When children experience the satisfaction of thinking and listening to others, they are not afraid to have ideas, to

enter into a discussion, and to solve their own problems and the problems of their class by using their brains.

Once an atmosphere of thinking, discussing, and problem solving is established, and it can be established rather quickly, situations that ordinarily would cause serious disturbances in class and that might cause a child to be sent to the principal's office can be handled effectively within the class. Children learn that their peers care about them. They learn to solve the problems of their world. Then it is easy to accept the teacher who says, "We have a problem; these two boys are fighting. At our next class-meeting time we are going to discuss the fight, but now would you boys be willing to stop fighting and wait for the meeting?" This simple request has proved to be effective. The boys stop fighting and wait because they know there is a reasonable alternative to their misbehavior — a solution from the meeting. When they believe that even if they stop fighting they will be punished or expelled from the class, they often continue to fight because the alternatives offered aren't any better than fighting. Classroom meetings can serve to siphon off steam in the class by providing a better alternative. Often the problem is dissipated before the meeting, and the children agree it would be a waste of time to discuss it. The availability of the meeting allowed the children to use the normal ways children have to solve problems.

This excerpt serves as an introduction to the rest of the readings in this chapter. It should be read as a vicarious experiment and experience in offering students a large measure of freedom. What happens when you remove visible signs of limits? That is the question you can think about while reading about Herndon's experiences. Coming from a background of very successful creative teaching, Herndon and his colleague started a junior high "English" course by removing every limit they could imagine. For the result, read the excerpt. Then, make two analyses. First of all, what might they have done if they had followed Dewey's or Holt's advice more closely? Secondly, what do the teachers in the following readings do differently that creates both a sense of freedom and limits?

JAMES HERNDON

EXCERPT FROM *HOW TO SURVIVE IN YOUR NATIVE LAND*

About a month before the end of one school year, Frank Ramirez and I invented a course for the next year. We thought

Copyright © 1971, by James Herndon. Reprinted by permission of Simon and Schuster.

up a simple notion. We wanted a two-hour class, and we wanted to both be there at the same time. We wanted the class to be free of certain restrictions — those regarding curriculum, those regarding grades and those regarding school behavior rules, mainly the ones about leaving the classroom.

Frank had been working at the school for perhaps eight or nine years. In the two or three years I'd been there, I learned from watching him how to conduct yourself as a regular teacher in regular classes in a regular school. How you could teach and work there without driving yourself nuts with boredom, rage, a sense of your own hypocrisy, without unending uproars with the administration and parents and without getting fired, which was important to me. Frank was the best at this I ever saw. He filled his room with art materials, even though he was supposed to be teaching English and social studies to seventh graders. While other teachers were complaining publicly how difficult it was in the short time of nine months to "get through" the "material" in the texts, Frank announced that the stuff you were supposed to teach in a year could be handled easily in six weeks or so, and you had the rest of the time to do other things you might care to do. He figured the other teachers dragged out the teaching of Egypt or math all year because they didn't have anything else they wanted to do or cared about, or because they were afraid of the kids once the threat of the curriculum was called off.

In Language Arts, he showed the kids how to diagram sentences, pointed out the parts of speech, showed them where to put commas and semicolons — all in quite a short time. He was the only man I've ever heard give a good answer to that old question, Why do we have to make these diagrams?

Why? Because they are beautiful, said Frank. What Frank understood, or knew how to work, or knew how to involve the kids in, or something . . . was a kind of inter-relationship between studies, which were supposed to be real, and fantasy, which was supposed to be not-real. So that if they were "studying" some place which was an island, they studied it O.K., read the book, answered their questions on ditto sheets, and then the kids would find themselves with big pieces of paper inventing an island, drawing and painting in its geography, describing its people, its kings and rulers, the way the people ate, or what they lived in, or how they celebrated Christmas. Or they went to the library and got books and wrote to the authors, and put the authors' answers up on the board, telling where they were born and how they got the idea of writing such and such a kid's book. Then Frank might give some letters to other kids, who would write secret answers as if they were the authors and these would go up on the board too. He took kids to the Golden Gate Bridge, where they dropped off bottles with fake notes in them into the outgoing tide and the answers to these notes, from points up and down the California coast, went up on the board too, along with "environments" made from junk in cigar boxes and illustrations from books or stories which he made the kids paint left-handed with big brushes on small pieces of paper so their technique or lack of it wouldn't get in the way.

I joined him in this kind of work. In my class we wrote to the Peace Corps and got real information about the problems of various countries and the straight dope on what the Corps hoped to do in these countries, how they would work, and so on. The kids, pretending to be Peace Corps workers themselves, wrote imaginary journals of stays in Africa and South America; the idea was that they would use the official information in their writing and would solve a lot of problems. In fact, though, their journals were full of first-class air travels to and from the countries, drinking cocktails and making it with stewardesses or *white hunters* in the *bush,* torture by *natives,* escapes, liaisons with chiefs' daughters, buried treasures and elephants' graveyards. Little attention was given to the raising of chickens, the building of irrigation systems, or the growing of flax. Medical care was brought in only as accessory to a needed miracle — the chief's son cured by a shot of penicillin just when the Corpsman was about to be eaten up by head-hunting pygmies.

In English, I had the kids begin inventing languages. They wrote down lists of common words and when we had the lists we'd start making a picture or symbol to stand for it, just like them Egyptians did.

Then we'd choose the best symbol and make lists of those and after we had a couple of hundred or so we'd start translating simple fairy tales into our new language, or making up stories to write in it, and put the stories on huge decorated pieces of paper and send them over to Frank's class to see if they could decipher them, as if they were Linear B. . . .

We went on and on with it. Too much! I thought to myself all the time, full of excitement and pride, it is a great lesson. We are inventing, we are learning parts of speech and puns and structure of language and intricacies of grammar — all participating, with fun, uproar, excitement, consultant approval, letters from the superintendent saying as how Frank and I were creative teachers, A's for the kids, Frank and I coming to work feeling good and ready to go, happy parents — and we all lived through a kind of Golden Age of Rooms 31 and 45 at Spanish Main School. I mean we were a big success — more importantly *I* was; Frank had already been one for some time.

In this marvelous confident mood we approached the beginning of the year in Creative Arts. We had more ideas than you could shake a stick at.

For most of that year Frank and I agreed that CA — as the school soon began calling it — was absolutely the worst class we could have imagined. Nothing worked right. We had a lot to blame it on, griping to each other, commiserating together,

telling each other it wasn't our fault. It was the administration's fault for one thing, scheduling things wrong. Then it was the kids' fault, for not being the right kind of kids. It was also the school's fault, for manifesting an atmosphere in which you wouldn't do anything unless you were made to.

In fact, another two main things — of a quite different nature, and yet quite firmly connected — were at fault. The first was what had seemed to us a detail and concerned leaving class. On the very first day we issued Permanent Hall Passes, each with a particular kid's name on it, and told the kids they could come and go in and out of our classrooms at any time, without asking permission or leave, and they could go anywhere around the school grounds. If stopped they had only to show their passes. We announced this casually; it seemed simple and obvious to us. One of the biggest drags in a school is the fact that whenever a kid wants to go anywhere, or whenever you want to send a kid somewhere to get something or do something, you have to stop and write out a pass, sign it, date it, put down the time and his expected destination. If you didn't, then the kid was sure to get stopped by some adult in the halls or wherever he was and get in trouble for being in the halls without a pass. Then the kid would come back to you, sometimes with the adult in question or with some goofy Rally Boy or Rally Girl who was On

Duty at the time, and demand that you save him from detention or calling his mom for this sin, and you'd have to say Yeah, I sent him out, or Yeah, I said he could go . . . then like as not the kid hadn't gone where you said for him to go or where he said he was going, and so you had to go into that, and in the end everyone was mad and nothing had been accomplished, except maybe the kid had gotten his smoke in the bathroom, supposing that was what he wanted.

Being smart, we got around all that with the Permanent Hall Passes. The kids were ecstatic, and spent quite a bit of time that first day interrogating us as to what we really meant. They kept it up so long I finally got mad and yelled that it meant they could leave anytime, go anywhere on the grounds, that yes, once and for all yes, that was what it meant and if anyone said another word about it I was pulling back these passes and it was all off. Then they believed it.

The second thing was that all the great notions we had, all the ideas for things to do, all our apparatus for insuring a creative, industrious, happy, meaningful class didn't seem to excite the kids all that much. Most of the kids didn't want to do any of them at all, anytime. They didn't want to write to the Peace Corps, they didn't want to bring cigar boxes and make avant-garde environments, they didn't want to make plaster statuary, they didn't want to write stories, they didn't want to paint left-handed or make up new languages . . . they didn't want to do a fucking thing except use that fucking Permanent Hall Pass in the way it was supposed to be used, namely to take it and leave the class, roam around, come back in, leave again, roam around and come back in. When they went out they would say *There's Nothing To Do Around Here,* and leave, and when they came back they would say *There's Nothing To Do Out There* and everyone would agree and say that awhile and bitch about the number of adults and narc Rally Boys who made them show their pass and brag to each other about how they told off the chicken-shit narcs of all sorts . . . and for the first few days we were besieged by teachers and Rally Boys asking were those unbelievable *Permanent Hall Passes* valid and we'd say yes, and then for a few more days we were visited by kids who had invented excuses to get out of class in order to drop by and ask us urgently if it were really true that we had given out *Permanent Hall Passes* to *Every Kid* in our *Class,* and we'd say Yes! . . . and after those gripes and narratives had run out of interest someone would remember to say There's Nothing To Do In Here again, and out most of the kids would go.

Well, as a lesson plan, there is nothing I can recommend quite so highly as a Permanent Hall Pass. After a while, Frank and I, on the edge of complete despair, began to figure out what was wrong with the ideas that had worked so well in our regular classes. It was very simple. Why did the kids in regular class like to do all that inventive stuff? Why, only because it was better than the regular stuff. If you wrote a fake journal pretending to be Tutankhamen's favorite embalmer, it was better than reading the dull Text, answering Questions on ditto sheets, Discussing, making Reports, or taking Tests. Sure it was better — not only that but you knew the teacher liked it better for some insane reason which you didn't have to understand and you would get better grades for it than you were used to getting in social studies or English. But that only applied to a regular class where it was clear you had to (1) stay there all period and (2) you had to be doing something or you might even get an F. Take away those two items, as Frank and I had done in all innocence, and you get a brief vision of the truth.

Here we find Dennison discussing at length one student in The First Street School. He compares the experiences of a girl who was having difficulty in public school and in The First Street School. In general, the girl's behavior is very aggressive. Dennison shows with examples that authority used in the child's prior schooling did not help her to learn about limits. He argues that limits necessarily refer to the border between individual and social needs and that an interactive environment is needed for each person to learn this for himself. Limits must be personal and incorporated in-

ternally. Dennison gives examples to show how they can be learned through realistic interaction with peers and teachers. As you read this excerpt, try to imagine how you would deal with a similar problem.

GEORGE DENNISON

EXCERPT FROM
THE LIVES
OF CHILDREN

I have been stressing the fact that the idea of freedom, to be intelligible, must be stated in terms of actions and individuals; and I have just mentioned that children at play support one another's ego growth. Let me describe Maxine's experience — both at the public school and at First Street — in terms of the behavior that most deserves to be called symptomatic; and let us see how the different environments affected her, and what role was played by the children themselves.

Maxine was a great "tester of limits." Like most neurotic behavior, this testing was self-defeating. She would scream and quarrel over some object which in fact meant little to her; or she would antagonize the teachers when in fact she wanted their friendship. This behavior was

From *The Lives of Children*, by George Dennison. Copyright © 1969 by George Dennison. Reprinted by permission of Random House, Inc.

clouded and obscure, it was not functional in the immediate situation. Yet it concealed a tendency that *was* functional — or that might be, if only it could be clarified. This is worth spelling out, for the behavior that is described loosely by the phrase "testing the limits" is often misinterpreted by writers on education. Children who engage in it are not interested in license. Nor are they wasting their time, though certainly they are in a dilemma. The chief source of misunderstanding is this: that the idea is often applied exclusively to the child, as if it described a characteristic, or character trait, whereas it is meant to be applied to the child *in* his particular environment. It describes the dynamics of a situation, not the behavior of an individual.

Maxine was somewhat frightened by her own impulses. She needed to know in what way she could rely upon others — children and teachers both — to handle the impulses she could not handle herself. But she was also frightened of the other children, not physically, but as competitors and rivals, for in her eyes her age-mates were far more mature than she was. And so she needed to know what special privileges she might obtain, and where she might establish her own security. Hence she needed to know exactly where the power lay. It was as if she were asking herself on what terms she could be part of a group, on what terms have her personal wishes gratified. What good thing might be offered her in return for giving up her infantile desires? She wanted to know,

too, which aspects of her teachers' behavior constituted the true authority of adult life. Which aspects could be trusted, and which persons, for she was far too necessitous to allow herself to relate to merely capricious behavior. All this was the meaning of her testing the limits; and it is worth mentioning here that such testing is quite normal at an earlier age (and therefore looks vastly different) and occurs routinely in the family circle. The goal of all this activity, though Maxine herself might have sensed it only in the most disorganized way, was precisely what any adult would agree was necessary to her growth: the organization of self and world — a self that might be more than impulse, social activity that might be more than constraint. Her needs were so extreme that she tried to make every occasion answer them. And here we see why such behavior is especially disturbing, for the needs that Maxine experienced in extreme forms are in fact basic in every child's life, to say nothing of the lives of the adults, who experience them in moments of severe temptation. Her antics touched deep chords in her classmates and teachers. She was irresistible. If one were to draw back and take a comic view of the situations she created, the figure that would emerge would be precisely that of Harpo Marx.

The word "limits," then, does not mean rules and regulations and figures of authority. It refers to the border line at which individual and social necessities meet and merge, the true edge of necessity. This is as much as to say that the question, Who am I? belongs to the question, Who are you? They are not two questions at all, but one single, indissoluble fact.

How did Maxine ask this dualistic question? She asked it by stealing Dodie's soda pop, and by shouting some loud irrelevancy when Rudella was trying to question her teacher, and by taking all the magnets from the other children and kicking her teacher in the shins, and by grabbing Eléna's cookies at lunchtime. And what answers did she receive? But let me describe the public-school answers first, for she had done the very same things in the public school. She had stolen someone's cookies, but it was the teacher who responded, not the victim; and so Maxine could not find out the meaning of her action among her peers. Nor could that long and subtle chain of childrens' reactions — with all their surprising turns of patience and generosity — even begin to take shape. And when Maxine confronted the teacher directly, shouting in class and drowning her out, she was punished in some routine way and was again deprived of the individual, relational response which would have meant much to her. Yet she kept pressing on, creating crisis after crisis, always insisting upon relation.

Now the other half of testing the limits becomes clear. For what were the limits? The teacher herself was constrained by orders from above and by the inexorable demands of the schedule. She had to earn a living, had to secure herself with superiors and observe many regulations which violated her own better judgment. She could not express her feelings or act upon them, and was forced to cultivate a patience that often resembled mere inhibition. One would say that she herself was in a quandary of limits. Where did the edge of necessity lie? Was she sacrificing herself to an unworthy notion of social demands? Who held the power? The UFT? The supervisors? The parents?

The quandary of the teacher affected Maxine. It deepened her confusion and deprived her of relation. And it frustrated — precisely — her need for limits.

The forms of necessity are the same for children as for adults. Necessity cannot be argued with; it is overwhelming in one way or another, which is to say that it possesses a superior rationality, a persuasive function, an unanswerable force, the power of numbers. Let us imagine Maxine searching for the edge of necessity. She understands that her teacher is compromised, for she sees that her judgment has no scope and that she rarely acts upon either insight or feeling. The teacher is an instrument in other persons' hands. But who are those other persons? And what power does the teacher have? For Maxine wants security, and she must know. What, too, are the demands of the group? But then what is the group? There seems to be none, for the children are not allowed to establish real relations among themselves. We know that Maxine feels herself to be a little odd and guesses that her needs are special. How shall she bring this to anyone's attention? Whose attention? And what can they do?

The testing goes on and on . . . and the reason does not lie in Maxine, but in the fact that under such conditions as prevail in the public schools — or in any highly institutionalized way of life — there is simply no such thing as limits in the true social and psychic sense. Everything is arbitrary.

At First Street Maxine tested the limits and arrived — lo and behold! — at limits. She snatched up Dodie's soda pop and proceeded to drink it: one swallow, two . . . Dodie gapes at her wide-eyed . . . three swallows . . . "Hey!" Dodie lunges for the bottle. Maxine skips away, but Dodie catches her, and though she does not strike her, she makes drinking soda pop quite impossible. Maxine has much to think about. Apparently the crime is not so enormous. Dodie allowed her two swallows, but was obviously offended. More than that Dodie will not allow. An hour later they are playing together. Dodie did not reject her. You can play with Dodie, but you can't drink up all her soda pop. She runs fast, too, and I bet she'll hit me some day. (Dodie did finally hit Maxine one day . . . and they still remained playmates . . . and the days of stealing soda pop were long gone.)

Maxine takes Eléna's cookies. That's over in a minute. Eléna throws her to the floor and kicks her in the rear, cursing at her in Spanish. The kicks don't hurt, but they're kicks all the same. This is no source of cookies! But Eléna is impressive in her ardor, and perhaps she's a source of security, a really *valuable* friend. An hour later they are playing in their "castle." Eléna is the queen, and Maxine, for several reasons, chooses to be her baby.

Maxine shouts while Rudella is speaking to Susan, her teacher. Rudella is disgusted. "Why don't you shut up, Maxine! You're always makin' so much *noise!*" Other voices second her. "Yeah, Maxine!" "Shut up, Maxine!" No one punishes her. Susan says, "What is it, Maxine? If you're in such a hurry, go ahead and tell us." Or Susan, too, gets angry and yells at her. In any event, Maxine again has much to think about. Susan's anger is immediate and personal; nothing lies beyond it. Susan takes herself seriously, and Maxine must take her seriously, too. As for the kids, when they are all yelling at her together, they are too much even for her own formidable powers of resistance. While she can absorb endless numbers of demerits, endless hours of detention, endless homilies and rebukes, she must pay attention to this massed voice of her own group. She needs them. They are her playmates. But her need of them is balanced by their need of her. There is a basis here for give and take. Too, Maxine's own peculiar needs have been accepted, not that they will be answered necessarily, but they have been accepted as her very own attributes. Her anxieties are out in the open. So, too, are the many impulses she has such difficulty in mastering; and wonder upon wonders!

— the others can handle them, can actually handle them in the exact form in which they arise! Maxine heaves a sigh of relief. She can do her worst and she'll still have a social group around her, because people really *can* take care of themselves. And she knows now where the power lies. It's right there under her nose. The kids have some of it and the teachers have the rest. And they really have it, because there's no principal, no schedule, no boss. Why even the teachers blow their lids! George spanked her the other day when she took all the magnets and kicked him in the shins. Just like Eléna, only worse because the spanking hurt. Yet they played together half an hour later and he wasn't mad any more.

Given the radical environmental change at First Street, the inherent rationality of Maxine's testing gradually came to the surface and achieved its purpose. For the limits were there to be discovered, the true border line, in all its particularity, at which Maxine's unorganized self met the more organized demands of the people who made up her group. Her need for relation was answered, and with it her need for security. Nor was she obliged to feel so very special in the oddities of her needs, for *all* the kids were special, all spoke in distinctive ways and had immediate access to the teachers and to each other. No one had to wonder what mysterious hierarchical necessities lay beyond the teachers' words and actions. There was no ulterior power. Good sense arose in the occasion, as did everything else: feel-

ing, judgment . . . even the day-to-day conception of the appropriate tasks of learning.

Daniels, working with junior high school students, gives examples of how psychodrama and role playing can be used to help students internalize limits. He describes these kinds of informal acting and shows how they bring a new level of awareness to age-old problems. Awareness does not magically stop students from breaking classroom rules, forming gangs, or cutting school, but it does bring teacher/student interaction into a new and sometimes refreshing arena. The techniques themselves provide students with a large measure of freedom within a specific context. In addition to their specific utility, they can also be used as a model for planning other activities that create freedom through new kinds of limits.

STEVEN DANIELS

EXCERPT FROM
HOW 2 GERBILS,
20 GOLDFISH,
200 GAMES,
2,000 BOOKS
AND I
TAUGHT THEM
HOW TO READ

The activity that my students enjoy most . . . is role-playing and psychodrama. Psychodrama, the creation of Dr. J. L. Moreno of Beacon, New York, is a combination of sociological role-playing and psychological group therapy. It permits the students to get out their feelings toward me, school, one another, racism, gangs, sex, or any other subject. In classroom form, it calls for setting up a wide circle of chairs, with two chairs in the middle, on the "stage." All the students in the class sit in the circle, and any student who wants to talk, or in any other way act out his feelings, is free

From *How 2 Gerbils, 20 Goldfish, 200 Games, 2,000 Books and I Taught Them How to Read,* by Steven Daniels. Copyright © MCMLXXI, The Westminster Press. Used by permission.

to come and sit in (stand, walk around) one of the middle chairs. He can ask someone else to sit in the other chair, or the other chair can remain empty. On occasion, more chairs are moved into the center. The lighting and staging effects are controlled by a director (usually myself). Audience participation is encouraged at all times, and the only restriction governing psychodrama in my room is that there be no physical violence.

The most exciting psychodrama I personally participated in occurred with Stanley Frazier during my first year. Of all the control problems I had that year, Stanley was the biggest. Incessantly talking, leaving the room as though it were a movie house and he wanted more popcorn, chewing gum until I was convinced he'd need false teeth. (A year later, recalling that there were some college classes I couldn't get through without a cigarette, I changed my mind about the value of chewing gum.)

On a Monday in the middle of the year, lights dimmed, Stanley moved to one of the center chairs. He asked me to share the stage with him. Then he loudly announced that he was going to be the teacher, and that I should act as Stanley. I agreed, walked over to one of his classmates, asked for a stick of gum, and returned to my chair. Then, as elaborately as possible, I unwrapped the gum, stuck it in my mouth, and threw the wrapper on the floor. Stanley, acting very much the teacher, stood up, approached my chair, and said, "Spit it out." I continued chewing. "Spit it out!"

he said, pointing a finger at me. I did nothing. He wheeled, walked over to the corner of the room, brought back the wastepaper basket and with all the authority he could muster, firmly spoke: "Stanley, I want you to pick up your wrapper, put your gum in it, and throw them in this basket!" Still, I did nothing. Stanley looked at his classmates in the circle, then looked back at me. There wasn't a sound in the room. Quietly he put the wastepaper basket back in the corner and returned to his seat in the circle.

An impressive lesson. Without physical force, you can't make a ghetto student do something which he vehemently refuses to do. Superficially, I learned that teacher-baiting can be fun, and Stanley found out what it was like to be faced with a Stanley in his class. Not suprisingly, his misbehavior through the end of the year was minimal.

Another psychodrama concerned gang wars. Two members of one gang sat across from and confronted two members of another gang. Since physical violence was against the rules, the language was pretty strong. Though most of the interplay centered around who had the stronger gang — regardless of who was playing which role — it came out in one long exchange that one of the reasons most kids join gangs is fear: fear that they will be socially ostracized if they don't, and fear for their physical safety if they remain independent.

While a few psychodramas in one classroom didn't stop gang wars in Philadelphia, the lesson that joining gangs is a product of weakness and not of strength is something I could never formally teach.

Role-playing, while not as psychologically involving as psychodrama, is just as stimulating. One Monday during my second year the room was turned into Municipal Court no. 407. The defendant, Alan Jenkins, was an extroverted, good-looking boy. He was charged with cutting school for two days (which was true). Alan wasn't particularly embarrassed at being singled out for this offense, as most kids cut at one time or another during the year. If anything, he was a little proud of it.

After Alan was sworn in, Robert Coleman, the prosecuting attorney, started the interrogation: "How come you cut? You know you can't get a job without an education."

Alan didn't say anything.

Robert (more impatient): You ain't gonna get nowhere if you cut. Man, if you skip school —

Defense attorney Keith Morton interjected: "You don't learn nothin' at school. You can learn more outa here. How do you know you can't get a job, huh?"

Robert: Listen, I know.
Keith: How do you know?
Robert: Listen, man, I know!

After two minutes of this the judge, another student, quieted everybody down. Then he leaned over his desk and queried Alan directly:

Judge: Whad'ja learn outa school?
Alan: Nothin' much.
Judge: Whad'ja do?
Alan: Walked around and played sports.
Judge: Don'cha know it's against the law to cut school?

Finally, the case went to the jury, which was composed of the rest of the class. They returned a verdict of "guilty as charged," but recommended probation. They further ordered that if Alan cut again, he "be made to stay after school one hour a day for a week," in effect making up the time he was out.

This warning proved effective. Either Alan didn't cut again or he had the sense to have the same person forge all his absence excuses.

————————————

This article by Norman Newberg brings together the ideas and problems of this chapter by looking at both freedom and limits theoretically and practically. In one example, the boundaries are blurry and the teachers do very little to adapt their teaching styles to the new kinds of freedom they imagine they are offering. In a second example, we see a teacher who is experimenting with new ways of guiding his students authoritatively (rather than using an authoritarian approach). The result is real freedom within limits that the students regard as clearly necessary, fair, and helpful. As Newberg says, "Teachers are paid

to serve students." After reading this, ask yourself how you might serve your students in ways that would increase their freedom.

NORMAN A. NEWBERG

SHARING RESPONSIBILITY FOR LEARNING

I recently visited an experimental project within a public high school in Cambridge, Mass., in which the stated goals of the teaching staff were to establish nonauthoritarian role relationships with students. The faculty hoped that students would then be more responsible for their own learning; they would use each other as resources and would see teachers as nonthreatening colleagues. The project is now in a state of crisis because the teaching staff has been made acutely aware by many of the students and parents that the atmosphere in the school is neither conducive to learning, nor psychologically and

This article was specially prepared for this book. Copyright © 1976 by Norman A. Newberg.

physically safe for children. The teaching staff's response to this indictment was to establish a clear set of criteria for expelling students from the program.

I was present at a house meeting in which two teachers presented their criteria for expulsion. The atmosphere of the meeting was exceptionally tense. Students were angry because they had not been consulted in establishing these criteria. The teachers responded that students were always asking teachers to take more responsibility, and when they finally did, students were dissatisfied because they felt excluded. The students retorted that they had always been told, and especially at a point of crisis, "Look, this is your school; what happens here is your responsibility." Another student replied, "I cut eight times before I was caught, what can I do now." Implicit in both statements is the realization among students that they were very much alone in this process of creating a new contex for learning, that the boundaries were entirely blurred, and that they had no givens or outer limits that they could rely on. Now the teachers were beginning to crack down and the students were shocked. They did not want to return to an authoritarian rule. Several basic confusions in role relationship seem apparent here. The teacher must sort out the differences among three basic roles: an authoritarian, an authority figure (i.e., in loco parentis), and a master who speaks authoritatively.

Although very few students today will submit to an authoritarian relationship, they do want some sense of structure in their educational context. Chaos is as frightening to children as it is to adults. Children do expect parents to protect them from physical and psychological harm. They also need to learn how to take care of themselves. In a school as teachers, which is not unlike being in a home as parents, we face the uncertainty of how to strike a balance between dependence, independence, and interdependence. We can learn something from each mode of behavior; the trick is not to become stuck in one mode and thereby impoverish our repertoire for experiencing life. Unfortunately, many so-called liberated teachers reacting against the authoritarian teachers they experienced as students refuse to set any limits. Some even refuse to share what they know with some sense of authoritativeness for fear of stifling the students' response. If that way of operating persists, those teachers will be guilty of creating a cultural jungle in which it will be necessary to discover the wheel rather than reinvent it. Teachers are paid to serve students. Students expect teachers to provide reliable information and the processes for solving problems.

What they do not want is to play the game of "the correct answer" inside the teacher's head. The problem for the teacher, then, is to say — with a sense of authoritativeness — "These are my expectations of you"; or "This is the Pythagorean Theorem"; or "Let's imagine the wheel has not been discovered; how would you go about inventing the wheel?" Those statements provide information the student needs to know if he is to cope in his society. He also needs experience in coping with ambiguity and relativity. To that end, the teachers need to shift roles into a collaborative relationship where together they search for an unknown answer or answers. The problem teachers face is not the authoritarian versus democratic style of teaching. Rather, it is one of intellectual and emotional integrity. Students expect teachers to see them as people first — responsive to their human concerns. And human concerns are complex and at times ambiguous; one mode of operating cannot answer them.

I would like to describe in detail one class period in which a high school teacher prepares a context for "student-directed" learning. I believe that you will recognize that these students have command of particular processes for directing their own learning. Student-directed learning does not happen simply because teachers or students affix the word FREE in front of the word school. Student-directed learning occurs as students are prepared to take responsibility for their own learning. For this to occur, new roles must be learned by students and their teachers.

What follows is a description of a classroom that I visited at Olney High School in Philadelphia. Olney is an integrated high school that had experienced very intense racial strife. The classroom I will describe is a social studies class which is participating in an effective approach to the study of the city. The particular program is called "urban affairs" and it is a part of the Philadelphia Affective Education Program. The teacher in this classroom is Mr. Jack Fein.

When I enter the room, Mr. Fein informs us that his class has recently completed a unit using the Fenton Social Studies Series. The Fenton Series focuses on important social and human relations issues in contemporary society. He tells us that this work has proceeded rather slowly and student involvement with the Fenton materials has been moderately successful. Now Mr. Fein is moving the class to a more self-directed program and he has had considerable difficulty encouraging these students to take responsibility for their own learning. Earlier this week he had his class videotaped and played the tape for his students so that they might analyze the dynamics of their classroom behavior.

On this particular day he plans to make the class a student-directed experience. Students have had some prior experience with taking responsibility for running the class. Mr. Fein has been working with a concept developed by my colleague, Dr. Terry Borton, called "the learning group," and these students are familiar with some of the roles that exist in a learning group. For example, they know the role structure of a Navigator. A Navigator is selected by the class to keep the group in touch with its goals or goal and to help the group navigate through the complexities of inter-

personal difficulties or various problems in solving a particular task.

As the class enters the room Mr. Fein asks them to group themselves in a corner of the room. The students form a circle and Mr. Fein says, "I'd like you to take out a pencil and paper and think about the following question: What makes me different from the other students in this classroom? How am I being perceived by my classmates? Now I would like you to make a list of about five questions that you would like to ask of your classmates that would give you more information about how you are perceived in this classroom." At this point, about half of the students are seen to be writing particular questions that they would like to ask. The other students are talking among themselves, and the atmosphere in the classroom is quite informal.

When most of the students have finished the assignment, they start talking again, and at one point a student speaks directly to Mr. Fein. Two girls say, "Jack" ("Jack" is Mr. Fein's first name), "what do we do now?" Mr. Fein does not respond. After another pause, a second student, Sondra, asks Jack Fein this question, "Are we supposed to take over the class today?" Mr. Fein does not respond. The student turns from Mr. Fein and addresses her classmates. "I think we're supposed to take over the class today." There is some laughter about that and another student asks, "Who is going to be the Navigator?" A girl volunteers to be the Navigator and the class appears organized to move ahead

with the problem that was stated at the beginning of the class. The Navigator says, "Who wants to go first? Who wants to ask some questions about themselves?"

Student: How do you see my personality?
Pat: I see you as an honest person. I like the way you talk. Everytime you say something everybody gets quiet, but when Tyrone talks we get noisy.
Tyrone: Do I get on your nerves?
Sharon: You don't get on my nerves, but you upset me.
Sandi: You upset yourself. *(Speaking to another student)* She does.
Charlie: I think you're funny, Tyrone.
Bill: Hey, Jack *(speaking to Mr. Fein),* can I get a drink of water?
All the students say "no."
Bill: Jack, can I get a drink of water?
Jack doesn't respond to the student's request.
Jack: (To the entire class) At this point if you would like to use a barometer, perhaps he might be helpful to this process. What the barometer will do is tell you when he thinks you're not taking the problem seriously. If he feels that you're not taking the problem seriously, he will raise his hand. If he thinks you are taking the problem seriously, he will not raise his hand.
Pat: John, how come you don't talk very much? You've been with us now for a couple of months. Seems like you should feel more comfortable.

John #1: Everytime you have a debate, I'm trying to figure out how I can give the right answer.

Tyrone: Instead of answering yourself?

John #1: I'm trying to figure out what's right or wrong.

Pat: It's just your opinion. Why not take a chance?

Lydia: Do you all think I'm distant, away from this class?

Sandi: (Not speaking to Lydia) She used to always give her opinion; now she doesn't.

John #2: Do I seem lost or with the class? *(A lot of laughter at this question; some kids yell out alternately "you're lost," "you're with it.")*

At this point the Barometer raises his hand. The Navigator recognizes the Barometer's intervention and says to her classmates, "Hey, we're not being serious."

Linda: How can I be more active?

Sandi: She whispers a lot. Linda, say it outright.

Charlie: Where do you think my mind is at?

Pat: I don't think you're being straight now.

By this time the tone of the class is serious and personal. At the beginning of the class at least 50 percent of the students were uninvolved. By the end of the class there was a quiet concentration among the students periodically punctuated by warm laughter and some teasing. At this point the teacher decides to intervene with the class. Mr. Fein says, "I'd like to see if you can evaluate today's class for yourselves. If you think that today's class was an example of how you'd like the class to be regularly, group yourselves at the end of the room" (pointing to the north end of the room): "If you feel that today's class was least like you'd like it to be regularly, group yourselves near the south end of the room. You may group yourselves along a line which indicates that it was more like you want it to be or less like you want it to be. So you may also distribute yourselves around the middle and points from the middle." The students moved to group themselves. Three quarters of the group grouped themselves around the middle of the room spreading out to the north with the greatest concentration near the midpoint of the northern end. A few students grouped themselves near the mid-point of the southern end of the continuum and two students were situated at the extreme south portion of the classroom. Judging by this scale the majority of the students favored this particular classroom format over a traditional teacher-directed class.

This was an exhilarating class to observe. We sensed that the students and their teacher were developing a fresh contract for learning. What processes did each party use to negotiate this contract? How did a different context emerge in which new roles were available to these students and their teacher? Obviously Mr. Fein has struggled with a variety of approaches. His distant objective from the beginning of the school term has been to move this class to the point where class members will take more responsibility for what happens in the class. Mr. Fein began the term by using imaginative texts like the Fenton Series and achieved some small return in limited student participation in classroom discussions. Generally speaking, his class was still dependent on him as a prime generator of ideas and strategies. Mr. Fein then introduced the notion that each class member, including the teacher, plays many roles — some implicit, others explicit. By observing their behavior played back via videotape, students were able to gain some objectivity in seeing *how* they operated in this class. Mr. Fein had also introduced a new student role — the Navigator, which is now a part of the class repertoire.

The preceding comments illustrate the kinds of strategy that Mr. Fein used to activate student responsibility in this class. Now let's take a second look at Mr. Fein's behavior in the class to see how he has redefined his own role to compliment the new changes in student behavior. In his first statement to the class, Mr. Fein states the problem: ". . . Make a list of about five questions that you would like to ask of your classmates that would give you more information about how you are being perceived in this classroom." Then, he withdraws to the sidelines and creates a leadership vacuum that must eventually be filled by students. Mr. Fein is very clear about what he will and will not do. When a student asks him a direct question, "May I get a drink of water?", he ignores the question and lets the group handle the student's diversionary tactics. From the time he sets the problem he intervenes only two more times: once to add a second role of the Barometer and again when he structures a final evaluation of the class. In addition to the master teacher role, Mr. Fein now has a substantially different way of relating to students through a role of facilitator. In the fifty-minute period we described, Mr. Fein made three statements consuming about five minutes of class time.

When Mr. Fein refuses to fill the leadership vacuum by playing teacher, the students rightly assume that it's their class. Contrast this situation and the one we described in the experimental "school within a school" in Cambridge. In the Cambridge high school, students were angry and resented the fact that teachers used the students' desire for freedom as a whip to admonish them into responsibility. In that example, teachers had abdicated responsibility for teaching new roles or new behaviors. In the Cambridge school, the faculty assumed that an egalitarian spirit would in itself generate the desire for cooperative, responsible learning and teaching. Quite the opposite turns out to be true. Our experience shows that each person needs to learn and be taught the processes of listening, sharing, leading, and

being accountable for his actions. If the teacher relinquishes his authority before students have learned how to organize themselves, chaos and bitterness are the only products they can produce. Of course it is possible for teachers to browbeat students into a dumb show of democratic process. Teaching and learning are subtle arts; it's easy to pervert an ideal into a cliché. The essence of creating a genuine alternative to the traditional factory model classroom is to be certain that both teacher and student are learning and practicing new roles.

projects
and
activities

THE
"I-MESSAGE"
CIRCLE

Limits and boundaries are not only the teacher's concern; they are the student's concern as well. Moreover, students tend to follow rules and regulations more rigorously when they have had a hand in shaping them. Many teachers recognize this tendency but make the mistake of rushing into class meetings and community rule-making. They overlook the fact that, often, students need time to share feedback with each other and with their teacher before they can make just and flexible rules. One way for students and teacher to become more aware of the effect of their behavior is by a technique called the "I-Message Circle." You can try this with students or with colleagues.

Background information

Most of the messages we send to people about their behavior are "you-messages" — messages that are directed at the other person and have a high probability of putting them down, making them feel guilty, making them feel their needs are not important and generally making them resist change. Examples of you-messages are usually orders or commands ("Stop doing that"; "Get into the corner"; "Stop tapping that pencil"; "Leave him alone"), or blaming or name-calling statements ("You are acting like a baby"; "You are driving me crazy"), or statements that give solutions ("You should ———"; "You'd better ——— "), thereby removing the responsibility for behavior change from the other person. Perhaps the worst of all you-messages is the if-then threat ("If you don't ——— then I will ——— ").

An "I-message," on the other hand, allows a person who is affected by the behavior of another to express the effect it has on him and, at the same time, leave the responsibility for modifying the behavior with the person who demonstrated the particular behavior. An *I-message* consists of three parts: the specific

This activity was written by Marc N. Levin, Teacher Training Coordinator, Philadelphia Affective Development Program, and is reprinted here with his permission. "I-Message" is a term used by Dr. Thomas Gordon in his book *Parent Effectiveness Training* (1971). See the reading by Gordon ("Six Steps of the No-Lose Method," pp. 268–271) for a discussion of the technique.

behavior, the feeling you experienced as a result of the behavior, and the tangible effect on you. Thus a teacher might say to a student:

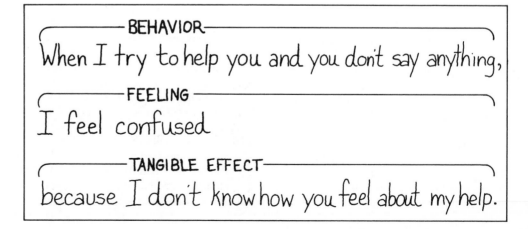

BEHAVIOR
When you tap on your desk with your pencil,

FEELING
I feel upset because

TANGIBLE EFFECT
I get distracted and have difficulty teaching.

or

BEHAVIOR
When I try to help you and you don't say anything,

FEELING
I feel confused

TANGIBLE EFFECT
because I don't know how you feel about my help.

In effect, the I-message allows the sender to say implicitly, "I trust you to decide what change in behavior is necessary." In this manner I-messages build relationships and, equally important, they do not place the sender in the position of enforcing a new behavior as is frequently the case with the you-messages discussed above.

For all these reasons it would be helpful for teachers to have I-messages become the norm for expressing dissatisfaction about another's behavior. There are two ways to introduce I-messages into the classroom as a norm. One, of course, is for teachers to begin using I-messages to express their own feelings and dissatisfactions. Another is the I-message circle.

Procedure

Gather the students in a circle. Explain to them what an I-message is and prepare a few examples so they can hear what they sound like. It might be helpful to give them a few hypothetical situations and have them volunteer some I-messages. For instance, what would you say to a student who keeps bothering you when you are interested in the lesson, or to a teacher who hasn't returned composition papers in a long time? Explain to them that for the next ten minutes (it helps to set a time

limit) we are going to send I-messages to each other, following three rules:

1. Only those who wish to send an I-message need to do so.
2. No one can respond to a message sent to them.
3. All messages should contain at least the behavior and the feeling. (For the I-message circle the tangible effect portion of the message may be omitted: this mainly serves to clarify the relationship between behavior and feeling.)

At this point it would be helpful for the teacher to write the formula for I-message on the blackboard. When you *(behavior)* I feel *(emotion, feeling)*. The teacher should keep in mind several rules:

1. Participate yourself. Receive some messages and remember not to respond to them. If the students begin to send all their messages to you, explain that you are only one member of the group and it is not fair for everyone to send you messages.
2. Be aware if any student begins to receive many messages. It is not fair for him to be "dumped on." If you see this beginning to happen, you might want to introduce a new rule saying that no one should receive more than two messages before everyone else has received one.
3. Remind the students when only two minutes are left. You might point out that it is common for people to think of something they would like to say and then decide to hold it. Tell them if they don't share it now, they will have to wait for another time.

4. Intercede only when necessary. In some situations, however, when the class is first using the I-message circle, it is helpful for the teacher to intervene. In the beginning it is usually difficult to make the behavior and the feelings very specific. The teacher can help by indicating when the feelings and behaviors presented are general or when the I-message refers to a point in time rather than a behavior (When you were talking about ——— I felt ———). Also students will often describe a thought that occurs to them or try to analyze the behavior rather than reporting a feeling of their own (When you ——— I feel that you're upset). Again, it is important to remind the students of the formula and encourage them to give a specific feeling and a specific behavior.

5. When the exercise is over, check with students to see if they found it valuable. If you found it valuable, share your reasons with them. If they are willing to try it several more times, you might institute it as something to be done for 10 minutes a couple of times a week. The result may be a class that has more awareness about its individual and group behaviors and more understanding about the feelings behaviors produce. They may begin to feel better about and closer to each other and be more willing to share responsibility for the class's success or failure with you. No less important, it may help them to see you

in a different light and generally improve your relationship with them.

WHO DECIDES?

One of the issues that teachers confront is clarity about the responsibilities they wish to maintain and the decisions they are willing to leave up to students. If teachers are not clear about this, they often wind up resentful when students do not take responsibility for themselves or when they feel free to decide things about which the teacher has definite preferences. The following activity is designed to help you clarify this matter.

Procedure

1. Fill in the blanks below. When deciding where to put each decision, consider all areas of classroom life, such as managerial rules and regulations, scheduling, curriculum content, seating arrangements, evaluation, small group composition, and use of materials. Be as specific as possible.

Decisions I want to make

_____

_____

Decisions the students can make

_____

_____

_____

_____

_____

Decisions the students and I should make together

_____

_____

_____

2. If you are presently teaching, you might want to find out how your students perceive your preferences. List for them all the decisions you thought of and ask them to guess for each one whether they think you would like to make this decision yourself, leave it to them, or share the decision-making. You might also ask them which decisions *they* prefer to make themselves and which they would want to leave in your hands or discuss together.

RESOLVING CONFLICTS

As Thomas Gordon so neatly expresses it, many conflicts between adults and children are solved by "win-lose" methods. Either the adult or the child emerges victorious instead of both parties being satisfied. In order to change to a "no-lose" situation, it is necessary to generate possible alternative solutions to the conflict and find one that is acceptable to both the adult and the child.

Procedure

1. In each of the role-playing situations below, there is a conflict between the teacher and the student. Role play each situation twice. The first time, both the student and the teacher should be out to "win," but the second time they should work together to find the best mutually acceptable solution. If time permits, come up with some situations yourselves.

— A student wants the teacher to finish the second half of a short story she is writing. The teacher doesn't think it would help the student if he did the writing for her.
— The teacher is going to hold a class discussion on the causes of inflation. Prior to class, a student approaches the teacher and says that she is upset about an argument she just had with her boyfriend and doesn't want to participate in class today. The teacher is sympathetic, but also feels that the student would benefit from the discussion.
— Two students are fighting over the use of a microscope. The teacher wants them to work out their problem by themselves, but each student refuses and wants the teacher to intercede on his behalf.

As a guideline, the six steps of the "no-lose method" are provided here:

a. identifying and defining the conflict
b. generating possible alternative solutions
c. evaluating the alternative solutions

d. deciding on the best acceptable solution
e. working out ways of implementing the solution
f. following up to evaluate how it worked

2. After each scene is role played the second time, observers might interview the "teacher" and "student." Questions like these might be asked:

a. Did you ever feel like you were losing? What happened to make you feel that way?
b. Was the conflict resolved so that you both felt like winners?
c. What was done to facilitate "getting together?" or What was blocking the resolution of the conflict?

EXAMINING YOUR CLASSROOM RULES

Because a classroom is a social organization, rules are necessary. Without rules, classrooms, like games, turn into chaos.

This activity originated in a "boundaries workshop" conducted by the Philadelphia Affective Education Program, Norman A. Newberg, Director We appreciate their permission to adapt their activity for this book.

Although many rules can be determined by the class members themselves, every teacher has his or her own. This exercise will help you to get feedback on the rules you intend to make when you become a teacher, or the rules you currently have with your students.

Procedure

This procedure will work with groups of ten or less.

1. Make a careful list of *all* the rules that are either explicit or implicit for living or working within your classroom. (Don't put your name on it but do indicate grade level.) Use the language you actually use or would use. Be honest!
2. Collect all the lists. Shuffle, and redistribute them so that no one gets his own paper back and no one knows whose list he has received.
3. Each group member should take a turn reporting to the others the rules on the list he has received. He should then assume that he is a student in that person's class and should soliloquize about the following: What kind of teacher makes these rules and demands? What do I think his reasons are for them? Which rules are clear to me? Which ones sound flexible? Which seem realistic? Which rules would I find hardest to agree with? Which would be hardest to follow? Keep in mind that the goal of this activity is to allow each person to see how his rules "come across" to students.

---

4. Allow time for group members to reinforce or contradict the feedback given and to discuss general learnings from this experience.
5. If possible, follow up this activity by giving real students your list of rules, and asking them the same questions.

ROLE MODELS

Besides deciding what limits we need to place on students, we also need to examine the style we use in setting limits. There are ways of saying no which students can respect, and there are ways they may resent. The following activity allows you to explore the ways people in your past influenced your style of setting limits.

Procedure

1. Pair off with another person. Each of you should take some time to select a person, in your life, who had a good way

This exercise originated in a "boundaries workshop" conducted by the Philadelphia Affective Education Program, Norman A. Newberg, Director We appreciate their permission to publish this exercise.

of setting limits and boundaries and one who had a bad style. The former should be someone who could place restrictions on you or make complaints about your behavior without causing resentment. The latter should be someone you found offensive when he or she placed limits on or criticized your behavior. If you cannot select two people in your past who meet these criteria, choose someone who, at times, had a positive style and at other times, had a negative style.

2. Take turns to talk while the other listens. Try to describe and, if you can, imitate the voice, gestures, looks, tones, mood, and attitudes of the negative role model. After a while, switch to a description of the positive role model. See if you can identify specific behaviors you appreciated or resented.

3. Discuss with your partner the following questions:

a. Which model was easier to describe and imitate?
b. How much of either of these people is in you?
c. When have you acted like the positive role model and when have you acted like the negative model?

4. Last, get together with other pairs of people and collectively share your learnings. One way to do this is to develop a group list of behaviors and attitudes you appreciate and resent when someone is dealing with you.

A DEBATE
ON CLASSROOM
DISCIPLINE

Debates are often unproductive. Issues become polarized, and people become narrow-minded. Whenever a group develops a strong bias on an issue, however, it is helpful to take the other side so that ideas are not frozen. If you sense that your group has developed a bias during its work in this chapter, try this activity. If the time limits and procedures suggested are not feasible, alter them to suit your purposes.

Procedure

1. The debate is concerned with this statement: "Resolved: A teacher must bribe, coerce, threaten, and punish to manage a classroom."

2. The total group should divide themselves into an even number of small groups. Try to keep the small groups no larger than four. Half of the small groups are assigned the pro position and half are assigned the con position. Take about a half an hour preparing arguments in the small groups.

3. Each small group should select one of its members to be on the debate team. The resulting debate team for each side should not be less than three nor more than five (if they are, make adjustments in the number of representatives chosen).

4. Steps of the debate.

a. Each team has ten minutes to make its case. Its presentation can be in any form desired.
b. Each team member gets one minute of rebuttal time. It is best to alternate rebuttals between opposing teams. You can rebut any point presented previously by the other team.
c. For five minutes, each team can interview the other team, asking them any "press conference" questions they wish.
d. There is a ten-minute break in which each team huddles and prepares its final argument.
e. Each side has five minutes for its final argument.

During the debate, people in the audience are encouraged to pass notes to their debate representatives with views they want expressed. Debaters are encouraged to use proverbs, quotations, and humor in the debate.

5. When the debate is over, the group can discuss learnings derived from this experience.

additional resources

BOOKS AND ARTICLES

Ashton-Warner, Sylvia. *Spearpoint: Teacher in America.* New York: Knopf, 1972.

Castan, Frances. "Alternatives to Corporal Punishment," *Scholastic Teacher,* September, 1973, 21–27.

Craig, Eleanor. *P.S., You're Not Listening.* New York: Baron, 1972.

Dennison, George. *The Lives of Children.* New York: Random House, 1969.

Dewey, John. *Experience and Education.* New York: Macmillan, 1938.

Dreikurs, Rudolf. *Psychology in the Classroom,* 2d ed. New York: Harper and Row, 1968.

Dreikurs, Rudolf; Grunwald, Bernice B.; and Pepper, Floy C. *Maintaining Sanity in the Classroom: Illustrated Teaching Techniques.* New York: Harper and Row, 1971.

Ginott, Haim. *Teacher and Child.* New York: Macmillan, 1972.

Glasser, William. "A New Look at Discipline," *Learning,* December, 1974, Vol. 3, No. 4, 6–11.

Glasser, William. *Schools Without Failure.* New York: Harper and Row, 1972.

Gordon, Thomas L. *Parent Effectiveness Training.* New York: Peter H. Wyden, 1970.

Gordon, Thomas L. *Teacher Effectiveness Training.* New York: Peter H. Wyden, 1974.

Hart, Harold, ed. *Summerhill: For and Against.* New York: Hart, 1970.

Herndon, James. *How To Survive in Your Native Land.* New York: Simon and Schuster, 1971.

Holt, John. *Freedom and Beyond.* New York: E. P. Dutton, 1972.

Johnson, Lois V., and Bany, Mary A. *Classroom Management.* New York: Macmillan, 1970.

Kohl, Herbert. *36 Children.* New York: New American Library, 1967.

Kounin, Jacob S. *Discipline and Group Management in Classrooms.* New York: Holt, Rinehart and Winston, 1970.

Editors of Learning Magazine. *Resolving Classroom Conflicts.* Palo Alto, Calif., 1975.

Lederman, Janet. *Anger and the Rocking Chair.* New York: McGraw-Hill, 1969.

Neill, A. S. *Freedom — Not License!* New York: Hart, 1966.

Redl, Fritz. *When We Deal With Children.* New York: Free Press, Macmillan, 1966.

Rogers, Carl. *Freedom to Learn.* Columbus, Ohio: Charles E. Merrill, 1969.

Ryan, Kevin, ed. *Don't Smile Until Christmas: Accounts of the First Year Of Teaching.* Chicago: University of Chicago Press, 1970.

FILMS

Children as People. Polymorph Films, 331 Newbury Street, Boston, MA 02115. Presents a school in which children have radical avenues of freedom.

Dealing with Discipline Problems. Media Five, 1011 North Cole Avenue, Suite F, Hollywood, CA 90038.

William Glasser outlines and illustrates a six-step process for helping children to discipline themselves.

Joshua in a Box. Stephen Bosustow Productions, 1649 Eleventh Street, Santa Monica, CA 90404.

An animated cartoon which explores reactions to psychological imprisonment and freedom.

Teacher Effectiveness Training. Media Five, 1011 North Cole Avenue, Suite F, Hollywood, CA 90038.

Thomas Gordon demonstrates active listening, "I" messages, and the "no-lose" method for resolving conflicts.

Why Class Meetings? Media Five, 1011 North Cole Avenue, Suite F, Hollywood, CA 90038.

William Glasser presents a rationale for class meetings and outlines techniques that contribute to successful class discussions.

chapter
six
_____
building
active
teaching
roles

initial experiences

METAPHORS

Teachers work out how they will relate to their students in many ways. The following list provides a rough indication of the multiplicity of roles teachers might assume. (For example, a teacher who tries to act as a guru will be very different from someone who presents himself as a resource person.)

— guru
— resource person
— disciplinarian
— engineer
— doctor
— bureaucrat
— social worker
— therapist

— coach
— camp counselor
— travel agent
— parent
— Zen master
— missionary
— honest peddler
— jazz musician

1. Discuss these roles with others. Consider these questions:

a. How do you define these words as they apply to teaching?
b. What are some differences among the metaphors in the list?
c. Can you think of teachers in your past whom these labels fit?
d. Which metaphors describe your teaching style?
e. Can you add other metaphors to the list?
f. Which metaphors suggest attractive and unattractive teaching roles for you?

2. Try role playing some of these teaching styles. One way of entering a role-playing situation is to imagine it is the first day of class. How might different teachers present themselves to students in this situation?

EVALUATION EXPERIENCES

Evaluation should mean more than grading. Because it often does not, almost any activity connected with evaluation can create an overriding sense of a teacher's authority. Ordinarily, teaching involves a judgmental relationship. The intensity of the relationship will vary according to the personal effects it has on each student.

Many teachers have experimented with alternatives to traditional grading, and probably most of us as students have imagined methods of evaluation that would have a more positive effect. To ensure the success of this experimentation, one needs to think about what aspects of learning are important to evaluate. This activity is designed to help you explore some of the effects of evaluating different aspects of learning.

1. In groups of about ten, hold a gripe session. Share your worst evaluation experiences as a student. Talk about tests, papers, teachers, final grades, and anything else that relates to your personal aggravation from being evaluated at any level of your schooling. As you progress, refocus on the aspects of learning you wish teachers would aim their evaluations. Next, split the group in half and come up with one good design — from experience or imagination — for innovative evaluation. Specify the level of schooling, a course of study or the actual work, and the kind of information or experience that would be used as a basis for making a judgment. The remainder of the time can be used to share the ideas that have come from the small groups. If you are currently enrolled in a course, would they apply? How do other people in the class react to the potential effects of the design of your group?

2. The following individual project can be undertaken if time permits. Evaluate a learning activity in which you will soon be involved, as a student or as a teacher. Beforehand, make the following decisions in writing:

a. What will mark the beginning and ending of the learning activity?
b. What are your personal goals? Include consideration of cognitive, affective, and social factors.
c. What data, information, or experience should be used as the basis of evaluation?

Evaluate the activity for yourself as a student or, if you are a teacher, evaluate it for your students. Write a one-paragraph evaluation and share it and your reactions with others who have completed this task. What aspects of learning were evaluated?

introduction

Should a teacher teach? — that is the question that is being seriously raised by many teachers today. The readings thus far have indicated that many aspects of teaching do not require active communication of information, and that, at times, it is important to deemphasize leadership aspects of the teacher's role. The physical nature of an environment alone, through the instructional materials that are made available, can stimulate curiosity and allow for active self-directed learning. The development of inquiry skills requires a great deal of independent student activity. Emotional growth seems to be highly dependent on programs in which the active transmission of cognitive information has a relatively low priority. And, certainly, the development of skills for working in small groups often requires teachers to deemphasize objectives for learning specific knowledge and their own leadership role in the students' activities. But, when the concept of "not teaching" is pushed to extremes, many difficulties can arise. As we have seen in the discussion of freedom and limits, a classroom can too easily become a kind of institutional chaos which is aimless and sometimes destructive. Assuming the intelligent exercise of authority, however, we still need to know when a teacher can initiate, pursue, and evaluate ideas and experience. To be in real dialogue with students, a teacher must have active avenues of self-expression. Where does active teaching come into the picture?

We see three avenues for developing active teaching roles. First, learning can be structured in ways that do not negate student direction. Initial activities that develop common goals, and joint teacher-student planning efforts can make a big difference in the success of learning experiences. Strong teacher influence can often be exercised much more fairly at the outset of a classroom activity or in a committee planning an activity than after independent student inquiries are underway. Similarly, the kinds and quantity of choices a teacher offers can express some of his or her own points of view. Second, teachers can use a variety of roles to guide learning that is in process. A teacher may have many different images: guru, resource person, disciplinarian, engineer, doctor, travel agent, trainer, therapist, coach. Each of these images (and any others you might think of) offer possibilities for fruitful interaction between teacher and students. Some of them point to ways for providing very direct teacher guidance. Others suggest ways in which teachers can facilitate group learning, and yet others suggest the manner in which independent inquiries can be encouraged. Third, different kinds of evaluation can be introduced, for use by the teacher and the students, to determine whether the goals of all concerned are being accomplished. We tend to think of evaluation only in terms of a teacher giving grades for student performance, but this is obviously an inadequate conception of teaching. Evaluation must have a broader meaning. It can include means for making judgments about both the students' and the teacher's goals. It can be focused on the process of learning as well as the outcomes. And it can involve subjective as well as objective judgments. Thus, teachers can take active roles (even in an open classroom) through structuring, guiding, and evaluating learning experiences. If the learning outcomes are not predetermined, these roles can be effective and teachers will enhance, rather than endanger, the dynamic dialogue that is the mark of good teaching.

The readings in this chapter deal with these three avenues of teacher initiative.

Structuring learning experiences. Teachers who want to establish some degree of student direction in their class need to think about structuring open-ended learning experiences. Since most of us were educated in traditional ways, such experiences may not be easy to imagine. The possibility of student involvement, however, will be enhanced by personal approaches to the theories and ideas presented in the readings. At this point, you may be thinking about many issues that are difficult to put into words, but perhaps some reflection on the following questions will bring into focus your particular concerns: What kinds of experiences have helped you develop common goals with other people? In what ways could a teacher meaningfully plan learning experiences with students? How do open-ended activities personalize learning?

Guiding learning experiences. Somehow, once a teacher is actively engaged in teaching, he or she seems to need a kind of magic to do all that is needed and not to do too much. It is almost as if what one does as a teacher at any particular moment depends on what happened the moment before. All is not hopeless. A person can learn to act in many different ways. These ways can be used when and where they make the most sense. Also, a teacher can honestly act one way one day and an entirely different way the next if he or she truly feels differently. Some questions that might help you personalize these ideas are: What experiences have you had in which you felt like an entirely different person from one situation to the next? How can actors play very different roles and strike us as essentially honest people? What are some very different roles, which teachers have used in your experience, that have been particularly helpful to you? How does flexibility differ from inconsistency?

Evaluating learning experiences. Evaluation necessarily involves judgment, but there are many different kinds of judgment. Some might simply involve checking to see what's going on: Are students actually doing what you, the teacher, think they are doing? Some might primarily involve subjective data: How do I feel about this learning experience? Yet other evaluation may be based on information and work that has involved a lot of careful effort to produce. Different kinds of evaluation serve many different purposes, and they all raise important questions such as: How do *you* feel about being judged? What are some fair and helpful ways through which you have been evaluated in your experience as a student? How do you imagine teachers could be evaluated?

Allender's article can serve as introductory reading for this entire chapter. Assessing teaching and learning depends on what we expect of teachers and students. Traditionally, "assessing" means judging how much knowledge students have learned (at least temporarily), but humanistic concepts of education require a broader view of evaluation. This article describes goals such as the development of common meaning, cooperative planning, and offering and making choices. Other articles in this chapter suggest how teachers and students might evaluate achievement of goals like these.

JEROME S. ALLENDER

THE ROLE OF THE TEACHER IN STUDENT-DIRECTED LEARNING

In designing an educational environment on the basis of a theory of student-directed

Adapted from "New Conceptions of the Role of the Teacher" by Jerome S. Allender, in Melvin L. Silberman, Jerome S. Allender, and Jay M. Yanoff, *The Psychology of Open Teaching and Learning* (Boston: Little, Brown and Company, 1972). Copyright © 1972 by Jerome S. Allender.

learning, the initial problem is to determine how conflicts between teacher's and students' meaning can be resolved. In the traditional classroom, such conflicts are minimized because the teacher is expected to make all decisions concerning goals, materials, rules, etc. But when a teacher begins to consider the possibility of teacher-student planning, as one would within the context of an open classroom, a set of problems different from those traditionally experienced is created. The inclination has been in the operation of open classrooms to solve such problems intuitively. It is feasible, though, to anticipate the kinds of conflicts that are likely to occur and to create a classroom environment which is conducive to their resolution.

A general view of the problem reveals that uncertainty is caused by open-ended environments; this is in contrast to the traditional classroom where the roles of the teacher and the student are relatively well defined. For the teacher, the goals that he has, his ideas about relevant subject matter, and the minimum rules that he thinks students must follow to function within a group have to be open to discussion, challenge, and change. And the student in such a situation has to be willing to articulate what is meaningful for him: his goals, his interests, and his ideas about rules. The resolution of conflict between these two viewpoints depends on the existence of common goals, mutual interests, and agreement about the social conventions that are to be followed. It is reasonable to believe that an educational environment which is designed to help teachers and students reach these kinds of common meaning has to have specific structures within which they can be developed.

What is significantly missing in any uncertain social context is an automatic basis for trust. The underlying basis of trust is to withhold the use of the testing mechanisms in the mind that judge the value of one's relationships with others. When a person discovers that he has some important meaning in common with another person, this is the way in which he can enhance the quality of subsequent interaction. Equally important, however, is the need for people to suspend judgment of each other, if only temporarily, in an effort to *develop* common meaning. The process appears to be cyclical, and out of it, it should be possible to arrive at teacher-student goals, commitments concerning time and work, and an assurance that the methods of evaluation will not be unfair to students (or the teacher) if the commitments are fulfilled. This does not mean that extensive trust can be created instantly, but it is a context within which it can be deliberately built up.

It might be argued that conflicts could easily be minimized if a teacher were willing to help students plan without imposing his own expectations; this is no more tenable, though, than asking students to place complete trust in their teachers and not to bring their personal expectations to the learning process. A more realistic approach to the resolution of conflicts in meaning requires a willingness to modify one's expectations and an interest in finding areas of commonality. It begins with an awareness of the determinants that seem to be given and a sharing of expectations with the purpose of uncovering underlying conflicts. This can be partially accomplished through discussion, but it would seem to be facilitated by activities which are based on temporary commitments. The teacher's role would be to initiate the learning experience within the context of some minimally agreed-upon goals. The student would need to not judge the experience while participating in it and he would have to allow himself to become involved. A successful *initial experience* might broadly define an area of subject matter, cause positive feelings of tension, and/or provide the opportunity for sensing relevant problems. On the basis of this experience, a teacher and his students could also engage in a dialogue searching for new areas of commonality. The process can be appropriately viewed as initiating teacher-student planning, and it should be generally helpful toward building trusting relationships.

The practical application of initial experience to teaching will be hindered mostly by disagreements over the pressure of time. Without agreement on overriding broad goals as to what needs to be accomplished in a given period of time, either the teacher or the student can easily create a failure situation by prolonging unduly any aspects of the initial process. There is a limit to how much can be communicated in an orientation to students just as an excessively long presentation of a teacher's expectations can make a discussion meaningless. Similarly, students' unwillingness to follow basically the instructions that have been prepared for an initial experience can delay its completion and deflate the tensions and interest in an inquiry that it was meant to produce. These kinds of problems are not foreign to the teacher in a traditional classroom, but they are much more critical in the context of an open classroom. For one, if there is a commitment to cooperative planning, the authority to keep the process moving is no longer completely in the power of the teacher. Secondly, initial experiences facilitate only the beginning of an inquiry; if adequate time is not allowed for other phases of inquiry, the total process is undermined.

The success of an initial experience seems to depend on a teacher's ability to design an activity which is within the range of the students' interests and to obtain a loose agreement concerning what has to be done to complete the activity. How often a teacher might provide such initial experiences is an open question just as is the determination of its particular nature for any given learning situation. Initial experiences will probably be quite different for times when one is first meeting a group of students compared to times when one is simply introducing a new subject-matter area. With these questions in mind, though, a practical hypothesis is tenable: that adequate common meaning to serve as a basis for meaningful teacher-student planning can be established through the combination of a short orientation, a sharing of expectations, participation in an initial experience and a discussion of that experience.

A decision to encourage cooperative planning also creates a number of difficult problems for the teacher. In one way, they are not intrinsically different from those associated with the establishment of common meaning. Planning is basically the creation of a relationship of long-range trust and this means that the two processes are very interdependent. The kinds of activities, however, involved in planning are different and their potential for tangible and immediate consequences is greater. In addition, where the initiation of learning can depend on the usual willingness of people to engage themselves in temporary commitments for a while, the prospect of longer-range commitments tends to make people wary. The most basic problem has to do with closed-mindedness on the part of both the teacher and the students. Such closeness is not unusual for the teacher in the traditional classroom, and it is not automatically dissolved for someone who is trying to create a new educational context. Mainly, it interferes with a teacher's ability to value and build upon a student's past experience and current thinking, and it supports any tendency that students have within the freer context of an open

classroom to disregard a teacher's knowledge and experience. The latter is an important part of what the teacher has to offer his students, and the planning process is greatly handicapped without it. This problem, from either side, causes an imbalance in the dialogue that leads to cooperative planning, and it would seem to necessarily impede the process.

Should a productive dialogue actually be established, other problems can come into focus. A teacher and his students may agree on their overall goals and still be in conflict over the specific direction that plans take. Even when their views of relevant subject matter are not in conflict, the evaluation of plans in terms of their probability of success can differ significantly. Of equal importance, a willingness to become involved in a learning activity can be frustrated by a plan which is only capable of generating high initial interest and unable to sustain it for the extended time that the plan might require. The solution of these problems usually falls solely to the judgment of the teacher; structures are needed to create a context within which teacher and students can make them together.

Theoretically, planning learning activities, particularly when they are related to the teaching of inquiry skills, is a kind of problem formulation. The unique characteristic of cooperative planning is that common formulations are formed in the minds of the teacher and the students. The functional difference between individual and group formulation of plans has to do

with the subprocesses that are involved. For the teacher who plans by himself, there is no need to allow systematically for every aspect of information processing that is important to problem formulation. With a little awareness, it is possible to coordinate aspects of planning that are related to the subject matter, the learning process, and the likelihood of student interest. In cooperative planning, though, because the processing of information is going on in many minds at once, it is easier to avoid subprocesses and/or to not allow for the increased need for time that is involved in the formation of common formulations. One individual should not have responsibility for judging the utility of the process in which the group is engaged.

It is necessary, therefore, that time be allocated for each subprocess that is considered to be critical, and they need to be kept somewhat distinct. First of all, there must be an adequate opportunity for the input of information into the planning process. For the teacher, this means that he has a responsibility to create an awareness of the different ways in which relevant problems can be formulated and the kinds of information, including the range of materials and activities, that can be made available. For the students, this means that there is an opportunity to formulate and reformulate problems sensed in initial experiences, to raise questions that will facilitate an inquiry into these problems and to propose activities that will be helpful for resolving them. Secondly, there must be points at which a teacher and his students can negotiate between their two positions. There are an unlimited number of planning problems that might develop, but it is assumed that working agreements can be reached on the basis of a reasonable amount of time spent negotiating. For example, when the formulation of a plan by students requires materials that a teacher is unable to make available, he would ask them to reconsider it. Or, if a teacher judges that a proposed activity is too difficult to undertake, his students might insist that he help them plan a comparable activity that is easier. Thirdly, time needs to be allowed for formalizing plans. Depending on whether students were working individually, in small groups, or as a class, their structure might differ widely, but they would be helpful, in any case, for students and teachers alike. A completed plan for students serves as a detailed guide for a sequence of learning activities, and, for the teacher, such plans direct his preparation and allow for meaningful evaluation.

The application of the theory is easiest if it is actually conceptualized in terms of planning activities. Their order and number might be varied according to differences in subject matter, students, and teachers, but invariably there seems to be a need for the three kinds of activities that have been distinguished. From the input

of information, students would gain an overview of the subject matter in a short period of time. From the negotiation, there would result a new level of common meaning — one that is conducive to immediate action. The completed plans of the students and the teachers can almost be considered as an end in themselves. The activities, which logically can be thought of as *pre-formulation, negotiation,* and *post-formulation,* constitute structures that are hypothesized to facilitate the planning process. These structures are not likely to be found in a present-day school, and their practical development will surely be enhanced by experience and research. Their strangeness, though, might begin to be undone by looking to models outside of education. Cooperative planning is basic to democratic institutions and there could not be a more appropriate model in our society for the design of this aspect of an educational environment.

The design of an educational environment to provide for choice is the least difficult to imagine and implement. Part of the ease is related to the experience of traditional education. Although the overriding goal for most teachers may be the direct transmission of information, it is not always assumed that only a single channel of communication should be used. It is doubtful, indeed, that any challenging classroom environment is devoid of choice. Many teachers are able to make available several channels of communication at the same time, and over the period of a day,

a week, or a semester, a child has a fair opportunity to match what he is learning with his interests. This demonstrates how, when a variety of different kinds of relevant information are provided, students' learning of specific knowledge and skills can actually be facilitated. Advances in the development of individualized materials and technology also make problems connected with the provision of choice less of an obstacle than they might appear at first.

For goals of teaching that include the development of inquiry skills, other new developments and changes in emphasis make the offering of appropriate kinds of choice feasible. A context like that of an open classroom is expected to promote learning how to learn and, hopefully, directly help children learn thinking skills. Ordinarily, the kinds of choice that have been offered in schools would not accomplish these goals, but some of the new self-instructional materials are helpfully focused on problem solving and creativity tasks. Another problem, in connection with direct inquiry experience, has to do with the quantity of information that is needed. Much more must be on hand when children are encouraged to engage in high-level information processing than would ever be offered in a traditional classroom. The problem is beginning to disappear, however, because of the introduction of a wide range of inexpensive techniques for reproducing information and new means for reducing the amount of space required for storing it. A related problem has to do with the need for open-ended materials. This is more a matter of mental set than one of technology. If one looks to the total body of information that is readily and practically available in our society instead of to that which is usually used in schools, there is no shortage of materials that can be used to raise questions and serve as pools of data necessary for open-ended inquiries.

Toward a radical reconceptualization of the classroom, a general approach to design along these lines is missing only a theory for the organization of choice. All the problems that have been identified are related to students' finding information. This is equally true for learning specific knowledge and skills, for learning general thinking skills, and for engaging in a personal inquiry. The solution is not to create a special organizational structure for each of the different kinds of goals that are involved. The essential element is the opportunity for search activity. What is necessary is an overall structure that facilitates searching for information at as many levels as possible. Thus we come to the idea that the classroom should be designed like a learning center. Two overlapping concepts serve as a basis for accomplishing this kind of reorganization in its most radical form. The first involves recognizing that there are different basic sources of information and it is appropriate for a teacher to use all of them in an effort to make the maximum amount of

choice available. The second shows how difficult kinds of information can be offered at the same time. The clarification of these two concepts, involving sources and kinds of information, illustrates how they might be applied.

It is reasonable to regard *experience, observation,* and *knowledge* as the primary bases for obtaining information in place of conceptualizing the teacher as the major source of information for his students. There is nothing unusual about a teacher who is willing to share his own experiences — particularly as they relate to the learning activities of his students. It would be equally helpful, though, for students to have an opportunity to gain their own relevant experience as it relates to their studies, either in the school or in the community. The significance attached to laboratory work and the history of apprenticeships and work-study programs make this idea less foreign than it might initially seem. Similarly, the extensive expansion of the idea of field trips might make systematic observation of any aspect of society or nature an important source of learning. Its general relevance to science is an argument for its value to education. Obviously, the most important source of information in school usually will be knowledge; it is an error, though, to assume that the teacher is its largest storehouse. No person can vie with the amount of knowledge that can be stored and transmitted via recorded communication. Highly innovative educational technology

aside, books, programed texts, all other printed instructional materials, and audiovisual aids are so integral to teaching that their unique role can be missed. In addition, a student's previously acquired knowledge and his ability to generate new knowledge through his own thinking can be too easily dismissed. Recorded communication, the student, and the teacher are all valid sources of knowledge upon which to draw.

A look at how different kinds of information can be useful to students reveals a second dimension. Where the student has identifiable questions or skills that he wants, for which established knowledge exists, it would be foolish to look elsewhere for such information. To do otherwise is what makes "discovery learning" a phony process. Similarly, during the planning of an inquiry, it is relevant to directly learn strategies that are equivalent to broad thinking skills and information that are necessary for initial experiences. They may need to be restructured in terms of a student's personal information processing style, but they clearly are the simplest means for facilitating an inquiry. Yet a third kind of information is needed to create pools of data toward which the search phase of an inquiry can be directed. This would be an unusual kind of material to find in a classroom because it can include relatively disconnected information which only acquires meaning to the extent that it becomes a part of a student's search activity. These categories are not mutually exclusive; there is a need to plan for each of them separately, though, if they are all to be included in an educational environment.

In general, if care is taken to muster as many opportunities for experience, observation, and gaining knowledge as possible, and a broad view is taken concerning the kinds of information that are relevant, a teacher will have an excellent basis for providing a wide variety of choice. The teacher's minimal role would be to make available a sufficient range of sources and kinds of information to allow for plans that have been negotiated. With the accumulation of materials and experience, though, it is easy to imagine a classroom environment which would actually begin to stimulate searching for information. Sometimes a teacher would be called upon, as a resource within that environment, to transmit knowledge directly; the teacher's main role, though, in relation to search activity, would be to continue developing the design of the environment and to keep it organized.

An attempt has been made to show how to develop a structured open classroom by designing an environment on the basis of a theory of student-directed learning. From this vantage, new kinds of structures would be introduced with the specific aim to facilitate the establishment of common meaning between a teacher and his students, to encourage the cooperative planning of learning activities, and to make as much choice of materials and activities available to students as possible.

Flanders describes "interaction analysis," a technique that involves analyzing one's own classroom verbal behavior on the basis of an observer's record or a tape recording. He discusses, in detail, ways of interpreting the data collected by using this technique. He also discusses two contrasting styles of teacher behavior — direct and indirect — and their typical effects on students. His article is extremely useful for developing alternative ways of responding to students.

NED A. FLANDERS

INTENT, ACTION, AND FEEDBACK: A PREPARATION FOR TEACHING

THE PROBLEM

The point is that much of what is learned in education courses is neither conceptual-

From The Journal of Teacher Education 14, no. 3 (September 1968): 251–60. Reprinted with permission.

ized, qualified, nor taught in a fashion that builds a bridge between theory and practice. Education students are only occasionally part of an exciting, systematic, exploration of the teaching process, most infrequently by the instructor's example. How can we create, in education courses, an active, problem-solving process, a true sense of inquiry, and a systematic search for principles through experimentation? At least one factor favors change, and that is the lack of solid evidence that any thing we are now teaching is clearly associated with any index of effective teaching, with the possible exception of practice teaching.

A great many factors resist curriculum change in teacher education. Perhaps the most important is that genuine curriculum innovation, to be distinguished from tinkering with content and sequence, would require that existing faculty members, old and new alike, think differently about their subject matter, act differently while teaching, and relate differently to their students. For some this is probably impossible, for all it would be difficult. Yet changes do occur when enough energy is mobilized and convictions are strongly held.

It is a serious indictment of the profession, however, to hear so many education instructors say that their students will appreciate what they are learning *after* they have had some practical teaching experience. What hurts is the obvious hypocrisy of making this statement and then giving a lecture on the importance of presenting material in such a way that the immediate needs and interests of the pupils are taken into consideration. Such instances reveal a misunderstanding of theory and practice. To be understood, concepts in education must be verified by personal field experiences; in turn, field experiences must be efficiently conceptualized to gain insight. With most present practices, the gorge between theory and practice grows deeper and wider, excavated by the very individuals who are pledged to fill it.

One stumbling block is our inability to describe teaching as a series of acts through time and to establish models of behavior which are appropriate to different kinds of teaching situations. This problem has several dimensions. First, in terms of semantics, we must learn how to define our concepts as part of a theory. We also need to organize these concepts into the fewest number of variables necessary to establish principles and make predictions. Too often we try to teach the largest number of variables; in fact, as many as we can think of for which there is some research evidence. Second, in terms of technology we must develop procedures for quantifying the qualitative aspects of teaching acts so that our students will have tools for collecting empirical evidence. Third, in terms of philosophy, we must decide whether our education students are going to be told about teaching in lectures and read about it in books or if they are going to discover these things for themselves. This paper will be devoted to these three issues, in reverse order.

A PHILOSOPHY OF INQUIRY

When Nathaniel Cantor (1953) published his nine assumptions of orthodox teaching, there was little evidence to support his criticisms. Must pupils be coerced into working on tasks? In what way is the teacher responsible for pupils' acquiring knowledge? Is education a preparation for later life rather than a present, living experience? Is subject matter the same to the learner as it is to the teacher? The last decade has provided more evidence in support of Cantor's criticism than it has in defense of existing practice.

H. H. Anderson and his colleagues (Anderson, 1939; Anderson and H. Brewer, 1945; Anderson and J. Brewer, 1946; Anderson, Brewer, and Reed, 1946) first demonstrated that dominative teacher contacts create more compliance and resistance to compliance, that dominative teacher contacts with pupils spread to the pupil-to-pupil contacts even in the absence of the teacher, and that this pattern of teaching creates situations in which pupils are more easily distracted and more dependent on teacher initiative.

Flanders and Havumaki (1960) demonstrated that dominative teacher influence was more persuasive in changing pupil opinions but that such shifts of opinion were not stable since inner resistance was so high.

A research team in Provo, Utah (Romney et al., 1961) believes that patterns of spontaneous teacher action can be identified and that more effective patterns can be

distinguished from less effective patterns. The difference is that more dominative patterns are less effective.

Our own eight-year research program which involved the development of interaction analysis as a tool for quantifying patterns of teacher influence lends further support to Cantor. The generalizations to follow are based on all teachers observed in our different research projects. This total is only 147 teachers, representing all grade levels, six different school districts in two counties; but these teachers came from the extremes of a distribution involving several thousand teachers. The total bits of information collected by interaction analysis are well in excess of 1,250,000.

The present, average domination of teachers is best expressed as the rule of two-thirds. About two-thirds of the time spent in a classroom, someone is talking. The chances are two out of three that this person is the teacher. When the teacher talks, two-thirds of the time is spent by many expressions of opinion and fact, giving some direction and occasionally criticizing the pupils. The fact that teachers are taking too active a part for effective learning is shown by comparing superior with less effective classrooms. A superior classroom scores above average on constructive attitudes toward the teacher and the classwork. It also scores higher on achievement tests of the content to be learned, adjusted for initial ability. In studies (Flanders, 1962) of seventh grade social studies and eighth grade mathematics, it was found that the teachers in superior classrooms spoke only slightly less, say 50 to 60 per cent of the time, but the more directive aspects of their influence went down to 40 to 50 per cent. These teachers were much more flexible in the quality of their influence, sometimes very direct, but on more occasions very indirect.

To describe the classrooms which were below average in constructive pupil attitudes and in content achievement (they are positively correlated), just change the rule of two-thirds to the rule of three-fourths plus.

The foregoing evidence shows that no matter what a prospective teacher hears in an education course, he has, on the average, been exposed to living models of what teaching is and can be that are basically quite directive. After fourteen or so years he is likely to be quite dependent, expecting the instructor to tell him what to do, how to do it, when he is finished, and then tell him how well he did it. Now it is in this general context that we turn to the question of how we can develop a spirit of inquiry with regard to teaching.

Thelen (1960) has described a model of personal inquiry, as well as other models, and the question is whether teacher education can or should move toward this model. He describes this model as follows:

. . . [Personal inquiry] is a process of interaction between the student and his natural and societal environment. In this situation the student will be aware of the process of which he is a part; during this process he will be aware of many choices among ways he might behave; he will make decisions among these ways; he will then act and see what happens; he will review the process and study it with the help of books and other people; he will speculate about it, and draw tentative conclusions from it. (Thelen, 1960, p. 89.)

Returning to the education course, the student will be aware of the learning process of *that* classroom, he will confront choices, he will make decisions among the choices, he will act and then evaluate his actions, and then he will try to make some sense out of it with the help of books, the instructor, and his peers. This is a tall order, but who knows, it may be the only route to discovery and independence for the prospective teacher.

Occasionally we hear of exciting learning experiences in which education students attain a sort of intellectual spirit of inquiry. A unit on motivation can begin with an assessment of the motivation patterns of the education students. The same assessment procedures can then be used at other grade levels permitting comparisons and generalizations. Principles of child growth and development can be discovered by observation and learned more thoroughly perhaps than is possible with only lecture and reading. But this is not what is meant by inquiry.

Inquiry in teacher education means translating understanding into action as part of the teaching process. It means experimenting with one's own behavior, obtaining objective information about one's own behavior, evaluating this information in terms of the teacher's role; in short, attaining self-insight while acting like a teacher.

Procedures for obtaining self-insight have been remarkably improved during the last decade in the field of human relations training. Two characteristics of these training methods seem relevant to this discussion. First, information and insights about behavior must become available in a way that can be accepted and in a form that is understood. Second, opportunities to utilize or act out these insights must be provided. Our ability to accept information about ourselves is a complex problem, but it helps if we believe the information is objective, valid, and given in an effort to help rather than hurt. Our understanding of this information will depend a great deal on our ability to organize the information conceptually. Freedom to act at least requires freedom from threat or embarrassment.

From all of these things, a spirit of inquiry develops.

THE TECHNIQUE OF INTERACTION ANALYSIS

Interaction analysis is nothing more and nothing less than an observation technique which can be used to obtain a fairly reliable record of spontaneous verbal statements. Most teacher influence is exerted by verbal statements and to determine their quality is to approximate total teacher influence. This technique was first developed as a research tool, but every observer we ever hired testified that the process of learning the system and using it in classrooms was more valuable than anything else he learned in his education courses. Since interaction analysis is only a technique, it probably could be applied to teacher education in a fashion that is consistent or even totally inconsistent with a philosophy of personal inquiry. How it is used in teacher preparation is obviously as important as understanding the procedure itself.

The writing of this manuscript followed the completion of a terminal contract report of a U.S. Office of Education-sponsored, in-service training program based on interaction analysis as a tool for gathering information. How we used interaction analysis is illustrated by the conditions we tried to create for the fifty-five participating teachers, most of whom represented about one-half of the faculties of two junior high schools:*

* Interaction analysis as a research tool has been used ever since R. F. Bales first developed a set of categories for studying groups. Most of our research results can be found in the references for this paper. Its use as a training device is more recent. Projects have taken place in New Jersey, Philadelphia, Chicago, and Minneapolis. Systematic evaluation is available in only the Minneapolis project.

1. Teachers developed new (to them) concepts as tools for thinking about their behavior and the consequences of their behavior. These concepts were used to discover principles of teacher influence. Both types of concepts were necessary: those for describing actions and those for describing consequences.
2. Procedures for assessing both types of concepts in practical classroom situations were tried out. These procedures were used to test principles, to modify them, and to determine when they might be appropriately applied.
3. The training activities involved in becoming proficient in the assessment of spontaneous behavior, in and of themselves, increased the sensitivity of teachers to their own behavior and the behavior of others. Most important, teachers could compare their intentions with their actions.
4. By avoiding a discussion of right and wrong ways of teaching and emphasizing the discovery of principles of teacher influence, teachers gradually became more independent and self-directing. Our most successful participants investigated problems of their own choosing, designed their own plans, and arranged collaboration with others when this seemed advantageous.

Five filmstrips and one teacher's manual have been produced and written. These materials would have to be modified before they could be used with undergraduate students. Before asking how interaction analysis might be used in teacher preparation, we turn next to a description of the procedures.

THE PROCEDURE OF OBSERVATION

The observer sits in a classroom in the best position to hear and see the participants. At the end of each three-second period, he decides which category best represents the communication events just completed. He writes this category number down while simultaneously assessing communication in the next period and continues at the rate of 20 to 25 observations per minute, keeping his tempo as steady as possible. His notes are merely a series of numbers written in a column, top to bottom, so that the original sequence of events is preserved. Occasionally marginal notes are used to explain the class formation or any unusual circumstances. When there is a major change in class formation, the communication pattern, or the subject under discussion, a double line is drawn and the time indicated. As soon as the total observation is completed, the observer retires to a nearby room and completes a general description of each separate activity period separated by the double lines, including the nature of the activities, the class formation, and the position of the teacher. The observer also notes any additional facts that seem pertinent to an adequate interpretation and re-call of the total visit.

The ten categories that we used for in-teraction analysis are shown in Table 1.

The numbers that an observer writes down are tabulated in a 10 × 10 matrix as sequence pairs, that is, a separate tabula-tion is made for each overlapping pair of numbers. An illustration will serve to ex-plain this procedure.

Teacher: Class! The bell has rung. May I have your attention please! [6] *(During the next three seconds talking and noise diminish.)* [10]

Teacher: Jimmy, we are all waiting for you. [7] *(Pause)*

Teacher: Now today we are going to have a

Table 1. Categories for interaction analysis

Teacher Talk	Indirect influence	1.[a] Accepts Feeling: accepts and clarifies the feeling tone of the students in a non-threatening man-ner. Feelings may be positive or negative. Predicting or recalling feelings are included.
		2. Praises or Encourages: praises or encourages student action or behavior. Jokes that release ten-sion, not at the expense of another individual, nodding head or saying, "um hm?" or "go on" are included.
		3. Accepts or Uses Ideas of Student: clarifying, building or developing ideas suggested by a student. As teacher brings more of his own ideas into play, shift to category five.
		4. Asks Questions: asking a question about content or procedure with the intent that a student answer.
	Direct influence	5. Lecturing: giving facts or opinions about content or procedures; expressing his own ideas, asking rhetorical questions.
		6. Giving Directions: directions, commands, or orders with which a student is expected to comply.
		7. Criticizing or Justifying Authority: statements intended to change student behavior from nonac-ceptable to acceptable pattern; bawling someone out; stating why the teacher is doing what he is doing; extreme self-reference.
Student Talk		8. Student Talk — Response: talk by students in response to teacher. Teacher initiates the contact or solicits student statement.
		9. Student Talk — Initiation: talk by students which they initiate. If "calling on" student is only to indicate who may talk next, observer must decide whether student wanted to talk. If he did, use this category.
		10. Silence or Confusion: pauses, short periods of silence and periods of confusion in which com-munication cannot be understood by the observer.

[a] No scale is implied by these numbers. Each number is classificatory; it designates a particular kind of communication event. To write these numbers down during observation is to enumerate, not to judge a position on a scale.

very pleasant surprise, [5] and I think you will find it very exciting and interesting. [1] Have any of you heard anything about what we are going to do? [4]

Pupil: I think we are going on a trip in the bus that's out in front. [8]

Teacher: Oh! You've found out! How did you learn about our trip? [4]

By now the observer has written down 6, 10, 7, 5, 1, 4, 8, and 4. As the interaction proceeds, the observer will continue to write down numbers. To tabulate these observations in a 10 × 10 matrix, the first step is to make sure that the entire series begins and ends with the same number. The convention we use is to add a 10 to the beginning and end of the series unless the 10 is already present. Our series now becomes 10, 6, 10, 7, 5, 1, 4, 8, 4, and 10.

These numbers are tabulated in a matrix, one pair at a time. The column is indicated by the second number, the row is indicated by the first number. The first pair is 10–6; the tally is placed in row ten, column six cell. The second pair is 6–10; tally this in the row six, column ten cell. The third pair is 10–7, the fourth pair is 7–5, and so on. Each pair overlaps with the next, and the total number of observations, "N," always will be tabulated by N–1 tallies in the matrix. In this case we started a series of ten numbers, and the series produced nine tallies in the matrix.

Figure 1 shows our completed matrix. Notice that in a correctly tabulated matrix the sums of the corresponding rows and columns are equal.

The problem of reliability is extremely complex, and a more complete discussion can be found in two terminal contract reports (Flanders, 1962, 1963) one of which will be published as a research monograph in the 1963 series of the Cooperative Research Program. Education students can

learn how to make quick field checks of their reliability and work toward higher reliability under the direction of an instructor.

Category	1	2	3	4	5	6	7	8	9	10	Total
1				1							1
2											0
3											0
4								1		1	2
5	1										1
6										1	1
7					1						1
8				1							1
9											0
10						1	1				2
Total	1	0	0	2	1	1	1	1	0	2	9

Figure 1. Completed matrix

THE INTERPRETATION OF MATRICES

A matrix should have at least 400 tallies, covering about twenty minutes or more of a homogeneous activity period, before attempting to make an interpretation.

Certain areas within the matrix are particularly useful for describing teacher influence. Some of the areas will now be discussed by making reference to Figure 2.

The column totals of a matrix are indicated as Areas A, B, C, and "D." The figures in these areas provide a general picture by answering the following questions: What proportion of the time was someone talking compared with the portion in which confusion or no talking existed? When someone was talking, what proportion of the time was used by the students? By the teacher? Of the time that the teacher talked, what proportion of his talk involved indirect influence? Direct influence?

The answers to these questions form a necessary backdrop to the interpretation of the other parts of the matrix. If student participation is about 30 or 40 per cent, we would expect to find out why it was so high by studying the matrix. If the teacher is particularly direct or indirect, we would expect certain relationships to exist with student talk and silence.

The next two areas to consider are Areas E and F. Evidence that categories 1, 2, and 3 were used for periods longer than three seconds can be found in the diagonal cells, 1–1, 2–2, and 3–3. The other six cells of Area E indicate various types of transitions between these three categories. Sustained praise or clarification of student ideas is especially significant because such elaboration often involves criteria for praise or reasons for accepting ideas and feelings. The elaboration of praise or student ideas must be present if the student's ideas are to be integrated with the content being discussed by the class.

Area F is a four-cell combination of giving directions (category 6) and giving criticisms or self-justification (category 7). The transition cells 6–7 and 7–6 are particularly sensitive to difficulties that the teacher may have with classroom discipline or resistance on the part of students. When criticism follows directions or direction follows criticism this means that the students are not complying satisfactorily. Often there is a high loading on the 6–9 cell under these circumstances. Excessively high frequencies in the 6–6 cell *and* 7–7 cells indicate teacher domination and supervision of the students' activities. A high loading of tallies in the 6–6 cell alone often indicates that the teacher is merely giving lengthy directions to the class.

The next two areas to be considered are Areas G and H. Tallies in these two areas occur at the instant the student stops talking and the teacher starts. Area G indicates those instances in which the teacher responds to the termination of student talk with indirect influence. Area H indicates those instances in which the teacher responds to the termination of student talk with direct influence. An interesting comparison can be made by contrasting the proportion G to H versus the proportion A to B. If these two proportions are quite different, it indicates that the teacher tends to act differently at the instant a student stops talking compared with his overall average. Often this is a mark of flexible teacher influence.

There are interesting relationships between Area E and Area G and between Area F and Area H. For example, Area G may indicate that a teacher responds indirectly to students at the instant they terminate their talk, but an observer may wish to inspect Area E to see if this indirect response is sustained in any way. The same question with regard to direct influence can be asked of Areas F and H. Areas G and H together usually fascinate teachers. They are often interested in knowing more about their immediate response to student participation.

Area I indicates an answer to the question, What types of teacher statements trigger student participation? Usually there is a high tally loading in cells 4–8 and 4–9. This is expected because students often answer questions posed by the teacher. A high loading on 4–8 and 8–4 cells alone usually indicates classroom drill directed by the teacher. The contrast of tallies in columns 8 and 9 in this area gives a rough indication of the frequency with which students initiate their own ideas versus respond to those of the teacher.

Area I is often considered in combina-

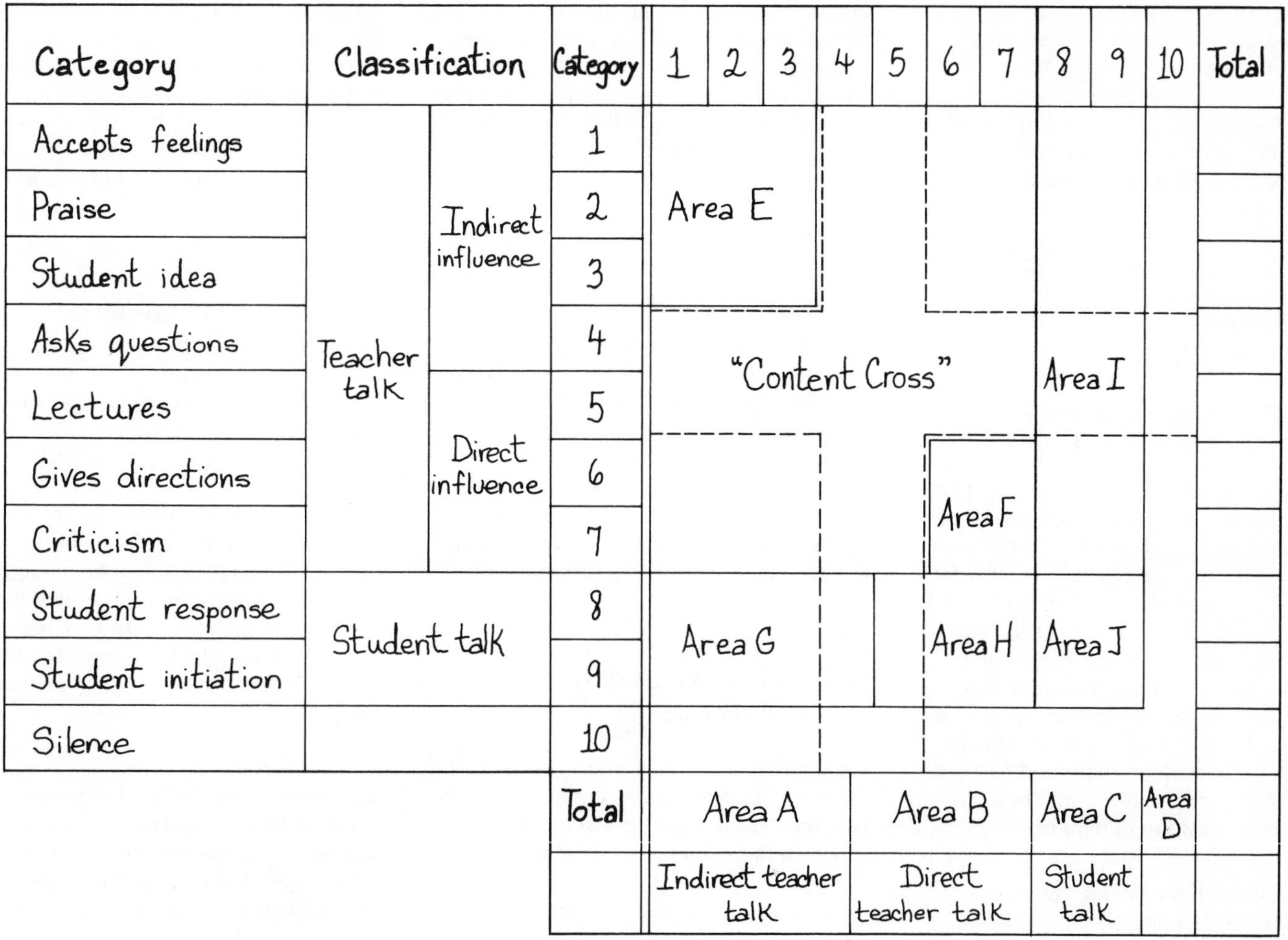

Category	Classification		Category	1	2	3	4	5	6	7	8	9	10	Total
Accepts feelings	Teacher talk	Indirect influence	1	Area E										
Praise			2											
Student idea			3											
Asks questions		Direct influence	4	"Content Cross"							Area I			
Lectures			5											
Gives directions			6							Area F				
Criticism			7											
Student response	Student talk		8	Area G						Area H	Area J			
Student initiation			9											
Silence			10											
			Total	Area A				Area B			Area C		Area D	
				Indirect teacher talk				Direct teacher talk			Student talk			

Figure 2. Matrix analysis

tion with Area J. Area J indicates either lengthy student statements or sustained student-to-student communication. An above-average frequency in Area C, but not in Area J, indicates that short answers, usually in response to teacher stimulation, have occurred. One would normally expect to find frequencies in Area E positively correlated with frequencies in Area J.

We turn next to concepts and principles of teacher influence before speculating about how this technique can be applied to teacher education.

CONCEPTS AND PRINCIPLES OF TEACHER INFLUENCE

It may be too early to determine what are the *fewest* number of concepts which, if organized into logically related principles, can be used by a teacher to plan how he will use his authority. Surely he will need concepts that refer to his authority and its use. He will need concepts to describe learning goals and pupil tasks. He will need concepts to classify the responses of students. He may also need concepts to characterize class formations and patterns of classroom communication. These concepts are at least the minimum.

CONCEPTS THAT REFER TO TEACHER BEHAVIOR

Indirect influence. Indirect influence is defined as actions taken by the teacher which encourage and support student participation. Accepting, clarifying, praising, and developing the ideas and feelings expressed by the pupils will support student participation. We can define indirect behavior operationally by noting the percent of teacher statements falling into categories 1, 2, 3, and 4.

Direct influence. This concept refers to actions taken by teacher which restrict student participation. Expressing one's own views through lecture, giving directions, and criticizing with the expectation of compliance tend to restrict pupil participation. We can define direct behavior operationally by noting the per cent of teacher statements falling into categories 5, 6, and 7.

Other concepts which we do not have the space to discuss include: flexibility of teacher influence, dominance or sustained direct influence, and intervention.

CONCEPTS THAT REFER TO LEARNING GOALS

Clear goals. Goal perceptions are defined from the point of view of the pupil, not the teacher. "Clear goals" is a state of affairs in which the pupil knows what he is doing, the purpose, and can guess at the first few steps to be taken. It can be measured by paper-and-pencil tests, often administered at different points in a problem-solving sequence.

Ambiguous goals. "Ambiguous goals" describes a state of affairs in which a pupil is not sure of what he is expected to do, is not sure of the first few steps, or is unable to proceed for one reason or another. It can be measured as above.

Other concepts in this area include: attractive and unattractive clear goals, pupil tasks, task requirements, and similar concepts.

CONCEPTS THAT REFER TO PUPIL RESPONSES

Dependent acts. Acts of dependence occur when a pupil not only complies with teacher influence but solicits such direction. A pupil who asks a teacher to approve his work in order to make sure that it is satisfactory, before going on to the next logical step, is acting dependently. This type of response can be measured by observation techniques and by paper-and-pencil tests on which he indicates what kind of help he would like from the teacher.

Independent acts. Acts of independence occur when the pupils react primarily to task requirements and are less directly concerned with teacher approval. The measurement of this concept is the same as for dependent acts.

Other concepts include: dependence proneness — a trait, compliance, conformity, counter-dependence, and similar concepts.

SOME PRINCIPLES THAT CAN BE DISCOVERED

We discovered in our research (Flanders, 1962) that, during the first few days of a two-week unit of study in seventh grade social studies and when introducing new materials in eighth grade mathematics, superior teachers are initially more indirect, becoming more direct as goals and associated tasks become clarified. We also suspect that these same teachers are more indirect when helping pupils diagnose difficulties, when trying to motivate pupils by arousing their interest, and in other situations in which the expression of pupil perceptions is helpful. On the other hand, the average or below average teacher did exactly the opposite.

Now the problem in teacher education is not only to create a situation in which education students could verify these relationships but could practice controlling their own behavior so as to become indirect or more direct at will. One place to begin is to have two, six-man groups work on a task under the direction of a leader. One task is something like an assembly line; it has a clear end product and sharp role differentiation. The other task is much more difficult to describe and does not have clear role differentiation. Now let the class superimpose different patterns of leader influence. Let them interview the role players, collect interaction analysis data by some simplified system of categories, and discuss the results. When undergraduate students first try to classify verbal statements, it sometimes helps to use only two or three categories. In one instance, the issue was the effect of using broad questions versus narrow questions. A broad question was one to which it was hard to predict the type of answer. A narrow question was one to which it was easy to guess at the type of answer. Which type of question was more likely to increase pupil participation? The students role-played this and kept a record of broad questions, narrow questions, and the length of the response. The fact that they verified their prediction correctly for this rather superficial problem was much less important compared with the experience that they gained. They learned how to verify a prediction with empirical evidence, and some had a chance to practice control of their own behavior for professional purposes.

There is no space here to list a complete set of principles that can be investigated by systematic or intuitive data-collecting procedures. The following questions might stimulate useful learning activities. Does dependence always decrease as goals become clear? Is the final level of dependence determined by the pattern of teacher influence when goals are first formulated? Are measures of content achievement related to the pupils' attitudes toward the teacher and the schoolwork? What effects can you expect from excessive and pedan-

tic clarification of pupil ideas and feelings? And many others.

APPLICATIONS OF INTERACTION ANALYSIS TO TEACHER EDUCATION

Suppose that before education students were given their practice teaching assignment, they had been exposed to a variety of data-collecting techniques for assessing pupil perceptions, measuring achievement, and quantifying spontaneous teacher influence. Suppose, further, that these skills had been taught in a context of personal inquiry as described earlier. What effect would this have on their approach to practice teaching?

One of their suggestions might be that two students should be assigned as a team to the first assignment. While one took over the class the other would be collecting information; the next day or so, the roles could be reversed. Together they would work out a lesson plan, agree on the data to be collected, go over the results with the help of the supervising teacher who might also have the same data-collecting skills. This situation could approach the inquiry model described earlier. The practice teacher might discover that his failure to clarify the pupils' ideas restricted the development of curiosity or that his directions were too short when he was asked for further help; both of these inferences can be made from an interaction matrix with reasonable reliability and objectivity.

Later on a student may wish to take a practice reading assignment by himself and turn to the supervising teacher for aid in feedback. In either case, the requirement is that the learner be able to compare his intentions with feedback information about his actions and analyze this information by using concepts which he found useful in his earlier courses in education.

There are some precautions that can already be stated with regard to the use of interaction analysis in such a situation.

First, no interaction analysis data should be collected unless the person observed is familiar with the entire process and knows its limitations.

Second, the questions to be answered by inspecting the matrix should be developed before the observation takes place.

Third, value judgments about good and bad teaching behavior are to be avoided. Emphasis is given to the problem being investigated so that cause-and-effect relationships can be discovered.

Fourth, a certain amount of defensive behavior is likely to be present at the initial consultation; it is something like listening to a tape recording for the first time.

Fifth, a consultation based on two observations or at least two matrices helps to eliminate value judgments or at least control them. Comparisons between the matrices are more likely to lead to principles.

Just how experiences of the type we have been discussing will fit into the present curricula is difficult to know. If activities of the sort described in this paper are valuable, are they to be superimposed on the present list of courses or is more radical surgery necessary?

Perhaps this is the point to risk a prediction, which is that teacher education will become increasingly concerned with the process of teaching itself during the next few decades. Instead of emphasizing knowledge which *we think* teachers will need in order to teach effectively, as we have in the past, we will turn more and more to an analysis of teaching acts as they occur in spontaneous classroom interaction. We are now at the point in our technology of data collecting at which procedures for analyzing and conceptualizing teaching behavior can be developed. Systems for doing this will become available regardless of whether they are similar or dissimilar to the procedures described in this paper. When this fine day arrives, the role of the education instructor will change, and the dichotomy between field and theory will disappear. The instructor's role will shift from talking about effective teaching to the rigorous challenge of demonstrating effective teaching. The process of inquiry will create problem-solving activities that will produce more independent, self-directing teachers whose first day on the job will be their worst, not their best.

These changes will be successful to the extent that the graduates of teacher education can learn to control their own behavior for the professional purpose of managing effective classroom learning. It will be the responsibility of the education instructor to help prospective teachers discover what their teaching intentions should be and then create training situations in which behavior gradually matches intentions with practice. Teaching will remain an art, but it will be studied scientifically.

Here we find discussion on other new concepts that add to the ideas presented by Allender (pp. 301–306). This article is especially helpful for developing ways of thinking about the role of a teacher. Wolfson contrasts two analogies — the teacher as a doctor and the teacher as a travel consultant — which do not precisely conceptualize the teachers' role but do clarify how individualizing instruction can be based on radically different styles of teaching and how the degree of open-endedness differs from one approach to the other. The article also contains a review of some of the studies on student-directed learning and brief descriptions of innovative teaching.

BERNICE J.
WOLFSON

PUPIL AND TEACHER ROLES IN INDIVIDUALIZED INSTRUCTION

We have been hearing a persistent call for better education. Yet, the people who join in making this appeal are far from agreement in their criticisms of present school conditions and in their views of what is required to effect improvement.

"Better education" may mean more up-to-date knowledge, faster achievement, better teachers, introducing new disciplines in the early grades, preparing every child for college, or, less often, changing education to make it more relevant to the lives of today's children. On the one hand, the emphasis may be on "more-and-better" of the school's traditional pattern and role. On the other hand, the focus may be on finding some new pattern for the institution and for the processes to occur within it.

From *The Elementary School Journal* (April 1968): 357–66. Published by The University of Chicago Press. Copyright © 1968 by the University of Chicago. Reprinted by permission.

WHY INDIVIDUALIZE?

With the second focus in mind, many of us in education are committed to the idea of individualizing instruction. Again, we find a variety of reasons for this commitment. Some of us hope to teach more efficiently than we have taught under some form of group instruction. We want children to achieve the same learnings we have been striving for but at different rates and possibly with greater amounts of enrichment. Others want to encourage greater individuality among pupils and a wider variety of learning outcomes. Still others perhaps want to go beyond our current view of the classroom to transform our present goals and ways of working into a new image made possible by individualized instruction. No doubt, there are additional purposes. But it seems to me that each of us must know why he wants to individualize instruction. What makes it a desirable thing to do?

Personally, I believe that individualizing instruction can enable us to change our educational direction. I would like to see less emphasis on conformity and more on initiative and individuality. I would like to see us break out of the box of "covering content" as defined in grade level steps or predetermined sequences. Particularly, I would like to see more opportunities for children to ask questions of real concern to them, to make choices and plans, to evaluate and think independently, and to develop individual interests and commitments. I am well aware that many thought-

ful and gifted teachers have sought to provide such opportunities with varying degrees of success. I believe that organizing to individualize instruction — or, more accurately, to encourage personalized learning — will strengthen efforts to move in these directions.

WHAT IS INDIVIDUALIZATION?

Even though we might develop some agreement about reasons for individualizing instruction, our definition of the process is not quite clear. In fact, observations in classrooms where teachers say that they are individualizing instruction reveal a wide variety of practices. Teachers may be using traditional textbooks and workbooks and allowing each child to work at his own pace. Teachers may have conferences with individual children. They may instruct small groups in particular skills. In some classrooms pupils may use programmed materials or textbooks assigned by the teacher on an individual basis, as she decides they are appropriate. In other classrooms small groups of children who share some common interest may work together, and individual children may select their own materials from the available resources.

It is not at all certain that these practices provide individualization. Take a pupil-teacher conference. This procedure obviously provides a one-to-one relationship. But the teacher may be doing the same thing that she would do in a directed reading lesson with a group. In fact, she may be doing what she does with many of the other pupils, one at a time. I would not consider these conferences examples of individualized instruction. The use of programmed learning materials and textbooks with individual pacing is not truly an example of individualized instruction. These materials provide for differences in rate of learning, but are not responsive to other kinds of variation among pupils, such as motivation, style of learning, energy level, attitudes, previous learning, and complex personality factors.

At present, the most popular interpretation of individualized instruction is that the teacher makes specific recommendations and assignments for each pupil. This interpretation rests on the teacher-as-doctor analogy, an analogy seriously in need of examination. According to this view, the teacher functions as a doctor, that is, she diagnoses needs, deficiencies, or problems and prescribes appropriate treatment.

Admittedly there is something appealing about this analogy. Part of its appeal is probably due to the high status doctors have in our society. To say that teachers behave like doctors is therefore seen as a compliment. However, I think that the attractiveness of this analogy is due mostly to the apparent simplicity, precision, and neatness of the model: One assesses the present condition, diagnoses the nature of the problem, prescribes the appropriate treatment, and a cure is effected.

However attractive this model may be, teaching really does not fit such a design. (And I doubt that doctoring does either.) Surely teaching is more complicated than doctoring, has more dimensions, and, in spite of intensive efforts, has not developed clear-cut criteria for treatment success.

Let us examine this model further as it might be applied in a hypothetical classroom. Consider the plight of the teacher who must diagnose and prescribe for thirty pupils in many subject areas over an extensive period of time. Does she really know what each pupil is ready for or what specific learning experiences he needs next? She may have some general hunches, and perhaps she could get some helpful suggestions from the pupil. But how would she make her diagnosis and prescription? She might decide that a pupil is ready for third-grade work or for subtraction or for addition with bridging. She might decide that he needs practice in recognizing beginning sounds. Or she might merely decide that he has successfully completed one section of his workbook and is ready to start the next section. In many so-called nongraded schools she would decide that he is ready to read at Level 11.

Most of these decisions, it seems to me, are arbitrary and often not relevant to the pupil's understanding of his world. Somehow I do not believe that these are meaningful ways of planning for individual, continuous learning. Furthermore, since the teacher is the chief source of evaluation, her relationship with the pupil is necessarily judgmental and the pupil continues to be dependent on her evaluation of his efforts. Finally, the inappropriateness of this model becomes clearer when we recognize that the teacher as a diagnostician is led to focus on needs, disabilities, and problems instead of attending to the pupil as a person who is constantly growing and learning. If the doctor analogy is inappropriate, what analogy might be more fitting?

Recently, I have been exploring the notion that the teacher is more like a travel consultant. Suppose you want to take a trip to the Orient. You tell the travel consultant what you think you would like to see. He will have some questions: How much time do you have? What are you most interested in seeing? How much money do you want to spend on this venture? How do you prefer to travel? He may suggest other possibilities you did not know existed. A good travel consultant will help you to plan loosely, so that you will not find yourself dashing from one place to another. He will also help you to plan flexibly, so that if you find a place that you particularly enjoy you can make arrangements to stay longer.

Among the interesting features of this analogy, at least as far as I have taken it, are the implications for outcomes. It seems to me that this analogy implies that the primary outcome is not simply to get to the Orient. The outcomes are the kinds of experiences you have along the way and while you are there. Some of these outcomes are completely unpredictable — the people you happen to meet, the experiences you could not anticipate. These unpredictable outcomes might be, in the long run, the most vital aspects of your trip — the ones you remember forever, in contrast to the general clear-cut objective of getting to the Orient or of seeing certain sights that you decided on in advance. Furthermore, other travelers can choose other destinations.

This analogy, in contrast to the medical analogy, is in large part open-ended, responsive to persons (rather than to deficiencies), and clearly allows for self-direction. Still, after all has been said, analogies are merely vivid pictures that may help us see new relationships but that necessarily fall short of describing the realities we are discussing. Instead of exploring analogies, then, let us consider how teachers and pupils might function to promote the kind of individualized and personalized learning that is truly responsive to, and supportive of, individuality.

BELIEFS WE CAN QUESTION

For a discussion of this kind we must first eliminate some of the constraints that inhibit our thinking about new roles. These constraints are both conceptual and institutional. The first conceptual constraint I would discard is the idea that there is a necessary sequence for learning certain skills, or a particular set of sequences that is best for all children. Also I would discard the idea that certain predetermined sequences are necessary to develop understanding in a content area. These two assumptions underlie programmed learning and the "structure-of-discipline" approach to curriculum. In addition, I do not believe that we know what knowledge and skills all children should have. Knowledge is neither certain nor permanent. As for skills, I think there are certain agreements in our culture. For example, in order to learn you have to be able to read, and reading involves a variety of interrelated skills. However, there is great difference of opinion as to what constitutes reading skill and how children learn to read. Commonly held assumptions inhibit our view of curriculum.

I would also discard the premise that the learner is primarily a receptive, reactive organism responding to stimuli presented by the teacher and by teaching materials, as well as to reward and punishment, or approval and disapproval, as meted out by the teacher. I would reject the view, still common among teachers, that intelligence tests measure the child's ability, or potential for learning, and that this potential is fixed and almost entirely genetically determined. Assumptions of this kind limit our perceptions of children.

I disagree with those who believe that grade level is a meaningful and useful way of organizing schools and curriculums. I do not believe that the teacher directly controls what is learned by the class. Nor do I believe that certain specific content or concepts must be covered during a school year. Finally, I cannot accept the current conviction that specific behavioral objectives provide the best guidelines for the planning of teaching and learning.

All these commonly accepted assumptions can, I believe, be challenged and rejected. Here I will discuss only the first assumption: that there is a best or desirable sequence for learning.

A study by Mager (1964) raises some interesting questions about learning sequences. Six adults were studying electronics in a learner-directed program. Each subject in this study was treated individually and took part in one to seven sessions that lasted sixty-five minutes on the average.

In the experimental group, the instructor's role was merely to respond to the questions and requests of the learner. These requests could be for information, for demonstration, for reviews, for whatever the learner felt he needed at the moment.

Some interesting findings emerged. The author reported: "Subject-matter commonality in the learner-generated sequences was greatest at the outset of instruction. As instruction progressed the learners moved into their areas of special interest in electronics. . . . The instructor-generated sequences began with an entirely different topic than did the learner-generated sequences. This suggests that the sequence most meaningful to the learner is different from the sequence guessed by the instructor to be most meaningful to the learner" (Mager, 1964, p. 3). In fact each learner pursued a different path of instruction. The instructor found it difficult to follow the questions of the learner. Mager commented: "If the instructor finds it difficult to keep up when the sequencing of content is controlled by the student, what kinds of obstacles must the student be facing when the instructor controls the sequence?" (Mager, 1964, p. 3).

Also, although the subjects were convinced that they knew absolutely nothing about electronics before this experiment, it turned out that they actually had a large body of relevant background information from which the instructor could draw. In addition, from the learners' behavior, the way they raised questions and used the information they got, it appeared that they "were continuously attempting to tie new information to information they already knew, whether correct or incorrect" (Mager, 1964, p. 3).

Finally, the author concluded, "The data suggest that the learner's motivation increases as a function of his control, or apparent control, of the learning situation. Subjects' comments indicated that they terminated their sessions because they felt unable to absorb more material rather than because they were bored" (Mager, 1964, p. 3).

Mager started out to compare the effectiveness of instruction using the traditional methods with the effectiveness of instruction using programmed materials. He found that he saved time when he used the program. However, he saved even more time when he used learner-directed instruction. This investigation, it seems to me, encourages us at least to question the conviction that we can determine the best sequence for teaching and learning.

ROLES REDEFINED

A willingness to question many commonly held assumptions will make it possible to visualize a new model of the classroom. We must, of course, be aware that the same actions at different times and in different contexts will have different meanings. We cannot say that behaving in a certain fashion is necessarily consistent with our goal of developing individuality. Furthermore, each classroom is a unique environment for learning. It could not be otherwise. Each teacher is unique, and each combination of individuals who make up a class is unique. The resultant mix of personalities, attitudes, interests, resources, and materials can never be duplicated.

How then might pupils and teachers, having discarded the old assumptions, function in these environments? I will describe some possible roles that I believe would encourage the individual development of the pupil.

Principally, the pupil could play a more significant role in determining his learning activities. He could be involved in significant decisions — not just in the unimportant ones we usually allocate to him. Within broad limits, he could choose what he will learn and in whose company. He could plan and evaluate for himself. He could be free to raise questions important to him and to explore his world outside the classroom as part of his planned learning. He could be encouraged to clarify his personal meanings and values. In short, he could be a self-directing, active learner, a role not often emphasized in today's schools.

The teacher's role would be primarily that of consultant and resource person to the learner. She would be a manager of the classroom environment, supplying a variety of materials and at times initiating new experiences. She would help pupils learn to plan, to evaluate, and to consider alternatives. She could bring her own interest and inquiry into the classroom. The main focus of her activity would be to promote self-direction (Wolfson, 1967). Of course, each teacher's approach is unique. But if a teacher does not intend to promote self-direction, she will not truly allow children to make choices. Her intent, therefore, will influence how she and her pupils organize their class.

In these classrooms there would be a flexible mix of individual activities, small-group activities, and large-group activities.

There would be frequent pupil-teacher conferences. Small groups might ask the teacher to confer with them. Temporary interest-centered groups would develop and disband as they completed their plans. At times the entire class would meet at the request of the teacher or a pupil. A wide variety of materials in many media would be available. Resources outside the classroom would also be used. The significant element in organizing and using resources would be the co-operative planning of pupils and teacher.

A word of caution is appropriate here. Many of the features I have been describing may be found in classrooms that are not focused on the educational purposes I have been emphasizing. Furthermore, we cannot conclude that the presence of these features will in themselves further individualized instruction and the development of self-direction. The intent and the functioning of the teacher will have an important influence on the pupils. Are they actually learning to be self-directing, or are they merely learning how to give the teacher what she expects? The teacher's attitudes, values, perceptions, and communications contribute to the formation of classroom climate and to the pupil's perception of his role in school.

NEW ROLES IN ACTION

Let us turn now to some examples of efforts to achieve the type of educational experience I have been discussing. Three projects seem to me to incorporate the spirit of this conception. There are undoubtedly other examples.

The first project was reported in an article called "Mississippi's Freedom Schools: The Politics of Education." In that article Florence Howe described her experience as a teacher and director of a Freedom School one August. Most of her work was with a group of eleven-to-fourteen-year-olds. Her description seems to communicate the realities of the situation. Take the following remarks about the teacher role:

The teacher's main problem was to learn to keep quiet, to learn how to listen and to question creatively rather than to talk at the students. He had to discard whatever formal classroom procedures he had ever learned and respond with feeling and imagination as well as with intelligence and good humor to the moods and needs of the group. Above all, the students challenged his honesty: he could not sidestep unpleasantness; he could not afford to miss any opportunity for discussing differences. (Howe, 1965, p. 155.)

These comments, it seems to me, convey an awareness of the need for "real" people as teachers. They also remind us that teaching consists of confronting problems. One cannot support a particular approach to teaching in the hope that it will eliminate all problems. Teachers and pupils must choose to confront the problems that they feel are meaningful. These are not necessarily the problems that other people consider meaningful.

A second example of an effort to achieve the type of educational experience I have been describing is an experimental high school in California. A report of the first year of the school describes the problems and the development of a school designed for "maximum student involvement and maximum freedom for individual growth" (Roberts and Schuetz, 1966, p. 1). In discussing curriculum and the related teacher-student roles the authors state:

In the classroom the student is shown that he should feel free to be himself. Our teachers try not to hide behind their teacher role; they, in turn, urge students not to hide behind theirs. They all begin their courses as students, the teachers only perhaps farther along in their questioning. Teachers encourage their students to formulate and share their own questions. By sharing in the inquiry, students will hopefully be drawn by their own natural curiosities into a search for the heart of each subject, and to the basic questions which draw disciplines together. They are made free to explore . . . the student learns to take more and more charge over his own education. By making choices available, by encouraging individual and small-group projects, by fostering an open, non-threatening atmosphere, by encouraging divergence of approach and opinion, by allowing ample room for unscheduled exploration, by aiding in the formation of individual goals, and by giving each student some personal attention and understanding, the teacher in the classroom makes constructive use of the individual learning pattern and goals of each student. (Roberts and Schuetz, 1966, p. 4.)

In this description, too, we can see an awareness of the need for teachers to be "real" people to their students. Admittedly, it is easy to describe an experimental school in glowing terms without providing corroborative evidence of its practices. I have spoken with the writers of this report, but I have not yet observed the school in action. Still, the direction of the effort clearly speaks to the kind of possibilities I am exploring.

For a third example, I would like to describe some observations made by teachers with whom I have been working, who teach in multiage, heterogeneous classrooms. As you can imagine, working with randomly assigned six-, seven-, and eight-year-olds (or nine-, ten-, and eleven-year-olds) in one classroom requires one to individualize instruction and to provide a wide variety of materials and learning opportunities.

In some of these classrooms I have seen evidence of extensive changes in teacher and pupil roles. Some teachers report that they experience a new kind of relationship with their pupils. At times, as pupils become increasingly self-directing, the teachers wonder how much they are needed. They note that pupils feel free to come to the teacher for help on various problems, but often the pupils also seek help from other pupils. Teachers express amazement at the capabilities of some of their pupils, capabilities that were completely unexpected. Some teachers also report that they

do relatively little direct instruction, and are surprised to see growth in skills on achievement tests without specific instruction.

In these classes pupils appear to learn to accept differences in other children and to work willingly with individuals who would ordinarily be in other grades. Many pupils pursue individual or small-group projects for an extensive period. One boy at the primary level spent much time studying continents and then proceeded to study air currents. Two boys (who would have been in third and fourth grade in a traditional organization) worked together for a long time studying about various animals.

I could give many examples (Wolfson, 1967) but to describe what one may see in a class of this kind, or to describe the activities a teacher and her pupils engage in, does not get to the heart of the matter. To provide the type of environment for learning I have been trying to describe, the teacher must have a view of man, and of children in particular, that allows her to see them as growing creatively, rather than as moving in predetermined paths. She must be able to interact honestly and realistically with her pupils. Living in schools can be real, not just playing the game of beating the system. To me individual and personalized learning means really living in school.

There is little research on the conception I have tried to develop. Most current research about teaching seems to me to be based on a mechanistic rather than an or-

ganistic model of man. The classroom observation and analysis research done in recent years by Anderson, Withall, Flanders, Smith, Hughes, Medley and Mitzels, and others (in Gage, 1963) have produced observation and category systems that purport to describe and analyze the teacher's behavior, mostly verbal behavior. The result of these efforts is a relatively superficial labeling or categorizing of the teacher's verbal acts. These categories describe a limited dimension of teaching behavior, but they are not really pertinent to what the teacher thinks she is doing. Nor are they particularly crucial dimensions of the teacher's actions. It seems to me that this type of analysis is equivalent to using the linear dimensions of an automobile and the names of some of its parts in an effort to describe and explain its functioning. Research of this kind assumes that the teacher's verbal behavior is meaningfully described by discrete units of activities in categories such as "asks questions" or "accepts feelings." This research also assumes that these bits, when added together in each category and examined for proportional distribution, will characterize some significant differences among teachers.

I have no objection to researchers who observe teaching and try to describe and even measure what they see. I would hope they might uncover some meaningful relationships. However, for the teacher of teachers and for the teacher herself, study of this kind has not yet yielded much useful information. I have already suggested that these studies fail because of the mechanistic nature of their analysis. I would also like to suggest that it is a mistake for the teacher to look to research for specific answers to her concerns as a practitioner. Like the aesthetician, who may possibly add to the artist's generalized thinking about art, but not directly affect how he goes about creating a painting, the student and researcher of teaching may possibly add to our generalized understanding about teaching, but not directly affect how we go about teaching.

HOW TEACHERS KNOW

It seems to me that our most vital questions as teachers cannot, at least at present, be answered by the researcher, the curriculum specialist, or the principal. Each of us must draw our working answers from our personal interpretation and integration of our current knowledge and experience. Indeed, our "tacit knowledge" (Polanyi, 1966) guides our actions whether in wisdom or in error.

I would like to close with the reminder that science is but one way of knowing, no doubt an extremely useful way but still, as Bronowski said, uncertain. Bronowski went on to say:

Not all experience is got by observing nature. There is a second mode of knowledge which differs from the procedures of science. In our relations with people, and even with animals, we understand their actions and motives because we have at some time shared them, so that we know them from the inside. We know what anger is, we learn an accent or the value of friendship, by directly entering into the experience. And by identifying ourselves with the experience of others, we enlarge our knowledge of ourselves as human beings: we gain self-knowledge. (Bronowski, 1966, p. 83.)

In my view of individualized and personalized learning, the teacher is working with her knowledge from the inside as well as with her observations from the outside. It is, I believe, through some combination of both kinds of knowledge that we must continue to search for the heart of the matter in struggling with the concepts of teaching and learning I have been discussing. The teacher cannot relinquish either focus, or indeed separate them, if she is concerned with her own and her pupils' personal learning.

Lederman explores with the reader the possibility of making subjective evaluations of students. There has been a long-standing assumption in our culture that only evaluation that strives to be objective is valid. In this reading, we find a challenge to this notion. Lederman assesses the work she and her aides have done with seven children. Judge for yourself whether you think other, more objective measures would add anything practical for the teachers and students involved. Do you think that some of the affective goals in education require more subjective means of evaluation? Combs (pp. 332–336) talks

about the need for different ways of assessing humanistic objectives. Is Lederman's approach a reasonable alternative?

JANET LEDERMAN

CONFLUENT LEARNING — PERSONAL VIEWPOINT

Often I am asked how I evaluate the "techniques" I use with children. How do I know what to do? How do I know if I am succeeding in my efforts to "teach" effectively? My first impulse is to answer, "I have no elaborate system of evaluation." I wonder if this is so. I am an affective being; that is, I have and use such emotions as love, anger, grief, and joy. I have a great deal of cognitive information stored and ready for use — information accumulated from study and experience. Therefore, when I am teaching I am affectively (emotionally) and cognitively (thoughtfully) encountering the child who is also

From *Human Teaching for Human Learning* by George Isaac Brown. Copyright © 1971 by George Isaac Brown. Reprinted by permission of The Viking Press, Inc.

responding both affectively and cognitively. The balance and the percentage of each component is a constantly changing sum within me and within the child. We are formed by both affective and cognitive domains as a sculpture is formed by both positive and negative space. There is no way in reality of separating the two without changing the "beast." Therefore, I use both in a continuing evaluation system.

I would like to take you with me, in reflection, as I expose my "system": my attitudes, my expectations, my intuitive responses, and my computations — my affective and cognitive domains.

I do not plan for children I have not met. How can I? I have no idea of "where they are" in either domain. I have enough teaching experience to be able to pass out paper; I have enough teaching experience to be able to create a lesson on the spot or lead a discussion or a game until the true needs of the children make themselves apparent. It is then that real educational environment begins to develop. With some children the time of waiting is almost nonexistent; with others the time of waiting is long. I will wait. The children come into a barren room. The room begins to fill as they begin to *live* within the environment we create together.

Now I ask the reader to enter inside of me and listen in to my senses, my intuition, and also my computations. I shall not address you now, for I am directing my attention to the children.

Roderick, you walk into the classroom. It is your first day. You hit every child in your path as you cross the room. There are several toys on the floor, and you step on each one of them. You do not sit in the circle with the other children. You sit just outside the circle. You are in touch with being "angry," and that you are able to communicate. You seem busy protecting yourself. I imagine you could use some help. I want to find ways of showing you I want to protect you. Words won't do. Then I imagine you will *allow* me to protect you (trust) and then perhaps some of your energy will be released for other things — like learning to write. Now you need to be a big shot or bully. This way you imagine you are safe. I won't get too close to you. I will give you space. I watch you until I discover something that you like to do. Something you do well. It takes a while and I wait. You like to work with wood. I ask you to saw many pieces for me. You do. I don't let anyone take the job away from you. I only ask you to do things in which you will succeed. Your experience with frustration is ample. One day after recess some bigger boy chases you into the room. I have no idea whether you provoked the situation. This is the time to protect you. I do. We don't talk about it. The action stands for itself. I am beginning to feel love for you. I enjoy your aggression. When you start to take over the class, I do not respond with pleasure. I do not tolerate your violence. I don't imagine you want that kind of power. You are testing to see if I am strong enough to take care of you. Yes, I am. We even wrestle to prove it to you. You are very much in your senses. Words have little meaning for you. I use very few words. My messages to you are through action. We will build words after our relationship has developed a meaning. How will I know? You begin to arrive at school on time. If you need to go play for a while, you put your lunch bag by the door for me to see you are here. You begin to call me by my name. You have your temper tantrum in the room instead of stealing something and running away. Your body begins to relax, and you smile now from time to time. You begin to work on numbers when I sit with you. You begin to learn to print when I sit with you. I am not going to push you to work away from me yet — not until you are ready. The first time I will ask you to work on something I know you can do and that *you know* you can do. How will I know you are ready? You will not mind if I am giving attention to some other child when you sit next to me. I might get up and move away for a few minutes, and you will keep working. I am watching you. I am listening with my eyes and ears, all the time thinking what the next step is to be. I watch for the first time you make a mistake and are able to go on instead of tearing up your paper. I assume you feel safe in the room when I see that you don't have to be a bully for the entire time. I begin to send you on small errands, and I give you points for returning right away. I mark down the time you leave and return so that you have some structure. I know you are beginning to trust *you* and me when you don't need that structure. And I imagine you trust me when you are in stress and ask for it back from time to time — before disaster strikes. I do not ask you to do things that are impossible for you. You have enough contact with frustration and you don't need more! You begin to trust that I will not ask the impossible of you; therefore, you begin to take a few risks — such as writing a story. I make sure you succeed. Soon you are willing to try arithmetic, and you find you love adding numbers. You do pages of adding. Then comes a crisis. You have been doing what you thought impossible and this scares you. How do I know? You become a bully once again. You try all your old techniques — almost to make sure that they are still there. I won't let you use them in the classroom any more. This time I tell you, "Roderick, I won't accept this kind of behavior any more. You needed it when you came. You knew no other way to behave. Now you do. I have seen you. I won't let you stay in class today." I send you home. You want to stay. You cry. I send you home and hope you get the message. The next day you return. You got the message. You left the bully outside the door. We don't talk about what happened. We go on. I felt you wanted someone to control that bully. You begin to use other things available to you in the room — puzzles, games, the chalk board. You sit with us in the circle. You like to sit next to me while I read stories. You like to select the book, and you begin to make your wants known

— not by fighting but by asking. You can even wait and take turns. You put your arms around me, and you allow me to hold and comfort you and play with you. You begin to say, "This is my teacher, my room, my school."

Stanley, you spent two years with me. I am remembering when you first arrived. You are sullen. You do no schoolwork. You steal things from the room. I say nothing yet. I give you time to be wherever you are. I will meet you there first. You cry a great deal. You have no friends. I am wondering if you remember this day? You are frowning and angry. You walk over to the chalk board and you write in large letters, "FUCK." You look at me. You see I am looking at you. I accept your message. You stand there for a time, then you slowly erase the word. You do not steal anything today. Thereafter you use that technique to show me your anger. Sometimes the letters are huge, sometimes they are very tiny. You start to print, and then you want to write stories. You love to paint and build boats. At the end of the second year you are ready to move on to a regular room. A room you have tested and found to be comfortable for you. You come back for visits. Your visits become shorter and shorter. Soon you visit only when there is a substitute teacher or when you are under stress. Then comes the time when I push you from the nest. I tell you, "Stanley, you are too big to visit during the school day. Come see me after school and tell me what you are doing." You are ready, and somehow that gives you more confidence in

yourself. Then comes the *day*, that wonderful day your teacher and I stopped you from reading. Your eyes were red-rimmed. Were you "reached," as they say? I think so. Do I have a systematic test to prove it? No!

Willis, on your first day you came in fighting. You ran away when you couldn't take charge of the classroom. You got frustrated the instant you made one mistake. You tore up your paper and found someone to hit. You tried to hit me, we wrestled, and you cried. When you calmed down, I gave you a hammer and nails and you fixed the tool cart. You could have thrown the hammer at me, but you didn't. For several months you only worked with wood. Oh, you built so many airplanes! You wouldn't touch a pencil. You loved to clean and organize the room. I arranged for you to work in the kindergarten, and you loved taking care of the small children. You were in the second grade, yet you still seemed to need the kindergarten experience, but with status. You never bullied the little children. You were gentle and patient. Gradually you began to work with a pencil. You wanted to practice your printing. You wanted to be perfect. You could not stand failure. With a community volunteer by your side you were able to get through your intense frustration. You have been in a regular room for a year. You still fight and you still get frustrated, but you can also wait and give yourself a chance before you tear up your work. You can now wait while the teacher gives directions. You are not removed from the classroom. You are there and you can learn.

Nora, oh, Nora! You have not talked for two years, ever since you started school. You talk at home and when there is no teacher around, but you will not talk in the classroom. That takes a great deal of strength on your part. You walk around, you go through all the motions of school, but you never talk. You pretend to write stories. You scribble. Soon you begin to learn to write your name and then other letters. You want to write a story. How can I give you the words you need when you won't ask for them? I see the frustration. But not talking is still more important. Today is your special day, a day I will always remember. Raymond comes over and socks you. Mrs. Chalmers, a volunteer, is working with you at the time. You look at Raymond. You have never hit anyone in the classroom before. This time you do. You sock him, and Mrs. Chalmers gives you a lollipop. You look shocked! You whisper your first words in school. I feel as though you just grew a head taller and put on ten pounds. Soon you begin to whisper the words you want for your story. You write stories every day. You begin to learn arithmetic. You begin to read. Your whisper is getting louder and louder. You are smiling more and more. You have been in a regular room for a year. Mrs. Chalmers keeps working with you twice a week. You don't need me at all.

Christine, you came into the room with a reputation for biting, and you fulfilled that expectation on the second day. Now, two years later, I point to my arm and we both start laughing. We were together for a year and a half. You used to be in a fight every day. Now you are in a regular room, and you have a delightful sense of humor. I enjoy our time together — we visit and talk. You have an occasional fight. You have a very live temper. You are very alive. You write interesting stories, you do lovely art work, you enjoy coming to school. You have been in two regular rooms, and you are making it.

George Henry, they threw you out of kindergarten. You beat up the kids. George Henry, the big bully of the kindergarten set. You wouldn't change activities every ten minutes like the other children. No, not you! You enter the room. You spend days just walking around. You explore. You talk with no one. I soon discover you have your very own rhythm and you are not about to sell it short. You sit and play with a hammer and nails for an hour, quietly and all-absorbed. You cannot print and you don't want to learn. You love to work puzzles, and you work with them for hours. You come in each morning and go over to a chair and eat half your lunch. If I stop you, you are impossible the rest of the day. For two years you eat half your lunch the first thing each morning. You learn to saw. You begin to build trucks and boats. You like to paint, and you continue working puzzles. You love music. You play with the toy piano, and you are very methodical. I learn that you enjoy staying with an activity you are interested in, and you do not like to change as often as most children your age. You stay with me until the end of the first grade. Now you love to print and practice words on the chalk board. You begin to write stories. You love to add, and you laugh with delight as you keep asking for more and more work. You enjoy going back to the kindergarten and working for your former teacher, and she enjoys having you there. You are helpful. Soon you become bored, but first you fully enjoy the pleasure of being the returning hero who made good.

As I reflect, I am also aware of the failures. Raymond, the school failed you. There is no one at home who wants you. Your needs are too great for the school. You have grown too big — you are eleven years old — and the school is too small. You cannot maintain yourself in a regular room, and the school has no facilities to care for you. The adjustment between home, streets, and school is too much. Several organizations are "trying" to find a twenty-four-hour youth facility that *can* provide the care you need. I do remember the times you came to the room for contact. You didn't like being away from school. We talked, and I let you stay for a while. Soon the younger children became frightened with you there. You began to demand more time than I had available. I asked you to leave. I know you have to return to the streets. I cannot be with you all the time. You are still a very hungry boy.

I could go on with each child as he came and went. But I feel that these examples are enough. Each relationship is unique in its intensity and depth; each relationship is unique in the "system."

William Bridges' article is a personal evaluation of his teaching over the last ten years. He has experimented with, experienced, and lived through the problems and ideas that were presented in the previous chapter on freedom and limits. His teaching has changed from informal, to nonexistent, to an interest in giving direction. Each change has been accompanied by a thoughtful weighing of the successes and failures he has experienced at each juncture. He sees the potential for teachers to err "in the direction of abandonment" and "in the misuse of authority." How do you imagine he judges these errors for himself? How would you judge for yourself?

WILLIAM BRIDGES

THOUGHTS ON HUMANISTIC EDUCATION, OR, IS *TEACHING* A DIRTY WORD?

Ten years ago I was dismayed to hear Carl Rogers tell a Harvard audience, "Teaching is, for me, a relatively unimportant and vastly overvalued activity." At the time, I was just beginning full-time teaching and struggling to be a good teacher. Having read *On Becoming a Person,* I even fancied that I was something of a Rogerian in the way in which I conducted a literature class. I was pretty informal and supportive, but I was still *teaching.* Stop *teaching?* My God, better to stop breathing!

Yet, in the next several years, I slowly stopped "teaching." As a result of reading, workshops, and my own experimentation, I gradually shifted to the role of facilitator — the one who helps students learn what they want or need to learn without "teaching" it to them. At the same time, I began to acquire (as all those workshop brochures promised that I would) a sizeable repertoire of techniques drawn from

From *Journal of Humanistic Education* 13, no. 1 (Winter, 1973): 5–13. Reprinted with permission.

Gestalt therapy, encounter, psychosynthesis, sensitivity training . . . you know the list. Each semester a higher percentage of my class meetings included some unexpected "experience" for the students. Most of my classes continued to be literature classes in name, but more and more time was spent on ourselves and less and less on literature.

Having spent a lifetime being sensible, level-headed, reliable, highly organized, and uncontroversial, I was startled (and shyly pleased) to find myself coming to be known as controversial and even radical. My colleagues began to treat me with the mixture of interest and mistrust that might come the way of someone whose hair has turned white over night. Before long, I had a kind of niche in the institution: There was the resident poet, the black militant, the ecology freak, and *me.*

I can't really say just when the whole thing began to pall, but I know that about a year ago I finally had to admit to myself that I wasn't at all clear any longer about what I was really doing in the classroom. What was my purpose? How were my class techniques serving that purpose? It was a very disturbing realization. Only a year earlier I was so sure of my vision of the educational promised land that I was ready to leave teaching entirely in favor of running The Center for Innovative Studies, an exciting but (fortunately) never-funded institute to set up programs to bring the *word* to the unredeemed. My *hubris*-level at that time was high, and if it had all happened 2500 years ago, the Gods probably would have made me fall in love with a seal, thus making a complete fool out of me.

To reiterate, this past year has been very different indeed; it has been a whole series of grudging acknowledgments of some of the serious problems of nonteaching, as well as an awakening to some other possibilities that I had not explored. At the same time, as coordinator of the AHP* Education Network, I have been talking and corresponding with many other teachers whose difficulties and desires are very like my own. It now appears crucial to take a critical look at some of the common assumptions about humanistic education, and this is precisely what I propose to do.

TRADITIONAL EDUCATION TODAY

The time is past when it is important just to turn teachers on and crack them loose from their unquestioned ways of doing things. Teachers in increasing numbers everywhere are already out of their ruts. It is astounding to find how many traditionally trained teachers — people who have used the same notes and class plans for years — are trying new and very unconventional approaches in their class-

* Association for Humanistic Psychology

rooms. From periodicals and books, from the example of free schools and free universities, from growth-center workshops and university extension courses come a flood of information on new classroom techniques. But in this welter of innovation some important questions are being bypassed.

Two of the key complaints against traditional education are (a) that it is prescriptively structured ("This is what you need to know, and this is how to learn it") and (b) that it is too exclusively cognitive in style and content ("Forget how you feel about it, just get the information accurate"). It is natural, then, that humanistic education has come to be associated with unstructured learning situations and the use of nonverbal techniques. The corollary of these characteristics of the humanistic classroom is the facilitator role for the teacher — the role of the "real" and unauthoritarian resource person who is there to help the students learn what they want to learn.

Put this way, there is hardly anything about the role that could be argued with. But, in fact, these ideas are full of various dilemmas and contradictions, some of which are elaborated upon in the following paragraphs.

1. There is an implicit conflict between the exhortation to be nonprescriptive and the desire to introduce to the class those wonderful "experiences" that one enjoys so much. For, actually, there is not much difference between saying, "Now, every-

one shut your eyes and I'll take you on a fantasy trip" and the old business of "Read pages 345–378 and do the exercises on page 379." When pressed to explain the justification for the fantasy trip, I used to say that it was an interesting rewarding experience that would provide students with another dimension of knowing. This was a dishonest answer though. For some students they *weren't* interesting rewarding experiences. And the latter part of the answer is simply a more sophisticated way of saying that these experiences are good for them — which I believe to be true, but which is also just what my fourth-grade teacher used to say about drawing all those stinking little spirals in penmanship class.

2. There is also an implicit conflict between the humanistic ideal of working with students *where they are* (as the real individuals that they are right now) and the fact of laying a very heavy trip on them (a set of expectations that masquerade as total freedom). To say to a class, "What do you want to learn? This is your chance to explore something that really interests you" is also to say, "Your difficulties in this situation reflect your difficulties in dealing with freedom." Now, that's true; but how painful such freedom really is is seldom acknowledged by the classroom teacher. Instead, the impression is left that it is only hung-up people who can't deal with freedom (i.e., who have trouble with my class). If a teacher is really ready to take on the exploration of the person's resistances to full awareness and his anxieties over the implications for his life of abso-

lute freedom, he is embarking on a long journey that quickly transforms the undertaking into something that he had better be more ready for than I was. Students are, of course, amazingly resilient as well as resourceful, so my concern is only partly for those for whom the class provides too little support in such an undertaking. My concern is also with the much greater number who size up the situation, find themselves unable or unwilling to risk so much, and then simply fake their way through the class with the same skill that they have faked their way through traditional courses for years. I have been startled to learn how many of my students have taken the latter route, saying and writing things that made me think that I was doing great things with them, when actually they were just figuring out what was appropriate to the situation and passing that off as their own experience.

3. The context in which it would be possible to freely explore this anxiety-laden experience would be a group context, and there are some classes led by some teachers that can profitably turn themselves into encounter or even therapy groups. For a while, I was willing to go this route and even encouraged it in my classes, but I do not do so now. There are many reasons for this decision. First, students enroll in classes for very different reasons (including its convenient meeting hour) from those which lead people to join groups. A person's presence in the class does not mean the same thing as his presence in a group, and there is not the same degree of com-

mitment to the sort of honesty and openness that makes a group work. Second, my particular field of literature does not justify turning the class into an encounter group in the same way that a course in, for example, interpersonal behavior would. The students whose genuine desire to learn involves the field of literature would rightly feel upstaged when the focus of the class shifted permanently to the group itself. And third, I really don't want to lead a group; I want to teach literature, which brings us back to "teaching."

INFORMATIONAL BIAS

Is teaching really such a damaging operation as I thought when I became a facilitator? As I have puzzled over this question, I have realized that humanistic psychology really represents a blending of two traditions. One of them mistrusts teaching, emphasizing nondirective work with others. It grew out of the field of clinical psychology on a one-to-one basis. The other tradition grows out of the idea of the spiritual discipline and represents a way of working with initiates toward new kinds of insight into the nature of things. In our day of instant gurus, this latter stream often seems polluted. But it is still an important one, for there are simply some very rewarding and growthful things that a person will not discover on his own.

The question of how to help people learn is complicated by the fact that each of these two traditions within the human-

istic fold is directed toward a different kind of "learning." Learning itself is a concept that covers quite different kinds of experiences. The facilitator role deals most adequately with two kinds of learning: the acquisition of information and personal learning ("I realize that I get anxious when I'm around angry people"). In each case, such learning demands assistance but not intrusion, and in neither case is it possible to impose one's own views without making the student's task more difficult. The teacher role, on the other hand, deals better with other kinds of learning, particularly those which involve training in a technique, procedure, or new kinds of discriminatory perception ("That blur on the X-ray plate is a rib, but *that* blur is a scar"). These distinctions between different kinds of learning are customarily distorted by our culture's bias toward the purely informational and the consequent tendency to convert things into informational form: "I am an obsessive person because of my early training"; "Clovis was a good king — true or false?"; "To carve a leg of lamb, turn it so that. . . ."

Perhaps I am the more conscious of this informational bias and the distortions of reality that it encourages because it is so strong in me that I am always running afoul of it. When I decided to learn to ski at the age of thirty, I did what only someone with a graduate-school education would do: I bought a book on skiing, read it through, buckled on my skis, and fell down. I was really offended at the thought that I needed a teacher, that I needed someone to say, "Hey, keep the weight on the downhill ski . . . tuck your tail in . . . bend your knees." I finally gave up and took classes, and I learned more skiing in the process. I realized how different it is to do something and *at the same time* get instruction. In my literature classes, people did things outside of class and then brought them in for instruction (or rather they did until I grandly swore off instructing for a while). But productive learning just doesn't happen after the fact; you need it while you are doing the thing. You read a line of a poem and misunderstand a word, or don't hear the sound, or miss a metaphor, and if someone can say right at that moment, "Well, I thought that he was saying . . . ," then something productive happens. This, incidentally, is not the stimulus-response phenomenon that the teaching-machine people are always talking about, because it's not saying, "Wrong, try again." It is saying something more like, "Keep your weight on the downhill ski and see how much better you do when you turn." The payoff is not in getting the right piece of information, the teacher's approval, or the machine's methodical advance to the next question. It is finding that you can do something that *works*.

This informational bias of which I have been speaking has confused discussions of teaching by leaving the erroneous impression that there were basically only two kinds of learning: experiential and personal learning of the sort that goes on in therapy or in an encounter group, and the acquisition of information about the extra-personal world. If you accept this view, it is natural to conclude that teaching gets in the way of learning because it predetermines the information and precludes intrapersonal encounter. But if you are seeking to work with the other kinds of learning that are left out of this falsely polarized picture — something beyond the facilitation of natural processes — some other sort of teaching is required. This is a crucial point because if humanistic education is falsely dichotomized into personal learning and the acquisition of information, a great deal is lost. What is lost is learning to do and to perceive in ways that unlock the innate human potential and provide the person with a great deal of pleasure.

This dichotomization of learning burdens the educational process in another way as well by suggesting that the solution must be found in the classroom rather than in the institution. If working with the student's authentic need to know is the basis of the humanistic endeavor, then the institution's task is to provide him with access to learning situations. Today's institutions don't do that. They provide him with access to "courses" — chunks of academic work that only faintly correspond to his actual situation. It would be interesting to speculate whether the heavy emphasis on warm and accepting teacher-student relations within the classroom doesn't result from the fact that so few of the students in a class have anything vital to relate to besides the teacher. This occurred to me recently when I asked for and received a lesson in tree pruning from a man who broke all the rules of humanistic education. He was judgmental, compulsive, and impersonal; he talked down to me, made light of my reactions, and taught me to prune an apple tree, which is what I wanted to learn. This apparently technical operation had deep personal significance for me, for it was part of my growing interest in a more land-related, self-sustaining, and integrated way of living. This interest is carrying me into fields of information and technique that I would have found terribly boring five years ago, fields on which books are written and in which universities offer courses. But if I were an undergraduate today, I would have to try to convert these interests into a schedule of classes that told me more than I wanted to know about subjects only vaguely related to my interests.

PROBLEMS OF HUMANISTIC TEACHING

Clearly, the problems facing the humanistic teacher come partly from this institutional situation. The student who is longing for a new mode of living naturally, and who wishes he knew how to prune an apple tree, shows up in my poetry class. I ask what he wants to learn about, and he says that he's into tree pruning. Well, I can be as unstructured as the next teacher, so he develops a project on tree pruning (in poetry, of course) and leads a class on it. But that falls flat because the class is made up of people who are into I Ching and black nationalism and creative writing and impeaching Nixon and astrology and computer programming. Of course, I can bring them together on a purely interpersonal level (except for the I Ching girl who doesn't relate well and the black nationalist who thinks that self-exploration is white, middle-class bullshit). And I can give them some growth-oriented experiences that fill up the class periods. But I can't really give them what they need, because the institution insists that we convert needs into three-unit, semester-long classes that don't conflict with one another. Until we can restructure institutions to become educational resource places, we will mistakenly, but understandably, be trying to do the impossible — make each individual classroom what the institution ought to be.

I suspect that one reason so many out of my generation of teachers have been swayed toward this willingness to try to meet every student's needs is that we have lost our faith in the importance of what we have learned and of what we have to offer others. Traditional teachers, like my tree-pruning mentor, have a profound advantage on us in this matter. They care about and feel the importance of what they know. Often I mistrust them, feeling that the certainty is bought at the price of awareness, and sometimes I fall into the despair that William Butler Yeats must have felt when he wrote,

Things fall apart; the centre cannot hold;
Mere anarchy is loosed upon the world,
The blood-dimmed tide is loosed, and everywhere
The ceremony of innocence is drowned;
The best lack all conviction, while the worst
Are full of passionate intensity.[1]

These lines remind me that what is needed is not faith in some subject or procedure or value system, but a centeredness, a rootedness in the place/time where we stand. They serve to make me remember that the drift I have experienced is not an uprootedness (for my old faith in which I knew was a rootless clinging) but a detachment from connections which provided safety though lacking sustenance. So I can see the drift in positive terms as the opportunity to home in on a genuine standpoint, the place from which my profession (which comes from the Latin word for confess or acknowledge) will be authentic.

As detachment from extrinsic values, this rootlessness provides the opportunity for a homecoming. Yet, it is also a state of anguish, and one that I and others have too often misrepresented and rationalized as a positive state in which we can help

[1] Reprinted with permission of Macmillan Publishing Co., Inc. from *The Collected Poems of W. B. Yeats* by W. B. Yeats. Copyright 1924 by Macmillan Publishing Co., Inc.. renewed 1952 by Bertha Georgie Yeats. Also by permission of M. B. Yeats, Miss Anne Yeats and Macmillan of London & Basingstoke.

others without laying our trip on them. In fact, we too often lay a very heavy trip on others when we work with them in this condition. We are living vicariously through them as they search for the meaning that we have not ourselves been able to find. It is not just that we project our own confusions onto them in the name of liberating them from the false; it is that we project onto them the hope of and responsibility for finding the relation to reality that we ourselves cannot find.

The fault here does not by any means lie in the humanistic ideal of each person's discovery of his own angle of vision — an ideal that I dearly cherish. It is simply that the ideal provides an unfortunately convenient rationale for abandoning the learner to his own devices. If we are all lost, it is indeed a good idea to be lost together. But the value of that experience begins with the acknowledgment that it is in fact the case, not with misrepresenting it as a guided experiment in freedom and self-discovery.

The humanistic ideal in education is gravely endangered by this situation, but the ideal itself remains for me the only hope in a world where traditional value systems and the myths that embody them have lost their hold on our imaginations and, hence, their power to connect us to the living reality. The humanistic goal of self-knowledge and of what Emerson called "an original relation to the universe" can only be reached by providing people with several different kinds of educational opportunities. We must create institutions which are truly resource centers, networks of persons and libraries and non-written resources to which we can turn whenever we know what we need to learn. Profoundly alienated from ourselves, however, many of us do not yet know what we need, so we must devise ways in which to enable ourselves to recover that experiential center from which our own situations and their demands on us are revealed. To do this we must draw upon both of the great humanistic traditions mentioned earlier — the tradition that emphasizes nondirective assistance in discovering one's personal reality, and the tradition that emphasizes the masterly unfolding of new ways of doing and perceiving. Each path is perilous, the former liable to degeneration into abandonment, the latter liable to degeneration into authoritarian control. But the dangers come from misuse rather than use.

Had I been addressing this article to a traditionally oriented audience, I would have spent far more space on the dangers of the model of the teacher as master. It is all too obvious that for every teacher who errs in the direction of abandonment, 10 err in the misuse of authority. Until recently it has seemed to me unnecessary to worry about a scale that was already so heavily weighted in the "wrong" direction: any change would be beneficial when things are so bad. But now I feel differ-

ently, and it is the very successes of the humanistic thrust that make me feel this way. It is time to set our own house in order, to stop measuring ourselves against an obviously decrepit status quo, and to begin to look critically at our own assumptions and accomplishments.

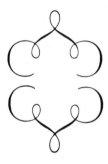

In this article, Combs uncovers some of the basic difficulties of evaluating the goals of education. Many new kinds of objectives have been formulated, essentially humanistic objectives, and they are not amenable to direct measurement. They are holistic, affective, human, and involve personal meaning. Moreover, openness means that specific ends are not predetermined. Combs suggests that the solution can be found in evaluating the <u>processes</u> that are used in learning. He concludes his argument by pointing to the importance of human judgment. Although the scientific value of humanistic goals has been questioned, we see that they are important. In the final analysis, the comparison of values is a matter of personal judgment.

ARTHUR W. COMBS

EDUCATIONAL ACCOUNTABILITY FROM A HUMANISTIC PERSPECTIVE

The humanist approaching educational accountability finds himself in a difficult spot. On the one hand he finds it necessary to resist the distortion produced by preoccupation with performance based criteria as educational outcomes. Behavioral objectives, however, have such apparent simplicity and straightforwardness and create such an illusion of business-like precision that the humanist finds himself regarded as soft, unscientific, fuzzy minded, and generally opposed to progress. On the other hand, the humanist finds himself unprepared to offer immediate or simple solutions to the processes of accountability because the problem as he sees it is: (a) so large and so complex that behavioral objectives can deal only with the simplest, most primitive aspects of educational goals; (b) humanistic goals do not readily

From *Educational Researcher* 2, no. 9 (September 1973): 19–21. Copyright, 1973, American Educational Research Association, Washington, D.C.

lend themselves to traditional modes of assessment; and (c) the humanist movement in education is still so young it has not yet developed sophisticated techniques for assessing outcomes in humanistic terms. As a consequence, the humanist position is often tough and lonely.

The issue is one of overall goals. Methods of assessment have inevitable indirect as well as direct effects upon the educational settings in which they are employed. Such side effects cannot be ignored. They must be clearly perceived and taken into account in the design of accountability models lest the cure turn out to be worse than the disease it was designed to correct. Millions are spent each year in the pharmaceutical industry to test the side effects of drugs. In education we cannot do less and educational accountants must, themselves, be held accountable for the effects their techniques impose on our educational system.

I have outlined elsewhere (Combs, 1972) my reservations about the behavioral objectives-performance based criteria approach to accountability. Here, let me outline some of the characteristics of humanistic objectives for education.

HUMANISTIC OBJECTIVES

Humanistic objectives: (1) are largely holistic. They have to do with such matters as intelligence, problem solving behavior, creativity, adaptability, responsibility for self and others, positive self concepts, feelings of identification, values, attitudes, self actualization, and the discovery of personal meaning; (2) are concerned with affective aspects of learning that determine the expression of information in action; and (3) are directed to the qualities that make us human — internal states like feelings, attitudes, beliefs, understandings, perceptions. Any comprehensive approach to educational accountability must deal with these important goals. Our society can get along with a bad reader. A bigot is a danger to everyone.

Humanist objectives for education cannot be readily assessed by current behavioral, performance-based techniques primarily because they are matters of personal meaning. Meanings are internal. They lie inside of persons and are not open to direct investigation. Since they do not have a direct one-to-one relationship to behavior, neither can they be adequately assessed by the familiar psychometric techniques on which most of us cut our teeth. For the humanist, behavior is a function of meaning. It is not the cause, but symptom, and the attempt to understand human beings on the basis of symptomatology is likely to be no more successful for psychologists than it is for physicians. Behavior, in and of itself, is nothing. It has significance only in terms of its meaning to the behaver and to the receiver.

Whatever a person's behavior, it is always a function of the personal meanings existing for him at the moment of action — especially, how he sees himself, how he sees the world in which he is moving, and

the purposes he has in mind at that moment. Perceptions are expressed in behavior, to be sure, but this relationship is not one-to-one. A given set of perceptions may produce many varieties of behavior. With a little imagination, for example, any child who wants to upset a teacher can find myriad ways to do so. How a person behaves at any instant is a function of what is going on inside him — especially his beliefs, feelings, values, attitudes, personal meanings, purposes, and goals. Permanent change in behavior is only likely to occur when these causative factors within the individual are changed. Concentrating on behavior thus puts attention on the wrong dynamic. Except in the case of comparatively simple skills, it is an inefficient road to behavior change. A given perception in the student may lead to hundreds of behavioral expressions. Or, a given behavior may be the product of a vast number of personal perceptions. Change in behavior with no change in perception is unlikely to remain very long. On the other hand, a change in perception may result in many behavior changes. To be sure, sometimes when a behavior change has been manipulated, perception also changes and the behavior may become permanent. However, this is a roundabout haphazard approach to changing behavior, like taking an unnecessary detour.

To deal with the problems of perception, a new psychology is called for, not to replace behavioral approaches but to supplement and extend that frame of reference to deal with problems it cannot readily handle. I believe this humanistic psychology is at hand in the work of persons like Carl Rogers, Abraham Maslow, and others, including myself. Out of such thinking guidelines for achieving humanistic objectives can be discovered and means for assessing outcomes developed. If behavior is a function of meaning, it will not be necessary for us to measure behavioral outcomes with the precision demanded by current systems approaches if we can find ways to assess the personal meanings which lie behind behavior. The value of such approaches is especially evident applied to the assessment of holistic goals that do not lend themselves readily to measurement in terms of specific behaviors.

ASSESSMENT OF PROCESS

Behavioral objective approaches to accountability are essentially closed systems of thinking. The paradigm goes: (a) set objectives in behavioral terms, (b) establish the machinery to achieve those ends, then, (c) test whether in fact they were actually achieved by assessment in behavioral terms. The measurement of long term educational goals, whether humanistic or not, by this procedure is always hampered by the question of who or what was responsible for the measured outcome. Students do not only go to school; they are affected by everything that happens to them. The attempt, therefore, to isolate the peculiar stimuli responsible for remote outcomes is thus a study in futility.

The closed system of thinking required by behavioral objective approaches to accountability runs head on into the open systems generally characteristic of humanistic practice. Open systems do not call for specific ends determined in advance. Instead, they are problems oriented with ultimate goals established only in very general terms if at all. Operating in this way teachers and students together confront a problem, and together seek solutions which neither knows precisely in advance. It is not surprising, then, that the imposition of behavioral objectives upon persons working in this frame of reference should be met with resistance.

Open systems direct the practitioner's attention to processes rather than ends. The goal is to confront students with problems that constantly keep them stretching and to join or assist them in the discovery of appropriate answers. The educator's emphasis is thus on the creation and maintenance of process rather than ends, and the effectiveness of the practitioner must be judged in terms of his success or failure in establishing effective processes. Such a goal, it should also be observed, is basically consistent with the democratic principle that "When men are free they can find their own best ways." Professionals operating in the open system are bound to find themselves in conflict with accountability practices that require precise definition of behavioral outcomes determined in advance. Such demands cannot be met without surrender of their basic beliefs about effective teaching.

As a professional worker the humanist can and must be held responsible for the processes he uses. It is the very essence of professional responsibility that whatever professional workers do, they do for good reasons. This is an aspect of accountability that teachers can and should be held accountable for. It also offers an alternative approach to accountability directed toward the assessment of process. This is no mean contribution and has several important advantages. For one, it is much simpler to accomplish. For another, it concentrates teacher attention on what and how and why he is doing whatever he does. Such a focus is more likely to result in innovation and change than concentration on behavioral outcomes subject to unknown degrees of influence by forces outside the teaching situation.

Whatever is done in the name of accountability must be couched in terms consistent with the frame of reference for teaching within which the teacher is operating. To demand that he be accountable for goals he is not seeking or outcomes he cannot describe in precisely defined behavioral terms is not only grossly unfair but downright destructive to humanistic goals and purposes. One could reverse the coin and demand that closed system teachers be held totally accountable for processes rather than ends but that would be equally unfair and destructive for them. It seems to me the only rational resolution of this dilemma is to recognize that there are *two* ways of looking at the accountability question, each appropriate to its own unique goals and purposes, and *both* systems of thinking must be included in any comprehensive plan for accountability.

Understanding the validity of the humanist position opens at least two new avenues for exploration of accountability problems. Accountability can be achieved through the assessment of process, as we have just been observing. It can also be achieved through an understanding of professional responsibility. The antithesis of professional responsibility is mindlessness. Professional workers can and should be held responsible for being able to demonstrate some rational basis for whatever they do, be it research, logical thought, experience, consistency with theory or whatever. This is an aspect of accountability that all teachers can and should be held accountable for. It also opens another avenue for assessment of the educational process, especially in those instances where objectives have to do with change in internal states or broad, holistic kinds of behaviors projected well into the future.

THE ACCEPTANCE OF JUDGMENT IN ASSESSMENT

If the heart of learning is the personal discovery of meaning, then the assessment of personal meaning should be at the very heart of accountability. At the present state of our assessment technology this can only be accomplished through the use of some form of human judgment. Unfortunately, human judgment is held in very low esteem by specialists in educational research. It is generally regarded with suspicion and looked upon as too imprecise, vague, and mystical to be accepted as valid indication of what is happening in the educational process. But judgment is what both education and science are all about. The purpose of both these endeavors is, in the final analysis, the refinement and improvement of human judgment. Judgment frees us to extend our observations beyond the immediate and the palpable. Its use is absolutely essential for successful operation in our daily lives and lies at the very heart of effective professional activity. Regarding human judgment with disdain and contempt undermines the very basis of what the profession is all about. Rejection of the use of human judgment for assessing educational outcomes will result in failure to measure the most important aspects of our educational objectives, on the one hand, and contribute to further destruction of teacher morale on the other.

Human judgment, of course, can be fallible. It can also be highly reliable when subject to the same tests of credibility utilized in the physical sciences. Among these are such tests as internal and external reliability, predictive power, internal consistency, the test of fit in mental manipulation, and agreements with expert judg-

ment. Judgment is a necessary and useful tool for the professional worker. Indeed, in our research on good and poor teachers at the University of Florida (Combs, et al., 1969) we have found repeatedly that objectivity correlates negatively with effectiveness.

Since humanistic objectives like values, feelings, beliefs, understandings, attitudes and personal meanings lie inside people they cannot be effectively measured by any devices we now possess except through some form of inference. But inference, like human judgment, is generally regarded as unscientific, mystical, and unreliable by persons concerned with assessment of educational outcomes. This is a pity, for such an attitude closes the door on highly fruitful and valuable resources for achieving accountability goals. Even the physical sciences use inferential techniques to deal with problems not immediately observable. To reject it for educational purposes is most short sighted.

Internal personal meanings can be defined and assessed by a simple process of "reading behavior backwards." If it is true that a person's behavior is a function of his internal beliefs, attitudes, values, and the like, then it should be possible to infer these events from adequate samples of the individual's behavior. As a matter of fact, that is precisely what all of us do every day in trying to understand the behavior of people around us. We call it sensitivity or empathy, and inferences made in this fashion provide effective and useful bases for the control and direction of our own and others' behavior. Inferences made in this fashion are basic tools of the clinical psychologist, the teacher, social worker, and counselor. Like human judgments of any kind they can also be subject to accepted tests of scientific credibility.

TWO TOOLS ARE BETTER THAN ONE

It is fashionable in some quarters to regard behavioristic and humanistic approaches to understanding human beings as opposite poles on a continuum. Such dichotomies are downright destructive to thinking and practice because they unnecessarily handicap our efforts at dealing with what is already a difficult task. Let us draw on an analogy from mathematics. When in the course of man's history men needed to deal with countable things they developed arithmetic. Later on it was no longer enough to deal with observable countable things; men also needed to deal with unknown numbers, matters that could not be directly observed and counted. To meet this need they invented algebra. Algebra did not deny arithmetic. It built upon and extended beyond to deal with problems that could not be handled in the original frame of reference. This is the current situation for behaviorism and humanism. Humanism does not deny behaviorism. Instead, it provides a valuable tool to deal

with those problems the behavioristic approach is unable to handle so effectively and efficiently.

It does not make much sense to dig a ditch with a teaspoon or to stir coffee with a steam shovel. The tools we use to accomplish a task must be appropriate to the tasks we confront. The professional worker who insists upon approaching all problems from a single frame of reference must necessarily seriously impede his own effectiveness and the accomplishment of his objectives. Just so, the search for accountability that ignores humanistic objectives and insists upon exclusive use of behavioral approaches must necessarily provide a limited and distorted understanding of educational processes.

It is time we regarded humanistic objectives and humanistic assessment as important in accountability. This will necessarily require allocation of time, money, and human energies to the humanistic aspects that have been discussed. The price of not making such allocations will be further dehumanization of an educational system already in serious trouble for lack of relevance and for alienation of students who opt out, cop out, and drop out at ever increasing rates. If we fail to recognize and utilize the best we know about humanizing education, we will have failed everyone — ourselves, the schools, parents, children, and society itself.

This excerpt from Seif's book on open education provides practical ideas for all those who are trying to evaluate their students and their teaching. Seif first stresses careful assessment of individual student work. He follows this with a variety of realistic suggestions including the use of work schedules, work sheets, student folders, student notebooks, individual conferences, student diaries, informal observations, diagnostic tests, and more. What is particularly interesting about these ideas is that they are generally already part of the ongoing business of good teaching. Seif helps us recognize their value for systematic evaluation of students and programs. When you finish reading his suggestions, try to think of several more of your own.

ELLIOTT SEIF

FORMAL AND INFORMAL EVALUATION IN THE OPEN CLASSROOM

Observation

In one first-grade class the children who were seated at their desks, were told to finish a workbook assignment. Some children finished

From *Success with Open Education: A Manual for Educators and Parents*, by Elliott Seif (Belmont, Ca.: Fearon Publishers, 1975). Reprinted with permission.

early. They became fidgety and restless. The teacher had a rule — they must sit in their seats until everyone was finished. No child was even allowed to get out of his seat to get a book to look at or read. What an incredible waste of time!

When observing an open educational environment, one is struck almost always by the movement, talking, and apparent lack of restrictions. Students are usually, at some times during the day, moving about from one activity to another. One somehow gets the feeling that there is a lack of educational accountability in the system — that somehow teachers and students are not accountable for what a child is doing and learning or not learning. That is precisely one of the biggest complaints about an open educational environment.

In my judgment, in order for an open educational environment to work, there has to be a strong measure of accountability built into the system. But just to say that may be deceptive, for my notion of accountability is different from the typical translation of educational accountability. Usually when one thinks of educational accountability, one thinks about teacher accountability for what a child learns. In my definition, educational accountability refers to *teacher and student accountability both for what is learned and what a student does with his time.*

The open educational environment has as one of its basic assumptions that students must take more control of, and consequently have more responsibility for, what they do at school and in classrooms. Thus, to a greater extent than in traditional classrooms, students keep records of what they do and are more accountable for what they learn. This does not mean that there is no educational accountability for the teacher, but that the nature of that accountability changes from a teacher responsible for the amount of learning that every child must learn in a given period of time to one who: (1) is responsible for creating a structured environment in which children can and do learn on their own and in which many things to be learned are introduced to children; (2) is responsible for diagnosing and helping students diagnose educational problems and needs; and (3) is responsible for seeing to it that students are responsible for their time within the open environment.

How can these be fostered? Many open education teachers have devised systems to enable these types of accountability to occur. In some classrooms, for example, work schedules and work sheets are developed on which a child himself writes down the activities performed, at what times they were performed, and when they are completed. At the beginning of the day or week, students are provided with an opportunity to explore the daily or weekly schedule and develop their own schedules. They check off these activities as they are performed.

Also in many classrooms students keep records of the activities, evaluations, and other assessments in a folder or notebook. The folders or notebooks can be kept for skill areas, such as reading and math, or they can be kept together with all work that is done by a student during the week.

Teachers in these classrooms also schedule individual conferences with children during the week often enough so that a teacher can see a child at least on the average of once a week (less if the class is large and the teacher does not have enough help to schedule individual conferences often during the day). During these conferences, the teacher and the child look at the work the child has done, and the teacher suggests activities in skill areas for the child to do. The teacher also may discuss any problems the child is having in the class and suggest solutions. Other work may also be checked.

Another form of assessment is a diary, which the children may be asked to keep about their day. Each afternoon, there may be a time period of about fifteen minutes set aside for diaries, in which a child writes down what he did during the day, how he felt about it, etc. These diaries may be private; they are also very helpful to stimulate writing. However, if a child agrees, a teacher may use the diaries as a basis for a conference for they can give a teacher insights into the way a child thinks and even into skill problems which a child is having.

Another important means of assessment is the informal observations and descriptions a teacher makes during the course of the day. During the day a teacher has the opportunity to observe the children in a variety of academic and social situations, and to assess skill development and social concerns informally. The teachers in many open classroom settings try to use this in a more formal way by actually keeping written notes of what is observed under each child's name. The teacher carries a small notebook and jots down pertinent information about the children which is later transferred to cards for each child. Another way to pursue this informal kind of observation is to choose one or two children a day to watch and observe and note. Then the teacher can concentrate on really getting to know that child and his or her strengths and weaknesses. A teacher might even want to have informal conferences with each child the day after that child is observed. This has the advantage of allowing more depth to a conference, since the teacher's notes are only one day old and fresh in her mind.

There is a myth normally associated with open educational environments — that there are no tests. Many open educational environments I have observed do have tests — but the tests are used in a different way. For example, I have observed classes in which a child might be working on his own or reading comprehension and skill development. At the end of each reading exercise, there is a comprehension test. The child has instructions to read each story during the scheduled reading time and then take the comprehension tests at the end of each story. The student also keeps a record of how well he did. During the conferences, or informally, the teacher checks on the comprehension level of the child via the test scores. He or she *does not give a grade;* rather the teacher tries to talk about the strengths and difficulties the child is having and to suggest continued work, some other task instead, etc. The teacher also keeps records of work completed and work correct.

Thus the purpose of the testing is not for grading or to expose the weaknesses of the child; rather, the test is used diagnostically by both the teacher and the student to determine the strengths and weaknesses of a student's ability and to determine future tasks and goals for the student. The diagnostic tests can be pre-tests, designed to determine how much a child knows *before* tasks are developed, and post-tests designed to determine how much a child has learned and to assess strengths and difficulties of the child at a given point in time. All children do not have to take tests at the same time: each activity has self-tests built into it, and as a child completes a task, he or she takes the tests on his own. If the tests measure what it is the child is supposed to be learning, there is no reason why another child or the teacher cannot help the student take the test — this help will facilitate learning for the child. It is to the child's advantage to take the test honestly — otherwise the activities he or she will be doing will be too difficult and unrewarding — in other words, not "fun" like the other children's activities.

Some open classroom schools operate with "contracts" — in other words the student contracts to complete a certain amount of work and activities and to take the tests associated with them according to his own interests, abilities, speed of work, levels, etc. If a student finds he or she cannot complete the work, then the contract is renegotiated. Where students seem to have difficulty working on their own and concentrating on their work, a point system contract can be developed. Students and teachers together devise contracts in which each task is assigned a certain number of points. In order to receive the points, the student must complete tasks on the contract and have the final products accepted by the teacher. The tasks are developed so as not to be impossible for the student, but to be challenging. As the student begins to be rewarded for the completion of a task and as students are able to work on their own, the point system is dropped.

Finally, most open educational environments have changed, or are trying to change, their report card systems. Some utilize, instead of report cards, individual conferences with parents and children. Some have report cards which are completely open-ended and descriptive, simply divided into the various subject areas like reading–language arts, social studies, etc., with spaces for written comments. Some are divided into levels of abilities and the children are scored according to their levels, particularly in reading and math. The important thing is that there is an elimination of grades and an attempt to devise a system which enables a teacher to report growth of the child rather than to report that child's standing compared with others.

Some teachers also use a form of self-evaluation. Teachers, in conference with the students, discuss the student's own evaluation of himself and his abilities and then try together with the student to write down what should be on a report card or what the parent should be told.

ASSESSING SCHOOLS AND CLASSROOMS

These ideas are designed to bring into the open educational environment a strong measure of accountability for a student's use of time and learning, and also to provide a more humane type of assessment which allows a teacher to continuously monitor the strengths and weaknesses of students, to allow students to monitor their own strengths and weaknesses, and to emphasize each individual's own growth and learning and not their failures. Such a system of accountability may include any or all of the following:

— student work schedules and work sheets
— work done kept by students in folders or notebooks
— individual conferences between teachers and students
— student diaries
— teachers recording daily informal observations and descriptions
— pre- and post-task diagnostic tests
— contracts
— "open ended" report cards and/or parent-teacher conferences

Featherstone is a journalist who has written extensively about schools in Great Britain. In this article, he expresses his concerns that open classrooms have become a sudden fad in America and that American educators have overlooked many aspects of the long British experience with informal education. The most valuable part of this reading, in our opinion, is Featherstone's discussion of the mistaken notions teachers hold about their role.

JOSEPH FEATHERSTONE

TEMPERING A FAD

Word of English schools reaches us at a time of cultural and political ferment, and the American vogue for British reforms must be seen as one element in a complex and many-sided movement. Within our schools, there is nearly a pedagogical vacuum. Few reformers have come forward with practical alternatives; even fewer have

From an excerpted version of *Informal Schools in Britain Today: An Introduction* by Joseph Featherstone. Copyright © 1971 by Schools Council Publications. Reprinted by permission of Schools Council Publications, Macmillan London & Basingstoke, and Citation Press, a division of Scholastic Magazines Inc.

deigned to address themselves to working teachers. The grass-roots nature of the English reforms, with their emphasis on the central importance of good teaching, has a great appeal for people who are victims of the general staff mentality of our school reformers and managers. Blacks and other minorities are interested in new approaches simply because they reject all the workings of the schools as they stand; some of the best of the community control ventures, such as the East Harlem Block Schools, have been promoting informal methods, as have some of the parent-controlled Headstart programs. And there are growing numbers of middle- and upper-middle-class parents in favor of "open" and "informal," not to mention "free," schooling, even though they are vague on the pedagogical implications of these terms.

The most cogent chapters in Charles Silberman's *Crisis in the Classroom* are a plea for American education to consider the English example. Silberman's book is interesting as a cultural document, as well as a statement in its own right. For it registers an important shift in opinion. Silberman is arguing that too many American schools are grim and joyless for both children and teachers. What was once said by a handful of radical critics is now very close to being official wisdom. Silberman, it should be added, distinguishes himself from many critics of the schools in that he is deeply sympathetic to ordinary classroom teachers and has a clear sense of the crucial importance of the teacher's role in creating a decent setting for learning.

By now I've visited a fair number of American classrooms working along informal lines. The best are as good as anything I've seen in England; the worst are a shambles. In the efforts that look most promising, people are proceeding slowly, understanding that preparing the way for further improvements and long-term growth is more important than any single "innovation." (As I've noted, there are too few entire school environments run along informal lines.)

Understanding the need for slow growth and hard work with teachers and children, many of the informal American practitioners I've talked to are alarmed at the dimensions of the current fad for "open" schools. There are reasons for skepticism. From today's perspective, which is no doubt morbid and too disheartened, it seems that our successive waves of educational reform have been, at best, intellectual and ideological justifications for institutions whose actual workings never changed all that much. At the worst, the suspicion is that past reform movements, whatever their rhetoric, have only reinforced the role schools play in promoting social inequality. The realization that schools alone cannot save the social order — which should have been obvious all

along — has prompted some to despair over ever getting decent education.

Added to these sobering reflections is a fresh sense of dismay over the outcomes of the past ten years of "innovation." For we have finished a decade of busy reform with little to show for it. Classrooms are the same. Teachers conduct monologues or more or less forced class discussions; too much learning is still rote; textbooks, timetables, clocks set the pace; discipline is an obsession. The curriculum reform efforts of the '60s brought forth excellent materials in some cases — materials still essential for good informal classrooms — but they took the existing environment of the schools for granted. Perhaps because so many were outsiders, the reformers failed to engage teachers in continuous thought and creation, with the result that the teachers ended up teaching the new materials in the old ways. Being for the most part university people, specialists, the reformers were ignorant of classrooms and children: of pedagogy. They concentrated on content — organized in the form of the standard graduate school disciplines — and ignored the nature of children and their ways of learning. Too often children were regarded as passive recipients of good materials, and teachers as passive conduits. The reformers lacked a coherent vision of the school environment as a whole. It was characteristic of the movement that it ignored the arts and children's expressiveness.

In the philosophical chaos of the curriculum projects, the proponents of pre-

cision had a debater's advantage. They were able to state their goals in precise, measurable, often behavioral terms. For a time this false precision encouraged a false sense of security. And for a while the behaviorists and the education technology businessmen were allies: they imagined that a new era of educational hardware was dawning, promising profits commensurate with those in the advanced defense and aerospace industries. Now that the bubble has burst, it seems evident to more and more people that this curious alliance had all along been talking about training, not education. Training means imparting skills. It is an aspect of education, but not all of it. I suggest a reading example: if I teach you phonic skills, that is a kind of training. Unless you go on to use them, to develop interests in books, you are not educated. This ought to be the common sense of the matter, but it isn't. Our technicians conceive of reading as a training problem on the order of training spotters to recognize airplane silhouettes. If a sixth-grader in a ghetto school is reading two years below grade level, as so many are, the problem may not be reading skills at all. A fourth grade reading level often represents a grasp of the necessary skills: part of the problem is surely that the sixth grader isn't reading books and isn't interested.

Another reason why some practitioners are dubious about "open" education reflects a further skepticism about the evangelical American mode of reform, with its hunger for absolutes and its weakness for rhetoric. Our "progressive" education movement often neglected pedagogy and the realities of life in classrooms and instead concentrated on lofty abstractions. It will be essential in promoting good practice today to abandon many old ideological debates. Yet the English example is now part of a whole diverse American cultural mood, which means that it is already ranged on one side of an ideological debate. The American milieu is polarized culturally and politically; this polarization conditions American responses to accounts of informal teaching. The responses tend to fall into the stereotyped categories of a cultural cold war raging between the hip, emancipated upper middle class and the straight middle and working class. It is class and cultural conflict, and it takes the form of battles between those who see life as essentially a matter of scarcity — and defend the virtues of a scarce order, such as thrift, discipline, hard work — and those who see life as essentially abundant — and preach newer virtues, such as openness, feelings, spontaneity. Hip people like the idea of open classrooms, because they seem to give children freedom; straight people fear the supposed absence of order, discipline and adult authority.

If I portray this conflict in highly abstract terms, it is because it seems to me remote from the concerns of good American and British practitioners actually teaching in informal settings. Take the issue of freedom, for example. Letting children talk and move about is helpful in establishing a setting in which a teacher can find out about students; it helps children learn actively, to get the habit of framing purposes independently, using their own judgment. But this freedom is a means to an end, not a goal in itself. As a goal, freedom is empty and meaningless — "a breakfast food," as e. e. cummings once put it.

There are always those who argue that freedom is something negative — freedom from — and those who argue that freedom is positive. From authoritarians like Plato to libertarians like Kant and Dewey, the second line of argument has linked freedom with knowledge — the free use of reason or intelligence and, sometimes, action with knowledge. Whatever the merits of the positions in this fascinating, perpetual debate, it is surely more appropriate for educators of the young to conceive of freedom in the second sense, not a momentary thing at all, but the result of a process of discipline and learning. Informality is pointless unless it leads to intellectual stimulation. Many children in our "free" schools are not happy, and one suspects that part of the reason is that they are bored with their own lack of intellectual progress. As William Hull remarks in a trenchant critique of the current fad for "open" education: "Children are not going to be happy for very long in schools in which they realize they are not accomplishing very much."

Or take the issue of authority. That it *is* an issue is a mark of deep cultural confusion, as well as a reflection of the frequent misuse of legitimate authority in America. Whatever their politics, good practitioners assume as a matter of course that teachers have a responsibility to create an environment hospitable to learning, that there is what might be called a natural, legitimate basis for the authority of an adult working with children. In his superb little book, *The Lives of Children,* George Dennison outlines some aspects of this legitimate authority: "Its attributes are obvious: adults are larger, more experienced, possess more words, have entered into prior agreements with themselves. When all this takes on a positive instead of a merely negative character, the children see the adults as protectors and as sources of certitude, approval, novelty, skills. In the fact that adults have entered into prior agreements, children intuit a seriousness and a web of relations in the life that surrounds them. If it is a bit mysterious, it is also impressive and somewhat attractive; they see it quite correctly as the way of the world, and they are not indifferent to its benefits and demands. . . . [For a child] the adult is his ally, his model — and his obstacle [for there are natural conflicts, too, and they must be given their due]."

Disciplinary matters and the rest of the structure of authority in American schools work against the exercise of legitimate authority. And thus, in reaction to the schools, the education opposition movement foolishly assumes that all adult guidance is an invasion of children's freedom.

Actually, in a proper informal setting, as John Dewey pointed out, adults ought to become more important: ". . . Basing education upon personal experience may mean more multiplied and more intimate contacts between the mature and the immature than ever existed in the traditional schools, *and consequently more rather than less guidance.*"

If you remove adult authority from a given group of children, you are not necessarily freeing them. Instead, as David Riesman and his colleagues noted in *The Lonely Crowd's* critique of "progressive" education, you are often sentencing them to the tyranny of their peers. And unacknowledged adult authority has a way of creeping back in subtle and manipulative ways that can be more arbitrary than its formal exercise.

Another fake issue in the debate on open education is the distinction between education as something developed from within and education as something formed from without, the old, boring question of whether to have, as they say, a child-centered or an adult-directed classroom. There are, to be sure, certain respects in which the best informal practice is child-centered. The basic conception of learning, after all, reflects the image of Piaget's child-inventor, fashioning an orderly model of the universe from his varied encounters with experience. The child's experience *is* the starting point of all good informal teaching. But passive teaching has no place in a good informal setting, any more than

passive children do. Active teaching is essential, and one of the appeals of this approach to experienced teachers is that it transforms the teacher's role. From enacting somebody else's text or curriculum, the teacher moves toward working out his own responses to children's learning. The teacher is responsible for creating the learning environment.

Still another confusion on the American scene lies in the notion that liberalizing the repressive atmosphere of our schools — which is worth doing for its own sake — will automatically promote intellectual development. It won't. We need more humane schools, but we also need a steady concern for intellectual progress and workmanship. Without this, it is unlikely that we will get any sort of cumulative development, and we will never establish practical standards by which to judge good and bad work.

Some American practitioners question the utility of slogans such as the "open school," or "informal education." The terms are suspect because they become cliches, because they don't convey the necessary values underlying this kind of teaching, because they suggest a hucksterized package and because they divide teaching staffs into the "we" doing the open approach and the "they" who are not. Some imitate the philosopher Charles Saunders Pierce, who changed his "pragmatism" to the much uglier-sounding "pragmaticism" — in order, he said, to keep his ideas safe from kidnappers. They prefer an awkward and reasonably neutral term like "less formal." A brave few are

modestly willing to march under a banner inscribed "decent schools."

This suspicion of slogans can be carried to ludicrous extremes. But at the heart of the evasiveness is an important point: educating children or working with teachers is an entire process. A good informal setting should not be thought of as a "model" or as an "experiment," but as an environment in which to support educational growth in directions that have already proved sound.

Some observers fear the manner in which our schools implement reforms in a way that destroys the possibility for further development of teachers. (There are already instances where principals have dictated "open education" to their staffs.) There is a deep — and I think altogether justified — mistrust of the conventional channels of reform from the top down: pronunciamentos by educational statesmen, the roll of ceremonial drums, the swishing sound of entrepreneurs shaking the money tree. Most of the serious American informal practitioners are self-consciously local in their orientation. They are interested in planting themselves in Vermont, Philadelphia, New York City, North Dakota or wherever, and working at the grass roots. They imagine that it will take a very long time to get good schools, and they do not believe that big-wig oratory or White House Conferences on Education are any substitute for direct engagement with teachers and children in classrooms.

The changes they are starting are small but they have large implications. All teachers, no matter how they teach, suffer from the climate of our schools, and every serious attempt at reform will soon find itself talking about lunchrooms, toilet passes, the whole internal control structure of the schools, relationships to parents, relationships to supervisory staff, the ways in which supplies are ordered, the links between an individual school and the central bureaucracies; ultimately issues of politics, power and money.

As schools move in informal directions, there will be an increasing criticism of our system of training and credentialing teachers and administrators. (Here, with the exception of outstanding institutions like London's Froebel Institute, the English do not have examples to emulate; their teachers colleges are improving, but they have trailed behind the work of the best schools.) The training of administrators will come under attack, and in some places separate training programs for administrators will be abolished. The inadequacy of teacher training will also become more evident, although it is far from clear how to improve it. What we do know is that theory has to be reunited with practice. Without a solid grounding in child development, much of our informal teaching will be gimmickry; and without a sound base in actual practice in classrooms, theory will remain useless.

The enormous variety of the American educational landscape makes it difficult to speak in general terms. In certain areas, education schools willing to restore an emphasis on classroom practice may unite with school systems ready to move in informal directions. In other areas, where the education schools are unable to change their mandarin ways, school systems will have to assume more and more of the responsibility for training and credentialing teachers. Whichever the pattern, a central feature of successful programs will be periods of work in good informal settings. Thus a prerequisite to any scheme of training will be the existence of good schools and classrooms to work in. The single most important task is the reform of schools and classrooms, for good informal classrooms provide the best teacher training sites.

Whether the current interest in informal teaching leads to cumulative change will depend on many things. Two are worth repeating: whether enough people can understand the essentially different outlook on children's intellectual development which good informal work must be based on, and whether our schools can be reorganized to give teachers sustained on-the-job support. I'm somewhat optimistic about the first: the ideas are in the air, and many teachers, on their own, are already questioning the assumptions behind the traditional classroom. The second question will be much harder to answer satisfactorily. In some places, the schools are ripe for change; in others change will come slowly and painfully, if at all; and in others the chances for growth are almost zero. Those promoting informal teaching ought to be wary of suggesting good practices to teachers working in institutional settings where real professional growth is out of the question. In such a setting, all obstacles mesh together to form what people rightly call the System. Right now it seems unlikely that the System in our worst school systems will ever permit teachers to teach and children to learn. But things may have looked that way to some British educational authorities in the '30s, too.

A final word on the faddishness of our educational concerns. The appearance of new ideas such as the clamor for open, informal schools does not cancel out old ideas. "Open education" will be a sham unless those supporting it also address themselves to recurring, fundamental problems, such as the basic inequality and racism of our society. The most pressing American educational dilemma is not the lack of informality in classrooms; it is whether we can build a more equal, multiracial society. Issues like school integration and community control have not disappeared, to be replaced by issues like open education. The agenda simply gets more crowded. It will be all the more essential, however, to keep alive in bad times a vision of the kind of education that all wise parents want for their children.

We hope you will agree that Newberg and Levin's article is a very appropriate one for ending this chapter and the book. Although theoretical in form, it will allow you to bring together many of the diverse ideas that have been presented into a sin-

gle framework. Cognitive, affective, and group learning can be conceptualized, respectively, as public, personal, and interpersonal knowledge. Of particular interest for this chapter, a variety of teacher roles are recommended and interconnected with three approaches to evaluation— all considered important. Newberg and Levin argue that students need to be, at different times, independent, interdependent, and dependent. They also argue that evaluation can be, at different times, done by the teacher, by peers, and by oneself. The thrust of the authors' argument is that not one new view, but several views of content, teaching style, and evaluation are needed for meaningful and successful teaching and learning.

NORMAN A. NEWBERG
AND
MARC N. LEVIN

THE CLASSROOM
AS A
LABORATORY
FOR LIVING

We are presently living in an unsettling time. Spiralling inflationary trends encour-

This article is published for the first time in this book. Copyright © 1976 by Norman A. Newberg and Marc N. Levin.

age us to question and worry about our financial security. Energy needs force us to ponder the limits and uses of the world's resources. Technology alters the job market yearly. These concerns influence the world of education too, as educators imagine the future for which they are preparing young people.

Currently administrators, teachers, and parents are engaged in a healthy questioning of the basic purposes of education. For some, this search has led to creating alternative structures for the learning process in the hope of personalizing education; hence all the interest in free schools and informal and affective education. In this article we propose a model that the school community can consider as a guide toward achieving its educational goals. We do not advocate a particular kind of educational structure, and we have no particular investment in open or closed, traditional or experimental learning environments. We do however, advocate the use of variety of contexts purposely chosen to better prepare students to operate in the social, political, and economic environments in which they live.

From an examination of the various environments in which we work and play, it is apparent that there are three different styles of behaving. Occasionally, we must be *independent;* we are on our own. We have decisions to make that affect only us and for which we are responsible, and we have activities that we must do alone. At other times we need to be *interdependent.* In these instances, we work with others with whom we share a task or re-

sponsibility. In such interdependent situations we must balance our personal needs with the needs of others in a group. At yet other times we rely on others to do things for us, to provide us with information or to give us permission or approval. In these situations we function *dependently.*

Each of these styles demands different behaviors. Our task as educators is to provide students with explicit experiences so they can learn when each style is appropriate and which behaviors are required for functioning effectively in each style.

For many years educators have been saying that the purpose of education was to help students become independent learners. We hoped that students would become self-generating, self-motivating learners who would eventually take responsibility for *what* they learn and *how* they learn. Unfortunately, very few students reach this goal. Most remain dependent upon others to stimulate and organize their learning for them. That should not surprise us since historically most teaching in the United States has been structured in ways that tend to create dependent learners. We emphasize lectures, question and answer sessions, questions at the end of chapters in textbooks, and generally place the teacher in the role of the controller and owner of all knowledge.

The eminent sociologist, Erving Goffman, in his book *Asylums,* ironically suggests that such disparate institutions as prisons, hospitals for the mentally ill, and schools — each designed to develop independence in people — place the subjects of their attention in dependent roles and relationships. Although all of us are dependent on others to some extent, and the skills related to functioning in a dependent relationship are valuable indeed, students learn only submission from the traditional, implicitly dependent model. As a result, they receive little or no experience in developing the sense of self and self-direction that would allow them to function independently.

Recently, much interest has been shown in a variety of models designed to develop student independence, which are broadly designated by the term "open classroom." Those models, which help teachers create environments in which students are given increased responsibility for making decisions, asking for help, and determining their own learning pace in an explicit way, are providing an important structural alternative for teachers and students. We need to develop an even greater repertoire of ways for individualizing instruction and allowing students to learn by themselves and for themselves. These models fall short, however, when they underestimate and ignore the value of both dependent and interdependent experiences.

Although important changes are gradually appearing in schools, especially in the lower grades, to provide students with greater opportunities to develop independence, the opportunities for students to value and use interdependent skills by working in cooperative learning relationships are still rare. All schools, of course, preach that cooperation is important in human relations, but the message learned is that competition rewards the individual. Students are pitted against one another for scholarships; they compete for the limited number of high grades a teacher is willing, or allowed to give; and they are given numerous awards for the best this or the best that. The message is clear: he who looks out for himself, and competes successfully, wins. Rarely do students learn that pooling resources produces a more complex opinion or solution and that complex problems are often solved by people working together, especially in fields such as science and medicine. No better example exists than the cooperation of thousands of minds and skills that allowed us to place a man on the moon. No one group or agency could conceivably have accomplished this task. Nevertheless, other than in extracurricular activities such as athletic teams, dramatic productions, and musical ensembles, students rarely get the experience necessary to learn the skills needed to work cooperatively. We could correct this deficiency by using a greater variety of groupings in the classroom and assigning team tasks in which students have the opportunity to work on a program together, be responsible to and for each other, and see the class as a group.

THE THREE CONTENTS OF EDUCATION

Just as we have overemphasized the dependent style of teaching and learning to

the detriment of adequately developing the independent and interdependent, so have we overemphasized public knowledge — the traditional academic content areas — to the neglect of personal and interpersonal knowledge as legitimate areas of scholastic inquiry. Although all schools intend to educate the "whole child," most only impart the disciplines of English, math, or science, leaving to chance the development of an understanding of oneself, the behaviors we use in relating to others, and the relationship of these two areas to the culture we have inherited — public knowledge.

Although the acquisition of academic skills may help us attain greater economic success, certainly our security and happiness as persons depend also upon our ability to develop a realistic self-image and our ability to relate to others in a way that makes it possible for us to create and maintain satisfying relationships. Thus, studying the content of the *personal knowledge* area provides an opportunity for students to learn about themselves as persons — their feelings, values, strengths, vulnerabilities, and ambitions. Such considerations should help students establish realistic self-concepts which, in turn, should aid them in making more satisfying personal decisions with regard to careers, military services, schooling, marriage, and issues of similar importance.

Equally important is the study of *interpersonal knowledge*. Included in the curriculum would be issues such as how individuals in a group interact with each other, the helpful roles we can assume while working with others, and how we negotiate the conflict between being an individual and being part of a group.

Studying content in the public knowledge area — the traditional subject matter of schools — remains vital. It becomes more significant if seen as the shared information and values of our culture, the mastery of which allows a student to function effectively within it. This emphasis would allow teachers to choose curricula with greater confidence of purpose and permit students to develop a healthy respect for the authority and experience that public knowledge represents. In addition, students could recognize the pull that is exerted between the traditions of the past and the constant need for cultural redefinition.

If we create a grid with the styles of teaching and learning on the left and the three content or knowledge areas on the bottom, we have a visual model of the preceding discussion (Figure 1).

This model brings the interrelationship between the styles and contents into focus and makes clear the desirability of enabling students to experience and learn each of the content areas in each of the learning styles.

Thus a student studying a unit on working in groups would be working on interpersonal knowledge. If the teacher wanted the student to have an opportunity to learn in all three styles he might use activities such as the following:

Dependent
— Teacher gives 20-minute lecture on the way groups operate.

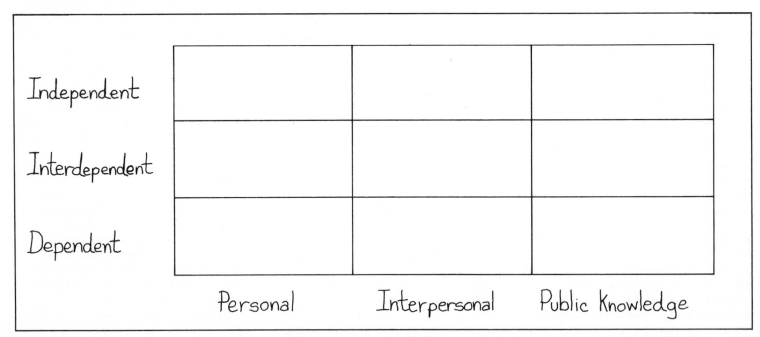

Figure 1.

— Teacher assigns a reading on group roles.
— Teacher shows film on cooperation in China and has student answer certain questions.

Interdependent
— Students work on project in groups of five or six; after completing the project they examine the way they worked and list the behaviors and statements they found useful and the behaviors and statements that they found not helpful.

Independent
— Teacher instructs students to choose a novel, poem, play, or other reading in which people work in groups and find a way to analyze how the characters or subjects operate as group members.

It is important to note that the determination of the content block in which an activity should be placed is determined by the primary purpose of the lesson. If this lesson was a social studies lesson on China, it would be appropriate to place the film in the public knowledge area. However, since this was a lesson on working together in groups, the cooperation theme was the important factor and, therefore, the film is placed in the interpersonal knowledge area.

Similarly, in determining the proper style block, the important element is the style in which the student is learning the information and not who initiated the activity. In this example, although the teacher structured and assigned the tasks in the interdependent category and the independent category, the learning was not determined by him. In the former, the students create the list of helpful statements and behaviors that become part of the knowledge base of the class as a result of their own experience, and in the latter, the students choose the novels and provide the analyses. In the dependent example, however, the teacher has not only selected the material to be studied but has determined what is to be learned as well.

Although we do not suggest that we must structure students' work over the year so that one-ninth of all the learning experiences fall into each block, we do suggest that the grid be used as a tool in evaluating how well we have provided a balanced experience for our students and in planning how we might do so in the future. Of course different classes have different needs, and some teachers will choose to provide some classes with more independent experiences, others with more interdependent activities. However, if each of us takes the time to achieve a balance among the different contents and styles that is appropriate to our students' needs, we will be greatly improving their preparation for life.

EVALUATION

Evaluation is another vital issue closely tied to the styles and contents concerning us here. Perhaps no other element has so pervasive an influence. Students experience so many teachers who use evaluation as a

weapon that it destroys trust and becomes the end, rather than the means of education for many. If we look again to life situations to see what our students will need in the way of evaluation skills, we find that we must sometimes take responsibility for evaluating our own selves and work, whereas at other times it is our peers, parents, teachers, or other authority figures who properly own an evaluative function. Now we can expand our grid to include evaluation and identify the three evaluation opportunities we can take advantage of in the classroom. We can continue to evaluate students when the expert's experience and knowledge is obviously needed. When this is not the case, students can evaluate themselves and evaluate each other when appropriate. Sharing the responsibility for evaluation seems necessary to create an atmosphere of trust and develop the student's responsibility for his own education.

In several centers in the United States, work is being done to expand content beyond public knowledge, and teaching styles beyond the dependent mode. At the University of California in Santa Barbara, George Brown in the Confluent Education Program seeks to relate a student's personal knowledge and feelings to public knowledge. At the University of Massachusetts, Amherst, Gerald Weinstein, in the Center for Humanistic Education, stresses personal knowledge through teaching a course called Education of the Self. Weinstein asserts that the Self is a neglected area in education and must be made legitimate for exploration. The Affective Education Program in Philadelphia works with teachers in an urban setting and attempts to develop designs and approaches in all three content areas and in all three styles. After working for several years emphasizing the interdependent and dependent modes and the interpersonal and public knowledge content area, the program has more recently included personal knowledge and the independent style in its work.

All of these content areas, styles, and evaluation techniques are present to some degree in classrooms all the time. The difference between what we are proposing and what occurs in most classrooms appears in the teacher's conscious, explicit use of all three styles, all three content choices, and all three evaluation methods to both meet the needs of the students and to expand the variety of their experience. Increasing the variety not only will heighten the students' capacity to learn and increase their commitment, but will also give them the skills their real world demands.

DRAW
A TEACHER
IN AN
IDEAL CLASSROOM

Earlier in the book (p. 65), we asked you to draw a picture of a classroom. Now we ask you to try out your artistic skills again, in the space provided on the next page, to see if they have improved.

Procedure

1. In the space provided, draw a teacher as you imagine he or she would appear in an ideal classroom. Use stick figures if your artistic talents are still limited. If you wish, turn the book sideways for your drawing.

2. In a small group, look at each other's pictures. How are they the same? How are they different? Does any of the sameness reflect stereotyped thinking about teaching? How do the differences reflect different roles for the teacher — and the students? How much do you think your pictures represent your present conception of what teaching means to you?

3. Following the presentations and discussions, try to imagine as a group what a composite picture would look like. If there is time, draw one.

REAL
LEARNING

How can you tell if you really understand something? Here we list seven things a student can do if he has surely learned. Use these criteria to evaluate your own learning.

Procedure

Study or restudy the article by Combs (pp. 332–336) and with someone who has also read the article, do the following:

1. State the argument of the article in your own words.
2. Give examples of the main points.
3. Imagine how his ideas would apply to other roles besides teaching (for example, a policeman).
4. Relate the author's ideas to the ideas of others or your own.

projects
and
activities

5. Suggest an application of the ideas.
6. What might be the outcome of such an application?
7. Argue an opposite point of view.[1]

[1] Adapted from John Holt, *How Children Fail* (New York: Pitman, 1964), pp. 103–7.

Together, come up with an overall evaluation on how well you understand the article. When you are finished, share your reactions as to the effectiveness of this kind of evaluation. How meaningful was it for you? How could you use this idea in a classroom?

FACING STUDENTS

Despite a teacher's conceptions of his or her role, the real expression of a teacher's role takes place in face-to-face contact with students. In the situations presented below, you will be confronted with decisions about your role. With what ways of acting as a teacher do you seem most comfortable? Are there approaches to teacher-student relationships which you would like to master but, as yet, find difficult?

Procedure

This procedure works with groups of six to eight people. Two people should role play each of the following situations while others in the group watch. Allow only a few minutes for each situation. Then choose which scene you, as a pair, found most difficult or intriguing and reenact it. Take as much time as you like. Other pairs should repeat the same process. When everyone has had a turn, compare and contrast the "roles" people played in these situations.

1. The teacher senses a problem about which the student seems to be unaware. The student has chosen books to read whose level of difficulty is clearly beyond his ability. The teacher is concerned be-

cause the student has done this before and the results were unproductive. The student, however, feels gratified that he has found materials in which he is genuinely interested. The teacher begins by looking at the books and commenting on them. The student responds to the teacher's comments.

2. The teacher has reviewed a student's work on a project that is about half-finished. She feels the work is interesting, but not exciting. The main problem, however, is that the plans to complete the project are impractical. The student feels that she has worked very hard on what has been done and that it will turn out to be an important learning experience for her if she can complete the project. The student should try to talk about these feelings. The teacher should try to hold to her "own" opinion *and* see the student's point of view. Her first response should be to try to emphasize with the student's feelings about her project thus far.

3. The roles here involve a student who works very fast and a teacher who feels that the student should consider more alternatives. The result of the student's work is that he has developed a clever but not very useful method for solving a set of math problems. The teacher feels that the student's quick thinking (usually helpful in other areas) is creating his difficulties in math; he doesn't check his process; he doesn't do problems in alternative ways; he doesn't try to understand the logic of the procedure. The student begins by showing the teacher his method and by

talking about how he feels. The teacher responds in any way she can to get the student to be more open-minded.

OBSERVING AND EVALUATING STUDENTS

The following excerpts are from observations of six- and seven-year-old children in classrooms in a London primary school. Imagine, as you read the excerpts, that these children were your students. Through the eyes of an objective observer, what can you learn about your students?

1. Seven-year-olds. In one section of the room, five children are writing and drawing, each one working on his own project, though they exchange occasional comments. Postures are relaxed and casual. Three are working on a table; one is sprawled on the floor, writing; one is on a chair, with knees up, writing. All are working on a story-report titled "A Mouse Swimming." They apparently conducted an experiment with a mouse in a tank of water earlier in the day, following a card of instructions. Each is now writing up what he saw, on his own, but there are some words spelled out on a small chalkboard nearby: dog paddle, steer, wiggle, etc. They are not obliged to use these words; they are there as references, if needed. When a child finishes, he takes his work

to the teacher, seated across the room and working with some other children. The teacher reads the report and makes some comments and corrections. Two children go to the teacher with questions while they're working, and he stops for brief responses each time. When a child finishes the story, he begins to work on a drawing to go with it, though one child is doing both at the same time, working a bit on one, then going to the other.

2. Seven-year-olds. Picture stories, drawn, made up, and written by the children are tacked up on display. They are cut out in many forms, obviously designed by the children themselves: fish, house, plane, bat, griffin, etc. Each has the child's story written around its outline in the child's own writing. Some examples:

Heart shape: "I am your heart. I am pink and liver in you I get fid up inside you. Because I keep pumping and I am never asleep."
Rocket shape: "I am Apoolo 11 rather fat and big. My mom is Apoolo 2 she is on the moon. I am going to the moon and my daddy is Apoolo 6. I am on the moon it is suny."
Number 13: "I am number 13. I'm a wicked number because I'm an unliked number."

3. Six-year-olds. Teacher gathers twenty children together. They are in "teams" and she asks what each team did last time in math, then redirects them to something new. A group of three boys and a girl is sent to weighing. They come over to a table with a balance scale, boxes with collections of stones, peas, chestnuts, etc. in them and a group of cards with questions and procedures written on each. Children take cards and begin to read. Cards ask such things as "How many shells balance 12 peas. Guess first." They are to write down their esti-

mate, carry out the procedure, then write the results in their notebooks. One girl and one boy get started, but run into trouble about using the balance. Both want it at the same time. The girl is more insistent and gets her material in. The boy watches. A second boy sifts stones and peas through his fingers and a third boy wanders off and joins another child cleaning his gerbil cage. The girl has written her prediction that 3 stones don't balance 2 chestnuts. She weighs them and says happily, "I was right! The stones are heavier." She moves to another card and begins pouring rice. The boy wants to use the balance but her material is in again and she says, "No, I have to. I'm telling Miss ———." He protests, but she continues to threaten, leaving her material in the balance while she records results and repeats, "I'm telling!" He frowns and retreats. Through the rest of the observation, the girl works steadily, the boys are elsewhere, stepping back to watch but never carrying out weighing exercises.[1]

Procedure

Find a partner. Clarify with him or her what is happening in each excerpt. Then discuss all the things you think you could learn about the children in these situations. Don't restrict yourself to cognitive skills. Consider group process, affective themes, and any other skills that come to mind. In some cases the behavior of the children is sparsely reported. You will thus need to imagine what behavior might have occurred which would be worth assessing.

[1] Observations made in March 1972 by Patricia Minuchin. Reprinted with permission.

INTERACTION ANALYSIS

Interaction analysis allows for an examination of the verbal interaction of students and teachers. It also helps to suggest to teachers specific patterns of behavior that might prove useful for their personal goals. The following activities are provided to help you learn this technique.

Procedure

Consult Flanders' "Intent, Action and Feedback: A Preparation for Teaching" (pp. 306–316) for background information to carry out the following exercises:

1. Write the digits of your telephone number down the lefthand margin of a piece of paper. After each digit, write a teacher or student statement which would qualify as an example of that numbered category in Flanders' system. Try to make the resulting teacher-student dialogue convincing. Example (using our telephone number at Temple University):

— 7 *(Teacher gives criticism):* I'm really annoyed with your behavior.
— 8 *(Student reply):* Oh, yeah?
— 7 *(Teacher justifies authority):* I've really no choice.
— 7 *(Teacher gives criticism):* You don't seem to be applying yourself.

— 2 *(Teacher praises):* I know you can do a good job.
— 1 *(Teacher accepts feelings):* This is tough work.
— 5 *(Teacher gives opinion):* But, I think it is important to learn this as well as possible.

2. Reply to the student statements in the following dialogues with as many teacher statements you can think of within the category given.

Teacher: Who has been called the father of our country?
Student: Christopher Columbus.
Teacher: (3 — *accepts ideas of students*)

_____

_____

_____

_____

_____

_____

Teacher: What's wrong, Bill?
Student: I just can't do this problem.
Teacher: (1 — *accepts feelings*)

_____

_____

_____

_____

_____

_____

_____

Student: I don't think we should get grades in this course.
Teacher: (4 — *asks questions*)

_____

_____

_____

_____

_____

_____

3. In a group, role play the following situation. The person who plays the teacher

should think over Flanders' categories and decide which behaviors would be most helpful in the situation.

You have just finished a unit of study on the Reconstruction Period in American History. For evaluation of this work, you are prepared to give a test or accept papers. You want the students to decide. The class is now meeting with you to resolve the question.

When the role playing is completed, the teacher should tell the group what behaviors he or she was trying to perform and ask for feedback on how it went. Other people should take a turn being the teacher and going through the same process.

4. A high school English teacher has been displeased with the lack of involvement and development of ideas in class discussions. On the basis of the interaction analysis matrix shown here (derived from observation in the teacher's classroom) what helpful feedback could you give this teacher to improve her leading of discussions? Derive your information from an examination of the frequencies of (1) each major category (for example, the number of times the teacher praises students is equal to the number of tallies in row or column 2); (2) particular cells (for example, the number of times the teacher's questions are followed by silence is reflected in the 4-10 cell); and (3) specific areas of the matrix (for example, the way a teacher responds to students is revealed in rows 8 and 9 through column 7).

	1	2	3	4	5	6	7	8	9	10
1				1						
2				3	3	1	1		2	
3					4					
4								10		7
5				10	12	4			9	6
6								8		4
7								4		6
8		6	4	2	9	3	1	2	1	
9	1	4		1	6	1	4		5	2
10					7	3	4	4	7	
Total	1	10	4	17	41	12	10	28	24	25

A COLLAGE OF MY VIEWS ON TEACHING

As you are bringing your inquiry into making learning real to a close (for now), it might be useful to reflect on your personal identification with the role of a

teacher. What aspects of teaching do you want to encourage yourself to undertake or reinforce, and what do you wish to avoid?

Procedure

One way to express these personal decisions is to make a collage which reflects the teaching qualities you wish to build within yourself and the qualities you wish to suppress. Gather together magazines and other glueable items. Cut out words and pictures which symbolize for you positive and negative aspects of a teaching style. If you can not find the material you want, try to draw the ideas you wish to express. Place the negative symbols on the left hand side of your collage and the

positive symbols on the right hand side. Share your collage with others and use it as a basis for describing your views on teaching.

additional resources

BOOKS AND ARTICLES

Amidon, Edmund J., and Flanders, Ned A. *The Role of the Teacher in the Classroom: A Manual for Understanding and Improving Teacher Classroom Behavior.* Minneapolis: Paul S. Amidon and Associates, 1963.

Amidon, Edmund J., and Hunter, Elizabeth. *Improving Teaching: Analyzing Verbal Interaction in the Classroom.* New York: Holt, Rinehart and Winston, 1966.

Barth, Roland. *Open Education and the American School.* New York: Agatha Press, 1972.

Blitz, Barbara. *The Open Classroom: Mak-It Work.* Boston: Allyn and Bacon, 1973.

Bremer, John, and Bremer, Anne. *Open Education — A Beginning.* New York: Holt, Rinehart and Winston, 1972.

Conroy, Pat. *The Water is Wide.* Boston: Houghton Mifflin, 1972.

Curwin, Richard L., and Fuhrmann, Barbara Schneider. *Discovering Your Teaching Self: Humanistic Approaches to Effective Teaching.* Englewood Cliffs, N.J.: Prentice-Hall, 1975.

Dunkin, Michael, and Biddle, Bruce J. *The Study of Teaching.* New York: Holt, Rinehart and Winston, 1974.

Dunn, Rita, and Dunn, Kenneth. *Practical Approaches to Individualizing Instruction.* Englewood Cliffs, N.J.: Prentice-Hall, 1972.

Fader, Daniel, and McNeil, E. *The Naked Children.* New York: Macmillan, 1971.

Featherstone, Joseph. *Schools Where Children Learn.* New York: Liveright, 1971.

Flanders, Ned A. *Analyzing Teaching Behavior.* Reading, Mass.: Addison-Wesley, 1970.

Frymier, Jack R. *A School for Tomorrow.* Berkeley, Calif.: MuCutchan, 1973.

Gross, Beatrice, and Gross, Ronald, eds. *Will It Grow in a Classroom?* New York: Dell, 1974.

Hapgood, Marilyn. "The Open Classroom: Protect It from Its Friends." *Saturday Review* 21 (September 18, 1971).

Hassett, Joseph D., and Weisberg, Arline. *Open Education: Alternatives Within Our Tradition.* Englewood Cliffs, N.J.: Prentice-Hall, 1972.

Hayman, John L., Jr., and Napier, Rodney W. *Evaluation in the Schools: A Human Process for Renewal.* Monterey, Ca.: Brooks/Cole Publishing, 1975.

Jackson, Philip W. *The Teacher and The Machine.* Pittsburgh: University of Pittsburgh Press, 1968.

Kirschenbaum, Howard; Napier, Rodney W.; and Simon, Sidney B. *Wad-Ja-Get?: The Grading Game in American Education.* New York: Hart Publishing Co., 1971.

Kohl, Herbert. *The Open Classroom: A Practical Guide to a New Way of Teaching.* New York: A New York Review Book, 1969.

Kozol, Jonathan. *Free Schools.* Boston: Houghton Mifflin, 1973.

Kryspin, William J., and Feldhusen, John F. *Analyzing Verbal Classroom Interaction.* Minneapolis: Burgess, 1974.

National Association for the Education of Young Children. *Open Education: The*

Legacy of The Progressive Movement, 1834 Connecticut Avenue, N.W., Washington, DC 20009, 1970.

Postman, Neil, and Weingartner, Charles. *The School Book: For People Who Want to Know What All the Hollering Is About.* New York: Delacorte, 1973.

Rasberry, Salli, and Greenway, Robert. *Rasberry Exercises: How to Start Your Own School and Make a Book.* Freestone, Calif.: Freestone Publishing Co., 1971.

Rathbone, Charles H., ed. *Open Education — The Informal Classroom.* New York: Citation Press, 1971.

Silberman, Charles E., ed. *The Open Classroom Reader.* New York: Vintage, 1973.

Stephens, Lillian M. *The Teacher's Guide to Open Education.* New York: Holt, Rinehart and Winston, 1974.

Sterling, Phillip. *The Real Teachers.* New York: Random House, 1972.

Thelen, Herbert. *Education and the Human Quest.* New York: Harper and Row, 1962.

Wolfson, Bernice J. *Moving Toward Personalized Learning and Teaching.* International Center for Educational Development, 16400 Ventura Boulevard, Suite 339, Eucino, CA 91316, 1969.

FILMS

Choosing to Learn. Educational Development Center, 39 Chapel Street, Newton, MA 02160.

Alternative elementary school in Rochester, New York.

The Humanity of Teaching. Media Five, 1011 North Cole Avenue, Suite F, Hollywood, CA 90038.

Several famous educators share their views on the importance of feeling good about yourself as a teacher.

The Open Classroom. Media Five, 1011 North Cole Avenue, Suite F, Hollywood, CA 90038.

A documentary study of various forms of

open education in operation in several public schools.

The Who, What & Why of Authority. Media Five, 1011 North Cole Avenue, Suite F, Hollywood, CA 90038.

Comments by famous education critics on the teacher's role, and discussion of Dennison's concept of natural authority.

They Can Do It. Educational Development Center, 39 Chapel Street, Newton, MA 02160.

The development over the school year of an open classroom in an urban elementary school.

Overview, pages 1–7

Yanoff, Jay M. "The Effects of Open Teaching Styles on Involvement and Inquiry Activity of Elementary School Children." Ed.D. dissertation, Temple University, 1972.

Silberman, Melvin L., and Allender, Jerome S. "The Role of the Teacher in Student-Directed Learning," U.S. Department of Health, Education, and Welfare, Office of Education, Project no. 1-C-009 (Washington, D.C.: GPO, 1973).

CHAPTER 1

Initial Experiences, pages 10–12

Rosenberg, M. B. *Diagnostic Teaching.* Seattle: Special Child Publications, 1968.

Melvin L. Silberman, "What Schooling Does to Children," pages 17–22

Adams, Raymond S., and Biddle, Bruce J. *Realities of Teaching: Explorations with Video Tape.* New York: Holt, Rinehart and Winston, 1970.

Brenner, Anton; Hofmann, Helmut; and Weddington, Rachel. "School Demands." *Elementary School Journal* 64 (1964): 261–64.

Dreeben, Robert. *On What Is Learned in School.* Reading, Mass.: Addison-Wesley, 1968.

Feshbach, Norma D. "Student Teacher Preferences for Elementary School Pupils Varying in Personality Characteristics." *Journal of Educational Psychology* 60 (1969): 126–32.

Friedenberg, Edgar Z. "The Modern High School: A Profile." *Commentary* 36 (1963): 373–80.

Hawkes, Thomas H. "Structural Constraints Upon Interpersonal Communication in the Classroom: A Study of Reciprocal Sociometric Choice Dyads." Paper presented at the American Educational Research Association, February 1968.

Henry, Jules. "Attitude Organization in Elementary School Classrooms." *American Journal of Orthopsychiatry* 27 (1957): 117–33.

Holt, John. *How Children Fail.* New York: Pitman, 1964.

Jackson, Philip W. *Life in Classrooms.* New York: Holt, Rinehart and Winston, 1968.

Jackson, Philip W., and Wolfson, Bernice J. "Varieties of Constraint in a Nursery School." *Young Children* 23 (September 1968): 358–67.

Kallet, Anthony. "Two Classrooms." *This Magazine Is About Schools* 1 (1966): 45–59.

Kohl, Herbert. *36 Children.* New York: New American Library, 1967.

Lippitt, Ronald, and Gold, Martin. "Classroom Social Structure as a Mental Health Problem." *Journal of Social Issues* 15 (1959): 40–49.

Maslow, Abraham H. *Toward a Psychology of Being.* 2d ed. New York: Van Nostrand Reinhold, 1968.

Minuchin, Patricia. "Solving Problems Cooperatively: A Comparison of Three Classroom Groups." *Childhood Education* 41 (1965): 480–84.

Rosenthal, Robert, and Jacobson, Lenore. *Pygmalion in the Classroom.* New York: Holt, Rinehart and Winston, 1968.

Abraham H. Maslow, "Defense and Growth," pages 22–28

Anonymous. "Finding the Real Self." Letter with a foreword by Karen Horney. *American Journal of Psychoanalysis* 9 (1949), p. 7.

Wilson, F. "Human Nature and Esthetic Growth." In *The Self*, edited by C. Moustakas. New York: Harper, 1956, p. 213.

Zuger, B. "Growth of the Individual's Concept of Self." *American Journal of Diseases of Children* 83 (1952), p. 179.

Carl R. Rogers, "The Interpersonal Relationship in the Facilitation of Learning," pages 31–36

1. For a more extended account of Miss Shiel's initial attempts, see Rogers, 1966. Her later experience is described in Shiel, 1966 .

Appell, M. L. "Selected Student Reactions to Student-centered Courses." Mimeographed manuscript, 1959.

Ashton-Warner, Sylvia. *Teacher*. New York: Simon and Schuster, 1963.

Axline, Virginia M. "Morale on the School Front." *Journal of Educational Research* 38 (1944): 521–33.

Bull, Patricia. Student reactions, Fall 1965. Mimeographed manuscripts. State University College, Courtland, New York, 1966.

Jackson, P. W. "The Student's World." Mimeographed. University of Chicago, 1966.

Rogers, C. R. "To Facilitate Learning." In NEA Handbook for Teachers, *Innovations for Time to Teach*, edited by Malcolm Provus. Washington, D.C.: Department of Classroom Teachers, NEA, 1966.

Shiel, Barbara J. "Evaluation: A Self-directed Curriculum, 1965." Mimeographed, 1966.

Jerome S. Bruner, "The Will to Learn," pages 36–43

1. For a further account of the functions of early curiosity, see J. S. Bruner, "The Cognitive Consequences of Early Sensory Deprivation," *Psychosomatic Medicine* 21, no. 2 (1959): 89–95.

2. R. W. White, "Motivation Reconsidered: The Concept of Competence," *Psychological Review* 66 (1959): 297–333.

3. Ruth H. Weir, *Language in the Crib* (The Hague: Mouton, 1962).

4. David C. McClelland, *The Achieving Society* (Princeton, N.J.: Van Nostrand, 1961).

5. R. Freed Bales, "The 'Fixation Factor' in Alcohol Addiction: A Hypothesis Derived from a Comparative Study of Irish and Jewish Social Norms" (Ph.D. diss., Harvard University, 1944).

6. Mark Zborowski and Elizabeth Herzog, *Life Is with People: The Jewish Little-Town of Eastern Europe* (New York: International Universities Press, 1952).

7. Pauline Sears, "Attitudinal and Affective Factors Affecting Children's Approaches to Problem Solving," in *Learning About Learning*, ed. J. S. Bruner (Washington, D.C.: U.S. Office of Education, 1963).

8. Roger Barker, "On the Nature of the Environment," *Journal of Social Issues* 19, no. 4 (1963): 17–38.

Projects and Activities, pages 60–67

1. For more information about the administration, scoring, and research results of this instrument, see Melvin L. Silberman and Jerome S. Allender, "The Course Description: A Semi-Projective Technique for Assessing Students' Reactions to College Classes," *Journal of Higher Education*, 45, no. 6 (June 1974): pp. 450–57.

2. For more information about the administration, scoring, and research results of this instrument, see Melvin L. Silberman and Jerome S. Allender, "The Role of the Teacher in Student-Directed Learning," U.S. Department of Health, Education and Welfare, Office of Education, Project no. 1-C-009 (Washington, D.C.: GPO, 1973). Available from authors, Department of Psychoeducational Processes, Temple University, Philadelphia, PA 19122.

CHAPTER 2

Jay M. Yanoff, "The Functions of the Mind in the Learning Process," pages 77–84

Allender, Jerome S. "A Theory for the Teaching of Inquiry." Paper read at American Psychological Association Meeting, September 1967, at Washington, D.C.

Bartley, S. Howard. *Principles of Perception*. New York: Harper and Row, 1969.

Bush, Wilma Jo, and Giles, Marian Taylor. *Aids to Psycholinguistic Teaching*. Columbus, Ohio: Merrill, 1969.

Getman, G. N. *How to Develop Your Child's Intelligence*. Luverne, Minn.: Author, 1962.

Hebb, D. O. *The Organization of Behavior*. New York: Wiley, 1949.

Hill, Winfred F. *Learning: A Survey of Psychological Interpretations*. San Francisco: Chandler, 1963.

Kephart, Newell C. *The Slow Learner in the Classroom*. Columbus, Ohio: Merrill, 1960.

Miller, G. A.; Galanter, E.; and Pribram, Karl. *Plans and the Structure of Behavior*. New York: Holt, Rinehart and Winston, 1960.

Osgood, Charles E. *Method and Theory in Experimental Psychology*. New York: Oxford University Press, 1953.

Penfield, Wilder. "Consciousness, Memory and Man's Conditioned Reflexes." In *On the Biology of Learning*, edited by Karl Pribram. New York: Harcourt, Brace, Jovanovich, 1969.

Piaget, Jean. *The Mechanisms of Perception*. New York: Basic Books, 1969.

———. *The Construction of Reality in the Child*. New York: Basic Books, 1954.

Pribram, Karl. "Neurological Notes on the Art of Educating." In *Theories of Learning and Instruction, NSSE 63rd Yearbook, Part 1*, edited by Ernest Hilgard. Chicago: University of Chicago Press, 1964.

Simpson, Dorothy M. *Learning to Learn*. Columbus, Ohio: Merrill, 1968.

Kenneth R. Conklin, "Wholes and Parts in Teaching," pages 84–88

1. The discussion of wholes and parts, personal knowledge, and the manner in which focusing on parts can hinder their integration into a whole is based on Michael Polanyi's theory of knowing, found in his books *The Tacit Dimension* (Garden City, New York: Doubleday, 1966) and *Personal Knowledge* (London: Routledge and Kegan Paul, 1958). Gestalt psychology also supports what is said here: see George W. Hartmann, *Gestalt Psychology* (New York: Ronald Press, 1935). For a more thorough explanation of how knowledge is communicated, and why a teacher cannot deliver knowledge to a pupil in finished form, see Kenneth R. Conklin, "Knowledge, Proof, and Ineffability in Teaching," in *Educational Theory*, forthcoming.
2. Lewis Carroll, "*Through the Looking-Glass:* The Jabberwocky Poem," in *The Annotated Alice*, ed. Martin Gardner. (New York: Bramhall House, 1960), pp. 191–97.

Lee S. Shulman, "Psychological Controversies in Teaching," pages 95–104

Bruner, Jerome S. *The Process of Education*. Cambridge, Mass.: Harvard University Press, 1960.

Bruner, Jerome S. *Toward a Theory of Instruction*. Cambridge, Mass.: Belknap Press, 1966.

Gagné, Robert M. *The Conditions of Learning*. New York: Holt, Rinehart and Winston, 1965.

Gagné, Robert M. "Contributions of Learning to Human Development." Address of the Vice-President, Section I (Psychology), American Association for the Advancement of Science, December 1966, at Washington, D.C.

Gagné, Robert M. Personal communication. May 1968.

Jennings, Frank G. "Jean Piaget: Notes on Learning." *Saturday Review*, May 20, 1967, p. 82.

"Pain & Progress in Discovery." *Time*, December 8, 1967, pp. 110 ff.

Shulman, Lee S., and Keislar, Evan R., eds. *Learning by Discovery: A Critical Appraisal*. Chicago: Rand-McNally, 1966.

Worthen, Blaine R. "Discovery and Expository Task Presentation in Elementary Mathematics." *Journal of Educational Psychology Monograph Supplement* 59, no. 1, Part 2 (February 1968).

Al Rodriguez, "Mathematics for the Human Classroom," pages 115–118

1. "Measurement: How to Say How Much." *First Things: Mathematics. Sound Filmstrips for Primary Years* (Pleasantville, New York: Guidance Associates).

CHAPTER 3

Harold Bessell, "Awareness," pages 147–152

1. Weston La Barre, *The Human Animal* (Chicago: University of Chicago Press, 1954). Theodosius Dobzhansky, *Mankind Evolving* (New Haven: Yale University Press, 1965) (esp. Chap. 12, pp. 319–48).

2. Alfred Adler, *Practice and Theory of Individual Psychology* (New York: Harcourt, Brace and Co., 1923).
3. Harry Stack Sullivan, *Concepts of Modern Psychiatry* (W. A. White Psychiatric Foundation, 1947).
4. Otto Fenichel, *The Psychoanalytical Theory of Neurosis* (New York: W. W. Norton, 1945).

Gerald Weinstein, "The Trumpet: A Guide to a Humanistic Psychological Curriculum," pages 178–185

1. Gerald Weinstein and Mario Fantini, *Toward Humanistic Education: A Curriculum of Affect* (New York: Praeger Press, 1970).
2. Roberto Assignoli, *Psychosynthesis: A Manual of Principles and Techniques* (New York: Hobbs Dorman, 1965).
3. Daniel I. Malamud and Solomon Machover, *Toward Self-Understanding: Self-Techniques in Self-Confrontation* (Springfield, Ill.: Thomas Publishing Co., 1965).
4. Frederick Perls, *Gestalt Therapy Verbatim*. (Lafayette, Calif.: Real People Press, 1969).
5. Robert S. DeRopp, *The Master Game* (New York: Dell Publishing Co., 1968).
6. For more opposite exercises see Perls, Goodman and Hefferlane, *Gestalt Therapy* (New York: Dell Publishing, 1965).

CHAPTER 4

Introduction, pages 200–203

1. We are indebted to Richard and Patricia Schmuck for this notion. For an excellent treatment of these four dimensions of the

peer community, see their book, *Group Processes in the Classroom* (Dubuque, Iowa: W. C. Brown, 1971).

Richard A. and Patricia A. Schmuck, "A Practical Guide to Group Development," pages 209–221

Gardner, John. *Self-Renewal: The Individual and the Innovative Society.* New York: Harper and Row, 1963.

Kohl, Herbert. *The Open Classroom: A Practical Guide to a New Way of Teaching.* New York: A New York Review Book, 1969.

Parsons, Talcott, and Bales, Robert. *Family, Socialization and Interaction Process.* New York: Free Press, 1955.

Watts, Alan. *The Book.* New York: Collier, 1961.

Elizabeth Hunter, "Improving Group Productivity," pages 221–227

1. This material is based on the work of K. D. Benne and P. Sheats, "Functional Roles of Group Members," *Journal of Social Issues* 4, no. 2 (Spring 1948): 42–47. The listing of group task and group maintenance roles can be found, in somewhat different form from the way they are presented in this chapter, in the *Reading Book of the NTL Institute for Applied Behavioral Science,* 1201 Sixteenth Street, N.W., Washington, D.C., 1969, pp. 22–23.

2. There are many variations of this game. This particular one was introduced to me by Dr. William Gellerman, an independent consultant in New York City.

Jack R. Gibb, "Defensive Communication," pages 227–231

1. J. R. Gibb, "Defense Level and Influence Potential in Small Groups," in *Leadership and Interpersonal Behavior,* eds. L. Petrullo and B. M. Bass (New York: Holt, Rinehart and Winston, 1961), pp. 66–81.

2. J. R. Gibb, "Sociopsychological Processes of Group Instruction," in *The Dynamics of Instructional Groups,* ed. N. B. Henry. Fifty-ninth Yearbook of the National Society for the Study of Education, Part 2 (1960), pp. 115–35.

CHAPTER 5

William Glasser, "Social-Problem-Solving Meetings," pages 271–273

1. Two excellent articles support these points. The first, "Whose Fault Was It?" by Charles I. Gragg, *Harvard Business Review,* January–February, 1964, discusses the futility of fault finding. The second is a chapter, pp. 62–67, from *The Human Side of Enterprise,* by John Haberman, McGraw-Hill, 1960. This article deals with an unusual labor-relations program that eliminated punishment completely and that was highly successful. Theoretically, it followed almost exactly the ideas of Reality Therapy as expressed in Chapter 2 of this book.

CHAPTER 6

Ned A. Flanders, "Intent, Action and Feedback: A Preparation for Teaching," pages 306–316

Anderson, Harold H. "The Measurement of Domination and of Socially Integrative Be-

havior in Teachers' Contacts with Children." *Child Development* 10: (June 1939) 73–89.

Anderson, Harold H., and Brewer, Helen M. *Studies of Teachers' Classroom Personalities, I: Dominative and Socially Integrative Behavior of Kindergarten Teachers.* Applied Psychology Monographs of the American Psychological Association, no. 6. Stanford, Calif.: Stanford University Press, July 1945.

Anderson, Harold H., and Brewer, Joseph E. *Studies of Teachers' Classroom Personalities, II: Effects of Teachers' Dominative and Integrative Contacts on Children's Classroom Behavior.* Applied Psychology Monographs of the American Psychological Association, no. 8. Stanford, Calif.: Stanford University Press, June 1946.

Anderson, Harold H.; Brewer, J. E.; and Reed, M. F. *Studies of Teachers' Classroom Personalities, III: Follow-up Studies of the Effects of Dominative and Integrative Contacts on Children's Behavior.* Applied Psychology Monographs of the American Psychological Association, no. 11. Stanford, Calif.: Stanford University Press, December 1946.

Cantor, Nathaniel. *The Teaching-Learning Process.* New York: Dryden Press, 1953. Pp. 59–72.

Flanders, N. A. "A Terminal Contract Report on Using Interaction Analysis for the Inservice Training of Teachers." To be submitted to the U.S. Office of Education, N.D.E.A., Title VII. Available from the author, University of Michigan, after April 1963.

———. "Teacher Influence, Pupil Attitudes, and Achievement." Research Monograph, Cooperative Research Program, U.S. Office of Education, 1963.

Flanders, N. A., and Havumaki, S. "Group Compliance to Dominative Teacher Influence." *Human Relations* 13: 67–82.

Romney, G. P., et al. *Progress Report of the Merit Study of the Provo City Schools.* Provo, Utah, August 1958. XIX + 226 pp. See also *Patterns of Effective Teaching: Second Progress Report of the Merit Study of the Provo City Schools.* Provo, Utah, June 1961. XII + 93 pp.

Thelen, H. A. *Education and the Human Quest.* New York: Harper Brothers, 1960. Pp. 74–112.

Bernice J. Wolfson, "Pupil and Teacher Roles in Individualized Instruction," pages 317–323

Bronowski, J. *The Identity of Man.* Garden City, N.Y.: The Natural History Press, 1966.

Gage, Nathan L. *Handbook of Research on Teaching.* Chicago: Rand McNally, 1963.

Howe, Florence. "Mississippi's Freedom Schools: The Politics of Education," *Harvard Educational Review* 35 (Spring 1965):144–60.

Mager, Robert R. "On the Sequencing of Instructional Content." Reported by Millicent Alter in *Programmed Instruction* 4 (November 1964): 3–4.

Roberts, Raymond J., and Schuetz, Carolyn. "Monte Vista High School — The First Year." Mimeographed. San Ramon Valley Unified School District, Danville, California, 1966.

Wolfson, Bernice J. "The Promise of Multiage Grouping for Individualizing Instruction." *Elementary School Journal* 67 (April 1967): 354–62.

Arthur W. Combs, "Educational Accountability from a Humanistic Perspective," pages 332–336

Combs, A. W. *Educational Accountability: Beyond Behavioral Objectives.* Washington, D.C.: Association for Supervision and Curriculum Development, 1972.

Combs, A. W., et al., *Florida Studies in the Helping Professions.* Social Science Monograph no. 37. Gainesville, Fla.: University of Florida Press, 1969.